BOOKS WRITTEN OR EDITED BY

Alan F. Westin

PRIVACY AND FREEDOM   1967

VIEWS OF AMERICA   1966
(*with Julian H. Franklin, Howard R. Swearer and Paul F. Sigmund*)

POLITICS IN THE SOVIET UNION: SEVEN CASES   1966
(*with Alexander Dallin*)

POLITICS IN EUROPE   1965
(*with Gwendolyn Carter*)

POLITICS AND GOVERNMENT IN THE UNITED STATES   1965
(*with E. Redford, D. Truman, A. Hacker and R. Wood*)

FREEDOM NOW: THE CIVIL RIGHTS STRUGGLE IN AMERICA   1964

POWER AND ORDER: SEVEN CASES IN WORLD POLITICS   1963
(*with John Stoessinger*)

AN AUTOBIOGRAPHY OF THE SUPREME COURT   1963

THE CENTERS OF POWER   1963
(*with Louis Koenig and H. D. Price*)

THE THIRD BRANCH OF GOVERNMENT   1962
(*with C. Herman Pritchett*)

THE SUPREME COURT: VIEWS FROM INSIDE   1961

THE ANATOMY OF A CONSTITUTIONAL LAW CASE   1958

PRIVACY AND FREEDOM

Alan F. Westin

PRIVACY AND
FREEDOM

Foreword by Oscar M. Ruebhausen,

CHAIRMAN OF THE SPECIAL COMMITTEE ON SCIENCE AND LAW,
THE ASSOCIATION OF THE BAR OF THE CITY OF NEW YORK

ATHENEUM   NEW YORK
1967

Portions of Chapters 2, 3, 13, and 14 were previously published in different form in "Science, Privacy, and Freedom: Issues and Proposals for the 1970's" by Alan F. Westin, Columbia Law Review, June and November, 1966, copyright © 1966 by Directors of the Columbia Law Review Association, Inc.

"The Lie-Detector Era" by Dwight Macdonald, quoted on pages 151–2, was published in The Reporter, *June 8, 1954, copyright 1954 by The Fortnightly Publishing Co. Quoted by permission.*

Published simultaneously in Canada by McClelland & Stewart Ltd.
Manufactured in the United States of America by H. Wolff, New York
Designed by Kathleen Carey
First Printing June 1967
Second Printing September 1967
Third Printing October 1967
Fourth Printing December 1967

To my mother, Etta Westin,
and the memory of my father, Irving Westin

Foreword

EVER SINCE Prometheus first stole fire from the gods, man has been fascinated, and a little anxious, about the magic of science. Though centuries have passed, the hint of alchemy still lingers; and the word Frankenstein persists as a chilling symbol.

Yet the basic posture of modern man toward science is not fearful but proud. Intuitively, at the least, he sees the systematic collection and classification of knowledge as central to his dignity, the process of adding to knowledge as elevating, and the contributions of science as an essential part of the lives he leads and the joys he takes.

With each passing year, however, the pace of obsolescence in old knowledge seems to quicken. New data, new concepts and techniques seem to press upon the structure of our lives with ever accelerating force.

For the first time it appears to be coming within the reach of man to exercise on a large scale powers often previously believed to be the province of the great Creator: the conquest of space, the control of genetics, the synthesis of life, the deferment of death with artificial organs, influencing the weather, the pollution and purification of air and water, the probing of the cosmic forces in our solar system, and the shaping of human values and behavior. The catalogue is long and provocative. Nor is it wholly free of terror.

Survival, it is clear, depends on the rapidity with which such new knowledge is mastered. This is an axiom for industry and commerce, as well as for biologists. It is no less axiomatic—only somewhat less explicitly accepted—for our social and political institutions.

In a simpler society the pace of new knowledge, and of the technology which adapted it to the uses of man, was slow. Thus it was easier for society to accommodate its laws and its culture to the wondrous new ways. The "revolutions" of the steam engine, electric power, the wireless, and the gasoline engine spent their initial force over decades of time. Institutions, such as the family, the professions, government, and the several priesthoods of society, both religious and secular, were thus

afforded sufficient breathing space for accommodation to the new technology. These institutions were, therefore, quite effective in exploiting
the new data and the growing wisdom, while minimizing the dangers
which always accompany an advance in knowledge or technique.

With our complex and dynamic society, however, the advent of
new knowledge can be traumatic. Especially is this true when the pace
of advance is rapid and the initial force of radical discoveries must be
cushioned and accommodated in a relatively short interval of time. It
is no surprise that our social and political institutions are now sorely
pressed to find the flexibility to utilize new technology effectively while,
at the same time, preventing its abuse.

As we approach the year 2000, therefore, it is plain that the new discoveries of science cannot be accommodated successfully to our already
intricate social and biological mechanisms unless more laymen have
better perceptions and anticipations of both the potentials and limitations of science than they have ever before enjoyed. And our ingenuity
will increasingly be challenged to create the cultural institutions competent to make the most of what science is providing. Nothing less will
do if the new revolutions of science are to serve the well-being of man
and the dignity of his existence.

In this spirit, and with that end in view, the Association of the Bar
of the City of New York organized in 1959 its Special Committee on
Science and Law. This action was born of its experience, a decade earlier,
in establishing the first committee of lawyers to concern themselves with
atomic energy.

The role of this Special Committee was in many ways unique. The
scope of its concern was as broad as the whole interface between the
disciplines of science and the aspirations of society. Unlike many conventional bar-association committees, it did not concern itself primarily
with substantive legal issues or with their resolution, but, rather, with the
interrelationships between man, science, and society and the concessions
which each sought to exact from the others. It was, we felt, out of this
complex interaction between human goals and modern science that
fresh social challenges and new legal problems would arise.

With this concept as its guide, the current problems that were the
most clearly apparent were not of paramount interest to the Special
Committee. A problem perceived was, we thought, probably already
being attacked on a variety of fronts—the battle lines drawn, the scholars
committed, and lobbyists in position.

In contrast, the Committee on Science and Law sought to anticipate and identify the embryonic issues that might later mature into
problems. Attention called to a latent issue, we were convinced, meant
a better prospect for either avoiding or resolving a future problem. It
would be "preventive law" in a very positive sense if the Committee

could in any way contribute to a climate of understanding out of which public decisions could wisely evolve. We also held the notion that new insights and fresh perspectives in terms of new problems might lift the vision and redirect the energies of those already long locked in combat on related and familiar issues.

It was a central part of our approach to reach out to scientists who might be willing to share their concerns with lawyers in an interdisciplinary experience. The spirit of our examination was relaxed and cooperative. There was little of the purposeful legal inquiry. Our test of success was not measured in terms of blueprints for reform or technical proposals for legislation. We sought rather to widen our own perceptions and, possibly, those of the scientists who collaborated with us.

This shared experience was productive. It suggests a model for wider use not only by the bar, but by all the professions. Cooperative interdisciplinary examination, by practitioners, not just scholars, into items of common concern could be rewarding in a large number of areas. A dialogue between the working lawyer and the religious leader, the practicing accountant and his legal counterpart, between the priest and the physicist, the moralist and medicine, are suggestive of the richness of the opportunity.

In this spirit we proceeded. Initially, a look was taken at weapons technology and its implications for war and peace, and for democratic institutions. Some thought was given to the pace and pervasiveness of federal programs for the support of scientific research. The possibilities of communications satellites and the institutions to cope with them were reviewed. A similar look was taken at computers and their associated phenomena; and the consequences of an "irreversible experiment" in outer space were explored.

Gradually we came to an appreciation of the remarkable advances in electronic, optical, acoustic, and other sensing devices. The rapidly developing capability to observe, record, and broadcast actions and conversations that are conventionally assumed to be private was thought to signal some problems of potential concern. Of paramount importance was the challenge perceived to individual privacy. Not only privacy from unscrupulous, criminal, or pathological persons. Not alone privacy from aggregations of public or private power, but privacy also from simply the aggressive, or the curious, who may be tempted to use the new techniques. If, as it seemed, the new technology was on a collision course with the values of personal privacy and human dignity, could the collision be averted? Could a system be devised to identify and permit beneficial uses of the new technology and yet, at the same time, preclude those uses that most men would deem intolerable?

Such queries prompted the Committee on Science and Law, early in 1962, to propose a more formal study. Thus, it sought, and obtained, the support of the Carnegie Corporation of New York for an inquiry into the impact of modern technology upon privacy. That support, thrice supplemented, was surely an act of faith in the fine tradition of one of the most creative of foundations.

Hence, the birth of this volume. Alan F. Westin, Professor of Public Law and Government at Columbia University, and the author of this book, was selected to organize the Committee's studies and to direct its research. In this both he and the Committee were assisted by a large number of consultants, some of whom participated actively in Committee meetings, some did research at our suggestion, others joined a two-day Conference at the Onchiota Conference Center in the spring of 1964, and all whose names are listed in the Acknowledgments by the author gave to him and to the Committee insight and encouragement.

The more than four years committed to this project had three discernible phases. First there was a survey of the privacy-invading capacity of modern science, the capabilities of the technology, and the range of the available hardware. This phase was both the shortest and quite the simplest. The second phase centered on the nature and meaning of privacy—a concept that proved ro be part philosophy, some semantics, and much pure passion. True to our methods of proceeding, we reached out for the reflections and advice of anthropologists, psychologists, biologists, physicists, historians, and psychiatrists, as well as philosophers, lawyers, and laymen. We held meetings and we sponsored research. The third, and still continuing, phase has concentrated on analysis of the interaction of three forces: one, the individual's claim to a private personality; two, society's need to acquire information and to control individual behavior; and, three, the inexorable reality of the available new technology.

What we have been examining is one facet of man's struggle for a human dimension in a highly structured society, for dignity notwithstanding dependence. Science has vastly complicated this elemental contest.

The work of the Committee has had, as anticipated, a "ripple" effect. What was not anticipated, however, was the serendipity with which the ripples would exert their influence. While some of the consequences of the Committee's project may never be known to it, a rewarding number of them have been direct and apparent.

Thus, courses or seminars on science and law, and on the contest between privacy and society's other values, are finding their way into the curricula of our leading educational institutions at both the graduate and undergraduate level. Directly responsive, too, are the administrative revisions being made by colleges and research institutions throughout the country in the procedures for supervising and taking responsibility for the conduct of behavioral research. And government is re-examining its own responsibility in this area as well as in law enforcement.

Symposia, conferences, keynote addresses, and panels on privacy are now blossoming all over the cultural landscape. In many of these the Committee or its members or Professor Westin have been privileged to participate. The literature, both popular and scholarly, and even the theses submitted for doctoral degrees are proliferating with privacy. Much of this output has been directly supported, shaped, or influenced by the Committee's effort.

What is worth a special word is that while the Special Committee has yet to issue recommendations or testify before Congress—the traditional format for bar-association groups—several members of the Committee have been moved to independent work and have published scholarly material of more than passing importance on aspects of privacy.

In all of this there were several surprises. First, perhaps, was the realization that the problems for privacy were at the present time not significantly posed by esoteric new discoveries. Rather, they were raised most sharply by the familiar and increasingly pervasive items: the miniature, battery-powered microphone, the extension telephone, the portable (and concealable) tape recorder, and the small, high-resolution camera.

Second, midway through the project the general public began to "discover" the new technology and the extent of its abuse. This sharply shaped the direction of our effort. For with the public alerted, the need and, no less important, the temptation to sound the tocsin in simplistic terms of alarm were thoroughly removed. This development enabled the Special Committee, and the author of this book, better to concentrate on the complexities of the competing claims and their underlying, adversary values.

Even more significant was our discovery that the claim to privacy was little understood though widely honored. The functions of privacy seem never to have been systematically explored. Few monographs analyzed the role of privacy or the tolerable limits upon its invasion. A very few did precisely this, however, with gleaming flashes of insight and scholarship.

Until the nature of privacy and its uses was reasonably understood, there was little prospect that the Committee project could contribute to devising a system under which the new technology and the individual claim to the dignity of a private personality could live in productive partnership. Hence, the nature of privacy inexorably became a central concern of the project and of this volume by Professor Westin. As a by-product there will also be a companion, historical volume by Professor Westin, to be published later in the year, on privacy as it was nurtured or neglected in various periods of history.

Although these books are in a very immediate sense a result of the Special Committee's four-year project, the research, the authorship, and the scholarship are Professor Westin's. He has conducted the first comprehensive exploration of privacy and of the interaction between it and the competing claims of society. Legislators, lawyers, administrators, jurists, and laymen will find this work essential in distinguishing the tolerable from the intolerable intrusions upon the dignity of man.

Oscar M. Ruebhausen

DECEMBER, 1966

Acknowledgments

THIS BOOK would not have been written, at least in its present scope and comprehensiveness, were it not for two organizations. First is the Special Committee on Science and Law of the Association of the Bar of the City of New York, which sponsored, guided, and reviewed the study that led to this volume. I profited greatly and often from the counsel of the Committee members—Edward J. Bloustein, John W. Brumbaugh, George H. P. Dwight, Kenneth R. Frankl, Everett L. Hollis, Daniel James, John M. Kernochan, William A. W. Krebs, Jr., Arthur W. Murphy, Bethuel Webster, and Adam Yarmolinsky. A special debt is owed to the Committee's gifted chairman, Oscar M. Ruebhausen, and its energetic secretary, Bevis Longstreth. The second godfather of this volume is the Carnegie Corporation of New York, whose interest and support sustained the work. To John Gardner, James Perkins, Alan Pifer, Fritz Moser, Margaret Anderson, Margo Viscuzi, and to the Carnegie Board of Trustees goes my appreciation for acts both fiscal and intellectual.

During the research stage, the following persons served as continuing consultants or advisers to the project: Paul Bator, William M. Beaney, William O. Baker, Ralph Brown, Norman Cantor, Charles C. Hughes, Yale Kamisar, Stanley P. Lovell, Robert J. Lifton, Arnold Simmel, Paul S. Visher, and George E. Valley, Jr. Leo Beranek, Francis Weiner, and Charles Dietrich, of the firm of Bolt, Beranek, and Newman, provided reports as consultants on physical-surveillance technology, as did Nathan Kline, Eliot Chapple, Herbert Spiegel, and Peter Wotton, on psychological-surveillance issues.

I was fortunate in having a talented group of research assistants throughout the life of the project. Gordon M. Stevenson and Heather Feldman worked on the whole study and contributed to it continuously. On its legal side, I drew on the efforts of Edward R. Bendet, Michael Curzan, Robert Z. Dobrish, Robert E. Easton, William D. Friedman, Stephen Gardner, Harvey J. Goldschmid, Richard Goldsmith, Charles L. Grimes, Lawrence D. Horowitz, Mary V. Magilligan, Perry W. Morton, Stephen M. Nassau, John D. Niles, Michael R. Parnes, Jonathan E. Perlow, Arthur Schatten, Richard F. Scott, Martin Self, and Shoshana Tancer. In studying the functions of privacy, I was aided by Elinor Berlin, Barbette Blackington, Virginia R. Boehm, Caren Goretsky, Thomas Gregor, George Latimer, Patricia A. Lee, Jane Shapiro, and William J. Sittig. Work on aspects of privacy in Western history was aided by Taylor Albert, J. Paul Blum, Stephen Cole, David Flaherty, Marvin E. Gettleman, Louis Menashe, Ronald Moe, and Alan Posner. A small but important grant from the Columbia University Council for Research in the Social Sciences aided in several of the research activities in which the above-named assistants were engaged.

Into a group whose members offered intellectual encouragement and helpful suggestions to the project I would put David F. Cavers, Lee J. Cronbach, Samuel Dash, Charles R. DiCarlo, G. Everett De More, Louis L. Jaffe, Harry Kalven, Jr., Franklin A. Lindsay, Francis J. McCarthy, J. Robert Oppenheimer, Dwight C. Smith, Jr., Robert C. Sprague, Herbert Wechsler, John W. Wade, and Carroll L. Wilson. Colleagues within the Association of the Bar were continually helpful, notably Harry H. Almond, Jr., Granville M. Brumbaugh, Herbert Brownell, Dudley Bonsal, Mark N. Donohue, Paul B. De Witt, Orison S. Marden, Russell D. Niles, Samuel I. Rosenman, and John S. Walker.

While data were being gathered, I either saw or had aid through correspondence from a considerable number of government officials, organizational leaders and staffs, and specialists in particular fields. Because I think some of those I interviewed would prefer not to be mentioned, I have omitted a few names, but the following were most helpful: Sam Archibald, David C. Acheson, Ben H. Bagdikian, Bernard S. Benson, Frank Bartimo, Howard F. Cerny, Norman B. Cornish, Edward E. David, Julius C. C. Edelstein, Bernard Fensterwald, Jr., Robert R. J. Gallati, Frank Hogan, Najeeb E. Halaby, Evin Jenkins, Benny L. Kass, Nicholas DeB. Katzenbach, Spurgeon Keeney, George W. Lindberg, Eliot A. Lumbard, Horace P. Moulton, John McNaughton, Alice Miller, John Pierce, Emanuel R. Piore, John Quisenberry, Philip J. Ruffo, Richard M. Scammon, M. R. Schroeder, Alfred J. Scotti, Walter T. Skallerup, Jr., Arnold Sagalyn, Paul Schrade, Theodore J. St. Antoine, Glenn E. Watts, Eric Witt, David Worgan, and Kenneth Young.

In two areas, I asked specialists to read my first drafts and criticize the discussion developed there; though I profited from these reactions, the following have no responsibility for the shortcomings that may still remain in these sections. In the area of personality testing, I am grateful to Gordon W. Allport, Richard S. Barrett, George K. Bennett, Charles P. Bowen, Jr., Isidore Chein, Walter V. Clarke, John D. Dole, Edwin W. Davis, Robert L. French, Leo Goldman, Stephen Habbe, Raymond A. Katzell, Harry Levinson, Robert N. McMurry, Perry L. Rohrer,

Floyd L. Ruch, Charles K. Rudman, Harold Seashore, Ross Stagner, King Whitney, Jr., Allen V. Williams, and Arthur A. Witkin. In the field of data collection and computers, I was aided by Franz L. Alt, Paul Baran, Edmund C. Berkeley, Orville Brim, Jr., S. D. Conte, Robert B. Forest, Roy N. Freed, Bernard A. Galler, Robert M. Gordon, R. W. Hamming, A. R. Hibbs, A. R. Householder, George Kennard, Robert Patrick, R. E. Pickett, Jr., L. T. Rader, Gordon D. Sikes, Norman Statland, Louis Sutro, John Todd, H. W. Trimble, Jr., C. H. Wacker, Arnold K. Weber, Stanton Wheeler, and Burton R. Wolin.

The section on the functions of privacy was aided by the thoughtful readings contributed by Conrad Arensberg, Charles C. Hughes, Robert J. Lifton, Robert K. Merton, Robert F. Murphy, and Kurt H. Wolff.

After the manuscript was completed, it was read by Alice Kwartler and Mary O'Melveny, both of whom helped to clarify thought and improve language. My wife, Bea, and my sister-in-law, Elinor Miller, were subjected to the readings-aloud and "what-do-you-think-of-this-approach?" which authors inflict on those too near and dear to turn them away. They always gave me the lift I needed and let me drop when the performance did.

During the writing of this book, I was able to try out the ideas being developed at a number of conferences and before various professional groups. The most important of these, sponsored by the Special Committee on Science and Law, was a conference on "The Impact of Technological Progress on Privacy," held at Onchiota Conference Center, Tuxedo, New York, on May 24–26, 1964. Those attending this stimulating and fruitful meeting were W. O. Baker, Alan Barth, William M. Beaney, Simon Michael Bessie, Edward J. Bloustein, Eliot Chapple, E. E. David, George H. P. Dwight, Kenneth R. Frankl, Stanley H. Fuld, Stuart Hampshire, Frank S. Hogan, Everett L. Hollis, Daniel James, John M. Kernochan, Nathan Kline, William A. W. Krebs, Harold D. Lasswell, Lee Loevinger, Bevis Longstreth, Robert S. Morison, Arthur W. Murphy, John deJ. Pemberton, Jr., Alan Pifer, Rt. Rev. James A. Pike, Samuel Rosenman, Oscar M. Ruebhausen, Stephen I. Schlossberg, Edward A. Shils, Herbert Spiegel, Harris B. Steinberg, George E. Valley, Jr., Ralph V. Ward, George T. Washington, Bethuel Webster, William Webster, Joseph Wershba, and Adam Yarmolinsky.

Other groups before whom I appeared and tested some of the ideas in this book included the Center for the Study of Democratic Institutions, Santa Barbara, California; the Anglo-American Legal Conference, Ditchley House, Enstone, Oxfordshire, England; the Biennial Conference of the American Civil Liberties Union; the Brookings Institution Conference for Federal Investigative Officials; and the Harvard University Program on Technology and Society. I also ran the gauntlet of professional groups in almost all the fields that I had the temerity to advise about invasions of privacy. These included the American Psychological Association, American Personnel and Guidance Counselors Association, American Orthopsychiatric Association, American Political Science Association, and American Federation of Information Processing Societies.

Finally, a special word of appreciation is owed to the firm of Debevoise, Plimpton, Lyons & Gates, of which Oscar M. Ruebhausen is a member, and to its partners, associates, and staff, whose time, facilities, and equipment lent continuous support to the writing of this book from its inception.

Contents

PRIVACY AND FREEDOM

Prologue

TO ITS PROFOUND distress, the American public has recently learned of a revolution in the techniques by which public and private authorities can conduct scientific surveillance over the individual. In chilled fascination the press, television programs, and popular books have described new means of telephone tapping, electronic eavesdropping, hidden television-eye monitoring, "truth measurement" by polygraph devices, personality testing for personnel selection, and growing dossiers of personal data about millions of citizens. Some of these accounts of new surveillance technology have gone on to speculate uneasily about future developments in the next decade, from data surveillance by computer systems to drug-aided interrogations and the possibility of brain-wave analysis. As examples mount of the uses made of the new technology, worried protests against "Big Brother" have set alarms ringing along the civic-group spectrum from extreme left to radical right. Reflecting this concern, "invasion of privacy" has become a leading topic in law-review articles and social-science journals, as well as the subject of legislative and executive investigations at the state and federal levels and of a growing number of exploratory judicial rulings throughout the country. As the late 1960's arrived, it was clear that American society had developed a deep concern over the preservation of privacy under the new pressures from surveillance technology.

This condition suggests that the thoughtful reader has little need for further ringing denunciations of "Big Brother in America" or popular volumes devoted to documenting the spread of privacy-invading practices in our society. That job has been accomplished. The real need is to move from public awareness of the problem to a sensitive discussion of what can be done to protect privacy in an age when so many forces of science, technology, environment, and society press against it from all sides.

Such an analysis seems to call for at least four inquiries. First, privacy must be defined rather than simply invoked, and its psychological, sociological, and political dimensions must be described on the basis of leading theoretical and empirical studies. Second, the new techniques of surveillance, their present uses, and their future prospects must

3

be described, forsaking Orwellian imagery for hard facts. Third, the ways in which American society has reacted to the new surveillance techniques must be examined in depth to see what has been happening to our norms of privacy during the past two decades and whether there are trends in interest-group and general public opinion that may help to guide American policy-makers. Finally, there should be a discussion of how American law has dealt with the issue of privacy and surveillance, as the backdrop for an analysis of specific measures that public and private authorities might take to ensure the continuation of privacy in the 1970's as a cornerstone of the American system of liberty. Exploring these four topics does not guarantee wise policy decisions, but it is hard to see how we can come to grips with the dilemmas of privacy and freedom unless these are the problems we study.

PART ONE

The Functions of Privacy and Surveillance in Society

Few values so fundamental to society as privacy have been left so undefined in social theory or have been the subject of such vague and confused writing by social scientists. This is emphasized by the fact that most commentators assume that privacy is a distinctly modern notion, possibly emerging as an idea in the late eighteenth century, with Protestantism and early capitalism, but really maturing in the late nineteenth or early twentieth centuries.

In my view, the modern claim to privacy derives first from man's animal origins and is shared, in quite real terms, by men and women living in primitive societies. Furthermore, the approach to privacy taken by Americans today developed from a tradition of limiting the surveillance powers of authorities over the private activities of individuals and groups that goes back to the Greeks in Western political history.

Since these ideas ought to raise the hackles of at least some of those reading this book, it is important that I define at the outset what I mean by privacy before setting out to prove these points. Privacy is the claim of individuals, groups, or institutions to determine for themselves when, how, and to what extent information about them is communicated to others. Viewed in terms of the relation of the individual to social participation, privacy is the voluntary and temporary withdrawal of a person from the general society through physical or psychological means, either in a state of solitude or small-group intimacy or, when among larger groups, in a condition of anonymity or reserve. The individual's desire for privacy is never absolute, since participation in society is an equally powerful desire. Thus each individual is continually engaged in a personal adjustment process in which he balances the desire for privacy with the desire for disclosure and communication of himself to others, in light of the environmental conditions and social norms set by the society in which he lives. The individual does so in the face of pressures from the curiosity of others and from the processes of surveillance that every society sets in order to enforce its social norms.

The test of these general statements is obviously in their explanation and application, which represent the task of the three chapters that make up Part One.

7

CHAPTER ONE

The Origins of Modern Claims to Privacy

Privacy in the Animal World

MAN LIKES TO think that his desire for privacy is distinctively human, a function of his unique ethical, intellectual, and artistic needs. Yet studies of animal behavior and social organization suggest that man's need for privacy may well be rooted in his animal origins, and that men and animals share several basic mechanisms for claiming privacy among their own fellows. Within the past year these points have been made in two excellent books for the general reader that report recent findings in biology, ecology, and anthropology—Edward Hall's *The Hidden Dimension*[1] and Robert Ardrey's *The Territorial Imperative*.[2] Thus we begin our analysis of man's patterns of privacy at the chronological starting point—man's evolutionary heritage.

One basic finding of animal studies is that virtually all animals seek periods of individual seclusion or small-group intimacy. This is usually described as the tendency toward territoriality, in which an organism lays private claim to an area of land, water, or air and defends it against intrusion by members of its own species.[3] A meadow pipit chases fellow pipits away from a private space of six feet around him. Except during nesting time, there is only one robin on a bush or branch. The three-spined stickleback guards an invisible water wall around him and attacks any other stickleback that swims into his territory. Antelopes in African fields and dairy cattle in an American farmyard space themselves to establish individual territory.[4] For species in which the female cannot raise the young unaided, nature has created the "pair bond," linking temporarily or permanently a male and a female who demand private territory for the unit during breeding time.[5] Studies of territoriality have even shattered the romantic notion that when robins sing or monkeys shriek, it is solely for the "animal joy of life." Actually, it is often a defiant cry for privacy, given within the borders of the animal's private territory to warn off possible intruders.[6]

These territorial patterns have been found by scientists to serve a cluster of important purposes. They ensure propagation of the species by regulating density to available resources. They enhance selection of "worthy males" and provide breeding stations for animals that require male assistance in raising the young. They also provide a physical frame of reference for group activity such as learning, playing, and hiding, and provide contact for group members against the entry of intruders. The parallels between territory rules in animal life and trespass concepts in human society are obvious: in each, the organism lays claim to private space to promote individual well-being and small-group intimacy.

Animals and man also share elaborate distance-setting mechanisms to define territorial spacing of individuals in the group. The distance set between one non-contact animal and another (illustrated by the spacing of birds on a telephone wire) has been called "personal distance."[7] Among species such as birds and apes, there are rules of "intimate distance" regulating the space held between mates or between parents and their young.[8] "Social distance" links members of the animal group to one another and sets off the group from others,[9] while "flight distance" is the point of approach at which an animal will flee from an intruder of another species.[10] Though man has eliminated flight distance as a regular mechanism of his social life, Hall's studies indicate that man sets basically the same kinds of personal, intimate, and social distance in his interpersonal relationships as do mammals in the animal world.[11] In addition, man still relies heavily on his "animal" or physical senses—touch, taste, smell, sight, and hearing—to define his daily boundaries of privacy. What is considered "too close" a contact and therefore an "invasion of privacy" in human society will often be an odor, a noise, a visual intrusion, or a touch; the mechanism for defining privacy in these situations is sensory.

Ecological studies have demonstrated that animals also have minimum needs for private space without which the animal's survival will be jeopardized. Since overpopulation can impede the animal's ability to smell, court, or be free from constant defensive reactions, such a condition upsets the social organization of the animal group. The animals may then kill each other to reduce the crowding, or they may engage in mass suicidal reductions of the population, as with lemmings and rabbits.[12] Experiments with spacing rats in cages showed that even rats need time and space to be alone.[13] When rats were deliberately crowded in cages, patterns of courting, nest building, rearing the young, social hierarchies, and territorial taboos were disrupted. Aggression and fighting increased and sexual conduct became more sadistic. Experiments also showed that wild rat populations would stabilize at about 150 when the rats were placed in an open quarter-acre pen, even though the females there could have produced 50,000 progeny in the test period. However, if rats are given individual quarters in pens two feet square, 5,000 rats could thrive in the same area, and 50,000 in the same space in eight-inch cages. This suggests that when private space is provided, density does not necessarily produce social disorganization or diseases. Studies of crowding in many animals other than rats indicate that disruption of social relationships through overlapping personal distances aggravates all forms of pathology within a group and causes the same diseases in animals that overcrowding does in man—"high blood pressure, circulatory diseases, and heart disease." [14]

Crowding in animals can also produce what has been called "biochemical die-off." For example, a deer herd on an island near the coast of Maryland had increased gradually to 300, about one deer to an acre. Food was adequate for all, and there was no evidence of infection. Yet between 1958 and 1959 more than two thirds of the deer simply died, in apparently fine physical health. A study of the "die-off" concluded that crowding had created such metabolic stress that an endocrine reaction set in, producing a process of natural selection and reducing the population.[15]

A final parallel between animal and human societies is the need for social stimulation which exists in animals alongside their needs for privacy. As Ardrey has written:

> In species after species natural selection has encouraged social mechanisms which seem ultimately to exist for no reason other than to provide conditions for antagonism and conflict and excitement. We may comprehend the evolutionary necessity for bringing together a breeding community. . . . But why must it live in a dense, disturbing, challenging, competing, squabbling, argumentative mass? If it is not to avoid boredom, then why must the animal demand for privacy stand cheek-by-jowl with the urge to plunge into the largest available crowd? [16]

Even though food supplies are adequate for living in seclusion, even though natural enemies may be manageable alone, and even though pairs could have their sex and family activities alone, animals consistently return to the group after being apart. The work of leading scientists such as Darling,[17] Fisher,[18] and Wynne-Edwards[19] shows that it is not security per se that brings animals of the same species together, but a desire for the stimulation of their fellows.

What the animal studies demonstrate is that virtually all animals have need for the temporary individual seclusion or small-unit intimacy that constitute two of the core aspects of privacy. Animals also need the stimulation of social encounters among their own species. As a result, the animal's struggle to achieve a balance between privacy and participation provides one of the basic processes of animal life. In this sense, the quest for privacy is not restricted to man alone, but arises in the biological and social processes of all life.

Privacy in the Primitive World

Even though man shares some needs for privacy with most animals, the dominant anthropological "lesson" about privacy seems to be that our contemporary norms of privacy are "modern" and "advanced" values largely absent from primitive societies of the past and present. For example, Dorothy Lee, whose work as a cultural anthropologist has focused on the relation between freedom and culture in various societies, has drawn a sharp contrast between privacy in American society and interpersonal life among the Tikopia of Polynesia.[20] In child rearing, Americans concentrate on teaching the child to be "himself" and "self-dependent," preparing him for his individual struggle in life and also giving the mother important privacy during child rearing.

> Now the child grows up needing time to himself, a room of his own, freedom of choice, freedom to plan his own time and his own life. . . . He will spend his wealth installing private bathrooms in his house, buying a private car, a private yacht, private woods and a private beach, which he will then people with his privately chosen society. The need for privacy is an imperative one in our society, recognized by official bodies of our government.[21]

Life among the Tikopia, Mrs. Lee notes, with their greater emphasis on social rather than individual values, produces very different practices.

> [T]he Tikopia help the self to be continuous with its society [rather than separate from it]. . . . They find it good to sleep side by side crowding each other, next to their children or their parents or their brothers and sisters, mixing sexes and generations; and if a widow finds herself alone in her one-room house, she may adopt a child or a brother to allay her intolerable privacy. . . .
> Work among the Tikopia is also socially conceived and structured; and if a man has to work alone, he will probably try to take a little child along. In our culture, the private office is a mark of status, an ideal; and a man has really arrived when he can even have a receptionist to guard him from any social intrusion without his private consent.[22]

Margaret Mead's famous study of Samoa deals with another society in which the basic American concepts of privacy are unknown.[23] In the Samoan house there are no walls, and only mosquito netting separates the sleeping quarters of the married couples, children, and old folks. Adults wear little clothing and children none. Bathing in the sea is performed without clothes. The beaches are used openly as latrines. No privacy is claimed or provided for the processes of birth and death; even the children stand about watching these moments of intimacy. In all these areas, Dr. Mead notes, "there is no privacy and no sense of shame." In Samoa, "little is mysterious, . . . little forbidden."

To give one last example from another area of the world, Livingston Jones has written of the Tlingit Indians of North America:

> There are no skeletons tucked away in native families, for the acts of one are familiar to all the others. Privacy is hardly known among them. It cannot be maintained very well under their system of living, with families bunched together. . . . The Tlingit's bump of curiosity is well developed and any thing out of the ordinary, as an accident, a birth, a death or a quarrel, never fails to draw a crowd. . . . They walk in and out of one another's homes without knocking on the door. A woman may be in the very act of changing her garments when Mr. Quakish steps in unannounced to visit her husband. This does not embarrass her in the least. She proceeds as if no one had called.[24]

One could compile a long list of societies, primitive and modern, that neither have nor would admire the norms of privacy found in American culture—norms which some Americans regard as "natural" needs of all men living in society. Yet this circumstance does not prove that there are no universal needs for privacy and no universal processes for adjusting the values of privacy, disclosure, and surveillance within each society. It suggests only that each society must be studied in its own terms, focusing sensitively on social customs to see whether there are norms of privacy called by other names, and recognizing all the difficulties in making cross-cultural comparisons. The analysis must also recognize the fact that there are psychological ways of achieving privacy for the individual or the family as well as physical arrangements, ways which are crucial in those societies where communal life makes solitude or intimacy impossible within the living areas.

Most of the work on cultural universals has been based on studies of about 200 to 300 non-literate societies, providing us with a fairly representative cross-section of the 3,000 to 4,000 people with distinctive cultures who have lived on the earth.[25] Based on the leading general works of anthropology and sociology, a survey of the major ethnographic studies, and the relevant categories of the Human Relations Area Files at Yale University, I suggest that there are four general aspects of privacy which apply to men living together in virtually every society that has been systematically examined.

Needs for individual and group privacy and resulting social norms are present in virtually every society. Encompassing a vast range of activities, these needs affect basic areas of life for the individual, the intimate family group, and the community as a whole. Privacy norms for the society are established in each of these three areas. The individual seeks privacy, as well as companionship, in his daily interactions with others; limits are set to maintain a degree of distance at certain crucial times in his life. The family-household unit also institutes limitations on both members of the unit and outsiders to protect various activities within the household. Finally, significant rituals and ceremonies in the larger community are also protected by customs which prescribe privacy for these rites within the group. As we will see, the norms vary, but the functions which privacy performs are crucial for each of these three areas of social life.

Anthropological studies have shown that the individual in virtually every society engages in a continuing personal process by which he seeks privacy at some times and disclosure or companionship at other times. This part of the individual's basic process of interaction with those around him is usually discussed by social scientists under the terms "social distance" and "avoidance rules." [26] Although it is obviously affected by the cultural patterns of each society, the process is adjusted in its finer degrees by each individual himself. A sensitive discussion of this distance-setting process has been contributed recently by Robert F. Murphy of Columbia University.[27] Murphy noted that the use of "reserve and restraint" to provide "an area of privacy" for the individual in his relations with others represents a "common, though not constant" factor in "all social relationships." Indeed, Murphy says, it is one of the key "dialectical processes in social life." The reason for the universality of this process is that individuals have conflicting roles to play in any society; to play these different roles with different persons, the individual must present a different "self" at various times.[28] Restricting information about himself and his emotions is a crucial way of protecting the individual in the stresses and strains of this social interaction. Murphy also notes that creating social distance is especially important in the individual's intimate relations, perhaps even more so than in his casual ones. Precisely because the intimate relationships are the most emotional and ambivalent for the individual, they are "most demanding of expressions of distance, however elusive and ambivalent these may be."

Murphy's work among the Tuareg tribes of North Africa, where men veil their faces and constantly adjust the veil to changing interpersonal relations, provides a particularly visual example of the distance-setting process. Murphy concluded that the Tuareg veil is a symbolic realization of the need for privacy in every society. "The social distance set in some societies by joking and respect or avoidance behavior toward certain specific categories of relatives is accomplished here through the veil." The eyes and the mouth are instruments that "expose" the individual and diminish his psychological privacy; thus Tuareg men shield the eyes and mouth. Murphy notes that the Tuareg custom is only a more physical and exaggerated rendition of the privacy-protecting "masks" found in many societies, such as the use of the fan by women to cover the mouth and eyes when establishing their relations with men, or the use of dark glasses today among high personages in the Near and Middle East, Latin America, or Hollywood.

Examples of distance-setting techniques and avoidance rules from other primitive societies could be presented at length. The point is that kinship rules and interaction norms present individuals with a need to restrict the flow of information about themselves to others and to adjust these regulations constantly in contacts with others. This need is fundamental to individual behavior with intimates, casual acquaintances, and authorities.

The claim to individual privacy gives rise to some other limits on interpersonal disclosure. Virtually all societies have rules for concealment of the female genitals, and restrictions on the time and manner of female genital exposure; only a handful of societies practice complete nudity.[29] Though Murdock lists "modesty about natural functions" as a trait found in all societies,[30] the openness with which people in most nonliterate societies engage in evacuation makes this a "public" affair in contrast to modern norms in a society like the United States. Similarly, the individual's moments of birth, illness, and death are considered taboo and are secluded from general view in many societies,[31] but as some peoples conduct these affairs in casual view, they cannot be considered universal matters of privacy.

Needs for privacy do appear in the intimacy of sexual relations (the "pair territory" discussed by Ardrey). There are only a few exceptions to the norm that men and women will seek seclusion for performance of the sexual act. In their survey of sexual patterns in 190 societies, Ford and Beach note that "human beings in general prefer to copulate under conditions of privacy." [32] Only in a few cultures, such as the Formosan and among Yap natives of the Pacific, is the sexual act performed openly in public. Even here, Formosans will not have intercourse if children are present, and Yapese couples are generally secluded when intercourse takes place, though they do not seem to mind the presence of other persons who may come on the scene.[33]

The location of sexual intercourse in various societies sheds further light on norms of privacy in society. Where the household contains a nuclear family (husband, wife, and their children), or where it includes various other relatives but furnishes physical arrangements that provide opportunities for privacy, the sexual act takes place within the household. But where the household is crowded, or when there are communal households of large numbers of families sharing the dwelling, the sexual act is usually performed outside, so that privacy can be obtained, in bush, field, forest, or beach.[34]

As A. R. Holmberg wrote in describing the situation of the Sirionó Indians of eastern Bolivia:

> Much more intercourse takes place in the bush than in the house. The principal reason for this is that privacy is almost impossible to obtain within the hut where as many as fifty hammocks may be hung in the confined space of five hundred square feet. Moreover, the hammock of a man and his wife hangs not three feet from that of the former's mother-in-law. Furthermore, young children commonly sleep with the father and mother, so that there may be as many as four or five people crowded together in a single hammock. In addition to these frustrating circumstances, people are up and down most of the night, quieting children, cooking, eating, urinating, and defecating. . . . Consequently intercourse is indulged in more often in some secluded nook in the forest.[35]

Norms of privacy are also found in the family-household settings of primitive life. Whether the primitive household is nuclear or extended, most societies have rules limiting free entry into the house by non-residents, as well as rules governing the outsider's conduct once he enters.[36] Even in those societies where entry is fairly free, there will usually be rules limiting what a person may touch or where he may go within the house. There will also be norms limiting family conversation or acts performed while the outsiders are present.

Clearly there is less privacy for the individual or pair in an extended household than in the nuclear one, based on the criterion that more people see and exercise influence over each other's behavior in the extended household. But even here there are usually rules of avoidance, based on the kinship system, to govern who speaks to whom and which relatives may be in the same room with each other. These avoidance rules have the effect of ensuring certain levels of psychological privacy in the midst of crowding.[37] Restricting the flow of information about oneself in an extended household is often accomplished by covering the face, averting the eyes, going to one's mat, or facing the wall. The respect given to these claims to withhold information are part of the way social structure is defined in all societies.[38] Writing of the Papago, whose households contain ten or more people living and sleeping in a one-room house, R. M. Underhill notes that their avoidance rules are such that "they maneuver without touching one another where Europeans, who have more privacy, are continually doing so." [39]

The subtlety with which norms of privacy operate in the household has been described in a paper by Clifford Geertz comparing household-privacy practices in two Indonesian societies, Bali and Java.

In Java people live in small, bamboo-walled houses, each of which almost always contains a single nuclear family—i.e. mother, father, and unmarried children. Once in a while an aged grandparent may be present, but almost never anyone else. The houses face the street with a cleared front yard in front of them. There are no walls or fences around them, the house walls are thinly and loosely woven, and there are commonly not even doors. Within the house people wander freely just about any place any time, and even outsiders wander in fairly freely almost any time during the day and early evening. In brief, privacy in our terms is about as close to nonexistent as it can get. You may walk freely into a room where a man or woman is stretched out (clothed, of course) sleeping. You may enter from the rear of the house as well as from the front with hardly more warning than a greeting announcing your presence. Except for the bathing enclosure (where people change their clothes) no place is really private, and that is open above the shoulders and below the knees. . . . The Javanese have literally almost no defense against the outside world of a physical sort.

The result is that their defenses are mostly psychological. Relationships even within the household are very restrained; people speak softly, hide their feelings and even in the bosom of a Javanese family you have the feeling that you are in the public square and must behave with appropriate decorum. Javanese shut people out with a wall of etiquette (patterns of politeness are very highly developed), with emotional restraint, and with a general lack of candor in both speech and behavior. It is not, in short, that the Javanese do not wish or value privacy; but merely that because they put up no physical or social barriers against the physical ingress of outsiders into their household life they must put up psychological ones and surround themselves with social barriers of a different sort. Thus, there is really no sharp break between public and private in Java: people behave more or less the same in private as they do in public—in a manner we would call stuffy at best—and maintain the privacy of their personal life by the same means as they deal with others in their public life. . . .

Now, in Bali people live in houseyards surrounded by high stone walls into which you enter by a narrow, half blocked-off doorway. Inside such a yard lives some form of what anthropologists call a patrilineal extended family. Such a family may consist of from one to a dozen or so nuclear families of the Javanese sort whose heads are related patrilineally: i.e. father, his two married sons, his two married brothers, *his* father, and the unmarried children of these; or a set of cousins with their families who are sons of two brothers, etc. . . .

In contrast to Java, nonkinsmen almost never enter one's houseyard (except on ceremonial occasions, etc. when they are invited to do so). Within the yard one is in one's castle and other people know better than to push their way in (if they wish to see you they will send a child to fetch you, etc.). Other patrilineal relatives of yours may come around in the early evening to gossip and in some cases a close friend or two may do so, but except for these when you are in your houseyard you are free of the public. Only your immediate family is around.[40]

While the emotional atmosphere of a Javanese house is "stuffy," Geertz said, the Balinese house is marked by "a tremendous warmth, humor, [and] openness. . . . As soon as the Balinese steps through the doorway to the street and the public square, market and temples beyond, however, he becomes more or less like the Javanese."

Privacy for certain group ceremonies is another characteristic of primitive societies. One major example involves the rites of passage, by which girls and boys, as they come of age, are withdrawn from the whole group, go into seclusion, participate in special ceremonies, and then re-enter as "adults." At the first onset of menstruation, for instance, girls in most societies go to secluded places away from the village for periods ranging from several days to several months; in the privacy of this all-female society (men are forbidden to visit the area), the girls receive sexual instruction and marriage information from older women. A similar secluded period for boys in many societies involves subjecting the youths to ordeals designed to test their manhood; after these ceremonies the boys are given sexual instruction.[41]

Margaret Mead suggests that the enforcement of privacy for the ceremonies of various sub-groups in the community rests on the feeling that the presence of "spectators" would affect the psychological feeling of unity and belonging of the participants. Speaking of the night dances among the Samoans, which usually end in openly promiscuous relations, Mead writes:

> [C]hildren and old people were excluded, as non-participants whose presence as uninvolved spectators would have been indecent. This attitude toward non-participants characterised all emotionally charged events, a women's weaving bee which was of a formal, ceremonial nature, a house-building, [and] a candlenut burning.[42]

Whatever the reasons given, virtually every society holds ceremonies for special groups from which various segments of the whole tribe or community will be barred—ceremonies for warrior males, cult members, women, and the like. Strict sanctions are imposed on invasion of the privacy of these occasions. In addition, there are taboos forbidding anyone other than priests or some special elite from entering sacred quarters or going to sacred places.[43]

PRIVACY AND ISOLATION

The ways in which human beings perceive their situation when they are alone, in a state of privacy, is another important area in which to compare primitive and modern aspects of privacy. The data suggest that fear of isolation leads individuals in human societies to believe that they are never wholly alone, even when they are in physical solitude. Especially in pre-literate societies, men are convinced that they are in the presence and under the observation of supernatural forces, some protecting the individual, some threatening or tempting him, and some simply watching to judge him for a future purpose, perhaps his fate after death.[44] "The longing to communicate with the supernatural" has been said to be "common to all races of mankind." [45] It arises from such factors as the need for protection, the desire for identity, and spiritual longings. Both the idea of being watched and the need to communicate are found in contemporary Judeo-Christian, Moslem, Hindu, and Buddhist systems as much as in the beliefs of primitive peoples about ancestors, spirits, witches, and gods.

In primitive societies a man who was truly alone when he was away from fellow humans was a man in terrible peril, since hostile spirits were believed to be all around—in the bodies of animals, in trees or rocks, in shadows, and even in the air.[46] While primitive man follows various taboos and performs various rituals to avoid offending or disturbing such spirits, they remain all about him, and his prime protection lies in the friendly spirits that go with him and protect him if he retains their favor.[47]

Whatever the manner in which the individual establishes initial contact with the spirits or gods,[48] he will seek privacy in order to communicate with his guardian spirits. Among primitive peoples, this situation usually rests on fear that enemies would locate his spiritual guardian and appropriate it or cause it to go away.[49] In modern societies, periods of seclusion, whether for minutes or days, are assumed to be essential to create the contemplative and holy mood for religious communication. Thus when man seeks to reach his guardian spirit, he seeks privacy—usually by physical solitude in forest, beach, or church but also by psychological isolation through self-induced trance or reverie, or even dreams,[50] if the individual cannot escape the physical presence of others.

The significant point is that men in most organized societies have a belief that they are watched by gods or spirits even when they are physically alone, and that personal communication with guardian spirits requires either physical or psychological privacy if it is to be most effective.

Curiosity and Surveillance

The third element of privacy that seems universal is a tendency on the part of individuals to invade the privacy of others, and of society to engage in surveillance to guard against anti-social conduct. At the individual level, this is based upon the propensity for curiosity that lies in each individual, from the time that as a child he seeks to explore his environment to his later conduct as an adult in wanting to know more than he learns casually about what is "really" happening to others.[51] Again, this is not a phenomenon restricted to man. Studies of monkeys have shown that even when experiments take away such possible motivations as hunger, fear, sex, comfort, and the like, monkeys will actively take things apart, poke their fingers into holes, and exercise active curiosity.[52] Though the degree to which action will be taken to satisfy human curiosity varies according to cultural and personality factors, men and women in all primitive societies try to find out what has been happening to members of their own family, other villagers, other tribal members, and so forth. Gossip, which is only a particular way of obtaining private information to satisfy curiosity, seems to be found in all societies. People want to know what others are doing, especially the great and the powerful, partly as a means of gauging their own performances and desires and partly as a means of vicarious experience, for by satisfying curiosity the individual experiences a sense of pleasure from knowing about exciting or awesome behavior in others.

It has been noted that the tendency to curiosity varies widely among individual members of any society. William McDougal has written that "these differences are apt to be increased during the course of life, the impulse growing weaker for lack of use in those in whom it is innately weak, stronger through exercise in those in whom it is innately strong. In men of the latter type it may become the main source of intellectual energy and effort." [53] And, of course, each society can encourage or discourage such curiosity in its members.

The conduct just described might be called simple curiosity, the day-to-day inquisitiveness or search for explanations that is usually acceptable or even considered beneficial in most societies. There is also "anti-social" curiosity, the phenomenon that takes place when curiosity leads individuals to break the taboos of their society and penetrate the sacred worlds. This is the well-known "insatiable" craving to discover the secret things —to watch the forbidden ceremonies, visit the forbidden places, eat the forbidden fruit, utter the forbidden names. Some persons will take great risks to satisfy this craving.

The commonness of this phenomenon (and the need to control it) is illustrated by the myths in many societies about men and women who have lost precious things, or destroyed themselves, or injured their community because they did not control their curiosity. Western society's cautionary tales of Lot's wife, Pandora opening the box, Eve tasting the apple, Bluebeard's wives opening the forbidden room, Orpheus looking back to Hades, Psyche almost losing Cupid, and others,[54] all have their primitive counterparts, as in the Australian bush myth that death came to mankind because a woman went to a tabooed tree.[55] When normal curiosity is placed alongside the desire of some members of society to penetrate the secrets, it becomes clear that the notion of societies in which people happily "mind their own business" and "let everyone alone" is a fantasy of some libertarian's imagination, not the condition of men in either primitive or modern societies.

Curiosity is only half of the privacy-invading phenomenon, the "individual" half. There is also the universal process of surveillance by authorities to enforce the rules and taboos of the society. Any social system that creates norms—as all human societies do—must have mechanisms for enforcing those norms. Since those who break the rules and taboos must be detected, every society has mechanisms of watching conduct, investigating transgressions, and determining "guilt." In these processes each society sets socially approved machinery for penetrating the privacy of individuals or groups in order to protect personal and group rights and enforce the society's rules and taboos. Society also requires certain acts to be done in the presence of others, in recognition that visibility itself provides a powerful method of enforcing social norms.[56]

The importance of recognizing this "social" half of the universal privacy-invading process is similar to the recognition of individual curiosity—it reminds us that every society which wants to protect its rules and taboos against deviant behavior must have enforcement machinery. Until a society appears in which every individual obeys every rule and taboo and there is no ambiguity to create choices and tensions, there will be family heads, group leaders, religious authorities, and tribal-national authorities who will engage in surveillance to see that private conduct stays within a socially determined degree of conformity with the rules and taboos of that culture. Any discussion of privacy must recognize this fact.

Privacy and the Movement from Primitive to Modern Societies

Finally, the anthropological literature suggests that the movement from primitive to modern societies increases both the physical and psychological opportunities for privacy by individuals and family units and converts these opportunities into choices of values in the socio-political realm. Some anthropologists, such as John Honigmann, have expressed this concept in terms of an increase in the scale of life.

> Increase of scale . . . though necessarily involving greater centralization produces not less but more freedom in personal relations. . . . The freedom of a primitive man is limited at every point by the pressure of neighbors and kinsmen, living and dead, from whom he cannot escape. He has little privacy. His position in society is largely fixed by sex, age, and blood. The freedom of the civilized man from neighbors and kinsmen, and from the immediate past, is much greater than that of the primitive; not only does he live relatively aloof in his house, but he can escape the living by moving.[57]

The developments associated with the rise of modern industrial societies—such as the nuclear family living in individual households, urbanization and the anonymity of city life, mobility in work and residence, the weakening of religious authority over individuals—all provide greater situations of physical and psychological privacy than do the milieu and belief-systems of primitive man. But modern societies have also brought developments that work against the achievement of privacy: density and crowding of populations; large bureaucratic organizational life; popular moods of alienation and insecurity that can lead to desires for new "total" relations; new instruments of physical, psychological, and data surveillance, as discussed in this book; and the modern state, with its military, technological, and propaganda capacities to create and sustain an Orwellian control of life. This suggests that the achievement of privacy for individuals, families, and groups in modern society has become a matter of freedom rather than the product of necessity.

Privacy in Western History: The Struggle to Limit Surveillance by Authorities

The point just made is illustrated concretely by the evolution of Western political and social institutions from Greek and Roman antiquity to the contemporary era.[58] This development has been marked by two competing traditions. One, associated primarily with phenomena like the democratic city-state in ancient Greece, English Protestantism and common-law traditions, and American constitutionalism and property concepts, has been a trend to place limits on the surveillance powers of governmental, religious, and economic authorities in the interest of privacy for individuals, families, and certain social groups in each society. A competing tradition in Western history, associated with societies such as Sparta, the Roman Empire, the medieval Church, and the continental nation-state, continued very broad powers of surveillance for governmental, economic, and religious authorities. The socio-political balance of the former tradition expanded, in each society, the opportunities of individuals and groups to enjoy substantial opportunities for privacy as that was conceived in the particular era. The socio-political balance in the second tradition created a restrictive setting and instilled a competing set of values in its citizenry. Of course, the two traditions sometimes competed within particular societies, as alternative trends, but it is remarkable how constant the dominant themes have been.

It is beyond the scope of this brief summary to describe how the leading elites, general citizens, and the poor and unfree in each of the Western societies studied conceived of privacy, enjoyed or had none of it, and balanced the values of privacy, disclosure, and surveillance in their civic life. The point that can be made, however, is that no society with a reputation for providing liberty in its own time failed to provide limits on the surveillance power of authorities. In this sense, American society in the 1970's faces the task of keeping this tradition meaningful when technological change promises to give public and private authorities the physical power to do what a combination of physical and socio-legal restraints had denied to them as part of our basic social system.

CHAPTER TWO

Privacy in the Modern Democratic State

Privacy and Political Systems

IT IS OBVIOUS that the political system in each society will be a fundamental force in shaping its balance of privacy, since certain patterns of privacy, disclosure, and surveillance are functional necessities for particular kinds of political regime. This is shown most vividly by contrasting privacy in the democratic and the totalitarian state.

The modern totalitarian state relies on secrecy for the regime, but high surveillance and disclosure for all other groups.[1] With their demand for a complete commitment of loyalties to the regime, the literature of both fascism and communism traditionally attacks the idea of privacy as "immoral," "antisocial," and "part of the cult of individualism." This attitude is most strongly expressed in the consolidation phase of a new totalitarian regime.[2] Autonomous units are denied privacy, traditional confidential relationships are destroyed, surveillance systems and informers are widely installed, and thorough dossiers are compiled on millions of citizens. Most important, the individual is not allowed to gain security by conforming without opposition and quietly doing his job. The regime demands active and positive loyalty.[3] These policies, by creating fear and distrust, tend to foster a sense of loneliness and isolation in the citizen; for relief, he turns to identification with the state and its programs so that he may find the satisfactions of affiliation and achievement.

Once the regime has consolidated its power and a new generation has grown up under totalitarian rule, some of the anti-privacy measures are relaxed. A degree of privacy is allowed to families, church, science, and the arts, and police terror is reduced. However, the public has been well conditioned by the old methods, and occasional punishment of those who use their new privacy too aggressively is sufficient to restore

23

the required amount of regime control. Furthermore, the primary surveillance systems of paid and volunteer spies, eavesdropping and watching devices, and strict records control are retained to keep the regime on
its guard.

Just as a social balance favoring disclosure and surveillance over privacy is a functional necessity for totalitarian systems, so a balance that
ensures strong citadels of individual and group privacy and limits both
disclosure and surveillance is a prerequisite for liberal democratic societies. The democratic society relies on publicity as a control over government, and on privacy as a shield for group and individual life. The
reasons for protecting privacy tend to be familiar to citizens of liberal
democracies; thus the specific functions that privacy performs in their
political systems are often left unexpressed.[4] The discussion that follows
will treat these functions briefly.

Liberal democratic theory assumes that a good life for the individual
must have substantial areas of interest apart from political participation
—time devoted to sports, arts, literature, and similar non-political pur-
suits. These areas of individual pursuit prevent the total politicizing of
life and permit other models of success and happiness to serve as alternatives to the political career and the citizenship role. Personal retreats for
securing perspective and critical judgment are also significant for democratic life. A liberal democratic system maintains a strong commitment
to the family as a basic and autonomous unit responsible for important
educational, religious, and moral roles, and therefore the family is allowed to assert claims to physical and legal privacy against both society
and the state. As a result of religious diversity and ideas of toleration,
most democratic systems make religious choice a "private" concern; both
law and custom forbid government controls over the nature and legitimacy of religious affiliations and allow maximum privacy for religious
observance and for religious examination of public policy issues.

Because of the central role played by groups in a democratic society
—they provide opportunities for sociability, expression of independent
ideas, resolution of community conflicts, criticism of government, and
formation of a consensus on public policy—citizens are given wide freedom to join associations and participate in group affairs. To this end,
privacy of membership and intra-group action are protected. Associations themselves are given substantial organizational privacy to achieve
their objectives efficiently and responsibly. Liberal democracy recognizes
the special needs of scholars and scientists to be free of constant community and government examination so that paths to truth and discovery
can be pursued even in directions that offend dominant opinion. Liberal
democratic systems ensure maximum freedom for political choice by
providing a secret ballot to protect the voting process and by forbidding
governmental inquiries into a citizen's past voting record. Through a

network of constitutional, legal, and political restraints, democratic societies protect the individual's person and personality from improper police conduct such as physical brutality, compulsory self-incrimination, and unreasonable searches and seizures. Finally, liberal democratic societies set a balance between government's organizational needs for preparatory and institutional privacy and the need of the press, interest groups, and other governmental agencies for the knowledge of government operations required to keep government conduct responsible.

The functions of privacy in liberal systems do not require that it be an absolute right. The exercise of privacy creates dangers for a democracy that may call for social and legal responses. Private-life commitments can produce such indifference to political and governmental needs on the part of citizens that society must work to bring its members back to participating responsibility. In some situations claims to organizational privacy can give rise to anonymous influences over public life, can overweigh the organized sectors of the citizenry, and can foster the growth of conspiracies that will threaten the democracy's survival. Persons who venture into public debates or civic life sometimes claim an unjustified right to privacy from fair reply or fair criticism. Rules protecting the privacy of the person by forbidding new but not necessarily unreasonable law-enforcement methods can seriously impede protection of the public from crime and lessen the nation's internal security. Privacy may also frustrate the public's "need to know," important behavioral research, and effective administration of government and business. An overly strict cloak of privacy for governmental affairs can cover manipulation of the public, misuse of office, and aggrandizement of power by government agencies. Thus the constant search in democracies must be for the proper boundary line in each specific situation and for an over-all equilibrium that serves to strengthen democratic institutions and processes.

No one has written more sensitively on this problem than the political sociologist, Edward Shils:

> Democracy requires the occasional political participation of most of its citizenry some of the time, and a moderate and dim perceptiveness—as if from the corner of the eye—the rest of the time. It could not function if politics and the state of the social order were always on everyone's mind. If most men, most of the time, regarded themselves as their brother-citizens' keepers, freedom, which flourishes in the indifference of privacy, would be abolished.[5]

Shils sees the "first principle of individualist democracy" to be "the partial autonomy of individuals and of corporate bodies or institutions."

> Autonomy involves the right to make decisions, to promulgate rules of action, to dispose over resources and to recruit

associates in accordance with criteria which the individual or organization deems appropriate to its tasks. The principle of partial autonomy assumes that, by and large, an individual's or a corporate group's life is its own business, that only marginal circumstances justify intrusion by others, and that only more exceptional circumstances justify enforced and entire disclosure, to the eyes of the broader public, of the private affairs of the corporate body or individual.[6]

Shils makes an important distinction between privacy and secrecy. In secrecy, he notes, law forbids the disclosure of information. In privacy, disclosure "is at the discretion of the possessor, and such sanctions as laws provide are directed only against coercive acquisition" by persons to whom the individual does not want to disclose.[7]

In over-all terms, the goal of a liberal society is to achieve a state of political "civility," which Shils defines as a condition in which there is enough privacy to nourish individual creativity and group expression; enough publicity of government affairs to let the public know the facts necessary to form judgments in political matters; and a small area of secrecy for government to preserve the integrity of certain secret information and the privacy of internal policy-making processes.

Variations in Privacy Balances Among Western Democracies

It is important to realize that different historical and political traditions among contemporary democratic nations have created different types of over-all social balances of privacy. Britain has what might be called a "deferential democratic balance," based on England's situation as a small country with a relatively homogeneous population, strong family structure, surviving class system, positive public attitude toward government, and elite systems of education and government service. This combination has produced a democracy in which there is great personal reserve between Englishmen, high personal privacy in home and private associations, and a faith in government that bestows major areas of privacy for government operations. There is also a tradition of tolerating non-conformism which treats much deviant political and social conduct as permissible private action. The balance among privacy, disclosure, and surveillance in Britain is one in which disclosure or surveillance of associational and governmental activities occurs less frequently than would be the case in democratic nations where the patterns of deference toward and trust in the Establishment were not so strong.[8]

West Germany today has what might be called an authoritarian democratic balance. The Bonn Republic defines privacy in a nation where the traditions of democratic self-government came late; authoritarian patterns are deeply rooted in German family structure and social life; both law and government are permeated by high public respect for officialdom and experts; and neither German law nor government showed high capacity, until the post-World War II period, to enforce a meaningful system of civil-liberties restraints on government surveillance practices or harassment of dissent. The result is a democratic state in which privileged elements having the authority of family, wealth, and official position often enjoy substantial privacy and government enjoys great rights of secrecy; but the privacy of the critic and the non-conformist is still not secure in West German life. As the government midnight raid in 1962 on the offices of the *Spiegel* magazine and its acceptance by the German courts illustrate, respect for the privacy of person, home, office, and press still gives way to the claims of official surveillance and disclosure in the German political tradition.[9]

Where does the United States fall in this spectrum of socio-political balances of privacy? I would term it an egalitarian democratic balance, in which the privacy-supporting values of individualism, associational life, and civil liberty are under constant pressure from privacy-denying tendencies toward social egalitarianism, personal activism, and political fundamentalism.[10]

American individualism—with its stress on unique personality in religion, politics, and law—provides a major force for privacy in the United States. This attitude is derived from such factors in American national experience as frontier life, freedom from the feudal heritage of fixed class lines, the Protestant religious base of the nation, its private-property system, and the English legal heritage. Along with the individualist stress has gone a complementary trait of associational life—the formation of numerous voluntary groups to pursue private and public goals. An outcome partly of our heterogeneous immigrant base and partly of the American's search for group warmth in a highly mobile, flexible-status society, associations have long been a distinctive aspect of our culture, with well-established rights of privacy against government surveillance or compulsory public disclosure. A final value supporting privacy is the American principle of civil liberty, with its belief in limits on government and private power, freedom of expression and dissent, and institutionalized mechanisms for enforcing these rights, particularly the legal system and independent courts.

Were these the dominant values of the American socio-political tradition, the privacy balance in the United States might be called wholly libertarian. But, from colonial days down to the present, foreign and native analysts have observed other powerful tendencies in American life that press against privacy and support restrictive rules of disclosure and surveillance. The classic American belief in egalitarianism and "frontier democracy" gives rise to several trends: a denial of various "status rights" to privacy that once were attached to European aristocratic classes and are now claimed by elite groups of culture, intellect, and science; a propensity toward "leveling curiosity" in social and political life that supports a muckraking press and inquisitive interpersonal relationships; and a demand for external conformity of a high order, in the name of a middle-class system in which the blessings of equality and opportunity carry with them a heavy burden of ideological and social conformity.

Pressure on privacy is increased by the American credo of personal activism. Because Americans believe deeply in social progress, especially material progress, and because they are a highly sociable people who like to be psychologically open to others and involved in group affiliations, there has always been a heavy "go-getter" quality to American life. Those who actively "produce" are our heroes (even among professors, religious leaders, and intellectual critics), with public suspicion falling on solitary types, "unsociables," and on contemplation for its own sake unless it is the temporary contemplation of those preparing to produce.

Finally, political fundamentalism has been a major limiting force on privacy in American culture.[11] In one sense this is our nativist tradition, with its elements of xenophobia, religious and racial prejudice, and isolationism. In another facet this is "populist" fundamentalism, the belief that American democracy requires such "open" politics and government that there is no right of privacy for associational groups or government processes. Political fundamentalism also rests on aspects of the American Puritan heritage, with its moral absolutism, censorial watching over the private lives of community members, and the Puritan approach to social welfare, which violates the privacy of the poor and unfortunate in the name of the "good" being done them.

The United States is thus a democracy whose balance of privacy is continually threatened by egalitarian tendencies demanding greater disclosure and surveillance than a libertarian society should permit. For example, the basic balance of privacy in America was clearly threatened during the late 1940's and early 1950's, when American fear over the cold war, atomic holocaust, and internal subversion united with the fundamentalist tradition to produce the McCarthy era.[12] By the late 1950's, however, American society had restored the equilibrium with the containment of radical-right anti-communism.

Variations in Privacy Patterns by "Sensory Cultures"

Privacy also differs from nation to nation in terms of the impact of culture on interpersonal relations. The idea that notions of privacy vary widely from culture to culture has been treated by anthropologists,[13] psychologists,[14] and sociologists,[15] but the most extensive recent work on this theme comes from the cultural anthropologist Edward Hall, who states that people in different cultures experience the world differently not only in terms of language[16] but also with their senses. They "inhabit different sensory worlds," [17] affecting the way they relate to one another in space, in matters ranging from their concepts of architecture and furniture arrangement to their setting of social distance in interpersonal contact.

To compare these differences, Hall studied a number of contemporary cultures to see how their notions of sensory pleasure and displeasure affected their definitions of interpersonal space. First, he compared the dominant norms of American society, as set by the white middle and upper classes, with three European cultures with which the American middle and upper classes are most closely linked historically and culturally—Germany, England, and France. Germans, Hall found, demand individual and enclosed places to achieve a sense of privacy. This need for individual "Lebensraum" is expressed in closed doors to business and government offices, fenced yards and separate closed rooms in the home, discomfort at having to share facilities with others, and strict "trespass" rules regulating the person-to-person distance on social, business, and ceremonial occasions. In addition, in defining private space around each individual, or around a group talking in public, or in the areas surrounding a private home, Germans assert a larger sphere of private territory than cultures such as the American or British. This need is symbolized by the German law which forbids photographing strangers in public without their consent. In contrast, Americans are happy with open doors in offices, do not require fencing or screening of their homes to feel comfortable, and are far more informal in their rules of approach, order, and distance. An American does not feel that a person walking close to a group or a home has "intruded" on privacy; Germans will feel this a trespass.

English norms of privacy, Hall found, lie between the American and the German. The English accomplish with reserve what Germans require doors, walls, and trespass rules to enforce. Because English children in the middle and upper classes do not usually have separate rooms but share the nursery with brothers and sisters until they go away to boarding school and live in dormitories, the Englishman grows up with a concept of preserving his individual privacy within shared space rather than by solitary quarters. He learns to rely on reserve, on cues to others to leave him alone. This habit is illustrated in later life by the fact that many English political and business figures do not have private offices; members of Parliament, for example, do not occupy individual offices, and they often meet their constituents on the terrace or in the lobbies of the House of Commons. Englishmen speak more softly and direct the voice more carefully so that it can be heard only by the person being spoken to, and the eyes are focused directly during conversation. Where an American seeking privacy goes to a private room and shuts the door, an Englishman stops talking, and this signal for privacy is respected by family, friends, and associates. By contrast, when an American stops talking, it is usually a sign that something is wrong among the persons present, and silence is often a signal for punishment in American relations. Hall terms the English pattern an "internalized privacy mechanism" in contrast with the "physical privacy screen" of the American. Furthermore, where Americans use privacy to define social status (the private office, the private secretary, and the like), the English social system firmly determines a person's position, and privacy is not needed for this purpose. Similarly, Americans "neighbor" heavily by propinquity—who lives next door or down the block—while the English neighbor by class and set firm barriers against overtures from persons who merely reside close by.

Hall found that the influence of Mediterranean culture set the French apart from the American, English, and German patterns. Mediterranean peoples pack more closely together in public, enjoy physical contact in public places, and are more involved with each other in sensory terms than more northern peoples. On the other hand, while the American brings friends and acquaintances into his home readily, the French home is reserved for family privacy and is rarely opened to outsiders, even co-workers of long standing or acquaintances from social functions.

The work by Hall and others makes it clear that the way individuals define interpersonal privacy is heavily affected by each culture's conceptions of sensory relations. This holds true even of sub-cultures within one country. Attitudes toward privacy on the part of lower-class Negro-Americans, Puerto Ricans, and American Indians make these groups much more involved with one another in sensory terms than middle- and upper-class Americans. We do "inhabit different sensory worlds," and a contact between two persons that is "too close" in one culture may be "too remote" in another. What "respects privacy" in one can "intrude" in another.

Privacy and Individual Life in Western Democracies

Recognizing the differences that political and sensory cultures make in setting norms of privacy among modern societies, it is still possible to describe the general functions that privacy performs for individuals and groups in Western democratic nations. Before describing these, it is helpful to explain in somewhat greater detail the four basic states of individual privacy that were mentioned briefly in the Introduction to Part I: solitude, intimacy, anonymity, and reserve.

The first state of privacy is solitude; here the individual is separated from the group and freed from the observation of other persons. He may be subjected to jarring physical stimuli, such as noise, odors, and vibrations. His peace of mind may continue to be disturbed by physical sensations of heat, cold, itching, and pain. He may believe that he is being observed by God or some supernatural force, or fear that some authority is secretly watching him. Finally, in solitude he will be especially subject to that familiar dialogue with the mind or conscience. But, despite all these physical or psychological intrusions, solitude is the most complete state of privacy that individuals can achieve.

In the second state of privacy, intimacy, the individual is acting as part of a small unit that claims and is allowed to exercise corporate seclusion so that it may achieve a close, relaxed, and frank relationship between two or more individuals. Typical units of intimacy are husband and wife, the family, a friendship circle, or a work clique. Whether close contact brings relaxed relations or abrasive hostility depends on the personal interaction of the members, but without intimacy a basic need of human contact would not be met.[18]

The third state of privacy, anonymity, occurs when the individual is in public places or performing public acts but still seeks, and finds, freedom from identification and surveillance. He may be riding a subway, attending a ball game, or walking the streets; he is among people and knows that he is being observed; but unless he is a well-known celebrity, he does not expect to be personally identified and held to the full rules of behavior and role that would operate if he were known to those observing him. In this state the individual is able to merge into the "situational landscape." Knowledge or fear that one is under systematic observation in public places destroys the sense of relaxation and freedom that men seek in open spaces and public arenas.

Anonymous relations give rise to what Georg Simmel called the "phenomenon of the stranger," the person who "often received the most surprising openness—confidences which sometimes have the character of a confessional and which would be carefully withheld from a more closely related person." [19] In this aspect of anonymity the individual can express himself freely because he knows the stranger will not continue in his life and that, although the stranger may give an objective response to the questions put to him, he is able to exert no authority or restraint over the individual.

Still another kind of anonymity is the publication of ideas anonymously. Here the individual wants to present some idea publicly to the community or to a segment of it, but does not want to be universally identified at once as the author—especially not by the authorities, who may be forced to take action if they "know" the perpetrator. The core of each of these types of anonymous action is the desire of individuals for times of "public privacy."

Reserve, the fourth and most subtle state of privacy, is the creation of a psychological barrier against unwanted intrusion; this occurs when the individual's need to limit communication about himself is protected by the willing discretion of those surrounding him. Most of our lives are spent not in solitude or anonymity but in situations of intimacy and in group settings where we are known to others. Even in the most intimate relations, communication of self to others is always incomplete and is based on the need to hold back some parts of one's self as either too personal and sacred or too shameful and profane to express. This circumstance gives rise to what Simmel called "reciprocal reserve and indifference," the relation that creates "mental distance" to protect the personality.[20] This creation of mental distance—a variant of the concept of "social distance"—takes place in every sort of relationship under rules of social etiquette; it expresses the individual's choice to withhold or disclose information—the choice that is the dynamic aspect of privacy in daily interpersonal relations. Simmel identified this tension within the individual as being between "self-revelation and self-restraint" and, within society, between "trespass and discretion." The manner in which individuals claim reserve and the extent to which it is respected or disregarded by others is at the heart of securing meaningful privacy in the crowded, organization-dominated settings of modern industrial society and urban life, and varies considerably from culture to culture.[21]

The Functions of Individual Privacy

This analysis of the various states of privacy is useful in discussing the basic question of the functions privacy performs for individuals in democratic societies.[22] These can also be grouped conveniently under four headings—personal autonomy, emotional release, self-evaluation, and limited and protected communication. Since every human being is a whole organism, these four functions constantly flow into one another, but their separation for analytical purposes helps to clarify the important choices about individual privacy that American law may have to make in the coming decade.

Personal Autonomy. In democratic societies there is a fundamental belief in the uniqueness of the individual, in his basic dignity and worth as a creature of God and a human being, and in the need to maintain social processes that safeguard his sacred individuality.[23] Psychologists and sociologists have linked the development and maintenance of this sense of individuality to the human need for autonomy—the desire to avoid being manipulated or dominated wholly by others.

One of the accepted ways of representing the individual's need for an ultimate core of autonomy, as expressed by such theorists as Simmel, R. E. Park, Kurt Lewin, and Erving Goffman,[24] has been to describe the individual's relations with others in terms of a series of "zones" or "regions" of privacy leading to a "core self." This core self is pictured as an inner circle surrounded by a series of larger concentric circles. The inner circle shelters the individual's "ultimate secrets"—those hopes, fears, and prayers that are beyond sharing with anyone unless the individual comes under such stress that he must pour out these ultimate secrets to secure emotional relief. Under normal circumstances no one is admitted to this sanctuary of the personality. The next circle outward contains "intimate secrets," those that can be willingly shared with close relations, confessors, or strangers who pass by and cannot injure. The next circle is open to members of the individual's friendship group. The series continues until it reaches the outer circles of casual conversation and physical expression that are open to all observers.

The most serious threat to the individual's autonomy is the possibility that someone may penetrate the inner zone and learn his ultimate secrets, either by physical or psychological means. This deliberate penetration of the individual's protective shell, his psychological armor, would leave him naked to ridicule and shame and would put him under the control of those who knew his secrets. Autonomy is also threatened by those who penetrate the core self because they do not recognize the importance of ultimate privacy or think that the casual and uninvited help they may be rendering compensates for the violation.

Each person is aware of the gap between what he wants to be and what he actually is, between what the world sees of him and what he knows to be his much more complex reality. In addition, there are aspects of himself that the individual does not fully understand but is slowly exploring and shaping as he develops. Every individual lives behind a mask in this manner; indeed, the first etymological meaning of the word "person" was "mask,"[25] indicating both the conscious and expressive presentation of the self to a social audience. If this mask is torn off and the individual's real self bared to a world in which everyone else still wears his mask and believes in masked performances, the individual can be seared by the hot light of selective, forced exposure. The numerous instances of suicides and nervous breakdowns resulting from such exposures by government investigation, press stories, and even published research constantly remind a free society that only grave social need can ever justify destruction of the privacy which guards the individual's ultimate autonomy.

The autonomy that privacy protects is also vital to the development of individuality and consciousness of individual choice in life. Leontine Young has noted that "without privacy there is no individuality. There are only types. Who can know what he thinks and feels if he never has the opportunity to be alone with his thoughts and feelings?" [26] This development of individuality is particularly important in democratic societies, since qualities of independent thought, diversity of views, and non-conformity are considered desirable traits for individuals. Such independence requires time for sheltered experimentation and testing of ideas, for preparation and practice in thought and conduct, without fear of ridicule or penalty, and for the opportunity to alter opinions before making them public. The individual's sense that it is he who decides when to "go public" is a crucial aspect of his feeling of autonomy. Without such time for incubation and growth, through privacy, many ideas and positions would be launched into the world with dangerous prematurity. As Robert MacIver has stated, "Everything that grows first of all does so in the darkness before it sends its shoots out into the light." [27]

Summing up the importance of privacy for political liberty, Clinton Rossiter has also stressed the feature of autonomy:

> Privacy is a special kind of independence, which can be understood as an attempt to secure autonomy in at least a few personal and spiritual concerns, if necessary in defiance of all the pressures of modern society. . . . [I]t seeks to erect an unbreachable wall of dignity and reserve against the entire world. The free man is the private man, the man who still keeps some of his thoughts and judgments entirely to himself, who feels no over-riding compulsion to share everything of value with others, not even those he loves and trusts.[28]

Emotional Release. Life in society generates such tensions for the individual that both physical and psychological health demand periods of privacy for various types of emotional release. At one level, such relaxation is required from the pressure of playing social roles. Social scientists agree that each person constantly plays a series of varied and multiple roles, depending on his audience and behavioral situation.[29] On any given day a man may move through the roles of stern father, loving husband, car-pool comedian, skilled lathe operator, union steward, water-cooler flirt, and American Legion committee chairman—all psychologically different roles that he adopts as he moves from scene to scene on the social stage. Like actors on the dramatic stage, Goffman has noted,[30] individuals can sustain roles only for reasonable periods of time, and no individual can play indefinitely, without relief, the variety of roles that life demands. There have to be moments "off stage" when the individual can be "himself": tender, angry, irritable, lustful, or dream-filled. Such moments may come in solitude; in the intimacy of family, peers, or woman-to-woman and man-to-man relaxation; in the anonymity of park or street; or in a state of reserve while in a group. Privacy in this aspect gives individuals, from factory workers to Presidents, a chance to lay their masks aside for rest. To be always "on" would destroy the human organism.

Closely related to this form of release is the need of individuals for respite from the emotional stimulation of daily life. For most persons the constant experiences and surprises of active life are what make it worth living; indeed, we all search for richer and more varied stimulation. But the whirlpool of active life must lead to some quiet waters, if only so that the appetite can be whetted for renewed social engagement. Privacy provides the change of pace that makes life worth savoring.

Another form of emotional release is provided by the protection privacy gives to minor non-compliance with social norms.[31] Some norms are formally adopted—perhaps as law—which society really expects many persons to break. This ambivalence produces a situation in which almost everyone does break some social or institutional norms—for example, violating traffic laws, breaking sexual mores, cheating on expense accounts, overstating income-tax deductions, or smoking in rest rooms when this is prohibited. Although society will usually punish the most flagrant abuses, it tolerates the great bulk of the violations as "permissible" deviations. If there were no privacy to permit society to ignore these deviations—if all transgressions were known—most persons in society would be under organizational discipline or in jail, or could be manipulated by threats of such action. The firm expectation of having privacy for permissible deviations is a distinguishing characteristic of life in a free society. At a lesser but still important level, privacy also allows individuals to deviate temporarily from social etiquette when alone or among intimates, as by putting feet on desks, cursing, letting one's face go slack, or scratching wherever one itches.

Another aspect of release is the "safety-valve" function afforded by privacy. Most persons need to give vent to their anger at "the system," "city hall," "the boss," and various others who exercise authority over them, and to do this in the intimacy of family or friendship circles, or in private papers, without fear of being held responsible for such comments. This is very different from freedom of speech or press, which involves publicly voiced criticism without fear of interference by government and subject only to private suit. Rather, the aspect of release concerned here involves commentary that may be wholly unfair, frivolous, nasty, and libelous, but is never socially measured because it is uttered in privacy. Without the aid of such release in accommodating the daily abrasions with authorities, most people would experience serious emotional pressure. Even Presidents and other high public officials have been well known, under the strains of office, to lash out momentarily in angry commentary that they really do not mean. Their privacy in such moments is respected because society knows that these occasional outbursts make possible the measured and responsible speech that is produced for public presentation.

Still another aspect of release through privacy arises in the management of bodily and sexual functions. American society has strong codes requiring privacy for evacuation, dressing the body, and arranging the body while in public; and privacy for sexual relations is deeply rooted in our culture. Though poverty may produce crowded conditions which deny privacy for bodily and sexual functions, it is not accidental that surveillance of such functions by outsiders is practiced with social approval only in what sociologists call "total institutions" [32]—such as jails, mental institutions, and monasteries—or on volunteers in medical or behavioral-science experiments. Even then, prisoners and patients usually complain about being watched and seek ways to escape the constant surveillance of guards.[33]

Finally, emotional release through privacy plays an important part in individual life at times of loss, shock, or sorrow. In such moments society provides comfort both through communal support by gatherings of friends and through respect for the privacy of the individual and his intimates. A similar need is often felt by individuals in public life who have suffered defeats or loss of face and need to retire from public view to regroup their psychological forces. Reporters, legislative committees, and social scientists do not always respect the claim of restorative privacy by public figures in temporary distress, but it is striking how often the rules of "decency" do provide substantial privacy in these circumstances. Privacy also performs a protective function at moments of less intense stress, during the periods of anxiety and uncertainty which are part of daily life.

Self-Evaluation. Every individual needs to integrate his experiences into a meaningful pattern and to exert his individuality on events. To carry on such self-evaluation, privacy is essential.

At the intellectual level, individuals need to process the information that is constantly bombarding them, information that cannot be processed while they are still "on the go." Alan Bates has written that privacy in such circumstances enables a person to "assess the flood of information received, to consider alternatives and possible consequences so that he may then act as consistently and appropriately as possible." [34]

Privacy serves not only a processing but a planning need, by providing a time "to anticipate, to recast, and to originate."[35] This is particularly true of creative persons. Studies of creativity show that it is in reflective solitude and even "daydreaming" during moments of reserve that most creative "non-verbal" thought takes place. At such moments the individual runs ideas and impressions through his mind in a flow of associations; the active presence of others tends to inhibit this process.[36] For example, the Yale studies of "brain-storming" found that group-think sessions produced fewer ideas quantitatively than periods of individual, private work by the same number of people.[37] Many studies and autobiographies have described the "creative loneliness" needed by artists and writers to produce their works.[38]

The evaluative function of privacy also has a major moral dimension —the exercise of conscience by which the individual "repossesses himself." While people often consider the moral consequences of their acts during the course of daily affairs, it is primarily in periods of privacy that they take a moral inventory of ongoing conduct and measure current performance against personal ideals. For many persons this process is a religious exercise. Religious contemplation, said Coe, was a time for "organizing the self,"[39] and William James called religion the experience of "individual men in their solitude."[40] Thus, periods for rumination over past events and for communication with oneself have been said to be "institutionalized in all societies."[41] The tradition of religious retreats is another means of providing a time and setting for moral inventory. Even for an individual who is not a religious believer, privacy serves to bring the conscience into play, for, when alone, he must find a way to continue living with himself.

A final contribution of privacy to evaluation is its role in the proper timing of the decision to move from private reflection or intimate conversation to a more general publication of acts and thoughts. This is the process by which one tests his own evaluations against the responses of his peers. Given the delicacy of a person's relations with intimates and associates, deciding when and to what extent to disclose facts about himself—and to put others in the position of receiving such confidences—is a matter of enormous concern in personal interaction, almost as important as whether to disclose at all.

Limited and Protected Communication. The greatest threat to civilized social life would be a situation in which each individual was utterly candid in his communications with others, saying exactly what he knew or felt at all times. The havoc done to interpersonal relations by children, saints, mental patients, and adult "innocents" is legendary.

In real life, among mature persons all communication is partial and limited, based on the complementary relation between reserve and discretion that has already been discussed. Limited communication is particularly vital in urban life, with its heightened stimulation, crowded environment, and continuous physical and psychological confrontations between individuals who do not know one another in the extended, softening fashion of small-town life. Reserved communication is the means of psychic self-preservation for men in the metropolis.[42]

Privacy for limited and protected communication has two general aspects. First, it provides the individual with the opportunities he needs for sharing confidences and intimacies with those he trusts—spouse, "the family," personal friends, and close associates at work.[43] The individual discloses because he knows that his confidences will be held, and because he knows that breach of confidence violates social norms in a civilized society. "A friend," said Emerson, "is someone before . . . [whom] I can think aloud." [44] In addition, the individual often wants to secure counsel from persons with whom he does not have to live daily after disclosing his confidences. He seeks professionally objective advice from persons whose status in society promises that they will not later use his distress to take advantage of him. To protect freedom of limited communication, such relationships—with doctors, lawyers, ministers, psychiatrists, psychologists, and others—are given varying but important degrees of legal privilege against forced disclosure. The privacy given to the religious confessional in democratic societies is well known, but the need for confession is so general that those without religious commitment have institutionalized their substitute in psychiatric and counseling services. Confessional relief also comes through the stranger, to whom communication is limited because what he is told will not be repeated in the "home sphere" of the person who has confided in him. For this reason, certain places where the real world is seemingly held in suspension "outside"—such as trains, boats, and bars—lend themselves to free conversation.

In its second general aspect, privacy through limited communication serves to set necessary boundaries of mental distance in interpersonal situations ranging from the most intimate to the most formal and public. In marriage, for example, husbands and wives need to retain islands of privacy in the midst of their intimacy if they are to preserve a saving respect and mystery in the relation. These elements of reserved communication will range from small matters, involving management of money, personal habits, and outside activities, to the more serious levels of past experiences and inner secrets of personality. Successful marriages usually depend on the discovery of the ideal line between privacy and revelation and on the respect of both partners for that line.[45] In work situations, mental distance is necessary so that the relations of superior and subordinate do not slip into an intimacy which would create a lack of respect and an impediment to directions and correction. Thus, physical arrangements shield superiors from constant observation by subordinates, and social etiquette forbids conversations or off-duty contacts that are "too close" for the work relationship. Similar distance is observed in relations between professor and student, parent and child, minister and communicant, and many others.

Psychological distance is also used in crowded settings to provide privacy for the participants of group and public encounters; a complex but well-understood etiquette of privacy is part of our social scenario. Bates remarked that "we request or recognize withdrawal into privacy in facial expressions, bodily gestures, conventions like changing the subject, and by exchanging meaning in ways which exclude others present, such as private words, jokes, winks, and grimaces." [46] We learn to ignore people and to be ignored by them as a way of achieving privacy in subways, on streets, and in the "non-presence" of servants or children. There are also social conventions within various sub-groups in the population establishing fairly clearly the proper and improper matters for discussion among intimates, workmates, persons on a bus, and other groups. And, as James Thurber showed so engagingly, the individual can simply go off into mental privacy when he needs to, as the Walter Mittys of society work off their aggressions and dream their fantasies.[47]

The Individual's Quest for Intra-Psychic Balance

So far, the discussion has stressed the individual's need for privacy and the functions privacy performs in his personal life. But privacy is neither a self-sufficient state nor an end in itself, even for the hermit and the recluse. It is basically an instrument for achieving individual goals of self-realization. As such, it is only part of the individual's complex and shifting system of social needs, part of the way he adjusts his emotional mechanism to the barrage of personal and social stimuli that he encounters in daily life. Individuals have needs for disclosure and companionship every bit as important as their needs for privacy. As ancient and modern philosophers agree, man is a social animal, a gregarious being whose need for affiliation marks his conduct in every society. Thus, at one hour a person may want lively companionship and group affiliation; at another moment, the intimacy of family or close friends; at another, the anonymity of the city street or the movie; and at still other times, to be totally alone and unobserved. To be left in privacy when one wants companionship is as uncomfortable as the inability to have privacy when one craves it.

This balance of privacy and disclosure will be powerfully influenced, of course, by both the society's cultural norms and the particular individual's status and life situation. In American society, for example, which prefers "activism" over contemplation,[48] people tend to use their leisure time to "do things" rather than to rest, read, and think in privacy. And, in any society, differences in occupation, socio-economic level, and religious commitment are broad conditioning factors in the way each person allots his time and tunes his emotional wave length for privacy.

This fact raises an interesting question about "status tensions" and privacy in America. Many claims to privacy or expectations of receiving privacy arise out of certain statuses—rich man, university professor, corporation executive, lawyer, and the like. Privacy rights and roles grow out of the legitimacy and prestige of these statuses. Yet, as noted earlier, American society from its inception has had a commitment to egalitarianism and social democracy that presses against the kind of privacy rules that are so well defined and well observed in European systems, which developed out of feudal traditions and still have definite class lines. In the United States this situation means that both the individual who occupies a high-status position and the low-status persons who come in contact with him are not always sure of what privacy rules ought to apply, of where proper reserve and discretion begin. This egalitarian-democratic ethos accounts for the "openness" and disregard for privacy in so many areas of American interpersonal life, but it makes the individual's adjustment of his intra-psychic privacy balance a more experimental and fluid matter than in most other systems, including most European democracies.

In general, however, all individuals are constantly engaged in an attempt to find sufficient privacy to serve their general social roles as well as their individual needs of the moment. Either too much or too little privacy can create imbalances which seriously jeopardize the individual's well-being. Too much privacy can be a result of social or physical conditions that lie largely beyond the individual's power to control. Thus, it can come from forced physical separation from society, as in the experiences of children raised by animals away from human society or the reactions of volunteers in sensory-deprivation experiments. More relevant is the solitary confinement of the prisoner or the isolation of explorers and disaster victims; memoirs and scholarly studies document the depression, hallucinations, and even mental collapse that such isolation can create.[49] Or it may be the effect of life in complex, impersonal, industrial societies; many studies testify to the sense of rootlessness, anomie, and psychological isolation that this evokes in segments of the citizenry.[50] Although the individual has no control over the conditions creating too much privacy in these situations, whether or not he adapts successfully depends on his own emotional capacities.

Too much privacy can also result from the individual's failure to adjust his own life situation to achieve a healthy emotional state, even though he enjoys "normal" social conditions. Karen Horney has described the individual who invokes an unnatural degree of privacy because he cannot relate successfully to daily life as one of the three major types of neurotics in our society.

[This type of neurotic] is like a person in a hotel room who rarely removes the "Do-Not-Disturb" sign from his door. Even books may be regarded as intruders, as something from outside. Any question put to him about his personal life may shock him; he tends to shroud himself in a veil of secrecy. A patient once told me that at the age of forty-five he still resented the idea of God's omniscience quite as much as when his mother told him that God could look through the shutters and see him biting his fingernails.[51]

At its extreme, this state produces the total privacy of the mental patient, alone in a self-sealed world as only the mad can be totally alone in the midst of society.

The opposite pole of imbalance is too little privacy. Here, too, some factors beyond the individual's effective control limit his opportunities for a "normal" privacy balance. These may be environmental factors such as crowded and noisy living conditions; economic factors such as poverty that make privacy less important than the satisfaction of more basic family needs; political factors such as widespread government surveillance of speech and communications; business and social factors such as intrusions into the home by telephone solicitors, door-to-door salesmen, and opinion surveyors; or cultural pressures such as the ethic of activism and the pressure on middle-class persons to participate in group affairs. Such limits on privacy in democratic societies require the individual to adjust his psychological balances, to find sufficient privacy *despite* these limiting factors. Thus, people in crowded living quarters find privacy outdoors—in the streets of cities, in the corners of bars, in motion-picture houses, and in a host of "public" places where the necessary solitude, intimacy, anonymity, and reserve can be found. Individuals find ways to bypass governmental surveillance of their private messages. Householders slam doors on solicitors or put "No Trespassing" signs on their property. These attempts to secure privacy even under hostile social conditions illustrate the quest for intra-psychic balance at work.

Too little privacy can also be present as a result of the way individuals manage their own lives. Nervous breakdowns and physical collapses from overwork often have as one major ingredient the lack of that emotional relief from stimulation which is a function of privacy. This factor is often much more basic to the collapse than physical strain. Psychiatrists have described the mental conflicts created by individuals who deliberately avoid solitude because they do not want to confront themselves with the moral implications of their own conduct; constant activity is an attempt to silence conscience by those who are abnormally afraid of being alone.[52] A similar phenomenon takes when people reject normal levels of intimacy with those close to them.[53] In another type of neurotic conduct the individual, to avoid "threatening" normal intimacies, immerses himself in group activity; this is a retreat into public life.

The basic point is that each individual must, within the larger context of his culture, his status, and his personal situation, make a continuous adjustment between his needs for solitude and companionship; for intimacy and general social intercourse; for anonymity and responsible participation in society; for reserve and disclosure. A free society leaves this choice to the individual, for this is the core of the "right of individual privacy"—the right of the individual to decide for himself, with only extraordinary exceptions in the interests of society, when and on what terms his acts should be revealed to the general public.

The Functions of Organizational Privacy

Having discussed privacy thus far in terms of individuals, we turn now to privacy and group life. The approach adopted here involves making two judgments about the issue of "organizational privacy." First, the legal and social claims to privacy given to organizations by American society are more than a protection of the collective privacy rights of the members as individuals. Organizational privacy is needed if groups are to play the role of independent and responsible agents that is assigned to them in democratic societies. Among these are the satisfaction of needs for affiliation in large-scale society; the expression of basic interests felt by sub-groups in the community; the operation of civic enterprises by private rather than government management; criticism of government policies; and measurement of public sentiment on issues and policies between elections. Just as with individuals, and subject to the same process of social limitation, organizations need the right to decide when and to what extent their acts and decisions should be made public. The need to protect society from the "multiplier effect" of concerted activity by large numbers of individuals affects the setting of the balance, but does not eliminate the legitimate claim to group privacy.

Second, the term organization will be used to include public as well as private bodies. All organizations—from law firms and fraternal groups to political parties, courts, juries, legislatures, and executive agencies—are similar in that they have an organizational purpose, a separate entity, and internal rules and procedures. Government agencies have the same basic need to be free from constant and immediate public exposure as do corporations, unions, universities, religious bodies, and civic groups. Each government agency must also resist intrusions into its privacy by other government agencies under our separation-of-powers, checks-and-balances system of government. Though the traditional democratic belief in an open governmental process should operate to weight the balance between privacy and disclosure in favor of earlier disclosure and greater visibility for certain aspects of government's decisional process, it should not be seen as denying the claim to privacy.

The most helpful way to analyze the functions privacy performs for organizations in a democratic society is to apply the same four categories used for individuals and test these for the organizational setting.

ORGANIZATIONAL AUTONOMY

The lack of privacy for certain core secrets can threaten the independence or autonomous life of an organization much as it does that of an individual. The diplomatic, military, economic, and scientific secrets of government agencies are protected by law because public disclosure of such information under conditions of international conflict could threaten national security and survival. Business groups often have trade secrets—special processes or formulas—on which their commercial success rests. The law will usually protect these secrets against disclosure to competitors by former employees or through business espionage, and against demands for access by labor unions or legislative committees. Wilbert Moore and Melvin Tumin have noted that privacy for confidential business decisions is an absolute requirement of a competitive economic system; without such privacy, business units could not function with the individual autonomy that our anti-trust laws demand.[54]

Membership privacy represents a core secret for many civic organizations, especially those advocating controversial ideas. Forced public disclosure of members' names could lead to social sanctions against the members and, therefore, to wholesale defections that could destroy the organization. In democratic societies a legal right to privacy for membership lists and officers' names has been given to labor unions, religious and political bodies, and civil-rights organizations, especially when these groups were facing hostile community pressures. Such a right is often denied to organizations which are considered "illegitimate" in democratic theory, as with groups using violence (such as the Ku Klux Klan) or conspiratorial groups linked to foreign powers (such as Communist and Fascist parties).

Still another aspect of privacy for organizational autonomy involves the secret rituals of private groups. Many legitimate organizations, particularly the fraternal and social type, have secret rituals that provide the bond of acceptance and cohesiveness within the group. For outsiders to obtain and publish these rituals would undermine the sense of exclusiveness and identity that the ritual provides to the organization's members. Of course, if the ritual involved unlawful acts (such as torture or obscenities) or was itself seditious (such as burning the American flag), the press and government would be justified in investigating such acts. In the normal circumstance, however, privacy of ritual is respected because it provides an important psychological satisfaction in certain types of organization that fill approved social needs.

Government policies of non-interference with the internal executive and disciplinary procedures of such private organizations as societies, clubs, churches, and associations is based on a belief that autonomy for these groups furnishes experience in self-government and acts as a check on government power. Allowing private self-government also avoids the necessity of continued government involvement in the internal regulation and factional disputes of private groups unless these decisions have so great an effect on public interests that government must intervene.

Where to set the boundaries of organizational privacy remains a continuing topic of debate. "Full exposure" has been advocated by commentators who believe that the identities of those who attempt to influence public policy, such as organized lobbyists, ought to be known to the public in a free society. Claims to membership privacy have at times been rejected by the courts, the decision turning on the illegitimacy of those organizations' goals and methods of operation.[55] Yet this requirement of visibility has been rejected in other areas where it too narrowly constricts organizational autonomy, as in the labor-union, civil-rights, and political-lobbying areas. These rulings indicate that society must constantly set a balance between those ultimate secrets it feels may legitimately be kept private and those it does not. An enterprising press or social-science study may increase public wisdom by the penetration of the "inside affairs" of groups, but too much exposure can create distrust and hamper group activity. Permitting too much classification of information by government agencies can jeopardize democratic control over public policy; but too little may endanger national security.

RELEASE FROM PUBLIC ROLES

Just as individuals need privacy to obtain release from playing social roles and to engage in permissible deviations from social norms, so organizations need internal privacy to conduct their affairs without having to keep up a "public face." This involves, in particular, the gap between public myth and organizational reality. For the same basic reasons that standards of moral expectation are set for individuals, society builds images of how universities, churches, labor unions, corporations, and government agencies ought to operate. These idealized portraits are usually based on notions of rational decision making, fair-minded discussion, direct representation of membership viewpoints by the leadership, dedication to public over personal interest, and orderly control of the problems assigned to the organization's care. In fact, much of the behavior of both private and public organizations involves irrational decision-making procedures, harsh and/or comic discussions of "outside" people and causes, personal motivations for decisions, and highly disorderly procedures to cope with problems seen by the organizations as intractable or insoluble. Despite press and social-science exposures of the true workings of organizations,[56] society at large persists in believing that these are departures from a norm and that properly led and dedicated organizations will adhere to the ideal procedures.

Given this penchant of society for idealized models and the far different realities of organizational life, privacy is necessary so that organizations may do the divergent part of their work out of public view. The adage that one should not visit the kitchen of a restaurant if one wants to enjoy the food is applied daily in the grant of privacy to organizations for their staging processes. Privacy affords the relaxation which enables those who are part of a common venture, public or private, to communicate freely with one another and to accomplish their tasks with a minimum of social dissembling for "outside" purposes. Without such privacy the operations of law firms, businesses, hospitals, welfare agencies, civic groups, and a host of other organizations would be seriously impaired.

The arguments for operational privacy made by public executive agencies are often criticized by legislative overseers as "undemocratic" and in contrast to legislative "openness." It is helpful, then, to note that legislative bodies themselves have such a need for privacy and exercise it constantly. From 1953 to 1960, between 30 and 41 per cent of the sessions of congressional committees were closed "executive" meetings from which press and public were excluded.[57] Robert Luce, an experienced observer of legislative behavior, has noted:

> Behind closed doors nobody can talk to the galleries or the newspaper reporters. Buncombe is not worthwhile. Only sincerity counts. Men drop their masks. They argue to, not through, each other. That is one reason why it would be a calamity if the demand for pitiless publicity of committee deliberations should ever prevail. . . . [P]ublicity would lessen the chance for concessions, the compromises, without which wise legislation cannot in practice be secured. Men are averse to changing their positions or yielding anything when many eyes are watching. It is in the conference room that agreements are reached, results accomplished.[58]

In the judicial sphere, American law institutionalizes privacy for jury deliberations, and judicial practice provides private conferences for opposing lawyers at the bench or in the judge's chambers. Judicial decisions are reached in privacy, and the refusal to tell the press or other government agencies what went on at the judges' conference has been fundamental to our judicial system. Even the publication of intra-conference discussions years later by scholarly biographers has been condemned by many commentators as a threat to the proper functioning of the judicial conference. "[T]he free give and take of a secret conference may dry up," John P. Frank has written, "if the justices feel that what may be highly biased accounts by some of their brothers are going to find their way into the history books." [59]

Of course, society decides that certain phases of activity by some organizations are so charged with public interest that they must be carried out in the open, with full visibility. This is illustrated by rules requiring public agencies or private organizations to conduct certain proceedings in public (such as regulatory-agency hearings or union elections), to publish certain facts about their internal procedures (such as corporate accounting reports and other public-record requirements for private groups), and to open their premises to representatives of the public for periodic inspection of procedures (such as visiting committees of universities and government inspectors checking safety practices or the existence of discrimination in personnel policies).

EVALUATIVE PERIODS FOR DECISION MAKING

Just as individuals need privacy to evaluate what is happening to them and to decide how to respond, so organizations need privacy to plan their courses of action.

Planning by organizations involves both periods of reflection for considering long-range implications of organizational policies and the frank process of internal debate needed to reach day-to-day decisions. In both situations privacy is essential if the individuals involved are to be able to contemplate and to express their views with primary loyalty to the organization. If all written memos and policy discussions were subject to immediate publication, or if private organizations knew themselves to be under continuous monitoring by government agents, much of the debate would automatically become formalized. Gradual accommodation of divergent views within the organization would be hampered.

It is useful to recall that the Constitution of the United States was itself written in a closed meeting in Philadelphia; press and outsiders were excluded, and the participants were sworn to secrecy. Historians are agreed that if the convention's work had been made public contemporaneously, it is unlikely that the compromises forged in private sessions could have been achieved, or even that their state governments would have allowed the delegates to write a new constitution. Once the constitution had been drafted, of course, it was made public and its merits were freely debated and discussed as part of the ratification process. A generation later Madison's notes of the debates within the convention appeared and the record of who said what was finally disclosed.

The privacy involved in the writing of the American Constitution suggests the importance of confidentiality of organizational decisions until agreement has been reached, and confidentiality for a reasonable time thereafter of the way in which they were reached. Today this issue is most often discussed in terms of the federal executive branch and the question of legislative power to compel disclosure of policy positions taken by executive officials. President Eisenhower expressed the view of chief executives since Washington's time when he wrote in 1954:

> [I]t is essential to efficient and effective administration that employees of the executive branch be in a position to be completely candid in advising with each other on official matters. . . . [I]t is not in the public interest that any of their conversations or communications, or any documents or reproductions, concerning such advice be disclosed.[60]

In one of the recent public debates over the propriety of publishing former presidential aides' accounts of recent intra-executive positions, Adolf A. Berle, Jr., has written:

> A President must talk to his staff. He can get the best from them—and they can best function—only when exchange is wholly candid. In the reviewer's experience, great decision-making usually boils down to a tired chief of state on one side of the desk and a trusted friend or aide on the other. If at that point the chief of state must consider not only the decision involved but also the possible effect of revelation of himself, his emotions and his thinking—concerning men, political effects of possible measures, his personal hopes and fears—frankness will necessarily be inhibited.[61]

Obviously, the issue has its counterpart in the staff relations of law clerks to judges, of military aides to commanding officers, and of legislative assistants to Senators and Representatives. What law there is on the matter remains confused, because at heart the question is usually one of reasonableness, the nature of the issue involved, and the give-and-take of the checks-and-balances system.[62] Time is obviously an important factor in striking the practical balances, since what is an invasion of a former superior's privacy in a memoir today may not be so five or ten years from now. Staff advice must, in the usual case, be kept private for a reasonable time if men are to make government work.

The other aspect of privacy for organizational decision making is the issue of timing—when and how to release the decision—which corresponds to the individual's determination whether and when to communicate about himself to others. Groups obviously have a harder time keeping decisions secret. The large number of persons involved increases the possibility of leaks, and the press, competitors, and opponents often seek energetically to discover the decision before the organization is ready to release it. Since most organizational decisions will become known eventually, privacy is a temporary claim—a claim of foundations, university administrations, political parties, and government agencies to retain the power of deciding for themselves when to break the seal of privacy and "go public."

While the timing problem is not unique to government (advance news of a corporate decision is worth a great deal in the stock market and may harm the company's plans), its scope is greatest in governmental life. A major need is to prevent outsiders from taking unfair advantage of a government decision revealed through secret surveillance, careless leak, or deliberate disclosure by a corrupted government employee. The rulings of courts and regulatory agencies are particularly sensitive in this regard.[63] Another concern is to prevent improper pressure on government agencies, such as federal and state regulatory commissions, by persons who learn prematurely that certain actions are proposed. Privacy is also necessary when the degree and timing of disclosure of the government's views are vital to the application of responsible policy. Adam Yarmolinsky has stressed the need for freedom from "premature exposure" in the international area of "signaling."

> There has been a good deal of discussion in recent international crises of the importance of signals being transmitted to an adversary by particular actions that the U.S. chooses to take. In the Cuban missile crises, for example, we were much more concerned about the way in which the Russians would read our actions in imposing a naval quarantine than about the physical consequences of the actions themselves. Living as we all do under the threat of nuclear destruction, our ultimate reliance is on a policy of nuclear deterrence, which means if we have to use our nuclear weapons our policy has failed. In every confrontation below the nuclear level, therefore, our words and our actions are at least as important for what they signal about our ultimate intentions, as for their more immediate effects.[64]

Similarly, in domestic situations, government is constantly involved in taking actions or making statements which are primarily designed as signals of ultimate intentions. Civil-rights confrontations are a case in point. If such signaling is not to be misunderstood, government officials need freedom to decide when their statements to Southern officials or civil-rights leaders remain a matter of executive privacy and when they should be made public.

The basic point is obvious: privacy in governmental decision making is a functional necessity for the formulation of responsible policy, especially in a democratic system concerned with finding formulas for reconciling differences and adjusting majority-minority interests. Nevertheless, drawing the line between what is proper privacy and what becomes dangerous "government secrecy" is a difficult task. Critics have complained that the public often has a right to know what policies are being considered and, after a decision is taken, to know who influenced the result and what considerations moved the governmental leaders.[65] Apart from the broad jockeying for position that underlies privacy conflicts between the legislature and the executive or between elected and appointed branches of government, there is also the problem of manipulation of the privacy claim by government agencies to secure what is really unfair advantage. An effective legislative or press campaign may be needed to compel responsibility when an agency makes a partial disclosure of information to advance its own interests or invokes the privacy principle to shield wrongdoing by public officials (as in the Dixon-Yates affair during the Eisenhower administration).[66]

PROTECTED COMMUNICATIONS

The organization's need to communicate in confidence with its outside advisors and sources of information and to negotiate privately with other organizations corresponds to the individual's need for protected communication. At the governmental level this necessity ranges from the so-called "informer privilege" (by which American law recognizes the need of the executive branches, especially the law-enforcement and security services, to keep secret the identities of persons who report wrongdoings in confidence) to the situation of private persons who give confidential advice to the President and to executive departments. For example, in refusing to release a private citizen group's confidential report on the adequacy of national defenses, President Eisenhower in 1958 explained that the willingness of citizens to give advice to the government was heavily dependent on protecting the privacy of these communications.[67] Society sets limits on this privacy for informational sources, such as the requirement that informers be produced if the government wants to use their statements in criminal prosecutions or that information "volunteered" to executive and regulatory agencies by private citizens—when it is really advocacy of their economic interests—be placed on the record.

Another aspect of privacy for confidential communication involves the information that organizations acquire from individuals and other organizations. Private agencies such as life-insurance companies, credit bureaus, employers, and many others collect reams of personal information, sometimes under the compulsion that the benefits offered by the organization cannot be had unless the information is provided. Government departments, in their capacities as law-enforcement, regulatory, money-granting, and employment agencies, collect even more personal data, and much of this, too, is compelled—by a legal duty to respond to the government inquiry. Normally, this issue is discussed as a matter of individual rather than of organizational privacy, because of the individual's interest in ensuring that personal information which he gave for one purpose is not used for another without his consent. But organizations also need to protect such information against many of the claims to access made by the press and other private and public agencies if they are to continue to get frank and full information from reporting sources. This fact makes confidential treatment of the data an independent organizational need, not an assertion of privacy solely on behalf of those furnishing the information.

Many private organizations have developed confidentiality policies to govern this issue. Government usually tries to safeguard confidential information through statutes or regulations prohibiting unauthorized disclosures by government employees of information acquired in their official capacities or contained in government files. Census data, for example, are legally restricted to the statistical purposes for which they were acquired and no other government officials may examine the census returns.[68] Income-tax data are also restricted; they may be used beyond revenue purposes only for limited governmental inquiries.[69] Pressures on the privacy of governmentally obtained data arise when business, the press, or other govermental agencies claim the right of "the people" to have access to such information, creating an important area of struggle over executive privacy.

A final aspect of confidential communications involves the privacy of negotiations among organizations in society. In many spheres of American life, private organizations are expected to negotiate and agree among themselves on matters that affect the common interests of their various memberships. Leading examples of this method are labor-management negotiations over working terms, negotiations among political parties and factions over political affairs, and the bargains struck by civic groups of all kinds on matters of community relations. Unless the representatives of the negotiating organizations can debate and work toward such bargains in privacy, without premature exposure either to their respective memberships or to the general public, there cannot be a successful process of accommodation and compromise.

A typical illustration of this factor at work was reported in a *New York Times* account of a series of community fact-finding conferences on local problems held in New York state during 1964. Several "open" meetings for local group spokesmen were conducted, then a session was scheduled for off-the-record statements. The *Times* reporter noted that the open meetings had been marked by "a lack of candor," since "many who took part . . . did not want to discuss the city's racial situation in public." However, when the meeting was closed, permitting "civic, business, labor and civil rights leaders to express themselves without fear of being quoted in the newspapers," the *Times* reported, the participants felt that they were discussing realities, and leaders spoke frankly for the first time.[70]

Government agencies have a similar need to engage in negotiations with other governmental bodies to arrive at joint decisions. Examples are the conference committee meetings at which differences between Senate and House versions of legislation are reconciled; meetings of representatives from various executive agencies to arrive at a unified policy for the executive on defense or foreign-policy matters; and, of course, many of the most critical negotiations among national governments. "Open covenants openly arrived at" is a Wilsonian precept that has definite limits in the realities of international affairs, especially in negotiations between nations with different ideologies, cultures, and basic international objectives.

The foregoing discussion of organizational behavior suggests that privacy is a necessary element for the protection of organizational autonomy, gathering of information and advice, preparation of positions, internal decision making, inter-organizational negotiations, and timing of disclosure. Privacy is thus not a luxury for organizational life; it is a vital lubricant of the organizational system in free societies.

CHAPTER THREE

Intrusions on Privacy: Self-Revelation, Curiosity, and Surveillance

THE PREVIOUS chapter has already discussed several aspects of intrusions on privacy, from curiosity and social control surveillance as universal elements in society to the individual's own search for a personal balance of privacy within his society's general framework of environment and norms. But there are three topics involving intrusion that deserve special treatment in terms of contemporary American society and the problem of privacy: the degree of self-disclosure that involves a threat to the libertarian definition of privacy; the problem of voyeuristic curiosity; and the effects of surveillance by authorities in group and community life.

Self-Revelation and Interpersonal Relations

Georg Simmel found a basic aspect of privacy in the individual's exercise of reserve and the use of discretion by others. The analysis of invasion of privacy properly begins with "self-invasion," the lack of reserve through which an individual fails to observe his own minimum boundaries of privacy. By this failure, Simmel felt, the individual reveals so much about himself to those around him that his relationships deteriorate and he ceases to have a private life.[1] Obviously, if enough individuals lose their reserve, the sense of discretion in others would be affected; those who tell all prompt others to ask all. A particular aspect of many of the new drugs, such as LSD-25, is that they may greatly affect the individual's daily personal balance between what he keeps private about himself and what he discloses to those around him. Widespread use of

52

such drugs could profoundly alter our traditional interpersonal sense of privacy.

Some recent writers on privacy have lamented that self-invasion is growing dangerously in American society, especially in people's responses to public-opinion pollsters and behavioral researchers. What will happen to respect for privacy, it is asked, when people blurt out their views, personal histories, and intimate behavior so freely to such inquiring questioners, instead of saying, "It's none of your business"? [2]

Actually, the attack on disclosures of personal information to pollsters and researchers overlooks the distinction between the reserve which should govern the setting of privacy with intimates and acquaintances and that required for relations with the stranger and for anonymous disclosures. To verify this point, I wrote to the leading survey organizations and asked them about trends in the past two decades in people's willingness to disclose personal information—such as information about their income, sexual conduct, political and religious beliefs, and criminal records. The areas of highest resistance to questioning are income and money (about 10 per cent refusals), age for women respondents, and educational background when questioning persons with little formal education.[3] The responses were uniform in saying that the American public was overwhelmingly willing to disclose intimate information to reputable survey organizations. This willingness had grown steadily in the past two decades. The main problem today for those seeking information is not that people fear an invasion of privacy but that they are angry at salesmen who use false surveys for merchandising purposes.

Such self-disclosure to survey researchers is not a uniquely American characteristic, however. Dr. George Gallup, whose organization, The Gallup Poll, has affiliated polling organizations in twenty-five foreign nations, reported that "the number of persons refusing to be interviewed is extremely small and about the same in all nations. . . . [P]eople the world over react about the same way when put in the same situation." [4] Why? Reputable polling and survey organizations, it must be remembered, always tell their subjects that all information will be treated as confidential and that the subject's identity will never be disclosed; this guarantee of anonymity has been respected. Furthermore, the interviewer and the polling agency he represents are strangers to the respondent and will remain so; this is not the surveillance of government, the boss, neighbors, friends, or intimates. The respondent knows that he will not be hurt by disclosing his private thoughts, his past conduct, or his future intentions; nothing will be used against him. Indeed, not only will he not be influenced by self-disclosure, but the interview offers him as well an unusual opportunity to influence others—the manufacturers, television programmers, advertisers, government agencies, and others who will read and study what the respondent says. As George Gallup observed, this situation creates an "eagerness" to respond, especially in a democracy which "doesn't give the typical citizen much of a chance to participate or to have a feeling that his views have any significance." Finally, Elmo Roper has noted that the individual always has the right to refuse to answer, and with that guarantee intact, "the limits of privacy" in a free society "are defined by what people are themselves willing or unwilling to talk about."

The other side of self-disclosure is what individuals are willing to reveal to those who do continue in their lives, particularly to family and close friends. Clearly, the age we live in is shaped by many factors expanding the desire to reveal, from the effects of Freud and the popularization of psychiatry to the American tradition of interpersonal openness. What kinds of "private" fact Americans are willing to reveal in this context has been the subject of recent studies experimenting with a "self-disclosure questionnaire" developed by the psychologist Sidney Jourard.[5] This form contains twenty-five questions about personal facts divided into the basic areas of personality, body, attitudes, tastes, work, and money. Individuals given the questionnaire were asked to indicate, anonymously, whether they had lied or misrepresented, told nothing, given general information, or revealed full and complete details on each of the aspects of themselves to various persons on a checklist: mother, father, spouse, male friend, and female friend. Jourard's tests with the questionnaire during the past ten years with diverse groups of subjects have shown that money, personality, and body were low-disclosure items, while attitudes, tastes, and work were high-disclosure items. No significant difference in self-disclosure was found according to the intelligence or academic achievement of test subjects. The basic patterns that emerged are that white Americans disclose more to their intimates than Negroes, and females more than males. Jewish males reveal more than Protestant and Catholic males, but Jewish females do not differ significantly from other females. Unmarried American white and Negro subjects of both sexes disclose more to mothers than to any other on the checklist; married persons disclose most to their spouse, and in more intimate detail than they did to mothers before marriage. Jourard's broadest conclusion was that self-disclosure to intimates is systematically related to mental and possibly to physical health. Psychologically and physically healthy subjects were the most free in self-disclosure.

Intrusions Through Curiosity Pressures

A companion to the issue of self-invasion of privacy is that of discretion—the willingness of people to respect the privacy of others. This factor has always been subject to the propensity for curiosity that seems to be a universal human trait, as we saw in the discussion in Chapter 1.

Though curiosity varies considerably in its intensity among individuals and cultures,[6] it serves a number of important functions in all societies—it helps, for example, to provide vicarious experience, to circulate information, and to promote group and community norms. In its usual forms, curiosity operates as part of family, neighborhood, and organizational life; in the form of gossip, it expresses the desire of persons in any social unit to know what is "going on" and to be privy to the "inside" and "secret" aspects of behavior. The basic stock in trade of the press is to satisfy curiosity through radio, newspapers, television, magazines, and books; and the press often stimulates public curiosity to maximum levels by reportorial techniques that override the privacy claims not only of "public figures" but also of anyone who happens to be touched by a "public event." As one commentator has put it, "There is a hermit spirit in each of us," but there is also "a snooper, a census taker, a gossipmonger and a brother's keeper."[7] This is why *casual* eavesdropping is such a regular part of most people's daily life, and why they derive such normal satisfaction from it. "Show me a man who doesn't eavesdrop," one writer on curiosity has written, "and I'll show you a man with a serious hearing problem."[8]

Though curiosity is a constant element in social life, and even gives rise to aggressive efforts to penetrate other people's secrets,[9] many social scientists have observed a rise in recent decades of a particular and dangerous form of curiosity, to which the term "voyeurism" has been applied. As a clinical term employed in abnormal psychology, voyeurism refers, of course, to an individual's desire to obtain sexual gratification by viewing another's sexual organs or the sexual intercourse of others.[10] Psychological literature attributes voyeurism to parental repression of curiosity impulses about sexual matters during adolescence or to the young adult's fears of inability to obtain satisfaction through heterosexual relations.[11] The voyeur's excitement comes in part from doing something forbidden and in part from watching persons who do not know that they are being observed. The "peeping Tom" of English history is the most common form of voyeur.

As used in its social rather than its clinical sense, voyeurism refers to the tasteless pursuit and aggressive exposure of the privacies of personal life, especially sexual conduct among the socially prominent. Such invasion of privacy for its own sake as a stimulant to those who do not find direct social satisfactions is commonly seen in the mass circulation of confession and fan magazines; in a certain semi-salacious style of exposé journalism (*New York Confidential, Washington Confidential, U.S.A. Confidential,* and so forth); in the "Candid Camera" type of peeping into the situations of persons experiencing embarrassing troubles; and in the style of television reporting that thrusts a microphone under the chin of a woman who has watched her child being injured and urges her to tell the viewers how she feels. The intimate relations that are captured and disclosed by wiretapping, camera surveillance, or personality testing find an avid market in the voyeuristically inclined segment of the public.

The dangerous appeal to voyeuristic urges is illustrated by increasingly open and offensive newspaper and magazine advertisements and retail-sales outlets of firms distributing devices for surreptitious listening and watching. Among the most offensive of the advertisements are those found in the various "men's" magazines. For example, one recent ad offers a miniature device that can be inserted in a small hole drilled through a wall. A lens in the device provides a view of most of the room on the other side of the wall. The advertiser points out that "people who relax in 'privacy' have no way of knowing that you can *see everything they do!*" It is suggested that the device, dubbed "Super-Spy," has applications limited only by its owner's imagination, including use in bedroom walls to "keep an eye on the kids while they take their naps," and in bathrooms to "avoid the embarrassment of barging in while it's occupied!" The advertisement recommends purchase of the device by anyone who finds it "fascinating or profitable . . . to know what people do when they don't know they are being watched." Using what is perhaps especially revealing language, the advertiser urges the reader to "order *spares* so you're never denied the thrill of sudden or unexpected opportunities." An advertisement for a similar device in the same magazine is illustrated with a drawing of the device being used to peer into a bedroom occupied by a young woman sitting on the bed and a young man standing beside her.[12] Such ads, openly inviting customers to eavesdrop for fun and profit, contribute to the erosion of public moral standards. Television programs that show sophisticated bugs and closed-circuit TV being used regularly by police, intelligence agencies, and private investigators have certainly not slowed this erosion process.

There are other relations of voyeurism to the problem of surveillance. Some observers of law enforcement believe that wiretapping and eavesdropping assignments, the private-detective business, the polygraph profession, and similar activities frequently attract voyeuristic types. This circumstance is illustrated by the polygraph operators who deliberately use "embarrassing personal questions" on female subjects, despite scientific opinion that this procedure upsets the whole polygraph examination, and the wiretap experts (both police and private) who save tape recordings of intimate conversations and play these to their friends for entertainment.[13]

Invasion of Privacy in Group and Community Life:
The Concept of Surveillance by Authority

Surveillance is obviously a fundamental means of social control. Parents watch their children, teachers watch students, supervisors watch employees, religious leaders watch the acts of their congregants, policemen watch the streets and other public places, and government agencies watch the citizen's performance of various legal obligations and prohibitions. Records are kept by authorities to organize the task of indirect surveillance and to identify trends that may call for direct surveillance. Without such surveillance, society could not enforce its norms or protect its citizens, and an era of ever increasing speed of communication, mobility of persons, and coordination of conspiracies requires that the means of protecting society keep pace with the technology of crime. Yet one of the central elements of the history of liberty in Western societies since the days of the Greek city-state has been the struggle to install limits on the power of economic, political, and religious authorities to place individuals and private groups under surveillance against their will. The whole network of American constitutional rights—especially those of free speech, press, assembly, and religion; forbidding the quartering of troops in private homes; securing "persons, houses, papers and effects" from unreasonable search and seizure; and assuring the privilege against self-incrimination—was established to curtail the ancient surveillance claims of governmental authorities. Similar rules have evolved by statute, common law, and judicial decision to limit the surveillance powers of corporations, unions, and other private agencies.

Though this general principle of civil liberty is clear, many governmental and private authorities seem puzzled by the protest against current or proposed uses of new surveillance techniques. Why should persons who have not committed criminal acts worry whether their conversations might be accidentally overheard by police officers eavesdropping on public telephone booths or at public places used by suspected criminals? Why should truthful persons resist verifying their testimony through polygraph examination? Shouldn't anyone who appreciates the need for effective personnel placement accept personality testing? And aren't fears about subliminal suggestion or increased data collection simply nervous responses to the new and the unknown? In all these instances, authorities point to the fact that, beyond the benefits of the surveillance for the organization or the community, the individual himself can now prove his innocence, virtue, or talents by "science" and avoid the unjust assumptions frequently produced by "fallible" conventional methods.

The answer, of course, lies in the impact of surveillance on human behavior. This impact can best be understood by distinguishing three main types of modern surveillance. First is surveillance by observation. Writings by leading social scientists[14] have made it clear that observation by listening or watching which is known to the subject necessarily exercises a restrictive influence over him. In fact, in most situations this is exactly why the observational surveillance is set up—to enforce the rules. When a person knows his conduct is visible, he must either bring his actions within the accepted social norms in the particular situation involved or decide to violate those norms and accept the risk of reprisal. Sociological writing has stressed that there are degrees of observation in various types of group (work forces, government agencies, and the like) which will prevent the particular group's members from performing effectively. Robert Merton has explained this phenomenon as follows:

> Few groups, it appears, so fully absorb the loyalties of members that they will readily accept unrestricted observability of their role-performance. . . . Resistance to full visibility of one's behavior appears . . . to result from structural properties of group life. *Some* measure of leeway in conforming to role-expectations is presupposed in all groups. To have to meet the strict requirements of a role at all times, without some degree of deviation, is to experience insufficient allowances for individual differences in capacity and training and for situational exigencies which make strict conformity extremely difficult.[15]

Even though the authorities may accept evasion of the rules, the experience will be "psychologically taxing" on both the observed person and the authorities, since the latter must decide whether or not to act against the non-complying person and must measure the effects of not acting on the group perception of authority.

> What is sometimes called "the need for privacy"—that is, insulation of actions and thought from surveillance by others—is the individual counterpart to the functional requirement of social structure that some measure of exemption from full observability be provided for. Otherwise, the pressure to live up to the details of all (and often conflicting) social norms would become literally unbearable; in a complex society, schizophrenic behavior would become the rule rather than the formidable exception it already is. "Privacy" is not merely a personal predilection; it is an important functional requirement for the effective operation of social structure. Social systems must provide for some appropriate measure, as they would say in France, of *quant-à-soi*—a portion of the self which is kept apart, immune from social surveillance.[16]

Though the destructive effect of near total observation and compulsory public confessions is associated in the public mind with totalitarian systems, as depicted with chilling effect in Huxley's *Brave New World* and Orwell's *1984*, the histories of utopian community experiments also document the disintegrative effect of complete observation over individual and group life. Robert Owen's famous community of New Lanark contained what Owen called a "silent monitor" system to watch the conduct of workers.[17] This feature of life in several utopian communist communities of England and America in the nineteenth century led Charles Nordhoff to observe in 1875 that the absence of the "precious" thing called "solitude" was one of the key factors in the failure of these experiments.[18] In his leading work on the Israeli kibbutz, Melford Spiro has noted that the early settlers' deliberate rejection of personal privacy gave way in the established kibbutz, and especially among the second kibbutz generation, to a demand for privacy in family and living arrangements that had to be satisfied to keep the loyalty of the kibbutz members.[19] It is revealing that the attempt to use total observational surveillance and to require total self-revelation to the group or to authorities takes place either as part of efforts to run perfect societies, such as utopias, or perfect sub-societies, such as monasteries or convents. In the Jesuit order, for example, brothers in training must keep themselves under a total monitor, keep a record of their improper thoughts and actions, and report themselves each day to their superior. In addition, each week all the brothers must report anything they have heard their fellow brothers say or do that breaches the rules. Only those who can sustain an absolute commitment to the ideal of perfection can survive total surveillance. This is not the condition of men in ordinary society.

Sociological analysis of observability explains why the prospect of total physical surveillance is so psychologically shattering to the individual. If a factory is wired completely with listening and watching devices, workers know that every station cannot be monitored all the time. Yet no individual has any way of knowing when he is under observation and when not. The particularly dehumanizing feature of this situation is not the fact that the surveillance is done by machine techniques rather than by direct human observation, but that the person-to-person factor in observation—with its softening and "game" aspects—has been eliminated. The same element is present in data surveillance—the maintenance of such detailed daily and cumulative records of each individual's personal transactions that computerized systems can reconstruct his acts and use such data for social control even without direct physical surveillance.

On the other hand, surveillance may be such a vital means of providing physical security, as in our public places, that properly controlled use of new watching and listening devices may be desirable. This point was made by Margaret Mead in a recent essay. After noting that city life offers "extraordinary possibilities" for anonymity from neighbors, relatives, and community controls, Mead stated that the desire for "personal privacy" is being confused with a notion of "privacy from the law." This confusion is based on the erroneous assumption that there is no obligation to create institutions of social protection in cities to replace the public safety provided by social surveillance of known persons in small communities. New listening, watching, and recording devices in apartment buildings, police street monitoring, and similar situations are to be welcomed. "[T]he devices we have rejected because they can be (and have been) used to invade individual privacy can also be used to ensure the public safety, without which privacy itself becomes a nightmare isolation." [20]

A second main type of surveillance is extraction—entry into a person's psychological privacy by requiring him to reveal by speech or act those parts of his memory and personality that he regards as private. Earlier discussion of the individual's need for autonomy explains the threat this procedure poses to the individual in a free society. American society has understood well that such extraction through torture, test oaths, self-incrimination, and governmental inquiries into religious belief is antithetical to civil liberty, and our law has forbidden such official surveillance.

It is not such traditional methods of extraction that are causing the present debate over privacy, of course, but less direct methods, such as polygraphs and personality testing. The issue of personality testing for personnel selection by industry and government provides a useful subject for studying the social effect of extraction.

The basic objection on privacy grounds to the typical personality test used in personnel selection today—with its questions on such topics as sex and political values—is that many individuals do not want to be sorted and judged according to standards that rest on the unexplained evaluations of professional psychologists in the employ of "institutional" clients. Liberals fear that a government or industrial psychologist will enforce conformist or elitist norms. Conservatives fear that school or government testing might not only "reward" liberal ideology and penalize conservative ideas but also "implant" ideas through the testing process itself. Negroes are concerned that psychologists might enforce standards of personality that penalize minority groups and that the personality test might enable the "white power structure" to accomplish covertly discrimination it can no longer carry out openly. In all these situations the assertion of privacy serves to say to those in power: "If you make evaluative decisions openly, questioning me directly and justifying your decisions openly, I can fight out publicly your right to judge me in a certain way, and American society will decide our conflicting claims. But if you invoke 'science' and 'expertise' and evaluate me through personality tests, the issue becomes masked and the public cannot judge the validity and morality of these evaluative decisions. Thus, where such basic issues as political ideology, religion, and race are at stake, the selection process must be objective and public, and I assert my right of privacy to close my emotions, beliefs, and attitudes to the process of job evaluation in a free society."

In addition, the basic aim of test psychology is admittedly to search for norms of conduct and to use these for judgment in "trait" and "prediction" matters. The intellectuals who lead the anti-personality-testing campaigns know how far they themselves are from any type of "bland" normality, how many conflicts and personal disturbances lie behind their social masks, and yet how useful they are in their area of work, whether it is business, law, government, teaching, or the ministry. Many intellectuals are aware of the test psychologist's answer that he does not advise the selection of "normals" only, that the tests can reward imagination, initiative, and other traits. But, knowing how fundamentally emotional tension and creativity are linked in the individual, intellectuals are not willing to submit themselves or the majority of their fellow citizens to the judgment of psychologists on that point. One of the basic functions of privacy is to protect the individual's need to choose those to whom he will bare the true secrets of his soul and his personality. The counseling and clinical psychologists have long been among the handful of those professional groups in whom many Americans have been willing to place such intimate trust. If civic reactions of the 1960's are any sign of developing public trends, many will not accept the test psychologist, working for an institutional client, in such a role.

Finally, from the literature of psychology and psychiatry, as well as from personal experience, critics of personality testing know that many individuals go through life with personal problems and conflicts that they keep under control. These "managed" conflicts may involve sex, struggles over self-image, careers, and similar matters. Most of these people can grow old without having these conflicts become serious enough to impair their capacities at work, in the family, or as citizens. If these capacities are impaired, of course, the individual needs help; he may seek it himself, or it may be offered to him when his difficulties become observable. The problem presented by the spread of personality testing is that it may, by the pressures of testing and of rejection in selection, bring to the surface personality conflicts that might otherwise never have become critical in the individual's life, and may thus precipitate emotional crises. It can be argued that it is healthy to bring such problems to the surface and to lead the disturbed individual to professional help. Perhaps we are moving toward an age of preventive mental health by personality testing, when individuals will get their emotional "check-up" just as they have their bodies, eyes, and teeth checked. Before we accept this trend in American life, however, we had better be more certain than we are now that we can cure the wounds opened by such a process, or that awareness is a good thing even though a cure is not always possible. Until then, resistance to such extraction will be invoked as a way of saying, "I want to go on managing my problems myself; and what might force me to a self-confrontation that I do not want invades my privacy in the deepest way."

A third type of surveillance, which has not yet been studied by social scientists because of its recent development, is what I would call reproducibility of communication. Through the new recording and camera devices, it is now simple to obtain permanent pictorial and sound recordings of subjects without their knowledge. This may be done by the person with whom the subject is talking or acting, or a secret recording may be made by a third party. The special character of this surveillance is that it gives the person who conducted the surveillance the power to reproduce, at will, the subject's speech or acts. When a person writes a letter or files a report, he knows that he is communicating a record and that there is a risk of circulation; thus he exercises care and usually tries to say what he really means. But in speech that is overheard and recorded, all the offhand comments, sarcastic remarks, indiscretions, partial observations, agreements with statements to draw out a partner in conversation or to avoid argument, and many similar aspects of informal private intercourse are capable of being "turned on" by another for his own purposes. The right of individuals and organizations to decide when, to whom, and in what way they will "go public" has been taken away from them. It is almost as if we were witnessing an achievement through technology of a risk to modern man comparable to that primitive men felt when they had their photographs taken by visiting anthropologists: a part of them had been taken and might be used to harm them in the future.

When surreptitious recording and filming was limited primarily to security or law-enforcement agencies or to private investigations into misconduct such as employee pilfering, the risk to society may not have been great. Now that such recording devices have become general commodities—and are spreading so rapidly into the business, governmental, and personal worlds—we must consider the impact of their use on our freedom of private expression, and the widespread public assumption that important conversations are being recorded, whether they are in fact or not.[21] Secret recordings *are* being made by federal executive agencies (wholly apart from security matters) and other government bodies, and such recordings *are* being used to exert pressure on individuals by playing back to them comments which would be embarrassing if revealed publicly. Such use in corporate life is not yet as widespread, but if the history of surveillance practices teaches us anything, it is that business will not lag far behind government for long.

PART TWO

New Tools for Invading Privacy

THE EFFORT to limit official surveillance over man's thoughts, speech, private acts, confidential communications, and group participation has for centuries been a central part of the struggle for liberty in Western society. This search for personal and group privacy has been waged against kings and legislatures; churches, guilds, manor lords, and corporations; sheriffs, welfare investigators, and political police.

When the American Republic was founded, the framers established a libertarian equilibrium among the competing values of privacy, disclosure, and surveillance. This balance was based on the technological realities of eighteenth-century life. Since torture and inquisition were the only known ways of penetrating the mind, all such measures by government were forbidden by law. Physical entry and eavesdropping were the only means of penetrating private homes and meeting rooms; the framers therefore made eavesdropping by private persons a crime and allowed government to enter private premises only for reasonable searches, under strict warrant controls. Since registration procedures and police dossiers were the means used to control the free movement of "controversial" persons, this European police practice was precluded by American governmental practice and the realities of mobile frontier life.

Since World War II, spurred primarily by wartime development and government projects in the cold-war era, a series of scientific and technological advances has taken place that threatens the classic American equilibrium on privacy, disclosure, and surveillance. The tiny listening "bugs" and closed-circuit TV eyes, discussed with alarm in the mass media and legislative halls in the past two or three years, are only part of a larger revolution in surveillance technology. Further developments are possible that could pose wholly new and unprecedented intrusions into the emotions and mind of the citizen in the future. This technology has been developed at a time when socio-cultural changes in American life have produced an acceptance of these surveillance techniques by many private and public authorities, disseminating the new techniques rapidly through the society and outstripping the classic legal and social

67

controls over "unreasonable" surveillance.

The first response to this situation, obviously, must be careful factual analysis. What is this new technology? How is it being used to invade personal and group privacy? And what realistic prospects lie ahead in the next decade, if present scientific trends are projected forward or if break-throughs are made in areas currently stalemated?

For a clear discussion of these topics, the field of surveillance can be divided into three general parts. First is physical surveillance, the observation through optical or acoustical devices of a person's location, acts, speech, or private writing without his knowledge or against his will. In this area lies the greatest present threat by new technology to individual and group privacy. Second is psychological surveillance, the use of oral or written tests, devices, or substances to extract from an individual information that he does not give willingly, or does not know that he is revealing, or reveals without a mature awareness of its significance for his private personality. Last is data surveillance, the collection, exchange, and manipulation of documentary information about individuals and groups by data-processing machines (primarily computers) which, if enough detailed data is accumulated and collated, can produce such knowledge of an individual's or group's transactions that privacy may be seriously threatened.

It is obvious that none of these types of surveillance is brand new. Eavesdroppers and paid surveillance agents go back to antiquity. Torture, sex, alcohol, opium, hypnotism, primitive "lie" tests, and tests for proper "personality" are also ancient ways of unlocking minds, extracting information, or implanting suggestions. As for data surveillance, many societies in the past required registration of residences, movements, and transactions, and used elaborate dossiers and permits as a mechanism of administrative social control. What is new today is the marriage of advanced scientific technology to these classic surveillance methods.

CHAPTER FOUR

The Listening and Watching Devices: New Techniques of Physical Surveillance

Locating the Individual [1]

A MAJOR ASPECT of privacy for individuals (though something lost by celebrities) is the ability to move about anonymously from time to time. Because a major aspect of physical surveillance depends on knowing where the "subject" is at all times, and especially where he goes when he wants to be alone, physical shadowing has been a technique of surveillance since antiquity. What the new technology adds is ways to "tag" persons so that they can be followed more efficiently and with less risk of discovery. At least three major ways of tagging individuals have been developed.

Fluorescent powders or dyes have been produced which are applied secretly to a person's hands, shoes, clothing, hair, umbrella, and the like, or can be added to such items as soap, after-shave lotion, and hair tonic which an individual applies to himself. Although these substances are invisible under regular light, they register as "glowing" substances on the person being followed when he is illuminated by an ultraviolet-light source carried by the investigator.[2]

A second locating device is the miniature radio-signal transmitter, smaller than a quarter. This is used at close ranges without antennae or is equipped with twelve to fifteen inches of thin wire antennae for longer-range shadowing.[3] It can be secreted on a person, his clothing, car, or briefcase, or other articles that he carries. The transmitter sends out a signal which registers on a receiver tuned to that frequency, enabling the investigator to keep his quarry located, especially if two operatives are assigned to surveillance and a "cross-fix" can be utilized. The places available for hiding such transmitters in a car are so plentiful that secret

69

installation rarely presents a problem. In addition, surveillance manufacturers have built special auto-tagging equipment in the form of standard spotlights or rear-view mirrors.[4]

Tagging transmitters can also be built into eyeglasses, hearing aids, and wrist watches for close-range shadowing. Longer-range transmitters (requiring some sort of antennae) have been made to match coat buttons, the antennae being sewed into the collar or piping of the garment. Shoes with shoelace antennae, tie-clasps with tie antennae, hat emblems with hatband antennae, and buckles with belt antennae are examples of how "tagging" the individual has been carried out by resourceful investigators. The range of the signals with antennae is several city blocks.

Technology has recently contributed another advance on this front through the "radio pill" developed for medical research.[5] This emits a signal sufficiently strong to be followed at fairly close ranges—five to twenty yards today, with greater ranges expected in the near future. Thus, if a person takes large-sized anti-histamine or anti-allergy pills and an investigator can fill his medicine bottle with radio pills, a tag can be lodged in the stomach of the subject himself. It will eventually be passed out of the body without the individual's suspecting that he has been converted, for a time, into a living electronic beacon.

Third, substances of low radioactive levels can be placed on a person's clothing or belongings, while the investigator uses small Geiger counters or scintillation detectors to obtain signals from the radiation. The radioactive material comes in powder and liquid forms and is not visible under normal physical inspection.[6] In addition, tiny quantities of gamma-ray-emitting substances, put into a person's food, drink, or medication, are enough to "tag" a person by indications on radiation detectors. Such a quantity of material would not cause immediate effects on the subject, though it might eventually be harmful to the person's health.

Observation and Photography of Physical Acts

The physical activity of a person when he is within the closed areas of his home, office, or apartment, or in the private rooms of public facilities such as hotels, or in places such as the bathrooms of stores or factories, has traditionally been a prime target of those applying physical surveillance.

Today special "screens" can be installed in the walls of a room that seem opaque to persons inside but permit an observer in the adjoining room to look through and photograph everything taking place. At the simplest level this is done by the well-known technique of using glass which seems to be a mirror or screen in the room under observation.[7]

A far more sophisticated technique made possible by new technology is the use of special substances that seem to be wall panels and appear solid from both sides. These do not permit regular light to pass through, but transmit infra-red light—light with extra-long wave lengths —enabling investigators to take infra-red photographs or observe actions visually through an infra-red viewer. The infra-red-light source does not have to be placed within the room; it can be supplied by a beam sent from the observation post itself.

Secreting cameras within a room has been a growing technique of the past two decades. Miniature "still" cameras can be hidden within a room to take films on electronic signals from outside, at periodic pre-set intervals, or when triggered by a light switch being turned on or a file drawer opened. They can also be set off by the entrance of persons into an empty room, by means of antennae that sense changes in a room's electronic balance. Electric eyes in these hidden cameras provide shutter changes to take account of light factors. Such cameras, ranging in price from $100 to $300, are easily hidden behind air-conditioning and heating grills, in wall clocks, in the speaker section of television sets, and many other vantage points. One radio-controlled model now in use by police and private detectives can take more than four hundred 35-millimeter frames without reloading, from control distances of up to one mile.[8]

Probably the most useful device in visual surveillance is closed-circuit television, since this provides continuous observation and permits instant response by the investigator to what is seen. "Television eyes" now come in small units (3 inches by 9 inches) commercially available at about $500.[9] These can be hidden on the premises and can send a picture of the room to a remote receiver located a block or two away. TV cameras have also been developed with light pipes, or optical fibers, which can bend light around corners. Thus the camera can be installed in another room and only the optic fibers need be placed in the room under surveillance.[10] TV cameras able to fit into a vest pocket and featuring an "eye" the width of a cigarette have been built ever since the late 1950's[11] and probably for government surveillance work as well. Closed-circuit television has been widely used to check assembly-line progress, guard warehouses at night, protect tenants in apartment elevators or lobbies, prevent subway-car assaults, supervise prison cell blocks, survey stores with high shoplifting records, watch gambling tables in Nevada, and the like. Some police forces have already experimented with street surveillance by TV units mounted in lamp poles and parking meters to prevent thefts and provide riot control. This technique appears likely to increase in coming years. A few police forces have hidden TV cameras monitoring all incoming air flights, to identify organized-crime leaders coming to their city.

The uses closest to our area of concern have been the secret installation of TV eyes in business offices, in hotel rooms, and in homes, for police-investigation work or private-surveillance purposes. Such installations present few serious technical problems. In addition, video-tape units to record what is seen by closed-circuit TV are now on the general market at prices from $500 to $1,000.[12]

When persons are in a dark room, they may assume themselves to be immune from surveillance. The truth is that concealed cameras equipped with infra-red film can photograph actions in a dark room if an invisible infra-red-energy source has been placed within that room. One way this is done is by putting special bulbs in overhead fixtures or lamps. To the naked eye the bulb seems to be unlit, since no visible light is transmitted; but it is actually flooding the room with infra-red light and will provide the basis for clear snapshots or film. Of course if the windows are bare, cameras outside the premises can photograph inside by projecting infra-red illumination into the room. Other cameras have methods of amplifying very small visible-light sources. One closed-circuit television camera operates with such sensitivity (and without the need of infra-red energy) that it can transmit clear pictures of an entire room from the illumination of a cigarette lighter.[13]

While some persons seek privacy in closed or darkened rooms, others go out along public streets or parks or place themselves considerable distances away from other persons or objects. Several types of camera devices enable investigators to handle these situations. Miniature still cameras costing less than $100 have been made in the form of cigarette lighters or match boxes; with these, or a regular miniature camera concealed in the palm of the hand or in a hat, a casual passerby or a man sitting across the aisle on a bus can take pictures of his "subject" without detection.[14]

Telephoto-lens cameras will produce a clear picture of a person 100 yards away. Special lenses with extra-long focal length (costing $1,000 or less) can produce recognizable pictures of persons from 500 to 1,000 yards away.[15] One popular investigative tool combines binoculars, camera, and telecamera elements into one compact instrument.[16] The binocular and camera are synchronized so that both normal-range pictures and telephoto shots can be taken in either color or black and white up to 1,000 yards away while the binocular focuses on the view. As every newspaper reader knows, these are crude ranges compared to the camera capabilities presently used in "spy satellites" and other photo-reconnaisance systems. Camera surveillance for distances of *miles* is clearly possible now.

Photography outdoors in the dark presents few problems when the investigator uses infra-red energy and special film. The World War II sniperscope viewer is now available in police equipment with a viewing range of 500 feet or more, at a cost of $150.[17] Military sniperscopes used in Vietnam illuminate a man in darkness at 700 *yards*.[18] More important still, a new image-intensification system has been developed which uses starlight radiated by the night sky.[19] With this system, objects in apparent blackness can be clearly observed and photographed. Since no light source from the photographer shines on the object, as in infra-red observation, the surveillance cannot be detected by devices for locating infra-red rays. This intensification device is also in current use on rifle sights for the military services.

Listening To and Recording Speech

The transmission of verbal information from one person to another, either directly in face-to-face conversation or over a telephone, radio, or television "line," is a major target of physical surveillance. Other targets are the highly specialized voice-transmission channels, such as microwaves and laser beams, which are used by governments to transmit speech on security matters, whether "straight," in code, or "scrambled" electronically. When such conversations are obtained, through technological means, by someone who is not a party to them, or is not known to be listening by both parties involved, this is known as "third-party eavesdropping." The new electronic technology is now able to break through long-standing physical barriers to such third-party audial eavesdropping and can provide sophisticated means for extracting speech from closed locations or transmission lines and sending it to secure listening posts. Apart from such non-technological aids to surveillance as lip-reading, a bulging arsenal of new or improved techniques for vocal surveillance has been developed since World War II.

The investigator's dream is to make his subject a walking radio transmitter, enabling the investigator to hear everything the subject says to anyone else, or even what he mutters aloud while he walks along the street. This can be done by wiring a person's clothing. A leading method is to build a microphone into one button of a suit coat, a sub-miniature transmitter into a second button, and the batteries into a third. The thread with which the special buttons are sewn in is of conductive wire, carried through the seams of the coat or jacket to make up the antenna. Access to the subject's coat for a few minutes is all that is necessary to install these devices. Common points of contact—the tailor shop, the dry-cleaning establishment, the restaurant checkroom, and the like—are often available. An example of the installation possibilities of existing micro-miniature transmitters is provided by a transmitter so small that it has been mounted as a tooth in a dental bridge.[20]

Because of the expense and frequent difficulty of wiring the person, plus the fact that the place of conversations to be overheard is often known in advance, wiring the premises is the most common form of eavesdropping. Developments in electronics and miniaturization in the past two decades, moving from the vacuum tubes of the 1930's to transistors and the latest "chip" integrated circuits,[21] have reduced bugging devices to ultra-miniature sizes. Microphones the size of sugar cubes ($10) or special "pea" units ($100) are presently available to secrete in rooms, offices, autos, chairs in hotel lobbies, tables at bars and restaurants, and so forth.[22] By 1966 micro-miniaturization had reduced high-quality microphones to match-head size.[23]

Any of the tiny mikes presently available can be attached by adhesive to the underside of furniture or by magnetic force to metal objects. They can also be installed inside telephones, intercoms, doorbell units, radios, TV's, water coolers, desk sets, clocks, picture frames, lamps, mattresses, flower pots, ash trays, cellophane-tape dispensers, bulletin boards, air conditioners, and a hundred other common objects within the room.[24] A special microphone and transmitter have been built into a light bulb so that the transmitter begins broadcasting when the light switch is turned on and stops when it is turned off.

Usually microphones are attached to the regular electrical wiring system or have their own wires connected to a receiver outside the room. Common models of this type have a range of one to three city blocks and cost $135 to $250. At the listening post the eavesdropper can monitor the conversation and make a tape recording of the parts he desires. Battery-operated portable tape recorders provide one to six hours of recording time without change of tape. Special equipment is available which activates a tape recorder automatically when voices are heard in the room and shuts it off when conversation ceases; this makes it unnecessary to "man" a listening post.[25] Tape recorders with twenty-four hours or more of recording time are used by surveillance specialists.[26] Miniature tape recorders providing a full hour without changing the reel have been reduced to cigarette-pack size.

Where utmost security is called for, investigators use trails of electrically conductive metallic paint from the microphone, along the walls or baseboards, and out to the receiver location or a place safe enough to connect to regular wires. The paint trails can be sprayed with artificial dust so that they don't look fresher than the old paint surfaces.[27]

Where the installation of any kind of wiring is too dangerous, even electrically conductive paint, FM microphones are available with their own built-in battery-operated radio transmitter. One unit on the commercial market is less than two cubic inches in size and sells for $90 to $150.[28] Government units are even smaller.

Electric sources already in the room can also be used to power the microphone for transmission. One such source is the handset of the telephone, which can be converted in simple fashion into a live microphone that broadcasts speech in the room to an outside receiver, whether or not the telephone is off the hook. Another source is the intercom system used in most offices and many middle-class homes. The built-in microphones of these units can be altered to make them broadcasting stations to outside receivers. Indeed, many of the intercoms and public-address systems manufactured today are already equipped for listening in, without notice, from the master console unit.

In all the "bugging" situations described so far, the microphones were added to existing premises. However, a whole building or suite can be wired for eavesdropping during its construction, and with great ease. One ingenious device developed recently allows investigators to activate, by remote control, a bug placed in the telephone of the person under surveillance. After the bug is secreted in the telephone, drawing its power from the telephone line, the eavesdropper calls the bugged telephone from any place in the world. Once the line rings, either before the person answers or after he hangs up, the eavesdropper sends out a harmonica tone on the line. This activates the bug inside the person's telephone and enables the eavesdropper to listen on that telephone line to everything said in that room within a range of fifty feet until the investigator hangs up. The remote-control tone device sells for $400, and its inventor reports that he has sold "lots of them." [29]

The laser has contributed another new technique for taking sound out of rooms. One available portable laser microphone sends out an invisible infra-red beam only a quarter of an inch in thickness. The power of a laser beam to remain focused over long distances allows it to go for miles from the point of transmission to a target room. There it strikes a two-inch mirrored modulator planted in the room by the investigator, which sends the laser beam back to its original source miles away. Since the returning beam has been modulated by the sound waves produced by speech in the room under surveillance, a photo amplifier at the listening post allows the investigator to transform the returning light into sound. [30]

All these listening devices are installed inside the room under surveillance. Where entry is impossible or impractical, a contact microphone can be used to add electronic power to the "ear on the wall" principle. When sound waves generated by speech strike the walls, floors, and ceiling of a room, they set up measurable vibrations. The contact microphone, a vibration-sensitive transducer priced at $40 (available in lima-bean size for $50) is attached to the opposite side of a vibrating surface and picks up enough of the vibration to permit listening and recording with accuracy. [31] Where the walls are too thick or where separate panels are mounted on studs and trap too much air space, a $50 contact microphone known as a "spike-mike" is used. Here the walls or ceiling of the room under surveillance act as a sounding board.

The acoustical vibrations triggered by conversations in the room are transmitted through thin metallic shafts, or spikes, to contact microphones, and are then recorded by portable magnetic-tape recorders.[32]

Vibrations set off by speech in a room can be carried for considerable distances along the steel-and-concrete frames of a structure, especially in modern light-frame office and apartment construction. Speech vibrations are carried even more strongly along air-conditioning ducts, heating vents, and water pipes. A contact microphone attached to these frames or pipes can pick up speech hundreds of feet from the source. This technique is more effective in a single-family dwelling or small office building than in large apartment houses or city office structures, where a myriad speech vibrations bombard the structural and electrical fixtures.

If a room is not closed completely—as when a window is open—directional microphones are able to zoom in and pick up speech at a considerable distance—across a city street, for example. Simple and easily operated parabolic microphones with eighteen-inch discs are advertised in the general press today as "toys" and have tested out as effective for ranges of 500 to 600 feet. These cost $15 to $20. Larger directional microphones increase this range considerably.

In addition to beaming through windows into rooms, directional microphones are used to listen to conversations outdoors—for example, on park benches or in fields hundreds of feet from any other object. Conversations in rowboats on a lake, as parties walk along a street, or as people dine at an outdoor restaurant terrace have been recorded through use of directional microphones. A special gun developed for American military authorities can shoot a small dart containing a wireless radio microphone into a tree, window pane, clump of bushes, awning, or any other object near people whose conversation the investigator wants to overhear.[33]

Speech vibrations in a room have a particularly strong effect on glass windows, window walls, and light-weight wallboard, even though an average-weight curtain may be hung over these surfaces. Speech produces "ultra-sound" vibrations on the outside surface which can be taken off and transformed back into sound. An ultrasonic generator is used which sends an airborne wave over space to the window or thin wall. The wave, modulated by the vibrations present, is then reflected back to the sending apparatus. The range of such eavesdropping depends on atmospheric conditions and winds. A Döppler radar microphone disguised as an automobile spotlight can beam its signal to window panes and obtain a returning beam from a mile or more away.[34] Other methods of "reading vibrations" include replacing one window pane with glass covered by a transparent film of tin oxide, causing it to be electrically conductive and enabling continuous-wave radar devices to convert vibrations into speech. It is also possible to attach a strip of metal foil to the window pane for removal of vibrations. The easiest situation of all for the eavesdropper occurs when a window already contains a foil strip as a burglar-alarm device, so that the eavesdropper installs nothing.[35]

An even more sophisticated technique for recovering speech from a closed room is by means of a tiny device using a reflector made of a thin diaphragm and microwave antenna. When a microwave beam is sent into the room from outside (this goes through solid wall barriers, with a range of a city block) the device is activated, sending its acoustic signal to an outside receiver.[36] An example of the effectiveness of this type of surveillance came to light in 1952, when State Department security officers discovered that conversations in the American Embassy in Moscow were being "overheard" by Russian agents through an ultra-miniature continuous-wave radar unit installed in a hollow part of the wooden Great Seal of the United States hanging in the Ambassador's study. A piece of metal with an attached spring-steel vibrator was activated by Soviet radar receivers across the street and enabled Soviet agents to pick up the vibrations set off by sound waves in the room.[37]

Finally, there is the telephone tap. Even though any reader of newspapers knows that wiretapping goes on in the United States, it is still almost impossible to conduct a business, engage in politics, participate in civic groups, or even run the Mafia without resorting to the telephone. As many confessional accounts in the past two decades have stated, even foreign espionage agents operating in this country have found it necessary to use the telephone (usually public pay phones) to arrange meetings or pass along code instructions, even though they are aware of wiretapping by government counter-intelligence services. What is even more important, radio-telephone conversations from field to office, picturephone conferences, long-distance copying and reproduction of documents by telephone line, and transmission of business and government data by high-speed dataphones—all new uses of the telephone—point to the growing rather than lessening importance of privacy for telephone communication.

Any of the techniques already described for eavesdropping on room conversations will obviously pick up the speech that goes into the telephone receiver. But it is often important for the eavesdropper to know who is on the other end and what that person says. Such two-way eavesdropping requires some means of entry into the telephone circuit.

Long before World War II (in fact, before World War I) direct cuts into telephone wires and splices into a set of earphones permitted eavesdroppers to overhear both sides of telephone conversations. Such "direct taps" could take place anywhere between the voice piece of the telephone and the main telephone exchange. However, these physical taps sometimes interfered with clear service and were subject to discovery by physical inspection.

The major innovation in wiretapping before 1941 (and still the leading technique) is the induction coil. A two-cubic-inch induction coil, priced at $10 to $15,[38] is placed a few feet from the telephone instrument or near its various connecting wires at any point before it is mixed with other lines. No cutting or breaking into the telephone wires or equipment is required. The coil, being in the magnetic field carrying the voice signal, draws off a very small amount of that signal and carries it to a receiver that permits listening or recording of the entire conversation. In addition to their use as "planted" devices, induction coils can be used as portable devices when kept in a pocket and wired to a pocket recorder. In this way, calls have been tapped by investigators sitting in waiting rooms outside business, law, and government offices, from rooms adjoining those of hotel guests, and even from the street outside a building when a phone is near the sidewalk.

Physical Surveillance of Records

In an age of reports, records, and data flow, individuals and groups are constantly concerned with protecting the privacy of their written communications from surveillance by those not entitled to examine them. Apart from the "non-technological" physical search of premises, there are several techniques of physical surveillance that have been applied to obtain private documents and data.

Powerful binoculars, long-range telephoto cameras, and "zoomar"-type television cameras have been used with great effectiveness in recent years to look through windows at important papers lying face-up on desks, at models of new products and designs, and at charts displayed at conferences. These techniques have become so common in certain areas of industrial espionage, such as the automobile industry, that elaborate security precautions are taken to keep designs and models in windowless rooms and to keep blinds drawn at all times in certain offices. Modern window-wall office buildings have made the job of observers much easier than it was in the era of concrete-and-brick buildings, and surveillance operations from building to building by camera have become a common technique.

Another area of record invasion involves the safes and storage vaults that most people rely on to keep records confidential. "Safe-cracking" has long been a criminal and espionage art, traditionally conducted by sandpapered fingers, dynamite charges, powerful drills, and the medical stethoscope. New electronic technology has added sensitive listening devices—one is widely advertised at $39.50 and a more sophisticated unit at $113—which are readily available to police and private detectives.[39] These permit the investigator to hear the clicking of tumblers as a rotary lock is spun and thereby to discover the combination. The typical rotary safe—the kind used by most offices and homes, though not in banks or security installations—can be easily opened in this manner.

A third aspect of privacy for records involves the growing volume of important business and governmental information transmitted by teletype and telephone ("dataphone") systems. Sales orders, production figures, costs, bid quotations, and many other confidential business items are now sent regularly by these processes. Since the machines originating this flow and those receiving it are located in the offices of subscriber corporations or government, many of the extraction techniques discussed under vocal surveillance (tapping the teletype by radio, for example, and feeding the signal into readily available, second-hand teletypewriters) can be used to secure the signal carried on these circuits. The great majority of data sent by teletype and dataphone today, while in electrical pulse form, is *not* "scrambled" (as secret government transmissions are).

Another area of surveillance over records involves letters and the postal service. Congressional investigations have recently publicized the practice of "mail covers," by which the Post Office copies the return addresses on letters delivered to a given person or organization under investigation for postal or general crimes. If private parties manage to get access to letters (before, during, or after they are in the hands of the Post Office), such mail can be opened secretly by steaming the adhesive seam open, reading the contents, and re-sealing the envelope. Modern technology has added to these existing situations the possibility of passing visible light or reflected infra-red energy through an envelope and taking pictures of the contents. These pictures can then be read—or, more properly, deciphered—by persons skilled in reading handwriting or typing where lines are inverted and superimposed. There is also available today a needle-thin "flashlight" that can be inserted in a sealed envelope to "light it up" for quick reading by a trained investigator. Where more than one or two sheets of paper are in the envelope, or where a random pattern has been printed on the envelopes to make them opaque, this type of surveillance is greatly reduced or even prevented.

A major new field of physical surveillance concerns tapping the computer. The vital records of businesses, government agencies, and other large institutions are increasingly being put into computer tapes and programs. Until recently little thought had been given outside the national security agencies to the possibility that computers could be "tapped"; many computer experts assumed either that such a procedure was impossible or that the information would be valueless to the tapper if he could obtain it. However, there are several ways that the computer can be subjected to surveillance. One method is the direct tap, by which a line is added to the computer and then fed out to the eavesdropper's computer nearby. If the slight power drain is compensated for by special equipment, such a direct connection would be noticeable only through physical inspection. However, direct connection is usually difficult to install and continue without observation. A more effective technique is to tap the electrical signals that operate the "print-out" mechanism of computers, enabling the tapper to reproduce on his own printing equipment the same data the computer's owner is generating. Acoustical as well as radio tapping of the printing mechanism is also technically possible with many computers in general use. Military and defense contracts now require special shielding and other security methods for computers used in security operations, in recognition of the vulnerability of the computer to tapping, electronic sabotage, and deliberate alteration of programs.

Another type of electronic data surveillance is a commercial device, perfected in 1964, for measuring television audience choices.[40] This permits a person within a range of three or four city blocks to learn whether a television set is operating within a home and to which channel it is turned. Since the TV set gives off signals that are known as horizontal oscillators, radar-type equipment in a truck or nearby building can pick up those signals, compare them with the particular signal produced for each channel, and identify the one in use, all within a fraction of a second. The developers say that they can also count radio signals and identify the stations. It might be possible for such equipment to be adapted to obtain other signals transmitted from a home or office—such as signals in teletypewriters or teleprinters or even tape recorders—and to reproduce the messages transmitted. There has also been talk recently about equipment capable of eavesdropping on electric typewriters and transmitting the signals to a parallel typewriter on the eavesdropper's premises making instantaneous copies.

The Present Limits on Physical Surveillance

So far, this description of the capabilities of new physical surveillance technology may suggest that unbounded power has been transferred to the eavesdropper. It *is* true that scientific advances have limited the security that was once attached automatically to enclosed places, open spaces, and communication media; that miniaturization has made the task of installing transmitting and recording devices much simpler than it has ever been; and that the creation of unwitting "human broadcasting stations" is a new addition to the eavesdropping art. But any balanced account of physical-surveillance technology must note that objective conditions and deliberate counter-measures pose problems for eavesdroppers. Electrical equipment such as fluorescent lights or air-conditioners sometimes frustrate successful "bugging" of rooms by causing a "hum" on the circuit. Distance or physical obstacles will sometimes defeat parabolic microphones or telephotography. Noises created by traffic, heavy winds, or typewriters and mimeograph machines within offices can make it impossible to hear conversations from one office-building window to another across the street. Gaining entry undetected to homes, offices, or hotel rooms to plant eavesdropping equipment, or securing a room above, beside, or below a subject's quarters in a hotel or motel is not always as easy as it seems in movie or television scenarios. Nor is it always simple to obtain a listening post within range of the place under surveillance where the operator can stay for long periods of time without creating suspicion about his presence. Voice recognition is always a problem to the eavesdropper. Running wires from induction-coil wiretaps or coaxial cables of closed-circuit television cameras without detection is often difficult or even impossible in some situations. Limitations imposed by darkness can make some camera devices ineffective. Rapid movement by persons seeking to throw off possible surveillance is still more effective than the devices designed to "tag" individuals, since there are countless ways to get onto subways, trains, and planes at the last minute or to melt away into crowds of people on the streets.

Yet most of these hazards of surveillance operations are "technical problems" to be overcome by patience and ingenuity, rather than basic limits on the use of new surveillance technology. Where private investigators utilize the methods of disguise and impersonation (of telephone repairmen, street-construction crews, delivery men, city inspectors, dispensers of free samples, and the like), they can usually gain entry and secrete their equipment. With sufficient time and the use of powerful devices, they can also overcome noise and distance problems. A person may sometimes "shake off" followers, but with good tagging equipment he will be followed more often than he is able to slip away. Furthermore, when the eavesdropping or observation is authorized by the owner of the premises—whether a factory, business office, hotel, home, apartment house, restaurant, club, store, garage, government installation, or other place—problems of access, location, and recovery of equipment are eliminated. Such surveillance with the "owner's" consent, as will be shown, has become a rapidly growing part of eavesdropping in America. Viewed as a whole, then, "natural obstacles" are not a *major* limitation on the new physical surveillance.

Counter-measures are a different matter. It is a classic adage of warfare that one weapon advance quickly begets a counter-weapon. Every "ultimate weapon" in history has proved to be only a transition to a new system of balances. This analogy holds true in one important sense for the physical surveillance field, since anti-surveillance technology and professional "anti-surveillance" specialists have become increasingly important in recent years. To protect speech or acts from surveillance, five

basic sets of counter-measures are available: checking the site of the conversation to make sure it is free from "internal" devices; jamming the
electronic field to prevent transmission of signals; shielding conversations
against surveillance from outside; speaking in code; and sending speech
by special communication media.

The presence of most microphones and transmitting devices within
a room can be discovered and the premises can be "de-bugged" through
a variety of special equipment.[41] After a physical search, experts use
metal-locating devices (patterned after the mine detector) to detect microphones "concealed in wood, plaster, textile, plastic, or flesh surround-
ings," as one supplier company puts it. A "radio-frequency probe" de-
tects hidden radio-frequency and carrier transmitters by sweeping along
the band of usable frequencies to see whether any are being used by
equipment within the room. A "tone generator" and "low-impedance
test leads" are used to check all wires in a room; if a microphone is connected to any of these, an audible tone reveals the presence of a "bug."
"High-impedance test leads" enable the expert to check the telephone
without dismantling it, to see whether equipment has been installed inside it, converting the telephone into a two-way tap or a room microphone. This is the so-called third-wire tap system. A "radio-detection
probe" indicates the presence of a radio-frequency field such as that
given off by pocket-sized transmitters hidden on a person in the room or
within inanimate objects. This device is also available in miniature, so
that security officers can verify, without revealing that a radio probe is
being conducted, whether anyone in the room is carrying a concealed
transmitter. A highly simplified device marketed by some electronic
firms specializing in "counter-measure equipment" allows a person to
talk in the room while listening on a set of earphones to a receiver that
can sweep the frequency band; if the searcher hears his own voice over
the earphones, he knows that a bug is broadcasting from the premises.
Electronics and detective firms now offer electronic sweeps and "bug
searches" as a regular commercial service for businessmen, lawyers, and
others. They have a rapidly growing clientele.[42]

Whether more sophisticated listening devices developed by the Sovi-
ets—and, presumably, our own government—can be detected by these
sweep techniques is a matter of dispute. There have been reports of
ceramic and plastic equipment that will not register on metal probes.
The transmitter placed by the Russians in our Moscow Embassy had no
local power supply and no circuitry to register on detection equipment;
such transmitters are supplied by power from outside only at short, unpredictable intervals.

A good deal of protection against ordinary bugs and FM transmitters is possible through jamming devices that send out electronic signals
which prevent radio-transmitter pick-up of speech. A portable "vest-

pocket" jamming device was introduced in 1965 for general sale by one manufacturer at a cost under $100. More powerful units are available for installation in offices or as desk-size models.[43] However, these do not jam direct-wire taps or bugs, or those using electric currents, and the anti-bugs will create interference with many appliances in the area in which they are used.

There still remains the situation in which, though there are no bugs or taps within a room, conversation can be extracted by taking vibrations off the walls, windows, wiring, heating ducts, pipes, or doors by direct contact with those surfaces, by planting equipment fairly close to them, or by beaming in on them from considerable distances. To prevent such surveillance, government security measures call for completely portable "floating rooms," which are assembled by security experts immediately before a meeting, inside a larger room which is also checked thoroughly. The portable rooms may be made of sound-proof materials, or they may even be constructed entirely of glass to reveal the presence of any devices in the portable walls, floors, ceiling, and attaching mounts. For those outside of top-secret government and industrial circles, a "confidential room" can be built without windows, with sound-deadening shields, and with self-contained lighting, heating, and cooling equipment. In 1966 an assistant FBI director was granted a patent for a commercial "bug-proof" room-within-a-room, with transparent walls and furniture, including an air space between the walls full of "masking sound." Light is supplied through the transparent ceiling, eliminating all need for wires, and an electrically conductive radiation shield surrounds the room.[44]

There are readily available on the commercial market several devices (at $200 to $300) that scramble conversation going into one telephone receiver and unscramble by the "twin" device at the other end.[45] While passing over the telephone wire, the message is garbled and will not be intelligible to a wiretapper. Similar equipment is available for use with radio transmitters; police, for example, use this to avoid interception of police radio calls by criminals.[46] Given enough time and equipment, however, an eavesdropper can record the intercepted conversation and put it through a series of scrambling-unscrambling patterns until he finds the right code.

On highly secret telephone lines, elaborate precautions are taken to foil potential wiretappers. The lines are run in a tricoaxial cable, consisting of a central wire surrounded by two flexible conducting tubes, all individually insulated. The telephone connection is surrounded by a field of high-level electrical noise which prevents inductive contact with the inner cable. Scrambling can be carried out through the use of speech inverters which reverse speech frequencies, causing a simple phrase like "telephone company" to sound like "playafiend crinkenfell."

Another scrambling device known as band-splitting utilizes filters which split the speech signals into narrow bands that can be rearranged in many different combinations altered according to prearranged codes.[47] While speech inverters may give some protection against private eavesdroppers, a professional group can often obtain low-pass filters, balanced modulators, and audio oscillators which could duplicate the unscrambling apparatus at the receiving end of the line.

In addition to these three basic types of counter-surveillance technique, there are ways in which persons seeking to prevent eavesdropping on room conversations can defeat accurate listening even if an inside or outside device is monitoring the premises. Talking in very soft voices close to the other person while a radio, phonograph, or television set plays loudly will defeat even a dual-track or three-location bug, unless it is literally under the noses of the speakers.

However, several classic techniques for avoiding wiretapping or bugging can often be overcome today. Talking close to running water in a sink or shower will not prevent eavesdropping (unless the sound is so loud as to drown out the soft speech) since the "white sound" of the water can be filtered out electronically from a recording to leave only the speech. Tapping the telephone speaker-receiver with a pencil while conversing is also useless, unless the bug is inside the telephone speaker-receiver itself and is damaged by the concussion. If the parties to the call can hear it, the tapper can also. So-called "tap-proof cables" for telephone conversations, based on shielding the line in lead casings and checking the pressure level of helium gas in the cable to reveal punctures, have been overcome in tests utilizing sophisticated induction devices, careful entries into the cable, and pressure-maintenance systems. And, of course, such cables are not available for the average businessman or citizen.

Courses on anti-surveillance measures have advised government personnel during top-secret conferences to write down on scratch pads names of persons, key facts and figures, times and dates, (while also shielding them from possible camera observation), so that eavesdroppers will lack the basic ingredients of the conversation and will have only the narrative. Bringing in sheets of paper with numbered parts and referring only to numbers at key points in the conversation is another recommended practice. Such techniques are the least costly and most effective anti-intrusion measures on the market.

Finally, conversations can be sent between two points on pencil-thin beams produced by infra-red communicators or on laser beams.[48] RCA recently announced the development of a supersensitive light detector which could be used for laser communications, noting that someday all radio, television, and telephone conversations in the United States in a single day could be put on one laser light beam.[49] In addition, there is meteor-burst radio communication, by which radio signals are sent on the ionized air trails left by the trillions of meteors that strike the earth's atmosphere daily. Many of our security communications today use just such transmissions, since interception is extremely difficult if not impossible.[50]

In one sense, therefore, counter-measures which are either elaborately technological or as simple as writing down key facts are available to those who have reason to fear that their conversations or acts are under surveillance. Therefore the weapon-counter-weapon idea has some validity. But it should be noted immediately that we are talking not about wars (and only in the smallest way about surveillance in international espionage) but about conducting business in America, working in factories, handling labor-management relations, attending civic meetings, staying at hotels and clubs, eating at restaurants, running local and national government, and carrying on our political and personal lives. If the effective minimum in counter-measures calls for a $400 search kit, trained experts to use the equipment (at $25 to $50 per search, per room, each time), and the self-consciousness to talk in hushed tones over blaring music while writing down key words, then we are talking about counter-measures that, to be successful, would alter profoundly the entire physical and psychological pattern of affairs in the United States. In this sense, not only the initiative but also the power to capitalize upon the normal patterns of American society has passed, at least for the present, to those who use the new physical-surveillance technology.

Physical Surveillance in the Next Decade

So far, we have been describing existing technology. Yet the pace of change in electronics, optics, and microminiaturization is already so swift that the latest "existing" methods are outmoded almost before a book about them can be published. If society and law are to be ready for the future, we must examine what the coming decade may bring. The best way to do this is to separate those possible developments directly aimed at conducting secret physical surveillance from those possible changes in communication and record keeping by our society which would affect the present surveillance-and-privacy situation.

In the field of locating individuals and following their movements, signal-transmitter "tags" promise to become steadily more powerful and less expensive. As the microelectronic circuits and microminiature components now available in space work and laboratory experiments filter into general use, such tags will become available in much smaller sizes, increasing still further the possibilities for secreting them in an individual's clothing or his personal and professional accessories. Receiving or scanning units will also grow more powerful and smaller, making it easier for investigators to carry them in concealed form on their persons.

Will it be possible to go from the present "radio pill" that passes temporarily through the digestive tract to new long-duration or even permanent implacements of "tagging" devices on or in the body? Invisible magnetic-ink tattoos might be applied (for example, to babies at birth) to provide permanent identification of every individual; these might possibly be used also for locating a subject. Existing microminiaturized transmitters the size of a pinhead might be coded with an identification number, enclosed in a permanent capsule, and implanted under the skin by a simple and painless surgical operation. Once in place, this tag would do no damage to the body, but when "interrogated" electronically by an outside beam, it would emit an identifying number. Experimental work has been reported in which such units have been made and tested successfully to monitor the continued presence of people in a two- to three-mile radius.

It is also possible that, for their limited lifetimes, such implanted units can be made to transmit the speech sounds vibrated through the body (especially by the bone structure) when the subject is speaking and is within microwave-beam range. Such a possible "body tag" or "body mike" has some obvious limitations for clandestine surveillance. It would have to be implanted surgically, though this could be done while the subject was rendered unconscious and its presence might not be noticed without an electronic check of the body. A greater limitation lies in the fact that a long-life or lifetime battery for such a microminiature unit is not presently available. However, it is possible that low-level electrical charges generated within the body or other bodily power sources, such as body heat or pressure changes, might be harnessed to provide the operating energy.

In the field of visual surveillance, miniaturization promises to reduce the size of cameras further and to make their concealment on premises or on the investigator's person even easier. The next decade may well see wireless, battery-operated television "eyes" the size of buttons, which would transmit by microwave to three-inch portable television receivers. These could be in the form of either closed-circuit TV for secret surveillance or pick-ups by TV reporters for even more "candid" broadcasting. In addition, the trend toward building in closed-circuit television during construction of new apartment houses and factories will probably be greatly spurred as unit costs for the cameras decrease and their size is reduced. Where built-in listening devices are now employed, built-in TV devices will be a "natural" surveillance growth.

Long-range photography in visible light has been advanced to cover incredible distances, as the U-2 flights over Cuba showed dramatically. Reconnaissance satellites now used by the United States and the Soviet Union provide continuing electromagnetic surveillance from space.

Russia's Cosmos satellite circles the earth at 18,000 miles per hour at a distance ranging from 300 to 120 miles, and it is presumed to carry high-resolution aerial cameras as well as electromagnetic receivers which record radio and radar signals on magnetic tape. The United States Samos satellite also carries magnetic tape and cameras with the capacity to identify ground objects in the Soviet Union only two feet long. It can also literally tap Russian long-distance telephone calls by using sensitive receivers to intercept their inter-city microwave telephone links. Another spy-in-the-sky project is the Midas satellite, which carries out infra-red surveillance.[51] Infra-red photography increases the range of surveillance, registering objects by the warmth they give off. "Night eye" long-distance surveillance techniques make night-time photography and television viewing without infra-red illumination practical for substantial distances. Some of these techniques in adapted forms will be likely to filter out into the police and private sectors in the coming years.

One leading application for speech surveillance will come from the more sophisticated techniques of using light. Experiments have shown that an infra-red light beam transmitted by a five-inch reflecting telescope with a sensitive photocell at its focal point (available at World War II surplus stores) can pick up speech uttered thirty-four miles away.[52]

The use of laser technology is another technique which may see rapid advances.[53] It may be possible to increase the effectiveness of laser beams so that pick-ups from window-vibration surveillance could be raised well beyond the present ranges. One corporation has announced the development of a laser TV system which allows subjects in complete darkness to appear on the screen as if in daylight brightness, since the beam is invisible.[54] Night-time surveillance would be greatly aided by this type of operation.

Another type of speech surveillance which might be accomplished is the use of high-speed computers to search eavesdropping tape recordings to locate a specific speaker in a large mass of different voices. If a speaker's previously recorded "voice-print" [55] (a spectogram can provide cue words that identify a speaker with great accuracy, much as does a fingerprint) could be fed into the computer as the object to be found, the computer could monitor telephone conversations or search masses of tapes, printing out only where the conversation included the voice-printed subject. It may also be possible to use phoneme sounds (bits of speech sound into which language can be broken, such as "th," "sh") to enable computers to spot particular words in oral communications, such as "atomic," "Pentagon," "Rockefeller," or "Cosa Nostra," and to take off only conversations containing these signals.

One prospect for both visual and speech surveillance that promises to become a major instrument in the next decade is the aerial viewing and listening device. Already demonstrated to the American and Canadian military by several firms in both countries,[56] this is a unit with two counter-rotating rotor blades which is sent to hover aloft, attached by cable to ground-control equipment. About three to four feet in diameter and weighing forty to fifty pounds, the surveillance unit now carries closed-circuit TV equipment that transmits pictures of objects at ranges of one mile or more. It could carry listening equipment just as easily. The unit hovers at altitudes of 100 to 2,000 feet and rotates 360 degrees for tracking purposes. At present the tethered platform is being developed for military reconnaissance in the field—for example, to allow a patrol to scan what lies over the ridges of hills without having to cross them, or to conduct close-search operations for nearby enemy installations. However, several American companies plan to develop commercial models for use in property protection (to scan railroad freight yards or large open-air depots), police work (for riot control observation), and related private situations. Since the hovering and guidance systems are simple to operate, any person with such a unit could watch, photograph, and listen to activity within a mile or more of his own property, without ever entering the physical air space of his neighbors.

Though this particular hovering surveillance unit is now attached by cable to the ground for television scanning, a cable-free unit (six feet in diameter) driven by wireless microwave has already been built by an American company. The size of such units could be drastically reduced by microminiaturization in the future. If so, sky-colored surveillance units the size of baseballs may be produced in the next decade to be sent aloft and hover outside windows, over park benches, and along streets, to conduct both sight and sound surveillance.

The other way to consider the future of physical surveillance is to look ahead to over-all changes in the communication and record-keeping processes of American society. For example, it is clear that there will be far more field-to-office and car-to-office communication by devices of the radio-telephone and "wrist-radio" types in the next decade. Mailing of letters, reports, and data may be cut sharply as data-phone and photo-transmission systems are adopted for use within units of a company or government agency. The present picture-phone conversation, in which individuals see as well as hear each other, will probably be expanded so that units will be in homes and offices, not just at special telephone centers. Television conferences that join persons at various separate locations for business, political, and governmental purposes will become commonplace and will include international conferences carried by the communication-satellite system. Military and diplomatic business will be carried out by direct conversations between field commanders and the Pentagon or by ambassadors and the White House, again through communication-satellite relays.[57] Signaling devices have been produced already[58] (and will become smaller and more powerful) by which persons within a building or miles away can be buzzed to let them know that they are wanted or that they should call in: these systems might also be used for locating individuals. A similar use would flow from the telephone-registry system (thoroughly feasible in the future) by which a person moving about a city would punch his code number into the telephone where he was visiting, so that computers could scan telephones in the city to locate him for the receipt of calls.

Many more prospects for new communication channels could be mentioned, but the basic point is thoroughly clear. Our society is taking more and more to the air—for speaking, for meeting, and for the exchange of written data. To this extent, the question of physical surveillance will become an even more important concern than it is at present. The older physical barriers of wall, file cabinet, and open space will offer even less protection than they do now. The concluding chapter of this volume will discuss new ways in which science and technology might be harnessed to the protection of speech, acts, and records. For the moment, however, the vital point is that the balance of power in the struggle over individual and group privacy in the electronic age has shifted unmistakably in favor of those conducting physical surveillance.

CHAPTER FIVE

Private and Government Use of Physical Surveillance

The Spread of Surveillance Technology Since 1945

ANY LITERATE American realizes that wiretapping, bugging, and camera surveillance are widely used in the United States today. Before presenting a detailed portrait of who is watching and listening to whom, and for what purposes, it is helpful to explain how the physical surveillance technology made its way to users so quickly, and to private as well as law-enforcement agencies.

FACTORS ACCELERATING PRIVATE USE OF THE NEW DEVICES

The basic factor advancing private use of eavesdropping is the growth of the private-detective trade since World War II. Today about 20,000 private detectives are doing investigative work in their own firms, for large detective agencies, for insurance and credit companies, or as corporate security officers. Most of these men are former government law-enforcement agents or military-intelligence veterans, trained in electronic eavesdropping techniques in government schools.[1] One Washington, D.C., private detective firm proudly advertises this fact: "Our staff and associates include former investigators of the Department of Justice, War Department, Naval Intelligence, Treasury Department and others of unusual qualifications. Secret electronic sound and evidence recording, transcription, mobile radio and complete laboratory equipment." In addition, private detectives make extensive use of former telephone-company employees, whose $75 to $100 a week salary as telephone linemen can rise to $200 to $300 weekly as "wiremen" for a busy private-detective agency.[2]

The factor that has done most to spread tapping and bugging throughout the private-detective profession has been the simplification

of equipment and techniques, coupled with aggressive promotion of the
new equipment by manufacturers who specialize in selling to private
investigators. Though new companies spring up continually, leaders in
this trade during the mid-1960's have been WJS Electronics of Hollywood, California; Tracer Investigative Products Corp. of Palm Beach,
Florida; C. H. Stoelting of Chicago, Illinois; R. B. Clifton of Miami,
Florida; Mosler Research Products Inc., of Danbury, Connecticut; Solar
Research Corp. of Oakland Park, Florida; Emanuel Mittleman of New
York City; and the Fargo Company of San Francisco, California. Such
firms mail out thousands of catalogues showing tapping devices, miniature microphones, and cameras, and will offer detailed instructions for
the installation or use of the devices. "Take advantage of the progress in
Space Age Electronics," one producer exhorts; "improve the efficiency
and effectiveness of your Investigation and Security efforts." [3] R. B. Clifton tells investigators, "Many new ideas are born from the requests we
get from people like yourself. So, if you have need for anything unusual
in Electronic Equipment, please write." [4] At conventions of groups such
as the American Society of Industrial Security Officers, manufacturers put
on extensive demonstrations of surveillance devices; display tables and
booths overflow with the latest in "surveillance hardware." [5] In September, 1965, for example, the annual meeting of the Council of International Investigators featured demonstrations of microphones hidden in
cigarette lighters, clasps of ladies' handbags and cigarette packs; two-inch
"palm" cameras; and similar equipment. "The main reason I came," one
investigator told reporters, "was to see the latest in electronic listening
devices." [6]

Just as surveillance-equipment manufacturers promote their wares
energetically to detectives, so the private detective agency now actively
solicits clients for electronic-eavesdropping work. For example, Montclair Technical Services, located in Bloomfield, Connecticut, sends out
letters to lawyers throughout that state, introducing itself as a service
"which specializes in matters requiring the use of electronic listening and
recording equipment." Montclair boasts that its arsenal of devices and
extensive experience "enable us to intercept and record conversation in
virtually any physical situation." Attorneys were assured that Montclair
was discreet, kept all its charges to the attorney confidential (so that the
attorney's charge to the client was a "private matter" between them),
and that names of attorneys or clients using Montclair were never given
out as references. "[S]pecial care is taken to ensure privacy." [7]

In addition to solicitations aimed at special groups, such as lawyers
and businessmen, private detectives are boldly advertising their surveillance skills to the general public. During 1964 and 1965, I examined the
classified telephone directories for several cities in each of the fifty states
and the District of Columbia. In eighty-six cities, located in thirty-nine

SURVEILLANCE ADVERTISEMENTS FOR PRIVATE-DETECTIVE AGENCIES IN 86 COMMUNITIES (1964-65) FROM CITY CLASSIFIED TELEPHONE DIRECTORIES

CITIES WITH AGENCY ADS (By Alphabetical Order of States)	SOUND SURVEILLANCE			VISUAL SURVEILLANCE				
	"Compact Transmittor Microphones" "Secret Microphones"	"Latest Electronic Recording Devices"	"Recorded Evidence"	"Motion Pictures" "Still and Motion Pictures"	"Infra-red and Ultra-violet Work"	"Telephoto Work"	"Closed-Circuit Television"	"Photographic Evidence"
	1	2	3	4	5	6	7	8
Birmingham, Ala.		X		X				X
Phoenix, Ariz.	X	X	X					X
Tucson, Ariz.	X		X					
Fort Smith, Ark.		X					X	X
Hot Springs, Ark.				X				X
Little Rock, Ark.				X				X
Fair Oaks, Folsom & Rio Linda, Calif.		X						X
Kern County, Calif.	X	X	X	X				X
Los Angeles, Calif.	X	X	X	X	X			X
Oakland, Calif.	X	X	X	X				X
Orange County, Calif.	X	X	X	X				X
San Francisco, Calif.		X	X	X				X

City	1	2	3	4	5	6	7	8
Denver, Colo.	X	X						X
Bridgeport, Conn.				X				X
Hartford, Conn.		X	X	X				X
Washington, D. C.		X	X	X		X		X
Wilmington, Del.				X			X	X
Greater Hollywood, Fla.		X						
Ft. Lauderdale, Fla.		X	X	X				X
Jacksonville, Fla.			X	X		X		
Atlanta, Ga.			X	X		X		X
Honolulu, Hawaii		X		X				X
Belleville, Ill.	X	X		X				X
Chicago, Ill.			X					X
Springfield, Ill.		X						X
Indianapolis, Ind.				X				
Topeka, Kansas				X				X
Wichita, Kansas		X		X			X	X
Lexington, Ky.								X
Baton Rouge, La.	X	X		X				X
New Orleans, La.					X			X
Shreveport, La.			X					
Baltimore, Md.		X		X			X	X
Boston, Mass.		X		X			X	X

SURVEILLANCE ADVERTISEMENTS FOR PRIVATE-DETECTIVE AGENCIES IN 86 COMMUNITIES (1964–65) FROM CITY CLASSIFIED TELEPHONE DIRECTORIES

CITIES WITH AGENCY ADS (By Alphabetical Order of States)	SOUND SURVEILLANCE			VISUAL SURVEILLANCE				
	"Compact Transmittor Microphones" "Secret Microphones" 1	"Latest Electronic Recording Devices" 2	"Recorded Evidence" 3	"Motion Pictures" "Still and Motion Pictures" 4	"Infra-red and Ultra-violet Work" 5	"Telephoto Work" 6	"Closed-Circuit Tele-vision" 7	"Photographic Evidence" 8
Lynn, Mass.			X					X
Springfield, Mass.			X	X				X
Battle Creek, Mich.	X			X				X
Detroit, Mich.			X			X		X
Flint, Mich.			X	X		X		X
Grand Rapids, Mich.			X					X
St. Paul, Minn.								X
Kansas City, Mo.		X		X				X
Springfield, Mo.			X					X
St. Joseph, Mo.			X					X
Omaha, Neb.			X	X				X
Las Vegas, Nev.		X	X	X	X			X
Reno-Carson City, Nev.	X			X				X

City	1	2	3	4	5	6
Nashua, N. Hamp.		X				
Hudson County, N. J.	X		X		X	
Newark, N. J.	X					
Plainfield-Somerville, N. J.	X		X		X	
Albuquerque, N. Mex.	X		X		X	
Santa Fe, N. Mex.	X		X		X	
Albany, N. Y.	X					
Buffalo, N. Y.						X
Newburgh, N. Y.	X				X	
Syracuse, N. Y.	X			X		
Troy, N. Y.	X					
Asheville, N. C.					X	
Charlotte, N. C.	X				X	
Greensboro, N. C.	X				X	
Winston-Salem, N. C.	X				X	
Akron, Ohio	X		X	X	X	
Cincinnati, Ohio	X				X	
Cleveland, Ohio	X			X		
Oklahoma City, Okla.	X			X		
Tulsa, Okla.	X	X				
Portland, Ore.	X	X	X	X	X	

SURVEILLANCE ADVERTISEMENTS FOR PRIVATE-DETECTIVE AGENCIES IN 86 COMMUNITIES (1964–65) FROM CITY CLASSIFIED TELEPHONE DIRECTORIES

CITIES WITH AGENCY ADS (By Alphabetical Order of States)	SOUND SURVEILLANCE			VISUAL SURVEILLANCE				
	"Compact Transmittor Microphones" "Secret Microphones" 1	"Latest Electronic Recording Devices" 2	"Recorded Evidence" 3	"Motion Pictures" "Still and Motion Pictures" 4	"Infra-red and Ultra-violet Work" 5	"Telephoto Work" 6	"Closed-Circuit Tele-vision" 7	"Photographic Evidence" 8
Philadelphia, Pa.		X						
Providence-Pawtucket, R. I.		X	X					X
Columbia, S. C.		X		X				X
Knoxville, Tenn.		X						
Memphis, Tenn.		X						X
Nashville, Tenn.			X					X
Austin, Texas			X					X
Corpus Christi, Texas			X					X
Dallas, Texas	X	X	X					X
El Paso, Texas	X	X					X	X
Houston, Texas			X					X
Salt Lake City, Utah	X	X		X		X		X

Norfolk, Va.					X
Roanoke, Va.	X			X	
Richmond, Va.			X		X
Seattle, Wash.	X	X	X		X
Spokane, Wash.	X	X	X	X	X
Milwaukee, Wisc.			X		X

states and the District of Columbia, I found under the headings of "Detectives" and "Investigators" advertisements that offered prospective clients a full range of electronic-eavesdropping and camera observation. (A spot check in 1966 showed that the same pattern still prevailed.) Discreet ads state that the firm will secure "Photographic and Recorded Evidence" or that "Evidence is Preserved by Photographic and Recorded Means." Others speak more plainly, advertising "Electronic Surveillance" and "Automatic Electronic Recording Devices." Some ads even include illustrations of agents with head sets listening to telephone calls or placing contact microphones against the walls of adjoining rooms. Still other ads offer prospective clients a complete catalogue of the surveillance services available through its operatives. Argus Investigation Service of Tucson, Arizona, lists: "Electronic Recording Equipment," "Motion Pictures and Still Camera Work," "Closed Circuit Television," and "Compact Transmitter Microphones." Confidential Investigations in Los Angeles, California, provides this catalogue: "Competent Investigators Equipped with Modern Electronic and Photographic Equipment. Portable Listening Devices, Wireless Transmittors, Recorders, Cameras, Mobile Two-way Mirror Units, etc. for Any Fact-finding Assignment. Secret Microphones Installed. Your Premises Searched for Listening Devices." The Legal Investigation Service of New Orleans, Louisiana, announces: "We are Trained in Modern Methods of Investigations such as Polygraph (lie detector), Electronic Surveillance by Aircraft, Telescopic Photography, Infra-Red and Ultra-Violet Photography, and Black Light Marking."

Another major factor in the spread of private use of surveillance devices is the distribution of the new equipment to the general public with aggressive promotion urging retail customers to purchase the hardware with which to become secret observers of private events. This public promotion has grown more blatant and openly voyeuristic each year of the mid-1960's. The "Memocord" pocket recorder, advertised in major newspapers throughout the country, stresses the "easily concealed tiny pin microphone [that] lets you record conferences and interviews." [8] Department and toy stores feature "The Bird," a stuffed parrot on a wooden base that comes equipped with a built-in tape recorder; buyers are urged to turn it on secretly, leave the room, and find out what "your company and friends say about you when you are gone." [9] Advertisements for "The Big Ear" and "The Snooper," two long-distance (over 500 feet) disc-reflector listening devices equipped with stethoscope earphones, have appeared in leading novelty catalogues, the Diner's Club Magazine (circulation 700,000) and many others. "The best part," the ads state, "a regular tape recorder can be plugged into the back [of the listening unit] to take everything down. Have fun!" Similar ads offer a "confidential pocket camera" as used by "the French Sureté" and a tiny

"10 X monocular" device "fine for outdoorsmen, snoopers, etc." [10] The Concord 330, the "world's first [commercially marketed] fully automatic voice-operated portable tape recorder," is advertised in national magazines with the recommendation that it can be used for "Secret Recordings . . . for investigations, interrogations, gathering of evidence. Works unattended. Voice starts and stops it." [11] Several varieties of the "new listen-in Monitor" are advertised for hearing and recording two-way telephone conversations "without touching or picking up the receiver. Sent with easy instructions." [12] Literature for the Miles "Walkie-Recordall" (a listening and tape-recording unit built into an ordinary-looking leather briefcase) stresses that "left unsupervised, W-R with an optional attachment silently turns itself on at the first word spoken in the room or on the phone and turns itself off after the voices stop. . . . It can even operate undetected in a locked safe or desk drawer." [13] American Geloso Electronics features an "Attaché case Secret Recorder"—"A private ear for the private eye and others"—for "investigators, attorneys, law enforcement agencies, personnel directors, interviewers, etc."—"looks like an innocent attaché case. . . ." [14]

The most blatant campaign aimed at the general public is the activity of the Continental Telephone Supply Company, with stores in such cities as New York, Philadelphia, and Miami, and national direct-sale newspaper advertising. Continental features telephone monitors ("Just think of the uses . . . !") and miniature recording devices ("to record unobserved and secretly"), equipped with "tieclasp microphone." [15] When a Continental Telephone Supply store opened recently in Miami, its invitation read:

> Big Brother is going to have his own department store. You are cordially invited to attend the opening of a unique new store designed to cater to members of our suspicious society. . . . This new retail outlet offers the very latest in telephone bugging devices, spy cameras, probes that can pick up voices through walls, lamps that are actually radio transmitters, disguised tape recorders and a host of other electronic privacy invaders.

"An automobile or a gun is neither moral nor immoral," the store owner said, "but the people who own them are. Whether we sell them or someone else sells them, they're going to be sold." [16]

Another spur to "amateur" activity is the advertising aimed at electronics hobbyists and self-appointed "detectives." These ads range from fully detailed articles (with plans) such as "Build the Shotgun Sound Snooper," in *Popular Electronics* for June of 1964 ("endless applications . . . construction is easy . . . the cost is reasonable. Don't delay!")[17] to the mail-order ads that appear monthly in the half-dozen leading popular magazines of applied science and electronics (with combined circulations in the millions), such as *Science and Mechanics, Popular Science,* and *Popular Electronics.* A typical ad during 1965 and 1966 aimed at investigators and the public read:

> *Investigators—Detectives—Industrial Security Officers:* New 1966 line of Electronic Surveillance Devices. Incorporating most advanced subminiature design. . . . Foolproof wireless sets are extremely *simple to use!* You *do not* have to be an engineer to get *professional* results with this equipment. [New York City firm].[18]

One ad offered a complete course for the novice in surreptitious surveillance:

> *Be A Spy.* Correspondence course on wire tapping, bugging, telescopic sound pickup, recording techniques, microphotography, and invisible photography. Lessons in surveillance, tailing, and use of equipment. Complete course. $22.50. [Hollywood, California, firm].[19]

None of these suppliers limit their sales to law-enforcement officers or licensed private detectives. Simply by putting a rubber-stamp address marked "Beach Personal Services Agency, Miami Beach, Florida," on plain white stationery, I was able to get catalogues, place orders, and receive the $22.50 "Be A Spy" course, nor was the slightest question raised by anyone as to who I was or what I would do with the equipment.

The impact of such readily available devices and voyeuristic promotion has already been felt in a rise of private "amateur" eavesdropping and clandestine filming. For example, three teen-agers in Chico, California, with a strong interest in electronics decided to test what they had been reading about wiretapping in popular magazines. Using stolen telephone-company equipment, they climbed a telephone pole near the home of the local police chief, rigged up their tap, and listened in on his calls for some time until their activities in the area drew suspicion from local residents and they were apprehended.[20]

In 1961 it was disclosed that a group of electronics enthusiasts at the Groton School in Massachusetts had installed miniaturized listening devices in the office of their headmaster. The conversations were recorded on tape and were played back as entertainment at parties of the school boys. The surveillance leaked out only when one of the boys said something to the headmaster that indicated the occurrence of eavesdropping, and bit by bit the story was extracted.[21] In 1963 a twenty-nine-year-old man in Denver, Colorado, who said electronics was his "hobby," was discovered to have tapped the telephone-terminal box in the basement of the apartment house in which he lived. By wiring the circuits into his own telephone connection, he was able to note by a flashing bulb on a control board set up in his own apartment which tenant's phone was in use, whereupon he could listen to the conversation.[22] Another type of example involves landlords in New Hampshire and West Virginia who bugged the bedrooms of tenants.[23] A Des Moines, Iowa, man was arrested after he had installed five concealed microphones in the bedroom of a woman in an adjoining apartment. He had also installed an intricate series of reflecting one-way mirrors that enabled him to look down on the woman's bed from the ceiling of the adjoining apartment, which he had rented under an assumed name. From inside the woman's bedroom, the mirror looked like a glass light fixture.[24]

Private eavesdropping has also been spurred by basic cultural factors in contemporary life. In the first half of the twentieth century social conventions against eavesdropping managed to inhibit widespread use of wiretaps, dictographs, and hidden cameras, even though property owners had theft problems in those decades, men had just as much itching curiosity to know the secrets around them, and legal prohibitions were no stronger then than now. What is different is that today we live in the age of Superspy and scientific wizardry, and this has been eroding our mores against secret eavesdropping. Our press celebrates the eavesdropping exploits of the CIA and the FBI and applauds the scientific advances that made possible our U-2 camera flights and Samos spy satellites. The fact that our opponents are deep in the surveillance industry makes most Americans feel that our efforts must be not just as good, but better. On television, the men from U.N.C.L.E. and Sunset Strip, Honey West, Maxwell Smart, and dozens of other private and government sleuths regularly employ real and futuristic surveillance devices to fight villainy and to defend truth. Audiences would be astonished if bugs and TV eyes were not used by these heroes as standard operating procedure. Of course warrants are never obtained on these programs, no one is ever restrained from using surveillance devices, and there are no prosecutions for illegal eavesdropping. This atmosphere is further deepened by the James Bond spy novels and spy movies of the mid-1960's, as well as the children's toy industry, which has flooded the gift market with toy listening devices, secret cameras, and lie detectors. The $5 models of "The Big Ear" sold to youngsters with specific suggestions to "bug the neighborhood" make eavesdropping just good American fun.

Even the hundreds of articles written about the new surveillance devices in the press, and television programs on local stations and national networks have helped to spread private use of the devices. Conversations with surveillance-equipment manufacturers indicate that sales pour in after each "exposé" of business and private eavesdropping; articles about the activities of leading electronics specialists have a similar effect in stimulating clientele. The rise in sales is even more pronounced when a man such as Ben Jamil, president of Continental Telephone, is invited as a guest on the Johnny Carson show (in May, 1966) to display his line of surveillance devices and to justify their use, without the slightest demurrer from his smiling host.

A final factor that has contributed to the growth of private eavesdropping is the collapse of legal controls, which will be discussed in detail later in this chapter. The fact to note here, however, is that there are no federal or state controls today over the manufacture of devices designed for surreptitious listening or watching, or the advertisement or sale of these to the general public or to private detectives. The great majority of states do not have any modern statutes on wiretapping to encompass the new tapping devices of the 1960's, and an even larger majority of states have no prohibitions against electronic eavesdropping or secret camera surveillance. A study of state and local wiretapping and eavesdropping prosecutions during the past decade shows that most of the leading eavesdroppers—men such as Bernard Spindel, Russell Mason, and their associates—continually have their indictments dismissed or their convictions reversed because of the antiquated nature of existing statutes.

FACTORS ACCELERATING GOVERNMENT USE OF THE NEW DEVICES

When we turn to government acquisition of surveillance technology, we begin with the recognition that the equipment is readily available and actively promoted. In addition to small shops and electronic-parts stores, several dozen firms are manufacturing and selling surveillance devices to law-enforcement agencies.[25] Their catalogues go to thousands of such government offices, and their products are advertised extensively in law-enforcement journals such as *Police Chief* and *Law and Order*. One leading manufacturer, C. H. Stoelting, advertises its surveillance equipment line as follows:

> Complete coordinated systems used extensively by Government Agencies during investigations of highly classified nature are now available for use by all law enforcement agencies and industrial organizations. . . . The equipment is made so any average investigator can install and operate the equipment successfully without difficulty. No special radio knowledge is required beyond the very elementary home variety of electricity. Simple and complete instructions accompany each unit.[26]

In addition to providing demonstrations of this equipment to individual government agencies or at law-enforcement conventions, some of the suppliers put on special schools in surveillance techniques for law-enforcement clients. Ralph Ward, Vice President of Mosler Research

Products, has given a detailed, anecdote-filled, "how-to-do-it" lecture on "Surreptitious Listening Methods" for prospective Mosler clients. This describes the basic equipment for all types of listening, shows how to install the equipment when the investigator "has access to area" or when he does not, and also deals with self-wiring, auto-wiring, and bug detection.[27] Solar Research Corporation of Oakland, Florida, until its building was destroyed recently by a fire, ran several special courses in surveillance methods under its "National Intelligence Academy." A two-week basic course, which laid out fundamentals, was followed by a second two-week course that went into advanced application. The combined tuition price was $175. The courses, open only to full-time law-enforcement officers, were for men from "Police, Sheriffs, Highway Patrol, Attorney General's Office, District Attorney's Office, and similar agencies." [28]

As this new equipment has come on the market, police journals have run special articles and feature columns to describe the latest advances in each area of surveillance. These include detailed, "how-to-do-it" articles on telephone tapping, radio-beacon tailing, and long-term recording.[29]

Between the late 1950's and the mid-1960's, then, microminiaturization, simplification of devices, cost reduction, and widespread distribution greatly increased the level of governmental and private-detective eavesdropping in America and brought amateur activity to serious levels for the first time. Since charges of "widespread tapping and bugging" are often made without convincing documentation, it is vital to have some estimate of the real proportions of current physical surveillance in the United States. Between 1958 and 1961 I wrote to 125 newspapers, at least one in each state, asking for copies of their clippings on electronic eavesdropping in their areas. Almost every newspaper provided such clippings. Between 1963 and 1967 a professional clipping agency secured articles on electronic eavesdropping from 1,800 daily newspapers, 9,000 weeklies, and 4,600 trade and consumer magazines. A thorough search of legislative and administrative hearings, court records, police journals, technical magazines, and similar materials between 1958 and 1967 added to these primary sources. Finally, I held more than seventy-five personal interviews with local, state, and federal law-enforcement officials, private investigators, surveillance-equipment manufacturers, telephone-company officials, crime-commission staffs, state and federal legislative-committee members and staffs, federal executive officials, military officers, practicing lawyers, civic-group specialists, and behavioral scientists. There is no guesswork or loose estimation in the account that follows.

Physical-Surveillance Activity by Private Persons

Private use of hidden surveillance devices can be divided into eight main areas of American life in which surveillance has become sufficiently widespread to warrant serious concern: business affairs, labor relations, professional life, personal and family affairs, customer surveillance, civic and political affairs, government agencies, and surreptitious research observations.

LISTENING AND WATCHING IN THE BUSINESS WORLD

Surveillance technology has been felt in the business community in two ways: surveillance of competitors and surveillance by business of its own executives, employees, and production facilities. Surveillance by business competitors has been rising steadily since 1958.[30] In 1965, at a time when Schenley Industries was considering a highly confidential offer for the purchase of Schenley stock, details of private discussions leaked out in a manner that suggested eavesdropping had been used. Anti-eavesdropping experts called in to investigate found a tiny transmitter installed in the paneling behind the bar in a home workshop of the president of Schenley. In addition, wiretaps were found attached to the telephones of the president and other high executives in the firm's Miami offices.[31]

Wiretapping is particularly widespread in the construction industry, where competitive bidding information can mean success in highly prized contract awards. An executive from one large corporation gave the following account of his firm's experience:

Recently, we were involved in a competitive-bid contract. We had spent some considerable time and effort determining that our bid would be $80 million. At the opening of the bids, one of our competitors underbid us by only $200,000 and got the contract. It was highly unlikely in a contract of this nature that two bids would be so close. We were very suspicious . . . and hired an investigator who discovered that our telephones were being tapped at three different locations throughout the country.[32]

One anti-eavesdropping expert reported that "head offices of supermarket chains are prime targets for listening devices,"[33] along with chemical, drug, design, electronics, and certain consumer-product industries in which trade secrets play a vital role. Large real-estate firms experienced increased electronic espionage in 1966, according to a *New York Times* survey.[34] A case in 1962, involving a surplus-aircraft-parts company, was uncovered when a Hollywood, California, private detective was convicted for installing a miniature "parasite microphone" on the telephone line leading from the home of the company's owner. The detective, whose activities had been communicated to the police by an estranged lady friend, was found sitting in his car half a mile from the site of the wiretap, recording the long-distance business conference calls between the businessman and a Texas company.[35]

While these incidents involved telephone taps, the trend in business espionage has recently shifted to the planting of room microphones. The President of Southern Counties Gas Co. of Los Angeles, California, learned in 1963 that a miniaturized radio transmitter had been placed in his desk telephone. "We don't really know when or why it was put there or who did it," the president said, "but it apparently had been broadcasting my private conversations to someone's receiver outside.[36] In 1963 a bug was found taped under the office desk of the president of a large corporation in Florida which had been plagued by leaks of business secrets.[37] In Washington, D.C., in 1962, a cigarette-pack radio transmitter was found taped to the underside of a coffee table in a suite at the Mayflower Hotel. Meeting in the room were the executives and lawyers for the El Paso Natural Gas Company and the Colorado Interstate Gas Company, which were appearing before the Federal Power Commission in a hotly contested proceeding involving a pipeline route to Southern California. Three private detectives were convicted for installing and operating the device.[38] Even executives "on the move" have been monitored, as in the case of an engineer whose automobile was bugged by a radio transmitter under the front seat, to obtain information about a pending European business venture.[39] In another instance, a market speculator paid a sixty-three-year-old cleaning woman $2,000 a month to place a "bugged" pen-and-calendar set in the office of a rival speculator to obtain stock predictions and advance "dope" on the market situation.[40]

Camera devices of various kinds have been employed in business espionage. Everything from telephoto lenses to aerial long-range photography has been used in Detroit to gain information about new car models, specifications, and performance. *Business Week* described "one of the more notorious cases" as the "nine-camera television system" that was found "installed behind overhead ventilation louvers in a Detroit auto design room." [41] Nighttime photography through infra-red light has been used in efforts to see products on laboratory tables or work benches when daytime access would have been too hazardous.[42] One private detective revealed that he had used closed-circuit television (as well as a microphone) to enable a client to observe hotel meetings held by a competitor in the business-machines field, at which new models were displayed.[43]

The installation of listening or watching devices by businesses to survey their own executives and employees is another rapidly spreading use of surveillance in the business community. In a recent attempt to measure the extent of this type of eavesdropping, a survey of security officers was conducted in 1965 by an editor of the law-enforcement journal *Law and Order*.[44] The survey drew responses from eighty-seven industrial, business-office, retail store, and laboratory organizations, whose work forces ranged from 200 to 3,400 employees. The results established that twenty-three firms—26.4 per cent of the sample—engaged in eavesdropping. The industrial firms which used eavesdropping said that they placed miniature transmitter devices in conference rooms, hid microphones in rest rooms and lounge areas, and monitored "selected groups" of telephone extensions. Nine out of the fourteen retail stores surveyed said they "had employed hidden microphones in washrooms and dressing rooms." Three of the eleven laboratory groups indicated that they use "telephone monitoring, hidden microphones and 'other devices.'" The main purposes for which these companies used wiretap surveillance devices were to check on non-business use of company telephones, "gather information as to what opinions of the company the employees might be passing on to outsiders," and "discover if any employees were passing on trade secrets to competitors." Hidden microphones were principally used "to collect data on the number of people loitering in washrooms during working hours; to gather information about the opinions employees had about supervision and management; to listen in on the way stockroom personnel handled material orders; to find out how sales people talked to customers and customer reaction. . . ." The security-company officers interviewed for the survey said that "upper management" requested the eavesdropping in "the majority of cases."

There have been many examples of these uses in the press during the past six years. Dissident stockholders in a West Coast corporation had investigators tap the telephones of top management in a proxy fight.[45] In a major national talent agency, with offices in Hollywood, a new executive who had used wiretapping as an OSS officer during World War II became suspicious when he heard a superior mention something that could have been learned only through a bug in his office. A search turned up a miniature transmitter in the base of a floor lamp. When the executive disconnected it, he was fired, since all the offices in this firm were kept bugged, and all the telephones tapped, as part of the company's basic notion of personnel control.[46] "In one department store, in a small town outside Philadelphia," a leading wiretapping study has reported, "telephones of the executive personnel were bugged or tapped. The lines from the tapped phones were all brought into a listening post in the manager's office, where he could, by throwing various switches, hear over a loudspeaker the conversations on any of the phones involved."[47] This trend to include permanent listening-device installations when building new executive offices and conference rooms has been reported by many insiders, including some who do the installations.[48]

One factor stimulating companies to install permanent listening equipment in their offices and shops is the appearance of local electronics entrepreneurs who specialize in this "service" and promote it in their communities as an "up-to-date" method for "progressive" managements. In one southern city a construction company that had announced plans to erect a new "home office" building was visited by a well-dressed salesman from an "electronics company" who asked one of the managing partners whether the "listening contract" had been given out yet, explaining that he was referring to the contract to install listening devices throughout the building. "It's so much cheaper when you do it during the original construction," he noted, "than when you have to rip out paneling and snake in lines later. And you can decide whether you want the devices just in the executive quarters or in the employee areas also, and where the 'listening console' should go." The astonished company executive, before he showed the salesman out, was told that "many large firms in the area" had used the service and could be supplied as references for the "top work" done by the installer.[49]

The usual situation which occurs in cases of executive surveillance begins when the corporation chief executive or manager contacts an eavesdropper to cope with a leak of trade secrets, a theft, or an unusual situation in sales or bidding practices. After the problem is solved, the manager or owner becomes so delighted with the values of surveillance that he orders permanent installations of listening or watching equipment. A manufacturer of listening devices said in 1965 that the use of concealed bugs and recorders by industries in California to monitor meetings and conversations on their premises was increasing because it gave business leaders a feeling of security to have these systems.[50]

Regular monitoring of company switchboards and of the public pay phones located on company property has been growing as a theft-control system.[51] In 1964, in response to a request by the California Public Utilities Commission, the Pacific Telegraph and Telephone Company reported that fifteen Santa Clara County firms purchased devices to monitor employee calls. The telephone company estimated that it supplies such monitoring equipment to perhaps 1,000 California subscribers and reported that any subscriber could request such equipment for use on his own phone.[52] Telephone companies themselves have used microphones hidden in dummy desk calendars to monitor telephone-company employees in their relations with customers who come into telephone company offices.[53]

Wiretapping and microphoning of union activities by employers had been a regular practice of many corporations in the decades before the Wagner Act required collective bargaining in good faith with major-ity-elected representatives of the employees. While the legitimacy of such eavesdropping lessened in the post-World War II period, there are signs that employer uses of surveillance technology in labor dis-putes has begun to rise again since the late 1950's. In West Virginia, for example, in 1965, the telephone company was accused by the Communi-cations Workers Union of tapping the home phone of a CWA member during an organizing drive.[54] Microphones were installed in the kitchen of a famous night club in New York to overhear conversations about union activity,[55] and similar surveillance was carried out by a detective agency for the International Trailer Company.[56] In 1965 a public tele-phone used by shop stewards at the Southern Pacific Railroad was bugged by an electrician working for the railroad; the speaker from the bug led into the office of a Southern Pacific superintendent. The union officials brought a $40,000 damage suit against the railroad and the officials involved.[57] Also in 1965, a private detective was indicted for tap-ping the telephones of the General Freight Co. in Whittier, California, to overhear conversations between employees and labor-union represent-atives.[58]

Unions have increasingly complained that companies are using sur-veillance techniques to obtain continuous checks on production speed. Chevrolet management at a Baltimore plant installed a closed-circuit television system whose cameras covered all areas of the plant, enabling a company observer to sit in a central room and watch every worker.[59] An electronic-instrument company in Flushing, New York, was ordered by a labor arbitrator in 1965 to dismantle two television cameras that had been installed to watch the ninety-five employees on the production floor.[60] In Grand Rapids, Michigan, the Dochler-Jarvis division of Na-tional Lead Co. installed a "Tele-Control" system of red and green lights on machines and taped records of machine attendance. As a UAW official explained: "The tape measures the productivity of each employee in fractions of seconds . . . all day. If you were to leave your machine for one minute . . . [the tape] tells them that also." [61] A UAW official reported that a foreman used a four-way intercom system to listen to girls working at the assembly tables; the foreman would cut in to tell them that he did not approve of their topic of conversation.[62] Another case that received wide publicity in 1965 involved a camera which a security officer of American Telephone and Telegraph hid in an air-conditioning duct in the employees' men's room of the New York office to discover the culprit who put obscene scrawlings on the walls.[63] The employees' union, the Communications Workers of America, reported that some managements had used camera devices in ladies' rooms.[64]

Another aspect of labor-relations surveillance arises within unions themselves. Leaders of some unions have used surveillance technology to check the fidelity of their own subordinates (just as corporate presidents have done in regard to their executives) and to eavesdrop on the meetings of dissident union members (paralleling the proxy-fight campaigns of management). For example, James C. Petrillo, president of the American Federation of Musicians, had a private detective plant a microphone in the Los Angeles hotel room of a group of insurgent union officials who were planning to oppose Petrillo at the next union convention. When the delegates of the AFM met in Atlantic City, New Jersey, at their national convention later that year Petrillo played excerpts from the recordings to dramatize the "disloyalty" of his opponents.[65]

Many other instances of eavesdropping by unions on management and within union ranks during internal disputes have been cited during this period.[66] In fact, leading private electronic eavesdroppers, in describing their professional activities to legislative committees and the press, list "union jobs" or "labor union clients" as a standard type of work.[67]

EAVESDROPPING ON PROFESSIONALS AND IN EDUCATIONAL INSTITUTIONS

The effects of surveillance technology have also been felt by professionals such as doctors, clergymen, and lawyers. In 1965 a physician in Wichita, Kansas, had to hire an expert to uncover several bugs planted in his office after his patients (especially unwed expectant mothers) complained of receiving blackmail calls related to their medical problems.[68] Ministers active in "racial reconciliation" efforts in southern states have been the target of private detectives working for prominent segregationists.[69] (Examples will be discussed below, under civic affairs.) An Associated Press survey of wiretapping in 1958 stated that the phones of several prominent psychiatrists in Washington were tapped by private detectives to learn the names of their patients and to obtain clues as to what might be troubling them.[70]

Lawyers have been a prime target of surveillance, with incidents involving private tapping or bugging of lawyers' conversations with clients in business, labor, governmental, and personal affairs. Usually the surveillance is focused on the client's affairs, but sometimes attempts are made to eavesdrop on a lawyer's office just to see who comes and goes and what matters are discussed. Lawyers are also among the prime employers of private surveillance agents.[71] In a case involving two California law firms, an attorney staying at the Chula Vista Motel found a small microphone transmitter pushed through a hole in his motel bedroom wall from an adjoining unit while he was in conference with clients.[72] A private-investigating firm in Beverley Hills, California, that checks law firms for hidden listening devices reported that between January and October of 1965, it had discovered four active transmitters secreted in attorneys' offices or on the premises of the attorney's clients.[73]

The press in the United States has also been tempted by the possibilities of augmented surveillance, and some newspapers, magazines, and TV reporters have used the new instruments. As early as 1924 a Chicago *News* reporter placed a stethoscope on a thin wall in the Criminal Courts Building to overhear the Leopold and Loeb murder confessions.[74] More recently, the *Cleveland Press* secreted a camera in a brothel and snapped pictures of members of the Cleveland police force having lunch.[75] Usually, press surveillance situations involve "participant" rather than "third party" recording. In 1960 the Columbia Broadcasting System persuaded the Chairman of an "Ike Day" celebration in Chicago to wear a hidden, wireless microphone behind his tie when he greeted the President; Eisenhower, who was not informed of the mike's presence, found that his remarks were broadcast to the nation.[76] Another CBS use of concealed microphones took place in 1963 at an airport meeting between the governors of Oregon and New York. The CBS announcer told the TV audience that the films were "candid" shots, in which neither of the speakers was aware that the mike was at work.[77] Such long-distance sound pick-up obviously raises serious questions about press invasion of privacy on private premises and on private conversations at public gatherings. In June, 1965, a New York *Herald Tribune* reporter rented a room in the Astor Hotel adjoining the suite where Alex Rose, Vice-Chairman of the Liberal Party, was meeting with New York mayoral candidate John V. Lindsay. Rose charged that reports in the *Tribune* showed that the reporters had listened in on the conversation.[78]

Listening equipment has also been used by private educational institutions. In several cases reported recently, schools and universities have installed intercom and broadcasting equipment which allows the central console to tune in each individual unit without the knowledge of the persons in those rooms. The installation of such a system in the men's and women's dormitories at Coalinga College in California led to charges that the administration was using the system to spy on the students.[79] In Toledo, Ohio, student complaints that the two-way dormitory call system was being used for eavesdropping led to an official statement by the University administration that a louder beep would be used to warn the student that the connection to his room was "open."[80]

Several leading private investigators have estimated to the author that 40 to 75 per cent of the average private investigator's surveillance is done in "matrimonial" cases. In addition to checking on a marriage partner's activities for a suspicious husband or wife, investigators use the new surveillance methods to produce documentary evidence to convince the "guilty" party to consent to favorable divorce, custody, or alimony terms.

Because of the self-consciousness and secretiveness under which most marital infidelity takes place, advanced surveillance techniques are frequently required. Parabolic microphones aimed across streets into hotel rooms, long-range shotgun mikes and telephoto lenses used to record events on isolated beaches, infra-red photography to penetrate dark bedrooms, and special speech transmitters built into fountain pens, umbrellas, Kleenex boxes, and the upholstered bedboards of suspicious subjects —all these have been used by operatives in New York, Chicago, Los Angeles, Washington, D.C., Las Vegas, Miami, Dallas, and other cities.

Matrimonial cases in which electronic surveillance is initiated by one of the parties have become a commonplace item in the press, with clients drawn from the middle as well as the upper classes. In San Jose, California, a husband hired a detective to "gather evidence" to prevent his wife's getting permanent custody of the children in a pending divorce suit; the private detective was seen and arrested in the act of installing a recording device outside the wife's home.[81] Also in 1964 the librettist of *My Fair Lady*, Alan Jay Lerner, having asked for a divorce, was locked out of his New York town house by his wife after detectives she had hired found microphone wires installed behind a drawing-room stereo set.[82] In Alabama, a factory foreman being sued for divorce obtained a twenty-six-minute recording of his wife's conversations with a neighbor by attaching a tape recorder to an extension of his home telephone.[83] During August and September, 1965, alone, the press featured domestic eavesdropping cases in Cleveland, Ohio, Tampa, Florida, Birmingham, Alabama, and Springfield, Massachusetts.[84]

These domestic investigations can carry over into important business, political, and governmental affairs. In 1958, when the husband of a U.S. Congresswoman from Minnesota became suspicious that his wife was too friendly with her legislative assistant, he hired a Washington, D.C., lawyer, who brought a local investigative agency into the case. Their operatives placed tracer devices in the Congresswoman's car and listened to conversations in her apartment by means of a parabolic microphone. The fact that the Congresswoman's legislative and political affairs were overheard at the same time was typical of the "bonus" that can take place with surveillance in "personal" cases.[85]

In another area of personal life, brothels have frequently installed built-in listening devices throughout their establishments. In Las Vegas, for example, the proprietors of a bordello frequented by leading political, gambling, and business figures eavesdropped on the conversations of their clientele and then used the tapes for blackmail purposes without disclosing where the information had been obtained.[86] In July, 1965, Chicago police carried out a vice raid on a prostitution ring that operated in Chicago, New York, Dallas, Miami, and Houston, "following the convention trade." Every room in the apartment was found to have been wired with electronic listening devices—for the probable purpose of extortion of business customers, according to police.[87]

EAVESDROPPING ON CUSTOMERS AND THE PUBLIC

When people go into stores, hotels, restaurants, and other places of public accommodation, they do not expect solitude and total freedom from observation. However, they do not expect to be under secret surveillance, especially in those times and places for which social custom has set some norms of privacy, even in "public" situations. Yet such surveillance by owners of facilities has been rising steadily since the 1950's, for a variety of legitimate and illegitimate purposes.

Businesses have used hidden microphones to eavesdrop on customers' discussions and to check the quality of sales efforts. For example, a top executive of the Ford Motor Company has been reported to use secret microphones to see how aggressively Ford auto salesmen close a deal.[88] Jessica Mitford reported the discovery of a microphone hidden inside an undertaker's casket-selection room to eavesdrop on the private deliberations of the bereaved about the amount they were willing to spend.[89] In 1960 and 1964 respectively, Arthur Murray, Inc., and Fred Astaire Dance Studio were ordered by the Federal Trade Commission to stop using hidden listening devices in the course of conducting sales presentations for dancing instruction.[90] After stating that more than one hundred New York real-estate firms use electronic devices for listening, a surveillance manufacturer said that "a concealed tape recorder in a model house or apartment can provide a builder with candid insight into consumer reaction" and "also give the renting or sales agent a first-hand picture of the approach and effectiveness of his salesman."[91] In Syracuse, New York, a loan company and a large auto-sales company placed "bugged" pen-and-calendar sets on desks in "private" cubicles where customers (usually wife and husband) believed they were privately discussing their financial affairs. The salesman would retire to the listening post, overhear the husband tell his wife how much they could afford to pay, and then come back primed to close the deal.[92] The Better Business Bureau of Metropolitan New York issued a warning in 1965 against high-pressure sales firms using "bugged" sales rooms in the New York-New Jersey area.[93] The display booths of manufacturers at sales conventions and trade fairs have been bugged so that the "frank opinions" of customers and the public can be learned, and tables at restaurants have been "wired" to learn what customers think of the food and the service.[94]

Another major area of customer and visitor surveillance involves installation of hidden peepholes, closed-circuit television cameras, and two-way mirrors to control theft and shop-lifting in retail establishments. Department stores and supermarkets in many cities, such as New York, Boston and Los Angeles, use these methods.[95] Some department stores have two-way mirrors in fitting rooms, to catch persons who put on unpurchased garments under their own clothing.[96] Gambling casinos in Nevada use concealed TV and mirrors to watch their operators and the public at the gambling tables. The Sands in Las Vegas, for example, installed a $40,000 ten-camera system to watch the tables.[97] When the owners of public accommodations tap the public pay telephones located on their premises, primarily to control employee misbehavior of various sorts, the result is that the calls of all customers who use the phones may be overheard and recorded.

Hidden recorders and cameras have also been adopted by advertising agencies seeking product endorsement. This procedure has been undertaken often enough with shoppers, housewives, college students, housing-project tenants, and a host of others to warrant citation in this catalogue of major uses for new surveillance devices. As one example, during 1966 and 1967, a TV commercial proudly stated: "At Kennedy Airport, hidden cameras reveal reaction of customers to Sanka coffee . . . ," and the presence of these hidden cameras was prominently featured in the company's magazine advertisements.[98]

During the summer of 1966, a great furor was created by disclosure before a state senate investigating committee that telephones in the Boston area had been monitored by the telephone company.[99] In September, 1966, an official of American Telephone and Telegraph announced before Senator Long's committee that company employees had listened in on 36 million long-distance calls in 1965, as part of the company's program of supervising its employees.[100]

EAVESDROPPING IN CIVIC AND POLITICAL LIFE

Eavesdropping on civic groups or on the operations of opposing political parties or factions has been one of the prime uses of the new surveillance technology. In 1959, a wiretap connection was found on the telephone lines of Charles E. McGuiness two days after McGuiness had been defeated in a Democratic primary contest by Carmine DeSapio. McGuiness had suspected a wiretap throughout the campaign, when plans and strategy had leaked out and had been anticipated, yet several inspections of the line by telephone-company employees had revealed nothing. Only after the election did a closer check by a phone-company investigator locate a "very professional wiretap installation" in the loft of a nearby building.[101] In 1960 a security officer at the Democratic National Convention found a wiretap on the telephones of the Stevenson-for-President Campaign Committee.[102] In Pennsylvania in 1958 a state senator charged that doctored tape recordings of conversations by prominent political and business figures in Philadelphia were being used for pressure purposes in local politics.[103] Senator Ralph Yarborough of Texas, after winning a bitter primary battle against radio executive Gordon McLendon in May, 1964, stated that investigators called in by the Senator had found powerful electronic impulses on his phone which indicated a wiretap.[104] In March, 1964, two Los Angeles private detectives were jailed for allegedly putting taps on the phone of Lloyd Gummere, a resident of the "Leisure World" development who was leading a group protesting certain policies in the housing development. The eavesdropping was discovered when Gummere's neighbors noticed a man claiming to be a roof inspector crawling into the attic above his apartment. Seal Beach police found a "tap" in his attic and a second one outside the building.[105]

In October of 1965 John F. English, Democratic Chairman in Nassau County, New York, took reporters to an apartment near Democratic County Headquarters and showed them a headset attached to a tap line on the headquarters' telephone number. Several men representing themselves as telephone company experts and police officers had been using the vacant apartment. Two wire-splicing devices and a wire leading several hundred yards from the telephone pole outside English's home were also displayed to reporters.[106]

Both Democrats and Republicans have used wiretaps, bugs, and cameras in political surveillance; other political and religious groups have also been both clients and victims of eavesdroppers. For example, a liberal organization during the 1950's hired one of the leading electronic specialists in the country to investigate the meetings of an extreme right-wing group. When the investigator learned that an important session of the extremist group's executive committee was to be held in an uptown apartment in New York City, he gained access to the apartment in advance, wired the telephone to serve also as a microphone transmitter, and installed a recorder in a piece of luggage in the apartment. The recording was picked up secretly the next day, and its tapes produced details of the group's plans for the coming months, as well as the identity of some of its principal financial backers.[107]

A standard technique of right-wing groups is the recording of speeches by members of civic and political groups, either openly or secretly, depending on the situation. The Western area co-ordinator for the ultra-conservative Minutemen boasted to a *Newsweek* reporter that his men are adept at devising and planting tiny "snitcher" transmitters, filming secret meetings of subversives (he stated that the group had recently purchased three old Fritos corn-chip delivery trucks for such undercover work), and recording conversations with "shotgun" (long-distance) microphones.[108]

The struggle over segregation and civil rights has prompted considerable electronic surveillance of Negro and white integrationist groups by some private segregationist organizations in southern states. One case of this type that recently became public knowledge involved a wiretap set up by a private investigator in Baton Rouge, Louisiana, in 1961. The telephones tapped were those of Reverend Irvin Cheney, Jr., then pastor of the Broadmoor Baptist Church in Baton Rouge; Wade Mackie, local director of the American Friends Service Committee; and Rabbi Martin M. Reznikoff of the Liberal Synagogue in that city. The three men had been among fifty-eight local clergymen who had issued a statement earlier that year stating that discrimination on the basis of race is "a violation of the Divine law of love." A private investigator working for a prominent local businessman and a state senator installed wiretaps on the home telephones of the three clergymen and on the office telephone of the American Friends Service Committee. Altogether, the telephones of fifteen ministers who had signed the statement against discrimination were believed to have been monitored. Four six-hour tapes were seized on which various statements supporting integration and the Supreme Court's desegregation ruling were made by the clergymen over several months' time. The prime use for these tapes was to play them before groups of prominent church laymen in order to force the ouster of those ministers who had signed the anti-discrimination declaration. Reverend Cheney, one of the tap victims, had resigned because of such laymen's pressure a few months before the wiretapping was discovered. One Protestant minister in Baton Rouge issued a statement denouncing the tapping of ministers' telephones as especially tragic because "the most intimate problems of a troubled heart are brought to a pastor over the telephone." [109] In Georgia during the late 1950's the state Commission on Education (a special anti-integration agency) used its appropriation to buy such equipment as a "long-lens camera, wiretap recorder, pocket mikes," and used these to check into activities by Georgians against segregation.[110] And the telephone of a Catholic priest active in the Selma, Alabama, civil-rights struggle was tapped.[111]

Since advance knowledge of government decisions can be worth a great deal of money, and the temptation of the press or of political rivals to eavesdrop on the incumbent administration to expose its "wrongdoing" is often great, government has been a troubled victim as well as a beneficiary of the new surveillance technology.

Several instances during 1964–65 involved private wiretapping or bugging of the conversations of law-enforcement officials. In Oklahoma City, Oklahoma, in 1965 the County Attorney learned of bugs placed on his office telephones by certain private parties; several prosecutions involving prominent local civic and political leaders were mentioned as the likely sources of the eavesdropping effort.[112] In Reading, Pennsylvania, in 1964 the Mayor and local law-enforcement officials confirmed press reports that a team of private investigators from a national private detective agency had been operating in the town for almost two months, "are known to be using modern wire-tapping equipment and are believed to be listening in on conversations of local public officials, including the district attorney's office." The Reading newspaper reported that this enterprise might represent the effort by local rackets figures to learn about police moves in an on-going anti-vice campaign. Such a use of eavesdropping by criminals on police operations has been confirmed as a phenomenon in many major cities by a major wiretapping study in 1959.[113] In Delaware, the special "security" telephone of the Attorney General was found to be tapped during a routine maintenance check. The phone was used for confidential calls from police and private informants during a major vice investigation that the Attorney General was conducting.[114] The Attorney General of Alabama, Richmond Flowers, a sharp critic of Governor George Wallace's administration and of the Alabama Klan, discovered his private telephone "bugged" in 1965. "[I]t becomes a serious matter," he observed, "when the phone of the attorney general of a state is bugged." [115]

Other cases have involved taps on and by mayors themselves. In York, Pennsylvania, hidden electronic listening devices were installed by the Mayor in places that made local newspapers highly suspicious. The York *Gazette and Daily* reported that "microphones had been hidden around city hall in a water spigot in the plaza of city hall, on the bottom of a chair in the Civil Defense office, and in an air-conditioning vent in the police radio room." [116]

Other levels of government have also been subject to private surveillance. A prime example during 1963 involved campaigns by ultra-rightist groups to prove that public officials are part of the "Communist conspiracy." During a controversy over "subverting youth" and "attacking patriotism" in the school system of Paradise, California, local extreme-right groups accused one teacher of "running down" the United States and of being anti-religious. To obtain proof of her "attitudes," the son of one extremist leader brought into class a hollowed-out book in which a tape recorder had been neatly concealed. He asked the teacher various leading questions and was compiling a set of tapes of her answers when the school principal learned of his effort. When the incident was widely publicized, the student's father noted proudly to reporters, "We've got a vault full of tapes. Ty carries [the dummy book] around almost every day." [117]

SURVEILLANCE IN SCIENTIFIC RESEARCH

Systematic physical observation has long been a traditional tool of the anthropologist, psychologist, sociologist, medical researcher, and political scientist, as well as marketing and advertising research agencies. In its early forms, listening and watching technology was adopted widely for such research. Basic textbooks on scientific methods describe two-way mirrors and built-in listening devices to observe behavior of individual subjects and groups in observation rooms, for experimental studies, and for the training of students as social scientists.[118] Concealed microphones and recorders have been used to take down the discussions of patients with psychologists and psychiatrists, primarily to insure complete records for later study by the therapist and to allow him to give full attention to the patient. This listening and watching generally takes place with the knowledge and consent of the subjects, or of their legal guardians if children (or seriously ill persons) are involved. However, when knowledge of the surveillance would have the effect of destroying the "necessary spontaneity" of an activity that the social scientist is trying to study, or when a mentally disturbed patient might be made over-anxious if he were told of the recordings, many social and medical scientists have considered their use of surreptitious surveillance to be ethically justified. Their basic reasoning has been that no use would be made of information to harm the person observed or recorded.

However, the spread of the new miniaturized technology has led to several "gray area" applications by social and medical scientists. At recent conventions of several social-science disciplines, there have been displays of briefcases with built-in microphones and recorders, operated by voice actuation or by a turn of the outside lock. At one such meeting that I attended, the salesman at the display table explained that with his briefcase, academic researchers would be able to obtain complete recordings of interviews with government leaders, political party officials, and civic-group spokesmen without taking handwritten notes and "inhibiting" the interviewed persons. "People speak more freely when they don't think anyone is taking down what they say," the salesman noted.

The most celebrated instance of use of hidden recording devices by social scientists in recent years involved the "jury-bugging" experiment conducted by a University of Chicago team of lawyers and social scientists in 1954–55. For a major study of the jury system, the project directors needed to obtain a small sample of real jury deliberations to use as a control in judging a much larger group of "mock" jury deliberations conducted with persons called for jury duty who would agree to participate in a staged-trial setting and go through "regular" deliberations. With the permission of the judge and the attorneys in each case, the Chicago experimenters secretly recorded five jury deliberations in federal-court civil cases in Wichita, Kansas. The recordings were to be sealed for two years, and the identity of the jurors, lawyers, parties and court were to be disguised. When news of the project leaked out, criticism was intense and Congress swiftly enacted Public Law 99 in 1955, making it illegal for any person not a member of a jury to "observe, record, or listen to the proceedings of a United States jury while it is deliberating." [119]

Government Use of the New Technology

Government use of surveillance devices falls into a context very different from the private uses we have been discussing. In their publicly authorized responsibility to protect persons, property, and national security, government law-enforcement agencies have a legitimate claim to the use of physical surveillance, within limits set by law. From the earliest days of the American republic, law and public opinion have accepted such clandestine police techniques as shadowing, simple eavesdropping, using informers, and planting government agents in conspiracies, as well as physical searches and seizures where these were reasonable—limited in scope, specific in quest, and authorized by court order. As the twentieth century has increased the speed, mobility, communication, and coordination of criminal and subversive activities, government responses have had to keep pace. Scientific techniques such as ballistics, fingerprinting, spectrograph analysis, and x-ray tests of documents have been applauded as new methods which increase the accuracy of investigations and lessen reliance on third-degree practices without invading privacy. Once the government response moves into technological surveillance, however, the basic process of balancing public safety and individual liberty comes into play.

SURVEILLANCE AND FEDERAL USE

At least fifty different federal agencies have substantial investigative and enforcement functions, providing a corps of more than 20,000 "investigators" working for agencies such as the FBI, Naval Intelligence, the Post Office, the Narcotics Bureau of the Treasury, the Securities and Exchange Commission, the Internal Revenue Service, the Food and Drug Administration, the State Department, and the Civil Service Commission.[120] While all executive agencies are under federal law and executive regulations, the factual reality is that each agency and department has wide day-to-day discretion over the investigative practices of its officials, particularly in comparison to nations with unified national police forces, such as France or the Soviet Union.

Between World War II and 1958, three main characteristics distinguished federal electronic-surveillance activities. First, the leading federal agencies stayed well abreast of technological advances in listening and watching devices, developing or buying the latest "hardware," actively training their agents at special schools, and using what was called "technical surveillance" as a regular part of federal investigative activity. Such proficiency was concentrated in a few federal civilian agencies (such as the FBI and Treasury), the military intelligence agencies, and special agencies such as the CIA, while other federal agencies used electronic eavesdropping only occasionally and often with "crude" techniques. Second, because of the confused legal situation surrounding electronic eavesdropping throughout the 1940's and 1950's and the civil-liberty questions presented, federal electronic eavesdropping activities remained highly secretive. Third, there was no general public review of federal surveillance activities and practices by the President, the Attorney General, Congressional committees, federal grand juries, the Federal Communications Commission or any other governmental agency.

Since the late 1950's, as new surveillance devices spread throughout the federal investigative establishment and other federal agencies, the amount of federal eavesdropping by wiretap and microphone has increased substantially. The extent of FBI eavesdropping outside the national security, kidnaping, and "endangering human life" areas was revealed dramatically between 1965 and 1967 by a series of incidents and disclosures that cast grave doubt on FBI statements of its own surveillance activities. Justice Department attorneys admitted in court in 1965 that the FBI leased twenty-five telephone lines directly from the telephone company in Las Vegas, Nevada, to monitor telephones at the Desert Inn and other Las Vegas hotels. The lines were leased to the "Henderson Novelty Company," whose address was identical with that of the Las Vegas FBI office. The Justice Department attorney told the federal court that the FBI taps had been made in an investigation of alleged "skimming" of gambling receipts by Las Vegas gamblers to avoid federal gambling and income taxes. The monitoring lasted at least eighteen months and produced a two-inch-thick volume containing synopses of eavesdropped conversations. In addition, bugs were planted in the executive offices of the Desert Inn, one of which was produced and shown to Congressmen by Edward Bennett Williams, whose client, Robert Baker, was being questioned about business affairs with a Desert Inn executive.[121]

A similar episode arose in Kansas City, Missouri. In 1965 a Southwestern Bell Telephone Company official told Congressional investigators that the FBI had obtained "leased lines" from the telephone company to monitor telephones at eight different locations during the previous three years. These included a night club, a toy store, a jobbing company, a restaurant, a residence, and three commercial buildings. The residence turned out to belong to a gambler, Max Jaben, who pleaded no contest to income-tax fraud in 1964 and was sentenced to four months in prison. Another disclosure in 1965 was that an electronics specialist working for the Dade County Sheriff's Office had installed wiretaps for the FBI in Miami in a jewel-robbery case and an extortion case.[122] During 1966 there were additional disclosures of FBI microphone installations in tax evasion cases in New York, Milwaukee, and Boston.[123]

Additional light on FBI wiretapping practices was provided by Jack Levine, a former agent stationed in Detroit, who resigned under honorable circumstances from the Bureau and then wrote the Justice Department about what he regarded as improper practices within the FBI. Later, in a memorandum and several interviews, Levine stated that FBI agents did considerable wiretapping in cases other than those involving internal security and major crime, and that these were often done in the field offices without the knowledge of the Bureau in Washington. At the same time he stated that much Bureau-ordered wiretapping was not reported to the Attorney General and was not included in the statistics given to Congress. Levine confirmed the use of monitoring lines leased directly from local telephone companies, which made it impossible for a person to know that his telephone was being tapped, even by a physical inspection from telephone handset all the way back to the telephone-company building. Levine explained unreported wiretaps as a product of the "prosecutive personality" of the FBI and its complete emphasis on conviction statistics.[124]

The scope of FBI microphone listening was indicated in a carefully researched account of electronic eavesdropping in 1964:

[The FBI has] expertly bugged rooms spotted through leading hotels. When they want to tune in on a guest, they ask the hotel management to steer him to one of these sonic studios. If the guest balks, an agent needs only a few minutes to sneak up and secrete several bugs in the room assigned the visitor; then a team of technicians moves into the adjoining room to set up listening and recording apparatus.[125]

A sample of such FBI bugging was revealed in May, 1966, when the Solicitor General of the United States told the Supreme Court that, unknown to Justice Department or Tax Department officials, the FBI had bugged the hospitality suite maintained in Washington at the Sheraton-Carlton Hotel by Fred B. Black, Jr., a lobbyist. Black used the suite to entertain government, political, and business contacts. After Black was indicted for income-tax evasion, FBI agents listened to conversations between Black and his lawyers about their defense of the case and passed this information along to Justice Department attorneys in charge of the prosecution, though without indicating its source. The FBI stated that the planting of the bug in Black's suite was part of "a criminal investigation of various individuals" and that it had not been in connection with Black's tax-evasion case. As the *New York Times* account of this episode noted, the conduct "lent credence to charges of wholesale electronic snooping by the [FBI] in recent investigations." [126]

The import of these disclosures about FBI practices is that the Bureau's use of electronic eavesdropping and hidden cameras goes beyond the subject areas it has admitted to publicly, that the Attorney General does not exercise effective control over FBI wiretapping and bugging operations, and that FBI mores encourage field offices and individual agents to eavesdrop whenever they deem it useful in criminal investigations, down to the level of gambling operations.

The other federal civilian agency that had established a record of extensive electronic eavesdropping before 1957 is the Treasury. Ironically, Treasury regulations flatly outlawed wiretapping. A Treasury directive to all its bureaus in 1938, re-issued regularly in the 1940's, 1950's, and 1960's, stated that wiretapping was not a permissible means of investigation "regardless of whether any divulgence is involved." Bureau heads were instructed to inform their agents that such was Treasury Department policy.[127] As noted earlier, however, the chief wiretapper for the Treasury Department, William Mellin, stated in 1949 that he had installed more than 10,000 wiretaps in Treasury Department investigations between 1934 and 1948, the year of his retirement, an average of 666 yearly.[128]

During the 1950's and early 1960's occasional reports revealed Treasury agents' use of microphone devices. For example, Internal Revenue agents bugged a public telephone booth in the lobby of the Internal Revenue Service building in Washington in 1963 to get evidence on a woman accused of operating a lottery.[129] In 1960 Bureau of Narcotics agents, with the cooperation of the management of the Sherry Netherland Hotel in New York City, installed listening devices in a hotel room adjoining that reserved for a French businessman suspected of smuggling dope into the United States.[130] Apart from a handful of such reported bugging operations, there was little public information about wiretapping and microphoning by Treasury in the 1950's and early 1960's. Many Congressmen and Senators were convinced that Treasury agents did not wiretap or bug, but relied instead on undercover work and informers.[131]

This was the picture given to me when I interviewed a high Treasury official in February of 1964.[132] I was told that Treasury "does no wiretapping, period." As for the new miniaturized listening and transmitting devices, the Treasury official said that these were "too costly" for the Treasury's limited budget—"we can't even afford enough two-way radios for our men to contact each other. The manufacturers come and show us their gadgetry but we can't afford to buy it." Even if they could have afforded the purchase, he said, organized crime groups are so sophisticated that they hire specialists to do electronic sweeps, have their homes fenced and patrolled by dogs, search all visitors, and carefully inspect all meeting places. "We would get little from trying electronic eavesdropping," he concluded; "informers and planted agents" are the Department's methods. Furthermore, this official mentioned that a Treasury agent had been "busted" a few years previously for using wiretapping on his own authority, and several other agents were currently being sued for damages in a court action for listening in on a wiretap installed by a telephone-company employee. These episodes were cited as the rare exceptions to a well-enforced ban on wiretapping. Finally, I was given a copy of a Treasury directive dated December 17, 1963, which reiterated the Treasury's rule against wiretapping and reminded all personnel that this "long-standing Treasury policy" was to be adhered to until the law was changed by Congress.[133]

In light of informed comments by other federal law-enforcement officials and private detectives, and the history of Treasury wiretapping up to 1948, this portrait was simply not credible, especially in terms of the practices of Treasury agents "in the field." What Treasury was actually doing with electronic eavesdropping and visual surveillance in the 1960's was dramatically revealed in 1965, as a result of hearings by the Long Committee. First, the Treasury Department was forced to admit that since 1958 hidden microphones and two-way mirrors had been installed in offices of the Intelligence, Alcohol and Tobacco Tax, and Internal Security Divisions of the Internal Revenue Service in more than fifty-seven cities across the country.[134] Spokesmen for IRS stated that they eavesdropped, recorded, and watched only when "the criminal element" were questioned at IRS offices, or when criminal charges were going to be lodged in tax-evasion cases. However, the rooms themselves were used for conferences with many other taxpayers, and the equipment was not disconnected. Furthermore, in the so-called criminal cases, conversations between the taxpayer and his lawyer were overheard when the Treasury official left the room temporarily and the individual spoke to his lawyer in the belief that they were alone. A certified public accountant told the Senate Committee that while he was in such a room with his client, a picture of the Statue of Liberty with an American flag superimposed on it was accidentally knocked down to reveal a two-way mirror behind it. In other cases the mirror was behind the Treasury seal. The microphones were built into the walls.[135]

Second, it was disclosed that throughout the 1950's and 1960's Treasury maintained a school at its building in Washington in which IRS agents were taught how to tap telephone wires, build and plant radio-transmitter devices, and pick locks for surreptitious entry. This "Treasury Technical Investigative Aid School" conducted a two-week course, and one IRS official estimated that about seventy agents had attended such courses since 1959. In addition, some IRS agents attended an eight-week course on "technical" investigation given by Army Intelligence at Fort Holibird, Maryland. The IRS school gave instruction for the carbon, dynamic, and crystal microphones, including the use of the spike mike and the shotgun microphone. Treasury agents also admitted that their equipment in the field offices included induction-coil devices, briefcase recorders, penn registers (for learning which telephone numbers are dialed from a given phone), and electronic "intelligence kits" from manufacturers such as Fargo. Several offices also had second-hand trucks painted to look like telephone-company vehicles, which were used to avoid suspicion when installing telephone taps or to conduct surveillance through peepholes.[136]

Third, the Long Committee extracted from IRS agents and officials a series of accounts indicating that both telephone tapping and third-party eavesdropping had been used by Treasury agents in the field, often with the knowledge and cooperation of high officials in Washington headquarters. The hearings learned that Owen Burke Yung, who was trained in electronic eavesdropping by William Mellin in the early 1940's, and who had later been an instructor at the Treasury's surveillance school, had compiled the following tapping and bugging record by himself during the past ten years.

1964—three wiretaps and one penn register installed in Denver.
1963—a penn register in Houston.
1962—a gambler's conversations tapped and recorded for thir-

teen months in Miami from an overhead apartment.

1961—two wiretaps placed in Pittsburgh and one in Wheeling, West Virginia.

1959—two mikes and a wiretap put into two Dallas hotel rooms.

1958—a concealed mike installed in a Washington, D.C., apartment, and a tap on the phone of an IRS employee.

1957—a concealed mike put into the offices of the Buffalo, New York, IRS district director.

1956—eight phones tapped in the Chicago IRS building.

1954—four phones tapped in New York's Government Building.[137]

That this list did not represent one overzealous agent's disregard of Treasury regulations was indicated by the testimony of several others to the effect that it was commonly understood by agents that top IRS officials approved of using wiretaps against "racketeers," and that there was no policy at all against using microphones to eavesdrop on conversations in rooms and automobiles. Cresson O. Davis, head of the IRS Intelligence Division in Pittsburgh, testified: "They conducted schools in Washington where our agents were taught to wiretap, to plant microphones, and so forth. It was my understanding that it was the proper practice." Davis showed how the understanding worked by relating that in 1961, and again in 1964, when he wanted to tap the telephones of several suspected local racketeers, he called the Assistant Director of the IRS Intelligence Division in Washington, Robert A. Manzi, and two members of the Washington staff and requested equipment for the taps. On each occasion Washington sent Owen Yung to Pittsburgh with equipment for the taps. The disguised telephone trucks were sent out, and lines were run to the den of Davis' house, where agents recorded telephone conversations on three different lines for about four months. Washington also approved the purchase of the wiretap truck.[138]

Accounts of IRS wiretapping and bugging came from other cities as well. In Miami IRS agents maintained a sedan painted like a telephone company vehicle and admitted installing four wiretaps in 1963, one operating for almost a year. During one gambling investigation Miami IRS agents installed a transmitter in a public telephone booth.[139] In Kansas City, Missouri, two IRS agents admitted that they had persuaded a landlord to put an electronic transmitter under a tenant's couch and to let them listen in the adjoining apartment for a week. The agents stated that they persuaded the landlord to install the bug because it "would be trespass" if they had done it themselves. After listening to the tenant's conversations for a week, including his conversations at night with a lady, the agents found no evidence warranting prosecution on tax evasion and gambling charges, and the investigation was dropped. The suspect was admittedly a "small-time" rather than "big" operator.[140] Other Kansas City IRS agents borrowed bugging and telephone-tapping equipment from a Kansas City private detective for their work. In another case IRS agents entered the office of an attorney in Washington, Pennsylvania, and planted a microphone in his office bookcase for two weeks; the attorney was suspected of having connections with the Mafia. When asked by several Senators about the ethics of such breaking and entering and secret eavesdropping, the IRS agent said: "Those of us in the organized crime drive felt proud to be in it. Anything that would have been asked, I would have done it." Senate committee investigators have described entries into lawyers' offices by IRS agents to plant microphones as a "widespread practice" in cities across the nation.[141]

It is useful to note here that IRS eavesdropping in organized-crime cases was spurred by a confidential instruction reported to have been issued to IRS agents on February 24, 1961, as part of the Kennedy administration's drive on crime. Calling for "saturation" investigations of the tax returns of "major racketeers," this instruction noted: "In conducting such investigations, full use will be made of available electronic equipment and other technical aids." [142]

Federal-agency use of electronic devices for two-party recording—where one party to the conversation records it surreptitiously—was illustrated vividly by the post-1958 practices of the Food and Drug Administration. No evidence was presented at the Senate hearings that FDA agents used third-party eavesdropping or telephone tapping, but extensive use of recorders was made by FDA inspectors to secure documentary evidence. Typical situations were those in which the FDA inspectors wanted to record statements made in behalf of foods, drugs, or health processes at public lectures by their promotors; to establish that medicines were being dispensed in a commercial rather than professional fashion; or to verify that improper manufacturing practices were being followed in drug production. To accomplish these purposes, FDA agents concealed a microphone in an American flag stand to record public lectures by the promotor of a dietary supplement; recorded statements in behalf of a food supplement made by the promotor in the home of a volunteer "decoy," with the FDA agent posing as the volunteer's husband; used a briefcase recorder to take down promotional statements made during a supermarket demonstration of a milk substitute for persons allergic to milk; and carried hidden recorders on the persons of FDA agents during a "visit" and tour through a drug company plant in Yonkers, New York, with the company president.[143]

Surveillance activities by the investigative branches of two other federal agencies were revealed in detail by the Long Committee hearings of 1965. The Post Office was shown to have purchased a sizable amount of electronic and recording equipment: Minifon recorders, briefcases with built-in mikes and recorders, miniature transmitters and receivers, and miniature microphones. In addition, Post Office inspectors borrowed transmitters for short periods from several other law-enforcement agencies: the St. Louis police department, the Food and Drug Administration, and the Chicago police department.[144]

Other incidents in the 1960's revealed the use of electronic eavesdropping by officials in other federal agencies. In 1964 a Congressional committee forced the disclosure that State Department electronics experts had tapped the telephone of the Department's chief security evaluations officer, Otto Otepka, who was believed to be giving confidential department documents to the Senate Internal Security Subcommittee in protest against State Department loyalty-security policies. At first, a Deputy Assistant Secretary of State, John F. Reilly, his special assistant, and the chief of the State Department's Division of Technical Services denied flatly that any wiretapping had taken place. But when the Senate Internal Security Committee obtained evidence pointing to the contrary, Reilly and his assistant sent letters "correcting the record" and admitting that wires had been connected to Otepka's telephone and fed into a "laboratory listening post" in order to "survey the feasibility of intercepting conversations in Mr. Otepka's office." The officials claimed that no monitoring had actually been conducted and that no information had been obtained that figured in the disciplinary action against Otepka; for this reason the original "experiment" had not been mentioned to the Senate Committee.[145] Reilly's main assignment in the State Department was as its electronics security officer, in charge of a staff of some thirty electronics specialists charged with locating enemy bugs and taps on State Department facilities and personnel, particularly abroad. The Senate Internal Security Subcommittee also investigated reports that a private detective agency in Washington, staffed by former intelligence agents, was wiretapping for the State and Justice Departments, as well as for the CIA, and that this agency had been employed to tap Otepka's home telephone.[146]

There have also been statements by reporters strongly alleging that telephones in the White House press gallery must be tapped. A leading woman correspondent telephoned her newspaper from this gallery recently to report an exclusive tip about an impending judicial appointment. Half an hour later she received a call from a White House staff member telling her angrily that her information was false and that the report would be wrong. The newspaper officials swore that no one had been told about the story during the elapsed half-hour. In a column on the spread of political wiretapping in Washington, Robert S. Allen and Paul Scott stated that several other correspondents had similar experiences with what was being called the press "tap line." [147]

SURVEILLANCE BY STATE AND LOCAL GOVERNMENTS

The great bulk of crime in America and the primary work of law enforcement are both centered at the local level, where city, county, and state agencies share jurisdiction over the investigation and prosecution of criminal acts. In 1965 William Shaw, the electronics editor of *Law and Order* magazine, conducted a nation-wide random survey of electronic eavesdropping by such local law enforcement agencies. Forty-two agencies responded, seven from cities with more than 150,000 population, twelve from cities with more than 75,000, and twenty-three from towns with more than 20,000 residents. In all, 80 per cent of the agencies reported that they used wiretapping "occasionally"; almost 30 per cent said they used it "whenever possible." Over 35 per cent of the agencies said they used regular wire-connected or battery-operated hidden microphones. None would state that they were using the simpler and more popular wireless radio-transmitter bugs. (Shaw explained that police agencies know such bugs are now forbidden by FCC regulations.) Eighty-eight per cent of the agencies said their interrogation rooms were wired for eavesdropping.[148]

The *Law and Order* survey is confirmed by the extensive clippings on local law-enforcement eavesdropping which I collected between 1963 and 1967. The practice is now found in communities of all sizes and types across the nation. Wiretaps have been used from Boston, Massachusetts, to Jacksonville, Florida; in Oswego, New York; Shively, Kentucky; West Pittston, Pennsylvania; and Scottsdale, Arizona. Miniature microphones have been installed secretly on premises from Wichita, Kansas, and Norfolk, Virginia, to Mineola, Long Island, and Austin, Texas; from Portland, Oregon, to Miami, Florida, and Cranford, New Jersey.[149] A conservative estimate would be that more than 10,000 wiretaps and bugs are installed annually by local law-enforcement agencies throughout the country. There is no doubt whatever that government surveillance by electronic technology is here, now, in American local law enforcement.

What is important in the law-enforcement area is the *purposes* for which government agencies are using listening and watching devices, *how* they are being used, and *with what impact* on our patterns of individual and group privacy. The data show that local law-enforcement agencies are utilizing this technique in many serious criminal cases. Eavesdropping has played a key role in solving or preventing crimes involving murder, blackmail, kidnaping, robbery, burglary, arson, prison escape, jury tampering, forgery, political corruption and many others.[150] Police have also used electronic eavesdropping in distinctly minor matters, such as investigation of the theft of a television set, to see whether park wardens were using their cars only for official driving, and to find out which policemen were making personal remarks on the police radio system.[151]

In the spring of 1966 I was able to study the eavesdropping activities of one of the largest and most respected prosecutive offices in the nation, the Manhattan District Attorney's Office under Frank Hogan. Wiretap orders obtained by this office under New York law ranged from thirty-four new authorizations in 1955 to forty-nine in 1964, with a high of eighty-four in 1961. Twenty-four new orders for microphone installations were obtained in 1964, plus seven renewals and one amended order, for a total of thirty-two. These thirty-two bug orders covered a total of sixty-nine different crimes enumerated in the affidavits. These ranged from homicide, assault in the first degree, organized crime conspiracy, burglary, extortion, bribery, grand larceny, and corruption of public officials or labor-union representatives to such offenses as operaing a policy business, unlicensed check cashing, false claim to an insurance company, possession of burglar tools, and unlicensed money lending.[152]

In New York City, as elsewhere, most of the wiretapping is done by police departments, and the bulk of this police surveillance is on bookmakers, gamblers, and prostitutes. Police spokesmen defend the use of such a "large" weapon on such "small" crime by noting that vice operations are a major source of money and power for syndicate leaders and the criminal organizations that deal in serious crimes. In addition, police cite instances in which wiretaps on minor suspects in vice cases have produced information about serious crimes, such as corruption of the judiciary, assault, and even homicide.[153] On the other hand, gambling and vice operations are the type of investigation that sometimes prompted "free-lance" wiretapping by police detectives and plainclothesmen. Examples of this activity recently took place in Scottsdale, Arizona, where wiretaps were installed without approval of the police chief,[154] and in Arlington, Virginia, where two detectives tapped the apartment telephone of several men suspected of running a lottery without the required approval of the police chief, County Manager, and Commonwealth Attorney.[155]

The gambling, bookmaking, and vice cases have also been the major setting for misuse of taps and bugs by corrupt policemen to extract payoff money from those whose incriminating activities have been captured on tape. Such was the situation in 1959, when "personal" tapping by police in Brooklyn resulted in the indictment of a deputy police inspector and two plainclothesmen.[156]

Misuse of electronic eavesdropping for political purposes has also taken place. Surveillance of political opponents by incumbent administrations, attempts to learn the political plans of local party leaders, and surveillance of political protest groups that the police decided "need watching" were all found to be accomplished through electronic eavesdropping. In December, 1965, for example, the mayor of one Long Island community admitted to a grand jury that a microphone had been secreted in the roof of a public telephone booth in the village center hall in order to hear and record the conversations of a local doctor who was a sharp critic of the village administration.[157] In New Orleans, Louisiana, when a special city investigating committee was set up to inquire into links between organized crime and the local police, members of the city police department tapped the telephone of the committee's chief investigator to find out who was giving him information.[158] In New York City, the Transit Authority, a public agency that operates the subways and negotiates with the transportation unions, secreted microphones in the offices and the meeting hall of the Motormen's Benevolent Association for eighteen months to listen in on union discussions. Those included many lawyer-client conversations.[159]

Such misuses are clearly exceptional rather than typical features of law-enforcement wiretapping and bugging. In some instances corrupt policemen and detectives simply used eavesdropping as a tool of their corrupt schemes; if electronic devices had not been available, the rogue policemen would have used other means to accomplish their ends. In other instances, however, the added power that came with possession of electronic devices was used to penetrate legitimate labor union and political affairs, or to investigate the activities of suspected criminals in ways that were unauthorized.

While many agencies maintain their own surveillance experts and eavesdropping equipment, some law-enforcement offices use private detectives, telephone company employees, and sometimes the telephone-company management itself to accomplish wiretaps. In Kansas City, Missouri, in 1965 the security supervisor for Southwestern Bell Telephone Co. stated that he provided the Kansas City police department with the pair numbers and other information necessary to tap telephones whenever this was requested by the chief of detectives.[160] At other times telephone companies have run lines from tapped telephones directly into law-enforcement listening posts, making "field connections" or "field listening posts" unnecessary. As for use of private detectives, the Pennsylvania Bar Study found that the sheriff's office in Baton Rouge, Louisiana, relied on a local private investigator to place all its complicated wiretaps.[161] A leading New York private eavesdropping specialist was called in by the Boston District Attorney's office, the Massachusetts Attorney General's office and the Massachusetts State Police for their listening assignments; this man installed the wiretaps during the investigation of the famous Brink's hold-up case.[162] Private detectives were found to be used in similar fashion by some law-enforcement agencies in Los Angeles and San Francisco.[163] Sometimes the private detectives are paid, sometimes they perform as a favor for the police; most often they gain as their basic return the good will of the police toward the private investigator's own tapping and bugging activities.

Electronic devices are spreading to places beyond the "traditional" areas of home, car, and office. Public telephone booths have become a common target of tapping and bugging. In pursuing investigations, New York officials have tapped public phones or placed bugs in hotel lobbies, newsstands, railway and bus terminals, restaurants, taverns, stores, subways, and gas stations.[164] The police defend such actions on the ground that these are the places used for the conspiracy, or that the phones are being used by suspected criminals, to escape eavesdropping on their home and office phones. Bugs have been placed in a hospital room to hear a patient discuss bribery of city officials with a visitor; in lawyers' offices when the investigation centered on suspected illegalities by attorneys; and in judicial chambers and judges' desks when charges of judicial misconduct were being investigated.[165]

Another site coming under increasing sound and camera surveillance is the jail. Surveillance of inmates in their cells and during visiting hours by non-electronic methods has been a classic police measure. Now, police have added built-in listening devices in prisoners' cells; TV eyes covering corridors, cells, and public areas; and listening and watching devices in interrogation rooms (the Shaw survey in Law and Order magazine in 1965 found 88 per cent of the sampled agencies had wired interrogation rooms).[166] Civic protest has focused on the growing use of one-way mirrors and bugs in the rooms in which witnesses, detained suspects, and arrested persons talk with their lawyers and members of the clergy.[167] In Syracuse, New York, in 1964, for example, the County Bar Association inspected the Syracuse Public Safety Building and lodged a sharp protest when it was discovered that a new monitoring system allowed police to overhear and record surreptitiously both the visitors' rooms and the material witness' rooms in the building.[168] Similar conditions have been present in Nashua, New Hampshire, Denver, Colorado, Ramsey County, Minnesota, and other cities.[169]

A major increase in use by police of camera surveillance has been another new feature. Some of this consists of the filming of activities in "public places" to secure positive evidence of illegal activities. Such a practice is illustrated by the movie-camera filming by New York detectives of ticket speculators standing in line over and over again to buy tickets to Hello, Dolly,[170] and movie- and TV-camera filming in many cities of persons going in and out of brothels, bookie joints, and gambling centers. The secreting of film and TV cameras on private or semiprivate premises has been used to secure evidence in cases of theft, bribery, narcotics peddling, and other crimes where the camera can catch the criminal in the act.[171] An article in Law and Order for December, 1964, outlined for its law-enforcement readership the means by which TV cameras can be hidden in walls with sheet-rock and plaster construction, angled mirrors can be installed in front of the camera lens so that only a two-way mirror had to be visible in the room under surveillance, and how a two-way reflecting mirror can be mounted behind a wall clock or wall thermostat control in a home or office.[172]

The fastest-growing application of police film and TV surveillance is in investigations of the activities of sexual deviates, usually homosexual solicitations or acts committed in "public" restrooms.[173] California police have used camera surveillance in toilet booths at department stores and amusement parks. In Mansfield, Ohio, films were used in a city-maintained restroom.[174] As one law-enforcement official described the Mansfield installation: "A two-way mirror was installed in a towel dispenser on a door in which a hole had been cut so that the officers could observe the restroom area from a concealed position. [The toilet booths were closed on only three sides and had no doors.] Not only were the activities of deviates observed but colored films were taken of the criminal acts which were used both for identification and as evidence in subsequent trials of the offenders." In other cases in which there were doors to the toilet booths, visual and camera surveillance has been conducted through ceiling openings such as heating ducts or light fixtures.[175]

Another trend in local law-enforcement use of electronic devices has been "participant recording," in which one participant in a conversation or meeting, either a police officer or a co-operating party, wears a concealed device that records the conversation or broadcasts it to others nearby. This law-enforcement technique is used tens of thousands of times each year throughout the country, particularly in cases involving extortion, conspiracy, narcotics, gambling, prostitution, corruption by police officials (including investigations of police corruption), and similar crimes.[176] Recordings of the private and public meetings of suspect groups has been growing. Police in Miami, Florida, used a hidden transmitter on a police agent to record statements made at meetings of a right-wing extremist group suspected of planning acts of terrorism. In 1964 a police undercover agent obtained recordings of incendiary statements by the leader of a Communist splinter movement in Harlem, at private meetings and at a public rally, which served as the basis for his conviction for attempting to overthrow the state government. Officers of the Subversive Unit of the Alabama State Department of Public Safety attend civil-rights meetings and record the proceedings; a tape recording of remarks made by one of the two Negro students admitted under federal pressure to the University of Alabama in 1963 was the basis on which the student was expelled for improper criticism of university administrators. A *New York Times* story on the Alabama Subversive Unit related that state troopers were making still photographs and films of individuals "at every recent racial disturbance and many interracial gatherings in the state. This includes the photographing of virtually every white person who attended the funerals of four girls killed [in 1963] in the bombing of a Negro church in Birmingham." [177]

A pattern that was thoroughly documented by the Congressional hearings, court cases, and clipping sources was the great frequency with which police officials commit trespass into homes, apartments, offices, and businesses, without judicial warrants authorizing such entries, in order to install wiretaps and room microphones.[178] Aside from the conduct of law-enforcement officials operating under court orders authorizing entries to install taps or bugs, it is clear from the data that *most* electronic eavesdropping by local law-enforcement agencies involves illegal entry. Sometimes this is done by police officers themselves breaking into the premises secretly, but it is also done through the aid of janitors, landlords, and other persons having custodial care of rented premises, who admit the police officers and never ask for any display of warrant authority.[179] The reason illegal entries are so frequent is that, despite the growing sophistication of listening devices for hearing through walls and heating ducts or for taking sound off windows and the like, most police eavesdroppers still prefer, for optimum service and reception, to plant their mikes or tap and bug the telephone instrument in the room itself.

CHAPTER SIX

Probing the Mind:
Psychological Surveillance

UNDER PSYCHOLOGICAL surveillance are grouped those scientific and technological methods that seek to extract information from an individual which he does not want to reveal or does not know he is revealing or is led to reveal without a mature awareness of its significance for his privacy.

The heart of the privacy issue in psychological surveillance at present lies in polygraph and personality testing, which have been present on the American scene since the early twentieth century, but which were swept into greatly increased use for corporate and governmental purposes since World War II.

The polygraph—the most widely used of the various devices known popularly as "lie detectors" [1]—was developed in its modern form during the 1920's, as an instrument to aid police in the detection of crime. The theory behind the polygraph is that lying causes distinctive and measurable physiological reactions in a person who knows that he is not telling the truth. The polygraph operator asks questions in a special pattern while testing the subject's heart and pulse rate, relative blood pressure, breathing, and perspiration rate. (Some polygraph machines also test muscle tension, and it is common to photograph and tape-record the entire examination secretly for later study.) Bodily changes are recorded by pens on graph paper, producing "squiggles" resembling those on an electrocardiogram or seismograph. By interpreting these records, a trained polygrapher is supposed to be able to identify untrue responses to critical questions.

Several important technological advances in polygraphing were made during the late 1950's and early 1960's. Federal agencies developed techniques for administering lie-detection tests without the knowledge of the subject. These rely on a seemingly "normal" chair which has equipment built into it to register body heat, changes in limb volume, and nervous movements. Hidden cameras are also used in such covert polygraphing to measure changes in eye-pupil size as an indicator of stress during the interview.[2] There has been some doubt expressed whether maximum stress is generated when the subject is not told that he is being put under "scientific, machine measurement." However, the covert polygraph techniques are considered valuable for situations in which it is not feasible to require a polygraph test or even to let someone know he is under suspicion.

Another new technique is computer interpretation of polygraph tracings. Since the weakest link in polygraphing is admittedly the variations in readings of the test results among polygraph operators, computers have been used to provide more rigorous and "objective" interpretation of stress levels. Such computer readings are particularly useful for collating and comparing new sensors which can be added to the test, such as devices to measure blood volume in fingertip arteries by photoelectric cells, changes in blood color and pulse waves, eye-pupil dilation, body-temperature fluctuation, and even brain wave patterns (through electro-encephalograph helmets). One scientist has developed a means of taking off and measuring nineteen different channels of stress responses on a recording device.

Personality testing is the use of written or oral examination to discover traits of personality for purposes of judging an individual's psychological strength, especially to predict his future performance in some role such as employment. Such tests may be in the form of pencil-and-paper quizzes, in which the subject answers questions about himself, his emotions, preferences, values, and attitudes, or they may be "projective" tests, in which the individual is asked to draw a picture, interpret ink blots, comment on ambiguous pictures, or perform other acts that provide psychological clues to his personality.[3] In general, personality tests differ from tests of intelligence or aptitudes because the personality test does not measure more or less objective factors, such as language skills, logic, or physical dexterity, but seeks to measure emotions, attitudes, propensities, and levels of personal adjustment. In addition, personality tests traditionally include questions asking the subject to reveal his attitudes toward sexual, political, religious, and family matters, since these are considered the significant areas for distinguishing deviations from norms of belief in the population being tested. The issue of privacy obviously raised by both polygraphing and personality testing is whether employers or the government should be allowed to require individuals to have their inner processes probed through machine or test measurements. How widely personality tests and polygraphs are used today is sketched in the discussions that follow.

Personality Testing and Personnel Selection

During the first two decades of the twentieth century, psychologists, psychiatrists, and educators turned with great expectation to the "scientific" measurement of man's abilities. Tests were developed to gauge intelligence and aptitudes, and many of these, such as the Stanford-Binet "IQ" test, became widely used and helpful aids to such analysis. But the frequent disparity between test results and the actual success of testees in schools or factories led psychologists to seek ways to measure the personality characteristics that made persons achieve "above," "below," or "about the level" of their "capabilities." With this search the modern era of personality testing was launched.

A psychological test, to psychologists, is "an observation of a sample of human behavior made under standard, controlled conditions which results in a linear evaluation called a score." Tests of personality characteristics are simply one type of psychological test. In more popular terms, a personality test is a written or oral examination that goes beyond measurement of intelligence, skills, or aptitudes and seeks to measure traits of personality, emotional balances, beliefs or values, sexual adjustment, and various propensities, in order to understand present personality conflicts for therapeutic or counseling purposes or to predict future performance for occupational purposes.

During World War I, in addition to using the famous Alpha intelligence test for judging potential officer material, the U. S. Army attempted to screen out psychoneurotics with a Personal Data Sheet designed by Dr. R. S. Woodworth of Columbia University.[4] Follow-up studies found the results to be poor, but the concept of "self-administered," "objectively graded," "pencil-and-paper" tests of psychological characteristics achieved the respectability of government use. Between 1918 and the mid-1930's, university psychologists experimented widely with pencil-and-paper tests of personality traits and attitudes, developing a "civilian edition" of the Woodworth test and of various other tests designed by such leading professors of psychology as Allport, Thurstone, and Bernreuter; these tests were designed for classroom experiments or to counsel students on future career choices. In addition to the pencil-and-paper tests, the 1920's and 1930's saw the appearance of another type of psychological test, developed for clinical use—the "projective" tests, such as the famous Rorschach "ink blot" exercise, which were employed primarily by psychiatric practitioners to identify serious mental disorders.

It was during the 1930's that personality tests moved from the university, the clinic, and the army into the field of personnel selection. At first, psychological tests were adopted by factory managers to determine which production or clerical workers were bad hiring risks. Then, several personnel consultants formed "testing companies" to help business firms select salesmen or junior executives, and some corporations developed their own tests of desirable sales-executive personality, based on "composite profiles" of their most successful salesmen. However, personality testing in industry remained a relatively small-scale operation during the late 1930's.

World War II thrust the federal government again into the forefront of personality testing. Psychological tests of every style, from multiple-choice "interest" exams to clinically derived projective inquiries, were given to millions of servicemen. In addition, such agencies as the Office of Strategic Services developed special simulation tests that attempted to create situations comparable to those OSS agents would confront in their wartime assignments. As with the World War I experience, careful follow-up studies showed that the personality tests had not proved to be more predictive of actual performance than chance selection,[5] but once again personality testing acquired government respectability. Cadres of war-trained testers took their tools into the civilian areas after 1945.

Between 1945 and the mid-1950's, personality tests moved steadily into many public-school evaluation and guidance procedures, some state and federal employment processes, several professional-school screening programs (such as medicine), the selection of many Protestant and Catholic candidates for religious posts, and—the most extensive of all— selection and promotion of corporate employees. By the late 1950's and 1960's, the administering of personality tests had become a routine procedure in these areas of American life, and a new professional subgroup had come into being—the "test psychologist" working for institutional clients.

Though the use of personality testing in the schools will be discussed later in this book, this chapter will concentrate on the uses being made of personality testing for personnel selection in industry and by government. The amount of personality testing in private industry in the mid-1960's is a matter of dispute, with estimates of American companies who use such tests for some or all of their employee evaluations ranging from 40 to 70 per cent. To get some idea of the situation, I sent a questionnaire to 300 corporations of diverse size, location, and type of business, asking whether their firms used personality tests.[6] Personality tests were defined as "oral or written tests that go beyond measurement of intelligence, skills, or aptitudes and seek to measure emotional states, traits of character, socio-political beliefs or values, sexual adjustment, and general propensities, and to use these measurements to predict future performance." Replies came from 208 companies: 97 companies (46.4 per cent) reported that they were currently using personality tests; 111 companies (53.6 per cent) said they were not.

Among the 111 non-user companies were many of the nation's leading corporations, including firms with highly modern personnel depart-
ments. Among these were Aerojet-General, American Motors, Armco
Steel, Braniff Airways, Bristol-Myers, Bumblebee Seafoods, Cities Service, Colgate-Palmolive, Delaware Power and Light, Diamond Crystal
Salt, du Pont, Elgin Watch, Florida Power & Light, Foremost Dairies,
General Aniline and Film, Gimbel Brothers, A & P, Greyhound, Jonathan Logan, Inc., Kaiser Industries, Litton Industries, Loew's Theaters,
Metropolitan Life, Northern Pacific Railroad, P. Ballantine & Sons,
Radio Corporation of America, Time Inc., and Westinghouse.[7] The
non-users also included small and medium-sized companies throughout
the country.

Fifteen non-user companies reported that they had at one time employed personality testing but had abandoned the practice. The tests
were "expensively worthless," wrote the American and Foreign Power
Company; "did not give a true picture of the individual" (anonymous);
"too time consuming; also, lack of faith on our part in the value (or
validity) of available tests" (Gamble Skogmo, Inc.); "Company personnel could do a better job of evaluating an individual's potential for advancement and promotion based upon appraisal of his job performance
. . . ." (Mississippi Power & Light); "We feel that by using objective
type testing, by thorough check of an individual's experience and education and by soliciting opinions from individuals who have had professional association with the candidate, we can make the kind of judgments necessary to assure a competent staff" (American Machine &
Foundry). One of the most interesting reasons for discarding personality
testing came from the Friedman Marks Clothing Company: "As soon as
the test revealed that the boss was not suited, personality-wise, to his job,
all tests were dropped."

The letter asked: "Do you feel that there is a legitimate question of
privacy involved in the use of [these] tests by industry?" Fifty-two of the
non-users checked "Yes"; twenty-four non-users checked "No," usually
without further explanation. Thirty-five non-users did not answer the
question.

For many of the non-users, the particular aspect of privacy that
drew their comment was the "divulgence of results to too many others as
time goes by." If tests were kept as "inviolate" between employee and
psychologist as confidences between lawyer and client, wrote an anonymous respondent, they might have some value; "too often," however,
there is "misinterpretation and misuse of the data revealed by the test
. . . hurting both employees and employer."

The group of ninety-seven companies that reported they were currently using personality testing represents a set of companies just as
diverse, nationally known, and professionally managed as the non-users.

No apparent distinctions can be found in the nature of the industry, the size of the company, or its managerial style. Among the industrial users are Acme Steel, American Hardware, Champion Papers, Chesebrough-Pond's, Delta Airlines, Doubleday & Co., Dun & Bradstreet, Encyclopaedia Britannica, Equitable Life, Ford Motor Co., Fruehauf, General Foods, Gillette, Helene Curtis, Hershey Chocolate, Hinky Dinky Supermarkets, Hayden Stone & Co., J. I. Case, Johnson and Johnson, Kellogg, Lever Brothers, Owens Corning Fiberglas, Pet Milk, Trans World Airlines, Tidewater Oil, United States Envelope Company, and Warner Brothers. A full complement of small and regional firms are also on the list.

These user companies actually give tests only to a small percentage of their total employee or executive forces. Most of these respondents tested less than 20 per cent of their employees; almost half tested less than 4 per cent. For example, TWA tested 150 out of 23,000; Chris-Craft tested 5 out of 3,000; Pet Milk, 6 out of 10,000; International Textbook, 40 out of 1,200; South Carolina Electric and Gas, 30 out of 1850; and Lever Brothers, 175 out of 8,000. Only nine firms out of sixty-eight administered personality tests annually to more than 500 employees or applicants for employment with their organizations. Half a dozen companies specified that they were "using" personality inventories and measures only to "test the tests," not as a personnel technique that they had accepted and had made part of their regular procedures. However, the majority of the users made it quite plain that they were enthusiastic champions of personality testing as a selection technique.

Personality testing is used in these companies for selection purposes primarily for management personnel,[8] salesmen, and professional employees, and for promotion purposes primarily for management personnel. Of the ninety-seven firms, sixty used their own staffs for evaluating the tests, though only fourteen employed professional psychologists. The remaining users employed outside professional agencies. Half of the users preserved the results in general personnel files, while one-third placed test results in special files or had them kept by the company psychologists. Only four companies destroyed the results.[9]

Commentaries from the directors of personnel of companies using personality tests provide a helpful perspective on the attitudes of corporate users on the privacy issue. A number of companies indicated that they had considered the privacy question but nevertheless felt that properly selected and administered tests ought to be continued. Boeing Aircraft responded:

There will always be a "legitimate question of privacy" in any personnel selection or placement decision, whether or not tests are used. Good taste, social acceptability, and relevance are the standards by which we must decide how far we can "pry" into an employment applicant's background. Properly administered and *validated* tests probably constitute less of a threat to privacy than many less formalized selection techniques—e.g., interviewing applicant's spouse.

S. S. Pierce of Boston stressed their respect for "individual privacy": "We here do not probe emotions, socio-economic belief and personality characteristics. We feel the real danger lies with those who believe they are doing this and believe furthermore that they are qualified to do so." Strong defenses of personality testing by company spokesmen who did *not* consider that there existed any significant invasion of privacy tended to stress four main points: (1) personal interviews have been widely accepted, yet these are frequently far more probing than personality tests; (2) "proper placement" is crucially important for the well-being of both the employee and the company; (3) the use of such tests is not intended to invade privacy and should not be seen in that light; and (4) complaints about intrusion into privacy from employees taking such tests are very rare. These four points were woven together, for example, in the response received from Pepperell Manufacturing Company (Biddeford, Maine):

> An interview by a skillful, probing interviewer can piece up valuable information that could be termed as intrusive, improper, and violative of individual dignity. . . . We are not interested in an individual's private life, his beliefs, or disbeliefs, but we do think that if a person, for instance, enjoys diversity in his employment that he should not be saddled with a repetitive job or vice versa. . . . [W]e have never entertained the idea that we were violating the privacy of any individual because our prime interest is fitting an individual to a proper job. . . . After 13 years of experience with this type of test I have seen no adverse reactions that would lead us to believe that we were improperly using techniques detrimental to the individual seeking employment in our plant.

Company need was illustrated by a statement from Pfizer and Company: "If tests 'invade' privacy, they do so with more than just self-interest on the part of a company. Proper placement of an individual is important because improper placement is both a disservice to the individual concerned and a time-consuming and expensive experience for the company."

The third defense, a lack of desire to invade privacy, was presented in the response from Revlon, which stressed that it "frankly did not know" at what point a personality test, an investigation of past character, or an interview "began to invade privacy. . . . We can only say that our intention is not to invade his privacy but to make certain that everything has been done to assure a selection that will be successful for him as well as for the company."

A final defense often registered was that employees have rarely complained, suggesting that they do not feel their privacy is invaded by such tests. Campbell Soup Company wrote, "[W]e have had no indication that applicants find them objectionable. On the contrary, most applicants find the tests and the results quite interesting." A Borden Company executive stated, "I have talked with many men who have been tested. . . . Not one has ever indicated any feeling his privacy had been invaded." In a more general vein, the B. F. Goodrich Company noted:

> There are many kinds of information about a person which are private to the public, but which are of legitimate concern under some circumstances to other parties. A person may wish to keep his personality characteristics confidential, but he could well feel the same way about his abilities, job performance, medical data, financial affairs, school grades, age, credit rating and other matters. At a time when increasing emphasis is being placed on a company's obligation to provide for the welfare of its employees both on and off the job, it is not idle snooping to attempt to determine what a person is like before taking the risk of bringing him into the organization or assigning him to a responsible position. . . . We have reservations regarding the validity and relevance of available personality assessment procedures, but not the privacy of such information if the assessments are properly made and treated confidentially.

Government Use of Personality Tests

During 1964–65, I conducted a mail survey of federal and state agencies to see how widely personality tests were being used. From the responses to this survey and testimony before congressional committees, this was the situation in the mid-1960's.

For more than two million federal employees in the "competitive" or "merit" posts of the civil service, personnel practices are under the jurisdiction of the U.S. Civil Service Commission.[10] The CSC sets rules for the initial hiring of these employees. Once they are hired, their promotion or disability retirement is under the authority of the individual agency, following "Civil Service Commission guidelines." Based on Civil Service Rule 1 (1884) forbidding inquiry into religious or political opinions, the CSC established the rule that personnel techniques cannot call for information "concerning the political, racial or religious opinions or affiliations of any persons, or cover knowledge gained only through such affiliations."

Under these standards, the CSC had not installed personality tests for initial hiring purposes and had "strongly advised" against agencies' using them for promotion purposes. The CSC's official statement on this question had stated four grounds on which personality tests "fail to satisfy merit system precepts for employment."

(1) They were developed for clinical use, and are not designed to measure the specific characteristics needed by persons working in particular occupations.

(2) These tests are subject to distortion, either purposefully or otherwise. Therefore, the scores are undependable as a basis for employment decisions.

(3) The scores on such tests can easily be grossly misinterpreted and misapplied by persons who are not qualified psychiatrists or psychologists trained to interpret such test results in the light of the total study of the individual.

(4) In view of the character of the questions asked, if the results of personality tests are used for employment purposes, the individual's right to privacy is seriously jeopardized.

While this policy was strongly worded, it had not been enforced vigorously before 1965 for promotion and medical exams, and various agencies had used personality tests for "special screening" purposes as they saw fit. Then, prompted in part by public discussion and growing Congressional inquiries, the CSC on May 17, 1965, issued a "restatement" of its policy in which it flatly "prohibited" all agencies under its jurisdiction from using personality tests in any aspect of personnel work. The only exception stated was for "a qualified psychiatrist or psychologist" during "medical determinations for employment or fitness for duty." As examples of posts requiring such medical clearance, Chairman Macy cited air-traffic controllers and ward attendants in public hospitals, the former because of the pressure of the work and the latter to screen out sadistic or unbalanced persons. Chairman Macy announced that, as of May, 1965, his agency had no evidence from its inspection system that personality testing was being used by any federal agency under CSC jurisdiction, apart from special medical clearances.

However, CSC had no jurisdiction over diplomatic, military, or intelligence agencies, policy-making posts, or federally aided programs administered by state or private agencies. Thus the State Department began using personality tests in 1949 with the creation of its Medical Division.[11] Tests were used when individuals displayed concrete emotional or psychological disturbances and when an examining psychiatrist felt (and the Medical Division agreed) that psychological testing was called for to aid in the judgment of the case. Out of 4,000 such medical examinations in 1963, 175 required psychiatric evaluation, and of these, less than sixty received psychological tests. The employee was referred to a consulting psychologist, who gave the test in his private office, kept the test results in his files, and forwarded to the State Department psychiatrist only a summary judgment. The State Department was not told the questions asked. Employees were allowed to refuse to take the psychological tests altogether or refuse to answer "any questions he deems offensive or an invasion of his privacy." In March, 1965, prompted by two employee complaints that personality testing intruded into their privacy, and by some Congressional inquiries, the State Department brought in five psychologists to review its procedures. On April 20, 1965, it issued new regulations, making both the psychiatric and psychological evaluations "voluntary"; allowing the employee a choice in selection of the psychiatrist and psychologist; eliminating use of the Minnesota Multiphasic Personality Inventory because of its questions on religion and sex; and adopting a policy of explaining the "significance and interpretation of the tests . . . more fully" to the employee than had been previously undertaken. The State Department also gives personality tests to all code clerks and communications personnel because of the need for emotionally stable persons in such "highly sensitive" work. If an employee refuses to take the psychological test, he cannot do communications work, but, the Department states, it provides "another assignment." The State Department also administered personality tests for twelve federal agencies having overseas operations, including the Library of Congress, the Department of Agriculture, the Geodetic Survey, and the Bureau of Public Roads.

The Departments of the Army, Navy, and Air Force each state that they do not use personality testing for regular hiring or promotion of either civilian employees or uniformed personnel.[12] The basic reason given was the failure of personality tests to achieve the service's standards for "predictive validity." The Air Force adds that its rejection of the tests is also based on "controversies" about such tests. Each of the services indicates that it sometimes gives personality tests for special missions involving extra stress on the individual, such as Navy submarine crews and personnel for Operation Deep Freeze. As for the Department of Defense as a whole, Walter T. Skallerup, Deputy Assistant Secretary of Defense, has stated that personality testing is not used for routine hiring, promotion, or retirement of civilian personnel.[13] Civilian personnel taking on overseas assignments answer a Personnel Data Questionnaire developed by the Civil Service Commission, modified by the Air Force, and "validated" on Air Force employees. This questionnaire is being "reevaluated" by the Department of Defense in light of the new CSC policies on personality testing. As for military personnel, Skallerup stated that a physician administering a "fitness" medical to applicants can call for a psychiatric evaluation if he sees evidence of mental disturbance. The same may be ordered when the commanding officer and the medical officer of a nuclear-weapons unit find that an individual displays signs of mental or emotional disorder. In these cases of psychiatric evaluation, the psychiatrist uses (or has a consultant use) whatever psychological tests are considered proper. These might include the Minnesota Multiphasic, Skallerup said, but he did not see any privacy objection to its use in such a "clinical" situation. Information was not provided as to testing practices of the Central Intelligence Agency or the National Security Agency.

Several "exempt" federal agencies relied heavily on personality tests. In 1964 the Department of Labor used a personality test for 22,000 persons applying to be trained as youth counselors for work with state employment services under Operation CAUSE.[14] The test included questions such as "I think Lincoln was greater than Washington"; "I feel there is only one true religion"; "When a man is with a woman, he is usually thinking about things related to her sex"; "I often go against my parents' wishes"; "I hardly ever get excited or thrilled." Under pressure from some Congressmen, the Department of Labor announced that it would not administer such tests in the future for Operation CAUSE. The Job Corps has been making experimental use of its own personality test for volunteers in the VISTA job-corps program,[15] not for selection of the volunteers, but to help the counselor who works with the youths learn more about each of them. The test results are retained for "comparative" purposes.

Though the Department of Health, Education and Welfare does not use personality tests for general hiring, promotion, or removal of personnel, psychiatric exams are conducted on the commissioned Officers Corps of the Public Health Service (PHS) when they serve with AID-Vietnam and the Peace Corps overseas.[16] Also within HEW certain experimental personality tests have been administered by the Social Security Administration to judge the tests' reliability in particular situations. In 1964–65 one test was given to fifty employees of Social Security Offices to measure personal characteristics important to a "public contact" position. Personality testing programs were used for about 100 persons working for the Bonneville Power Authority (under the Department of Interior) and for all volunteers training for the Peace Corps. The questions used in these programs and the defense of the agency officials for using such tests are discussed fully in Part III.

A sample survey of civil-service commissions of eleven states, one territory, and four municipalities shows that state and local governments reject personality tests for general civil-service appointment and promotion but do use them for a few situations of special public importance or employee stress. For example, in Los Angeles, police candidates are interviewed by a psychiatrist as a part of the required medical examination.[17] In New York, in the case of police officers, the Police Department gives a "standard personality test" to all persons who have been appointed to the Police Academy as probationary patrolmen; similarly, the New York Department of Correction administers a personality test to all persons appointed as correction officers for the various prisons and correctional institutions.[18] In New York City, those are the only positions for which such tests are reported to be used as a regular part of the selection or probationary process.

The most widely given reason for state and local non-use of personality tests for general screening was typified by Arizona's response: "Have not learned of any [personality tests] the validity of which has been established to our satisfaction." [19] The director of the Wisconsin State Bureau of Personnel stated:

> We believe that commercial personality tests available are not valid enough to be used by our jurisdiction, that persons can "fake" many of the answers, and that the results probably would not be upheld by a court of law if appealed by a candidate who was not satisfied with his results on a personality test.[20]

The President of the New York State Department of Civil Service wrote:

> We do not use such tests as the Rorschach, the Kuder, the Bernreuter, etc. In fact, we know of no available personality tests which are presently satisfactory for use in the selection of personnel for the public service. Whether these tests are useful in selecting people for private employment is probably a matter of opinion, but, in any event, we do not think they are practicable or defensible in our work.[21]

Public reaction or potential reaction against personality testing was a factor in the decision of three governments against using the tests: Maryland and the cities of Detroit and Des Moines. The City of Detroit Civil Service Commission felt:

> Tests of this type should be used with extreme care, with consideration to any effect that they will have in the maintenance of public and professional relationships of the agency and with proper preparation of the parties of interest to reduce misunderstanding of the purposes of their use.[22]

Both Maryland and Detroit had made use of personality tests in the past but had dropped them.

In Massachusetts a prohibitive state law was cited as the reason for not testing employee personality. The Massachusetts Civil Service Law bars the use of questions relating to political or religious affiliations.[23]

The data in this chapter shows that personality testing is still used widely in industry, though perhaps the high tide of corporate enthusiasm has passed and a declining trend has set in. In government, such tests are not used in significant numbers in the local and state personnel programs or in the general federal service, but are being used by certain federal agencies such as the Peace Corps and some military departments which justify testing by citing the special stress involved in their operations.

The Spread of Polygraphing

More than half the police departments in the United States, including those of almost every major city, are presently using polygraphs in their investigative work.[24] One major reason for such wide use appears to be the polygraph's success in producing confessions from those told that they have "flunked" the test. New York City in 1963 joined those police departments that purchased their own equipment and were employing their own polygraph expert. Before 1963 New York had hired private polygraph specialists for specific occasions or had used a Brooklyn police lieutenant who owned his own polygraph set and did consulting work.[25] Among the many cases of police polygraph testing reported in the press in recent years have been investigations of murders, policy corruption, paternity complaints, "fixing" basketball games, first-degree robbery, rape, and drugging meatballs of racing greyhounds.[26]

To measure the extent of these police uses of polygraphing, newspaper accounts of police use throughout the United States were collected for a four-month test period, from February through May, 1964. These were provided by a clipping service that covers 1,800 daily newspapers, 9,000 weekly newspapers, and 4,500 magazines and journals.[27] The four-month sample showed 111 publicized cases in which police polygraphs had been employed. Over half of these involved either murder (41) or robbery (22). The other major categories were arson (9); assault (7); burglary (4); morals (3); police brutality (3); bribery (3); paternity (2); impeachment (2); and miscellaneous (15).

In the majority of these cases the local police agency performed the test and no more than two or three suspects were examined. In several cases, however, a larger number were tested. Following the sexual assault of a seventeen-year-old girl in Oklahoma, seventy persons were eventually examined by polygraph.[28] In 10 per cent of the cases, the persons tested said that they had volunteered to take the lie-detector test.

Though these 111 cases occurred in more than two dozen states, there were distinct patterns of concentration. Illinois was the location for 27 of them, and more than half the remaining cases came from seven other states: Wisconsin, Indiana, Ohio, New York, New Jersey, California, and Texas.

Executive-agency replies to a Congressional Committee questionnaire revealed that thirteen federal agencies used some 12,000 polygraph tests for criminal and security investigations during the fiscal year 1963, with 487 polygraph operators in service. The following table, adapted

AGENCY	PURPOSE [a]	TESTS IN 1963[b]	POLY-GRAPHS OWNED	AUTHOR-IZED POLYGRAPH OPERATORS
Army Military Police	"Criminal"	4,400	118	206
Air Force	"Security and criminal"	1,912	72	73
Defense Department	"Security, criminal and misconduct"	147	3	3
District of Columbia Police Dept.	"Criminal"	350	3	6
Federal Bureau of Investigation	"Security and criminal"	2,314	48	46
General Services Administration	"Security and misconduct"	10	1	0
Office of Naval Intelligence	"Security, criminal, misconduct, and personnel screening"	1,200	77	86
Marine Corps	"Security and criminal"	813	9	20
Post Office Dept.	"Criminal"	472	17	16
Coast Guard	"Criminal and misconduct"	189	9	13
Narcotics Bureau	"Criminal"	20	0	0
Secret Service	"Criminal and misconduct"	175	4	18
State Department	"Security, criminal and misconduct"	17	0	0

a. Some agencies, as indicated, did not report separate figures for criminal and non-criminal matters.

b. Includes both tests given by the agency and tests performed for the agency by others, either other government agencies or outside polygraph services.

from the data supplied by the agencies, indicates the largest users among federal agencies:[29]

In addition, various Congressional Committees have asked corporate officials, union leaders, government officials, and private parties to "volunteer" for lie-detector tests when open conflicts in testimony between witnesses at legislative hearings indicated the possibility of perjury. Witnesses who do consent to take such tests have had them administered by operators from the Secret Service, FBI, Office of Naval Intelligence, and various other agencies.

The Polygraph as Personnel Sorter

Before World War II, there were considerably fewer than 100 private polygraph "agencies," most of these one-man services. Their work was composed primarily of interrogations for law-enforcement agencies or for business firms seeking to test their employees in order to solve specific crimes, such as embezzlement or theft of materials from a storeroom. The small amount of pre-employment screening for banks or for industrial plants, where easily concealed inventory could be stolen, was a minor part of the polygrapher's activity.

Today more than 1,000 persons (apart from federal employees) are giving polygraph tests. Though there are a few national polygraph agencies with branches in various cities, most polygraph "firms" are still one-man operations. The total continues to increase yearly, especially as government-trained polygraph operators return to civilian life. The only requirement for entry into this field (in all but one state) is the cash to purchase a polygraph machine or the electronic skill to make up one's own lie-detector apparatus. Leading companies, such as the Keeler Polygraph Institute and John E. Reid & Associates, report that their business rose "eight to ten times" in volume in the decade from 1950 to 1960, and that it is still soaring.[30] One firm reports that it gives about 6,000 tests annually.[31] Truth Verification Inc. of Dallas gave 26,000 tests in 1963, and this rose to 42,000 in 1964.[32]

Since 1945 only a fraction of the work of most private polygraph agencies (estimated at 10 per cent or less) has been interrogation for solutions to specific crimes for police or business clients. The great majority of tests, usually described as "90 per cent," are now for business and government clients using this technique as a means of personnel sorting, security checking, and "trouble insurance."[33]

In the field of industrial and commercial usage, hundreds of leading companies in the country have turned to "preventive" testing since World War II, among them Montgomery Ward, the Palmer House, Lord & Taylor, McKesson and Robbins, Armour & Co., Thillens Checkcashers, Marshall Field, and the Chicago Lake Shore Bank.[34] One polygraph expert has estimated that between 30,000 and 40,000 business firms today use polygraph tests for personnel analysis.[35] The clients of one polygraph service include fifteen banks, six mail-order houses, nineteen hotels, and twelve department stores.[36] Some of these companies give lie-detector tests to all prospective employees, asking questions that range from whether they ever stole anything from a previous employer or lied on their personnel forms to inquiries whether they use narcotics, are pregnant, or intend to stay long with this company if hired. In some companies the job applicant must pay for the cost of the polygraph if he "flunks the test" and is not hired. Some companies holding classified government contracts have been administering "loyalty checks" by polygraph, using questions that examine the ideological outlook, organizational record, and acquaintances of prospective employees. A growing number of companies have their own polygraph equipment and retain trained polygraph specialists on the company payroll. McKesson and Robbins, for example, operates its own personnel polygraphing, seeking information with which to forestall thefts of drugs from warehouses and laboratories.[37] The extent of corporate use of polygraph tests for screening personnel varies widely from city to city. New York, for example, a strong union center, has always been a poor site for polygraph operations, whereas Chicago is probably the leading city in America for corporate use of polygraphs. As a result of the presence of John E. Reid & Associates in Chicago, and of successful pilot programs in the early 1950's that cut Chicago department-store pilfering substantially, a variety of Chicago companies have adopted polygraphing.

In addition to selection testing, many companies now maintain continuing "polygraph check-ups" for employees. *Business Week*, in a 1960 survey of corporate lie detecting, concluded that "periodic personnel checks" have become a "common industrial application":

> Some companies run regular tests on shipping and receiving personnel, purchasing agents, buyers, door-to-door salesmen, tellers, bookkeepers, and others in a good position to make off with money or goods. Auto, toy, dress, and other design-conscious companies check workers in sensitive jobs to guard against information leaks.[38]

A Texas agency (Employment Services, Inc.) estimated in 1962 that 5,000 Texas firms required their employees to take periodic tests. The polygraph agency tells its customers that the tests are really "moral vaccination"; without them, "people will take advantage of you." [39] Spokesmen for companies using continuous polygraphing say that it serves to keep employees honest; many employees who might be tempted to steal or sell company secrets after they had passed an initial polygraph test at hiring time are dissuaded from wrongdoing because they know that their annual or semi-annual "check-up" is coming. The *Wall Street Journal* in 1961 cited the case of the Chicago check-cashing firm Thillens Checkcashers. A Thillens employee was tested regularly each year from 1948 to 1957 but missed the tests in 1957 and 1958, having been excused because he was ill when the yearly tests were given. When he was tested again in 1959, his answers revealed emotional disturbances when he was asked about the commission of thefts, and a full investigation revealed that between 1957 and 1959 he had stolen $366,000.[40]

Still another use of the polygraph by corporations is in the standard battery of tests given to those being considered for promotion. The probing here goes beyond questions of possible past misconduct and often deals with attitudes toward the firm, toward business life, toward the particular job under consideration, and even toward socio-political attitudes that bear on the executive's "rapport" with management. A polygraph expert with the Burns Detective Agency office in Richmond, Virginia, explained: "[W]e try to find the real attitude of the executives, to discover any hidden hostility, whether he intends to leave his employer and if he thinks himself that he can handle a job with more responsibility." [41]

Finally, there are a variety of uses of polygraph techniques that can only be described as "miscellaneous," though the number of these applications is steadily increasing. In Miami, Florida, the Hialeah Hospital announced in 1963 that all its nurses and employees would thereafter be given "scientific personnel evaluation interviews" by the Hallmark Polygraph Service. "Often, employees unconsciously resent their employers," the hospital administrator told the press, and such tests will "uncover any resentments so the management can correct them." The tests would also "establish if workers are happy in their jobs." [42] In New York City a national television network hired the National Training Center of Lie Detection to test audience reactions to a proposed new TV show.[43]

In all these uses of administrative polygraph interrogation by corporations, from screening of applicants to tests of the happiness level of employees, the overwhelming trend is to impose sanctions upon those who will not consent to take the tests. Applicants who decline will usually not be considered at all. Employees who are hired are often required to sign contracts consenting to periodic polygraph check-ups; such employees will usually be fired if they decide at any point not to continue accepting the tests. One Hollywood, California, agency that does extensive pre-employment and periodic screening for corporations explains that each subject signs a paper in advance waiving "any and all rights of privacy that I have with reference to the taking of said test or the results thereof." Thus, the operator said, "we deprive no one of his constitutional rights," and companies can insist on consent to the tests as a condition of employment.[44]

Polygraph testing for personnel selection and administration at the state and local governmental level has grown swiftly during the 1950's and 1960's, especially in police, fire, and health departments. For example, police departments in Orlando, Florida; Stockton, California; Cincinnati, Ohio; Salt Lake City, Utah; St. Louis, Missouri; Evanston, Illinois; Miami, Florida; and the State Police of Maryland, among many others, have recently adopted polygraph screening for law-enforcement posts.[45] In Chicago 150 policemen were polygraphed in 1960 after a scandal involving police involvement in burglary activities.[46] The Stockton, California, test asks all police candidates "about 300 questions on previous work, loyalty, arrest and traffic record, physical and mental health, financial stability, use of liquor and narcotics, education, marital records and abnormal sexual behavior"; about 40 to 60 per cent of the candidates in the typical police-candidate testing are rejected as a result of the tests.[47] Some municipalities, especially those plagued by scandals affecting the police forces, have begun to give periodic tests and to use the polygraph when promotions are made, to test for past misconduct, corruption, and so forth.

As noted earlier, more than half the police departments in the United States employ polygraphs in their investigations of criminal offenses. Usually, the "police position" on polygraphing is that an innocent person should have nothing to hide and should welcome the opportunity to confirm his innocence by taking a polygraph test. Polygraphing of the police themselves has been another matter, however. For example, when the Denver Civil Service Commission announced polygraphing of all applicants for appointment and promotions on the city police force in 1961, following a scandal involving thefts by Denver policemen, local and national police spokesmen protested sharply. A traffic patrolman in Denver said, "By forcing a man to submit to such a test, you imply that he is guilty of a crime. This is contrary to our entire way of life." A police captain stated that if a man up for promotion "does poorly on the lie detector test, which is far from infallible, not only is he not promoted but he is also discredited." These attitudes were also voiced by the director of the Field Service Division of the International Association of Chiefs of Police. Interviewed in 1961, he said that he thought the task of weeding out unfit policemen and determining talent for promotion could best be done by personal observation and investigation, not polygraphing.[48]

In addition to such use of polygraphs for screening state personnel, local and state governments have begun to use the polygraph to test some persons licensed or regulated by the state, such as owners of liquor stores or racing-board licensees.[49] Since 1959 municipal authorities in Evanston, Illinois, have given lie-detector tests on a quarterly basis to all municipal parking-lot employees.[50] Several Illinois officials began a campaign in 1963 to have polygraph tests given to all attorneys proposed for appointment as circuit-court magistrates, to screen out corrupt persons.[51]

Alongside the rise of "personnel sorting" and "preventive screening" in business and by state and local governments, there has been a major expansion of polygraphing by the federal government for similar purposes, especially in the area of sensitive "security" employment. As a consequence, there has been a trend toward polygraph questioning that is not limited to specific past misconduct but probes into the beliefs and inclinations of federal employees, in order to try to predict future tendencies.

A look at this development as of the early 1950's was contained in a series of articles in the *Reporter* in 1954, written by Dwight Macdonald. Macdonald's primary focus was on the spread of "tendency" polygraphing in several important federal agencies, such as the State Department and the National Security Agency, and the impact of this practice on government personnel from the lowest to the highest levels. One of several examples Macdonald presented involved general security screening at the National Security Administration, where all prospective employees were put through polygraph tests.

Richard Roe took his test in the fall of 1951. . . . [H]e had been working for several months at NSA but had not yet been cleared. . . . [H]e is a college graduate—a political science major—and was interrogated by an examiner who may or may not have gone to high school. . . . "I was willing, even eager, to take the test because I believed in its scientific reliability," says Richard Roe. "But halfway through, I felt like someone being tried in a Moscow purge."

The third-degree atmosphere was established the minute he entered the room. "My examiner looked and acted like a desk sergeant. He fixed me with a suspicious stare, didn't shake hands, smile, or even introduce himself." . . .

One of the questions on the list the examiner presented to Mr. Roe was, "Have you ever been sympathetic to Communism?" It caused a good deal of grief to both of them. Mr. Roe explained, or rather tried to—"there was a total lack of empathy"—that he had studied Marxism in college and consequently found it difficult to answer this with a simple Yes or No. If by "Communism" the examiner meant Marx's doctrines, then he could only say he was sympathetic to some and unsympathetic to others. If the term was to be taken in its Russian context, then he felt obliged to say that he had once felt sympathetic to the Mensheviks but had never been sympathetic to the Bolsheviks. All of this passed over the inquisitor's head with a heavy, soughing sound like wind in the branches of a rainsoaked tree. "I got the impression that he considered anyone who had studied Marx to be *ipso facto* a security risk and also that he personally wanted me to fail."

The results were inconclusive, and Mr. Roe, a rather highstrung type, had to take the test three more times, each time with ambiguous results. After each test, his security officer tried to persuade him to resign quietly, thus avoiding the possible stigma of being fired. The security officer also seemed anxious to save the security division a lot of trouble and possibly to add a scalp to be displayed to inquiring McCarthys later on. Mr. Roe was finally dropped, much to everyone's relief, including his own. . . . Other veterans of the polygraph wars at NSA tell stories similar to . . . Mr. Roe's. The examiners seem to have violated just about every rule of proper polygraph technique. The questions were often extremely vague—"Have you ever done anything you were ashamed of?" "Are you now or have you ever been in sympathy with leftist ideas?" . . .

When a psychology major in college who is working on his doctorate in history got the one about "leftist ideas," he asked to have the question reformulated. "But the examiner refused —he couldn't see why if I was 'innocent' I found it hard to answer. We just weren't *en rapport* at all." Another NSA subject—or victim—has reported that at one point his examiner shouted at him, "Goddammit, you're lying! I know you're lying, the machine tells me so!!" . . . Although all the manuals urge the examiner to try to reduce rather than increase emotional tension, so that significant reactions are not masked by irrelevant ones, the NSA gang relied heavily on what is known unfavorably in the trade as the EPQ (Embarrassing Personal Question) technique. EPQs are generally directed to the more intimate aspects of the subject's sex life. Women are apt to resent being asked, by a strange man, questions like (to unmarried girls) "Have you ever slept with a man?"—at least one is reported to have walked out at this point—and (to married women) "Did you sleep with your husband before you were married?" [52]

The personnel screening practiced by agencies such as NSA in the 1950's was not a temporary or passing phase. In fact, polygraphing by such federal agencies increased in the next decades. In reply to Congressional questioning in 1964, both the NSA and CIA stated that they give a polygraph test to every applicant for a position with their agencies.[53] Neither agency supplied figures as to the number of active employees or of applications processed each year, but informed sources in Washington estimate polygraphing for more than 5,000 persons a year. The Army and Navy informed the Moss Committee that they both used polygraphs for "personnel screening." The Army gave 4,600 tests for this purpose in 1963 and the Navy listed 1,200 tests (without further breakdown) for personnel screening, security, criminal investigations, and misconduct. The Army gave 3,494 additional personnel-screening polygraph tests in 1963 for a special program of enlisting Cuban refugees into U. S. Army service.[54]

The questions asked by these agencies continue to be much the same kind as described by Macdonald in 1954, and subject to much the same type of individual objection in particular cases. The questions used in CIA polygraph tests, for example, include the following:

"Have you ever been sympathetic to the theory or practice of Soviet Communism?"

"Are you personally acquainted with anyone whom you believe to be sympathetic to Communism?"

"Since 15 (18) have you engaged in sexual activities with another man or boy?" (asked of male applicants)

"Since 18 have you engaged in sexual activities with another woman or girl?" (asked of female applicants)

Other questions ask about drinking "problems," addiction to drugs, and whether there are "any unfavorable incidents in your life which may have a security bearing on your employment here?" [55] What is even more significant than these "first" questions in each subject area is the fact that the slightest "blip" on the machine in response will require many additional "follow-up" questions, of increasingly greater detail and intimacy, to "get to the real trouble."

During Congressional hearings in 1964 Representative Cornelius Gallagher (Dem., N.J.) related an incident involving a seventeen-year-old girl seeking employment as a clerk-typist at NSA who became quite disturbed when she was asked a series of questions about homosexual activity by the male operator administering the test while the two were alone in the polygraph examining room.[56] Representative Gallagher said that some checking he did with fellow members of Congress revealed that other Congressmen had also received complaints from constituents about "humiliating" and improper sexual questioning they had encountered as part of polygraph examinations for federal employment in sensitive agencies.[57] "I regret to say," Gallagher commented, "that the thread of outright voyeurism runs throughout too many of the cases that have come to my attention regarding the use of the lie detector." [58]

Another condition disclosed by Congressional hearings in 1964–65 was the regular use by many federal agencies of hidden microphone devices and two-way mirrors to enable government officials to listen to and watch polygraph tests being administered in "privacy." Persons taking the tests were not told that they were being monitored, though the Army Provost Marshal explained that soldiers going into the Criminal Identification Division "know" that they are being observed, and that monitoring examinations of females was really a protection against abuse.[59]

Finally, the Congressional hearings of 1964 revealed that it was a basic principle of polygraph analysis that the individual must "bare his soul" and discuss fully every aspect of his personal history in each of the areas about which he is being tested for federal employment, especially sexual affairs, ideological background, illegal acts, and emotional problems. Polygraph experts explained that this is necessary to relieve any guilt feelings about matters other than those being searched for. When the subject has bared all his guilt, the machine operator can then say, "Now, apart from the acts you have detailed, have you ever . . . ?" Polygraph experts consider this the heart of their "confidential" confessional session.[60] From the standpoint of privacy, the "clearing" procedure demands that the individual do for the government—and with an impersonal, generally insensitive operator—what few individuals will ever do in their lifetimes for wife, minister, or best friend. The individual must bare himself, knowing—at least now, after recent press and Congressional publicity—that the confessional is usually observed, recorded, and even photographed from outside.

Future Prospects for Psychological Surveillance

Great hopes for increased surveillance techniques in the future rest on research with drugs, particularly the development since World War II of new chemical agents which affect consciousness and volition in ways that might be used to lead a person to reveal information he would not otherwise disclose. The so-called truth drugs, such as scopolamine, sodium pentathol, and sodium amytal, are relaxant agents which release inhibiting controls and often enable individuals to talk freely about matters they are normally unable to discuss for emotional reasons. Careful tests have shown that it is possible for persons under these drugs to lie or give self-serving answers to questions affecting their guilt or innocence, and for this reason the drugs are not regarded as reliable "truth testers" by either scientists or the courts.[61] Because they affect conscious controls over the emotions, memory, and mind, the use of such drugs as a measurement of guilt or a condition of employment has been resisted on grounds involving privacy as well as reliability.

The more recent developments in the drug field have involved several classes of new drugs that affect levels of consciousness and self-awareness. Some of these are tranquilizers and some are stimulants, some are antidepressants (such as iproniazid and imipramine), and some are psychotomimetics. The latter, such as LSD-25 and psilocybin, produce effects simulating psychosis. In varying degrees, all these drugs can cause freer than usual talk, ranging from mild euphoric conversation to the babble of severe hallucinatory states. Here, too, attempts to use such drugs as truth agents have been unsuccessful.[62] Persons under the influence of the drugs can give partial information, can furnish false information, or can slip beyond the capacity for rational recitation. Many people are also subject to high suggestiveness under "truth" drugs and will admit fervently to acts they never committed, probably as a means of releasing guilt feelings. Moreover, the drugs have different effects on different individuals. Despite some fairly intensive research by government agencies, the colorless, tasteless liquid which, when put into the enemy agent's water or coffee, would cause him to reveal his most guarded secrets, still appears to be beyond achievement.[63] Alcohol, sex, and brain-washing are still ahead of drugs in leading subjects to disclose what they are trying to keep secret.

It is worth noting carefully, however, that the effect on many individuals of taking steady doses of such psychotomimetic drugs as LSD-25 is to so alter the view of life and reality that they undergo radical changes in their notions of what matters they consider it important to keep private. Thus LSD users, like persons on narcotics, may disclose many more personal facts about themselves to others than would their peers who are not on drugs.

Another area of psychological surveillance—the reading of thoughts through interpretation of brain signals—is a *potential* development of the future. Great progress has been made in brain analysis in the past three to five years. A brain-wave monitor has been developed that does not have to be implanted in the brain or attached to the scalp of an inert patient, as in the conventional electroencephalograph. The new device is made of sponge-covered tin electrodes that pick up brain waves through the hair and permit normal movement of the head during monitoring.[64] Such monitoring has been done through a compact device in an astronaut's helmet.[65] At the same time, computer analysis of brain signals has made it possible to screen out random signals and identify certain characteristic brain signals produced by certain stimuli, enabling researchers to tell what color a person is looking at, with one identifiable pattern produced when a person is looking at red and another when he is looking at green.[66] Other research has identified a brain-signal pattern known as an "expectancy wave," produced in response to a stimulus that "warns" of the imminence of another stimulus that calls for a particular thought or action.[67] Computer reading of brain signals has also been used to time the brain's response to light flashes; the theory has been advanced that this provides a test of intelligence—the brain's response to light being a measure of its neurological efficiency—which is not affected by language, reading ability, cultural background, or psychological state during testing.[68]

These advances, and others that may not have been released yet, suggest that we have made fundamental breakthroughs in the identification and deciphering of certain types of brain signals and that this process no longer requires physical implantation of electrodes. It has been suggested that such readings may even be taken without any physical implantation or connection, even to the hair. There is some possibility that brain-signal research may lead in the foreseeable future to reading of certain emotional states in the individual under brain-signal analysis, identifying when he is experiencing pleasure or pain, perhaps even anger, fear, or sexual excitement. Correlation of other body monitors, such as pupil-size changes with brain signals, might provide the cross-checks to advance more refined readings of this type.

Whether these techniques could ever make it possible to read thoughts themselves is another matter. The brain activity involved in an idea or memory involves the simultaneous action of millions of nerve cells, each of which seems to have much more than one memory or idea "bit" stored in it. How to "tap" each of these millions of neurons and segregate the signal involved in a particular thought process, and to manage this tapping without affecting or impairing the neurons themselves, is beyond even theoretical capacities at present. In addition, it has been pointed out that thinking involves not only electrical processes but also chemical ones, and possibly other phenomena.[69] Whether thoughts can ever be read without deciphering these elements in the complex is not known.

While thought-reading does not lie within present or foreseeable technology, the controlling of human functions and emotions through microelectronic devices planted in the brain by surgery is quite possible. Experiments on rats, goldfish, and other animals have shown that pleasure, pain, aggression, passivity, and distinct personality changes can be accomplished by stimulation of specific areas of the brain through mild electronic impulses below the conscious-awareness level.[70] Limited experiments with humans have reported some similar effects.[71] In addition, drugs have been used to erase memory in goldfish and to enhance memory and learning in rats, leading scientists to believe that deeper knowledge of RNA (ribonucleic acid), which controls the production of protein in living cells, and DNA (dioxyribonucleic acid), which sets the master genetic patterns in individuals, may lead to chemical interventions in memory and thought patterns.[72] The moral implications of electronic or chemical control over memory or personality are enormous, and the intrusion into the individual's freedom of action, of which his privacy is one part, raises serious issues of "mind control" for consideration.

CHAPTER SEVEN

The Revolution in Information Collection and Processing: Data Surveillance

THE COMPUTER-BORN revolution in man's capacity to process data is obviously an enormous boon. In business, government, medicine, science, and a dozen other fields, men are now able to make more fact-based, more logical, and more predictable decisions than they could do before the age of electronic information storage and retrieval.

At the same time, as philosophers remind us in a different context, knowledge is power. The issue of privacy raised by computerization is whether the increased collection and processing of information for diverse public and private purposes, if not carefully controlled, could lead to a sweeping power of surveillance by government over individual lives and organizational activity. As we are forced more and more each day to leave documentary fingerprints and footprints behind us, and as these are increasingly put into storage systems capable of computer retrieval, government may acquire a power-through-data position that armies of government investigators could not create in past eras.

Monitoring Man's Transactions

To understand the current pressures on privacy created by the information processing revolution, we should note six basic trends at work. First is the general expansion of information-gathering and record-keeping in contemporary American society, even apart from computers. As our industrialized system has grown more complex, as government regulatory functions have increased, as large bureaucratic organizations have become the model in our private sector, and as social science has committed itself heavily to data-collection and analysis, we have be-

158

come the greatest data-generating society in human history. To help himself, to help science, and to help society run efficiently, the individual now pours a constantly flowing stream of information about himself into the record files—birth and marriage records, public-school records, census data, military records, passport data, government and private employment records, public-health records, civil-defense records, loyalty-security clearance records, income-tax returns, social-security returns, land and housing records, insurance records, bank records, business reporting forms to government, licensing applications, financial declarations required by law, charitable contributions, credit applications and records, automobile registration records, post-office records, telephone records, psychological and psychiatric records, scholarship or research-grant records, church records—and on and on. New forms of financial operations have produced the credit card, which records the where, when, and how-much of many once-unrecorded purchasing, travel, and entertainment transactions of the individual's life. Through miniaturization, previous physical limits on such data storage have been overcome; the microfilm of earlier decades has now given way to photochromic microimages that make it possible to reproduce the complete Bible on a thin sheet of plastic less than two inches square, or to store page-by-page copies of all the books in the Library of Congress in six four-drawer filing cabinets.[1]

Second, the mobility of persons and the standardization of life in mass society have led to the development of large private and governmental investigative systems whose function is the amassing of personal dossiers on tens of millions of Americans. This has become the method by which a large organization makes judgments about people when it wants to hire or fire them, lend them money, or give them passports to travel abroad. A recent Washington *Post* survey noted that the largest American private investigative agency, the Retail Credit Company, which rates persons for a wide variety of purposes including industrial security, has 7,000 investigators, maintains dossiers on forty-two million people, and grosses more than $100 million annually from its activities.[2] Credit Bureau Inc., the leading company in Washington, D.C., maintains dossiers on 2.5 million present and former residents of the city. The Department of Defense has fourteen million life histories in its security files, the Civil Service eight million, and the FBI an unknown number (though it admits to some 100,000 on Communist "sympathizers" alone). There are investigations and dossiers that people never even learn about. For example, the Federal Housing Administration has private agencies conduct investigations of more than a million annual applicants for FHA loans. One purpose of these probes is to report on the "marital stability" of applicants, based on the theory that there is more risk of foreclosure when divorce is threatening. Private firms specializing in loyalty checks for industrial corporations have millions of files on the personal lives and political attitudes of persons who work in companies having defense contracts.[3]

The dangerous aspect of such dossiers is that the raw facts about individuals take on added weight because they are part of an "official file" compiled by an investigative agency. Because individuals often do not know of the existence of many of the dossiers about them, or what is in those they do know to exist, there is usually no process to challenge the accuracy of fact, opinion, or rumor the files contain. As large private and public organizations come to take personal dossiers for granted, the facts in them begin to circulate from agency to agency. For example, the supposedly confidential reports done by private investigative agencies for the FHA, on marital stability of FHA applicants, can be bought by private mortgage lenders for $1.50 each. The "Welcome Wagon" which greets newcomers to local communities and hands out a bundle of small premiums does so in return for answers to a long list of questions about the new family—what the man does, what the family's religion is, what services they use. Without the knowledge of the new arrivals, these facts are then sold to commercial firms and credit services as informational leads. More significantly, the information given to credit agencies or in applying for charge cards and bank loans is often channeled to government and private industrial-security firms, so that disclosures made in confidence for one purpose can become bars to the individual's progress at major entry and progress points of his career.

Furthermore, the growth of dossiers creates a physical record file with which personnel officers and rating services must deal; the evaluators are no longer free to ignore or dismiss a piece of information as they might have done when it was a verbal report or an informal document. This situation creates a potential "record-prison" for millions of Americans, as past mistakes, omissions, or misunderstood events become permanent evidence capable of controlling destinies for decades. Out-of-date facts, such as previous political affiliations or nervous disorders, often go unrevised, and these can haunt a person's life. As this fact becomes known to more and more Americans, psychological conflict between official bureaucracies and their members can grow deeper and living one's life to "make a sound record" can become a preoccupying concern.

Third, general information gathering and the dossier have been radically accelerated by the advent of the electronic digital computer, with its capacity to store more records and manipulate them more effectively and rapidly than was ever possible before. The present-generation computer, with thin-film memory cores and ultra-high-speed tunnel diodes, can store millions of bits of information and perform calculations on these bits at speeds of billionths of a second. In 1966 more than 30,000 digital computers were used in the United States.[4] The federal government had more than 2,600, representing an investment of some $6 billion. State governments had 325 computers operating in 1966.[5] Together the federal, state, and local governments are spending $1.3 billion annually on computers and associated personnel.[6] Leading industries, such as transportation, oil, insurance, and finance, each maintain more than 1,000 computers.

The most significant fact for the subject of privacy is that once an organization purchases a giant computer, it inevitably begins to collect more information about its employees, clients, members, taxpayers, or other persons in the interest of the organization. The result may be to provide better service, make more efficient use of personnel, know more facts on which to base decisions, pinpoint wrongdoers, and the like. But the inevitable result is that the investigator acquires two or three times as much personal information from respondents as was ever collected before because of the physical or cost limits of acquisition. The impact of computers on organizational life is to destroy practical boundaries of privacy in record giving which were once as meaningful in this area as walls and doors were to conversational privacy before the advent of new physical surveillance technology.

Fourth, the development of many new public programs has produced a requirement for more personal data about individuals than in previous research or record keeping. The Civil Rights Act of 1964 requires the Census Bureau to obtain information on personal voter registration. Employers must keep and give the government racial data on employees to show compliance with equal-opportunity legislation, as must school districts to prove school desegregation. Government and private studies of the reasons for students' success in school require personal questions directed at the student throughout his school career and, often, interviews with his parents and friends. The result of such highly psychological and sociological approaches to public policy is a demand for more personal data from schoolchildren, employees, employers, organizations, and so forth. Some are sought in the name of research or purely "statistical" data, some for general enforcement of socio-economic policy, but all extract more detailed personal information from citizens than ever before in our history. The data are then stored in computer memory centers, usually with the individual's name attached.

Fifth, advances in the computer field are rapidly accelerating the sharing of data among those who use the machines. Standardization of computer languages and the perfection of machines that translate one machine language system into another have made it possible for computers to communicate directly with one another, so that data can flow in and out of separate systems. This innovation has led to information exchanges among units within the same large organization, such as police and health agencies in a state, or among independent organizations with common interests, such as life-insurance companies. A more significant aspect of this trend is the growth of central data pools in many important fields, from education and health to banking, civil defense, and social-science analysis. Such data pools are not only based on the desire to collect and collate all significant information about individuals or events in a particular field but are also a response to the technological development that allows remote-station access to central data banks.[7] In return for putting its data into the central pool, an organization is able to draw on the total collection by leased-line interrogation of the central system from the organization's own headquarters. In the law-enforcement field, for example, the New York State Identification and Intelligence System currently being put into operation will pool information about persons arrested for crimes other than traffic violations from the more than 3,600 separate law-enforcement and investigative agencies in the state.[8] The FBI has set up a National Crime Information Center which provides a random-access computer facility collating records from federal and local law-enforcement agencies on wanted persons, stolen cars, and other stolen property.[9] J. W. Macy, Jr., Chairman of the Civil Service Commission, has indicated that "direct tape-to-tape feeding" of information from one department to another could become common.[10] David Sarnoff has predicted that computers in the field of health will eventually establish total medical profiles on everyone in the country "from the hour of birth" and updated through life.[11] Each record will be almost instantly accessible to medical personnel.

Sixth, we have entered an era in which automatic data processing will gradually replace many of the cash transactions of the past, providing an increasing trail of records about significant transactions of the individual's life. The credit-card system that spread in the 1950's was the first stage of this process. Despite problems of identification and misuse, the credit-card system proved so valuable to the fostering of personal and organizational spending that more than 20 million Americans now participate in credit-card plans.[12] More and more types of transactions are being put on such credit cards—plane travel, auto rentals, hotel accommodations, dining, purchases of goods, and the like, all potential records for income-tax subpoena or criminal investigation. The next step was to eliminate the middleman, by means of direct computer connection between the point of expenditure and the customer's account or financial source. For example, the Automatic Canteen Company of America has developed a system to enable people to buy refreshments from vending machines through credit cards. The card is inserted into a vending machine equipped with a $150 optical scanning and electronic-control device which inspects the coded plastic card to insure that it is valid, then conveys its number and the amount of the purchase to a central record-keeping machine of a facility such as a factory or hotel.[13] In 1965 the Bank of Delaware in Wilmington inaugurated a pilot program through which a customer is able to make purchases at retail establishments that will automatically be recorded at the bank; the shopper's account is then debited or an installment plan is initiated for him. This system uses the Bell Telephone Company's new Touch-Tone card-dialing instrument as the communication link between the store and the bank. In 1966 the Bank of Delaware set up the same system with a supermarket and with bill-paying from homes themselves, all using the Bell card-dialing system.[14] The increase in records about personal life from such direct computerized transactions is apparent.

Future Prospects in Data Collection and Processing

These six trends represent the present era in data collection and computer processing of information. Pending proposals and prospective developments of the next decade promise to raise even broader issues of privacy. For example, several study groups and a presidential task force have been working on proposals for a central federal data bank, to collect records of twenty federal agencies, such as Treasury, Labor, Commerce, Agriculture, and Health, Education and Welfare. These agencies already have 100 million punch cards and 30,000 computer tapes containing information about individuals and businesses.[15] The data center would allow sharing of information within the federal government and access for other groups, such as businesses, research organizations, and state and local agencies. Material classified as confidential would not be given out, but what constitutes confidential material is far from clear and uncontested. Another computer facility under consideration by the federal government is a medical-data bank, holding tapes of the medical case histories of all Americans. Conceding its value for public-health purposes and for treating persons taken ill away from their home physicians, the question has already been raised as to who could press the button and get the medical print-out on an individual—his employer? a Congressional committee? the White House? Such a record would include such items as past mental or nervous problems, social diseases, sexual deviations, and the like, which could gravely compromise individuals if it came into the wrong hands. Another system recommended already by a federal study commission is a national, computerized job bank, with employment files on job seekers to match against job openings as these are reported in.

The likelihood of further computerization of financial transactions has been predicted by spokesmen of IBM, RCA, Bell Telephone, and many others. A typical presentation of what the system would be like in the 1970's was written by Stanley M. Humphrey, vice president of a leading management consultant firm.[16] Daily life would run as follows, he speculated, starting with the housewife's trip to the suburban shopping center. Here, a universal credit card would be presented at each store she visited. By inserting the card in a slot and pushing a button, the clerk would record the transaction without sales slips, credit checks, or presentation of cash or checks. From department store to grocery store, each item would be ordered by the same process. The merchandise would then be automatically routed by an electric cart to the housewife's car which she had previously parked (also billed by credit card).

Humphrey sees few problems in establishing such a system. Low-cost simple recording devices placed in each store would feed essential financial information to a central communication office in the shopping center. From there it would be automatically "transmitted downtown to the Second National Finance Utility of Metropolis" (the larger institutions that would replace banks) where the family's "fund account" would be charged for the purchases. No paper would be exchanged in the entire operation. Weekly statements from the finance utility would go to the stores and to the customers. Data processing accomplishes inter-utility communication as well, eliminating clearing house and transit operations between banks as we know them today.

Similarly, public utility charges—gas, water, telephone services—would all be billed and paid through monthly collections of meter readings at a central data center without human intervention. The consumer would learn of charges and payments only after the entire transaction had been completed. Installment payments of all types could also be handled with easy efficiency.

Recording of income would be just as automatic. Through internal and transit computer operations, the finance utility would credit the family's fund account with monthly salaries, stock investments and other income sources.

Humphrey sees the dial telephone as an integral part of this computerized system. From simple items like travel and hotel reservations to more complicated private financial transactions such as doctor bills and rental payments on individually owned property, the individual would merely have to dial the finance utility's data processer to record the information. For travel, of course, no tickets would be needed. For hotels, only advance registration required. "There will be no midnight wait at the registration desk—use of the credit card automatically ejects an appropriate key." Commuting via train or bus would require only the insertion of the credit card into a slot—no tokens, tickets, or change would be necessary.

In winding up his portrait, Humphrey could not help mentioning at least one unpleasant potential of the system:

Such an integrated communication and processing system as described above on a nationwide basis could have important benefits for state and federal governments. Certainly, the Bureau for Printing and Engraving could be almost entirely eliminated—very little cash would be required. Also, the Internal Revenue Department could dispense with its investigating agents, and income tax revenue would rise drastically. Why? Every financial transaction of any importance for every individual in the country would be recorded as it occurred. Consequently, you as an individual would no longer prepare an income tax return including generous allowances for charitable contributions, local sales taxes, and so on. Instead, your fund account at Second National would be automatically charged as a result of a governmental calculation on an exact, accurate basis (using Second National tapes) of your income tax liability. As I said, an important by-product—frightening, isn't it?

Another disturbing fact in this prospective universal credit system is that the life of individual would be almost wholly recorded and observable through analysis of the daily "transactions" of "Credit Card No. 172,381,400, Humphrey, Stanley, M." Whoever ran the computers could know when the individual entered the highway and where he got off; how many bottles of Scotch or Vermouth he purchased from the liquor store; who paid the rent for the girl in Apartment 4B; who went to the movies between two and four P.M. on a working day at the office; who was at lunch at Luigi's or the Four Seasons on Tuesday, September 15; and the hotel at which Mrs. Smith spent the rainy afternoon last Sunday. Where every dollar came from that a government official banked, and where every dollar went that was spent by each corporation and labor union would also lie in the great treasury house of the computer. There would be few areas in which anyone could move about in the anonymity of personal privacy and few transactions that would not be fully documented for government examination.

Still another technological prospect is the collection, in various functional master memory systems, of basic information about each major aspect of the individual's life, an idea that has strong advocates in the governmental, scientific, and professional communities. The individual's complete educational record from pre-school nursery to post-graduate courses could be in the educational master file, including the results of all intelligence, aptitude, and personality tests taken during his lifetime. The individual's complete employment record could be in another master computer dossier.

This record would include every job held, rate of pay, efficiency ratings, employer evaluations, personality tests, recommendations, outside interests, family relation to work, and so on, and would be available on instant point-out when the individual was being considered for new employment by a private organization or government agency. The master credit file could contain all the information needed to do a thorough financial analysis of the individual: his income, fixed expenditures, pattern of past discretionary spending, savings, investment, predicted expenses based on personal and family history, and predicted promotion levels, and the like. Other central dossiers could deal with health, civic activity, telephone records, and criminal records. Every person could have a personal identification number, and computer scanning of a card-holder's fingerprint or voice-print could control assumption of another's number or identity.

For the average citizen, even one well informed about public affairs and general scientific news, this must often seem to be so speculative and distant that it really belongs in the George Orwell file, with a due date of 1984. Used to thinking about the problems of storing and using written information, the citizen imagines future data centers as giant installations in huge rooms, with tens of thousands of reels of tape being lifted on and off machines by clerks, and time-consuming human operations required for any significant comparisons to be made of information about a given person scattered through the data bank. In this portrait, time, cost, efficiency, and the requirement of cooperation by considerable numbers of data-bank employees are assumed to provide real limitations on data surveillance. Nothing could be more mistaken, either in terms of the general growth predicted for the computer in America or of specific adaptations of computers to data-bank and dossier purposes.

The general trends of the next decade have been carefully outlined in several studies done for the RAND corporation by Paul Armer and W. H. Ware.[17] Between 1955 and 1965, the size of the central processing unit of the computer decreased by a factor of 10, from 1,000 cubic feet to 100 cubic feet. By 1975, fully integrated circuits will reduce this by a factor of 1,000, to one tenth of a cubic foot.

Between 1955 and 1965, the internal speed of computers increased by a factor of 200, from 25,000 additions per second to 5 million per second. By 1975, this will be increased another 200 times, making possible operations at the rate of a billion per second.

In terms of operational costs, the price of doing a million additions declined between 1955 and 1965 from $10 to about 3.5 cents. By 1975, this cost will be reduced by another factor of 300, to one two-hundredth of a cent.

If all this still seems to be limited by the amount of computing power available to perform these operations, this factor too must be eliminated as a source of hope for substantial limitations on data surveillance. In 1955, all the installed computers in the United States, working together, could do 500,000 additions per second. By 1965, this capability had increased by 400, to 200 million additions per second. If we take one of the more pessimistic forecasts of computer growth in the next decade, a mere twenty fold, computing power will increase by 1975 to a capability of 5 billion additions per second. If the same growth rate takes place in 1965–1975 as in 1955–1965, as many computer experts think quite possible, the increase in power would be by 400, for a capability of 250 *billion* additions per second.

What these estimates of computer speed, power, cost, and storage capacities mean for data surveillance may be made even more concrete by describing the world not of 1975 but of 1967. The Precision Instrument Company of Palo Alto, California, has developed and demonstrated the model of a new laser process that burns minute craters along parallel lines of the opaque coating of plastic tape.[18] By this process, 645 *million* bits of digital data can be put onto one square inch of plastic tape. (The present capacity for storage is 5,600 bits per square inch.) The laser used has a speed-recording rate of 12 million bits per second. Accuracy of recording is assured by a "light-pipe" system which takes the light passing through the clear spots in the tape, translates this into electrical impulses by a photomultiplier, and compares these with the input data to verify the recording. The tape is read by passing another laser beam across the tape as it rolls by the reader. The light passes through the holes (without altering them) and is translated into electrical pulses which are then fed to a computer, recorder, or print-out machine.

This laser memory process will permit unprecedented storage capacity and rapid retrieval of data. One small unit, containing one 4,800-foot reel of one-inch plastic tape, will be able to store in digital form about twenty pages of information (250 words of typing to the page) for every person in the United States, including women and children. Specific information from a person's twenty-page dossier on this reel could be retrieved in a maximum search time of four minutes, and the entire dossier could be printed out for dispatch to an inquiring source in a matter of a few more minutes. All of this, let us note again, on just one reel of tape, searched swiftly while on its moving mechanism, without platoons of clerks or shifting of storage reels from place to place to signal the operation. Ten such reels would make possible 200-page dossiers on every American, and a mere 100 reels would begin to offer real possibilities of a progressive life-record dossier of each American from birth to death.

For planning, efficiency, and social control, these government data centers, computerized transaction systems, and central record files of the future could bring enormous benefits to society. But unless safeguards for privacy are placed carefully in the planning and administration of systems that most computer experts feel to be inevitable developments of the next two decades, the growth in data surveillance will be awesome. Meanwhile the present dossiers and computerized information systems continue to increase, without many legal or administrative guidelines as yet to cope with the issues of privacy that they raise.

PART THREE

American Society's Struggle for Controls: Five Case-Studies

W HY DID new surveillance techniques spread so rapidly during the past two decades, especially in light of general public opinion today that seems to exhibit surprise and dismay at this trend? Was it a breakdown in legal controls and social norms, a failure of the public to know what was really going on, or general support by the public for such surveillance methods as long as they were not "abused"? What changes in law, social norms, and public perceptions have taken place as a result of the "anti-Big-Brother" campaign of the past few years?

To explore these questions, Part III presents five case-studies of American reactions to the new technology. Using both published sources and personal interviews, the case-studies reconstruct the debates in each field and the struggle over defining new rules. The first topic treated is wiretapping and electronic eavesdropping, the oldest problem, the one with the longest history as an unsolved problem of American public policy, and the area in which the new technology has had its greatest impact thus far. The other four studies then take up "lie-detector" polygraphs, personality testing, subliminal suggestion, and information-processing by computers.

In each study, the questions asked include the way in which the professional in each area came to take up the new technology (and with what ethical or professional debates); the role of the mass media, social critics, and "guardian" groups such as civil-liberties organizations and bar associations in raising the privacy issues; the interest-group activity in each area; ideological positions generated; the role of government as user and regulator; and the collision between claims of privacy and other social claims to justify use of the surveillance.

The concluding section of each case-study highlights the aspects of privacy involved in each area and tries to put the issue in long-range perspective for American society. Though some specific policy judgments and suggestions appear in these concluding sections, a full set of recommendations for the next decade has been saved for presentation in Chapter 14.

CHAPTER EIGHT

Dissolving the Walls and Windows

Public Response to Eavesdropping in the Pre-1960 Era

Physical surveillance by listening and watching devices did not spring up with cold-war technology, despite some illiterate commentary that seems to suggest such an origin. In the United States technology was used to survey persons, groups, and communications well back in the nineteenth century. Union and Confederate forces tapped each other's telegraph lines during the Civil War, and telegraph tapping to intercept stock-market information, racing results, and political messages was reported regularly in the American press during the 1860's and 1870's.[1] With the development of snapshot photography in the 1880's came the use of cameras to photograph persons without their knowledge or consent. One popular magazine in the 1890's advertised a bowler hat with built-in hidden camera, for private detective work.[2] When the telephone came into general use in the 1880's, telephone tapping followed almost immediately and flourished in the pre-World War I era. During these years private telephone tappers eavesdropped on sources of newspaper rivals, filched business information, and gathered divorce-case evidence. Government telephone tapping ranged from federal agents listening to the conversations of suspected enemy agents to New York City police tapping the calls of Catholic priests who were opposing the City Administration's program for regulating Catholic charities. Hidden microphones and dictograph recorders also came into widespread use in the pre-World War I period. In 1912, for example, the press described dictograph eavesdropping by private detectives in labor-relations cases, church disputes, divorce actions, and business rivalries, and police microphoning to obtain evidence used in trials for blackmail, fraud, and legislative graft.[3]

In the 1940's and 1950's—*before* the new surveillance equipment had made its general appearance—technological surveillance was a well-established technique of police and private investigation, a fact which was revealed frequently in press accounts, legislative hearings, judicial proceedings, and special surveys during these two decades.[4] For example, a thorough study of state and local governmental eavesdropping as of 1957, conducted by the Pennsylvania Bar Endowment, showed that wiretapping, bugging, tracking devices, and hidden cameras were widely used not only by urban police and prosecutive offices but also by suburban departments, sheriffs' offices, state troopers, highway patrols, and state attorney-generals' offices, as well as some state regulatory agencies and legislative committees.[5] Whenever an eavesdropping assignment was unusually complicated, or called for specialized equipment, state law-enforcement agencies had no difficulty in enlisting private wiretapping specialists to do the job.

At the federal level, published information showed the FBI, Treasury Department, and military-intelligence agencies to be well-equipped users of electronic eavesdropping. J. Edgar Hoover and Justice Department spokesmen testified publicly each year between 1945 and 1957 that the FBI had from 50 to 200 wiretaps in "national-security cases" in progress on the day of testifying.[6] Published accounts of FBI tapping, bugging, hidden cameras, and locating devices included the Browder-Foster fight in the American Communist Party in 1944, the Nazi saboteur investigations, the Judith Coplon case in 1949, and surveillance of Soviet agents in the late 1940's.[7] The FBI also stated that it wiretapped in kidnaping cases or "where a human life may be imperilled." [8]

The Treasury Department (with jurisdiction over prohibition enforcement, narcotics, counterfeiting, and the like) was another primary user of electronic eavesdropping. On his retirement from federal service in 1949, William Mellin, chief wiretapper for the Treasury, announced in the *Saturday Evening Post* that he had installed more than 10,000 wiretaps for the Treasury between 1934 and 1948.[9] A stream of disclosures during the 1940's and early 1950's revealed that electronic eavesdropping was used by other federal agencies, such as the Post Office, and by some congressional committees, and that intra-agency monitoring was employed by many federal executive departments.[10]

As for the private arena, there was no shortage of data to show that private detectives specializing in electronic eavesdropping and camera work were actively serving business clients, while marital investigations provided a major portion of the surveillance trade.[11] Articles were frequently published detailing the busy activities of the top private electronics specialists—such "listening deans" as Robert La Borde, Jim Vaus, Charles Gris, Bernard Spindel, Russell Mason, Harold Lipset, Kenneth Ryan, and Fred Otash.[12]

Throughout this period, from 1860 to the 1950's, as technological surveillance grew more efficient, American public opinion displayed a continuing ambivalence toward this practice. On the one hand, there was constant fascination at the scientific marvels that were being accomplished—the extension of man's sight and hearing beyond his natural senses and his new capacity to preserve and reproduce events through picture or sound recording. There was also admiration for the inventiveness and derring-do of the men who used the new devices imaginatively to combat spies, criminals, and other anti-social elements. On the other hand, the public also displayed a nervous awareness that surveillance devices, if used improperly or too widely by public or private authorities, could endanger legitimate personal and group needs for privacy in a free society and could concentrate a menacing amount of power in the hands of those collecting surveillance data.

Despite this concern, secret surveillance was tolerated because American public opinion believed that governmental authorities were limiting their surveillance to the hard core of serious crimes, and private eavesdropping was assumed to be affecting only marginal areas of American life, such as the marital affairs of the wealthy and a few "pirate" fringes of business and political life. Though there had been reports that FBI agents were using electronic eavesdropping to keep leading political and civic leaders under surveillance and to eavesdrop on lawyer-client conversations during important federal trials,[13] public faith in the FBI, the Bureau's legislative support in Congress, and internal security concerns of the 1940's and 1950's kept these charges from being fully aired in a thorough inquiry. Public disclosures of Treasury Department eavesdropping, state and local use of surveillance devices, and warnings that private eavesdropping was spreading closer to the core of American business and civic life also failed to draw the concern of more than a minority of American civic groups and legislators.[14]

These were the prevailing public attitudes toward electronic eavesdropping when the new technology arrived in mass production in the late 1950's. As of that moment, American law proved unable to exert effective controls over uses of the new technology, leaving not only private detectives but also government agencies outside traditional restraints against unreasonable invasions of privacy. To see how this deadlock developed, we must go back to 1928, when the Supreme Court set off the present train of confusion.

The Rise of Legal Confusion over Wiretapping

In 1928, in the famous *Olmstead* case, the United States Supreme Court ruled that police wiretapping was not an unreasonable search and seizure forbidden by the Fourth Amendment to the Federal Constitution. The majority felt that nothing tangible had been seized, that persons speaking on the telephone voluntarily projected their voices outside the home, and that there was no entry forbidden by the Constitution when wires were tapped from outside.[15] In 1942 the Court held that police use of a sensitive listening device to overhear conversations in an adjoining room was also not in violation of the Fourth Amendment when there had been no illegal entry or penetration of the place under surveillance.[16] Under these decisions, the questions of who should be allowed to intercept telephone calls or to eavesdrop on room conversations, for what purposes, and under what safeguarding procedures, became issues for Congress and state legislatures rather than judicial issues of constitutionality.

As early as 1918 Congress had been sufficiently alarmed by reports of wiretapping to ban the practice for the remainder of the war emergency.[17] But in the 1920's and early 1930's wiretapping by federal and state officials became commonplace, especially in prohibition cases and by employers' agents in labor affairs. Public pressure for some wiretap controls led congressional appropriation committees to question various federal officers about their agencies' use of this "immoral" practice, and when public enthusiasm for a dry America began to wane, in 1933 Congress specifically forbade the use of wiretapping under the Prohibition Act.[18]

This left unanswered the larger problems of wiretapping in the investigation of other crimes, or of wiretapping by individuals who were not law enforcers. Congress was presented with a perfect opportunity to consider these problems in 1934, when it established federal rules for the radio, telephone, and telegraph industries. However, no reference was made to wiretapping in the committee hearings or floor debates, and no specific provision on police use of wiretapping was included among the new sections added to the Radio Act of 1927, on which the 1934 Federal Communications Act was based.[19]

During the next four years increasing use was made of wiretapping by federal agencies, state law enforcers, private detectives, company police, and many others. While these practices were often deplored in the press and by many Congressmen, and while bills to outlaw or regulate wiretapping were debated in Congress steadily (as they had been periodically since 1928), Congress passed no legislation and eavesdroppers listened to conversations unmolested.[20]

In 1937 the Supreme Court stepped into this vacuum and decided the famous *Nardone* cases. These decisions forbade federal officers as well as private individuals to tap wires, and made wiretap evidence obtained by federal agents inadmissible in federal prosecutions. The Court rested its decision on the Federal Communications Act of 1934, in which the Justices found a section that had been carried over verbatim from the 1927 Radio Act, stating that "no person" who had not been authorized by the "sender" could "intercept and divulge" the contents of a "message." While the Justices admitted that there was no legislative history to support the view that Section 605 had been intended by Congress to deal with official telephone tapping, the Supreme Court stated that this fact would not prevent it from giving effect to "the plain mandate of the statute." [21]

With the Supreme Court having "legislated" for Congress, it appeared that the wiretapping dilemma had been resolved unless Congress wanted to repeal Section 605 or to legalize wiretapping by federal agents. Congress did neither, but the wiretapping problem proved far from settled. Acting under the direction of the Attorney General, who felt wiretapping to be essential to prosecutive functions, federal agents simply ignored the judicial rulings and continued wiretapping, secure in the knowledge that, while the Supreme Court declared the law, the Attorney General enforced it. And since federal agents were themselves tapping, the Department of Justice announced that it could not, "in good conscience," prosecute state police who intercepted telephone conversations. Section 605 thus became only a rule for excluding evidence in the federal courts. [22]

In 1940, prompted by reports of wholesale wiretapping, especially for political purposes, the Senate ordered a full-scale investigation. A blistering Interstate Commerce Committee report emerged, condemning such conduct either by police or private tappers and calling for tighter federal legislation. [23] Within a week after the report was issued, Attorney General Jackson announced that "the law on wiretapping is now clear" and the FBI would no longer tap wires. In less than a year if not sooner, however, the FBI was tapping wires again, under Attorney General Jackson's new ruling that Section 605 was a bar only to the "interception and divulging" of telephone communications, not to tapping itself. [24] The fact that federal wiretappers would divulge the information to other federal officials was considered unimportant, since the entire federal establishment was regarded as a unitary "person" for this purpose.

Congressional concern with wiretapping was heightened as the war in Europe spread during 1940–41 and attention focused on fifth-column activities within this country. In 1941–42 Congress staged a major debate over wiretapping for national-security purposes. Attorney General Jackson, J. Edgar Hoover, and President Franklin Roosevelt urged Congress to legalize interceptions in security investigations. Many civil-liberties and labor groups withdrew their opposition to all wiretapping and supported a bill with narrow authority in the security area and careful safeguards. The issues were fully debated and the areas of disagreement were narrow, but Congress did not legislate. The votes against the authorization bill came from a coalition of Republicans and anti-administration Democrats. Actually the specific problem being debated had been resolved earlier, secretly, and again from outside Congress. President Roosevelt had sent Attorney General Jackson a secret Executive Order in 1940 directing the use of wiretapping by the FBI "when necessary in situations involving national defense." [25]

After World War II federal legislative debate began again. Bills to legalize wiretapping were filed in Congress, championed by law-enforcement groups and their allies, opposed by liberal, labor and civil-liberties groups, and never passed. Illegal taps by law enforcers and privateers continued unprosecuted.[26] The Judith Coplon case made wiretapping a matter of national attention in 1948, when it was revealed that FBI agents had not only tapped her home and office telephones, but were also monitoring the calls between Miss Coplon and her attorneys during her trial for passing government information. In reversing her conviction because of these wiretaps, Judge Sylvester Ryan reminded the Justice Department that wiretapping by the FBI remained "unlawful and prohibited," despite the Attorney General's authorizations of these interceptions.[27]

The *Coplon* case set off a round of discussions and editorials about the degree of privacy available on the telephone, the wiretapping activities of the FBI, and the contradictions between federal law as defined by the Supreme Court and by the Department of Justice. A national sample of fifty newspapers showed widespread dissatisfaction with the existing law and practices of wiretapping, but strongly divergent notions of which sword to use to cut the Gordian knot.[28]

Reports began to spread during 1949 and 1950 that wiretapping in Washington was increasing. As in 1940, when the Senate Interstate Commerce Committee had investigated "political" wiretapping, the reports prompted a congressional investigation, this time by a District of Columbia Subcommittee under Senator Claude Pepper of Florida. After learning that congressional-committee staffs, District of Columbia policemen, state detectives, and self-appointed sleuths were busy listening on Washington telephones (one line had failed because too many wiretaps were drawing power from it), the Committee reported shock at "the ease with which unauthorized persons . . . can invade the privacy of telephone conversations." The report advocated strong legislation.[29]

Meanwhile the United States Supreme Court's rulings in wiretapping cases and related issues had the effect of deepening the stalemate. The Justices declined to hear the *Coplon* case, leaving the decisions of the two federal courts of appeals in force. Since the Supreme Court did not pronounce directly on the FBI wiretapping practices involved in this case, the Department of Justice continued to maintain its authority for "non-disclosure" wiretapping.

Legal controls at the state level were in a comparably bad state. By the 1940's thirty-eight states had enacted laws forbidding "any person" to intercept, read, or obtain the contents of a telephone or telegraph message intended for another person.[30] The difficulty with these seem-ingly clear statutes was that they had proved almost wholly ineffectual. Under state-court constructions of these laws, subscribers were allowed to have their own home or business telephones monitored by private detectives. None of the statutes had been held to cover police intercep-tions. The typical language of the statutes ("cut or tap into") bore little relation to the realities of induction-coil wiretapping of the 1940's. And, only two of the thirty-eight statutes[31] forbade disclosure in court or in public of information obtained by illegal wiretapping. There had been less than half a dozen convictions of private wiretappers in fifty years of state law. There had been *no* convictions of police listeners under these statutes, despite the well-publicized wiretapping activities of policemen across the country in these decades. Only one state, New York, provided a comprehensive system for police wiretapping under court-order super-vision, but here also there had been no convictions for illegal tapping by private or police tappers.[32]

State microphoning or eavesdropping laws were similarly weak and antiquated. By statute or judicial decision many states recognized the crime of "eavesdropping" as it had been defined in English law by Blackstone: "[listening] under walls or windows, or the eaves of a house, to hearken after discourse, and thereupon to frame slanderous and mis-chievous tales." A few states, such as New York and North Dakota, had written modern-language statutes forbidding the "secret loitering" about a building "with intent to overhear discourse . . . and . . . repeat or publish the same" to annoy or injure others. Two states, Massachusetts and California, had forbidden the use by *private persons* of a dictograph or dictaphone to accomplish this listening.[33] Like the state wiretapping laws, however, these statutes had failed completely to come to grips with technical surveillance. Police conduct was wholly uncontrolled, private prosecutions were rare, and evidence obtained by eavesdropping was al-lowed in state trials and law suits.

United States Supreme Court decisions on telephone and micro-phone eavesdropping by state officials provided no effective controls ei-ther. Having ruled in the *Olmstead* case that state wiretapping did not violate the constitutional prohibition against unreasonable search and seizure, the Justices' doctrines in the 1940's and 1950's also held that, even if state wiretapping violated Section 605 of the Federal Communi-cations Act, each state was free to decide whether it would admit ille-gally obtained evidence in state trials.[34] This finding was contrary to a Supreme Court ruling which had forbidden use in *federal* trials of evi-dence obtained illegally by *federal* officials, a policy adopted to control official misconduct and prevent the winning of cases by "tainted" evi-dence.[35] Since thirty-one states in the early 1950's did *not* follow the fed-eral exclusionary rule, wiretap evidence in these states was freely admissible. At the same time, state officials knew that there had been no federal prosecutions of state police for violations of Section 605.

An even greater absence of federal judicial standards was present in the field of microphone eavesdropping as practiced on the state level, where there was no applicable federal statute such as Section 605, but only the Fourteenth Amendment's command that state officials refrain from denying any person "due process of law." By 1953 the Supreme Court had framed a rule that only police conduct so outrageous that it "shocked the conscience" would constitute a violation of the due-process clause and serve to bar such evidence in state trials. State-police wiretapping and eavesdropping practices had never "shocked the conscience" of the Supreme Court majority in this way. In 1954, a five-to-four decision of the Supreme Court refused to require exclusion of wiretap evidence obtained when Long Beach, California, policemen, in a case of suspected bookmaking by an "independent" small-time operator, secretly entered a man's home several times without a warrant, installed a microphone in his bedroom closet, and listened to his conversations and those of his wife for more than a month.[36] Though the majority opinion denounced the California police practice as outrageous and "almost incredible," the Court would not apply the exclusionary sanction.

During these years there was little discussion in Congress or in the public arena of new techniques of surveillance. The most that was observed was that induction-coil tapping (a development of the 1930's) had made the "cut and splice" technique of telephone tapping obsolete, and that tape recorders had greatly extended the usefulness of wiretaps and dictographs. Thus the clash of values raised between police surveillance for criminal detection and privacy of individual conversations was perceived as essentially a continuation of the pre-World War II debate.

The Beginning of the Orwellian Debate

A broad civic discussion of wiretapping arose between 1953 and 1955, prompted by three main developments. First, several technical witnesses presented congressional and state investigating committees with a description of new devices that were "revolutionizing" the eavesdropping business. This testimony explained how parabolic microphones could beam in on conversations from hundreds of yards away, even to a rowboat on a lake or across a street from window to window of two office buildings; that wireless resonator radio transmitters the size of cigarette packs could be planted under a table or bed and could send conversations to receiving sets a mile away; that refined induction-coil devices or even metallic-paint connections could be used to tap telephones; that "television eyes" small enough to be hidden in a heating duct or light fixture could send an instantaneous image of events in that room to a viewing screen in a nearby building; and that tiny automatic cameras were able to photograph almost in the dark with infra-red film. One professional wiretapper, Bernard Spindel, demonstrated at the House Judiciary Committee hearings that he could sit in a Congressman's outer office reading a magazine while secretly recording all the telephone calls made from the inner office. Newspapermen covering the hearing reported that the Congressmen were "visibly shaken" by the demonstration, and the story was carried on the front pages of the nation's press. Articles on the arrival of the "Buck Rogers" technology were carried in leading national magazines such as *Collier's, Coronet,* and the *Reporter,* and television networks carried special programs about these developments. The general response was a mixture of technological fascination and civic alarm.

A second development was the exposure of widespread wiretapping activities by private detectives and police. In February, 1955, the public learned of a central wiretap station, set up by private detectives, that could monitor over 100,000 lines in the mid-Manhattan area.[37] In Las Vegas, Nevada, hidden microphones were installed by a private investigator at the direction of a newspaper editor who wanted to secure proof that prominent gamblers and state officials were in connivance; in the wake of this exposure it was disclosed that Nevada's leading brothels made a practice of wiring their rooms to collect useful facts about clients.[38] These *causes célèbres* made the front pages of newspapers not just in the states concerned but across the country. The public learned that wiretapping and microphoning were not confined to the "eavesdropping capitals" of New York and Washington, D.C., but were nationwide.

Third, concern over the new technology and its uses spread beyond the ken of civil-liberties organizations, law-enforcement spokesmen, and editorial writers. Two national television networks in 1955 broadcast programs about the new eavesdroppers. The Reverend Billy Graham's organization produced a movie called *Wiretapper,* portraying the religious conversion of a man whose previous occupation had been a leading "earphones man" for both criminals and the police in California. Stories in *Life, Reader's Digest,* and major newspapers featured debates over how widespread wiretapping had become. A series of articles in the *Reporter* describing the spread of wiretapping practices was reprinted widely, won several national awards, was discussed in Congress, and was reprinted by several civic groups.[39] Even Daddy Warbucks in the comic strip "Little Orphan Annie" learned, to his anger, that agents of "The Syndicate" were tapping his calls. Sensitive to this burgeoning public concern, both Democratic and Republican leaders in Congress predicted that wiretap-control legislation would surely be passed by the Eighty-fifth Congress.

In 1952 and 1953 several bills to authorize limited wiretapping by federal officials in national-security matters and to forbid all other telephone tapping had been sponsored in Congress by various Republican and Democratic Congressmen. These legislators pointed to the advancing wiretapping technology, the continuing conflict between the Supreme Court's reading of Section 605 and that of the Justice Department, the inability of the federal government to use wiretap evidence in court to convict spies and Communist agents, the lack of standards or controls in the states for police taps, and the flourishing private wiretapping that was going on as a result of this "hopeless muddle" in the law. In 1953 Attorney General Herbert Brownell announced that the new Republican Administration's proposed "emergency anti-Communist" legislation would include a bill to legalize wiretapping.[40]

Hearings on "Wire-Tapping for National Security" were held by a Subcommittee of the House Judiciary Committee in 1953. The line-up of witnesses before the Committee was a confrontation between liberal-labor groups and law-enforcement spokesmen. Testimony against any authorization of wiretapping was given by the American Civil Liberties Union, Americans for Democratic Action, American Jewish Congress, American Federation of Labor, Friends Committee on National Legislation, the Criminal Justice Committees of the Philadelphia and Pennsylvania Bar Associations, and similar groups. If any bill were passed, these organizations called for restriction to the FBI, the narrowest definition of crimes for which taps could be used, close federal court-order supervision, checks by the Federal Communications Commission or other agency on how the authority was being used, and other safeguards. Testimony in favor of wiretapping and of broader, more permissive bills was presented by the International Association of Chiefs of Police, the National Association of County and Prosecuting Attorneys, the United States Department of Justice, the national military services, and district attorneys from urban centers such as Manhattan and Philadelphia. In the spring of 1954 the administration's bill was reported to the House for debate.[41]

Its presentation marked a sudden change of position on the part of both its principal supporters and its critics within the House Judiciary Committee. In the hearings of May, 1953, Representative Kenneth Keating (R, N.Y.) had repeatedly declared that a system which gave the Attorney General power to authorize wiretapping at his discretion was inadequate, and that a court order was an essential safeguard to prevent "mere spying and fishing expeditions." The six-member subcommittee which Keating headed accepted the Keating court-order bill unanimously. Then, without warning, Keating withdrew his bill and offered as a substitute an Attorney General authorization system, with a new section which retroactively legitimated wiretap evidence already gathered by the Justice

Department. Requiring court approval, said Keating, would seriously hamper our law enforcement—so a last-minute conference with Attorney General Brownell and J. Edgar Hoover had convinced him. Keating explained: "Those who would destroy us are clever, resourceful, and unscrupulous. They will stop at nothing. They do not deserve kid-glove treatment." Thus, after a full committee vote on party lines, Representative Keating was found leading the fight for an Attorney General system of wiretapping.[42]

In May, at the wiretap hearings, Representative Emanuel Celler (D, N.Y.) vigorously attacked the court-order approach as faulty for reasons of speed, secrecy, and uniformity. "I have every confidence in the present Attorney General," Representative Celler declared, "and I would implicitly give this authority to the Attorney General without the slightest equivocation, without the slightest hesitation." Yet on April 7, 1954, Representative Celler was leading the Democrats in offering an amendment to require a court order in place of Keating's "substitute" Attorney General system.[43]

The explanation for this curious legislative situation was that the wiretapping issue had become tightly enmeshed in the loyalty-security debate of the mid-1950's and the sharp Democratic-Republican conflict over this issue. The Attorney General (whom Congressman Celler trusted completely in 1953) was the man who later that year had accused former President Harry Truman of softness toward Communism in his handling of the Harry Dexter White case. Moreover, the House Republican leader, Representative Charles Halleck, had announced that the administration's wiretapping bill was not a wiretapping bill at all; it was "an anti-traitor bill," and should be viewed in this light by all "loyal" Americans. Finally, the addition to the administration's bill in 1954 of a provision to legitimate decades of wiretap recordings stored away by the FBI was viewed by many Democratic Congressmen as a move by the Republican administration to secure dramatic material for reviving the Harry Dexter White, Alger Hiss, and other loyalty-security cases involving former Democratic officials. When the bill reached a vote, the Democratic court-order amendment was passed by a heavy bi-partisan vote. So amended, the "anti-traitor bill" passed with only ten opposing votes.[44]

During the House debates and while the bill was under hearings in the Senate, the press commented extensively on the issues of internal security and privacy that were at stake. Many newspapers ran three or four editorials on the federal wiretap fight as it developed. A survey of more than 100 newspapers, distributed nationally and of all sizes, showed that a substantial majority favored the court-order bill. Hardly any press opinion supported the Brownell-Keating version allowing Attorney General authorization, and many of the staunchest Republican newspapers deserted the party position on this question. A small but distinguished group of newspapers favored a total ban on all wiretapping.[45]

The over-all sense of uneasiness that marked the responses of both those who opposed any federal wiretapping and those who reluctantly supported it under court-order safeguards was reflected in the Senate Judiciary Committee when it opened hearings in 1954. Senator Patrick McCarran of Nevada, a man noted for his strong anti-Communist views, introduced a bill of his own that outlawed all private wiretapping installations, required a court order for all police wiretaps (whether evidence was desired for use in court or not), and contained several other strict provisions. This position by Senator McCarran, when endorsed by Representative Emanuel Celler in testimony before the Committee, led the Committee Chairman, Senator Alexander Wiley (R, Wis.), to express his wonder at "the Irishmen and the Jews fighting against something on the same side." That made a powerful coalition, Wiley said. Indeed, the coalition was strengthened by the pledges of several Senators, such as Wayne Morse of Oregon and Thomas Hennings of Missouri, that they would filibuster if any wiretapping bill reached the floor. In fact, no bill was ever reported out of the Senate Judiciary Committee in 1954, and the House bill died when the session ended. Though wiretap incidents were much in the news during 1955 and hearings were held again before the House Judiciary Committee, no bill passed either the House or the Senate in 1955. Though Congress was obviously aroused in the mid-1950's, gave the issue an enormous amount of committee attention and floor debate, and tried to frame a responsible statute that would bring order out of the legal chaos, Congress simply could not take positive action.

The Shift of Scene to State Debates

With Congress in deadlock over wiretapping legislation, and with the Supreme Court's doctrines providing few effective restraints, efforts by concerned groups to protect privacy from unlimited electronic eavesdropping shifted to the states in the 1950's. The states could at least control use of wiretaps and bugs by local and state officials and by private eavesdroppers within the state. In addition, a few leading states might fulfill the classic function of "little laboratories" in the federal system, adopting model laws that could then spread to the other states and, eventually, provide a reasoned choice for the federal government.

Between 1955 and 1957 there was considerable activity at the state legislative and judicial levels. Two states—Pennsylvania and Illinois—outlawed all telephone tapping by public officials as well as by private persons, and Illinois extended its ban to all forms of electronic eavesdropping. Four states—Nevada, Maryland, Oregon, and Massachusetts —joined New York by adopting a court-order system that outlawed private wiretapping but allowed law-enforcement officers to listen to telephone calls in specific cases under judicial authorization and following specified procedures. New York, Nevada, Maryland, and Oregon placed microphone eavesdropping under similar court-order controls. In other states, legislatures passed statutes making wiretap evidence inadmissible in court or adding bugging to the state anti-wiretap law, and there were several state court rulings extending existing state anti-wiretapping statutes to the police.[46]

To see the issues raised by these state debates over electronic eavesdropping controls in the late 1950's and the process by which action was taken—or not taken—we will examine three representative situations: Pennsylvania (a total-ban state); New York (a court-order state); and California (where no legislative controls were enacted).

OUTLAWING WIRETAPPING IN PENNSYLVANIA

When the national debates over federal wiretapping legislation were at their height, Pennsylvania was one of the few states that had no law on telephone tapping, leaving both private detectives and police officials unrestrained by statute. During the 1940's and 1950's the Philadelphia District Attorney's Office, the Philadelphia Police Department, and police in other Pennsylvania counties had used wiretapping in a wide variety of cases, from numbers-game operations to murder investigations. Since this information was never used directly in court, however, it was not publicly known. Thus it was not until 1954 that any movement to outlaw wiretapping began to become effectively organized. As a result of a Superior Court decision ruling that police taps on the line of a suspected bookmaker were legal because of the absence of any Pennsylvania law to prohibit police wiretapping,[47] a campaign for a state law banning wiretapping was begun. This combined the forces of two organizations, the Philadelphia Bar Association and the Greater Philadelphia American Civil Liberties Union, with support from various liberal and church groups, such as the Americans for Democratic Action, the American Jewish Congress, and the Pennsylvania Council of Churches. To counter this effort, the Philadelphia District Attorney, Richardson Dilworth, a liberal Democrat, drafted a bill which incorporated a ban on private interception with a limited-warrant system for law-enforcement wiretapping.[48] The Dilworth bill was supported by the Philadelphia Crime Commission,[49] and the lines became clearly drawn for a legislative battle in the 1955 session of the General Assembly between what had come to be known, to its advantage, as the "Bar Association bill" and the "prosecutors' bill."

\

Spurred on by news of a private-eye wiretap network in Manhattan which had received widespread coverage in the Pennsylvania press, the anti-wiretap campaign moved into high gear as the Bar Association bill reached the floor of the House. The Dilworth proposal was also introduced and supported by a statement from the Police Commissioner of Philadelphia, arguing that without the use of wiretapping "hundreds of crimes committed in Philadelphia would go unsolved." Expert witnesses for the Bar Association included state and county prosecutors whose testimony denied the necessity to wiretap for effective local law enforcement.[50] The House passed a wiretap ban by a wide margin, but the bill was not considered by the Senate and died at that legislative session.

The entrance of a new figure on the scene proved to be the turning point in a debate which might otherwise have ended there. Victor H. Blanc, another liberal Democrat, became the District Attorney of Philadelphia. Though an opponent of official wiretapping earlier, Blanc became convinced that it was a more important tool in a prosecutor's job than he had thought. During his first year as DA, Blanc's office had used wiretapping to investigate a dozen cases, ranging from teen-age vice activities to narcotics and racketeering offenses.[51] Had the recordings been used only for leads to physical evidence, or even presented when the cases came to trial, Blanc might have accumulated a record suggesting that wiretapping was being used with care.

However, in July, 1956, the Philadelphia daily newspapers received from the DA's office transcripts of records which had been made on the telephones of three racketeers involved in a campaign to seize control of a Hotel and Restaurant Workers' local. The Philadelphia *Inquirer* published extensive sections of the transcripts, triggering a strong and outraged protest by the ACLU and the Philadelphia Bar Association. Noting that publicity rather than prosecution was the purpose of issuing the transcripts, the protests condemned the irresponsible release of unconnected names, irrelevant conversations, and privileged communications between attorneys and clients. Hard on the heels of this revelation came a series of exposés in nationwide pulp detective magazines which included descriptions of wiretapping operations by Blanc's detectives and even verbatim transcripts of wiretapped conversations.[52]

When the controversy over publishing wiretapping recordings was at its height, a new liberal Governor, George Leader, announced that he strongly advocated legislation to outlaw wiretapping; he delegated his Attorney General, Thomas McBride, one of the original leaders of the anti-tap movement, to lead the administrative forces in this fight. As the 1957 session got under way, the Bar Association bill was again introduced, along with a warrant substitute. The issue attracted widespread public interest. Spokesmen for each side were vocal in the press, within their own organizations, and in pamphlets distributed widely throughout the state. During the entire debate Blanc and other opponents of the wiretap ban attempted to attribute support for the bill to "a small clique" of lawyers representing criminals and communists who were attempting to thwart effective law enforcement. Despite these charges, Governor Leader and his supporters were able to overcome the prosecutor's block in the legislature. The total ban bill became law.[53]

According to several leaders of the anti-tap campaign, the 1957 victory was achieved largely because of District Attorney Blanc's missteps—his use of wiretap recordings for publicity purposes, his failure to prevent leaks of transcripts in a vice case, and his decision to "play it dirty" by attacking Bar Association leaders personally.[54] Since the liberal community was divided over a total-ban or a court-order approach, it took Blanc's mistakes to unite legislative sentiment against the law-enforcement position. Some of the most pleasantly surprised people in Pennsylvania were those who had been protesting against police wiretaps for years without expecting to secure a majority at Harrisburg for their position.

The Pennsylvania act makes interception or divulgence of telephone communications by anyone, secured without the permission of the parties, a misdemeanor punishable by a year's imprisonment and a $5,000 fine. The person whose conversations are tapped can sue the tapper or any user of the recordings for "treble damages," which are set at a minimum of $100 plus attorney's fees. The term "divulge" is defined to include disclosure of wiretap information in judicial, legislative, or administrative proceedings, or by one employee to his colleagues in government or private enterprise. In its most ambitious provision, the Pennsylvania law stipulates that the "persons" forbidden to tap include federal officials as well as state and local officers, making it a crime for FBI or Treasury agents to install taps within the borders of the state.[55]

TIGHTENING UP THE COURT-ORDER SYSTEM IN NEW YORK

New York in 1955 was the one state with a wiretapping law defining police authority to intercept telephone communications. Section 813-a of the Criminal Code, as authorized by the 1938 New York Constitution, allowed police officials and district attorneys to tap wires for a six-month period (subject to renewal) upon satisfying a state judge, in an *ex parte* hearing, that there was reasonable ground for believing that evidence of crime would be secured by such interception. A general ban on private tapping passed in 1892 had been expanded in 1949 when it proved impossible to convict two private detectives caught just before they installed wiretaps in New York City Hall; the 1949 amendment made it a crime for a person to possess wiretapping devices in circumstances showing intent to use them unlawfully, even though he was not caught in the act itself.[56]

Such was the system New York had used for almost two decades. The use of wiretapping by law-enforcement agencies in New York was a constant feature in the state press, with accounts of the solution of crimes such as bribery in organized sports, labor racketeering, prostitution, narcotics, and murder. In addition, wiretap recordings furnished by the New York police were used in several important congressional hearings during the 1940's and 1950's.[57] However, there was little hard information on the issues of *how much* tapping was being carried on by officials, in *what types* of cases, and *how essential* wiretapping was to the solution of the crimes investigated. Law-enforcement officials were tight-lipped about their activities, publishing no figures and defending their conduct purely at the ideological level. No official investigation of wiretapping by a state agency had provided answers to these queries before the 1950's. An investigation of the Brooklyn Police Department in 1950, however, brought to public attention the existence of corrupt practices reaching into high police echelons, revealing that warrants to wiretap had often been obtained by misleading or false affidavits to the judges, that records of wiretap operations were not carefully maintained, and that the recordings were often used to obtain payoffs from Brooklyn bookmakers.[58]

State prosecutions of private wiretapping specialists, long active in the state, numbered only two before 1954, and efforts to prosecute had been virtually halted in 1950 as a result of the New York court decision in *People v. Appelbaum*.[59] The *Appelbaum* case had held that the right of a telephone subscriber to have his own wire tapped for business or marital interests was superior to the privacy right of any person speaking on that line.

The wiretapping issue attracted serious public concern in early 1955 after the sensational disclosure of a private-eye wiretapping network which blanketed mid-Manhattan. Attempts by the police to hush up the existence of the network resulted in the release of the information to the press by the Anti-Crime Commission and the conviction of the lawyer who had organized the wiretapping enterprise.[60] Also at this time the New York Secretary of State launched an investigation of the wiretapping activities of licensed detectives which revealed that twenty-six had accepted wiretapping cases, with seven agencies monopolizing the operations.[61]

Out of the debate over wiretapping in New York (and from congressional hearings to determine whether to outlaw state wiretapping), came the first factual portrait of official wiretapping operations in New York. It was learned that 70 per cent of all orders to tap obtained in

New York City in 1952 were obtained by the Police Department and the remainder by the five county district attorneys' offices. In 1954, when over 3.5 million telephones were in use, about 1,000 lines were tapped by the Police Department, resulting in some 400 arrests, mostly in "morals" cases.[62]

The New York County District Attorney's office between 1942 and 1954 averaged seventy wiretap orders yearly, about three for each thousand cases handled. Out of 336 investigations using wiretapping, almost half were in the area of larceny, fraud, and extortion. Organized gambling and bribery amounted to almost 20 per cent, and the remaining 30 per cent were scattered over a wide range of cases from homicide, subversive activities, robbery, and assault to prostitution, rent gouging, and ambulance chasing.[63]

In 1955 the New York Legislature voted to create the Joint Committee to Study Illegal Interception of Communications. Chaired by Representative Anthony Savarese, the Committee became the spearhead for the investigation and exposure of public and private wiretapping excesses.[64] After extensive press coverage and several hearings, the Committee issued a report and a detailed set of proposals for remedial legislation, which received wide support in both public and legislative arenas. In 1956 the Republican legislature passed three anti-eavesdropping bills which wiped out the *Appelbaum* ruling, rewrote the common law of eavesdropping to include telephone tapping and microphoning of conversations to which the listener was not a party; outlawed the use of illegally obtained eavesdropping evidence in state courts and punished its disclosure; and required law-enforcement officials to secure warrants before engaging in microphoning activities.[65]

Governor Averell Harriman, a liberal Democrat, vetoed the bills in 1956 and again when they were passed in 1957 because law-enforcement officials had convinced him that the bills would "seriously interfere with the functioning of law enforcement agencies." [66] Only after a conference among Committee members, administration leaders, and law-enforcement officials was a compromise version of the bill worked out, eliminating the warrant-requirement section for microphone "bugging." The general bill was then passed and signed into law; the first indictment took place in 1958.[67] Later that year a court-order bill for bugging was passed again (as well as one protecting communications between attorney and client),[68] and these became law when law-enforcement officials were given a right to use a "bug" for twenty-four hours without obtaining a warrant when time did not permit the application to the court.

In 1955, Section 640 of the California Penal Code provided criminal penalties for any person who tapped wires or made "any" use of wiretap conversations. However, despite publicized incidents revealing extensive use of wiretapping by California police agencies during the 1940's and 1950's, no prosecutions of law-enforcement officers had ever taken place under this statute. In addition, California's rule admitting illegally obtained evidence allowed the use of wiretap or microphone recordings in the state courts. The wiring of rooms and automobiles or listening through walls with super-sensitive equipment was used even more widely than telephone interceptions in California. Widely publicized cases of police eavesdropping went alongside cases involving private eavesdropping on political figures and Hollywood stars.[69]

However, California did have a law intended to regulate microphoning. In 1941 the California Legislature had added Section 653(h) to the criminal code, making it a crime for anyone, except a police official authorized by a department head or district attorney, to install a "dictograph" without the consent of the owner or occupant of the property.[70] Use of the narrow term "dictograph" left serious doubts whether detectives using microphones attached to tape recorders or radio transmitters would come under this provision.

In 1951 A. L. Wirin, counsel for the Southern California Branch of the American Civil Liberties Union, filed suit against Los Angeles Police Chief William H. Parker, asking the court to enjoin the Police Department from installing dictographs or other sound equipment, on the ground that such installations were illegal trespasses and unreasonable searches and seizures forbidden by the constitutions of California and the United States.[71] Before the *Wirin* case came to a hearing, however, the U.S. Supreme Court decided an important California microphoning case. Long Beach police had entered the home of a suspected bookmaker and installed a microphone in the hall of his house, re-entering several times during the weeks of recording to move the microphone to choicer locations; the police made no effort to obtain a search warrant for their activities. These recorded conversations were partly responsible for the bookmaker's conviction. The Supreme Court upheld the conviction, based on its earlier decision in *Wolf v. Colorado*, allowing the states to decide for themselves whether or not to exclude illegal evidence from their courts. However, the Court vehemently denounced the activities of the Long Beach Police Department and directed that the record and opinion in the case be sent to the United States Attorney General for possible action.[72] The biting opinion on California eavesdropping excesses created a wave of attention from the California press, civic groups and law-enforcement officials. In response, California Attorney General Edmund Brown ruled that eavesdropping by trespass violated state and federal constitutional rights and could subject officials to criminal and civil penalties.[73] Even more important, the California Supreme Court in 1955 reversed the state's rule admitting illegally obtained evidence. The opinion denounced sharply the "deliberate, flagrant" behavior of the police, and concluded that exclusion of all evidence seemed the only answer.[74]

In the wake of these judicial developments, bills were introduced in the state legislature to forbid private eavesdropping and set up a court-order system for police surveillance.[75] The real impetus for legislative activity did not occur, however, until California court rulings in 1956 allowed the use in court of eavesdropping evidence if this had been obtained without trespassing. Sentiment for action was further strengthened when it was disclosed that police were listening to the conversations of prisoners and their confidential advisors in jails and police stations. A state senate Judiciary Committee held a series of hearings in 1957 which exposed the vast range of eavesdropping and wiretapping activities in California.[76] Comprehensive press coverage of the "shocking practices" in California drew public opinion to the side of the legislative recommendations made by the Regan Committee at the close of the hearings, which included outlawing the installation by *anyone* of surveillance equipment on private property; prohibiting any person from monitoring conversations, even on his own property, without posting a notice; requiring private detectives to file sworn annual reports of their activities; and forbidding recordings of confidential conversations between prisoners and their advisors.[77]

The campaign by law-enforcement groups in California to prevent passage of such legislation was a vigorous and skillful one. District attorneys' associations, sheriffs, and other law-enforcement officials launched an attack which was so successful that it allowed only three rather mild measures to pass the legislature—requiring telephone companies to report wiretaps discovered, forbidding the recording of confidential prisoner communications, and requiring a posted notice for all monitoring. Even the latter bill, once passed, was vetoed by Governor Goodwin Knight.[78]

After the legislative session had ended, the California Supreme Court ruled that it would grant an injunction in the *Wirin* suit unless Chief Parker indicated that dictograph eavesdropping would no longer be authorized.[79] Parker indicated that he would comply, but the extent to which this ruling covered wireless-radio eavesdropping and other new techniques was not clear.

Thus, in California the prosecutors' bloc won the day. Through their influence in the governor's office and the legislature, and aided by a carefully planned campaign, they were able to ride out public concern, making California's reaction to the balancing of surveillance and privacy as unsatisfactory and unclear as the federal law. It was left to the courts to step into the vacuum, using their power to define admissibility of evidence as a final (and very partial) means of controlling government use of eavesdropping devices.

The State Reform Movement Withers

Viewed from the perspective of the late 1950's, the state reform movement of 1955–58 seemed to hold enormous promise for the development of new legal controls over physical surveillance technology. Now that the national-security issue was absent from the debates, broad agreement on the need to protect privacy from unreasonable surveillance developed between liberals and conservatives in the states enacting new eavesdropping laws. In Massachusetts, for example, law-enforcement officials hoping to defeat a court-order bill were dismayed to see the Boston *Pilot*, the official newspaper of the Catholic Archdiocese, endorsing the court-order bill alongside the Massachusetts ADA and ACLU. The public's obvious interest in eavesdropping hardware and the average man's chilled fascination with the "Big Brother" implications of the new technology guaranteed continuous treatment by the local press as well as by the national media. Powerful state legislative committees came forward in this period to produce hard facts about police and private use, to force executive and police officials to testify about their activities, and to build the necessary public support for legislative remedies. In the states enacting new laws, city and state bar associations also played a central role which might have led to action in other states.

Despite all these favorable forces, the cold fact is that California's stalemate was repeated in most of the states that held active debates over modern eavesdropping laws in the late 1950's and early 1960's. Only one other state—Illinois—adopted the Pennsylvania "total ban" law. Only four other states adopted the New York court-order model. Apart from a statute in 1959 extending the Maryland wiretap-order system to microphoning in that state, no other state passed basic electronic-eavesdropping control statutes between 1959 and 1964. As the nation moved into the mid-1960's, forty-three out of the fifty states had rusty or inadequate statutes on wiretapping and bugging. The state legislative momentum had run out.

This was not from any lack of publicity over physical-surveillance uses during these years. *The Eavesdroppers*, published in 1959, documented fully the widespread use of police and private electronic eavesdropping throughout the country during the 1950's. It also demonstrated that federal and state laws, including the New York court-order system as it had operated before the 1957–58 amendments, provided inadequate controls over tapping and bugging.

It was true that enforcement of federal and state laws against illegal eavesdropping increased in this period. Beginning in the mid-1950's, the United States Department of Justice used Section 605 to prosecute *private* wiretappers. By 1963 there had been fifteen federal prosecutions, involving twenty-five defendants, primarily private detectives. These prosecutions were scattered in federal districts throughout the country, including New York, New Mexico, Oregon, Texas, Louisiana, Ohio, California, and Georgia. Fourteen of the fifteen cases resulted in convictions, and sentences ranged from fines to two-year prison sentences. No police wiretappers were indicted, however; here the Justice Department's self-imposed policy barred action against fellow law-enforcement tappers. States with new eavesdropping laws also began to prosecute private and police violators of their statutes. A deputy police inspector and two plainclothesmen on the Brooklyn, New York, force were found to have engaged in "personal" wiretaps to obtain payments from gamblers. All three were dismissed from the police force and were also indicted under the New York law. The two plainclothesmen pleaded guilty, but the deputy inspector's trial ended in a hung jury.[80] Private violators were convicted in Illinois, California, and New York. When prosecutions were not possible because states did not have legislation covering the situation, executive or administrative action was sometimes taken. For example, when the police chief of St. Paul, Minnesota, caused a secret microphone to be placed in the meeting hall of the Policemen's Union, his resignation was demanded and accepted by the city authorities. In Baltimore, Maryland, a police inspector who engaged in illegal wiretapping as part of a corrupt operation was convicted of a more serious offense, obviating the necessity of trying the wiretap case.[81]

Since these were exactly the years in which the new miniaturized devices made their appearance and were enthusiastically adopted by police and private eavesdroppers, the enforcement actions just described had little effect in stemming the tide of secret surveillance. Two other factors also contributed to the failure of legal controls: the continued confusion of court rulings and the continued inaction of Congress.

The Federal Stalemate Continues, 1957–1964

In 1957 the Supreme Court held, in *Benanti v. United States*, that wiretap evidence obtained by New York police under legal authorization could not be used in a federal trial, even though federal agents had taken no part in the wiretapping.[82] This eliminated state wiretap evidence from

federal trials. However, the ruling also seemed to suggest that state officers might be violating Section 605 by divulging wiretap information in
state courts. Since this issue was not before the Court in the *Benanti*
case and the Court specifically refused to decide whether interception
without public divulgence violated Section 605, the exact meaning of the
ruling was unclear. Following this ruling, a few state-court judges in New
York said that they would no longer issue warrants to wiretap.[83] The
Federal Court of Appeals for the second circuit (which includes New
York) held that introduction of wiretap evidence in a state court constitutes a violation of Section 605; those who present such evidence commit a federal crime and may also be liable to civil damage suits.[84] After
this ruling, District Attorney Frank Hogan of New York County announced that he would not introduce any further wiretap evidence in
state trials, but would await what he hoped would be quick action by
Congress to permit the states to authorize wiretapping under proper
safeguards.[85] Cases against several hundred defendants in matters ranging from bookmaking to narcotics were dismissed in various New York
courts because they rested on wiretap evidence.[86] Despite a ruling of the
New York Court of Appeals in 1962 that wiretap evidence *was* admissible in state courts, at least until the Supreme Court of the United
States ruled more clearly on this point than its passing reference in the
Benanti case, many New York state prosecutors stated that they would
await congressional or Supreme Court clarification before presenting
wiretap evidence.[87]

No such judicial clarification was forthcoming. The Supreme Court
did not rule on the relation of state-authorized wiretapping to Section
605, and the confusion was deepened when the Court affirmed in 1961 a
lower-federal-court ruling that a defendant in a state trial who had been
indicted on the basis of wiretap evidence could not obtain an injunction
in federal court to prevent state officers from using wiretap evidence at
his trial.[88] Thus wiretap evidence continued to be used in some state
prosecutions. The Supreme Court did rule in 1961 that states could no
longer admit evidence obtained by state officers in violation of constitutional rights, but a 1963 ruling of the Court refused to declare that electronic eavesdropping violated such constitutional rights unless there had
been an illegal entry.[89] Any comfort that law-enforcement officials might
have drawn from this rule was dampened by another Supreme Court
ruling that the use of a "spike mike" in the air space and heating duct
between a suspect's apartment and that occupied by the police constituted an illegal entry when police had not obtained a warrant to eavesdrop.[90] The net result of these rulings was to leave both police and opponents of electronic eavesdropping in common dissatisfaction with the
confusion and ambiguity of judicial rulings.

The other hope for clear national law on the balancing of surveillance and privacy was Congress. Indeed, the difficulties the Supreme Court was obviously experiencing with the wiretapping problem had been caused primarily by the ambiguous wording of the Federal Communications Act, by Congress' failure to clarify it in any way during the 1940's and 1950's, and by similar congressional inaction on the closely related issue of microphone eavesdropping.

The 1958–64 period did produce considerable activity among congressional committees investigating the surveillance problem. Between 1958 and 1962 the Senate Subcommittee on Constitutional Rights first tried to define the extent of electronic eavesdropping and the law surrounding its use, then explored specific legislative proposals and collected expert opinion on the constitutional and policy questions involved. The most striking shortcoming of the Constitutional Rights Subcommittee was its inability to develop information about federal wiretapping and eavesdropping practices (no data was pried out of executive-department witnesses on this matter) or to develop independent data on state and local use of physical surveillance. However, the Subcommittee continued to publicize the gap between law and practice. And by treating the issue of wiretapping and electronic eavesdropping as part of a post-McCarthy inquiry into constitutional rights (rather than in the context of national security), the Subcommittee began the transition to later congressional investigations that would take the constitutional right of privacy as their direct theme.

Another set of inquiries into federal telephone monitoring was conducted by the Special Subcommittee on Government Information of the House Committee on Government Operations, under the chairmanship of Congressman John E. Moss (D., Calif.). On the basis of a questionnaire sent to thirty-seven federal agencies, requiring them to list the listening-in equipment they had purchased or rented, and follow-up interviews with agency spokesmen, the Moss Subcommittee established that a minimum of 4,790 transmitter cut-offs and 527 listening-in circuits were being used by thirty-three federal agencies to enable federal employees to record telephone conversations or have a secretary listen in and take down conversations without the knowledge of the other party to the call.[91] Federal agencies housed in the District of Columbia were spending over $30,000 annually to rent such monitoring equipment. Only eight of the thirty-seven agencies surveyed in 1961 had regulations to control such use of covert telephone recording. The Moss Subcommittee concluded that "Big Brother may not be watching you, yet, but his secretary probably is listening in on your telephone calls to government agencies." The Subcommittee recommended that every federal agency have written regulations banning entry of other persons on a telephone call and any recording of conversations unless notice is given in advance to the other party. By means of follow-up inquiries, the Subcommittee established that by 1962 forty additional federal agencies had adopted regulations for telephone monitoring and that 529 transmitter cut-offs and 193 listening-in circuits had been removed. However, of the forty-eight agencies that now had monitoring regulations, fifteen still did not require that advance notice be given when a third party listened in and nine federal agencies, including the Department of Justice, had refused to adopt monitoring regulations.

In 1962 the Senate Judiciary Committee conducted hearings on proposals to outlaw private wiretapping and to authorize limited law-enforcement taps, sponsored by the Kennedy administration and defended before the Committee by Attorney General Robert Kennedy.[92] At first the Kennedy bill would have given the Attorney General power to authorize FBI interceptions, but strong criticism of this plan led Attorney General Kennedy to change his proposal to require court orders. The 1962 legislative hearings brought out a full array of labor, liberal, law-enforcement, bar-association, crime-commission, and academic witnesses. The same factual and ideological confrontation arose as in 1940–42 and 1954–55 among opponents of all wiretapping, supporters of a limited court-ordered system, and those wanting executive control of law-enforcement taps. The "hard-line" personality of Attorney General Kennedy had the same effect in raising the fears of conservative Republicans and some liberals as the loyalty-security policies of Attorney General Herbert Brownell had exerted on Democrats and liberal Republicans in 1954–55. The result was that no wiretap legislation ever reached the floor for debate in either house during the Kennedy administration, despite an overwhelming sentiment in the press for new federal wiretapping controls.[93]

Federal Eavesdropping Goes Public, 1964–1967

The period from 1964 to the present marks a new stage of public awareness and concern over physical-surveillance technology in America. There are strong indications that, like the final stage of an atomic pile, the wiretapping-eavesdropping issue is at last becoming "critical" and that concrete action will take place soon. The developments that carried the electronic-eavesdropping problem to this stage are easy to catalogue. During 1963 and 1964 leading newspapers, such as the New York *Herald Tribune*, the *Wall Street Journal*, and the Chicago *Sun-Times* carried feature articles on the development, sale, and expanding use of the new miniaturized listening and watching devices.[94] In 1964 a full-scale alarm over the new surveillance threats to privacy was sounded by two books: Vance Packard's *The Naked Society* and Myron Brenton's *The Privacy Invaders*.

Television documentary programs followed, such as ABC's "Big Brother Is Listening" and NBC's "The Big Ear," as well as discussions on "Open End." Extensive local television coverage also focused on the problem, with, for example, a series by Channel 11 in Pittsburgh which featured programs on "Bugging in the Automobile World," "Telephones and Intercoms," "Motel Bugging," and "Out in the Open, But Not Safe." The spread of surveillance technology into the business world for purposes of industrial espionage was treated widely in the press in articles such as "Cloak and Dagger Tactics Invade American Business," "When Walls Have Ears, Call a De-Bugging Man," and "How Spies Steal Business Secrets." [95] In dozens of cities newspapers published surveys of tapping and bugging operations of local private detectives and police agencies, warning residents of these cities: "Bugged by Snoopers? No Detroiter Out of Reach of Electronic Prying"; "There's No Place to Hide from Snoopers" (San Antonio, Texas); "Shades of James Bond, Bug Business Booming" (Hollywood, California); and "Is Your Phone Tapped?" (Chicago). [96] Public concern over electronic eavesdropping was buttressed by congressional hearings and public debates over the impact on privacy of lie detectors and personality testing, making the issue of "vanishing privacy" and "Big Brother" a far more general problem than wiretapping by itself had ever become in earlier decades. The issue even penetrated the academic world as articles by social scientists such as Margaret Mead and Edward Shils attacked as unethical the growing use of surreptitious recording and watching techniques by scholars and scientists studying human behavior. [97]

All of these reactions received fresh and continuing impetus when the Senate Subcommittee on Administrative Practices and Procedures under Senator Edward V. Long (D., Mo.) began hearings in 1964 on surveillance activities by federal agencies. Until the Long Committee began its disclosures, there had been pitifully little hard evidence of *federal* tapping and eavesdropping. No previous congressional inquiry or private study had been able to penetrate the curtain of secrecy around the operations of Treasury, the FBI, the military services, and other federal departments with investigative functions.

The Long Committee began by studying the commercial catalogues on electronic equipment approved by the General Accounting Office for purchases by federal agencies and obtaining from the suppliers information about the equipment they were selling and to whom they were selling it. Having learned which federal agencies were buying, the Committee staff circulated a detailed questionnaire to these agencies asking what uses were being made of the devices, and they followed up the answers (or the refusals to give responsive answers) with interviews of federal officials. [98] Moving to public hearings, the Committee called the principal manufacturers, asked them to display their wares before the public, and documented the presence of a multimillion-dollar industry in surreptitious eavesdropping and watching devices.[99] Then the hearings turned to federal use. With a shrewd sense of timing and public relations, the Long Committee did not try to take on FBI eavesdropping, but concentrated first on tapping and bugging by the Treasury Department. The findings of widespread eavesdropping by Treasury agents in local "racketeering" and income-tax-evasion cases, the maintenance of eavesdropping schools for Treasury agents, and the use of two-way mirrors and bugs in Internal Revenue Service district offices have been described above, in Chapter 5. The false denials and evasions of many investigative officers of the Treasury Department, until pinned down by the Committee's data, and the use of eavesdropping in the sensitive area of income-tax enforcement convinced the press and public that there really was a menace from federal use of the new surveillance technology.[100]

The Long Committee also exposed the use of hidden recording devices by investigators of the Federal Food and Drug Administration[101] (again raising fears in the business community) and dug out the extensive use of "mail covers" by the United States Post Office, by which a record of who wrote to persons placed under such a mail watch was taken off the covers of first-class mail by postal authorities at the request of various local, state, and federal law-enforcement agencies. It was also learned that first-class mail was opened to search for clues to hidden assets in the cases of persons who had defaulted on federal taxes and against whom the Treasury had secured tax liens.[102] Post Office use of peepholes, observation galleries, and surveillance of employee rest rooms to observe postal employees and prevent mail thefts was also brought out by the Long Committee hearings. The FDA and Post Office revelations shocked conservative as well as liberal opinion, since these were not situations in which national-security crimes or threats to life were involved. If such trends continued, the likely end result appeared to be standard government enforcement of its regulatory as well as law-enforcement functions through unlimited eavesdropping.

During this stage of the Long Committee hearings, in 1965, information began to filter out on FBI practices as well. The Long Committee publicized FBI arrangements to secure leased lines from telephone companies to eavesdrop in "organized crime" cases, and reports of FBI use of bugging in Las Vegas, Washington, D.C., and other cities mounted during 1966. In May of 1966 the Solicitor General of the United States told the Supreme Court, in a pending tax-evasion case involving Fred Black, Jr., a professional lobbyist, that the FBI had placed a bug in the lobbyist's Washington hotel suite in 1963, in an "unrelated investigation," without the knowledge of the Justice Department. However, the bug had been in use while the lobbyist was being indicted by the federal grand jury on the tax-evasion charge. The FBI had overheard his conversations with his lawyer, and FBI reports of these conversations (without any indication of the bug source) had been given to the federal attorney prosecuting the case.[103] After these disclosures about FBI tapping and bugging operations, the time had come, as *The New York Times* and editorials in many other newspapers declared, to look into FBI eavesdropping practices.[104]

In 1965–66, while it continued its probe of federal uses, the Long Committee also turned to eavesdropping in the industrial area, collecting proof of taps and bugs for industrial espionage, in-plant eavesdropping by company security officers, and surveillance in labor-management relations.[105] In late 1966 the Committee added a probe of private detectives to its hearings, calling such leading national eavesdropping deans as Bernard Spindel to relate their activities.[106] Throughout 1964–66 many of the Long hearings received front-page newspaper and prime-time TV coverage across the country; they also stimulated hundreds of alarmed editorials expressing shock at federal practices and calling for remedial action.[107] Senator Long helped to keep the issue bubbling by rising on the floor of Congress and reading into the Congressional *Record*, as his "Big Brother item for today," a variety of news items, editorials, and articles about electronic-eavesdropping activities.[108]

The Growing Momentum for Federal Action, 1965–1967

Activated by this barrage of disturbing incidents and facing warnings from prestigeful commentators that "something must be done now," the American civic community displayed a growing readiness to support remedial action against unlimited physical surveillance. A survey I made of more than 300 newspaper editorials on electronic eavesdropping and privacy during 1964–66 showed virtually unanimous agreement that control measures were needed and that both private and public-official eavesdropping had reached proportions unbearable for a free society. The significant aspect of this press opinion is that it spans the entire ideological spectrum, from the *Nation*, the *New Republic*, and the New York *Post* on the left to H. L. Hunt's *Life Line*, *U.S. News and World Report*, and the *National Review* on the right.[109] Business and labor periodicals both featured worried articles and editorials about the use of electronic eavesdropping in their respective affairs, and shared a common alarm over federal "snooping." [110] Conservative editorial cartoonists such as Don Hesse joined liberal colleagues such as Herblock, Mauldin, and Feiffer in attacking the spread of electronic eavesdropping.[111] Liberal columnists such as Drew Pearson, Max Lerner, and Russell Baker were as angry as conservatives such as Paul Harvey, Barry

Goldwater, and William Buckley.[112] Since the liberal's position on this issue is fairly predictable, it is revealing to look at the comments of a "hard" conservative to appreciate how the threat of surveillance technology has brought liberals and conservatives to a common diagnosis of the danger. In his syndicated column, "On the Right," William Buckley wrote in June of 1965:

> Conservatives are presumptively opposed to the passage of laws telling people they can't do things. But here is a classic situation where the affirmation of the individual's right overpowers the presumption against the passage of laws and indeed dictates their passage. More and more it becomes plain that privacy is the key to liberty. Privacy considered in the larger sense, as the right not only to insulate yourself against the importunities of a bustling, hustling order, but to preserve to yourself the ground with which to manoeuver. . . .
>
> Let us, then, have yet another law. Rather, 50 state laws . . . forbidding the sale or purchase or ownership of anti-privacy devices, with a penalty attached that will guarantee to any miscreant user thereof the privacy of a jail cell for a couple of months.[113]

Given the range of this public concern over eavesdropping and privacy, it might be assumed that the very intensity of public feeling would exert checks on surveillance activity. Such has simply not been the case with private use of the new devices. Surveillance-equipment manufacturers such as Ben Jamil of Continental Telephone and Ralph Ward of Mosler Research Products have reported that their sales have shot up after each "exposé" of their activities by congressional committees, television documentaries, and press surveys.[114] Ben Jamil even advertises: "Here are the products you read about in *Esquire!*" Private eavesdropping specialists such as Bernard Spindel report a similar rise in clients after each wave of critical publicity given his work.[115] As several revealing articles have shown, the display of the new devices, the ease with which they can be concealed and operated, and the voyeuristic pleasure they provide have brought thousands of purchasers into the retail outlets. And these customers are *not* social outcasts. In the retail stores they have been the most respectable, well-dressed, well-spoken middle- and upper-class clientele, always with a nervous excuse—"We've got to watch the maid stealing" or "I just want to have some fun at parties." Nor are lower-income customers lacking. The surveillance devices advertised in the "men's magazines" such as *Man's Story, Debonair, War Criminals,* and *True Detective* offer a full range of listening and watching devices for order by mail.[116] The same ineffectiveness of public opinion applies in the area of government eavesdropping. The constant flow of reported incidents in 1966 involving government use of the electronic eavesdropping devices—sometimes with warrants in the five states permitting such activity and many more times without, at the federal level and in forty-five of the fifty states—shows that government use is still beyond reach of public opinion alone.

Reflecting this fact, 1965 and 1966 witnessed a rise in legal and private counter-measures against unlimited physical surveillance. At the federal executive level, President Lyndon Johnson supported the Long Committee hearings against charges that it was harming the government's drive against organized crime. Through his press secretary, Bill Moyers, the President stated in July, 1965, that the inquiry into Internal Revenue Service use of eavesdropping "is in the public interest." Moyers also disclosed that, on taking office, President Johnson had instructed his Cabinet members that all wiretapping by federal employees was banned except in national-security cases approved by the Attorney General. The President had made another "vigorous statement" to this effect at a Cabinet meeting in June of 1965, while the Long Committee hearings were under way. The President also issued a still unpublished, page-and-a-half "confidential memorandum" to the heads of all federal agencies covering the use of devices for telephone or room eavesdropping; it declared forcefully the President's distaste for eavesdropping and his firm commitment to the right of privacy, and re-stated his ban on the use of eavesdropping except in national-security cases. All agency heads were told to promulgate within their own agencies a ban on eavesdropping without the consent of one party to the conversation; to order that no eavesdropping be done without the approval of the Attorney General; and to report to the Attorney General a full inventory of all eavesdropping devices the agencies presently owned, along with a list of all interceptions being conducted currently and the reason for them.[117] In August, 1965, the Department of Justice announced that it was preparing a survey of federal use of electronic-surveillance devices and would set forth guidelines for their use in the near future. A year later these guidelines had still not been issued, and *The New York Times* strongly deplored this inaction after the disclosure of FBI bugging activities in the Fred Black case.[118]

Also at the federal executive level, the Federal Communications Commission issued an important order in February, 1966, prohibiting the direct or indirect use by private persons of any radio device for eavesdropping on "private conversations" unless *all parties* to that conversation consented to the use. Originally, when it had announced its proposed rules for such an order in 1964, the FCC had planned to permit radio-device eavesdropping if only one party to the conversation consented, following the prevailing rule in the federal and state courts and in the five states with court-order eavesdropping systems that a person "assumed the risk" of divulgence by someone he spoke to voluntarily. This proposal, the FCC stated in its 1966 order, was objected to in a brief filed before the FCC by the Special Committee on Science and Law of the Association of the Bar of the City of New York, which argued that the assumption of a risk that conversations might be repeated from memory did not include assuming the risk of overhearing and recording conversations by radio devices. "[U]pon further re-consideration," the FCC declared:

> we have decided that the objections to this view are well founded and that we should not sanction the unannounced use of listening or recording devices merely because one party to an otherwise private conversation is aware that the conversation is in fact no longer private. . . . We agree that the ordinary risk of being overheard is converted into another risk entirely when the electronic device is made the instrument of the intruder. Coupled to a recording device, this new eavesdropping tool puts upon the speaker a risk he has not deliberately assumed, and goes far toward making private conversation impossible. . . . We are commanded by the Communications Act to "encourage the larger and more effective use of radio in the public interest." . . . Upon reflection, we do not believe it to be consistent with the public interest to permit this new product of man's ingenuity to destroy our traditional right to privacy.[119]

The FCC order was an important conceptual breakthrough in its official recognition of the threat to personal and group privacy through what we have called "surveillance by reproducibility." This standard may well be adopted by the courts and legislatures. Already the Illinois Supreme Court has reached the same result in a case of one-party recording, based on language in the Illinois Anti-Eavesdropping Act of 1957. However, the FCC order itself had only mild enforcement prospects: the sanction for its violation was only a $500 fine; it did not apply to state and federal officials operating "under lawful authority"; and the FCC refused to define what constituted "lawful authority." Furthermore, since radio devices could be used for eavesdropping when conversations were not "private" (as when people are in "public or semi-public places or where they may reasonably be overheard by others"), the manufacturers and retailers of radio-transmitter devices have continued to hawk their wares just as aggressively as before. Now they simply say that the devices must be used only where "lawful" and not prohibited by "pertinent regulations." [120]

A related action at the state executive level took place in California in 1965, when the state Public Utilities Commission banned the use of equipment provided by telephone companies for institutional subscribers to monitor conversations on their telephone systems. The PUC order noted that such equipment, used by more than 500 business subscribers in California, did not give notice "to each of the parties" and was thus "inimical to the maintenance of privacy of communication over the telephone networks in California." For such equipment to be used in the future, the PUC ruled, a tone warning device must be added to indicate the monitoring, each telephone instrument capable of being monitored must be "clearly, prominently, and permanently marked" to that effect, and use of such monitoring "should be explained in telephone directories.[121]

Several federal executive agencies took action in direct response to pressures generated by their exposure before the Long Committee. In December, 1964, the Postmaster General ordered that peepholes in all women's locker rooms were to be boarded up and none built in the future.[122] Sheldon Cohen, Commissioner of Internal Revenue, announced that two-way mirrors and bugs in district offices of IRS would be removed, and he pledged to end wiretapping and eavesdropping by IRS agents. Whether this announcement would stop IRS agents in the field was open to question; indeed, one IRS official, in whose district wiretaps and bugs had been used extensively in the past, told the press in January, 1966, on taking up a new assignment as regional IRS commissioner in Chicago, that electronic eavesdropping devices would be used whenever necessary in the war against organized crime. "Will the IRS never be reformed?" Senator Long commented on learning of the statement, and promised to continue hearings on IRS practices.[123] Another executive reaction was a memorandum sent by the U.S. Attorney in Connecticut to all *federal* law-enforcement agencies in the state. The memo cited the Long Committee's findings of illicit taps and bugs in IRS offices and warned Connecticut branches of federal agencies to be sure that there was no wiretapping "unless and until Congress sees fit to make any changes" in the statute, no electronic eavesdropping that trespasses onto private premises, and no attempts to "overhear surreptitiously" conversations between a suspect and his lawyer.[124]

Alongside these executive actions have come several significant judicial rulings on electronic eavesdropping during 1965–66, though none from the U.S. Supreme Court. In New York the Court of Appeals held that a defendant against whom eavesdropping evidence has been used is entitled to inspect not only the court order which authorized the wiretap or bugs but also the law-enforcement agency's affidavits on which the court order was based. "A refusal to permit a defendant to examine the facts on which his privacy has been broken into amounts to saying that any search warrant or order is all right if a judge has seen fit to sign it." The need in wiretap cases, the Court held, was to define the "adequate factual basis" on which judges can decide "whether to issue such an order." [125] In several cases New York courts have already suppressed eavesdropping evidence on finding that the affidavits were insufficient.[126] This offers the first real basis for appellate control over the grant of wiretap and eavesdropping warrants in court-order states. A more far-reaching decision in New York came when a trial-court judge, Nathan Sobel, ruled in 1965 that the New York court-order system could not justify a physical intrusion onto private premises to install a listening device. This ruling was based on the judgment that an "electronic search" for conversations represented a search for "mere evidence," in violation of the warrant provisions of the Fourth Amendment, which required specifically described *things* to be seized.[127]

Several other state-court rulings helped to tighten controls on electronic eavesdropping. For example, the Illinois Supreme Court held that recorded telephone and room conversations were not admissible in evidence under Illinois' Anti-Eavesdropping Act when not all parties to the conversations or calls had known of and consented to the recording. The case involved recordings obtained by means of a concealed radio transmitter on the person of a town official, Robert Smith, who suspected other town officials of fraud and set out to obtain recordings of kick-back offers. In addition, a wiretap device enabled Smith to record both sides of telephone conversations.[128] A California District Court of Appeals held in 1965 that a California penal law forbidding any person to make connections to the telephone line without permission of the telephone company was violated when a subscriber hired two detectives to place an electronic wiretapping device on his own line to overhear his wife's conversations and secure evidence for a divorce suit. The conviction of the subscriber and his two employees was therefore upheld.[129]

In another state ruling the Washington Supreme Court held that electronic eavesdropping by sheriff's officers on conversations of a defendant and his attorney in the conference room of a jail violated the defendant's right to counsel and required dismissal of the indictment.[130]

At the federal-court level, a district court dismissed indictments against two alleged bookmakers because the Internal Revenue Service had made use of a recording device at the central telephone office which makes a record of the numbers dialed, though it does not record any conversations or even register whether the call is completed. Judge William Campbell held that the use of such a "penn register" device violated Section 605 of the Federal Communications Act.[131] A federal court-of-appeals ruling in 1966, while upholding the FBI's practice of viewing suspects without their knowledge through "two-way mirrors" and having witnesses listen to their voices, went on to say that if the suspects had made any damaging admissions during the viewings, it would be unconstitutional for such admissions to be used in evidence against them because of the surreptitious surveillance.[132]

Several other federal-court rulings rejected claims to privacy. One federal district court refused to suppress recordings made in jail between a defendant and a witness by means of a transmitter concealed on the witness' person by federal agents with whom he was cooperating, as well as by a concealed transmitter that federal agents placed in the county sheriff's office where the conversations took place.[133] The federal Court of Appeals for the Second Circuit, whose jurisdiction covers New York, held admissible evidence obtained by federal narcotics agents who taped a microphone over the keyhole of a common door between their hotel room and that of a suspected smuggler, after swinging aside the metal plate covering the keyhole on the agents' side of the door. The court refused to hold that the New York statute forbidding electronic eavesdropping by "any law enforcement officers" without court order applied to federal agents.[134]

At the state legislative level, there was considerable debate but little legislation in 1965–66. Massachusetts appointed a state legislative committee in 1964 to investigate electronic eavesdropping, but it had not completed its work as of the winter of 1967. In several states, such as California, Minnesota, and Illinois, there were full-dress legislative debates in 1965 over proposed court-order bills (sponsored principally by law-enforcement spokesmen and crime commissions) to authorize limited law-enforcement taps and bugs. The bills were defeated in each state after opposition from labor, liberal, and bar-association groups, and particularly strong testimony against legalized wiretapping by telephone companies, such as the Illinois Bell and Northwestern Bell Telephone Companies.[135] In Illinois the major newspapers were heavily against the court-order bill, but in Minnesota leading papers such as the Minneapolis *Star* favored it as a necessary protection of privacy, since there were no existing legal controls in that state.[136]

A prime reason for the defeat of the Illinois bill was the public release in the newspapers of transcripts containing recorded conversations which had taken place over a two-month period in the hotel room of a registered lobbyist in the state capital, Springfield. The recording equipment had been secreted there, by persons then unknown, to obtain evidence of bribery in the state legislature. During the final stages of the wiretap debate, state legislators told a story about a mythical visitor who told a downtown Springfield hotel clerk that he "preferred an unbugged room" and was told in reply, "That'll be fifteen dollars extra." [137] In several other states, including Florida, Kentucky, Rhode Island, and New Mexico, there were debates over the treatment wiretapping and microphoning would receive in new state constitutions to be adopted later in the 1960's.[138] In one of the few pieces of concrete legislation, Maryland in 1965 enacted a statute requiring the registration of all wiretapping and eavesdropping devices with the state police by persons other than law-enforcement officers and telephone-company employees. The Act forbids the manufacture, sale, or possession of unregistered devices. Sixty days after the Act went into effect, however, fewer than ten such devices had been registered.[139] In New York a bill passed by the state legislature in 1965 required notification to the district attorney when wiretap orders were obtained within his jurisdiction (except when his own phone might be tapped on court order), but this statute was vetoed by Governor Rockefeller on the ground that it could impair investigation of corruption by local officials.[140] In Pennsylvania the House unanimously passed a bill to extend the state's wiretapping ban to eavesdropping devices, but the Senate did not act on it, and the bill died.[141]

Government enforcement of existing wiretapping- and bugging-control laws against private eavesdroppers also rose during the 1964–66 period. Among the reported incidents of state prosecutions were the convictions of a Los Angeles doctor for tapping the phone of a woman who had filed battery charges against him, a telephone-company employee in Cleveland for tapping the phone of a wife for the husband in a divorce suit, and two private detectives in Houston for "speculation taps" in marital-infidelity cases. Two private investigators in California were tried for tapping phones in a local political fight over a community development project, a man was arrested for placing a wiretap on a phone booth outside a Tampa, Florida, supermarket, and two private detectives in California were arrested for using a bug to eavesdrop on conversations in a motel room between a lawyer and his clients in a pending lawsuit.[142] The "dean of wire-men," Bernard Spindel, was indicted in Massachusetts for tapping at a factory and at a restaurant in Springfield, along with a telephone-company employee and a member of the Springfield Redevelopment Authority who was alleged to have authorized the eavesdropping.[143] There were also several federal wiretapping prosecutions, such as that of a private detective hired by a corporation to intercept telephone conversations of plant employees and union representatives.[144]

In addition, private suits for invasion of privacy by electronic eavesdropping began to be more frequent in 1964–66. Some of these were against public officials, such as the $5 million damage suit brought by owners of the Fremont Hotel against Las Vegas FBI agents for installing listening devices in the offices of the hotel's president; and a $35,000 damage suit against two Austin, Texas, police officials for bugging a plaintiff's apartment and trailer-house.[145] In Illinois a suit was brought against the Illinois Bell Telephone Company for invasion of privacy when the company furnished a wife with an extension to her husband's phone in an answering service, without his knowledge, and used this to listen to his conversations for divorce-suit purposes. The telephone company was fined $50.[146] An employee of the Southern Pacific Railroad sued the company and two men for $40,000 for placing a bug in a public telephone booth used by railroad shopmen and connecting it to a speaker in the shop superintendent's office.[147] A lawyer in California whose conversations were bugged by private detectives working for a law firm on the opposing side of a pending lawsuit sued the law firm for $300,000 for trespass and invasion of privacy.[148] In Gilford, New Hampshire, a husband and wife sued the landlord of their apartment for $100,-000 when they found that he had installed a microphone in a heating duct near the headboard of the wife's bed, connected by wires to the basement and running underground to the house of the landlord some 700 feet away.[149]

All of this civic and legal activity was important and helpful, but none of it came to grips fundamentally with the tides of manufacture, distribution, and use of electronic eavesdropping and watching devices. Thus the eyes of the press and informed citizens remained fixed on two basic sites—Capitol Hill and the United States Supreme Court building. The congressional scene proved a disappointment in 1966. The Senate Judiciary Subcommittee held hearings in March on a court-order bill to forbid private wiretapping and to allow state law-enforcement officials to tap where permitted by state law under court-order procedures. Attorney General Katzenbach testified in favor of the bill (though seeking to have it amended to specify the crimes for which state tapping would be authorized). As for federal wiretapping, the Attorney General urged that the President be permitted to authorize taps "for national-security purposes," as he now does. The Attorney General stated that if the "compromise" embodied in such a bill could not be achieved, he would recommend that Section 605 be amended to prohibit *all* wiretapping except that authorized by the President in national-security cases, as the only way to control the illicit wiretapping that now exists.[150]

1967 began with a flurry of activity from the White House. In his State of the Union message, President Johnson delivered one of the strongest endorsements of privacy ever to appear in an official state message.[151] In a passage that received more Congressional applause than any other topic in the speech, the President stated:

> We should protect what Justice Brandeis called the "right most valued by civilized men"—the right of privacy. We should outlaw all wire-tapping—public and private—wherever and whenever it occurs, except when the security of the nation is at stake—and only then with the strictest safeguards. We should exercise the full reach of our Constitutional powers to outlaw electronic "bugging" and "snooping."

When the President submitted his crime-control bill to Congress in February, it included the ban on all wiretapping and eavesdropping, except in national-security cases, and a provision forbidding the manufacture, distribution, or advertisement in interstate commerce of wiretapping and eavesdropping devices.[152] Republican leaders in Congress responded with criticism of the Johnson position, and promised to introduce an alternative measure to allow taps and bugs in organized-crime investigations as well.[153] With Senator Long holding wiretapping hearings in the winter and spring of 1967, the Congressional scene promised to be an active one.

Privacy and the Physical-Surveillance Issue

"Who approves of wiretapping and eavesdropping on private conversations?" No one. "Who believes some limited tapping and electronic eavesdropping should be permitted in especially serious areas under proper safeguards?" A majority of the American public, of the writers of editorials for the national press, and probably of Congress. There is the nub of the physical-surveillance issue. At the height of Congressional exposés of bugged martinis and FBI eavesdropping in 1966, a national poll asked respondents whether federal law should permit the FBI to use wiretapping to catch "spies and foreign agents." 68.7 per cent said yes; 19.8 per cent said no; and 11.5 per cent had no opinion. When asked whether federal law should allow FBI wiretapping to catch "white slavers, dope peddlers, riot leaders, and extortionists," the percentage favoring use rose even further to 70.1 per cent, with 19.0 per cent opposed and 10.9 per cent with no opinion. Only when the question was put whether Internal Revenue Service agents should be allowed to use wiretapping on "tax cheaters" did the in-favor vote drop to 43.3 per cent, with 41.0 per cent opposed and 15.7 per cent with no opinion.[154]

The language used in these questions may not have been the most neutral (though it is the way most law-enforcement spokesmen would put the issue), and it would have been useful to test opinion on the kind of control system favored. But there is little doubt that the poll is accurate in its finding that a majority of the American public still believes wiretapping and electronic eavesdropping are necessary tools of law enforcement. Other polls during the past decade confirm this continuing position.[155]

Looking carefully at the structure of American opinion on this issue, then, it is important to distinguish support for bans on private eavesdropping, or bans on eavesdropping by certain kinds of law-enforcement agencies (Internal Revenue, local police, etc.), from the core issue of district-attorney and FBI eavesdropping in serious crime cases. It has long been clear that if this core issue could be brought to any legislative resolution, the private-ban and limited-agency provisions would be passed without serious dissent.

To analyze this central dilemma, we can distinguish the short-term situation as of the late 1960's from what may be our choices a decade from now. In the short run, it may be that the Congressional stalemate of the past fifty years may soon be brought to an end. Perhaps the disclosure of FBI bugs without the knowledge of the Attorney General, plus Mr. Hoover's weakening power position in Congress, means the end of one of the three major positions in the classic Congressional stand-off, the position favoring taps and bugs under executive authorization and without court-order supervision. If so, this would leave the direct clash in Congress between those favoring a total ban, except by federal officers in national-security cases, and those supporting additional eavesdropping authority for federal and state officers under court-order systems. There are some new approaches even on the latter front, such as Senator Long's proposals that law-enforcement officials be permitted taps and bugs when one party to the conversation consents and court approval is obtained, but not for the third-party type of tapping and bugging.[156]

If one inclines to the view that rational decisions are possible in a democratic society and straight ideological choices ought to be kept to a minimum, then there is a continuing source of dismay in the wire-tapping-eavesdropping conflict. On the one hand, law-enforcement spokesmen assert that certain types of serious crime simply cannot be solved without use of taps or bugs. Their practice, both under legalized systems and through eavesdropping secretly to get leads where this is outlawed, makes this an operating tenet of contemporary law enforcement throughout the nation, in agencies and communities of all types. On the other hand, critics of wiretapping, including some present and former law-enforcement officials, deny flatly that taps and bugs are essential. Eavesdropping is called a lazy man's weapon, and a waste of time, except to aid corruption in law enforcement.

Presumably, it should be possible to test these assertions, both by analysis of types of crime and the problems of investigation and proof that they pose, and by comparative studies of law enforcement in jurisdictions having eavesdropping with those where it is banned (and where the bans are actually respected). Yet no such factual study has been possible in the past decade. I proposed this to the Fund for the Republic in 1957, and the idea was taken up by the Pennsylvania Bar Endowment; they commissioned the Sam Dash study resulting in publication of *The Eavesdroppers* in 1959.[157] Dash's book documented unequivocally the widespread use of tapping and bugging, but it was not able to come to grips with the necessity question.

When the President's Commission on Law Enforcement and the Administration of Justice began its work in 1965, it commissioned a paper on the evidence-gathering process in organized-crime cases from Professor G. Robert Blakey of Notre Dame Law School. Blakey tried to answer this very question by going to the files of one leading district attorney's office and describing four types of case in which wiretapping was an indispensable ingredient of successful prosecution (political corruption, racketeer infiltration of business, organized vice, and union racketeering). Though his study of the investigative process is an outstanding piece of analysis as a whole, it does not convince in this section. His case-studies are too short, all of the information in the files was not made available to him, and the alternatives are not fully presented and analyzed, either as absolutes or even in a comparison of the time-and-cost factors involved.[158]

I suspect from the failure of two such intensive private efforts that it would take some kind of official investigation to dig out the facts and to subject opinions to hard questioning. Ideally, this is what a Congressional inquiry could and should do. But it has never been undertaken, partly because of the unwillingness of local or federal law-enforcement agencies to submit to such truly searching inspection and partly because of the presence of sensitive material in the relevant files. As long as this is not done, however, informed observers and the public alike must fall back on their basic value systems for the answer. Thus we have absolutely conflicting factual claims and ideological responses.

Since my own policy recommendations in this area are spelled out in Chapter 14, the other main point to make here involves the long-run prospects of physical-surveillance devices and privacy in the United States. One trend will be a growing use of TV cameras and listening devices in public places and in public accommodation facilities to provide physical security for individuals and allow greater efficiency in police-force responses to emergencies. With notice, such devices will come to be taken for granted in many places such as elevators, streets, and building lobbies.

The more basic question is whether the next decade will see such a change in the nature of law enforcement and crime prevention that the wiretapping-eavesdropping problem may be solved by lessening its assumed necessity. Though police work will always have in it the classic ingredient of "one guy in a uniform chasing someone else," there are some observers who predict that the arrival of large-scale computer intelligence systems will make possible the kind of analysis of trends and transactions that will spell the end of organized crime. To the extent that we move to the cashless society described earlier in this book, such a trend would greatly augment this possibility. Political corruption and embezzlement would become much more difficult as well. Thus, if data surveillance becomes effective enough, physical surveillance may become unnecessary. Man's transactions rather than his speech will become the crucial factor in establishing guilt or innocence.

If such becomes the case, it might represent a net gain for privacy and liberty, unlikely as this may appear at first glance. Despite all the court-order safeguards, wiretapping and eavesdropping will always be dragnet in nature, monitoring the conversations of all those who talk on a tapped line or walk into a bugged room. There will always be the revulsion that any American feels when the home is made a broadcasting station. For all its problems of control—and these are discussed in detail in Chapter 12—there is far more possibility of installing and maintaining protection of individual privacy in the computer information and intelligence systems than there is with wiretapping and eavesdropping. To that extent, the advanced technology which produced the physical-surveillance devices may render them expendable by a still greater advance in technology, the computer information system. And I wonder what George Orwell would have said about that.

CHAPTER NINE

Truth Through Stress

DEBATES ABOUT the polygraph can be grouped according to two main issues. The first is: should law-enforcement agencies use polygraphing to secure evidence for presentation in court in criminal cases? The second is: should public or private employers use polygraphing for personnel selection or administration?

The Argument for the Polygraph in Law Enforcement

Supporters of the polygraph contend that it is a highly accurate "diagnostic" instrument for determining guilt as long as three elements are present in addition to the proper equipment: a qualified examiner, a proper procedure, and a "fit" subject. Examiners must be honest and ethical, well trained in the mechanical use of the polygraph apparatus, and capable emotionally of administering an impartial and neutral examination; they must also have the proper psychological and physiological education to interpret correctly the test results. A proper procedure is one that frames questions for each test in a "scientific" manner that establishes "control points" from which to measure departures that indicate "lies." Subjects will be asked trivial questions ("Is your suit brown?") or irrelevant questions ("Do you ever smoke?") to record normal truthful responses. They will be asked about a fictitious crime to test oversensitivity to accusation, or about illegal activity that virtually everyone is presumed to have engaged in at some time ("Have you ever stolen anything?") to test awareness of guilt and moral responsiveness. Ideally, there will be questions about factual details of the crime that only the guilty party could know ("Was the diamond necklace stolen last week wrapped in a brown chamois cloth?"), mixed into a group of fictitious details. Interspersed in these questions will be the directly relevant and critical inquiry ("Did you steal the Jones diamond necklace?").

The final requirement, a "fit" subject, means that the person being examined is mentally "normal" enough to have guilt feelings and know that he is not telling the truth. (About 5 per cent of the population has been estimated to be "non-testable," according to polygraph spokesmen.) An ideal subject is someone who is aware that social sanctions will depend on the outcome of his testing and who believes in the scientific accuracy of the polygraph. Such a subject, if guilty, often breaks down and confesses under polygraph examination; if innocent, he should record clearly as such. It is claimed that through the careful manipulation of control questions, the polygrapher can detect virtually all efforts of a normal person to lie about specific questions of guilt. According to figures published by a leading polygraph firm and analyzed by them, tests over a five-year period were rated as accurate in 95 per cent of the cases, 4 per cent produced indefinite results, and 1 per cent were "possible error." [1] However, these figures have been challenged by university scientists and others and have never been subject to independent verification.

In terms of moral and ethical questions, the polygraph advocate assumes that innocent persons will have nothing to fear in taking the test once its operation has been explained to them and its accuracy demonstrated. The person accused of a crime is not forced to take the test against his will by the police or courts, though refusal to take such a test is often a factor in the mind of a prosecutor in bringing an indictment. When investigating crimes, the polygraph operator contends, he does not intrude into privacy any more than does the police officer who interrogates a suspect about his motives, whereabouts, or connection with the crime. While a police officer will have to depend on visual observation (or independent investigation) to determine whether a suspect is telling the truth, the polygraph operator feels he is able to interpret "scientific" data. Finally, the polygraph advocate rejects the idea that there is any invasion of privacy through loss of dignity or penetration of the "unconscious mind" in a lie test. The only difference between direct questioning and the typical polygraph session, it is said, is that a rubber tube is fastened around the chest, a band similar to that used in taking blood pressure is placed around the arm, and electrodes such as those used in an electrocardiogram are attached to the hands. There is no penetration of the body, as in a spinal tap; no withdrawal of bodily substances, as in a blood test or in stomach pumping; and no interference with full mental consciousness, as in the administration of drugs for narco-analysis. The test is usually administered in a quiet room, where only the subject and the operator (and sometimes a police observer) are present and where there is a minimum of environmental noise to distract the subject.

THE ARGUMENT AGAINST POLICE POLYGRAPHING

Critics of the polygraph in criminal investigations begin by noting that polygraph instruments do not measure lying, or even physiological states that accompany lying; what is measured is physiological change in the subject generated by emotional stress. This may be caused by many stimuli other than lying. For example, in criminal investigations persons may be fearful that their innocence will not be accepted. They may be angry at being suspected. They may be emotionally disturbed if the crime affected their loved ones or property. Or they may be hostile to efforts to solve the crime if it was one they approved or condoned. Moreover, lying is far from the unique, conflict-generating act that polygraphers assume it to be. It is said that everyone lies throughout his life, sometimes for socially approved reasons and sometimes not. Lying thus "can conceivably result in satisfaction, excitement, humor, boredom, sadness, hatred, as well as guilt, fear, or anxiety." From these facts critics conclude that a significant number of guilty persons will "beat" the lie detector and a significant number of "innocent" persons will be falsely accused by the very nature of the instrument used.[2]

Turning to actual error, the reliability figures cited by polygraph operators have been rejected in most scientific and legal journals. The 95-per-cent figure cited earlier has been found to be less than 70 per cent when derived from controlled laboratory tests by independent scientists, and may be even lower than 20 per cent in terms of any verification of the *truth* of confessions obtained.[3] Efforts to have different polygraph operators test the same subject to judge the reproducibility and independent validity of the polygraph have not been successful.[4] Further, scientists have said that conditions vary so much in the environment of the test room and the physical state of the subject that a series of tests by the same operator with the same subject will show very significant changes in the results.

In addition, a number of scientific studies have concluded that it is possible for some persons to "beat the machine" purposely. A study done for the U. S. Air Force in 1962 by a contracting university concluded that such a result could be accomplished by subjects who assumed an impersonal "faraway" attitude (comparable to the state achieved by persons practicing yoga).[5] It was accomplished also by persons who conjured up sexual daydreams while being questioned, flexed muscles vigorously under questioning, or adopted other techniques that created a false emotional "jamming" effect on the recording instruments. If a subject was "calm on the lies . . . and panicky with the truth," the polygraph was often left with "a sort of nerve-wracking chart that renders everything implausible."[6]

For all these assorted reasons, scientific groups such as a section of the American Psychiatric Association have warned against reliance on the polygraph's infallibility.[7] European police do not have faith in polygraphing and do not use it in their investigations.

Another factor cited by critics is the crucial interpretive element of the individual examiner and the low state of training and professional ethics prevailing in the polygraph field. Prior to 1963 there were no licensing requirements by law and no professional-association controls over all practitioners, with the result that many self-trained and even "shady" entrepreneurs were attracted to the field. One leading polygraph expert has estimated that not more than about 20 per cent [8] out of some 1,000 to 1,500[9] "practitioners" could be trusted to interpret a polygraph test accurately. Complaints about "polygraph quacks" have been made frequently by the established agencies.[10]

Finally, polygraph critics denounce the use of this instrument as a reversion to "trial by ordeal," with awesome scientific gadgetry playing the role once reserved for religious or primitive-magic devices. Indian tribes once forced accused persons to chew rice and "convicted" those whose "guilt" dried up their mouths so much they could not spit it out. Ancient princes would tell a group of suspects to enter, one at a time, a darkened room and pull the tail of a "sacred ass"; the ass was supposed to bray when the guilty person touched him; the person in the group who entered but did not pull the tail would not get the black powder on his hands that had been sprinkled on the animal's tail and was therefore adjudged "guilty." Such are said to be the "tricks" on which the polygraph is really based today, with the strong possibility that psychological maladjustments are registered as "guilt." As one of the originators of the polygraph technique remarked recently, "in many places, [it] is nothing more than a psychological third-degree aimed at extorting confessions." [11]

LEGAL REACTION TO POLICE POLYGRAPHING

The consistent position of the state courts since the 1920's has been against admission of polygraph test results as valid evidence in criminal trials.[12] Polygraph experts and their corporate clients voiced the continual hope during the 1950's and 1960's that increased use of the polygraph by police forces, the federal government, business clients, and private associations, when coupled with verification studies carried out by leading polygraph firms, would persuade the courts to reconsider their ban on polygraph evidence. Several trial courts in New York, New Jersey, Maine, and Illinois did accept polygraph results during these years, when both sides of the case consented to its use. Test cases supporting these revisionist positions were organized by state and national polygraphers' associations, but to date most of these hopes have been completely dashed. As recently as June, 1963, for example, the Massachusetts Supreme Judicial Court rejected a carefully prepared test case asking for a new permissive rule on polygraph admission. The court's opinion pointed to "well-documented articles" in scientific and legal journals that continued to raise grave doubts about "not only the techniques employed in the administration of the tests, but the very premises and assumptions upon which they rest." Despite the general willingness of American courts to admit scientific evidence—such as fingerprints and ballistics records, and blood tests for paternity and intoxication—the Massachusetts court held that such admission rested upon the "general acceptance by the community of scientists involved." Until "substantial doubts" about the polygraph were removed, its product could not be similarly accepted as evidence in court.[13]

Certain courts have also prohibited such evidence on grounds other than lack of scientific acceptance.[14] The major point in such decisions is that the use of such evidence would violate the "hearsay" principle, since the machine cannot be examined or cross-examined.

Some state courts, however, have made exceptions to the inadmissibility of polygraph evidence. In the 1962 case of *State v. Valdey*,[15] the Arizona Supreme Court held that under certain specific conditions the results of such tests were admissible in Arizona criminal cases. The particular conditions include (1) written stipulation for the taking of the test and entrance of results into evidence signed by the defendant, his counsel, and the prosecutor; (2) discretion of the trial judge as to final admission of the results, based upon the examiner's qualifications and conditions under which the test was given; (3) the right of both parties to cross-examine the polygraph operator; and (4) the judge's instructing the jury that such evidence only tends to indicate whether the defendant was telling the truth at the time of the examination and does not *per se* prove or disprove any element of the crime. Judicial opinion is clearly divided on this type of exception, though, and several courts have ruled that no agreement between the parties can render such evidence admissible when its validity is not accepted scientifically.[16]

Other courts have upheld the power of public agencies to discharge or discipline public employees who refuse to take lie-detector tests when investigations of specific misconduct or crime is under way. The California courts, for example, have upheld the right of municipalities to fire policemen who refused polygraph questioning after sums of money had been stolen from the police department's cash-bail safe. The ruling asserted a general obligation on the part of public employees to cooperate in such situations involving the fidelity of law-enforcement officials themselves, and rejected both self-incrimination and right-to-privacy grounds for refusal to take the tests while retaining public employment.[17]

The Use of Polygraphs in Personnel
Selection and Control

As we saw earlier in this book, use of the polygraph for personnel selection and control has been an increasing practice of public and private employers. As of 1966, no state or federal court had passed on the power of government to make submission to preventive polygraphing a condition of employment or of promotion when no specific misconduct was under investigation.

The authority of private employers to use polygraphs has been passed upon by both government labor agencies and by arbitrators appointed under collective-bargaining contracts. The General Counsel of the National Labor Relations Board ruled in 1959 that it would *not* be an unfair labor practice, forbidden by the National Labor Relations Act, for an employer to insist upon polygraph tests for employees as part of job applications or in investigating thefts of company property, as long as there was no motive to discriminate against the union or to interfere with employee representation by this process.[18] An example of such interference was a 1962 case involving the 7–11 Food Stores Chain in the Washington, D.C., area, operated by the Southland Corporation. Lie-detector tests were given to all prospective employees, and among the questions about indebtedness, accident record, and arrests were several about past activity in unions and the applicant's future intentions toward unions if he were hired. On May 17, 1962, an NLRB trial examiner ruled that such questions during a polygraph test were illegal coercion under the Taft-Hartley Act.[19]

Several arbitrators' decisions have made it clear that an employer cannot institute polygraph requirements suddenly without first engaging in "good-faith bargaining" with the union over this change in "the conditions of employment," even if the employees individually sign agreements to take the tests. And if discharge is provided for in the collective-bargaining contract only for "good cause," it has been held that an employee's refusal to take a polygraph test cannot justify a dismissal without other grounds.[20] While these rulings obviously rest on the representational rights of the union and the terms of specific contracts, it is important to note that the opinions of the arbitrators often stress broad grounds of privacy in support of their decisions. In one 1962 case, involving a drug company that fired an employee for refusing to take a lie-detector test after a burglary attempt at the company warehouse had been analyzed as an "inside job," the arbitration board commented:

> The Board is mindful of the serious financial problem confronting this Company as a result of pilferage. In view, however, of the overwhelming weight of impartial scientific

authority that these lie detector tests are not accurate and legal authority that they do not constitute competent evidence and invade the right of privacy and the constitutional rights against self-incrimination, this Board cannot uphold such a requirement in this case.[21]

In another case a company, finding that work reports had been falsified so that some employees were overpaid, deducted the overpayments from the later checks of all overcompensated employees who refused to take a polygraph test on the issue of their part in the falsifications. The arbitrator ruled this conduct improper, since there was no evidence that these employees had been involved. "The time has not come," he explained, "when management can consign to a machine the job of supervision, especially when this machine is to take the employee in its embrace and measure his most intimate vital processes." No formal accusation was made against the employees by the company, and the polygraphing proposed here represented an attempt to "seine up all the fish merely because a predatory fish or two is known to be at large in the pond." [22]

In many arbitration cases the issue has not been whether the employer can insist that an employee take a polygraph test but what weight to assign test results when these are obtained and are read by the operator to indicate "guilt." Recent arbitration awards have been uniform in holding that lie-detector tests *cannot* be used as "probative evidence" justifying discharge by themselves. In such cases, the evidence is either excluded or must be supplemented by independent evidence of the offense.[23]

Other public agencies dealing with regulation of employment relations have shared the hostility to lie-detector practices. For example, an Illinois state board held that three employees fired for refusing to take lie-detector tests were still eligible to receive unemployment benefits. One sales clerk had allegedly registered a sale for one dollar below the precise price, had refused the lie-detector test, and had been fired. The board held that "injury to the legitimate rights of the employee resulting from the industrial use of lie detector tests far outweighs the unsure benefit to the employer," so that the test refusal *per se* was not the type of "misconduct" that would prevent the employee from receiving jobless pay benefits.[24]

Far more important to the use of polygraphing for preventive screening by industry have been state legislative developments in the past five years. These seem to have been triggered originally by two developments. First has been the appearance in the late 1950's and early 1960's of articles in both mass-circulation magazines and specialized journals condemning the spread of polygraph screening in business and government. For example, *Newsweek* in April, 1963, printed a feature story, titled "The Lying Machine," which called this practice "folly" and a "dubious witness." [25] A long article in the *Harvard Business Review* for November, 1962, written by two Harvard University psychologists and a research aide, was titled "Don't Trust the Lie Detector." This study warned businessmen that the machines were not trustworthy or scientific, and that, wholly apart from questions of validity and reliability, the polygraph raised fundamental "moral questions" for "policy-making executives."

The use of polygraphic techniques either to detect or to avoid hiring certain persons constitutes a subversion of judicial processes to "trial by polygraph." An individual is persuaded by social pressures to testify against himself through a distorted, error-ridden medium; he may be denied the right to work without ever knowing the reason why; he may be "convicted" of certain "tendencies" without having committed an illegal act; and he has no defense against the operator's report, since it is unknown to him and he has no rights in the process by which it is drawn up and used.[26]

Rather than invade employee privacy and dignity with this "dubious" process, the authors called on businessmen to rely on "tests, questionnaires, interviews, and, probably best of all, first-hand observation of performance. These ways may be slower and more time-consuming, but in the long run they are still the best a company can use."

The second influence has been labor-union activity aimed at outlawing the use of compulsory polygraphing by employers. Beginning in the late 1950's, the Teamsters, the Warehouse and Mail Order Employees Union, the Retail Clerks Union, the International Longshoremen's Union, and many other unions publicly condemned employer use of lie detectors. Articles in the labor press branded use of the polygraph as "a form of coercion," replete with questions that improperly intruded into private and personal areas. (For examples, see the section on state legislation, which follows.) A typical statement was that of James Shourt, editor of the *Southern California Teamster*, who declared that unions opposed the polygraph on "moral, social, legal and ethical grounds." The device, Shourt said, deprived workers of their constitutional rights to face their accusers and to be free from compulsory self-incrimination. "From the standpoint of organized labor, we don't feel this should be a collective bargaining issue at all. People shouldn't have to give up money or work rules to get something they already have by constitutional right." Furthermore, Shourt said, union leaders "have also discovered the thing has been used by anti-union and anti-labor employers to screen out people they feel have any sympathies toward the unions." [27]

Across the country as a whole, the AFL-CIO has led a concerted union campaign for new polygraph legislation and contractual protections. An AFL-CIO 1964 Collective Bargaining Report warned its constituents that use of lie detectors was growing rapidly and advised all unions to demand contract prohibitions against requiring workers "to submit to this indignity." The report stated that the "voluntary" submission method is being used by an increasing number of employers, listing the following industries as among the major polygraph users: steel, copper, autos, meat packing, food processing, oil, electronics, mail-order retailing, and supermarkets. The process of "inducing the 'fear of the lie detector' " was making it "America's Mental Blackjack."

The AFL-CIO Report went on to explain:

> Unions cannot depend only on courts and arbitrators to prevent workers from being victimized by the "lie box." As already noted, the unsuccessful job applicant has no recourse to an arbitrator or judge. In addition, the damage to an individual may be an accomplished fact before a judge or arbitrator can rule. Failing a "lie detector" test frequently brands a worker as guilty not only by the company but, unfortunately, also by fellow workers who may have accepted the "myth of infallibility" created by "lie detector" purveyors. Prohibitions against the use of "lie detectors" included in labor-management agreements will prevent this danger. Workers should not be required to submit to this indignity.

The report suggested the following clause to protect both workers and applicants:

> "The company shall not require, request or suggest that an employee or applicant for employment take a polygraph or any other form of lie detector test."

The report went on to say:

> The fact that a particular company has not used or says it does not intend to use the "lie box" should not persuade a union to neglect closing the door before the approach to the lie detector seller. It may be much easier to negotiate a preventative clause than to convince a company to end its "lie detector" program.
>
> There have been suggestions that unions join with management in working out "rules of the game" governing the use of the polygraph in employment relations. The trouble is that, while some protective guarantees might reduce or even possibly eliminate some of the abuses detailed in this report, they cannot remove the basic inadequacies of the polygraph in its use as a "lie detector." [28]

On February 25, 1965, an official AFL-CIO Executive Resolution condemned the use of lie detectors in both public and private employment for the first time on "privacy" as well as "accuracy" and "dignity" grounds:

> We object to the use of these devices not only because their claims to reliability are dubious, but because they infringe on the fundamental rights of American citizens to personal privacy. Neither the government nor private employers should be permitted to engage in this sort of police-state surveillance of the lives of individual citizens.[29]

The Executive Council instructed President George Meany to appoint a special subcommittee to start a campaign of education, legislation and "other appropriate action" to discourage the use of lie detectors. The report went on to state that private employers were using lie detectors to ask union members about their union activities, personal finances, past employment and future job plans, drinking habits, physical condition, police record, driving habits, sexual activities, and political beliefs.[30]

In a recent survey article, the *Wall Street Journal* found that the following legislative activity was precipitated in substantial part by the AFL-CIO campaign: the passage of a Washington state anti-polygraph law for private employment; passage of similar bills by one house of the state legislatures in Illinois, Michigan, and Missouri; state senate passage of a similar bill in New York; anti-polygraph proposals before state senate committees in Ohio and Wisconsin; passage by the Akron, Ohio, City Council, under the direct urging of the United Rubber Workers, of a resolution outlawing the use of lie detectors in the municipality as a condition for getting or keeping either a public or private job.[31] In April, 1965, Shively, Kentucky, also banned the use of the polygraph for employment uses.[32]

In fact, the labor campaign against the lie detector is part of a broader campaign against wiretapping, electronic eavesdropping, mail covers, and the like. AFL-CIO President George Meany explained, in an article in the *Virginia Law Weekly* in May of 1965, that labor objected to both the incompetency of the average polygraph operator and to the unreliability of the general procedure and results, but labor's chief objection was to the invasion of personal privacy.[33]

Other labor organizations such as the Teamsters and Retail Clerks have engaged in state legislative campaigns.[34] Reflecting these labor efforts, a panel discussion on "The Polygraph and Labor Relations" was held at the tenth annual meeting of the American Academy of Polygraph Examiners in 1963 with representatives of labor and business as well as the polygraph profession participating. The panel showed that, although the bulk of the union movement was opposed to polygraphing,

some unions had resorted to the polygraph to help solve internal problems. For example, John Reid was quoted as saying that a number of his
cases involved polygraphing for unions to investigate union thefts; one
involved an innocent union man charged with robbing the union office
but cleared by a polygraph test.[35] The panel also revealed some differences in the positions of labor advocates on the question of legislative
proposals and tactics.

State Legislative Campaigns Against Personnel Polygraphing

Building on the anti-polygraph articles in the press and operating
primarily through state labor councils and civil-liberties group allies, the
anti-polygraph forces scored their first major success in Massachusetts in
1959. In that year the first "total ban" statute forbidding compulsory
polygraphing by private employers was enacted. The brief, one-para-
graph statute provided:

> No employer shall require or subject any employee to any
> lie detector test as a condition of employment or continued
> employment. Any person violating this section shall be pun-
> ished by a fine of not more than 200 dollars.[36]

This campaign was carried to other major industrial states, and by
1965 it had produced total-ban laws in five other jurisdictions: Oregon,
Rhode Island, California, Washington, and Alaska. In addition, in 1964
the Madison, Wisconsin, Common Council passed a resolution opposing polygraph tests as well as electronic eavesdropping, and the Cincinnati, Ohio, Civil Service Commission adopted a policy restricting the use
of the lie detector to problem situations involving the honesty of a city
employee, with the single exception of parking-meter-collection workers,
who still are examined periodically. In 1965 several cities banned the
polygraph technique for employment uses.[37]

Actually, the legislation from 1963 on was sterner than the 1959
Massachusetts model. In 1963, for example, a determined drive by Massachusetts labor leaders secured passage of legislation that extended the
1959 statute by banning all lie-detector tests (except those administered
by law-enforcement agencies) even when a person volunteered to take
them.[38] Another example is the 1963 Oregon statute, which punishes any
employer or his representative, private or public, who requires polygraph
tests for employees with a $500 fine or one year in prison, or both.[39]

The fight over passage of the California ban statute in 1963 provides
additional insight into the civic and political structure of this issue. A
flurry of articles appeared in the California press between 1961 and 1963

describing the spread of preventive polygraphing by California business firms. It was reported that some large retail chains such as groceries and drugstores, savings banks and loan firms, and some service stations and liquor stores in the Los Angeles area required pre-employment screening and periodic testing by polygraph. According to a survey by the Los Angeles *Times*, the polygraph was not used extensively "by major defense industries, such as aircraft manufacturing companies, or by the leading banks" in the area. It was estimated that more than 100 polygraphers were operating in the California area.[40]

The California bill, which would outlaw polygraph tests as a condition for employment or promotion, or in the investigation of theft or other employee misconduct, was promoted by California labor-union groups, led by the state Teamsters Union. It was sponsored in the state legislature by liberal Democrats and reported favorably after hearings by the labor committees of the two houses. Testimony was presented attacking the reliability of the polygraph instrument and calling it "unscientific, inhuman, and anti-labor," and cases of California employees fired because they refused to take the tests on "personal privacy grounds" were publicized to the legislators and public. Opposition to the bill came from the National Board of Polygraph Examiners (through its chairman, a Los Angeles polygrapher), who defended the validity of the tests, their lack of any insulting or degrading aspect, and the right of any employer to require such a test of a prospective employee just as he could insist upon a medical examination or intelligence test. In addition to polygraph and detective-agency objectors and some company security officers, a professor of police science at Los Angeles State College spoke out in opposition to the total ban and called for minimum standards and licensing by the state as the proper remedy for any abuses of this valid and scientific tool.[41]

Partly in self-defense and partly out of a genuine desire to raise the standards of the polygraphing profession, polygraph experts throughout the country began to press actively in the 1960's for state legislation to license polygraph operators and thus win state recognition as a legitimate "profession." Groups such as the National Board of Polygraph Operators, the Academy for Scientific Interrogation, and the International Association of Polygraph Examiners drafted model licensing bills, supported these measures at the state level, and wherever possible, mobilized business support for this approach to polygraph regulation.[42]

By 1963 Illinois, Kentucky, and New Mexico had passed such statutes for "The Licensing and Regulating of Detection and Deception Examiners." [43] These provide standards of character and training for examiners; forbid any non-licensed persons to give polygraph tests; prohibit unethical or improper practices by "deception examiners" (such as making false promises, or divulging information obtained in an examination without the consent of the subject, or using misleading advertising); require that every instrument for the detection of deception measure at least "cardiovascular and respiratory patterns"; and put authority to issue additional regulations and supervise examiner conduct in the hands of a special board of examiners or an existing licensing authority. Similar statutes have been debated recently in Wisconsin and Texas. The effect of the Illinois law, for example, was to permit about eighty polygraph examiners to remain in business in Illinois. By 1966 two additional states— North Dakota and Texas—had passed licensing statutes.

The specific provisions of the Illinois polygraph-licensing law require a college degree and six months of special intern training to qualify for a state operating license, with a special state licensing committee composed of police and polygraphers appointed by the governor.

A third approach to polygraph regulation—what might be called the "omnibus" statute—combines controls over the scope of polygraph use with licensing standards for the polygraph practitioners. In 1961 Senator Thomas Laverne, a Republican from Rochester, introduced legislation in the New York state senate to forbid employers to require polygraphing for job applicants or as a condition for continuing employment. Senator Laverne stated that he had filed the bill as a result of a labor dispute in Rochester in which an employee had been dismissed on the basis of a polygraph test indicating that he had been stealing. The employee insisted that he was innocent and demanded another test. This proved to be less conclusive on the "lies," and the employee was reinstated.[44] The Laverne bill was strongly endorsed by AFL, CIO, and independent unions in New York, was praised by the Republican Chairman of the New York Senate Labor Committee (who called compulsory polygraphs "a Gestapo deal"), and received praise from several leading Democrats and Republicans in the Senate. Opposition came from McKesson and Robbins, Inc., which used lie detectors extensively to screen employees handling drugs and narcotics; from national polygraph associations; and from the head of a New York City polygraph firm that does "morals-screening" of drivers for private and public bus services transporting school children. The Senate passed the ban unanimously, but it failed to pass in the House, and no action was taken in 1961.[45]

At the 1963 session of the New York legislature, Senator Laverne again introduced legislation on lie detectors, but this time his measure was a comprehensive system to outlaw some uses of polygraphing and regulate others. Designed as an amendment to the General Business Law of New York, the bill would make polygraphers a regulated profession in the same way that hairdressers, cosmeticians, or private detectives are licensed in New York. Under the proposed system:

1. The use of any instrument or device "to test or question individuals for the purpose of determining truthfulness" would require a polygraph license.

2. No instrument could be used by a licensed operator unless it were capable of measuring and permanently recording "at least the following three physiological phenomena: cardiovascular reactions, breathing, and galvanic skin response."

3. No polygraph examination could be conducted unless the person to be tested was told that the examination was wholly voluntary and that he could decline to take the test, and this refusal could not be made grounds for discharge from employment or a condition for continuing employment. The subject matter of the examination must be made known in advance, and all questions to be asked must be read aloud before the instrument is used. A written statement certifying that this procedure has been carried out must be signed by the subject; the statement then includes a provision giving the examiner permission to disclose the results of the test to other persons.

4. It would be unlawful for any employer to dismiss an employee on the sole ground of refusing to take a polygraph test, or to require the taking of such examinations as a condition of continuing employment. Violations would be punishable by a fine of $100 to $500 or one year in prison, or both.

5. To secure a license, operators would be required to have a bachelor's degree from an accredited college or university, to have passed 150 formal hours of approved course work in polygraph principles and methods, to prove good moral character and an absence of felony convictions, and to pass a written and oral examination to be administered by the New York Department of State.

6. Licenses would not be required for persons holding the Ph.D. degree from an accredited university who had engaged in polygraph testing before 1962, or former law-enforcement officials with five years of experience in polygraphing prior to 1962, but such persons could not refer to themselves as polygraph examiners without securing a license.

7. Full-time employees of law-enforcement agencies of the state of New York or any of its subdivisions and of the United States would not be covered by this act while conducting examinations in the course of official investigations.

During the 1963 consideration of the polygraph-control bill, the New York legislators had the advantage of learning about several disturbing instances of polygraph error. One case, which took place in St. Louis, Missouri, in 1962, had involved a large robbery at the Credit Union office of the Anheuser-Busch Company. Among the employees given polygraph tests were one man who registered as "clearly" being free from involvement in the crime and another who was found to be "nervous but truthful" in his denials. Later, both men confessed to participation in the robbery.[46]

A more important case disclosed in 1963 concerned a corporation executive whose life was almost ruined by a "false positive" on the polygraph. The case was described by Drs. H. B. Dearman and B. M. Smith of the University of Virginia School of Medicine, in an article for the *American Psychiatric Association.* The story was picked up by the United Press, was printed in many newspapers throughout the country, and drew extensive comment from polygraph critics.[47] The episode involved the vice president of a bank which had instituted periodic lie-detector "checks" for its executives and employees. When asked, "Have you ever stolen any money from the bank or its customers?" the executive's "No" caused the polygraph needles to jerk violently; the "lie" was promptly reported to the bank management. The books were fully audited, but no shortage could be found; another polygraph test was therefore administered. This time, under sharp questioning from the operator and warnings that the machine "couldn't be beaten," the executive "confessed." Yet another audit again showed that nothing was missing. At this point the bank president, who believed firmly in the innocence of the executive, sent him for psychiatric aid. These examinations showed that the only time he had lied was when he had "confessed" to taking money, and this lie had been prompted by the pressure of the polygraph situation. The fact was that the executive had deep-seated, unconscious hostilities in certain matters toward his mother and wife, both of whom were customers of the bank. Although he had done nothing irregular with their accounts and was carrying out his duties perfectly, questioning under the psychological stress of the polygraph had upset his nervous system and had caused him to register a "false positive." Drs. Dearman and Smith concluded in their article that many polygraph operators were incompetent and could not interpret difficult charts accurately. When they encountered "trouble," they would press to convince the subject that the machine was infallible and therefore he must be lying. The harm caused by "false positives" as well as "false negatives" "cannot be calculated," said the doctors, but it surely has undermined reliance on the polygraph for "scientific" results.

With much the same line-up of labor support and opposition from polygrapher groups and individual businesses, and floor speeches detailing spreading business use, the 1963 bills were passed by strong bipartisan majorities in both the House and Senate in New York.[48] In a surprising development, Governor Nelson Rockefeller vetoed the measure, however. His primary reason was a "technical defect" in the bill, which had been pointed out by the Association of the Bar of the City of New York, under which jurisdiction to try cases arising under the statute was not clearly given to courts in New York City along with those outside the city. This flaw could easily be remedied by the next legislature.[49] But the Governor's message also stated that the need for such polygraph regulation had not been shown, and this brief remark seemed to indicate more serious differences between the state legislature and the chief executive.[50]

Two additional factors are important in understanding the New York executive position. First, a good reason for opposing licensing is that polygraph operators could invoke the licensing mechanism as proof that government believes polygraphs are reliable and trustworthy, that the process is not an improper invasion of privacy, and that licensed operators are reliable and ethical persons to conduct such a mental examination. Second, there is the possibility that standards of conduct might be established by codes of performance within the polygraph profession itself, without resorting to "the crutch of a legislative solution." [51]

In New York the issue continued to be debated. In 1964, for instance, The Retail Clerks International Association, via the state AFL-CIO, advocated bills banning polygraph use as a condition of employment or continued employment.[52] Two similar bills introduced at the same time in the New York State Assembly died in committees. Similar legislative proposals were introduced in 1966 and met the same fate. Some influential groups favored delay of the passage of such bills until further study clarified the scope of adequate over-all supervision in the field of personnel testing. Thus the Association of the Bar of the City of New York disapproved the 1966 proposals even though it strongly favored eventual legislation in the area.[53] Its position was that such laws should be much broader than a simple ban on polygraph tests alone and that precise employer-employee standards should be developed to include all areas of psychological testing.

In addition to these major responses to the privacy problems in lie detection, Illinois in 1959 passed legislation forbidding judges in state or municipal courts to "require" either party in a civil suit to submit to polygraph testing, or to "require, request or suggest" testing to defendants in criminal trials. This measure was passed to curtail the practice of judges in the Chicago Municipal Court who had allowed polygraph results by John E. Reid and Associates to be used in civil suits when these were agreed upon by all the parties and in criminal cases as a supplement to probation reports.[54]

In 1965–66 proponents of state controls, spearheaded by AFL-CIO efforts,[55] continued to gain ground. New Jersey, Maryland and Delaware adopted lie-detector laws in 1966, bringing to ten the number of states banning polygraph tests by employers prior to employing an individual.[56] Persons violating these laws are subject to jail in four of the states and to fines ranging from $100 in Maryland to $1,000 in Alaska, Hawaii, and Washington.[57] In addition to state legislation, the city of Akron became in 1965 the first major city to ban the use of polygraphs as a condition for obtaining either public or private employment. This action by the Akron City Council was precipitated largely as the result of a campaign led by the United Rubber Workers Union.[58]

Debates over Federal Use of Polygraphs

In 1952–53 a series of articles in *The New York Times* and the Washington *Post* detailed the burgeoning use of polygraphs in general security screening and personnel checks for federal defense and foreign-policy agencies. Examples were published of privacy-invading questions, bullying tactics by operators, and decisions based on polygraph judgments of beliefs and inclinations. These were commented on by many other newspapers and magazines throughout the country. Other examples of polygraph practices were added by columnists such as Drew Pearson.[59] In a Senate speech, Senator Wayne Morse described the details of one case of polygraph probing and said this practice infringed "the basic guarantees of personal liberty and freedom set forth in the Constitution." The Senator concluded that the screening of applicants for government jobs by polygraph was a wholly improper technique. Unless the Executive Branch stopped this practice, he said, "I shall in due course of time introduce appropriate legislation . . . to protect free American citizens . . . from what I consider to be a repugnant, abhorrent, and outrageous procedure for hiring Government servants." [60] Such a bill to investigate the use of lie detectors by the federal government and to learn whether legislation was needed to protect employees was introduced by an upstate New York Republican, Congressman Edmund P. Radwan, at this time.[61] Secretary of Defense Robert Lovett and other high Defense Department officials were informed of anti-screening sentiment at a meeting of the Senate Armed Services Committee, in January of 1952, and Lovett replied that he would have an investigation made at once.[62] Assistant Secretary of Defense Anna Rosenberg announced after the investigation was completed that polygraph screening was not a fair method and should be banned; and an official announcement was made in February that lie-detector tests had been abolished by the Defense Department as a "repugnant practice." An unnamed Defense Department spokesman told *The New York Times* shortly thereafter, however, that the polygraph was still used on a "voluntary basis" as a "requirement" for certain sensitive posts.[63] Just what a voluntary requirement meant was not explained.

The question of federal use then dropped out of the news, attracting little Congressional or civic-group attention until 1962 and 1963. At that time a series of dramatic incidents focused public attention on federal polygraphing. A 1962 investigation of NSA procedures by the House Committee on Un-American Activities, following the defection of two NSA employees to the Soviet Union, led to a report criticizing NSA for placing "far too much importance on the polygraph as a means of determining the employee's security suitability." (The two NSA men *had* been given polygraph tests.[64]) In a similar action, the House Banking and Currency Committee criticized the Secret Service for relying too heavily on polygraph tests in investigating the disappearance of $7.5 million in American securities from the Federal Reserve Bank in San Francisco.[65]

Civil-liberties groups became concerned with the issue because of the publicity aroused in a double-homicide case involving an Air Force enlisted man named Gerald Anderson. Arrested as the prime suspect, Anderson was given several polygraph tests that reached opposite judgments as to whether he was practicing deception when he denied involvement in the crime. Anderson confessed, then repudiated his confession as one given under pressure, and was then held in jail for seven months awaiting trial. At this point another man confessed that he had committed the crime, and a polygraph test concluded that he was telling the truth.[66]

The most explosive incident involving federal polygraphing arose in March of 1963. An unidentified source in the Defense Department leaked to the Washington *Star* an unclassified but "confidential" memorandum, written by an Air Force officer, which asserted that the staff of a Senate subcommittee was "browbeating" some of the military witnesses testifying about the propriety of a contract award for the TFX fighter plane. Angered at the uproar caused by the leak, Secretary of Defense McNamara ordered a thorough investigation.[67] The investigators, under the direction of the Air Force Inspector-General, included in their operation a request that each official who had access to the memo sign a form consenting to a polygraph test to verify his statements to the investigators. This added up to 120 federal officials, including Deputy Secretary of Defense Roswell Gilpatric, Secretary of the Air Force Eugene Zuckert, and Secretary of the Navy Fred Korth. Four of the 120 persons declined, including a top Pentagon official, Assistant Secretary of Defense Arthur Sylvester. Though he gave full information "truthfully" to the investigating officer, Sylvester angrily refused "as a matter of principle" to give his consent.[68]

Publication of this news caused an uproar. Editorials across the country denounced such a requirement. Representative Cornelius Gallagher of New Jersey, a Democrat, announced that subjecting government employees to lie-detector tests was "a great affront to human dignity" and should be abolished.[69] President Kennedy announced at a press conference that he thought polygraphing high defense officials to be "a mistake"—unnecessary and inappropriate—and that the whole investigation would be called off.[70] The reaction of some journals, such as *The New York Times*, the *Saturday Evening Post*, and the *Reporter*[71] magazine, was to take the position that, while it was nice to know that Secretaries and Assistant Secretaries would not be "hooked up" to test their truthfulness, it would better suit a free society if the President had been able to say that no military officers or federal employees in such circumstances would be required to take such tests. The *Saturday Evening Post* editorial illustrates the tone of many of these reactions:

> Some of the things that have been happening in the Pentagon recently would be easier to believe if they were in a novel by Franz Kafka or George Orwell. . . . [T]he damage was only partly undone by calling off the investigation before the polygraph tests were given. We have no quarrel with the polygraph per se. It has proved itself a useful investigative tool when properly used by qualified personnel. But there is a time and a place for everything, and we submit that polygraph tests for high Government officials have no place in our democratic society." [72]

In April, 1963, the Chairman of the House Government Operations Committee directed its Foreign Operations and Government Information Subcommittee to undertake a full investigation of federal polygraphs. Under the chairmanship of Representative John E. Moss (Dem., Calif.), the "Moss Subcommittee" sent questionnaires to 58 federal agencies asking the following as their most important questions:

1. Does your agency possess or make use of polygraphs or other so-called lie detection devices? . . .
2. Briefly explain your agency's general procedures governing the use of such devices and answer the following specific questions. . . . ("For what purposes," etc.) . . .
3. Please enumerate, by job title and grade, all employees of your agency who are authorized to conduct polygraph or similar tests and list their salary costs for fiscal 1963. . . .
4. How many polygraphs and other so-called lie detection devices are the property of your agency? . . .
5. Please provide two copies each of all intra-agency directives, administrative orders, rules, regulations and/or instructions governing the use of such devices within your agency.[73]

Nineteen federal agencies were found to own 512 polygraphs, acquired at a cost of $425,000, with an annual operating expense of more than $4 million; approximately 19,000 polygraph tests were given in 1963.[74] After securing and analyzing the agency replies, the Moss Committee held seven days of public hearings, taking testimony from private polygraph examiners, a panel of scientists who had made studies of the polygraph, and representatives of the Army, Navy, Air Force, Post Office, and FBI. CIA spokesmen were heard in four days of closed sessions.

The consensus of the scientific witnesses was that the polygraph instrument had *not* been proved to be reliable by either the validation tests of polygraph agencies or by laboratory experiment, while government agencies had completely failed to keep records to provide a basis for judging the accuracy of the 200,000 tests given by federal agencies in the past decade. The core of the scientific position can be illustrated by the statement of Dr. J. F. Kubis, professor of psychology at Fordham University and author of a leading experimental study on polygraph results:

> The use of lie detectors is generally unwarranted. There are relatively few situations so critical that justify lie detection procedures. . . .
>
> The rapid growth of lie detection services is also dangerous because the attractive fee structure encourages the inexpert or quack to enter the field. Becoming an expert is almost synonymous with buying an instrument. There are no certification standards; and the competency of the ordinary lie-detector operator leaves much to be desired. Further, the instrument itself has yet to prove its worth under rigidly controlled conditions . . . . [I]n the hands of an ordinary operator, the lie detector is relatively unreliable. . . .
>
> The threat to use the lie detector on a continuous basis in industrial and business organizations is degrading. The fundamental dignity of man is the issue.[75]

Contrasts were developed between the military agencies—which used two-way mirrors and recording devices without notice to the person tested and which allowed only the testee and operator in the examination room[76]—and an agency such as the FBI—which did not use either recording or watching devices and which always included the FBI agent in charge of the case at the examination.[77] Because of J. Edgar Hoover's skepticism about the conclusiveness of polygraph readings, only the Director or one of his two Associate Directors can authorize the administration of a polygraph test, and these officials turned down 265 of the 858 field requests in 1964. In all, the FBI used polygraphs in 593 out of more than 600,000 investigative matters in 1964.[78] They reported 1,155 tests in fiscal 1964, while the Defense Department gave 13,669 in the same period.[79]

The polygraph examiners' challenge to the judgments of scientific critics[80] was expressed by the testimony of Professor Fred E. Inbau, of Northwestern University School of Law:

> Mr. Reid's experience in the testing of applicants for positions on police forces . . . have come up with some frightening disclosures as to the extent of thievery, narcotic addiction, and what-not of people applying for positions on police forces. . . .
>
> . . . [The critics, psychiatric and otherwise] do not go out in the field and find out how the instrument is working to the advantage of the public and the individual himself.[81]

The Moss Committee hearings were an example of the Congressional Committee process at its best. The Committee used its legislative authority and its investigative leverage to force federal agencies to reveal just what uses were being made of polygraphs and, under questioning by Committee Counsel Benny Kass and the Committee members, to show by the agency witnesses' own admissions how badly controlled the polygraph procedures of almost every federal agency really were. At the same time, the genuine security interests of CIA and NSA operations were carefully protected. In addition, the Moss Committee staff, under the direction of Sam Archibald, produced an excellent paper on the history and technical aspects of the lie detector, a survey of judicial decisions relating to the polygraph, and a detailed bibliography. Through the use of the "panel discussion" technique with polygraph experts and then with scientific experts, the Committee produced a far more careful and useful record of discussions than is sometimes possible with straight witness-by-witness questioning.

Throughout the hearings the eight Subcommittee members and the committee counsel indicated general skepticism about many of the uses of the polygraph by federal agencies and the whole procedure by which tests were drafted, administered, evaluated, and used by federal agencies. The report filed by the Subcommittee, and adopted by the full Committee on Government Operations on March 22, 1965, reflected this skepticism strongly. "There is no 'lie detector,' " the report stressed, "neither machine nor human. People have been deceived by a myth that a metal box in the hands of an investigator can detect truth or falsehood."

> The polygraph technique forces an individual to incriminate himself and confess to past actions which are not pertinent to the current investigation. He must dredge up his past so he can approach the polygraph machine with an untroubled soul. The polygraph operator and his superiors then decide whether to refer derogatory information to other agencies or officials.

As long as a notation is made in any official file that an individual refused to take a polygraph test, the examination is in no way "voluntary." The refusal too often is taken as a presumption of guilt; the file notation which follows an individual throughout his career often casts a dark shadow on his future.[82]

Based on these judgments, the Report recommended that the Federal Government:

Initiate comprehensive research to determine the validity and reliability of polygraph examinations.

Prohibit the use of polygraphs in all but the most serious national security and criminal cases.

Improve the training and qualifications of Federal polygraph operators.

Restrict the use of two-way mirrors and recording devices during polygraph examinations.

Guarantee that polygraph examinations be, in fact, voluntary.

Insure that refusal to take a polygraph examination will not constitute prejudice or be made a part of an individual's records except in the most serious national security cases.

The committee further recommends that the President immediately establish an interagency committee to study problems posed by the Federal Government's use of polygraphs and to work out solutions to those problems.[83]

It was significant that the Report did not contain any discussion of privacy as a concept, nor did it conclude that the polygraph was *per se* a device that should be barred by law or executive order. Reform rather than abandonment, but drastic reform, was the motif of the Committee Report in 1965; only one Subcommittee member, Representative Robert P. Griffin (Rep., Mich.), was recorded as considering "too sweeping" the Report's recommendation that polygraphing be limited only to "the most serious national security and criminal cases." [84] However, a full "privacy attack" on all federal polygraphing was presented in the form of "additional views" by Representative Cornelius Gallagher.[85] Gallagher had been one of the first to call for a Congressional inquiry into federal polygraphing, but he had not originally been a member of the Moss Subcommittee. During the hearings he had been prevented from questioning witnesses directly, because Subcommittee members resented Gallagher's intrusion into the hearings and possibly also his uninhibited statements to the press about the progress of the hearings and the merits of the issue. Gallagher had also stated at the hearings, none too gently, that he felt Subcommittee members were not always pressing polygraph examiners and user-agency witnesses closely enough.[86] Thus Gallagher had no part in the writing of the Moss Subcommittee's Interim Report. However, before the Report was adopted by the parent Committee, Gallagher was added by the Committee chairman as a full member of the Subcommittee. He had also been given his own subcommittee late in 1964 to look into invasion of privacy as a general problem of federal governmental operations.[87]

From this background Gallagher issued "additional views" to the Committee Report that called for a ban on all federal use of polygraphs.

In my opinion, lie detector tests constitute an insidious search of the human mind and are a breach of the most fundamental of human rights. They provide a vehicle of excursion into the most private recesses of the human mind. Even if the polygraph testing was trustworthy, there is still no possible justification for such "mental wire-tapping." I believe the lie detector test under any compulsion is a violation of the fourth amendment to the Constitution. Its use upon Federal employees and job applicants is especially repugnant and should be stopped now—today.[88]

The compelling fact, Gallagher declared, was that "the use of lie detectors by the Federal Government is a blatant invasion of privacy which free men everywhere should condemn if they want to see liberty continue." The investigation had proved, Gallagher felt, that the polygraph was not reliable, that it belonged in the category of reading "tea leaves" and "the entrails of sheep." But even if it were proved infallible, it would still be clear that polygraphing "is an unreasonable and unlawful search of a person's mind and an attempt to unlawfully seize his thoughts." [89]

The Moss Committee hearings produced extensive editorial reactions in the nation criticizing federal polygraphing practices as loose, improperly controlled, and another example of the growing threats to privacy unleashed by new technology. A check during the spring of 1964, at the high point of the hearings, showed editorials running twelve to one in support of the Committee's critical approach to federal polygraphs, and even those defending the federal uses acknowledged the need for new safeguards to control abuse. Many newspapers[90] used sharp terms to describe the abuses against the citizen's rights uncovered by the Moss Committee. A good example of editorial sentiment was the position taken by the Scripps-Howard chain, printed in the Washington *Daily News.* The editorial noted that a judicial warrant based on probable cause and specifying what will be searched for is required before a man's house can be searched, but no such "legal niceties" are limiting "the search of men's minds by lie detectors, nor the subsequent use of the material thus dredged up. This fact is beginning to disturb, profoundly, Americans who are concerned about the protection of freedom and right to privacy." [91]

What concrete changes did the Moss Committee hearings bring about in federal-agency practices down to early 1967? First, a special Defense Department memorandum was issued by Deputy Secretary of Defense Cyrus Vance on April 27, 1964, specifically addressed to the Army, Navy, Air Force and NSA.[92] The memorandum stated that no polygraph examination should be conducted without advising the individual (1) that he has a right to refrain from any action which might tend to incriminate him; (2) that the examination will be given only with his prior, written consent; (3) whether a two-way mirror or similar device will be used; and (4) whether the test will be recorded or monitored by any means, in part or entirely. In July, 1965, the Defense Department issued a broad directive dealing with polygraph operations in the entire department.[93] This document was worked out with the aid of the Moss Subcommittee staff and represented the first serious government effort to make uniform regulations controlling the use of the machine and the training of operators. It should be pointed out, however, that the Subcommittee had hoped for even more restrictions than the directive set forth, as well as for a broader coverage of government departments and agencies.

The DOD directive specifically limited the cases in which the polygraph could be used in the areas of crime and security to crimes punishable by imprisonment of one year or more, or by death, and only in "national security" matters. It would still be possible to use such tests in personnel screening of defense-contract employees handling security matters and of NSA employees. Twenty-four cases of use with defense-contract employees were reported in 1964.[94] In addition, the polygraph would continue to be utilized in intelligence matters when data could not be checked by other means.

As a result of the directive, approximately 150 persons in the Department are authorized to approve lie-detector tests, but only after providing a written order that other methods have been exhausted, that the purpose of the examination follows the criteria established, and that reasonable grounds exist for believing that the individual has information about the situation in question. The directive also orders that the person be informed if the test is to be monitored or if two-way mirrors are to be used, and it forbids investigation into political and religious beliefs as well as attitudes on social matters and legislative policies. The individual must also be informed as to his legal rights, be told that no adverse action will be taken upon his refusal to take the test, and be given a chance to confer with a lawyer prior to the test.

The directive also attempted to tighten controls over access to the test data. In certain cases, however, the results could be turned over to other federal authorities outside the Department, as well as to state law-enforcement officials.[95] The order also reflects an effort to tighten the qualifications of polygraph operators and to raise their training levels. The clause on qualifications, however, is so inclusive that most of the current 430 operators are protected.[96] Each military service was authorized to establish a separate training program, including at least six months of on-the-job training, to be followed by a probationary period. The directive stated, finally, that the private schools previously employed for training purposes would not be utilized in future and that a sum of $100,000 was tentatively set for fiscal 1966 to conduct further research into the effectiveness of polygraph techniques.

One civilian reaction came from the Post Office, which indicated that it would gather more careful information from its regional offices about the uses of its machines and would require that private operators used as consultants must meet the same qualifications the Post Office required of its own polygraph examiners.[97] This Post Office response was not exactly a thrilling reaffirmation of the citizen's right to privacy or a serious attempt to deal with the heart of the polygraph issue.

The lack of immediate remedial action by other federal agencies and the failure of the Moss Committee to urge a ban on all polygraphing prompted some critical response in the press. Richard Starnes, a columnist writing in the Washington *Daily News*, remarked angrily:

> The moral squalor steadily engulfing the nation will be amply documented for any future Gibbon who undertakes the dismal task of chronicling America's decline and fall.
>
> Hearings now in progress before a subcommittee of the House will provide a squalid little footnote to his work. It will show that one of the signs of the decay of our social structure was our docile acceptance of the shocking, degrading tool of psychological blackmail—the "lie detector." . . . The American Congress, as if determined to reaffirm its inability to come to grips with any problem, tried (unsuccessfully) to regulate the use of the lie detector. Apparently it did not occur to its leaders that any decent concern for human dignity required that use of the machine be forbidden by law.[98]

On July 15, 1965, Representative Gallagher introduced H.R. 9878 to forbid the use by any agency of federal funds to acquire or use a polygraph except for cases involving "extraordinary necessity in protecting the national interest." In such cases the head of the agency had to authorize the use personally in writing and to detail the reasons for such use. The AFL-CIO pledged its "unqualified support" of the Gallagher "ban" bill and promised to push for its enactment at the next session of Congress.[99] Meanwhile the Moss Committee itself continued the quest for tight controls and limited uses, by legislation if necessary.

President Johnson announced in December, 1965, the creation of a government-wide committee to study the problems raised in the current use of polygraphs and to develop guidelines for their future use.[100] The establishment of such a panel, to be headed by U.S. Civil Services Commissioner J. W. Macy, Jr., carried out the earlier recommendation of the Moss Committee, and a report was expected in 1967. A memorandum by the General Counsel of the U.S. Civil Service Commission expressed doubt that any general screening of applicants by lie detectors would be upheld as legal.

The Polygraphers Counterattack

In reply to their critics, polygraph examiners and many law-enforcement and business allies have begun to mount a counterattack on what one police official called the "polygraph knockers." An article in *Police Chief* attacked the following groups as the ones heading complaints against the polygraph: (1) "Those who knew very little if anything about it (e.g., most psychiatrists)"; (2) "Those policemen, including administrators, who apparently are basing their adverse opinions concerning the real worth of the instrument upon the performance of untrained or improperly trained examiners or from the hearsay of other polygraph knockers"; and (3) "the Communists, fellow travelers, and those who hate anything that exposes the 3 C's—crime, corruption, Communism— whether it be in business, unions, government, or general society." [101] Along the same lines, "The Polygraph's Enemies," an article in the police journal *Law and Order*, stated that: "Subversives, fellow-travelers, professional thieves, racketeers, and certain vocal, irritant groups have one thing in common—to discredit the polygraph by means of a smear campaign, which is apparently being directed and coordinated by a certain central organization." [102]

Members of the polygraph profession have recently begun efforts to organize themselves more thoroughly in self-defense. For example, *The Police Chief* recently printed a statement by the President of the American Academy of Polygraph Examiners describing tactics to be used in the various states to secure licensing laws with minimum standards for operators. He stressed the importance of enlisting the aid of the various police departments and state attorneys' offices, and suggested considering publicizing the number of people "who run clean" and are cleared of suspicion on the basis of polygraph examinations. In this manner, the support of the general public might be secured.[103]

One should realize that there are various schisms within the profession as to the length of training needed, methods of questioning, and definitions of "honesty." [104] John Reid and Associates has expressed concern that "quickie courses" are giving lie detection a bad name and are careful to contrast their theory of polygraph "interviewing" with that of others who "interrogate."

A significant development in 1964 was the creation of the *Council of Polygraph Examiners Newsletter*, to provide information about the progress of relevant congressional hearings, reports on the continuing attacks in the press and networks, and a rallying cry for a defense of the profession by its members.[105] The *Newsletter* also issued pleas for funds to begin to finance a public-relations counterattack: "Your profession is under constant attack. You should have begun to fight long ago before the anti-polygraph interests became so well entrenched. It's not too late, however, to fight back. You can do your share, and maintain your polygraph business by supporting the efforts of the Council. Your $25 check will give you a voice in the counter-attack of the polygraph profession." [106]

By 1966 widely read magazines such as *Reader's Digest* and *Saga* were running articles on "Invasion by Lie Detector" and "Lie Detectors Are Liars." [107] On a different level, however, the polygraph showed its arrival as an object of "pop culture" by joining the children's toy market along with juvenile secret cameras and listening devices. One advertisement featured a "sensational new lie-detector machine" which registers "emotions, feelings and reactions," for only $4.95.[108] Complete with instructions and sample questions, the ad claimed that the device could record changes in skin perspiration and register emotional reactions on an indicator which moved from "Could Be" and "Are You Kidding" to "Little Whopper" and "Big Whopper."

Privacy and the Polygraph

Reflecting this continuing scientific challenge to the reliability of polygraph measurement of truth telling, industrial arbitrators, labor boards, regulatory agencies, and the courts continue to rely heavily on the argument of scientific unreliability in rejecting the use of polygraph results as evidence or in considering how much weight to give a polygraph result in a non-judicial proceeding. Yet, as Professor Gerhard Mueller of New York University Law School has remarked about the judicial opinions in particular, the courts seem to be "merely using the scientific imperfection argument to avoid the issue of the ethical justification for probing man's innermost sphere." [109] In Europe, by contrast, the courts, legal codes, and authoritative commentators have long rejected the lie detector as an impermissible police technique, not on the ground of its error ratio, but because it is felt to violate the essential dignity, human personality, and individuality of the citizen. It was this formulation of the issue that led Pope Pius XII in 1958 to condemn the lie detector (along with narco-analysis for investigative purposes) as an intrusion into man's "interior domain," invalid morally even when used for governmental purposes.[110] The growing union campaign against employer polygraphing, the publication of two books in early 1964 treating the new uses of the polygraph by industry and government as an issue of *privacy*,[111] and the congressional position reflected by the work of the Gallagher Committee (in contrast to the Moss Committee) all point to the development of a privacy objection as the real core of civic protest.

However, just what the claim of privacy rests on has not been clearly established as yet. One of the leading American experts on scientific techniques in law enforcement, Professor Helen Silving, has characterized the essential vice of the polygraph process as the machine's penetration of "the unconscious." Any such process, Professor Silving has written, crosses the line into impermissible terrain for a democratic society, and violates the dignity of the individual.[112] Several legal and medical writers, including some as fervently opposed to polygraphing as Professor Silving, have questioned her reliance on the concept of "unconsciousness" with regard to the polygraph. It is pointed out that while narco-analysis, and probably hypnotism as well, reaches the unconscious, the polygraph evokes responses from a person fully conscious. If mental conflict is created by a question that asks whether the individual committed a certain act or believes a certain idea, this effect is not really a matter of "testing the unconscious," and clarity of analysis is not served by putting polygraphing in this category.

Since I agree that "unconscious" is not the best term, I suggest that the real issue of privacy raised by widespread polygraph screening is threefold. First is the attempt to penetrate the "inner domain" of individual belief, tendency, and inclination through the questions on such topics used so often in polygraph sessions. The American Constitution sets up a basic distinction between acts and beliefs, and the style of polygraph screening discussed in this chapter violates the injunction against inquiry into belief by government. Second is the interference with the individual's sense of personal autonomy and reserve created by machine sensing of the individual's emotional responses to personal inquiries in a formal, public proceeding. If individuals confess because they feel they have lost their basic autonomy, we may detect some personnel risks, but we will leave citizens stripped of what made them feel like independent persons in a free society. Third is the increased psychological power over individuals that authorities acquire when they can apply the full panoply of large black box, moving stylus, wires, two-way mirrors, formal interrogation, and so forth, to a citizen seeking to work for a corporation or a government agency in a free society. The system of due process in America has truth seeking as only one of its purposes; the other two basic rationales are to preserve individual dignity and to place limits on the use of power by government. A society in which government straps its employees to a machine and makes judgments about their qualities in such a manner, or allows corporations to do so, can scarcely be called a society that adheres to the basic ideals of due process. Such a practice may be tolerated for certain special situations, but these must be limited to the smallest possible number.

It is also important to understand the meaninglessness of such terms as "consent" and "voluntary" in the context of polygraphing today, and to reject these as tests for measuring the privacy interests at stake. Normally, consent of the individual to relinquish his rights of privacy closes the discussion of conflicting values. If for money, recognition, status, psychic needs, or ideological interest, a person waives his right to withhold consent, the law—and society—generally accept the individual's choice. In the new polygraph situation, however, the realities of coercing consent must be appreciated. Before World War II, when lie detectors were used primarily by official law-enforcement agencies or company security forces to investigate particular crimes, and when the test results were inadmissible in courts, the setting of these situations usually made the giving or withholding of consent a meaningful factor. Normally, only persons whose relationship to a crime (through motive, opportunity, inconsistent story, and the like) had raised tangible questions about their innocence would be asked to submit to polygraph verification of their statements to investigators. This created a situation somewhat analogous to the "reasonable grounds to suspect" factor present in official search or seizure. There was a meaningful link, at least, between the specific person asked to take the polygraph test and a particular crime that had broken the public peace. To be sure, there were instances of police coercion of suspects into taking polygraph tests, or employer threats after a theft to dismiss all employees who would not verify their statements by polygraph. But these were clearly exceptions to the norm before World War II. They called for remedial action as specifics, but not for banning the polygraph entirely.

Today, when "consent" is considered, it should be done in the realization that some nine million employees work for federal, state, and local governments; a conscription law passes a high percentage of American males through military service; and the blue-collar and white-collar working force for American corporations is more than forty million. Because of the trend toward polygraphing to provide theft security for companies and loyalty security for government service, most of the adult working population of the nation now comes within the potential reach of "preventive" testing if the use of the technique continues unchecked.

This is why "consent" has been redefined in the civic debates in the past decade, and properly so. When applicants for corporate or government service, normally well qualified, well recommended, and with no trace of criminality to raise questions, must submit to polygraphing or forsake these key sources of employment in American economic life, then "consent" is far from free. Or if, when once hired, an employee is required to "consent" to periodic preventive testing as a condition of continued employment, the employee's freedom of choice is substantially narrowed. No doubt these are the considerations that have stimulated civic commentators and have led state legislatures to pass bans on employer polygraphing requirements to override the companies' concerns over thefts and financial security. No doubt, also, these are the strongest considerations in congressional and state legislative pressures to hold preventive polygraphing by government agencies to situations of special conditions, such as psychological make-up of policemen or security for national intelligence operations. They have also led labor-union, civic, legislative, and judicial spokesmen to invoke the right to privacy of employees as workers in a free society as the central reason for banning polygraph screening.

The issue of consent takes on added importance in light of the fact —described earlier in this book—that techniques for testing galvanic skin response, breathing, pulse rate, eye-blink rate, and muscle tension *without* the knowledge and consent of the subject have been developed, have been used experimentally by government, and are used by some security agencies now in their screening operations. At the moment, the best scientific judgment is that such secret lie-detection methods, because they do not produce maximum stress in the subject, do not produce as "satisfactory" a set of measurements as a polygraphic test given with the knowledge of the subject. But as techniques under development primarily for testing the physical and emotional states of astronauts are carried over into the lie-detection field, measurements that can be administered secretly may come to be more effective. Here the factor of consent should provide a firm boundary line against corporate or government use of secret lie detection, and recent civic reaction to the coerced-consent situation suggests that American society will react in support of bans on such practices if they should develop.

Where the polygraph is to be used by government, there must be a fully elaborated set of rules and safeguards to protect the rights of individuals to privacy and due process. The Department of Defense rules of July, 1965, are an excellent foundation for such a program. These should be adopted as requirements for all federal agencies using the polygraph and for state government as well. What needs to be added, however, is some means of review, besides the user agency, by which an outside authority can pass upon the relevance of the questions, their proper scope in terms of the constitutional right to privacy of belief, and whether the elements of due process were satisfied in a particular polygraph interrogation. Such a review board might be set up as an inter-agency body within the executive branch. An independent, "ombudsman"-type executive office would be best to pass on questions of improper use in particular instances. And as experience develops and standards evolve, it is also desirable that judicial review be provided as an ultimate check on executive action and a guarantee of citizen rights.

CHAPTER TEN

Prove That You're Adjusted

FROM ITS EARLIEST years, personality testing generated sharp controversy within scientific and university circles.[1] Many psychologists challenged the basic premise of tests that depended on the self-inventory of testees, and that probed for such concepts as "interest," "values," "attitudes," "balance," and "ideology." In addition, the tests were used for purposes such as industrial and government personnel work that were fundamentally different from the educational-vocational guidance work for which "objective" tests were developed, or the diagnosis of mental illness for which "projective" tests were designed. The literature of psychology and proceedings of professional meetings in this period abound in criticisms of overenthusiastic test designers. Reports were published of experimental studies which challenged the reliability and validity claims of the leading personality tests. In addition, personality testing was a favorite target of those critics from medicine and natural science who disputed the fundamental principles and methodology of psychology as a whole, and who insisted that psychology should be understood as a social study into human behavior (like the disciplines of government, history, and economics) rather than as a true "science." On the other hand, there were many psychologists in the universities and in the field who championed personality testing, defended specific tests, published validity studies, and argued that tests, used carefully as one key indicator, represented a scientific instrument of great personnel value.

Criticism within scientific and academic circles did not impede the steady growth of personality testing in industry, the schools, and government. Occasional articles in the business and religious press between 1945 and 1955 described the use of testing in these areas, sometimes expressing concern over the ability of personality testers to fulfill their promises.[2] None of these discussions raised the issues of privacy or personal liberty, however, nor did the commentaries probe deeply into the nature of the tests and the qualifications of the testers.

General public protests against personality testing came in this decade almost entirely from the political extreme right, whose basic concern was with the use of personality testing in the public schools. Personality-test inquiries into the "personal lives of the pupils" and their family life at home were seen by this group as attempts by a left-wing school establishment to brain-wash American children and to force them into the gospel of liberal "life adjustment." Furthermore, as a pamphlet issued by one right-wing group complained in 1954, personality tests created in the children a "willingness to tattle on their parents," and allowed the school to "undermine parental and religious influence." [3]

Partly because of such attacks from the right, American liberal groups in the 1945–54 period defended personality testing as an "objective" and "unbiased" tool for evaluation of school children. [4] As a personnel-selection method in industry and government, it seemed a desirable alternative to informal choices by class, family, race, religion, political affiliation, "manners," elite educational background, or cultural "veneer." Use of tests to screen out sadists and neurotics from police forces also drew strong liberal praise. The basic idea of psychological evaluation had a humane and "therapeutic" appeal to liberals, as a method for getting a person into the educational level, career, or particular job assignment that best suited his "psychological nature," and avoiding the severe personal stress caused by "mislocation." In addition, personality tests that revealed deep distress could often be the basis for suggestions that the tested individual should seek professional help, thus tying into liberally supported ideas of preventive "mental health" inventories. The fact that personality tests rested on the twin pillars of psychology and psychiatry accounted for much instinctive support from liberal groups, which identified strongly with these professions. A final factor was that defense of personality testing in schools, the military, and government was frequently a defense of "liberalism's own," since the fields of guidance counseling, government personnel work, mental health, and applied psychology were heavily stocked with liberals.

At one point some liberal questions were raised about personality testing in these years—over the possibility that questions on religion in leading personality tests might be used by employers as measures of discrimination. For example one state's fair-employment-practices commission asked the Psychological Corporation to delete questions on religion from the Minnesota Multiphasic Personality Inventory. [5]

The First Wave of Public Debate, 1954–1963

For the most part, however, personality testing did not become even a minor civic issue in the United States before the mid-1950's. The first thrust against such testing to stir significant public attention was the publication in 1954 of an article on personality testing by William H.

Whyte, Jr., in *Fortune*. This was expanded in 1956 into a section of Whyte's best-selling book *The Organization Man*, a protest against the trend in organizational life in America toward "(1) idolatry of the system and (2) the misuse of science to achieve this." [6] Whyte documented the spread of personality testing in industry with a 1952 *Fortune* survey which indicated that one third of American companies were using such tests to select, promote, or fire some of their employees. Another survey in 1954 showed that 60 per cent of sixty-three firms polled had adopted personality testing.

Whyte's basic complaint against personality tests was that "the organization" was using them to gauge "normality" in individuals and to select "well-adjusted" employees. The reason companies were refusing to rely on intelligence and aptitude tests, life records, and job interviews was that "it is the whole man The Organization wants and not just a part of him. Is the man well adjusted? Will he remain well adjusted? A test of potential merit could not tell this; needed was a test of potential loyalty." [7] To document his case, Whyte published—for the first time to a wide audience—a full sample of the personal questions and "approved answers" from leading personality tests.

In terms of scientific accuracy, Whyte was convinced that personality tests attempted to rate "the immeasurable," since they tried "to convert abstract traits into a concrete measure that can be placed on a linear scale." [8] The subjective attitudes of the tester were more often the basis for evaluation of the key questions than the "answers" of the candidate. The questions themselves, far from being "clear" and "neutral," were highly ambiguous, Whyte contended, loaded with arguable assumptions about desirable ideology, interests, cultural outlook, sociability, degree of aggressiveness, sex life, and even humor. The "mathematical proofs" of validity, Whyte suggested, were "purely internal," comparing the results of one test with another or of one tested group with another group taking the same test. The only scientific proof would be verification analysis based on the subsequent behavior of the persons tested, and such studies had *not* been done in industry.[9] Finally, Whyte noted that personality tests depend on recognizing the necessary qualities for general executive ability or specific job assignments, yet neither companies nor testers really knew what personality traits produce success in these posts.

Having made these points against the scientific validity of personality tests, Whyte turned to what he called the "moral" issue. Even if it were assumed that these tests could "reveal the innermost self," that would only make the question of their use "even more pressing. . . . Is the individual's innermost self any business of the organization's? . . . How much more must a man testify against himself? The Bill of Rights should not stop at organization's edge. In return for the salary that The Organization gives the individual, it can ask for superlative work from him but it should not ask for his psyche as well." [10]

With this perspective, Whyte offered two suggestions. First, organizations should give up personality testing as a flawed and harmful system and return to classic methods of selection and evaluation; and, second, the individual tested should simply "withhold his psyche" and "cheat," following a semi-serious "pony" that Whyte put at the end of his volume. Whyte's book—one of the most widely read works of non-fiction in the 1950's—received praise in several liberal journals. Some saw it as proof that business was using psychologists for reactionary and conformist ends; others, in keeping with the perspective of *Fortune*, read it as a warning to businessmen to be more "hard-headed" about their personnel-selection processes. Yet Whyte's critique had little effect on the spread of personality testing in industry; all surveys show such testing to have increased in the late 1950's and early 1960's. And since Whyte had not discussed personality testing in schools or by government and the military, his book did not set off significant public discussion of personality testing in these areas.

However, between 1956 and 1962 discussion of industrial personality testing and privacy increased notably. Dr. Jay L. Otis, formerly president of the Division of Consulting Psychology of the American Psychological Association, warned that business firms were "often" purchasing psychological testing for "espionage" purposes, and that testers were really employed as "company spies." [11] Persons sent to the psychologist by an employer were subjected to a probing, projective test without being told the object of the investigation; the private disclosures were thereupon interpreted for the employer's interest, rather than for that of the job applicant. The issue whether such "psychological espionage" is consistent with the ethical and professional obligations of psychologists was ignored in the enthusiasm for personality testing in industry, Otis felt.

An article in *Personnel* in 1961 listed as a complaint against the usual personality tests the charge that they "pry unforgivably into matters that are none of management's business or anybody else's." But, the article concluded, this "abuse of privacy" came primarily from "the unscrupulousness or naïveté" of the testers, not from anything inherent in testing itself.[12] Other business articles discussed the privacy issue, but found a satisfactory answer in calls for proper handling of the test results. One survey conducted by *Industrial Relations News* in 1960 and reprinted in *Management Review* cited a memorandum issued by the medical division of the Caterpillar Tractor Company, stating that psychological information "is confidential and should be treated as such"; furthermore, it would be interpreted only by "qualified, trained persons who know what should be said and what is better left unsaid to the individual." [13]

An example from the liberal press was an article in the Catholic magazine *Commonweal* in 1960, by Professor John P. Sisk of Gonzaga University. Sisk noted that the individual under testing is torn between a feeling of approval for testing—for the "confessional thrill," the competitive trial, the evaluation by "experts," and the "initiation ritual" into the organizational club—and a feeling of deep resentment over the test's intrusion into his personal privacy. "We resent them not only because we feel that they invade our privacy but because [the organization and the testers] so blandly assume that we don't mind. For most of us believe, with Pope Pius XII, that 'the content of the psyche is the exclusive property of the person himself.' " [14]

These liberal concerns with industrial personality testing were sometimes buttressed by labor-union activity against reliance on test results for selection and dismissal purposes. One pilots' union forced a national airline to stop using psychological interviews for prospective pilots, and another airline was faced by a strike threat when the pilots' union learned that personality-test results were used as the basis for firing employees. [15]

At that juncture some right-wing publications began to criticize personality testing by American businessmen. In the *American Mercury* an article titled "Pseudo Psychos" attacked industrial personality tests as "a peculiarly American concept of brain-washing," through which the "spychology" profession and employers who feared individuality had joined to create a system designed to select only the "properly docile 'company man.'"

> The country is acrawl with professional crystal gazers glad to take any employer's money to compile and "grade" such tests. And each, with a sneer for his competitors, insists that *his* is the sharpest skinning knife for peeling back the psyche of the skewered victim, layer by layer, to "prove" just how unqualified the poor human guinea pig is to shuffle papers or pound a typewriter in your office . . . sell your goods or manage your office . . . or to be promoted to vice president or elevated to a new directorship. [16]

In addition, right-wing campaigns against school personality testing increased in the mid-1950's. An article in the *American Mercury* attacked "brainpicking" tests, "mental undressing of children," and "school-instigated sleuthing" into the child's personal, sexual, and family affairs. [17] In "The Fight for Your Child's Mind" the author noted that the "right to privacy" in American law limited physical searches, forbade compulsion in most government health surveys, and required parental consent before medical or psychiatric exams could be given children in the schools. It was time that such privacy protections of voluntariness and parental consent were added by law in the area of personality testing as well, the article concluded.[18] In all these critical articles it was assumed that the real purpose of school personality testing was not to help the child learn or perform better in school, but to indoctrinate pupils with "left-wing, one-world, UNESCO ideas" and to "undermine parental influence and religious values" among the children.

Right-Wing Pressures on School Testing

Alerted to the problem by these warning articles, parents and right-wing groups in many local communities between 1958 and 1962 began to protest the use of personality tests in the schools. A campaign in Baltimore, Maryland, during 1958 against "invasion of privacy" by "Talent Tests" led to cancellation of the test program by the Baltimore school authorities.[19] In Ogilvie, Minnesota, parents protested against the use of a highly Freudian projective test of sexual adjustment, named the "Blacky" test, in schools for handicapped children; they drew support from a national Catholic magazine and won their battle when the State Board of Education announced it would not administer any tests other than intelligence tests to handicapped children without securing prior parental consent.[20] At the national level, Senator Barry Goldwater (R., Ariz.) offered an amendment in 1958 to the National Defense Education Bill to forbid the use of federal funds for "personality check lists, problem check lists, psychological aptitude tests," and similar tests that ask deeply probing personal questions.[21] Senator Goldwater's effort was praised in some conservative Catholic and right-wing circles,[22] but his amendment was rejected by the Senate. During 1959 the Daughters of the American Revolution adopted a resolution opposing personality testing as an invasion of privacy,[23] and local right-wing campaigns against such school testing were waged in East Paterson, New Jersey; San Diego, California; and Houston, Texas.[24] In the Houston case, a five-to-one vote of the Houston school board ordered that 5,000 answer sheets to a series of personality tests given to ninth-grade students in the Houston schools be burned, and future use of such tests was forbidden.

Similar episodes took place during 1960–61 in Kent, Washington, and Artesia, New Mexico, where school authorities were forced by public objections to drop their psychological-testing program.[25] The New York *Daily News* ran a series of articles on "Snoopers in Our Schools" in June, 1961,[26] and *Information: The Catholic Church in American Life*, published by the Paulist Fathers, featured an article in its November, 1961, issue titled, "Have Personality Testers Gone Too Far?" The answer was "yes." [27]

In several states during 1960–61, including New York and New

Mexico, conservative political groups supported bills in the state legislatures to forbid personality testing in the public schools or to require prior
parental consent, but these were opposed by state educational associations and were usually smothered in committee.[28] Similarly, Senator
Goldwater's attempt in 1961 to have Congress forbid federal funds for
personality testing was also defeated.[29]

Given the right-wing nature of these protests between 1956 and
1962 and their wholesale assault on school administrations, it was natural
that the reaction of educational groups, teachers' associations, psychologists' organizations, and most liberal supporters of the public schools was
to view them as radical-right attacks on modern education. An article in
American Psychologist on the burning of test results in Houston called
for better public relations by psychologists as the basic answer.

> When the student of behavior works in a xenophobic and indi-
> vidualistic community, he cannot assume that his scientifically
> honorable intentions will be considered morally justifiable by
> those whom he seeks to help. Even though the scientist says, in
> effect, "I am studying you, and asking you these questions, for
> your own good," his subject may respond, "It is part of my
> 'good' that you desist from your intrusion of my privacy." [30]

In October, 1962, a sharp attack on personality testing by the jour-
nalist Martin L. Gross swept onto the best-seller lists.[31] *The Brain
Watchers* was a perfect specimen of the angry, social muckrake in the
Vance Packard–John Keats genre. Its central theme was that personality
testers were violating the individual privacy of "10,000,000 Americans"
employed in business, "from factory worker to senior vice president," as
well as "countless millions" of servicemen, school children, professionals,
and government employees. "[W]e have seemingly relinquished our
constitutional rights of protection against search and seizure when it applies to our minds instead of our properties," Gross complained.
"Apparently there is something more sacrosanct in the inviolability of
our split-level castles than in the private nobility of our brains." [32]

Far more than Whyte in *The Organization Man*, Gross quoted
from the works in which academic psychologists themselves attacked the
scientific claims of personality testing, though Gross usually added his
own free-swinging comments to the more measured scholarly quotations.

Why were millions of Americans willing to confess their most private thoughts, beliefs, and activities, not only in written tests but in
"depth-interviews" as well? Gross commented:

> The employee has already been conditioned by our culture to
> regard excessive personal privacy as somewhat Victorian. Con-

fessional articles [and] books; market motivational research which probes into his eating, buying, sex, and fantasy habits; public opinion polls; school guidance counselors; and credit checks have made the employee almost aggressively voluble about himself without too much prodding from the tester.[33]

Gross called for a total ban on personality testing, to consign it to the historical waste heap like "medieval bloodletting." This halt might take the form of laws against the illegal practice of medicine; administrative controls such as Fair Employment Practices Laws; new legislation forbidding this practice in schools; or strong professional action by psychologists.[34]

If the fight were not won now, Gross warned, even worse prospects loomed ahead.

[I]t should not be difficult for us to visualize a Central Personality Bureau of the near future, which will electronically store in each metropolitan area the personality and character traits of every resident. Like credit bureaus today, the record will be available to all interested parties—a man's employer or potential employer, his landlord, the state, his creditors, the criminal and civil courts, and perhaps his prospective bride, or her father —at a nominal fee ($10 or less). There might also be an opportunity every half-decade for an individual to "up psyche" himself by taking the Bureau's newest battery of tests and perhaps register the improvement that time—and the careful consideration of what society expects of him—has made in his personality.[35]

Reviews of *The Brain Watchers* in newspapers throughout the country treated privacy as the book's most important message. "Big Brother Knows What You Think" was the heading of the Washington *Star* review. Testing is a "massive assault on individual privacy," noted the Tampa *Tribune*, and the Louisville *Courier-Journal* considered it an "inexcusable invasion of the psychic privacy." [36]

The Brain Watchers also received a warm reception from both liberal and "hard conservative" circles. Gross's chapter on "The Search for the Square American"—describing the industrial tester's screening out of liberals, Democrats, persons who play tennis, like music, or enjoy reading—was reprinted in the liberal *New Republic*.[37] The book was praised by reviewers in such liberal journals as the *Saturday Review*, *The New York Times*, and the Louisville *Courier-Journal*, and in such highly conservative journals as the *National Review*, the Columbus (Ohio) *Dispatch*, the Arizona *Republic*, and the New Haven *Register*, and by the Reverend Daniel Poling, editor of the fundamentalist *Christian Herald.*[38]

But it was still only the "hard-right" groups that attempted to organize a political and legislative response before 1964. The DAR, which had condemned personality testing steadily since 1959, called in 1963 for firmer local action to check the increased use of "these obnoxious tests" and linked the problem to new technology. Their concern was that "the information garnered by these tests is stored in files or on electronic tape where it remains a threat of possible later misuse as blackmail by unscrupulous persons." [39]

Picking up this theme in 1962–63, four Congressmen introduced bills that would have forbidden the use of funds awarded by the Department of Health, Education and Welfare to support examinations in elementary or secondary schools on the "student's personality, environment, home life, parental or family relationships, economic status, religious beliefs, patriotism, sexual behavior, or attitudes, or sociological or psychological problems," unless all questions were previously disclosed to the parents and they gave permission for the tests.[40] Of the four Congressmen leading the campaign for this legislation in 1962–64, one was an announced Birch Society member and the other three were strong right-wing figures. The most vocal of this group was Representative John Ashbrook of Ohio, whose speeches gave the following samples of statements from leading school personality tests on which students were supposed to give their feelings: "My father is a tyrant. . . . I feel there's a barrier between me and my parents. . . . I'm ashamed of my parents' dress and manners. . . . I wonder if I am normal in my sexual development. . . . I want to know about venereal disease. . . . I think about sex a good deal of the time. . . . I'm bothered by thoughts of heaven and hell. . . . Is there a conflict between the Bible and my school subjects? . . . Is it wrong to deny the existence of God?"

Such questions "literally undress young people and interfere in private areas which would better be left alone." Still other questions, Ashbrook felt, forced students to make "difficult and impossible" choices on matters of values that were private and none of the school's business. For example, one test used in a school had asked: "Which is worse: (1) denying the existence of God; (2) laughing while the Star Spangled Banner is being played? Which of the following men contributed more to the progress of mankind: (1) St. Paul (in the Bible); (2) Abraham Lincoln?" [41]

Ashbrook was sure that the momentum behind such testing came from "Freudians," "World Federalists," "progressive educators," "the UNESCO crowd," and "socialists," all of whom saw personality tests as a way to indoctrinate youth "down the path to collectivism and internationalism whereby they gradually lose their loyalty to home and nation." [42]

Significantly, no liberal Congressmen advocated federal action against industrial testing, or provided liberally oriented legislative proposals on school testing to parallel Congressman Ashbrook's crusade against "Collectivist brain-picking." Similarly, state campaigns remained in the hands of right-wing conservatives and focused exclusively on the schools; no liberal legislators sought state legislation to bar employer personality testing, as liberal-labor groups had done to outlaw industrial lie detecting. Right-wingers campaigned against school personality testing in 1962 and 1963 in Hicksville, Long Island (where a candidate won election to the school board on a campaign to eliminate the "Blacky" test and "other brain-picking probes" from the schools); in Seattle and Tacoma, Washington; Waterford, Connecticut; Abilene, Texas; Boulder, Colorado; and Montgomery, Virginia, to name only some representative cases. [43]

The Debate Widens

The most significant development of 1962–63 was the debate about privacy and personality testing that arose in the business community and among professional educators. (There was little comment from government spokesmen because so little was published on government use of personality testing before 1965.) In the business community, some management spokesmen welcomed the new attack on personality testing with open arms, since it only confirmed earlier doubts expressed by these writers. In *Advertising Age*, columnist E. B. Weiss (a vice-president of Doyle, Dane, Bernbach, Inc.) devoted five columns to total attacks on personality testing. [44]

A more widespread position in business publications was agreement with the criticism of personality testing on the privacy ground but attribution of current excesses to such factors as the abuses of free-lance testers, the retention of ill-conceived and outmoded tests, and the failure of some well-intentioned testers to perceive the ethical issues involved.

Dr. Saul Gellerman, manager of personnel research at IBM World Trade Corporation, formerly head of the psychological staff of a testing firm, praised the recent criticism of testing as serving a useful purpose, but warned that some of the critics "are advocating not reform but abolition." Such a move was neither necessary nor wise, he felt, since there was "no suitable alternative" to tests properly conceived and properly administered. [45] Dr. Richard S. Barrett, Associate Professor of Psychology and Management Engineering at New York University, advising management how to avoid abuses of testing, listed invasion of privacy as one of the basic charges made against personality testing. He responded to the charge as follows:

The tendency to probe into the applicant's personal life stems from the diagnostic therapeutic tradition of many psychologists. A person who comes to a clinic or to a therapist for help in resolving his problems with his wife and mother, or to find relief from indigestion attacks (for which his internist can find no assignable cause), expects to talk about his most personal thoughts. In fact, he wants to, because they may hold the key to his problems; but I believe that the job applicant has the right to keep his troubles to himself without penalty. Executives, by asking that reports be confined to job-relevant issues, can help to safeguard the applicant's privacy.[46]

A third position voiced in the business press in great proliferation was a full defense of personality testing against its critics.[47] A *Management Record* article noted: "It is absurd to condemn all testing because ludicrous items have been found in certain personality inventories, particularly those published twenty or more years ago." However, the *Record* article went on to warn against "test packages bought 'off the shelf,'" to note that measurement of "motivation" is really "not possible today" in the present state of the art, and that "tests designed by clinical psychologists for use in hospitals or tests designed by experimental psychologists for use in laboratories seldom have application to business situations." [48]

Reaction and debates within the educational community followed two basic lines. Faced in local communities and state educational departments with the type of attack that originated with traditionally "anti-collectivist" school critics, school and educational associations often defended the tests being used and tried to explain the "highly limited" and "careful" uses to which the test results were put. They also faced a fight in Congress in 1963, when Senator Barry Goldwater was successful in persuading the Senate Labor and Public Welfare Committee to adopt an amendment to the National Defense Education Act (NDEA) stating that no personality testing could be undertaken under testing, guidance, and counseling programs financed for seventh- and eighth-grade students.[49] The amendment was passed by the Senate with the wording: "[N]o such program shall provide for the conduct of any test, or the asking of any question in connection therewith, which is designed to elicit information dealing with the personality, environment, home life, parental or family relationships, economic status, or sociological and psychological problems of the pupil tested."

Caught off guard by the Senate passage of the anti-personality testing amendment, educational groups, the American Psychological Association, and its state affiliates[50] appealed to liberal Congressmen and the Kennedy Administration to defeat the Senate Amendment in the conference committee. (No amendment had been passed in the House version of the 1963 NDEA bill.) Dr. Arthur Brayfield, executive officer of the APA, sent telegrams to Congressional leaders noting that "relevant questions concerning invasion of privacy, denial of freedom, and compulsion" were involved, as well as issues of "educational progress and achievement" and "freedom of scientific inquiry," [51] but the summary treatment given these issues by the Senate Amendment did not give Congress the proper opportunity to explore these issues. Dr. Brayfield called for withdrawal of the amendment and direct action on the issues by Congress under "systematic and informed analysis."

In a statement issued November 4, 1963, Commissioner of Education Francis Keppel noted that HEW regulations dating from 1961 already prevented federal funds from being used for testing or guidance that employed personality, adjustment, or projective tests.[52] These regulations, covering the first- to sixth-grade testing and guidance programs, would apply automatically to the seventh- and eighth-grade testing programs being added, and in light of these facts, Commissioner Keppel persuaded the Congressional leaders to delete the Goldwater Amendment.[53]

The second response among educators was to re-examine their own position on personality tests. At its annual meeting in 1963, attended by 700 college and school leaders, the College Entrance Examination Board warned its members that the risks involved in personality testing were too great to warrant their use in college admissions at this time, as some admissions personnel had been suggesting.[54]

A similarly negative position was adopted in a book sponsored by the World Federation for Mental Health in 1963, *The Selection of Personnel for International Service*,[55] designed as a guiding manual for governmental, religious, and private agencies operating in the international arena. The chapter on psychological testing, written by an American psychologist and including comments from two British specialists, concluded that tests of intellect, motor coordination, and related areas were well worthwhile, but that tests of general personality, either of the self-reporting or of the clinical variety, were unreliable and unpredictive and should not be used at present.

Specialized publications in the educational field showed much of the same diversity that had marked the business press. Articles written by non-psychologists or non-guidance counselors tended to endorse the fears that tests were invading the privacy of school children improperly.[56] Dr. Leo Goldman, Associate Professor of Education at Brooklyn College, warned that professionals had better "get to work and clean house," one cleaning-up aspect being to reconsider the privacy-invading qualities of personality tests.

> Most troubling of all is the question as to whether it is ethical for psychologists to consider the employer (or school) their client, and the individual applicant or employee or student as merely a subject, from whom they pump as much as possible of what the employer wants to know and in whom they seek whatever qualities the employer deems desirable. . . .
>
> . . . They compel us to ask whether some current practices are indeed an unconscionable invasion of personal privacy and a curtailment of the right to a job without regard to one's political or religious beliefs or his family squabbles. Perhaps in our role as testers we don't see things quite the way we would if these were our own children or friends being tested by people who were strangers to us, and about whose qualifications we had some reasonable doubt.[57]

Though some educators protested on privacy grounds, many school guidance counselors and testing-service officials defended existing personality tests and did not view the privacy issue as a legitimate concern.[58]

Among psychologists, some university scholars denounced the use of personality testing in personnel selection as "psychological espionage" and a thoroughly improper intrusion into personal affairs.[59] Indeed, it was a professor of psychology at Yale, John Dollard, who had welcomed Martin Gross's book in a *New York Times* review despite what Dollard called the "invective and slanted judgments" that marred it.[60]

The problem of privacy had further been discussed as an "ethical issue" in personality testing by the author of the leading textbook in the field, Dr. Lee J. Cronbach. In the 1961 edition of his text, Cronbach noted that any personality test "is an invasion of privacy for the subject who does not wish to reveal himself to the psychologist. . . ."

> Every man has two personalities: the role he plays in his social interactions and his "true self." In a culture where open expression of emotion is discouraged and a taboo is placed on aggressive feelings, for example, there is certain to be some discrepancy between these two personalities.
>
> The personality test obtains its most significant information by probing deeply into feelings and attitudes which the individual normally conceals. One test purports to test whether an adolescent boy resents authority. Another tries to determine whether a mother really loves her child. A third has a score indicating the strength of sexual needs. These, and virtually all measures of personality, seek information on areas which the

subject has every reason to regard as private, in normal social intercourse.[61]

Cronbach felt that the psychologist "is not 'invading privacy' where he is freely admitted and where he has a genuine need for the information obtained," as in clinical and counseling situations. However, the use of personality tests by employers for purposes such as detecting union supporters was ethically "unthinkable," since it was a means of punishing "unuttered thoughts." When attitudes are measured in this way for institutional testing purposes, tests become "a force toward conformity and standardization." [62]

At the organizational level, the American Psychological Association had tried to cope with the ethical aspects of personality testing in several pronouncements during the 1950's and early 1960's. Though most of their guiding comments dealt with other issues (qualifications of testers, the duty to avoid making sensational claims, and the like), some APA statements did touch on privacy. Principle 6 of the APA ethical code for psychologists cautions that "every effort should be made to avoid undue invasion of privacy" when obtaining information "concerning children, students, employees and others. . . ." Principle 7, on client welfare, advised the psychologist working in industry and education that individuals should be asked to "reveal personal information in the course of interviewing, testing, or evaluation" only after "making certain that the responsible person is fully aware of the purposes of the interview, testing or evaluation and of the ways in which the information may be used." [63]

The APA did not attempt to deal with the issue of personality testing's ethical basis per se in personnel selection, nor did it define what might constitute "undue" invasion of privacy in questioning. Thus, despite concern by many top APA leaders, the APA did not exercise a controlling or even considerable restraining influence on the use of testing for personnel processing.

To sum up the debate over personality testing between 1945 and 1963:

1. Between 1945 and the early 1960's personality tests were used more and more widely each year in industrial personnel testing, special screening (as with religious candidates), and in public-school test programs. Yet, how widely tests were used in these areas, at what levels, and under what conditions were not systematically studied or disclosed, nor had the personality testing being adopted increasingly by government agencies in this period.

2. There had been no significant protest in this period from the hundreds of thousands of individuals called upon annually to take the tests. Though critics of these tests always told a story or two about themselves or "a friend" who had complained or refused to be tested, it was

clear that there had been no large-scale revolt in the populace, on privacy grounds or any other. Furthermore, up until 1963 little attention had been given to this issue by Constitution-minded civic groups. Interest-group protest was limited to the extreme right, and its constant linkage of the privacy issue in public-school testing with fearful denunciations of "communist brain-washing" by "Reducators" was guaranteed to alienate moderate and liberal opinion.

3. Finally, there were no public-agency inquiries into personality testing in these years—no legislative hearings, no court proceedings, and no administrative-agency investigations. At the same time, despite the genuine concern of its leadership over "abuses" of personality testing, the organized psychological profession had not exercised significant controls over "misuse." More important, the profession's leadership had never really accepted the legitimacy of criticism of properly administered tests on the invasion-of-privacy ground.

A New Turn in the Debates, 1964–67

At one level, civic debates in 1964 continued much as they had during the previous decade.[64] Yet something happened in 1964–65 that shifted the direction of public debate over personality testing and privacy. Beginning in 1964, liberal forces in the United States took up the issue of personality testing and privacy and began to support efforts at adopting political, legal, and administrative controls over its intrusive aspects. At the same time the focus of public debate was shifted from its usual targets of industrial and public-school testing to personality testing by the federal government. The real "Big Brother" context had arrived.

It was during the early 1960's that several federal agencies turned to personality testing for personnel administration. Agencies such as the Departments of State and Defense used personality tests to screen individuals for "special stress" assignments and as part of "fitness-to-serve" medical examinations when an emotional problem seemed present to the examining physician. Several new federal agencies, especially those with social-welfare and educational characteristics, such as the Job Corps, the Peace Corps, and the Youth Opportunity Program (administered by the Department of Labor), turned to personality testing as the "objective," "scientific," and, indeed, the "liberal" way to gauge personnel.

Not every federal employee responded to these new testing procedures happily, however, and complaints from federal employees were made in 1963 and 1964 to the American Civil Liberties Union, labor unions, and members of Congress.[65] The American Federation of Government Employees stated that employee complaints to the Union over federal personality testing rose from none in 1963 to fifteen in 1965.[66] Both the Senate Subcommittee on Constitutional Rights (the Ervin Committee) and the House Special Subcommittee on Invasion of Privacy (the Gallagher Committee) were also appealed to by federal employees who were upset by their experiences with federal tests inquiring into their sexual feelings, religious ideas, and socio-political beliefs.[67] It was crucially significant that these complaints came just as the American public and its civic leaders were learning of the new technology of electronic eavesdropping and polygraphing and were beginning to re-assess the question of privacy. With popular articles and books such as Vance Packard's *The Naked Society* pointing out the connection, the press and civic leaders began to look more coldly at the testing of personality and the government's collection of personal data about individuals, and to ask whether this was not one more area in which the erosion of rights of privacy needed to be checked. As news of personality questionnaires by federal agencies filtered out of Washington, the first liberal reaction began. In September, 1964, for example, Russell Baker's "Observer" column in *The New York Times* described government personality testing and speculated, sardonically, that "the big brain invasion" was a sign of the coming society in which individual deviations eventually would be efficiently identified by trained psychologists while deviates were still "mere toddlers gumming their pablum." "The trouble with psychology," Baker concluded, "is that it doesn't care that reducing people to subjects is bad for people." [68]

By December, 1964, several articles in liberal magazines had protested against federal government use of personality tests.[69] An Illinois Fair Employment Practices Commission examiner who investigated a Motorola company "ability" test ruled in 1961 that the test had the effect of discriminating against a Negro applicant and constituted an improper personnel action.[70] Several incidents during 1965 demonstrated the rise of new liberal and labor campaigns against government testing. In San Antonio the local American Civil Liberties Union chapter conducted an investigation of forced "medical" resignations of employees at Kelly Air Force Base "after the administration of a few pencil-and-paper psychological tests." The cases were said to involve employees who had been in some conflict with supervisors, and the ACLU stated that the test findings conflicted with more thorough exams by off-base psychiatrists. The ACLU announced that it would take the discharges to court, noting that the employees had been "intimidated into submitting to examinations that are clearly invasions of their privacy without being provided with adequate advice as to their rights and protections under the law." [71] The International Brotherhood of Electrical Workers assigned a staff member to look into personality testing by industry, after several employees with seniority rights had been rejected for promotions on the basis of psychological-test results and after this action had been upheld in arbitration awards.[72]

The new protest over federal-agency use of personality testing was not restricted to liberal publications. In January, 1965, an autobiographical article titled "Adventures of a Test Taker" appeared in the *National Review*. It related the experiences of a woman who had refused, on privacy grounds, to answer the "complete-a-sentence" questions asked her by an unnamed major federal agency about such things as her sex life, her religion, and her parents' private lives. Though the woman was found by the personnel department to be excellent material for the job and she had already begun working, the medical department of the agency considered her refusal to answer all the questions as a psychological danger sign and ordered her to take a two-day battery of additional tests, ranging from the Minnesota Multiphasic to the draw-a-figure test and the Rorschach ink-blot test. She then was interviewed by three doctors, who assured her that the testing was all for her own good, and asked further questions about whether, being a Catholic, she saw visions or heard voices and how she handled her sex drives. When she maintained that the tests were invalid instruments, gave "phony results," and invaded her privacy (she had taken psychology courses in college and had read Gross's book), the head of the medical department, a psychiatrist, told her that the department would not let her "get away with this." The woman was dismissed from the agency on orders of the medical department, and in the course of being checked out, she was told of numerous other instances in which persons found to be wholly satisfactory by the personnel officers had been forced to leave by the medical division. The author concluded that the personality testers were tightening their hold over this agency and were pursuing a policy of forced self-invasions of privacy that posed a serious threat to the citizen and the nation:

> The basic question, of course, is whether, under any circumstances, any employer has the right to the intimate details of his employees' personal lives. There is a certain point beyond which we may not go in violating the privacy of an individual, even if we say we are protecting our security or increasing our efficiency. . . . We accept testing as voluntary. Yet even psychiatrists admit that the questions asked on psychological questionnaires are cleverly designed to trap the subject into revealing subconscious attitudes and reactions of which he himself may not be aware. Is this so different from the use of truth serum? Is it not the right to privacy and indeed, personality, which is really at stake? [73]

Congress Enters the Fray, 1964

In 1964, a series of employee complaints began to reach the Subcommittee on Constitutional Rights of the Senate Judiciary Committee, under the chairmanship of Senator Sam Ervin of North Carolina, which had as one of its major areas of concentration the constitutional rights of federal employees. On the basis of the complaints the Ervin Subcommittee initiated a survey of federal agencies to see where personality tests were being used and the nature of the questioning. In October and December, 1964, the Subcommittee began giving the press samples of the personal questions, experiences of employees who had reacted against the tests, and testing practices of agencies such as State and Labor.[74]

A second Congressional body entered the field in early 1965—the Special Subcommittee on Invasion of Privacy, of the House Committee on Government Operations, under the chairmanship of Representative Cornelius Gallagher of New Jersey. Representative Gallagher delivered a series of speeches in the House denouncing personality tests as "a gross invasion of privacy into the lives and thoughts of our public workers . . . an insidious and illegal search of the human mind." [75] "Mental wiretapping" must be seen "as part of a larger picture which includes lie detector tests, mail checks and seizures, peepholes, trash snooping, and electronic snooping," all practiced by the federal government, and all providing the potential for dictatorship "if evil men came to power." Gallagher called on the federal government to set the standard for private industry by eliminating personality tests and relying instead on educational and employment records, reference checks, employment interviews, and observation during a probationary work period.[76]

As a result of the complaints of employees and congressional critics, several federal agencies announced changes of their practices in early 1965. The Export-Import Bank issued an order on April 20 forbidding the continuation or future use of "psychological-personality tests" because they "include questions of an extremely personal nature bearing on sex, morality, parental relationships, and the like." On March 26 the State Department wrote the Ervin and Gallagher subcommittees that it would "discontinue" the practice of administering personality tests during "regular medical examinations" when this was thought useful by the medical officer. Instead, any employee found to be in need of psychiatric help would be allowed to obtain it from a doctor of his own choice, in a "personal relationship." [77]

During the spring of 1965 both the Ervin and Gallagher committees released sample questions from the personality tests used by federal agencies, to inform the press and the public just how "intrusive" these questions were. Some of the examples came from the Minnesota Multiphasic:

TRUE OR FALSE

I feel sure there is only one true religion.

My sex life is satisfactory.

During one period when I was a youngster I engaged in petty thievery.

I believe in the second coming of Christ.

I believe women ought to have as much sexual freedom as men.

I believe in a life hereafter.

Christ performed miracles.

Children should be taught all the main facts of sex.

There is very little love and companionship in my family as compared to other homes.

I loved my mother.

I dream frequently about things that are best kept to myself.

I believe there is a God.

Once in a while I laugh at a dirty joke.

There is something wrong with my sex organs.

Questions on other tests used by federal agencies asked the employee to indicate whether he was troubled by any of the following:

Deciding whether I'm really in love.

In love with someone of a different religion.

Wondering how far to go with the opposite sex.

Lacking in sex appeal.

Afraid of being found out.

Bothered by sexual thoughts or dreams.

Worried about the effects of masturbation.

Another test described by the Congressmen required federal employees to complete the following statements:

I feel ashamed when ————————————————.

God is ————————————————————.

I secretly ——————————————————.

My childhood ————————————————.

Love ——————————————————————.

I am ashamed ————————————————.

I love ————————————————————.

Still another test consisted of 225 pairs of statements, in which the employee was told to "choose the one that is most applicable to you." If he liked both, he still had to choose the one he "liked best"; if he liked neither, he had to choose the one he "liked least." Included in this test were such items as:

A. I feel depressed by my own inability to handle various situations.

B. I like to read books and plays in which sex plays a major part.

A. I feel like blaming others when things go wrong for me.

B. I feel I am inferior in most respects.

A. I like to listen to or tell jokes in which sex plays a major part.

B. I feel like getting revenge when someone has insulted me.

It was against the backdrop of these disclosures that the Ervin and Gallagher subcommittees both held hearings during June, 1965, into federal use of personality testing. The testimony they obtained from spokesmen for the Civil Service Commission, the Departments of State, Defense, Labor, and Health, Education and Welfare, the Peace Corps and Job Corps, the Export-Import Bank, and the Bonneville Power Authority, provided the public with its first general picture of the development and extent of federal personality testing.

The only spirited defenses of existing personality-testing programs came from spokesmen for two federal agencies, the Bonneville Power Authority (under the Department of the Interior) and the Peace Corps. Their defenses, and the reactions of the Congressmen, provide an excellent joining of issues on the privacy question in personality testing.

Personality testing at Bonneville was initiated in 1963 by Charles Luce, a lawyer and administrator of the Authority appointed by President Kennedy.[78] Luce stated that he first thought of using tests when he talked to private utility companies and learned how valuable they considered such testing; as an Episcopal vestryman, he also had experience with the personality testing recommended by the Episcopal Church for selection of religious candidates. Luce noted that his was not a mass screening program—105 persons were tested in two years—but was intended only for certain types of important officials. To protect the employee's right to privacy, Luce said, he had decided to use outside firms of psychologists to administer the tests. Thus no person at Bonneville other than the employee himself saw the test answers. The outside psychological firm evaluated the test results and sent Bonneville a report which was locked in the Deputy's safe after it had been read by the Administrator and Deputy Administrator. It did not become part of the employee's personnel file, and Luce stated that he would not turn it over to any federal investigator without an opinion from the Attorney General. When the Civil Service Commission issued its new order on personality testing, Luce directed that the tests be suspended, but he told the Congressmen that he planned to ask the Interior Department to submit the Bonneville testing program to the CSC for study and approval to continue. Luce said he had found the personality-test evaluations very valuable and thought they ought to be continued, though he was sure the Authority would not collapse if they were eliminated.

Luce was subjected to sharp questioning by Congressmen Gallagher, Reuss, Rosenthal, and Horton, and members of the Gallagher Committee staff. First, questions from tests used by the Bonneville consultant firms were read into the record:

"Taking the Bible as a whole, one should regard it from the point of view of its beautiful mythology and literary style, rather than as a spiritual revelation." True or false.

"Which of the following men do you think should be judged as contributing more to the progress of mankind, (a) Aristotle, (b) Abraham Lincoln?"

Choose the best of two answers:
A. I like to become sexually excited.
B. I like to accept the leadership of people I admire.

A. I like to kiss attractive persons of the opposite sex.
B. I like to experiment and to try new things.

Luce was further asked whether he did not think such questions were invasions of the employee's constitutional right to privacy. He emphatically said "No." Whether these questions were silly or not, or good or bad, was up to trained experts—psychologists—to decide, and he would not try to do so as a lawyer. Nor would he, as a lawyer, try to rewrite the tests to take out some items.

Luce's defense of testing as a standard practice among leading private utilities and churches also aroused the Subcommittee's members. Luce explained that the use of the tests by churches meant that there was no "moral issue" in asking these questions. Representative Reuss replied: "I think one of the troubles of the last twenty-five years has been that everyone has been too ready to accept the fact that somebody else is using it. For example, when I go to my fellow Episcopalians in a few days and say, 'Brethren, are we right in using this test,' they will say, 'Of course we are. Bonneville is using it.' And so the picture goes."

The Peace Corps representatives testified [79] that the Minnesota Multiphasic was required for each volunteer after he had been received for training (usually during the first week). About 9,200 volunteers yearly are taking the test. Though this was the only required personality test, the training institutions (such as universities) were free to use other psychological tests as they saw fit. (At Teachers College, Columbia University, for example, six other personality tests beside the MMPI are given to the volunteers.)[80]

Peace Corps spokesmen explained that Congress had directed the Corps to select volunteers of sound body and "mental health," and that the assignments presented situations of special stress, since volunteers were often required to live in isolated posts or in urban slums and to cope with great psychological pressures. Identification of personality disorders was thus of vital importance, not only to the Corps and the American government, but to the would-be volunteer as well. All applicants for the Peace Corps are told in the recruiting handbook that psychological tests are given; there had been practically no objections by volunteers. The profiles are seen only by the Field Assessment Officer, who administers the MMPI, and the Field Selection Officer (both psychologists) and the consulting psychiatrist if a psychiatric interview is warranted. The Peace Corps staff, locally and in Washington, does not see the results. (The Peace Corps also took the view that medical and psychological files were not available to government investigators unless ordered by the Attorney General.)

Peace Corps officials told the Subcommittees that three major changes in testing practices had been adopted in May as a result of a policy review prompted by congressional inquiries. First, test results would all be destroyed after final selection for overseas assignment. Next, the Peace Corps was negotiating to have a special printing of the MMPI that omitted the last 158 questions, since these were not scored in the Corps's scales. Many but not all the questions on religion, sex, and the like which Congressmen found objectionable were among these 158 (thus, some of the "intrusive" items would still be asked). Finally, the Peace Corps promised to give even stronger instructions than previously to inform the volunteers that they need not answer any questions they felt improper or too personal, and that such refusal would not lead to rejection for service. Peace Corps witnesses added that the MMPI was used as one indicator in a lengthy and multifold evaluation program, that it was not regarded as infallible, and that no volunteer had ever been dismissed because of his MMPI profile alone.

This testimony was given in substantially the same form to both the Ervin and Gallagher Subcommittees. In the Senate, the Peace Corps witnesses were given an easy reception, but in the House committee there was considerable debate over whether the MMPI really identified anyone who would not otherwise have been spotted as disturbed during training. (The Peace Corps witness stated that he knew of half a dozen such instances, but several Congressmen doubted that they really represented well-controlled test situations.) Representative Reuss expressed the hope that the publicity given by the hearings would lead most volunteers in the future to accept the Peace Corps offer to refuse to take the MMPI, a course that would end the difficulty once and for all, Reuss thought. Representative Rosenthal, still worried about the privacy and conformity aspects of the tests, observed:

> [W]hen we originally started, we acknowledged, all of us, that the Federal Government really sets the tone for society. If the Federal Government permits incursions and invasions into privacy, all the other organizations, commercial organizations, are going to think this is a standard they can follow. So that we have an additional responsibility, beyond efficiency within the immediate organization, which is to set this tone or standard of Constitutional preservation. . . ."

In September the Gallagher Subcommittee also held hearings into federally sponsored personality-test research projects in public schools. An earlier letter to the Committee from R. C. M. Flynt, Associate Commissioner for Educational Research and Development, disclosed that between 1959 and 1964 government units had spent over $399,000 for the collection and analysis of personality data.[81]

After listing the questions used in these inquiries, Gallagher stated that hundreds of thousands of elementary- and high-school students were being forced "to answer questions about their families, sex experience, religious views, their own personal values, and other matters normally regarded as solely the private business of the individual." The questions also intruded into family privacy, such as: "How often do your parents (one or both) go to church?" "How often do your parents quarrel or argue with each other?" "How happy do you think your parents' marriage is?" In response to the Committee's concern, Dr. Francis Ianni, Acting Associate Commissioner of Education for Research, announced that whenever questions of a sensitive nature are asked of children below college age in school research projects, parents should and would be fully informed of the testing in advance and given an opportunity to refuse permission for their child to participate.[82]

The disclosure and discussion of federal personality-testing practices was one highlight of the congressional hearings in June, 1965. The other highlight was the conflict of professional testimony about the technical and moral validity of such testing. The positive case for personality testing was begun by Dr. Arthur H. Brayfield, Executive Director of the American Psychological Association. Dr. Brayfield, who did not see any genuine issue of privacy posed by proper use of personality tests by trained psychologists, told the Congressmen that legislation was appropriate to "prescribe the roles and functions of psychologists in the federal government" but not to "dictate the methods and procedures for carrying out these roles and functions," which was "more properly reserved to professional judgments." He did recommend that the federal government might create interagency assessment committees, advisory panels, and a national task force to survey and evaluate current agency assessment practices.[83]

Dr. Zigmond Lebensohn, for the American Psychiatric Association, offered full support to the test-psychologist's position. "If we are going to find out something about human behavior that will serve to advance mankind, then obviously we have got to ask the right questions. We cannot settle for only those questions which might have been acceptable to our Victorian grandmothers." Lebensohn stressed that there should be more safeguards against abuse of testing, including freedom by the person being tested to refuse to answer questions as well as the recommendations made by Dr. Brayfield for closer study of tests and agency procedures. In answer to questions from the Senators about the possibility of leaving out questions about religion, sex, or political ideas to ensure protection of privacy, Lebensohn emphatically opposed such a step. "To me, it would be like doing a physical examination and omitting the rectal . . . like practicing medicine as you do in certain of the countries of the Middle East, in which the person, because of modesty and cultural habits, keeps himself clothed in his robes and permits the doctor only to examine that part which hurts. . . ." [84]

A defense of certain types of personality test was also made by Dr. George Bennett, President of the Psychological Corporation of New York, a leading publisher of psychological tests and national distributor of the MMPI, which he defended when stressful situations are involved, as with the Peace Corps, military missions overseas, and the like. He explained to the Congressmen that the MMPI is normally scored by machine, and scorers do not look at the particular answer of Mr. Doe; they just make up the profiles and, normally, destroy the test answers.[85]

Professional criticism of personality testing came from Dr. Karl U. Smith, professor of industrial psychology at the University of Wisconsin, who provided a lengthy critique of the theoretical and predictive shortcomings of both the paper-and-pencil and projective tests. To mention just some of his main conclusions:

> (a) psychological testing has no critical relations with experimental psychology or any other branch of experimental science and reflects none of the recent advances in scientific understanding of the mechanisms of behavior; (b) testing is based largely on estimating deviations from social norms and has no significant means within itself of dealing with the individual; (c) there are no objective scientific principles to guide test construction; (d) the criterion groups or population samples against which tests are originally validated by no means represent the population as a whole; that is to say, representative samples have never been used in this field; (e) test research in schools

and industry is rarely objective and unbiased, and test validation programs have rarely been free of the influence of on-going
personnel and administrative operations.[86]

The Congressional hearings also heard testimony from Martin
Gross, representatives from the American Civil Liberties Union and the
American Federation of Government Employees; Professor Monroe
Freedman of George Washington University Law School; and Senator
Edward V. Long of Missouri.[87] All these witnesses raised objections
against continued use of personality testing by federal agencies and
called on Congress to forbid the practice.

In 1966 considerable pressure was put on the U.S. Civil Service
Commission both by Congressmen and by interested groups. On May 16
the ACLU sent Civil Service Commission Chairman Macy a sharp
letter calling for elimination of the "Sixteen Personality Factor Test" by
the Federal Aviation Agency.[88] The ACLU noted that the test had been
given to approximately 20,000 air-traffic controllers and requested
strongly that on-the-job evaluation of each individual replace the tests.[89]
The ACLU pointed out that the CSC had not specified whether penalties would be imposed on individuals who refused to answer any questions or to take the test at all. Despite the government's statement of
disinterest in the individual answers given by the testee, serious constitutional problems were raised, as well as questions about the inhibitory
effect of such tests on the employee's *future* political participation and
activity. The ACLU concluded that the government should:

> return to the basic criterion of judging an individual on the
> basis of his individual merit, as demonstrated by his compe-
> tency on the job. Observation of a government employee under
> working conditions, including pressure situations, or a personal
> examination by a psychologist in demonstrably necessary in-
> stances are more realistic ways of determining the ability and
> reliability of an employee for the job than a written test pre-
> sented on a mass basis which is open to interpretation removed
> from on-the-job study.[90]

On May 24 Senator Ervin in a letter to Chairman Macy criticized
the use of the "Minority Group Status Questionnaire" to determine the
race and ancestry of both government employees and applicants for federal jobs.[91] Ervin's letter was in response to an earlier letter from Macy
which supported the use of such forms. The CSC Chairman had explained to Ervin that the use of such statistics was solely in determining
areas in which minority groups were being denied equal job opportunity,
that the individual giving of statistics was not mandatory for applicants,
and that the automated system for sorting the statistics had been created

to guard the identity of the individual. Senator Ervin, however, pointed out that provisions had been made for follow-up checks to increase individual participation and that there was a certain type of "economic coercion" in such activity, since future applicants would fear the loss of their job should they refuse to give the data. The Senator also noted that the questions were apparently inconsistent with a separate CSC rule which precludes any query about religious beliefs or race of employees or applicants, and pointedly asked Macy how the two could be reconciled. Ervin recognized the existence here of a problem of balancing of interests, but concluded that: "The goal of equality of opportunity for some citizens does not and should not encompass the denial of personal privacy to millions." [92]

Public reaction to the Gallagher and Ervin hearings was highly critical of federal personality testing. Judging from clippings of editorials across the country, the invasion of privacy through such tests was regarded as a dangerous and insupportable practice, except in special military, overseas, and medical situations.[93] *Time* and *Newsweek* both ran accounts that made considerable sport of the "brain-tester" proclivities of federal agencies.[94] Labor-union periodicals hailed the investigations,[95] as did most liberal commentators.[96] Significantly, conservative commentators also joined the supporting elements.[97]

The publication, in 1966, of *How to Beat Personality Tests*, by Charles Alex, was an interesting indication of how widespread the expectation had become that one had to deal with personality testers in many phases of life. Reminiscent of Whyte's "pony" at the end of his *Organization Man*, this new book appeared along with a spate of how-to-take-the-draft-test volumes and similar efforts. The author discusses a variety of tests and advises on precisely how to reply so as not to "flunk" the test. Important points include always selecting the most heterosexual responses to sex questions, showing no cultural interests, and stressing normality in all inter-personal relations. In regard to ink blots, Alex advises to try to see animals in motion and, above all, to avoid mentioning sex organs.[98]

There were other continuing conflicts over personality testing in 1966 to keep psychologists and civic groups aware that many of the issues were still unresolved. In New York City a storm was raised by the use of the MMPI for a test of 350 ninth-grade pupils as part of a federally aided research project into identifying potentially disturbed youngsters.[99] In Florida the state superintendent of schools appointed a committee to set standards to prevent the use in guidance work of prying questions about parental income, religion, employment, and adjustment, and overly personal questions about the pupils themselves.[100] The U.S. Office of Science and Technology appointed an advisory committee to study the issues of privacy involved in government-conducted or government-sponsored behavioral research and ordered the Chairman of the Civil Service Commission to review the use of personality tests by contractors conducting programs for the federal government.[101] Six contractors—two with the Defense Department and four for the Atomic Energy Commission— were found to be using the tests for personnel work (out of twenty-two contractors for Defense and thirty-five for AEC), and some were using the tests in ways that seemed to violate federal standards.[102] In the meantime, bills to forbid the use of personality testing in public schools were introduced in some state legislatures and in Congress to control such testing with federal funds. Congressmen also pressed the Office of Education to exercise stricter control over the questions asked in school testing programs conducted under federal grants or to supervise compliance with federal programs.[103] Use of personality testing by private industry continued on a large scale, though debates over its propriety became louder. Though all these were signs of healthy ferment, the issue of personality testing and privacy still awaited sharper clarification of standards before it could be considered under effective social or legal control.

Psychologists Take Up the Debate

During the mid-1960's civic debates over the privacy and liberty aspects of personality testing began to evoke serious discussion from psychologists themselves. One source prompting psychologists to reconsider their approach was the near-success of Senator Goldwater's anti-testing amendment to the NDEA statute of 1963. After the last-minute psychologist-led campaign defeated this amendment, Dr. Lee Cronbach circulated a letter to his colleagues warning that the 1963 episode was only a skirmish, that further efforts at restricting personality testing in the schools would be forthcoming, and that psychologists had better be prepared, particularly on the issue of invasion of privacy. The need was to "map the limits of proper questioning and then to explain to the public why it is proper within those limits to question captive subjects in school." [104]

An even stronger position was taken by Professor Starke Hathaway, one of the co-authors of the Minnesota Multiphasic test and president of the Division of Clinical Psychology of the APA. Writing in the clinical psychologists' Newsletter in 1964, he stated:

> Personally, I favor a more fundamentally aggressive position that asserts our sincere aims and desires to make genuine contributions toward happier personal and public lives. Our integrity and sincerity accepted, we should then be *expected* to invade personal psychological privacy as surely as physicians are ex-

pected to examine individual bodies and their intimate contents.

Hathaway helped launch the educational campaign personally by writing an article on "MMPI: Professional Use by Professional People," which appeared in the *American Psychologist* in 1964. Replying to a question whether the MMPI's questions on religion disqualified that test for use by local governments in selecting policemen, Hathaway noted that there were nineteen questions relating to religion on the MMPI; these were present not to learn the religious views of the job applicant, but to check for "depressed or otherwise mentally disturbed persons" whose symptoms "often largely center in religion." As for the argument that the MMPI was proper only for "the patient, the mentally-ill persons, not applicants to schools, high-school children, or to those being considered for jobs," Hathaway contended that our era was one in which "preventive health is being emphasized" and "general surveys with such psychological instruments as the MMPI" rest on the same basic justification. Individuals given the MMPI were always supposed to be told that they could simply leave unanswered any questions they did not want to complete, and Hathaway noted that such deliberate omissions of the religious questions were "frequent" in MMPI testing.[105]

During the same period legal rulings in New York and California requiring the disclosure of psychological information about the child in school files to parents or state authorities led the APA to appoint an ad hoc Committee on Confidentiality of Records.[106] Though its prime concern was to develop proper safeguards for this inspection process, the Committee report in 1963 called for the profession to "police itself to prevent abuses in gathering information." This Committee was then reconstituted under the new title of the Committee on Social Impact of Psychological Assessment and was charged with studying this problem for APA review.

A comparable beginning of professional action on the privacy issue in industrial testing took place between 1961 and 1964. In May, 1961, the Committee on Scientific and Professional Ethics and Conduct of the APA had appointed an ad hoc Committee on Ethical Practices in Industrial Psychology. This committee's report included a section on "Undue Invasion of Privacy."

> Our Committee had occasion to review a number of individual appraisal reports, prepared by industrial psychologists for submission to the top managements of their client firms. A few of these reports—fortunately, a very small proportion—seemed to us to be shockingly gossipy; they revealed matters about the individual being appraised which, we felt, had no place in such reports. We found such statements as these: "Mr. X had a very

unhappy childhood, and got along very poorly with his mother."
"Mr. X feels that the president of this company is a very capable man. However, he does not think much of Tom Jones, his boss, or of his colleague, Bill Smith." [107]

To meet this situation, the Committee proposed to the APA the addition to the ethical code of a new sentence on "Confidentiality": "Written and oral reports should present only data germane to the purposes of the evaluations; every effort should be made to avoid undue invasion of privacy." This statement was adopted by the APA in 1962.

The fall of 1964 witnessed several other significant comments and actions. An article by Professor James R. Barclay in *Personnel and Guidance Journal* for September, 1964, examined "The Attack on Testing and Counseling" and warned school counselors that some of the issues raised called for reform:

> Curiosity-seeking is also a problem in the naive counselor. Often he probes into areas of personal concern not so much to understand as to satisfy his own needs for vicarious experience. Sometimes he will develop questionnaires or adopt tests which are presented to him through misleading advertisement as panaceas of prediction. Curiosity to pry into personal experiences is an immature aspect of psychological sophistication. In its worst aspect it is akin to voyeurism. Counselors need to recognize that this kind of prying reveals their own adolescent development. . . . If they have this type of need, let them read novels! [108]

During this same year psychologists also began to participate in the growing civic debates over privacy and personality testing. Writing in a law-school symposium on privacy, Professor Raymond A. Katzell of New York University stated that, while a "substantial amount of privacy" was accepted by psychologists as "a necessary condition to mental and emotional well being" for individuals, he did *not* believe that current personality tests intruded unreasonably on these privacy needs, and he considered proposals to halt personality testing on privacy grounds as "an untenable, if not irrational position." However, he did point out several ways in which invasions of privacy might take place through misuse of tests, as when "psychological test data find their way to organization members who have no proper responsibility or competency for acting upon them" or:

> if the information collected by means of tests were not demonstrably relevant to the decision regarding the candidate. . . . I should hasten to point out that testing should not necessarily be limited to questions or procedures that *appear* to be ger-

mane. For instance, it might seem on the face of it that questions concerning an applicant's relations with his parents are just plain snooping, but in fact the answers may be quite illuminating on the important issue of how much this person is inclined to be authoritarian in dealing with others. . . .

Finally, a candidate should be given reasonably complete and accurate information about the purpose of a test and how its results will be used. We must be able to assume correctly that the examinee is a cooperative party to the test—that he has agreed to take it after weighing the pros and cons. If he has been misled, he may have revealed himself for reasons or in ways which he might otherwise have rejected. Such practices would surely come under the heading of unreasonable search and therefore invasion of privacy.[109]

One of the most thoughtful responses from the psychological profession came when the Board of Professional Affairs of the APA selected "Psychological Tests and Public Responsibility" as the topic for a general evening program at the 1964 annual meeting of the APA, the papers being published in the *American Psychologist* in February, 1965, and summarized in *Science* Magazine.[110] In one of these, Dr. Orville Brim, Jr., of the Russell Sage Foundation, reported his research into the social consequences of standardized testing. Though concerned with intelligence rather than personality tests, Brim noted "a growing concern to many persons because test data are a key part of the new concept of the career record or dossier, which will accompany a person throughout his life. But, who is to keep the record and who is to have access to it?" On the issue of privacy, Brim commented:

Psychologists have defended the use of personality inventories by claiming that the data would be confidential, its access limited to competent research persons. The fact is that confidentiality cannot be protected. Psychologists are misinformed in thinking that test responses have the character of a privileged communication. Test results are subject to subpoena by any group with proper legal authority and easily can become a matter of public record.

Therefore, many are concerned about the legal rights of the individual to refuse to give out information about himself. The concern is legitimate and we must listen. The issue is: Under what conditions can the state invade an individual's right to privacy? Where national security is at stake, the state can invade; for instance, conscription, and the psychological testing associated with it, is legitimate. Also justified is the use of intelligence and achievement tests in the nation's public education system, for it is a valuable diagnostic device helping the school system do a better job of educating the students.

But, even though testing by psychologists often is justified on the ground that it benefits the respondents, there are many occasions when the use of tests by psychologists invades privacy without justification. Indeed, one could question the legitimacy of asking the questions reported on subsequently in this paper —questions which were asked of a "captive audience" of public high school students. Perhaps one justifies it because of its eventual contribution to knowledge, on the assumption that the growth of social science knowledge is a public good. But is this really sufficient? A serious matter is involved here, and psychologists must work through their moral philosophy on this point and chart a new section in our code of ethics.[111]

Brim concluded that psychologists could not continue to regard testing in the abstract; they "must be concerned about the society in which tests are used" and the "social meaning" of test scores. These "have impact on man's self-esteem; they influence his life chances; they engage his deepest political and social attitudes." [112]

The other article in this symposium that dealt with privacy was by Dr. Samuel Messick of Educational Testing Service. Messick observed that criticism of personality tests had led some members of the profession to call for "self-regulation" to avert external controls.[113] But self-regulation was not such a simple matter, according to Messick. There is a conflict of values between the psychologist's commitment to the individual's "dignity and worth" (which points toward avoiding invasion of privacy) and his commitment to "increasing man's understanding of himself and others" (which leads him to pursue inquiries for advancing individual and general welfare). In addition, there is the problem of how to enforce control procedures against invasions of privacy, recognizing that there are already ethical standards which are not being enforced against those misusing tests. Messick ended without making any concrete suggestions, other than to warn that imposing a solution by vote of the profession in order to placate critics would be as unacceptable as having outside legislative controls.[114]

The note of self-examination that marked this symposium continued throughout 1965 and, indeed, spread to some other areas in which personality testing is used. For example, Dr. William W. Cumming, Associate Professor of Psychology at Columbia University, criticized Columbia College for giving the Minnesota Multiphasic test to freshmen. The test "left the student embarrassed and feeling naked before the psychology examiner." No "worthwhile purpose that will benefit either the student or the College" existed to justify the invasion of privacy in giving the test.[115]

One interesting and unusual reaction among some of the professional psychologists, however, involved the argument that if a machine of some sort did the actual evaluation of the test results, there would be no privacy problems. One suggestion, by J. W. Hamblen of the Computer Sciences Project of the Southern Regional Education Board in Atlanta, was for computers to pose the questions and evaluate the results, after which either the computer or the individual would destroy the actual answer sheet.[116] Another article, entitled "The Computer That Psychoanalyzes You," projected the use of computers programmed to "talk about family relations," "talk about sex," and the like.[117]

On the other hand there were indications in 1966 of deeper concern in an opposite direction, as shown in John Lear's "Do We Need New Rules for Experiments on People." [118] In this article, personality testing is treated as but one aspect or phase of a much larger problem area, running from experiments on the controlling of animal behavior through the problems of cancer-transplantation experiments on humans.

Concern among psychologists was heightened by the hostility to their profession which accompanied the congressional hearings of 1965.[119] Much of the press reacted by ridiculing personality testing, relishing the psychologists' "getting their lumps," and supporting the Congressional attacks on "prying" and "brain-picking"; a line of angry pickets even appeared outside the Washington offices of the American Psychological Association.[120] Because of the intensity with which the APA felt the danger of the Congressional hearings, a whole issue of the *American Psychologist*, for November, 1965, the largest in that journal's history, was devoted to "Testing and Public Policy." [121] Rushed into print by special efforts, this included highlights from the congressional testimony and special articles written by key professional, congressional, executive, and critical spokesmen. Dr. Arthur Brayfield, the executive officer of the APA, set the introductory theme: psychologists have exercised important privileges and power in American society; now, society wanted an accounting for that power.[122]

Industrial Test Givers' Attitudes Toward Privacy

Among those whose livelihood was centered on giving psychological tests, including personality tests, criticisms on grounds of invasion of privacy had not proved terribly persuasive. To learn the attitudes of these firms, I wrote to fifteen leading test firms or management services offering personality testing for industry.[123] The survey asked the test givers to discuss whether a legitimate issue of employee privacy was raised by the tests they were using, whether they thought some boundaries of privacy should be observed in questioning, and what their firms had done to limit questioning and to guard personal disclosures.

Fourteen of the fifteen replied that their tests did not raise any legitimate question of privacy, and the remaining firm was convinced that the way its tests were treated made them a reasonable intrusion into the applicant's privacy. The value of the responses came not so much in the formal positions recorded as in the discussion of what it was felt privacy did and did not involve in industrial or governmental personnel-selection testing.

The president of the Personnel Laboratory, King Whitney, Jr., wrote:

> Surely everybody's privacy is being invaded today in some way because we live and work in much closer proximity than in the past. It is, therefore, a question of the degree of invasion that we are all concerned about. I feel the individual's privacy is best protected from abuse in testing by having competent psychologists evaluate what he completes. . . . I do feel that there is a legitimate issue of employee privacy raised by the kinds of tests we use because they are generally regarded by psychologists as deep-probing techniques. And in the hands of uninitiated or malicious practitioners, the information these techniques reveal could abuse the privacy of the examinee. But I would maintain that the way we use these techniques offers little or no threat to the privacy of the individual beyond reasonable and accepted limits.

For the head of J. N. Farr Associates, the key issue was the relevancy of the questioning and the test standards.

> [O]ne of the more vital considerations in this problem is whether or not the elements measured by tests are job-relevant. If they are, then how can they be treated as private to the applicant when they surely will become evident to all after he is hired? If aggressiveness is a necessary personality quality for a job, there will be nothing private about a man's lack of it once he goes to work. Why then should it be private before he is hired—providing that reasonable attention is given to protecting content-privacy while making an assessment?
>
> All these things argue for, and I support, a need for better professional standards and a more mature approach to the use of tests. But it does not seem to me to support the concept that

personality is any more private than a man's intellect, his colon, or his eye-hand coordination.

Some replies stressed the importance of personality tests in *reducing* bias in selection, even though the tests were not perfect. Case and Co. replied:

It is my feeling that your committee needs to ask itself the question, "What would happen if personality tests were not used?"

I believe that the judgments that are made about people without tests may be more biased and harmful than the judgments that are made with the use of them.

Privacy and Personality Testing

This survey of American attitudes toward personality testing from 1945 to the present showed the rise of protest from its early right-wing attacks on school testing programs to the present protest from liberal, labor, conservative, and right-wing spokesmen. Since the determination of the type of questioning and testing that "invades privacy" is based on what citizens in general regard as reasonable or unreasonable intrusions into their personalities, intimacies, and dignity, this rising protest indicates a major development in American norms of privacy. Whatever may have been the state of American attitudes toward privacy in 1945, or when William Whyte wrote in 1955, it is no longer possible to accept the "nobody-complains-but-oddballs" position on personality testing.[124]

In Chapter 2 it was explained why intellectuals and other critics see personality testing as a form of surveillance by extraction that threatens key functions of privacy. This discussion stressed that conservatives, liberals, Negroes, and other groups see personality-test judgments as a means of applying covert ideological standards in the name of expert wisdom about "adjustment." The discussion also stressed that the invocation of science and expertise to make such judgments out of public view was seen as defeating American society's basic tenet that such decisions be made in the open, where they can be challenged and fairly debated. These points bear repeating here.

I believe that 1965 saw a turning point in the position of the psychological profession on the matter of personality testing. From a wholly defensive response to "know-nothing" critics, leaders in the profession moved to a fundamental re-assessment of who is testing whom, for what purposes, with what social impact, and with what effect upon the image of the psychological profession itself. Those familiar with the literature of the profession know that a re-assessment was actually already starting between 1961 and 1964, but it was a small-scale effort and was not broadly publicized. The bruising public battle of 1965 and the obvious threat of legal restriction that will be fought out in the late 1960's have now brought the university and organization circles of the profession to a recognition that the whole field of personality testing is in both disrepute and disrepair, and that scientific studies of personality-testing theory, field studies of practices at every level, and value discussions of the balances between privacy and inquiry are responsibilities of the profession that have high priority in its organized life. Much must be done. Test psychologists must start talking to their colleagues in social and experimental psychology, to learn more about the nature and functions of privacy and must ready themselves to answer questions such as those raised by Dr. Messick in his APA article of 1965.[125] Hopefully, the discussion in this volume on the functions of privacy and invasion of privacy will be of assistance in the quest. The series of studies sponsored by the Russell Sage Foundation, including a study of personality testing in industry under way at Yale University, may also provide sensitive standards.[126]

In conducting this intra-professional examination, one point on privacy is crucial. If test psychologists are to open the minds of responsible critics, they will have to explain far better than any witness from psychology has yet done in public or in the scholarly journals how a score based on answers to questions about religion, political ideology, or sex does not rest on the substance of those answers. For example, it has been said repeatedly that questions on the MMPI about religious belief and commitment do not measure religious belief and commitment but "personality disorders" reflected in the subject's response to questions about religious matters. Now, American society is unequivocally committed to the idea that religious notions are *private* and that no governmental or quasi-governmental authority (such as the corporation, or the secular private university) should decide what is "reasonable" in religious belief. Given this fact, how can the psychologist state that adding up this and that question about religious belief ("I am a special agent of God," "I believe in the second coming of Christ," and the like) to define personality disorders is *not* a judgment on what religious beliefs are "reasonable" and "not reasonable"? Apart from the loose charges of some immoderate critics from both the journalistic and academic camps, no responsible observer believes that the Peace Corps psychologists or those testing for police-force or industrial selection care—or even notice—that a given person is Jewish, Catholic, agnostic, or atheist. But that is not the problem, and the psychologist's good faith is not an answer. The problem is whether a scale based essentially on religious "reasonableness" is an invasion of the privacy and liberty of Americans. On this issue, psychologists have yet to speak clearly and to make their case with proper documentary and logical proofs.

Another crucial question must be considered by leaders of psychology in their scientific deliberations. Can personality tests be developed which measure factors such as problem solving, independence of analysis, or supervisory skills, *without* including on them questions about sex, religion, or ideology? The projective-test advocates would probably say "No," but that is not to be taken as a conclusive answer, because (1) society has a right, if it wishes, to forgo the "penetration" of projective tests in what are, realistically, compulsory tests for government and industrial employment; (2) part of the projective testers' argument is based on the fact that no scientifically objective, double-blind procedure tests have ever been done to compare the actual predictive power of either projective or pencil-and-paper tests with non-personality tests (such as the "in-basket" test of performance on simulated problems for executives) or with the type of personality test that does *not* include questions on sex, religion, and ideology, or with tests that do not rely on written performance at all (such as the Chapple Interaction Chronograph).

The usual answer of test psychologists is that, however badly conceived current tests were to begin with in their questions and their sampling techniques for the first subjects, and however ambiguous their semantic meanings and connotations to this generation, these tests at least have a decade or more of applications to "validate" them. This is also no answer. If time and money are needed to try personnel tests that will not intrude directly on privacy, then time and money should and must be found to pursue this goal. Until it is attempted, society has not had a "scientific" answer to what it is usually asked to allow on "scientific" grounds. If psychologists can work so diligently and so thoughtfully on "culture-free" intelligence tests (to prevent unintended discrimination against Negroes), is it asking too much to have psychologists give as much attention to developing "privacy-respecting" tests in employment?

One of the most promising avenues to explore is the role-projection or social-simulation test. If a person is asked to respond to a test problem as though he were a Peace Corps volunteer or Sears Roebuck salesman, he is being tested on his capacity to assume a role. This is very different from trying to probe his mind to find out whether his personality is the kind the psychologist believes to be suited to the role. One procedure respects the privacy of personality while calling for social skills. The other does not.

One final point is addressed equally to the psychologists, the critics, and the public. Some of the statements by psychologists in their journals and before Congress called for "law" to stay out of this area of personality testing and to let the profession of psychology define and police socially acceptable and scientifically progressive standards. At one level I share this view strongly: ethical self-regulation by the scientific and "user" communities in new scientific and technological developments is a highly desirable situation. And if the ethical sensibilities of the primary profession run actively counter to the law, the prospects for enforcing legal privacy guarantees are not bright, as the wiretapping situation has showed so painfully between 1938 and the present.

Yet state and federal laws are already setting selection standards for civil-service employees; administrative-agency rules apply these statutory standards (such as the United States Civil Service Commission rules on use of personality testing and the United States Office of Education Interpretive Rule on the use of personality testing in NDEA programs); Fair Employment Practices rulings such as the *Motorola* case in Illinois involve an aptitude test; and even court rulings on this point exist. In addition, law is being advocated on several other fronts. Bills have been introduced in Congress and in several state legislatures to outlaw personality testing by government agencies, or by school authorities without parental consent. It has been proposed by Professor John Dollard and others that a government agency such as the National Bureau of Standards be empowered to certify tests as to their validity, reliability, predictive uses, and other qualities.

Thus the cold fact that must be faced by the psychology profession is that there *is* law already, and there may well be more in the next decade. The challenge to psychologists, lawyers, and the public is the kind of law and the wisdom of these regulations. One can only hope that the profession of psychology, with its members' high commitment to civil liberties and concern for humane values, will actively lead the effort to develop selection techniques that do not undermine a central value of the independent spirit in an independent society.

CHAPTER ELEVEN

Tampering with the Unconscious

Subliminals Become a Public Issue, 1957

SUBLIMINAL suggestion—the projection of messages by light or sound so quickly and faintly that they are received below the level of consciousness—swept into the attention of the general American public suddenly in the fall of 1957. On September 12, 1957, a marketing and motivational-research specialist named James Vicary held a press conference in New York City to demonstrate what he called the "technique of the future" in advertising and communication.[1] This was *sub* (below) *limen* (threshold) suggestion, and Vicary's announcement stated that his company—Subliminal Projection Inc.—was now ready to offer this new process to clients.

Vicary told fifty reporters invited to a rented projection room that they would see a demonstration of special equipment which his firm had tested recently in a New Jersey movie theater. "Drink Coca-Cola" and "Hungry? Eat Popcorn" had been flashed on the theater's screen at 1/3000th of a second every five seconds during the performance of a film called *Picnic*, starring Kim Novak. The message was superimposed over the regular image of the film so quickly that it was apparently not visible to the audiences. During six weeks of testing involving 45,699 patrons, Vicary asserted, lobby sales of popcorn increased 57.7 per cent on the days "Hungry? Eat Popcorn" was flashed, and Coke sales went up 18.1 per cent on the alternate days, when "Drink Coca-Cola" was flashed.

Vicary further explained that the primary purpose of subliminal projection was to eliminate irritations caused by excessive advertising. He outlined its potential uses for this purpose in television, movies, and display advertising, as well as its possibilities for medical and educational purposes. After this presentation, the lights were dimmed and a color film about underwater life, *Secrets of the Reef*, was run off for the press. Despite much eye-straining by the reporters, no one saw the "Coca-Cola" trademark that was flashed 169 times over the swimming fish, except on the three occasions when Vicary deliberately projected the message improperly to let it become visible.

When the lights were turned on, Vicary was questioned extensively by the press. The dominant tone of the queries was represented by one reporter present as one of "hostility, resistance, and unease." When asked whether this was manipulation of the audience without its knowledge or consent, Vicary replied that his firm was disclosing the process before putting it into commercial use to permit just such airing of "ethical" questions and to allow for the consideration of safeguards. The word "manipulation" was inaccurate, he protested, because subliminal suggestion "reminds" rather than "induces." People who felt thirsty reacted to the Coca-Cola "reminder," and those who liked popcorn bought it. Those who were not thirsty or didn't like popcorn were unaffected by the messages.

However, Vicary provided an example later in the conference of subliminal suggestion that had gone beyond reminding and had *created* audience feelings. He described a university test of subliminal suggestion in which a neutral, unexpressive drawing of a man's face was projected onto a screen. With one group of subjects, the word "happy" was flashed subliminally over the drawing; with another group, the word "unhappy" was projected. When asked to describe the man's mood, a majority of the first audience wrote "happy" and of the second wrote "unhappy." According to Vicary, other tests in England and by psychologists in the United States confirmed this effectiveness. For example, persons who were flashed anagram answers subliminally solved the puzzles more quickly than those who had not been exposed to the subliminal solutions. In another test a group of men was shown pictures of beautiful girls, with the number "3" flashed subliminally over them; later in a series of questions, the men were asked which number between 1 and 10 "most appealed to them"—a majority chose "3."

As the news conference continued, Vicary stated that his company had patents pending for the subliminal-projection process, that negotiations were under way with manufacturers for production of the special projectors, and that a number of advertising clients had expressed keen interest in using the technique. Television was a particularly promising field, he suggested, because subliminal messages reinforcing the regular opening commercial would enable sponsors to cut down on "repeat" commercials during the entertainment.

Vicary's press conference made front-page news throughout the country.[2] All the major wire services carried the story; interpretive articles appeared in most of the major national magazines; and there was extensive radio and television coverage of the new technique.[3] The fact that national debate over the ethics and social impact of advertising *per se* was at a high point in 1957 contributed to public concern over subliminal suggestion. Some commentators called the process a potential "nuclear breakthrough" in advertising weaponry. *Newsday*, for instance, regarded it as "the most alarming invention since the atomic bomb." [4] The *New Yorker* stated that we had reached the sad age when minds and not just houses could be "broken and entered." [5]

The overwhelming editorial, political, and civic reaction to the first news of subliminal suggestion was a combination of fascination, outrage, and determination to "fight back." Typical of these comments with the theme of privacy at their forefront were columns in journals as ideologically diverse as the New York *Journal-American* and the *Saturday Review*. Phyllis Battelle, who had attended the Vicary preview, wrote in the *Journal-American*:

> I have just had my subconscious mind tampered with—by a group of gentlemen who, I solemnly believe, have no business meddling in my id. . . .
> Aside from my basic horror at the idea of being prodded into acting without all my wits about me, . . . I picture the invisible commercial as a direct route to incontinence. . . . Advertising, it seems to me, should aid a person in logically selecting products which will help him live a better life. In this form, advertising could make Americans more intemperate than we already are. It could stimulate more eating, drinking, smoking, and spendthrifteries than we've indulged in before. . . . I suggest that, to prevent complete mental mayhem and preserve the public peace of mind, it be stopped before it's started.[6]

The *Saturday Review*'s comment (a full-page editorial) denounced the promoters of subliminal messages as men who "coolly propose to break into the deepest and most private parts of the human mind and leave all sorts of scratchmarks. The subconscious mind is the most delicate part of the most delicate apparatus in the entire universe. It is not to be smudged, sullied or twisted in order to boost the sales of popcorn or anything else." Warning that "nothing is more difficult in the modern world than to protect the privacy of the human soul," the *Saturday Review* warned that the time had come to stop "surrendering our privacy without a fight" and "adjusting ourselves to all sorts of intrusions, violations and assaults." Federal and state prohibitory legislation was urged, though the *Review* felt the ideal solution would be "to take this invention and everything connected to it and attach it to the center of the next nuclear explosive scheduled for testing." [7]

While these reactions of the first weeks were unfolding, news stories disclosed an additional fact about subliminal suggestion. Another company, Precon Process and Equipment Corporation of New Orleans, was already in this field and claimed to have filed its patent application a year before Vicary's firm. Precon had been founded by two men, Robert E. Corrigan, a psychological consultant with Douglas Aircraft and formerly a lecturer in psychology at Tulane University, and Hal C. Becker, an assistant professor of experimental neurology at Tulane, who also had a degree in electrical engineering.[8] The two men had been experimenting with subliminal suggestion since 1950 and had formed Precon to distribute the projection technique for commercial and educational purposes.

Hostile civic reactions began to mount steadily. Nine major developments characterized the furor:

1. Each of the three major television networks—CBS, NBC, and ABC—announced individually that they would not accept subliminal advertising or employ the technique on their radio or television network productions. As the Columbia Broadcasting System announcement noted, the "legal, social and ethical implications" of subliminal broadcasting "precluded" its use, at least for the present when so little was known about the method and its effects.[9] The Canadian Broadcasting System released a similar assurance.[10]

2. The Code Review Board of the National Association of Radio and Television Broadcasters, which includes the three major networks and about 300 of the nation's TV stations among its membership, announced a temporary ban on subliminal advertising and directed that any future plans by members to use subliminals be referred to the Board for review and decision.[11]

3. Half a dozen Congressmen, led by Senator Charles Potter (R., Michigan) and Representative William A. Dawson (R., Utah), called on the Federal Communications Commission to investigate subliminal advertising, with the aim of either controlling or forbidding the practice. Senator Potter declared that if the FCC lacked such power, Congress would immediately provide whatever authority was needed to control this "revolutionary and frightening new development in the communications field." Congressman Dawson called on the FCC to prevent stations from experimenting with subliminal projection while the FCC study was pending.[12] In 1958, and again in 1959, Congressman James Wright of Texas, a former advertising man, sponsored a bill to forbid any device that was "designed to advertise a product or indoctrinate the public by means of making an impression on the subconscious mind." The proposed law would subject subliminal purveyors to a $5,000 fine and/or thirty days in prison.[13] Congressman Hosmer introduced a bill to amend the 1934 Communications Act (section 326); his measure would have forbidden television stations to transmit any message "intended to be received through subliminal perception . . . absorbing fleeting visual information without being aware of it." [14] All three bills were referred to the House Committee on Interstate and Foreign Commerce, but no

hearings were ever held on them.[15]

4. Several state legislative committees opened hearings on subliminal broadcasting or projection. The New Jersey Legislature, for example, passed a concurrent resolution in 1958 creating a state commission to study subliminal projection and report on measures that might be needed to control it. Testimony was taken and reports were obtained from scientific experts and civic spokesmen across the country, and the Commission report was filed in 1959. The report stated that, while opinions varied as to the effectiveness of subliminal influences, the evidence indicated agreement that there *is* perception below the threshold of awareness. The Commission concluded that "This evidence alone is sufficient to cause legislative recognition of the technique in the protection of the public right of privacy." However, since there was some evidence that it might provide a supplemental aid to existing methods in education and psychotherapy, the Commission felt that an absolute prohibition of its use would be irresponsible. Therefore, the Commission proposed enactment of a statute forbidding the use of subliminal messages without an immediately prior announcement disclosing such use.[16]

In New York, the State Senate on March 12, 1958, passed unanimously a bill banning subliminal advertising.[17] With the center of the nation's advertising industry on Madison Avenue and the headquarters of the national television industry in New York City, the State Senate bill threatened, if passed by the House and signed by the Governor, to have an effect far beyond that of one state's reaction. A similar bill was introduced and debated vigorously in California. None of these state measures became law, but they were a firm indication of public hostility to the spread of subliminals.

5. A Los Angeles independent television station, KTLA, announced that "to keep ahead in the development of new forms of television," it had signed a contract with Precon (the New Orleans company) to broadcast "public service" messages subliminally. KTLA explained that these would only be reminders of a high civic character, such as "Drive Safely," "Give Blood," and "Don't be a Litterbug." [18] However, the reaction to the station's announcement was an avalanche of hostile letters condemning the proposal and threatening a boycott of the station. This reaction, plus the management's "uncertainty" as to the FCC's position on transmission of subliminals, led KTLA to cancel the venture.[19] Advertisements in the press and announcements on the station assured viewers that no "hidden messages" would be used. However, several radio stations decided to use "subaudial" messages—those broadcast so faintly in volume as not to be consciously heard by most listeners. Some, such as WCCO in Minneapolis-St. Paul, aired public-service messages between November, 1957, and January, 1958, such as "Slippery Road" during icy weather and "Ike Tonight" when the President was scheduled for a na-

tionwide address.[20] Other stations moved to attract commercial sponsors. WAAF, in Chicago, for example, broadcast subaudials experimentally during 1958, offering these to advertisers at $1,000 for every 500 messages, or about a week's run. "Seven-Up Refreshes" and "Oklahoma Gas Is Best" were broadcast as a test; "Buy This Record at Little Al's Record Shop" was used on a commercial basis in February. These messages would come through pauses in recorded music.[21] In response to a letter in 1964, the General Manager of WAAF stated that, while the technique "still intrigues us," it was not being used presently by WAAF, primarily because of FCC restrictions on the number of commercial messages that may be aired per hour. As for audience response in Chicago to the 1958 use, WAAF recalled that this was "mixed": "some were amused and some felt abused." The idea of replacing "some of the stuff you hear on the air today" with "whispered short messages" was worth more consideration, the manager felt, but "before we get back into it again, we would have to have absolute approval from the Federal agencies involved, and perhaps even endorsement from the National Association of Broadcasters." [22]

6. A substantial number of national and state civic organizations condemned the potential uses of subliminals. The Women's Christian Temperance Union[23] and the Methodist Temperance Board [24] warned that subliminal ads by liquor and beer advertisers could cause heavier drinking by adults, could corrupt youth, and could seriously harm alcoholics trying to reform. Other groups were equally alarmed about invisible cigarette advertising. In California the state American Legion, the Federation of Women's Clubs, and other groups joined in protesting the political and commercial threats posed by this technique and urged that it be outlawed.

7. Many advertising-agency spokesmen entered the debate by flatly denying the suggestive powers of subliminal advertising. Dr. Arthur Koponen of J. Walter Thompson stated: "There is no experimental evidence available that shows subliminal projection can influence product sales on television or in the movies." [25] A survey of attitudes in the advertising and motion-picture industries, conducted by the *Christian Science Monitor* in early 1958, reported that "the adverse publicity in the past five months has discouraged movie enterprises from taking the risk of incurring public displeasure." The *Monitor* found that major advertising agencies were studying the claims of the promoters and running tests to verify the results, but had "adopted a discreet silence on the subject" and were not recommending any uses of subliminals as yet for their clients.[26]

However, some reports early in 1958 about prospective uses of subliminal suggestion reinforced the fears of critics and, indeed, set off a fresh round of civic complaints. A Los Angeles movie house run by

United Artists Theatre Circuit flashed "Buy Popcorn" ads subliminally on its screen during January and February of 1958 and announced that the process would be used in the 350 other theaters of United Artists if the tests were successful.[27] In February of 1958 *Television Age* ran an item entitled "Subliminals for Tavern Trade."

> Liquor advertising on TV may be in the offing. But the station won't be the source, and it won't be consciously seen. Subliminal, of course. Precon Process & Equipment Corp., New Orleans, reports it is designing a rig for tavern TV sets. Guzzling viewers would get a continuous, automatic hidden message overriding the nightly fights, quiz and drama. Local pub owners could flash appeals for a brand, a specific mix, or just signal customers to keep drinking. The message can, for instance, be flashed 30 times a second all night long—over program matter and commercials. A Precon man says it's ideal— "The audience is captive and sitting down."[28]

A promotional brochure put out by Precon stated that tests of a "pilot model, point of purchase stimulator" during August of 1958 had "*doubled* sales of nationally advertised beverage during two weeks test period."[29]

In March, 1958, a *Life* magazine story reported that Corrigan and Becker of Precon were planning to move into the area of display advertising.

> One of [the best possibilities], Becker feels, would be a new kind of billboard, showing a landscape illuminated normally while another light, hung overhead, would throw a subliminal message on it via unseen ultraviolet light. Becker has already built another version of this as a point-of-sale sales stimulator. Ostensibly presenting a pleasant picture in glowing color and placed on the counter in a hat shop, it could presumably be sublimmed "New hat?" to the feminine customers, do wonders for sales. Another variation might be a plain screen in a supermarket that would sublim a flashing arrow in the direction of a Corn Flakes display."[30]

The press reported that Precon had provided subliminal messages to "augment" the psychological tension levels in a Hollywood movie, *My World Dies Screaming*. When the villain was shown on the screen, a serpent was placed across his chest by subliminal image. When the heroine felt love, a Valentine-like heart was shown. The word "BLOOD" and then a skull were projected subliminally when the heroine saw a dead body. The producer, William Edwards, stated that subliminals had made the movie into a new and more powerful art form, the "psycho-rama." [31] Corrigan of Precon explained to the press at a Hollywood preview of the film: "This is an authentic and honest approach. I think we can increase the entertainment impact of the motion picture art." A second movie, *Date with Death*, with added subliminal effects, was released in 1959. Each film had a prologue demonstrating the process and explaining it, while the film credits stated: "Subliminal Communication by Precon." [32]

8. American attitudes were affected by reports in our press that the British Institute of Practitioners in Advertising had banned subliminal ads. The Institute established a special committee which undertook a six-month study of subliminal communication. In July, 1958, the Institute issued a report instructing its member agencies to refrain from using subliminals "in whatever form for advertising or sales promotion." [33] Australian advertisers also established a ban similar to that set by the British Institute. [34]

9. Letters to editors, editorials, and articles in the press and magazines continued to be heavily critical through 1957 and 1958, with protests still running an ideological spectrum from the "hard" conservative Los Angeles *Times* to the left-liberal New York *Post*, and from the *Nation* to the *Wall Street Journal*. The highly influential interdenominational Protestant magazine *Christian Century* issued a call to personal action in a serio-comic editorial:

> It does not take a Casper Milquetoast to see in this new device another giant step toward the robotization of man. Its brainwashing possibilities are so obvious that even its inventor recommends immediate controls. Massive retaliation seems to be in order. We have drawn up a little list, in case the monster is universalized: Don't go to the movies. Turn off TV. Buy no brands that do not display a "No Subliminal Projection Advertising" affidavit. [35]

These critical articles frequently discussed the danger that subliminals could be used in political campaigns. Television ads could flash, "Elect Harry Jones," "Republicans Fight Communism Best," or "Throw the Rascals Out." A foreign-affairs and Soviet specialist with the Research Institute of America, Dr. Arthur Barron, warned that the Soviet Union probably had subliminals already, or would have them soon, and could flash "Americans are warmongers" or "Only Russia brings peace" on TV broadcasts to uncommitted nations or could use the technique to improve the Soviet image in the satellite countries. [36]

Among the many television discussions and documentaries was an ABC interview by Mike Wallace of Aldous Huxley. Huxley's novel *Brave New World*, published in 1931, had described a futuristic entertainment called the "feelies," in which movie audiences experienced the same sensations of love, anger, fear, or happiness portrayed on the screen. In the interview, Huxley cited subliminal projection as one of the techniques of the mass media that could be a menacing step toward political totalitarianism, and he called for tight controls in a free society. "I feel very strongly," Huxley said, "that we mustn't be caught by surprise by our own advances in technology." [37]

Later, in his book *Brave New World Revisited* (1958), Huxley contended that if he were rewriting his famous fable in the late 1950's, he would "certainly" include subliminal projection as a major portent of the future. For the real world, Huxley strongly urged legislation "prohibiting the use of subliminal projection in public places or on television screens." [38]

Concern was even expressed in cartoon form in such diverse publications as the *Wall Street Journal, Playboy,* and *Consumer Reports.*[39] The *Playboy* cartoons, for example, included one of a woman in a peignoir sitting before a television set, her face lathered and razor in hand, preparing to shave. Another showed four tough-looking men in a bar watching Arthur Godfrey on television, all four sipping not whiskey but Lipton tea, Godfrey's sponsor.

The science-fiction magazines also joined the "protest voices." In *Fantasy and Science Fiction*[40] a story by Edward S. Aarons described "The Communicators." On the television screens in this fictitious American dictatorship, the usual heroes and villains played out their roles at the visible level, but superimposed on the screens subliminally was this message:

CITIZENS OF TEXAS

The Communicators
Are Your Friends!
Obey the Austerity Program
BE STRONG!
BE DISCIPLINED!
WORK AND OBEY!

The story's narrator explained that through these invisible messages, flashed at microseconds, the Communicators "fashioned puppets out of the millions who lived and worked and obeyed in reply to the tug of invisible strings."

While these critical reactions were mounting, both Vicary and Precon spokesmen defended their processes and tried to calm the civic spokesmen. Vicary said he had "expected a few bursts from the eggheads, but not this." [41] In several public statements, Vicary maintained that subliminals could not make people do anything they did not want to; they could not "turn a Republican into a Democrat." They were only "re-inforcement" or "reminder" advertising. Furthermore, their use would lessen the obnoxious aspects of advertising, not increase them; "Many nights I've tried to watch the Late Show movie on TV but just before John kisses Mary, some sewer-cleaning commercial interrupts the show." Acknowledging that this idea was not new, Vicary still felt that his "practical work" with the process would stimulate research in an important field and would thereby benefit society's knowledge. Finally, Vicary defended subliminal advertising as a protected right under a free press in America. "We have a freedom to communicate," he told a *New York Times* reporter. "If we get into a hassle [with government bans], we'll go to the Supreme Court." [42] However, Vicary also admitted in June, 1958, that his venture was making "slow progress" and "we expected more sooner." [43]

Professors Corrigan and Becker of Precon also made public statements and speeches defending the process and deploring "emotional outbursts in the press." [44] Subliminals, they said, appeal only to "the mind people use every day." The human mind is "self-censoring," and individuals could not be brainwashed by subliminals. What individuals like can be reinforced, but it *cannot* be made unpleasant. If a serpent were coiled subliminally around a lovely heroine, Corrigan asserted, it wouldn't make her seem ugly, hateful, or repulsive to the audience.[45]

The Debate on Effectiveness

The worried predictions of critics and the reassuring responses of the promoters set the boundaries of a debate that proceeded actively from 1957 to 1959 and, indeed, is not finished yet. The issue was the real effect subliminals had—or could have—on an audience. The disclosure of Vicary's company and its plans brought into the press and magazines accounts of the pre-existing scientific history of subliminal suggestion. The roots were described as going back to Leibnitz's account of "petit perception" and Freud's concept of the unconscious, but the most direct forerunner of the Vicary-Precon procedures was the work done in 1917 by the Austrian neurologist Otto Poetzl. In a *New York Times Magazine* article on subliminals in 1958, Dr. George Klein of New York University described the Poetzl experiment to a reporter:

> Poetzl exposed landscape slides on a tachistoscope for one-hundredth of a second and asked his subjects to tell what they saw. They didn't see much. But he told them if they dreamed anything that night he'd like to hear about it the next day. The next day some subjects told him the details of their dreams. Poetzl found that some of the material in the dreams included

details they had not consciously seen the day before in the landscape slides. In other words, information which registered without awareness, was enlisted by whatever process operates in the construction of dreams; and it was utilized in forming some of the content of the dream.[46]

After Poetzl's experiments, work on invisible or inaudible stimuli was conducted with increasing frequency in psychology laboratories. Studies published in the *Journal of Experimental Psychology* and in *Archives of Psychology* in the 1930's and 1940's showed that auditory or visual stimuli transmitted below the normal threshold were recognized by subjects more often than chance would allow.[47] Just what this phenomenon meant and how powerful the effect was were matters not clearly explained by the experiments, however, and the subject remained scientifically interesting but vague.

It was against this background that the British Broadcasting Company had participated in a scientific experiment on July 6, 1956.[48] During a science program which averaged 4.5 million viewers, subliminal projection was discussed and a four-word message—"Pirie Breaks World Record"—was flashed on the screen subliminally at 1/25 of a second, over a filmed ballet sequence. After the program was over, an announcer said that a news item had been displayed, and anyone who had seen it was asked to write the BBC. The replies totaled 430. Twenty persons repeated the message exactly; 130 had it almost right. Others wrote that they woke up that night with the word "break" on their mind, and one lady said that some time after the night of the experiment, while she was washing dishes, "she kept thinking about the runner Pirie, and his new record."[49]

Other tests, performed *after* the Vicary press conference, confirmed that subliminal suggestion did get through to some viewers or listeners. In January, 1958, the Seattle radio station KOL began to air subaudial taped messages "under" the recordings played by its disc jockeys. These included, "How about a cup of coffee?" and "Someone is at the door." The disc jockeys asked listeners whether they heard "something else" on the records. According to a report of the experiment,[50] "One listener reported he 'thought about' having a cup of coffee, and two women admitted they went to the kitchen and made coffee immediately after hearing the broadcast. 'That's odd, too,' said one of them. 'I never drink coffee.' Another housewife who was tuned in while the 'door' message was being given said that although she did not go to the door, she did go to the window and look out. A 10-year-old girl reported after hearing the broadcast that she checked all four outside doors in her home and was puzzled to find no one there." (Station KOL illustrated some of the more controversial uses of subliminals when it broadcast—as "a joke"

—several "anti-TV" subliminals. These included, "TV's a bore," and "Isn't TV dull?") Other radio stations also began experimenting with subaudials, with KYA in San Francisco transmitting "Write KYA today" subaudially between records on a disc-jockey show. No announcement was made that anything special was being done. In six days the station received eighty-seven responsive letters. One said, "I don't know what you want me to write about but I will write anyway." Another letter said, "I seem to hear on KYA these days to write so I am. What's up?" [51]

Other television tests proved more negative. In February, 1958, Vicary appeared on a Canadian Broadcasting Company panel program, "Close-up," to discuss subliminal suggestion with a Canadian TV critic and an executive from a large Canadian advertising agency. During the program Vicary's equipment was used to flash "TELEPHONE NOW" 352 times during the half-hour program, which had a normal audience in the hundreds of thousands. After the discussion ended, the host urged viewers to write in if they had experienced any urge to do something they would not normally do while watching the show. Almost 500 viewers responded, and 51 per cent of these claimed to have received the message. However, only one viewer described this as "Telephone Now." The others said they wanted to drink Coke, beer, lemonade, or water; to eat; to remove their shoes; to put on sweaters; to shift their chairs; and a variety of other responses. A careful check of telephone-company records showed no abnormal telephone activity of any kind, nor was there any at CBC switchboards.[52] A similar "flop" was reported by TV station WTWO in Bangor, Maine.[53]

Apart from the various tests attempted by radio and television stations, a number of scientists issued statements contradicting the alarmed assumptions of some anti-subliminal critics. First, experts noted that many—often most—of the subjects at a subliminal showing could not report anything or failed to identify correctly the message flashed.[54] This seriously undermined the "power" attributed to subliminal suggestion. Second, the power of subliminal messages was quite weak even when received and was far from the all-compelling force that some critics had assumed. The best it could do was induce people to do something they were about to do anyway, such as drink Coca-Cola or eat popcorn.[55] Third, experts stated that the human mind controls such stimuli as the subliminals, not vice versa, and that the stimuli are ambiguous and often misunderstood.[56]

Finally, some scientific commentators saw the protests over subliminal suggestion as silly and "hysterical." Dr. Israel Goldiamond, head of the Perception and Conditioning Laboratory of Southern Illinois University, after debunking the effectiveness of subliminals on the basis of eight years of work in this area, compared its public reception to earlier fears that unscrupulous men would use X-ray machines to "peer through women's clothing." [57] Dr. Richard P. Barthol of UCLA saw attacks on subliminals as "safe" and "scapegoat" protest; the real place to challenge "hidden persuaders" in American society, he held, was in the "one-party press" or in news magazines that secretly mold opinions by describing one sixty-two-year-old politician as "aging" and another as "mature." [58]

These analyses by scientific commentators were not wholly persuasive to many others, however. The fact that subliminals might reach only part of the viewing audience was no solace for those who were reached, especially if those who "got the message" were also the elements in the population most susceptible to outside influences. Furthermore, while the defenses of the mind against overt advertising were well known, how the mind received and "censored" subliminal suggestion was something that none of the scientific experiments could judge authoritatively, especially if there were to be long-term repetition and possibly themes that appealed to secret fears of the audience.[59]

Government Responds

Government reactions took place in the midst of this public debate, and the final decisions of government agencies as to the need for action were greatly affected by the way the advertising industries responded to the public outcry. Soon after the Vicary press conference, amid editorial and Congressional calls for federal action, the Federal Communications Commission announced that it would investigate subliminal projection fully to see whether FCC action was needed.

In November a preliminary FCC report noted that while the Federal Communications Act forbids censorship of the content or manner of presentation of programs and advertising, the Act also provides that advertisers must be identified. And in renewing licenses, the Commission could consider whether stations carrying subliminal messages were knowingly engaged in deceptive advertising.[60] Both of these were ominous warnings for would-be subliminal users.

On January 12, 1958, Vicary provided a demonstration of his process for members of Congress and the FCC, as well as for the press. Using closed-circuit TV at a Washington, D.C., television studio, the message "Eat Popcorn" was flashed invisibly at 1/20 of a second, in five-second intervals, over a portion of a film called *The Grey Ghost*. During the demonstration Senator Potter told a colleague, "I think I want a hot dog," but no one present identified or "saw" the popcorn message until Vicary masked off the movie film and projected just the subliminal line. Then the movie was resumed, but the message was changed, secretly, to "Fight Polio." No one present described the shift, but later Senator Potter said, "I wanted to donate to something." [61]

Vicary told government officials and reporters at the demonstration that he was not dismayed at the lack of conscious response. "Those who have needs in relation to the message will be those who respond," he said, and he added that many responses were not immediate but delayed, sometimes for days or weeks. Vicary asked again that the FCC, the Federal Trade Commission, or Congress itself set up "some rules of the road" for the use of subliminals.

The FCC issued a statement shortly thereafter, to the effect that no television stations were using the technique at present and that there seemed no need to issue a ban on the process until more was known about its uses and effects.[62] Congress and the FCC itself could act when more became known.

In 1960, Section 317 of the 1934 Communications Act was amended [63] to redefine the situations in which broadcast licensees must make sponsorship identification announcements, and again these were revised in 1963.[64] Although this revision was influenced more by the impact of "payola" and "plugola" practices than by subliminal-broadcast techniques, the changes, according to FCC Chairman E. William Henry, would control subliminal broadcasting as well. As for any further action, Henry said the FCC "has not found it necessary to institute rule-making concerning the use of 'subliminal perception' by our broadcast licensees because the broadcast industry itself has effectively banned use of this advertising technique." [65]

At the state level, hearings and legislative debates were held in half a dozen states during 1958 and 1959, but no legislation banning or regulating subliminals was ever enacted, probably because of the lack of proof of its danger as well as the effectiveness of civic "containment." [66] The latter was felt strongly by the promoters of subliminal processes. "I've been taking a heck of a licking," Vicary complained in late 1958.[67] Previously his clients in marketing research and name-testing services had included leading corporations, such as American Telephone and Telegraph, Family Circle Magazine, the Ford Motor Company, and B. F. Goodrich Chemical Co. But, after the "public shock" over subliminals, Vicary said, "my market research clients didn't give me a tumble." He had to fire his staff of fifteen, move to smaller quarters, and try to rebuild his market-research services.[68]

The *Wall Street Journal* also interviewed Corrigan of Precon. "We've really had to tighten our belts," he reported. "This whole field is suffering from a complete public misunderstanding of our techniques and intentions." All of the firm's advertising contracts "went down the drain," and only two movies used subliminals to heighten psychological effects. However, Corrigan said, his firm was still "eager" to develop subliminal projection as "a tool for teaching and in psychotherapy." [69]

However, it was not until 1962 that the way was cleared even for these uses. The Patent Office finally issued a patent to Precon for motion-picture projectors that screen subliminal messages. The equipment consists of two projectors, one for the regular film and the other to flash the subliminal words or pictures. The subliminal message is printed on a loop of film that goes around continually; a second loop controls the frequency of the messages, and a third loop regulates the light intensity. It is interesting to note that at first the Patent Office refused the application on the ground that its issuance would not be in the public interest. Attorneys for Precon finally convinced the Patent Office that subliminal perception could not hypnotize, brain-wash, or coerce anyone into doing something that he did not want to do.[70] It might influence him, they contended, only if he were neutral or favorably inclined already.

The Present Status of Commercial "SS"

No commercial uses of subliminal suggestion seem to be in current operation. A survey of motion picture theater associations such as Loew's, Skouras, and Paramount produced completely negative reports.[71] "This company had been approached on the use of subliminal advertising," the president of Skouras Theatres Corporation recalled, "but the management . . . did not deem it advisable to entertain its use." A survey of various types of advertising agencies produced unanimously negative replies[72] and some interesting explanatory comments. A spokesman for Ted Bates and Company probably expressed the dominant thinking among advertising agencies by remarking:

    1. Subliminal advertising was actually a "publicity stunt" by a little-known research organization;
    2. It had enough appeal to sweep the daily press;
    3. When tested by other organizations, it was found to be invalid and without foundation.[73]

One additional reason for the boycott of subliminal techniques by advertising agencies was expressed by the Coordinator of Creative Activities of Diener and Dorskind. "[We] have troubles enough getting across an advertising message liminally. As our clients are continuously haggling with us over the fact that a 35-line ad in the New York Times ran only 33½ lines—I shudder to imagine the economic complications that would arise in trying to evaluate the number of men's minds we have succeeded in tyrannizing." [74]

Subliminals and Privacy:
False Alarm or Civic Containment?

One possible view of public response to subliminals is to dismiss the episode as a tempest in a teapot. In this view, the initial claims of the promoters were overinflated, the outcry of editors and civic spokesmen was overcredulous and self-feeding, and public alarm was a rather silly fear over Madison Avenue's super-power generated by the extravagant exposés of journalist-hucksters such as Vance Packard.[75] Once scientific estimates and commercial tests indicated that subliminals would not deliver the viewing masses to Ivory soap or Buick, and that a hard-hitting spot announcement for Senator Smith left more of a deposit on the voter's mind than a subliminal flash, the market for subliminals simply collapsed. The real test of the privacy issue, according to this estimate, would have come if subliminals had worked as well as their opponents feared, and American law and society would then have had to choose between a working process and privacy.

There is some force in this argument. Had the subliminal process worked, there might have been educational campaigns to "soften up" the public to accept the device. There might also have been "intermediate" solutions, such as announcements preceding programs or movies to the effect that subliminal ads would be shown, or even a single visible projection of the subliminal message before the program. Political subliminals might have been banned, though product advertising would have been permitted. Rules requiring subliminals to be "positive only" might have been promulgated by the FCC or by legislation. (This step would have prevented a company from projecting its rival's name over pictures of Stalin, snakes, and the Mafia "black hand.") Had such "intermediate" solutions been chosen, the debate over subliminals would have paralleled the issues involved in choosing between total bans and legal controls for electronic eavesdropping, polygraph testing, or narcoanalysis. Certainly the absence of any "law enforcement" aspect to the subliminal issue made it an "easier" issue than the others just cited.

This view finds some support in a survey undertaken in May, 1958, in a series of studies at Stanford University on the spread of scientific knowledge in the general community.[76] On the premise that scientific tests might someday perfect subliminal suggestion and advertisers might want to launch a campaign to persuade the public to accept the technique, the survey investigated what the public really believed about subliminal suggestion in the wake of the hostile publicity during 1957–58.

Interviews were held with a cross-sectional sample of 324 respondents from San Francisco during two weeks in May, 1958. Subjects were asked: "Have you heard of the possibility of using advertising on TV where the ads would be so dim, or flashed so fast, that you would not be aware of their being there? (This is called subliminal advertising.)" Of the respondents, 41 per cent said that they had heard of this development; 59 per cent had not. Forty-one per cent of informed responses represents a *high* degree of awareness, not a low level, compared with other surveys of public knowledge about civic issues or world affairs.

Of those who had heard of subliminal advertising, 50 per cent thought it was "unethical or wrong." When the full sample was asked, "Would you continue to watch your TV set if you knew this kind of ad was being used?" 67 per cent said that they would continue to watch, and 33 per cent said that they would not. Even 19 per cent who had felt the process to be "unethical or wrong" said they would watch anyway.

Analysis of the respondents' backgrounds and values revealed that those who would boycott TV if subliminals were broadcast were "least anti-intellectual" and most "evaluative" of those answering. Those who thought there was nothing wrong or unethical in subliminals had the highest "anti-intellectual" scores. The conclusion of the author of the study about the protestors was:

> Perhaps it is this same group that is most resistant to any type of commercial advertising. If this is the case, the advertising industry need not invest too much in trying to convert them, since they are out of reach. The fact that half the people who had heard of subliminal advertising thought there was nothing wrong with it, in spite of the tenor of the current mass media attacks on it, shows that the man on the street is not so frightened of subliminal advertising as are the more intellectual writers.

Despite an element of truth in the minimizing analysis described here, I think the minimizing view misunderstood the basic motive underlying public reactions to subliminals. The San Francisco survey, for example, was highly limiting in its question, "Would you continue to watch your TV set if you knew this kind of ad was being used?" since many other types of protest were also possible, such as boycotting particular programs, refusing to buy those products, or campaigning for government controls.

A better perspective on the 1957–59 response comes from considering what would probably have happened had the protests not been so widespread. The most likely event would have been a move by movie-theater owners, television sponsors, display advertisers, and film makers to try out the new technique. In addition, the process would have been used by dramatic shows and political advertisers on television. After tests had been run to determine the proportion of audiences who actually received the messages, the short- and long-range effects of the stimuli, the accuracy of perception, and the like, some rough balance of dollar costs against presumed return-in-sales would have been determined by advertising specialists, and a similar judgment would have been made by political and civic users. Subliminals would have then become part of the communication arsenal.

At that point no television viewer, radio listener, or movie-goer would have known whether any given performance he was consuming had used subliminal messages. The possibility of constant self-analysis by Americans of their "urges" might have been one consequence of the development. Moreover, the projection of subliminals might then have spread to other areas, such as waiting rooms at train, bus, and air terminals; public carriers; on billboards; or on the walls of offices and factories whose managements wanted to suggest to employees: "Stop Stealing," "Work Harder," "Who Needs Unions?" "You Aren't Thirsty," or "I Love This Job."

Moreover, whether people can be forced to do things "against their will" by subliminals is not the real issue. It is whether stimuli could release or strengthen urges that are already in viewers or listeners, both the impulse-filled "normal" person and the mentally disturbed. It is also whether slanted "information" could be planted in the minds of unsophisticated persons, in the form of "facts" or "judgments," that would later be thought of as the person's own beliefs or knowledge.

This is not to paint an apocalyptic vision, nor is it to say that subliminals would have had a 100-per-cent effect, or even a 30-per-cent effect, in producing the action suggested. It *does* suggest that the psychology of the public could have been profoundly altered by the knowledge that subliminal suggestion was being used on it, with only the self-restraint of the users as a limit on the type of message. This sense of defenselessness could have created serious anxieties had no privacy-asserting reaction been imposed. If someone projects visibly a skull, the word "BLOOD," or a picture of a serpent on my television screen or at a movie I am seeing, I can simply turn off the set or walk out of the theater if these symbols disturb or revolt me. But if they are projected subliminally into my subconscious, they not only could have disturbing later effects on my mental health, but the very fact that I know that this process is going on creates a sense of unease and helplessness that could have profound effects on American society, already far from lacking in mass anxieties. What was threatened was the function of personal autonomy that privacy performs for the individual.

Another issue of privacy at stake in the subliminal debates was the democratic political process. Though the conduct of representative government is obviously different today than when Locke, Jefferson, Mill, and Lincoln wrote their descriptions of governing "by the people," it is still a basic tenet of our system that voters know and judge what government and private groups are putting forward in public debates. Despite an awareness of new means of mass propaganda, we are still committed to the belief that most issues of public policy can be put to such a test of rational debate, though it often takes a vigilant press and strong civic-group protest to get debates on sensitive issues before the public. The threat of subliminal suggestion to the democratic process in the United States was that a public which was not consciously aware of the facts and arguments projected into millions of minds could not continue to exercise its crucial function of judgment and criticism. The mechanisms of democracy themselves were thus threatened by subliminal programs in the areas of lobbying, party campaigning, and governmental promotion. This is what the leading spokesmen against subliminals sensed—and reacted against.

Beyond the issue of subliminal suggestion lies the entire range of forthcoming devices, techniques, and substances that enter the mind to implant influences or extract data. Experiments have shown that it is possible to hypnotize persons watching television and have them experience the same emotional states as persons hypnotized in face-to-face hypnotic sessions. Drs. Herbert Spiegel and James H. Ryan of the College of Physicians and Surgeons of Columbia University—who demonstrated the "TV hypnosis" experiments at the American Medical Association Convention in 1965—have warned that this possibility has serious implications for the viewing public's rights to privacy. American society and its lawmakers, they contend, should be sure that there are adequate controls over the use of hypnotic "demonstrations" and "performances" on television and radio, as well as over "personnel having access to public broadcasting systems." [77]

Similar possibilities loom ahead, such as the placing of consciousness-affecting drugs in food, water, or air supplies without the public's knowledge or consent. Laws may be needed against private individuals or government officials so tampering with private or public supplies without full notice to the public and a proper proceeding involving legislative authorization.

Thus, I suggest that the leading elites of American society, supported firmly by civic groups that ranged from "hard conservative" to "left-liberal," understood better than did some of the scientific doubters and civic minimizers what was really at stake in the use of subliminal suggestion. The public outcry against subliminals in commerce or politics, far from being an empty or trivial victory, was a significant assertion of privacy's domain against a scientific innovation that might have been capable of great harm to society. Moreover, this victory was won not by legislation or judicial intervention but by the force of civic and public opinion.

CHAPTER TWELVE

Pulling All the Facts Together

THE IMPACT OF the "information revolution" on American society has been the subject of energetic discussions for almost two decades. Debates over social implications of data processing have focused primarily on three issues: the effects of computer-spurred automation on employment levels and work patterns; the extent to which business and government leaders are asking computers to "decide" questions that call for value judgments rather than fact or trend analysis; and the effects of computerization on the psychological attitudes of citizens toward work.

These are complex and subtle issues, on which reasonable men can disagree both as to what is occurring and what steps should be taken. As a consequence, the debates have been continuous discussions, moving from focus to focus as experience has been accumulated and new developments have arisen. What is significant is that computer specialists, civic commentators, private groups, and government officials all have recognized that these "side-effects" of computerization require thoughtful analysis, empirical study, institutional awareness by private and public computer users, and, in some instances, legal or governmental action to cushion or channel change.

Early Stirrings on the Data-Surveillance and Privacy Issue, 1961–1963

During the 1940's and 1950's the topic of privacy was conspicuously absent from these debates over the social implications of computerization. A thorough search of popular and scientific literature during this period reveals no treatment of the possible effects of computers on areas of personal and group life that had hitherto remained private because the information about these areas had been too voluminous, too scattered, too non-comparable, and too expensive to be collected by government or private organizations.

Then, in the early 1960's, a few voices among computer specialists

298

began to warn—usually in brief, prophetic forebodings—that the acquisition of vast new stores of information, their rapid and inexpensive processing, and the convenient availability of the data to government agencies and large private organizations might carry with it some dangers to the free society.

In April, 1961, Bernard Benson, president of a computer-manufacturing company in California, raised the privacy issue in a speech to the annual convention of the Society of Technical Writers and Publishers. More and more information is collected about every American these days, Benson noted, each piece obviously helpful in maintaining health, fighting crime, aiding employment, and the like, but all adding up to an almost embarrassingly intimate picture of each citizen. Someday somebody—or some machine—will reach the "logical conclusion" that all these data should flow into one computer or one computer center. When that happens, Benson warned, individual privacy and liberty will be "at the mercy of the man who pushes the button to make the machine remember." On the tapes will be each individual's entire history— "your FBI record, your childhood diseases and the attitudes of your parents, your school records, employment records, tax records, contributions to charity and even the records of your charge accounts and credit cards." With this information, the men running the computer would have achieved a vast increase in power over the lives of Americans. "Where information rests is where power lies, and [electronically computed] concentration of power is catastrophically dangerous." [1]

In December, 1962, Dr. Richard W. Hamming, a senior scientist and computer specialist with Bell Telephone Laboratories, concluded a review of the computer's useful potential at a scholarly meeting with a warning about the hazards it was creating. With machines ingesting a growing amount of personal information—collected by Selective Service, Social Security, Internal Revenue, insurance companies, places of employment, medical services, and even airline companies—"how do we know that this is always being used for the benefit of the individual . . . ?" Who would make sure that the data was used only for the purpose for which it was given? [2]

Another concerned comment appeared in the May, 1963, issue of the trade magazine *Computers and Automation*. An editorial reported the speed with which Massachusetts police had processed state punch-card records of blue 1958 Chevrolets to turn up a murderer who had been seen driving away from the scene of a crime in such a car. The editorial also reported that public announcement of the fact that bank-interest payments would be fed into the Internal Revenue Service computers had produced a big surge in new taxpayer reports of interest income. "To a greater and greater extent, [such] electronic data-processing will permeate the nerve channels of a complicated society." While tyranny "is not a necessary outcome" of these developments, "tyranny can be tighter and more inclusive for more people, and more efficient and more inescapable, with the contribution of computers and data processors." [3]

To some extent these occasional doubts in the night among computer specialists were matched by vague stirrings in several newspapers and magazines during the early 1960's. Often these were reactions to the adoption of computers by agencies of the federal or state governments. When the Internal Revenue Service installed its 7074 computer, cartoons in the press showed taxpayers being "spied upon" by mechanical brains.[4] This theme was also illustrated by a *Time* article that reported on the operations of the IBM 1410 computer used by the Commerce Department's National Driver Register Service. The system collects the names and records of all drivers whose licenses have been revoked in the states for drunken driving or have been in a fatality-producing crash. States can then send in names of applicants for drivers' licenses for checking and can receive a reply in less than twenty-four hours. Conceding the efficiency of the system and its properly limited purpose under the present law, *Time* noted:

> Today's Americans are a submissive lot. A generation ago, when someone suggested collecting everyone's fingerprints and filing them with the FBI, the civil libertarians shrieked with rage. But these days, hardly any U.S. auto driver knows—or seems to care—about a big grey machine in Washington. . . . It is a step toward a computerized Big Brotherhood that may one day be keeping elaborate tab on everybody.[5]

Some implications of federal data-processing operations for privacy were discussed in 1961, by David Bergamini in a *Reporter* article. Looking at the spread of computers throughout the federal establishment during the Eisenhower years, Bergamini was impressed by the vastness of the data being gathered.

> Much of the information involved has to do with property, with tanks and thumbtacks, rockets and light sockets. But information about people is also increasing in availability. By consulting the data-processing machines of various state and Federal agencies, it has become theoretically possible to assemble an amazingly quick and complete file on any citizen, including, for instance, his age, birthplace, Social Security number, employer, dependents, investments, dividends, liabilities, insurance coverage, license number, veteran's status, security clearance rating—even such intimate items as hobbies, organizational affiliations, physical blemishes, medical history or ability

to speak French. As Representative James C. Oliver (R., Maine) is reported to have put it, after hearings last year on computers by the House Subcommittee on Census and Government Statistics: "It's my impression that these machines may know too damn much." [6]

Another embryonic concern in the early 1960's was the effect of computers on the "internal affairs" of business. As corporations rely more and more on the use of computers for their decisions, control of operations, and other activities, and as more and more information is filed on computer tapes or other storage devices, such circumstances could obviously facilitate the searches of government anti-trust investigators for illegal activities. There was also a problem of private suits by competitors and public agencies that would demand computer records. In an article titled "Your Computer—Witness for the Prosecution?" a leading legal authority on computers, Roy N. Freed, briefed readers of *The Management Review* on some of these perils.

> When companies have put their correspondence files as well as their business records onto computers (through information-retrieval systems) legal opponents can conduct far more effective "fishing expeditions" than previously.
> All he need do is to ask you for a description of the records available through your machine system, the searching or indexing system used, and the specific questions that you have fed to the machine to comply with the court order. Going further, he also might be able to designate additional index terms to be searched and force you to re-examine your files. These approaches are obviously much more effective than questioning file searchers to find out how hard they looked—the procedure to which [an opponent] is limited at present.

None of these increases in accessibility represents the greatest danger of computers to corporate privacy, Freed continued. Despite all company attempts to operate in wholly lawful fashion, there are times when company policies lapse into illegal behavior, "through inadvertence, carelessness, ignorance of the law, or faulty communication between management levels in the company." Today such policies "are not formalized to the extent of being put into writing." But computers must be given instructions in detail, and this makes all company policies matters of record. [7]

Given the general currents of popular and scientific thinking about the computer during this period, the 1961–63 stirrings were isolated and infrequent commentaries. They were also very vague warnings, without specific examples of how actual misuse of data was altering the citizen's relation to organizations or government. Furthermore, the criticisms contained no suggestions as to what should or could be done to safeguard privacy without adopting a Wat Tyler "break the machine" revolt. Thus, even though the early protests were in the classic pattern of Orwellian prediction, they had little impact on the opinion of the public, civic groups, or computer specialists.

In fact, what concerned computer developers and users at this time (and since) was resistance to "good" computer applications in the name of "vague" social values such as privacy. Throughout the 1950's and early 1960's, military services, medical agencies, industrial concerns, government bureaus, credit agencies, university administrations, and many others were caught up in an exciting challenge. Through computerization they could now know more about the factual universe of their records, operations, and performance than had ever been possible before. Because of this new knowledge, they could also use computers to provide major gains in efficiency and insight—better customer services, more effective production, better implementation of public programs, augmented law enforcement, and more accurate prediction of developing trends. All these were seen as possible, in the here and now, if a computer system could be designed and installed to accomplish these goals. On that score, though, computer developers and users knew that they had their work cut out for them, since "anti-machine," "anti-automation," and "privacy-liberty" arguments had already arisen in several key episodes to limit data-acquisition programs in these years.

Two incidents from the late 1950's will illustrate the privacy-based resistance that computer users had encountered. In planning for the 1960 Federal Dicennial Census, the Census Bureau—one of the largest users of computers and a prime beneficiary of additional data-collection capabilities through computerization—decided to explore the feasibility of placing a question about religion on the 1960 census.[8] Census Bureau spokesmen stated that the agency had received repeated urgings from "business, social welfare, education, research, housing, and planning groups" that the Census obtain such religious-preference data. In a sample test conducted in a four-county area in Wisconsin during 1956, the question "What is your religion?" was asked of all persons over fourteen. When "Protestant" was the reply, the denomination was also asked. Any persons who declined to answer were not asked to state their reasons for refusing, and were not instructed that they had to answer. Census Bureau figures on the test showed that there was no greater refusal rate on religious identification than the very low rate the Census normally encountered on such questions as family income and educational background.

However, in 1957 a number of religious and civil-liberties organizations raised protests against the proposal to add a religious question to the 1960 Census. The American Civil Liberties Union, the American Humanist Association, most Jewish groups (such as the United Synagogue Council, American Jewish Congress, Anti-Defamation League, and American Jewish Committee), Christian Science groups, the General Conference of Seventh Day Adventists, the Mormon Church, and a few Protestant groups (such as the Baptists) protested that such a religious question—keeping in mind the legal requirement that every citizen must answer Census questions—would be a violation of the First Amendment's guarantees of freedom of religion and separation of church and state and a direct invasion of privacy of conscience. A resolution of the United Synagogue Council, for example, said such an inquiry "would constitute an unwarranted infringement upon the privacy of Americans." Some protestors indicated they would object even if the response to this question were made "voluntary."

The census proposal received strong support from some political scientists, the American Sociological Association, and major data-collection agencies. Catholic groups were strongly in favor, led by the National Catholic Welfare Conference and the National Council of Catholic Men. A Minneapolis *Tribune* survey found more Protestant groups "for it or neutral than against it." Editorial positions were divided, but a substantial editorial opinion clearly disapproved of the proposal on privacy grounds. Newspapers taking this view included the Washington *Post*, Minneapolis *Star*, Detroit *News*, St. Louis *Post Dispatch*, Sacramento *Bee*, Hartford *Times*, the interdenominational Protestant magazine *Christian Century*, and the liberal Catholic weekly *Commonweal*. The *Christian Science Monitor's* editorial protest, reprinted in many other newspapers, called the Census Bureau proposal a threat to "another treasured privacy of the American citizen."

Facing this considerable opposition, the Census Bureau announced late in 1957 that the religious-preference question would not be included on the 1960 schedule; the Bureau also decided not to seek a congressional statute to make such a question voluntary. Bureau spokesmen noted that the decision to include a new question was always a matter of weighing the advantages to be gained against the cost, the public opposition, and the reliability of response to be expected. (In 1966 the Census Bureau told a congressional committee that continued opposition made it "unlikely" that a question on religion would be used in the 1970 Census.)

Not only was no question on religion put into the 1960 Census, but opposition to Census Bureau publication of religious statistics led to a ruling by the Secretary of Commerce in 1958 forbidding any publication of the results of a religious-affiliation question included in a March, 1957, survey—the regular Census sample of 35,000 households done as part of the monthly Current Population Survey; the addition of a religious ques tion had been ordered by Census officials as a test for the possible 1960 question. Again the protest was strong enough to limit government action, the Secretary of Commerce's decision being taken after White House consultation and congressional soundings.

A second instance of civic resistance to increased data collection in this period involved a far more important issue for the future of computerization—the universal personal-identification system. If data collection and data processing of information about individuals is to be truly accurate and extended into new areas, it is essential that every person in the country have one distinctive identifying number. Unless this is so, errors will be made because individuals have their names recorded in different forms ("Smith, John Wilson," "Smith, J. W.," and so forth), because identical names are held by more than one person, because individuals change their names or the spelling of their names during their lifetimes, and because of a variety of other bases for error. The Social Security number system is not an automatic answer, since everyone does not have such a number and a person can have more than one number, or different numbers under different names. Though the Social Security Law was recently amended to allow the number to be used for income-tax reporting, the number cannot be used for other purposes under existing regulations.

To provide a universal personal-identification system, the National Office of Vital Statistics and cooperating state and local records agencies proposed in 1948 a national Birth Certificate Number, to give every individual born after January 1, 1949, a unique lifetime identifying number. Though this proposal was vigorously publicized by government agencies and some private business groups as a badly needed and desirable measure for health, safety, and statistical purposes, the idea was denounced in 1949 and 1950 in many newspapers as a potentially regimenting "police state" measure, and angry cartoons raised the "Big Brother" argument. The opposition was sufficiently strong to persuade twenty-four states to reject participation in the plan and to cause Congress to drop legislative proposals that had been put forward to provide for federal participation in the system. As of the early 1960's, the Bureau of Vital Statistics and many other federal and state agencies continued to favor the creation of a personal-identification system, but were convinced that a more powerful publicity campaign than could be marshaled at that time would be needed to overcome public resistance to the invasion-of-privacy aspect of the program.[9]

Based on experiences such as the two just mentioned, the computer community was generally less concerned in the early 1960's with dangers to privacy than with the dangers which "invasion of privacy" sentiment in public and legal opinion posed to current computer projects. This was the conclusion reached in the Bergamini article in 1961. After describing the adoption of computers for federal income-tax enforcement that had just gone into effect, Bergamini discussed proposals being considered by computer specialists to use computers for government anti-trust and criminal-law enforcement, and even to feed records of financial transactions from private firms, such as banks, directly to Internal Revenue Service computers. Bergamini noted:

> The Utopian possibilities have evoked a good deal of silence from industrial and government computer men. They are encouraged in their silence by what one of them calls "the official eggs-in-the-mouth and eggs-underfoot public-relations policy of computer manufacturers" and by what another terms "the quick hysteria and deep ignorance about all things automatic" that is exhibited by "liberally educated journalists, politicians, and labor leaders." . . . Computer men are quick to agree, off the record, that the main obstacle for improved computerized law enforcement is political rather than technological or financial.[10]

Of course, this was the fundamental cleavage between the early critics on privacy grounds and the mainstream of the computer community. While the Bensons, Hammings, and Berkeleys were peering into the future and wondering what might happen to privacy in the New Society, most computer specialists looking ahead were so completely gripped by the technocratic delights of a society under total or near-total computerization that they had no time or patience for considering privacy balances.

The Data-Collection Process Becomes More Concrete

This situation began to change by the mid-1960's. The first major development was the spread of computerization into areas and applications that provided some specific issues of privacy to replace the "hypothetical" questions of the pre-1964 period. At the top of the list was the expanded use of computerization for local and state law enforcement. By 1964 more than eighty local police forces had installed their own computers to help in rapid analysis of the characteristics of a crime and identification of suspect fingerprints from millions on file.[11] (By late 1966 a third of the police departments in a 284-city survey were using electronic computers.[12]) Computers have also been adopted in large cities to help pinpoint potential trouble spots and to enable police to assign special patrols to such areas, as well as to help keep track of arrests, violations, stolen-property reports, gun licenses, and pawnshop records.[13]

How police data processing began to raise privacy issues was illustrated by two uses of computers in New York. In 1964 the State of New York announced plans for a State Identification and Intelligence System, located in Albany, to bring together in one place information on certain criminal activity from the 3,600 police forces, prosecutors' offices, criminal courts, and departments of probation, correction, and parole in the state. When it achieves its operative goals in the late 1960's, the new bureau will provide not only records of arrest and court disposition of cases, but also record files containing data about the criminal history, modus operandi, and social history of individuals gathered by the various agencies. The system was designed to relieve each local law-enforcement agency of reliance on its own criminal-identification bureau, with the hope that New Jersey and Connecticut and other states would set up similar central bureaus which might tie in with the New York system.[14] Such file service is obviously desirable from the perspective of combating organized and mobile criminal elements. But the development also raised questions as to whose name and what kind of personal data will go into such police files, how the information will be kept, and who will have access to it. An article in one law-enforcement journal describing the New York system to its readers remarked that "a major problem of setting up the system is to establish various levels of security so that a citizen's privacy is observed, while police have maximum access to information on the underworld."[15] Governor Rockefeller's aide in charge of developing the bureau, Eliot Lumbard, mentioned to me in 1964 that one of his main problems in talking to New York State law-enforcement officials was to persuade them to drop suggestions for putting "too much data, about too many people" into the system.[16]

Another example of the privacy issue posed by increased police use of computers in New York was "Operation Corral" (Computer Oriented Retrieval of Auto Larcenists), which can identify a lawbreaker among ordinary motorists in 1/92,000 of a second. Using this system, a patrolman radios the license number of any car he wants checked to the computer, which is programmed with the license numbers of 30,000 stolen cars and of 80,000 "scofflaws." If the passing car is one of the wanted ones, the information is radioed ahead to a police car on the route being taken by the auto in question. Using the same computer, the license numbers of the 140,000 uninsured New York cars could be programmed, as could the more than 300,000 auto registrations which have been suspended or revoked. From its first use in May to August, 1965, the system resulted in the arrest of persons wanted for armed robbery, general larceny, rape, forgery, and narcotics peddling.

However, the initial demonstration of the system by the New York police, with a full company of reporters and television cameramen on hand, produced as its first "public" success the arrest of a thirty-four-year-old housewife who had not paid one traffic fine in the required period and had thus been fed into the computer memory bank as a "scofflaw." Her pained and frightened response at being pounced upon in this way led *The New York Times* to write an editorial entitled, "Big Brother is Watching," and she is now suing New York City for invasion of privacy.[17]

Federal data-collection developments in the 1960's also began to focus public attention on some concrete privacy issues. Although the twentieth-century regulatory and welfare responsibilities of American government have led to a general rise in government information gathering, the contribution of the computer has been to spur the collection of new levels of information, and to spread it more widely throughout the entire government establishment. A congressional committee found in 1964 that federal expenditures for the collection and processing of statistical information had gone up 23 per cent between 1961 and 1963 and had tripled between 1953 and 1963.[18] As a Deputy Commissioner of the Internal Revenue Service remarked, his agency's computers "feed into our processing operations items of information that we could not otherwise utilize. Computers, of course, can then make more internal checks and, through storage of additional information in the master file, provide accounting and checking techniques much superior to any we could hope to employ otherwise." [19]

The fact that "machine-to-machine reporting" is spreading data from agency to agency through the federal system was also noted by a congressional study in 1963. For example, agencies such as the Veterans Administration and the Department of Health, Education and Welfare now give the Treasury magnetic tapes containing information about the checks they issue. The Census Bureau uses tapes of earnings statements acquired by the Bureau of Old-Age and Survivors Insurance, and the latter in turn receives data tapes gathered under the Federal Insurance Compensation Act.[20]

An incident that took place during a Senate Appropriation Committee hearing in 1964 illustrates one inter-agency data-exchange situation that aroused serious protests from the Senators present. In presenting the Federal Trade Commission's request for authorization to purchase a computer (rather than to continue renting computer time), an FTC witness mentioned that the computer would enable his agency to process more efficiently questionnaires sent out on the basis of names of manufacturing companies drawn from federal income-tax files. The questionnaires were to collect statistics on economic trends in the nation. One Senator called the practice "shocking" and "unconscionable," and another told the FTC chairman, "you are in an area which is none of your business. . . . If I have access to your income tax return, even supposing I am only going to look to identify the name, . . . I have a tremendous advantage economically and otherwise over you. . . . This is just something that the government never intended to put in the hands of anybody." [21]

Another trend noted in a congressional report in 1963 was the increase through electronic data processing of the data exchanges between federal and state governments in regulatory and statistical programs. The report concluded that "the likelihood is strong that such applications will grow in the future." [22]

The first major group to feel the pinch of this increased federal data collection has been the business community, which has had to pay the bills and to spend the time to complete the detailed new questionnaires and reports born of computerization opportunities. Business concern over this development lay behind a Presidential directive in 1964 for all federal agencies to re-examine their reporting requirements to simplify procedures and eliminate "unnecessary" reports. [23] Business concern was expressed during a set of 1964 congressional hearings picturesquely titled "The Federal Paperwork Jungle." During these hearings, business witnesses complained that the volume of required reporting was soaring (a Montgomery Ward spokesman said his firm now files 2,700 different kinds of federal, state, and local reports each year); that individual federal agencies had initiated astonishingly detailed and probing questionnaire inquiries (the Federal Power Commission requires natural-gas producers to answer a ten-pound, 428-page questionnaire which costs companies between $80,000 and $250,000 to complete); and that the three federal agencies which were the main pressures were the Census Bureau, the Federal Trade Commission, and the Internal Revenue Service. The privacy theme was also raised by business spokesmen at the 1964 hearings. A spokesman for the National Association of Manufacturers stated that American businessmen were "concerned about the ever-increasing amount of statistics [required by the federal government] both in breadth and depth and detail." [24]

Centralization of data by the federal government began to concern others besides businessmen in this period. Master systems for collecting security-risk and security-clearance data have been initiated by several agencies, such as the Central Index File system created by the Department of Defense in 1955 for industrial security clearances within the United States and in 1963 for company-representative clearances to NATO countries. [25] In 1964 the Aerospace Medical Division of Brooks Air Force Base, Texas, announced that it was seeking "capability information" from organizations interested in the "development and application of procedures for coding derogatory information." Qualified organizations were to be invited to Washington to select at random a number of cases from the OSI files and to develop a "procedure of coding derogatory information by type, source, and other pertinent factors." Firms accepted for the competition were to have access to materials classified up through and including "confidential," but no materials were to be taken from the premises of the OSI offices. The *Nation* reacted to this announcement with an article entitled "Computerized Slander."

> The purpose of this Orwellian research and development contract is to assist personnel workers in multiple and rapid employment of derogatory knowhow for "security clearance purposes." . . . [K]nowledge of the system's existence, say insiders enthusiastically, will encourage greater provision of such "data" and permit a more rational and guided discipline to be operative in evaluation procedures. One can imagine with what interest government agencies and private corporations, to name only two of the more prominent potential users, are awaiting the outcome of this R. & D.[26]

Debate over the creation of an Income Tax Account Number System also contributed to the developing concern. When the Internal Revenue Service went into its automatic data-processing procedures, unique personal identification numbers were needed to feed all the reports on income transactions for each taxpayer into his proper account. Rather than devise and install a new numbering system, with the public and congressional opposition this might have drawn, the IRS sought and obtained legislation to use the Social Security number, making provision of this number on income returns a legal requirement. Those persons who did not have a Social Security number were issued such a number for both social-security and tax-identification purposes. A Social Security Administration witness stated in 1964 that 160 million numbers had been issued by that date, about five million of these for tax identification rather than for Social Security purposes. In February, 1964, Congressman Arnold Olsen expressed concern over several aspects of this numbering system. As he enlarged on his feeling in a letter to me, Representative Olsen explained that "a number can never have the dignity and respect of a name, as our jailkeepers well know. It concerns all of us that mass processing techniques applied to an individual's personal data can lend themselves to various kinds of abuses and, in my opinion, it is in these potential abuses that the real danger lies." [27]

Also during the mid-1960's a variety of computer applications in private industry and forecasts of computer developments by leading computer scientists and manufacturers[28] began to show that the computerized trail left by the individual in his daily life was no longer a futuristic prediction.[29] In the credit field, Credit Data Corporation adopted computers to provide subscribing companies with checks on individuals within ninety seconds of a request for data.[30] By telephoning one of the Credit Data's "Central Computers," a subscriber can get information on the individual's opened, closed, and delinquent accounts, as well as on the "instability" of the individual, as judged by his record of late, early, or no payments. The average cost of this service is twenty-two cents for each inquiry. Credit Data expects to have a nationwide system in operation by 1970.

In the area of local government, Santa Clara County in California is developing an alphabetical person index, called LOGIC—Local Government Information Control. The system is to include the individual's name, alias, Social Security number, address, birth record, driver's-license data, vehicle-license number, whether he is a county employee, and other information, including his voter and jury status and property holdings.[31] In the medical field, Maryland law requires that a record be kept of all persons receiving psychiatric aid. In education, New York Institute of Technology announced in 1966 a new project to use computers for aiding students' development. Special students would be tested and interviewed, and the resultant data would be fed into an International Telephone and Telegraph Company computer facility. These machines would provide profiles of student capacities and needs, enabling prediction of future performance and placement in a specific program. The computers would further be used to assess continually the students' progress.[32]

As for the immediate future in computerization, the press bulged in the middle 1960's with predictions of "total system" developments.[33] In 1965 the chairman of the board of governors of the American Federation of Information Processing Societies wrote that there were already in the development stage computer systems "with low-cost terminals attached to the home telephone, permitting the housewife to press a few telephone buttons to order and automatically charge purchases from a supermarket or department store." [34] The same point was made in 1964 by David Sarnoff, chairman of the board of the Radio Corporation of America. Sarnoff predicted that the time was nearing when the individual "will possess a personal number to serve as his private code for making or receiving local or global television calls, for credit information and innumerable other purposes. The number would tend to become as important for him as his name." [35] Dr. Simon Remo shared this view, but predicted that computer identification of fingerprints would be the distinguishing personal input.[36] The likelihood that private financial transactions would be linked directly to federal tax-agency and regulatory-agency computer systems was also predicted by government reports.[37]

Reactions to the New Data-Collection Uses

Reacting to these trends in computer uses, discussion of the implications of electronic data processing on privacy began to develop in a newly concrete fashion after 1964. There is no doubt that the rising debates over electronic eavesdropping, psychological testing, and polygraphing—and the public concern over privacy under technological pressure—had an important influence on these discussions of data surveillance.

Leading scientists in the computer community as well as other scientists helped to raise these issues among their colleagues and to the public. In a paper discussing the social implications of computers, delivered to the American Orthopsychiatric Association, Thomas C. Rowan of the System Development Corporation observed:

> [T]he issue of privacy will become increasingly important as expanding applications of information processing make it possible to combine record systems relating to education, credit, income tax, law enforcement, welfare, military service, and the like. Nor is this problem related to the individual's desire to remain anonymous—it rapidly escalates, and we must deal with centralized record systems or "data banks" as they affect broad socio-political environment.[38]

Paul Baran of the RAND Corporation emphasized in 1966 that increasing numbers of people and institutions are learning to depend upon computerized data as these become more readily available. Every person is beginning to leave a more complete trail of records through his life. Baran projected the increasing availability of such data, stored and assembled by interconnected "remote access" computers. Pointing to possible dangers arising to individual data privacy, he underlined the potential development of "inferential relational retrieval techniques" which eventually determine the connections of any person, event, or organization to any other person, event, or organization. Finally, Baran predicted an acceleration of the developing practice of systematic searching for any defaming data about political candidates.[39]

Another RAND expert, M. R. Maron, warned in 1966 that there may well be no effective method for individual appeal of a decision about his employment, promotion, loyalty, and so forth, if this is based upon computerized data retrieval. He forecast a "natural tendency" to make use of machines to select or reject people automatically, according to certain programmed criteria, for educational loans, passports, Job Corps, Peace Corps, security clearances, and the like. Yet Maron noted:

> Each individual is different, each has certain extenuating circumstances, each has information which he believes to be rele-

vant to the selector's decision and which the system does not consider relevant. . . . If an individual does not have the opportunity to be judged on the circumstances of his own special (individual) situation, *then he is being treated as a machine!* [40]

A final example of concern came from Vice Admiral H. G. Rickover in a 1964 speech on "Liberty, Science, and Law." Rickover complained that modern man seems to be tamely submitting to technological developments, such as numbering and decision by data processing, without making an effort to control their increasingly serious ramifications.[41] In April, 1966, Dr. Orville Brim, president of the Russell Sage Foundation, and I each wrote a paper for the American Orthopsychiatric Association Convention which stressed the growing problems of "dossier banks" and their effects on privacy. Accounts of these papers were carried widely in the press, prompting worried editorials in papers such as the *Wall Street Journal* and a feature story in *U.S. News and World Report*, titled "A Government Watch on 200 Million Americans?" [42]

The Deepening of Legal and Social-Science Commentaries

A firm sign that the relation between computers and privacy had begun to "arrive" as a topic of serious concern was the appearance of articles on this topic in social-science journals and law reviews in the mid-1960's. A good example is furnished by the article "Records and the Invasion of Privacy" by Professor Stanley Wagner, a political scientist at Oklahoma City University. "There is a new social control mechanism in our industrial society," Wagner wrote, "the result of the accumulation of personal information on individuals." The aspect which has raised special concern for privacy is the trend toward drawing record information together and correlating it. "It is conceivable," Wagner felt, "that a standardized cumulative record file on individuals will be the basis on which employment and membership in social organizations will depend. The record will be in the possession of some official agency. And it will all begin as it has already begun through voluntary commitment and unconcerned objective accumulation. (Our future application will be, 'Please forward my file to X.')"

The danger to privacy and to American liberties in this development was that individuals who knew that all this information was being collected and stored and lay readily available in the machines would never be able to know when it would be used "against them" and for what purposes. This public awareness of potential use would lead to an "increase in behavior 'for the record' " and less freedom of action and expression. People will be concerned not only with the fact that they are going "on record," but also with how that record will "look" to those in authority who examine it. The whole purpose of privacy, Wagner added, is to allow for unguarded, experimental "release" behavior by individuals, and this outlet is just what our dossier-computer system is threatening. Wagner could only suggest that creative people should deliberately engage in more private and anonymous activities and that those in authority should be taught to accept "contradictions" in the record as part of man's basic nature and dignity. Wagner's article thus reached a pessimistic conclusion; the "traditional recourse to social legislation or a national popular movement against the increasing use of records would be doomed to failure." [43]

An extensive discussion of privacy and the computer was contained in the *George Washington Law Review* in 1964. Donald N. Michael, a member of the Institute for Policy Studies and author of a monograph on *Cybernation: The Silent Conquest* (1963), noted in "Speculations on the Relation of the Computer to Individual Freedom and the Right to Privacy" that major social trends such as increasing mobility and population growth were making the average consumer *want* "central data files" so that he can "acquire quickly those conveniences that flow from a reliable credit rating and an acceptable social character." Thus "we can expect a great deal of information about the social, personal, and economic characteristics of individuals to be supplied voluntarily—often eagerly." In addition, acceptance of personality testing for government and industrial service and the increase of persons in science, engineering, and social sciences trained in "social engineering" methods would facilitate data collection.

Another development would be that the computer programmers— who have to know many intimate details in order to set up the programs and supervise the rules for relationships among the data—will be consulted by executives to assist them in making difficult judgments. Such a situation would create a need for ethical standards on the part of programmers "which now are not considered prerequisites to their trade" and would "inevitably" produce "corruptibles among this group who will leak private information." Programmers could also misfile or misclassify data, by accident or design, and ruin an individual's data record. This contingency raises the problem of how the individual will be able to challenge the data-file "picture" of himself. When records were primarily written documents or photographs, copies of such documents were kept in various places; but with increasing reliance on tapes, magnetic codes, and molecular films, paper records will tend to shrink or disappear altogether, leaving the individual unable to establish "a past history different from that jointly provided by the programmer of raw data and the interpreter of processed data." There will also be "fewer opportunities to derive a public consensus on what the data 'is,' for there will be no public language in which the primary data will be recorded through which the public can verify the meanings and facts of the records."

Michael acknowledged that the computer could make privacy more secure in several areas:

> [C]entralization of private information and its preservation in computer memories may decrease illegitimate leaks of that information. Those who will have access to personal history will see much more of it than was usually the case when it was contained in printed records, but fewer curious eyes will have knowledge of any part of the private history of the individual.

On the whole, however, Michael saw far more privacy-limiting effects of computerization than he saw privacy-enhancing ones. After considering government use of other technologies, such as electronic eavesdropping, and the opening of income-tax records for law-enforcement and loyalty-security purposes, Michael was not optimistic about the immediate prospects for privacy and freedom, nor did he have any proposals for control of social uses of the computer.[44]

Newspapers and magazines also began to register sensitivity when it was revealed that data collected by government for one purpose were used by government or private agencies to erode the citizen's privacy in areas wholly unrelated to the purpose for which the information had been collected. In 1964, for example, *The New York Times* editorially attacked the contract by which the New York State Motor Vehicle Department sold to a private firm the right to copy information from records which every person seeking a driver's license in New York must complete.[45]

In July, 1966, the *Saturday Review* printed a symposium on "The New Computerized Age" which included an article by John Lear entitled "Whither Personal Privacy." [46] In his *Newsweek* column of July 25, 1966, Henry Wallich expressed the increasing uneasiness of some financial experts about the potential uses of mechanized "financial profiles" of individuals. The article ends with a call for controls over the misuse of personal financial data, noting again that there are neither adequate screening controls over private access to such information nor clear court-defined standards for access by government agencies.[47]

A classic index of rising public concern on any social theme is best-selling "social-protest fiction." This has been especially true in the area of science and privacy, where the works of Huxley and Orwell are basic scripture. The computer and privacy received this treatment in Fletcher Knebel's and C. W. Bailey's book *Convention*, published in 1964. The story centers around a fictional national Republican Party presidential nominating convention, at which representatives of certain military-industrial interests obtain highly personal data on the delegates' lives, families, and financial problems and feed these into a digital computer (named "Oscar"). The private information is used to bring pressure to bear on the delegates to support the candidates backed by the military-industrial interests.[48]

Like a similar best-seller, the late Eugene Burdick's *The 480*,[49] the Knebel-and-Bailey book drew its inspiration from the "Simulmatics" computer developed by several professors at Columbia, MIT, and Yale and used as an aid to the Kennedy forces in the 1960 presidential campaign. Defended as an unmysterious way of finding out scientifically what people seem to want in politics or consumer goods, the Simulmatics machine had also provided possibilities that Messrs. Knebel, Bailey, and Burdick considered foreboding.

Congress Enters the Debate

The growth of concern about privacy and the computer first began to be recognized "officially" in 1965 when a subcommittee of Congress, authorized to study the general subject of invasion of privacy, added the topic of records and computerization to its list of agenda items, along with such "established" matters as personality testing, electronic eavesdropping, lie detectors, mail covers, and loyalty procedures.[50] The chairman of the subcommittee, Representative Cornelius Gallagher (D., N.J.), remarked, after listing the more conventional means of physical and psychological surveillance which his subcommittee would look into, "the magic of computers is helping [federal agencies] gather such a wealth of information from such a variety of sources that all of us may someday stand psychologically naked."

Actually, the Gallagher Subcommittee hearings did not investigate computers as such in 1965; they dealt with data surveillance in terms of the types of survey questions asked by government agencies, which were so broad or personal that they amounted to an unnecessary infringement of the citizen's privacy. A discussion developed concerning the process by which the federal government decides what questions to ask the citizen in survey (as opposed to regulatory) situations. In general, it was shown that the department seeking to circulate a questionnaire first determined for itself whether the data were needed, usually after consultation with leading organizations representing the people in the field. Furthermore, questions from every federal agency had to be approved by the Bureau of the Budget, which had general supervisory authority over all surveys in which identical questions were asked of more than ten persons or companies outside the federal employment force.

The most significant discussion of privacy and government survey procedures came in the testimony of Budget Bureau witnesses. Congressman Gallagher had stressed that every agency had its own duty, in the first instance, to consider the privacy issue, but it was clear that the Budget Bureau could be—potentially—the most effective guardian of privacy if it chose to use its gatekeeper function of authorization in this manner. Thus it was especially interesting to hear the Clearance Officer of the Budget Bureau, Edward Crowder, explain the Budget Bureau's position on privacy considerations in review:

> [O]ur review of any questionnaire or report involves a weighing of benefits against burdens imposed on respondents and costs to the government. Among the elements of impact on the respondent, we consider the sacrifice of privacy and the degree of such sacrifice, taking into account the voluntary or mandatory character of the response.

Thus the Budget Bureau's reviewing staff "is quick to identify questions of an unusually intimate nature" and then applies the tests: "whether the question serves a legitimate purpose, is technically sound for accomplishing that purpose, and provides appropriately for confidentiality." As examples of standards, Crowder noted that the Bureau had approved the personal questions about drinking, arrests, employment experience, and so forth, that appeared on Standard Form 57, the basic application for government employment, but the Bureau concurred in the stand of the Civil Service Commission that "personality tests have no legitimate role in regular application procedures." Intimate questions are approved for research projects in personality and mental health, since "participation is entirely voluntary and it has been our view that the issue of invasion of privacy does not arise." To show that privacy considerations had been present in the over-all judgment of the Bureau, Crowder stated that his committee had disapproved requests to administer a well-known personality test to six-year-olds; eliminated about twenty-five questions on the socio-economic background of youth counselors; and eliminated questions on the religious and political affiliations of civil-defense local officials in a survey designed to learn what factors made for effective civil-defense activity and leadership. In all, Crowder noted, there are 4,600 "active forms" in use by federal agencies, some no longer than a postcard and some running to forty pages.

While Crowder's presentation was well received, it was still the feeling of the subcommittee that formal rules on invasion of privacy and a sense of vigilance on the privacy issue ought to be part of the Budget Bureau responsibility.

What brought the Long and Gallagher committees directly to the problem of the computer were proposals from social scientists and government officials to create various types of centralized federal data pools.

Early in 1965 the Social Science Research Council received a committee report proposing that the Bureau of the Budget establish a National Data Center to coordinate the preservation and use of socio-economic data. A Budget Bureau consultant, E. S. Dunn, Jr., prepared a report in 1965 which recommended implementation of such a national data center to facilitate the efficient retrieval of information as government branches out into the more complex areas of poverty, health, urban renewal, and education, which require new and different uses of data.[51] For example, the Census Bureau, according to the 1964 Civil Rights Act, must collect data in 1970 on voting habits and registration, to determine what types of people vote. The Dunn Report recommended that the Bureau consider requesting initial funds in the 1967 fiscal budget to begin such a data center, with an eventual expenditure of $10 million annually to maintain the center. Though the Report noted the question of confidentiality, it simply assumed that no violations of existing rules of confidentiality would take place as a result of the data service, nor would there be any harm from putting data from state and local public agencies in the system, or in being able to trace aspects of each person's life through time.[52]

Reaction in the press and magazines to these proposals for a federal data center were almost wholly negative and alarmed. *U.S. News and World Report* published an article titled "A Government Watch on 200 Million Americans?" "Your life story may be on file with the Government before long, subject to official scrutiny at the push of a button. That's the trend." The Washington *Post* interviewed Dunn and concluded in the story that "[a]pparently no secrets would be kept from the Data Center." A typical editorial in the local press warned its readers: "Certainly the prospect of some bureaucrat being able to produce the life history of every person at the press of a button has disturbing implications." [53]

It was in this setting that Senator Long's committee held hearings on the data center, with Dunn figuring as the key witness. At the same time, Long introduced into the *Congressional Record* critical articles on the data center, such as one in the Washington *Post* by Richard Harwood titled "There's a Dossier on You." [54] Dunn's testimony before the Long Committee noted that the data-center proposal was not yet official and was still under study. He brought out the fact that the type of data under consideration was not at the "privacy" end of the data spectrum; that is, it did not include educational or court records, nor wiretap, polygraph, or psychological-testing data. The information under consideration was typical demographic data, collected by the government for many years and which was now needed to implement more rapidly new legislative and administrative proposals and projects in such areas as health, education, civil rights, and urban renewal.[55]

One point of particular concern to the committee was the meaning of the phrase "disclosure by-passing," which appeared originally in the Dunn Report.[56] The committee inquired into Dunn's recommendation that the data center have the capability for "disclosure by-passing" whenever "requirements violate legislative or administrative regulations," and asked whether it meant that additional legislation was needed to guard individual or corporate privacy. Dunn replied negatively, implying that under the current rules it would be possible with more flexible servicing procedures, to "generate new classifications and aggregates of these individuals to serve special purposes without modifying in any way the application of those legal and disclosure restraints." [57] The testimony did not provide much clarification of the term. As Senator Long noted:

> The files of the Internal Revenue Service, the Social Security Administration, the Veterans' Administration, the Defense Department, the Federal Housing Administration, and the Agriculture Department, to name but a few, already contain about all there is to know on almost every American. To store all this information in a computer where it could be collected and retrieved at a moment's notice gives rise to serious questions relative to privacy.[58]

Dunn reiterated his conviction that the paramount problem was not potential invasion of privacy but the greater availability of relevant and traditional types of data for administrative program planning and evaluation. He reminded the committee that Social Security records had been used for several years for creating some types of general-purpose data. On the other hand, Dunn said that FBI records would probably not be included in a national data center. At the present time, he stressed, it would be both technologically impractical and economically unfeasible to incorporate all existing government statistics into such a center. The type of data-collection project which would be feasible was a center which might locate information on people employed in machine manufacturing in New York, or all those in a given area who make less than $3,000 annually. The point is that if such data is not available quickly and inexpensively, the implementation of a specific program may not be possible.[59]

In responding to persistent committee questions about the possible safeguards against abuse of such a system, Dunn stressed two major types of control. First, there are series of existing regulations banning divulgence of personal statistics; in other words, standard procedure has generally been to release data not in individual form but in aggregates, groups, or classifications of information, without individual identification of any sort. Such safeguards could be extended to cover a national data center. Second, a special type of code could be developed to make certain that any tapes of "private information" would not be individually identifiable; however, there would be some form of "translation code" between this "private" type and such public codes as the Social Security code. Any "translation code" would be safeguarded through a type of "fail-safe" agreement under which half a dozen individual signatures might be needed to use the translation codes legally for any unique purpose.[60]

Long's basic complaint was not alleviated by this testimony. He emphasized repeatedly the need for "proper safeguards." Despite the fact that there is no intention to use such a data center for direct dealings with citizens, it is clear that it would still be relatively easy, technologically, to assign each individual a number and to develop the data center into a central dossier bank. As Senator Long explained, "The assignment of numbers to people bothers me but not as much as the idea that some petty official, by pushing a few buttons, could obtain a comprehensive dossier on any individual." It is possible, for instance, that states may have data from credit bureaus which could eventually be fed into such a data center. The committee made clear that it felt the administrative units had not studied the potential ramifications thoroughly enough, and that its own thorough investigation into the "hard questions" would continue while the data-center project was in its formative stages.[61]

In July of 1966 the Gallagher Committee held its own hearings on "The Computer and Privacy," with the federal data-center proposal as its main topic. The committee was hostile to Dunn and Bowman, the Chairman calling the proposed data center a "monster," and "octopus," and a "great, expensive, electronic garbage pail." Mr. Eckler told the committee that the Census hoped to ask in 1970 for Social Security numbers so that in the future more data on income, family size, and residence could be compared. He indicated, however, that public pressure had probably precluded any question on religion.

As the Gallagher hearings progressed, several points became clear about the proposed federal data-bank. Administration witnesses and computer experts indicated that the identity of the individuals and businesses reporting the data would have to be kept in the system so that the validity of the data could be assessed, shifts in population could be checked for demographic studies, and further questions could be asked of samples at a later time in order to clarify trends on a longitudinal basis.[62] This eliminated the possibility that privacy could be assured rather simply by breaking all links between identity and data.

It also became clear in the hearings that there was a difference of opinion among the experts on whether a data-bank for statistical purposes, with identities preserved, should be considered in any way comparable to an intelligence or dossier system, or whether data-banks were always potential intelligence systems capable of being used for that purpose by those having access to them.[63]

The immediate problem of the federal data-center was more or less settled when Administration spokesmen assured Representative Gallagher that no action would be taken to initiate such a center without presenting a full-scale proposal to Congress for approval in terms of both authorization and appropriations.[64] Both the Congressmen and Administration witnesses agreed that safeguards of confidentiality and privacy ought to be designed into the system as well as written into law before any such center was initiated.

In the larger context, several witnesses stressed that the computer community had been unconcerned for far too long with the basic issues of privacy, Congressman Gallagher stressed that there seemed to be no dialogue among computer people, behavioral scientists, and constitutional experts, and the Committee members voiced the hope that the hearings would prompt such meetings in the future.[65] One result of this suggestion was the creation of a committee on problems of privacy and the computer within the American Federation of Information Processing Societies (AFIPS), and the holding of a symposium on the subject at the national AFIPS convention during April, 1967. This was preceded in March by a three-day seminar meeting of leading computer experts, social scientists, law-enforcement officials, constitutional lawyers, and specialists on privacy.

In October, 1966, the report of the President's Task Force on the Storage of and Access to Government Statistics (the Kaysen Committee) was made public.[66] Unlike the Dunn report, this discussion emphasized the issue of privacy heavily, called for legislation to forbid all regulatory or law-enforcement use of data collected for statistical purposes, and recommended advance studies of ways to ensure confidentiality of personal data by technological and administrative means. The report concluded that, with such safeguards, a national data center was a highly desirable project and recommended that the Administration move ahead with it.

A third Congressional development in this period came from the Senate Constitutional Rights Subcommittee, which directed its attention to the collection of personal information by the federal government through the forms and questionnaires it required of federal employees and job applicants. The inquiry dealt briefly with personality tests, in a kind of "mop-up operation" from the 1965 hearings, then went on to medical forms, personnel history forms, special surveys of race and religion for equality compliance purposes, and questions about financial holdings for conflict-of-interest purposes.[67] Senator Ervin said that his committee had never before received such a flood of complaints and protests from citizens on any issue as it had on the requirements that federal employees supply racial and religious designations. During 1966 and early 1967, Ervin announced various eliminations of personal inquiries by federal agencies under pressure from his committee, such as the dropping by the Civil Service Commission of its Medical History Form 89. This had asked federal employees questions about bed-wetting, pregnancies, homosexuality, and whether blood relatives had committed suicide, had been insane, or had suffered from hives. The Commission had been unable to defend the necessity of the form on medical grounds, and examples were documented of use of the form to discipline or discharge employees when the real reasons for such action had been non-medical.[68] With thirty-five other Senators as co-sponsors, Senator Ervin introduced a general bill to protect the privacy of federal employees from unreasonable invasions by government officials.[69] This bill covered personality testing, polygraphing, race-religion-and-national-origin questionnaires, and various other self-reporting inquiries as to income and political activity. Hearings on this bill were held in late 1966, but the real test of the measure was expected to come at the 1967–68 sessions of Congress.

The Computer and Privacy

By the late 1960's large-scale data collection and processing of information about individuals and groups had been added to the American public's list of serious problems involving technology and privacy. For some, like the conservative editors of *U.S. News and World Report,* the computer promised to advance such unhappy developments as economic regulation, welfare activity, and government civil-rights enforcement by making them more efficient and thus even more distasteful. For others, such as liberals who do not ordinarily shudder at large-scale government activity in these areas, fears were raised by the prospects of government loyalty-security and law-enforcement activity. Reaching to each other from opposite ends of the American political spectrum, conservatives and liberals united in alarmed reaction at "computerized Big Brother."

Yet the fundamental thinking necessary to come to grips with the problems of the computer and privacy had not yet reached the public arenas as of 1967. Let me try to illustrate this point by describing first the larger setting of data-processing in American society, then examining the possibilities of achieving control over information systems to protect privacy from unreasonable invasions.

One of the basic philosophical and practical assumptions of a society is its theory about social decision-making, which can be called its information theory. The classic eighteenth- and nineteenth-century information theory was of rational individual action based on personal interest, for which a relatively limited pool of facts was required to run the business, social, and political systems.

Beginning in the early twentieth century, we have moved steadily toward a more behavioral-predictive theory of information, which assumes the need for much psychological and organizational data in order to make the decisions of social science, business, and government. The more computers offer opportunities to simulate behavior, forecast trends, and predict outcomes, the more pressure is generated for personal and organizational information to be collected and processed. In a way we sometimes only dimly grasp, this is one of the great changes in modern society.

At the same time, and partly generated by this change itself, there has been a distinct rise in public fear of de-personalization and manipulation through collection and processing of information. Big government, big private employers, even big social science have replaced the softening, face-to-face aspects of social control of earlier times. In this setting, the private personality is the last defense of individuality, the ultimate shield of personal autonomy. To the extent that this public fear clashes with the new information theory adopted by the decision-making elites of the society, this produces a sharp conflict which puts special stress on a society that wants to support both science and liberty.

The first way we can try to come to grips with this problem is to develop a new way of classifying information, to identify what is private and "non-circulating"; what is confidential, with limited circulation; and what is public or freely circulating. This can also be seen as a distinction between the facts about ourselves that are intimate, those that are part of our life transactions (education, employment, family, etc.), and those that are formal public records. Such a classification system actually approximates the theory used by some holders of mixed-information files today, such as the system used by law-enforcement agencies which divides files into those of public record, case-files, and "raw investigative" files.

Any attempt of this kind to develop a new information theory must take several factors into account. The "facts" about individuals put into new information systems always involve evaluation, by the very selection of what to record, the language terms in which it is formulated, with what other facts it is associated or classified, etc. As our society relies more and more on central files, what is in these becomes the most significant "facts" about an individual in his relations with society. This has great effect on decision makers as well. The decision maker comes to regard making judgments on such recorded facts as the most rational and fair way to make decisions, and will be threatened in his own role within the bureaucracy if he by-passes the record and relies on personal-hunch factors.

In addition, what information about an individual is put in his files becomes part of his estimate of himself; it is how the wise and the powerful forces in his life see him. It takes a very strong personality, especially among children being recorded in the new information-worshipping society, to reject or fight the recorded judgment of who he or she "is." (Part of the value of privacy in the past was that it limited the circulation of recorded judgments about individuals, leaving them free to seek self-realization in an open environment.)

In addition, the new information systems are probably going to create new institutions. While we worry now about investigations by credit agencies, it is likely that the decentralized credit-giving system of retail operations is going to vanish, to be replaced by the central financial utility discussed earlier, in which each person will have a single account that handles all his financial transactions of every kind. If this occurs, these new financial utilities will have in their information systems a total picture of every transaction of each depositor. What legal and ethical controls will we have ready for such bodies?

As for government, the likelihood is that our federal system will become less of a federal-state-local system of competing and sometimes cooperating layers and will develop into functional "subject-area control systems." All the government agencies concerned with a problem, such as health, employment, education, etc., whatever their level of government, will be part of an integrated information system and will coordinate their information to make decisions. These clusters will also be linked closely to private decision makers, such as employers, educational institutions, insurers, and hospitals. What controls over information collection and circulation will we have ready for these new public agencies?

If these judgments are valid, then we are now in a last-minute position to plan for the transition from one type of information theory of society to another. We must analyze the kinds of information our private and public agencies now collect, recognizing that increased possibilities of collation and circulation raise the danger potential of information our society was used to acquiring under the old information system.

This analysis would then take us to the planning and development of the new information system. The basic fact to be seen is that, even though machines in a carefully designed system can be made to do a great deal to protect privacy, man can defeat the most carefully designed system. This means that law and ethical restraints must be the final safeguards in the new information system. With this appreciation, we can discuss the machine possibilities and the legal-ethical possibilities for control.

System design aspects can be divided into three stages: input, storage, and output. The input stage can be set up to limit those who are allowed to put information in (excluding certain types of informant); to have the machine reject tainted information (such as wiretap information, grand-jury minutes, etc.); to reject information classified as too sensitive for this particular system (personality-test results, sexual records, etc.); and to classify all information as it comes in according to a sensitivity code from public-record to top-sensitive. Encrypting can be used to protect the input process from third-party tapping or attempts to distort information during input.

In the second phase, storage, protections would include physical safeguards against outsiders tapping in or tampering with stored data; background investigations and normal security controls over computer personnel; storing all data in a minimum scrambled form to prevent simple printing out (or "dumping") operations by system employees; creation of random audit operations to check on the functioning of the password-security codes for users; and creation of a program in the computer to reject attempts to convert statistical information into intelligence information (as by setting a minimum number of persons who must be in each category before the computer will give out data, to prevent "one-person" statistical inquiries).

In the third phase, output, machine controls would include locks preventing the obtaining of any information without an appropriate password for the type or class of information sought, and special two- and three-person password-combination requirements for specially sensitive material. Information can be coupled so that the computer will print out only in combinations that ensure protection of the individual's rights; for example, in law-enforcement intelligence systems, arrest records could be obtained only along with notations as to dismissals and convictions, and in government security files, allegations of disloyal conduct could be obtained only with the employee's replies. A major safeguard would be to record automatically all inquiries for information, verify immediately that they come from the proper source, and then compile a roster of inquiries for periodic review by outside review authorities (such as Congressional committees or a general protective agency) as well as by the information-system management.

Despite all these possible system safeguards, the system could still be corrupted from within or penetrated from outside by concerted effort. Thus the other half of the privacy front rests on new legal and ethical policies. Since some of the specific things law might do with the computer systems we have today are sketched out in Chapter 14, it is the broader principles for the future that I am concerned with here.

First, personal information, thought of as the right of decision over one's private personality, should be defined as a property right, with all the restraints on interference by public or private authorities and due-process guarantees that our law of property has been so skillful in devising. Along with this concept should go the idea that circulation of personal information by someone other than the owner or his trusted agent is handling a dangerous commodity in interstate commerce, and creates special duties and liabilities on the information utility or government system handling it.

With personal information so defined, a citizen would be entitled to have due process of law before his property could be taken and misused by government or by agencies exercising such enormous public power that they would be held to the same rules as government. Allowing for certain exceptions (national security, for example, or when information was separated completely from identity for statistical use), an individual would have to be notified when information was put into key central files. He would be able, if he desired, to examine the information that had been put into his file, to challenge its accuracy in some kind of administrative proceeding (with court review), and to submit a reply or explanation that would be coupled permanently to the information. In some instances, he should have a right to challenge the very opening of a file on him in certain derogatory-information systems.

Such a system of information review by the individual, somewhat like the rights government employees now have to see and contest their efficiency rating or of military personnel to rectify their military records, would have the most profound effect on the information system itself. When the information keeper knows that the individual will be notified, can see, and can challenge the information, all the restraints of visibility of action will be on the keeper. His loss of anonymity will be the best guarantee of fairness and care in the information-keeping procedure.

As suggested before, review of these information systems should be set up in an independent regulatory agency with an ombudsman-type character: a watchdog agency. Legislative review would also be needed.

Remedies for improper conduct in collecting, storing, or circulating personal information could include the usual criminal penalties, damage actions, and injunctions, though there would be difficult problems to work out here. What should not be overlooked is that the strongest sanction of all would be to exclude any person or agency from the information system itself, on a partial, short-term, or permanent basis. This, like exclusion from use in court of evidence obtained illegally, may be the most powerful weapon of all against misconduct.

Ethical developments in the future would range from educating a socially conscious, professional group of information keepers to official licensing with high qualifications, as well as the development of a code of ethics for the computer profession. One of the most interesting and important problems is: what will happen to those watchdogs of ethical performance in our society, the press and mass media, in the future information system? Can they continue to play their traditional role when access to information will be increasingly difficult for them, as outsiders? Or will the organs of criticism get their own computers and try to monitor selectively the operations of the big public and private systems?

All of these descriptions and suggestions may seem like fantasy to the reader of the 1960's. Yet few persons knowledgeable in the computer field would think that we are more than a decade away from the conditions for which such planning is needed. The most precious resource we have as a free society now is the lead time to become aware and to prepare ourselves.

In conclusion, two points might be noted as the "message" of this discussion:

1. The strict records surveillance that was for centuries the conscious trademark of European authoritarian systems, and which the young American republic deliberately rejected out of libertarian principles, is now being installed in the United States, not through a deliberate turn toward dictatorial policies, but as an accidental by-product of electronic data processing for social-welfare and public-service ends.

2. There is no way to stop computerization. As Professor Robert M. Fano of MIT has remarked, "You can never stop these things. It is like trying to prevent a river from flowing to the sea. What you have to do is to build dams, to build waterworks, to control the flow."

PART FOUR

Policy Choices for the 1970's

HAVING LOOKED intensively at five areas in which American society has been gripped by the surveillance-privacy dilemma during the past two decades, it is time to draw back and try to suggest the ways we might approach protection of privacy as a general concept in our social system. To do this, it is necessary first to go back to the days of the Framers of the American Constitution and see how the concept of privacy was dealt with in our formative years as a nation. We will see that American law set up a brilliant framework for balancing the interests of privacy, disclosure, and surveillance in the pre-technological era of 1790–1880. What happened to that balance between 1880 and 1950, under the impact of the first era of technological change, and how American law has been developing from 1950 to the present, are the issues treated in the rest of this chapter.

With this general constitutional and legal account at hand, the final chapter restates the basic themes of the book and turns to the task of restoring the balance of privacy in our society. This involves a process of analysis for considering conflicts between surveillance and privacy, as well as specific suggestions for private and public measures to deal with the presently imperative issues. In a sense, this is an agenda for discussion at the concrete level for the coming decade.

CHAPTER THIRTEEN

Privacy and American Law

Privacy Law in the Pre-Technological Era, 1790–1880

When the Federal Constitution was drafted and the United States was launched as an independent government in the 1790's, American political thought rested on a series of assumptions—drawn heavily from the philosophy of John Locke—that defined the context for privacy in a republican political system. First was the concept of individualism, with its component ideas of the worth of each person, private religious judgment, private economic motives, and direct legal rights for individuals. Second was the principle of limited government, with its corollaries of legal restraints on executive authority, the rule of law, and the moral primacy of the private over the public sphere of society. Third was the central importance of private property and its linkage with the individual's exercise of liberty; to protect these twin values, property owners required broad immunities from intrusion onto their premises and from interference with their use of personal possessions. Each of these guiding ideas had a common purpose: to free citizens from the unlimited surveillance and control that had been exercised over "subjects" by the kings, lords, churches, guilds, and municipalities of European society.[1]

The technological realities of eighteenth- and early nineteenth-century America limited communication to direct speech or letter. Eyes and ears were the only instruments for physical surveillance; penetration of the mind was possible only by torture or compelled testimony; and there was little extensive record keeping about individuals. Given this setting, American constitutional, statutory, and common law concentrated on establishing shields of privacy to protect individual and organizational autonomy, ensure personal and family privacy in the home, and safeguard confidentiality in the basic modes of communication.

"The laws inspect our actions," Crèvecoeur wrote about the American system, "our thoughts are left to God."[2] The foremost legal guarantee of this freedom was in the First Amendment to the Federal Constitution and its state counterparts. In his classic work *Commentaries on the Constitution of the United States*, Justice Joseph Story wrote in 1833 that the First Amendment's guarantees of free speech, press, assembly, and religion were intended to secure the rights of "private sentiment" and "private judgment." [3] Francis Lieber, one of the leading writers on American public law in the pre-Civil War period, contended in 1853 that the First Amendment was meant to ensure "freedom of communion," including "liberty of silence" (the right not to have to speak) and "the sacredness of epistolary communion." This safeguard was crucial to American civil liberty, Lieber explained, since no one could have liberty or exercise his "inextinguishable individuality" if "his communion with his fellows is interrupted or submitted to surveillance" by "the powerholder," government or private.[4] As one government official put it in 1855 when speaking of privacy for letters in the mails:

> The laws of the land are intended not only to preserve the person and material property of every citizen sacred from intrusion, but to secure the privacy of his thoughts, so far as he sees fit to withhold them from others. Silence is as great a privilege as speech, and it is as important that every one should be able to maintain it whenever he pleases, as that he should be at liberty to utter his thoughts without restraint.[5]

Furthermore, as Lieber noted, the freedom of communion given by the First Amendment included the right to form associations freely and to conduct affairs without surveillance by "the spy, the mouchard, the dilater, the informer, and the sycophant" of "police government." [6] It also encompassed restraints on police surveillance of public meeting places, such as coffeehouses and cabarets, in the offensive manner of European "police states." Since there were no significant Supreme Court interpretations of the First Amendment's free-speech and free-press provisions before the Civil War, the views of such men as Story and Lieber are our best sources for an understanding of what the First Amendment was thought to mean in the early decades of the nation.

The First Amendment and its state counterparts also protected individuals in the practice of anonymous publication. Contrary to the principle of seventeenth-century English licensing laws, which had required books and pamphlets to bear the name of the author and printer, the First Amendment's right of free press protected both anonymous and pseudonymous expressions. One historian has estimated that between 1789 and 1809 six Presidents, fifteen Cabinet members, twenty Senators, and thirty-four Congressmen published unsigned political writings or writings under pen names.[7]

Following the First Amendment's protection of individual and associational privacy was the Third Amendment's prohibition against the quartering of troops in private homes during peacetime without the owner's consent. The "plain object" of this Amendment, Justice Story held, was "to secure the perfect enjoyment of that great right of the [English] common law, that a man's house shall be his own castle, privileged against all civil and military intrusion." [8]

The Fourth Amendment, with its guarantee that "the right of the people to be secure in their persons, houses, papers and effects, against unreasonable searches and seizures, shall not be violated," was obviously a key element in American guarantees of privacy. Justice Story called the clause "indispensable to the full enjoyment of the rights of personal security, personal liberty, and private property." [9] The key to its meaning, he noted, was its reasonableness clause, requiring that warrants had to be issued on the basis of probable cause, be supported by oath or affirmation, and describe specifically the place to be searched and the person or objects to be seized. Lieber held that the Fourth Amendment's guarantees had two basic objects: they told each citizen, "Be a man—thou shalt be sovereign in thy house," and, simultaneously, they expressed the "direct antagonism" of Anglo-American law to continental "police government," where a policeman "enters at night or in the day any house or room, breaks open any drawer, [and] seizes papers or anything [he] deems fit, without any other warrant than the police hat, coat, and button." In the United States every schoolboy had in his reader Lord Chatham's speech against general warrants, to inculcate in Americans the principle that privacy in the home was guaranteed.[10]

This principle was re-stated in 1868, in the context of life after the Civil War, in Judge Thomas Cooley's *Constitutional Limitations*, probably the most influential constitutional treatise of that day. Cooley placed the citizen's "immunity in his home against the prying eyes of the government" alongside protection from "arbitrary control of the person" as the two foundations of personal liberty. The detailed limitations on the issuance and scope of search warrants that courts enforced, and the "very great particularity" required before "the privacy of a man's premises" could be invaded by government agents, were the bedrock of this guarantee. Speaking of legislation that might be proposed to allow searches of houses to discover evidence of certain crimes, Cooley voiced the sentiment on which Holmes would base his dissent in the *Olmstead* case sixty years later: "[I]t is better sometimes that crime should go unpunished than that the citizen should be liable to have his premises invaded, his desks broken open, his private books, letters, and papers exposed to prying curiosity, and to the misconstructions of ignorant and suspicious persons." For Cooley, it was unthinkable that "ministerial officers" in America should "take such liberties, in endeavoring to detect and punish offenders, as are even more criminal than the offenses they seek to punish." He cited the use of spies and informers, "prying into private correspondence" by postmasters, and disclosure of telegraph communications.[11]

Though no important federal cases on the Fourth Amendment are on record before the 1880's, state cases exist in this period on the comparable search-and-seizure clauses of state constitutions. These show that official entries were closely examined by judges to see whether probable cause was present to justify a search of private premises and to ensure specific descriptions in the warrant of the objects to be seized. In many of the reported cases, plaintiffs won trespass or damage suits against government officers for acting without warrants or on the basis of overbroad warrants.[12] And even though individuals had suffered no financial loss in such searches, it was held that money damages could be recovered because of the injury to reputation and character caused when government agents broke into "domestic repose." [13]

The Fifth Amendment's privilege against self-incrimination was another major legal bulwark for personal privacy, since it forbade the torture of individuals to compel testimony or to coerce confessions in criminal trials. However, it is a revealing fact that Lieber discussed "liberty of silence"—the right of persons and groups not to have to speak in public —under the First Amendment's guarantees, not those of the Fifth Amendment,[14] suggesting that leading commentators in the early decades of the Republic saw the First Amendment as providing a basis for privacy of opinion.

These constitutional protections of privacy were buttressed by common-law doctrines enforced at the local level. Under the law of nuisance, courts prevented unreasonable noises or smells that interfered with the "quiet enjoyment" of property by its owners. The law of trespass forbade any entry onto a man's land without his permission, and especially any entry without consent into a house, office, or other private building. In addition, trespass actions were the basic mechanism for challenging entries by public officials. When a citizen believed that his right to be secure in his house, papers, and effects had been violated, he tested the reasonableness of the official search by suing the entering officer for trespass. Since the officer's defense would be that he had a lawful warrant, it was in trespass cases, measuring physical "entries," that the judges examined whether a warrant was proper.

Eavesdropping prosecutions provided another common-law remedy. In upholding an eavesdropping charge against a man who watched a married woman through the window of her house and then circulated discreditable tales about her, a Pennsylvania judge commented in 1831:

> I consider this as a serious kind of offense. Every man's house is his castle, where no man has a right to intrude for any purpose whatever. No man has a right to pry into your secrecy in your

own house. There are very few families where even the truth would not be very unpleasant to be told all over the country. . . . [I]t is important to all persons that our families should be sacred from the intrusion of every person.[15]

Furthermore, the doctrines of relevance and necessity in determining the admissibility of evidence in civil proceedings were important protections of individual privacy. In discovery proceedings in the courts of equity, judges performed very much as they did when passing on the necessity for a search warrant. Bills in equity which tried to use discovery to secure information in which the plaintiff "had no interest, to gratify his malice, or his curiosity . . . would most aptly be denominated a mere fishing bill," wrote Justice Story.[16]

Privacy for the core secrets of business associations was protected under common-law doctrines such as trademark and protection of business confidences. Justice Story noted that "courts of equity will restrain a party from making a disclosure of secrets communicated to him in the course of a confidential employment. And it matters not, in such cases, whether the secrets be secrets of trade, or secrets of title, or other secrets of the party important to his interests." [17]

American law also established in its early decades the right of government agencies to claim privacy for certain internal proceedings. Even at that time, however, the line between appropriate government privacy and disclosure for public scrutiny was a difficult one for a republican system. The Constitution of 1787, of course, had itself been written behind closed doors; no reports were published, and all participants were sworn to secrecy, "to preserve the fullest freedom of discussion." [18] Though opponents of the Constitution denounced the "secret conclave," historians agree that a constitution would probably never have been issued if the convention's work had been publicized at the time. Privacy for the proceedings of jurors, judicial conferences, and legislative committees was questioned only rarely. The main struggle arose between the legislative and executive branches, especially at the federal level, with the press often aligning itself behind the legislative branch in defense of "the people's right to know."

Beginning with the first congressional session in 1790, Congress called on the President to supply papers dealing with acts of the administration.[19] When such a call was made in 1792 for the papers on General St. Clair's defeat by Indians, Washington speculated to his Cabinet that there might be papers "of so secret a nature that they ought not to be given up." Subsequently the President and the Cabinet agreed on the principle "that the Executive ought to communicate such papers as the public good would permit, and ought to refuse those the disclosure of which would injure the public." [20] Throughout the 1790's some calls were honored, such as that for the St. Clair papers; others were refused, such as the call for papers involved in the negotiation of Jay's Treaty. Later President Jefferson did send on a letter subpoenaed by Chief Justice John Marshall for use in the Burr treason trial, but he added this comment: "With respect to [Executive] papers, there is certainly a public and private side to our offices." Proclamations, grants, commissions, and the like were public papers, but other documents were "more executive proceedings," and "all nations have found it necessary that for advantageous conduct of their affairs some of these proceedings at least should remain known to their executive functionaries only." The President, "from the nature of the case must be the sole judge of which of them the public interest will permit publication." [21] Set by this broad framework, and with no rules put down by the courts, a struggle of relative institutional power and public relations between Congresses and Presidents became the rule.

Privacy of communication received legal protection in several ways other than those which flowed from the constitutional, statutory, and common-law rules already described. Legal recognition of privacy for communications between husband and wife and between lawyer and client had been firmly established since Colonial days, to preserve frankness and trust in these special confidential relationships. However, while priest-penitent confidences had not been given the same protection, American law did protect the privacy of the priest-penitent relationship. The most important case was an 1813 New York decision in which the court accepted a Catholic priest's refusal to relate the name of a person who had confessed a crime of robbery to the priest and had then given him the proceeds to return to its owner.[22]

The definition of privacy in other confidential relationships took place alongside the expansion of the privilege against self-incrimination in the early decades of the nation. Confidential communications between employer and employee were held not to be entitled to privacy, and testimony was required, for example, in cases involving clerks. The same rule was applied by the courts in cases involving doctor-patient confidence until, in 1828, New York enacted a statute making communications between doctor and patient privileged just as were those between lawyer and client. Other states followed the New York example, and eventually two thirds of American states adopted this privilege.[23]

Privacy of letters in the mail was firmly declared by congressional statute, first by an act of 1792 forbidding any person in the postal service to open a letter, then in an 1825 federal statute forbidding anyone to open a letter while it was being carried in the mail "to pry into another's business or secrets." There was no provision in the statute for opening of letters by government officials, by executive order or judicial warrant. Though leading political figures had many difficulties in the early decades of the Republic in preventing political postmasters from opening their letters, privacy for letters in transit was well secured through expansion of mail volume and official enforcement measures by the 1830's and remained so throughout the nineteenth century. No intercepted letters were used in federal court cases or congressional hearings, and none appear even to have been offered for use, in these decades. Furthermore, many states in this period added their own sanction to the federal penal law by passing statutes making it a crime for any person to read, open, or publish any sealed letter not addressed to himself without authorization from the writer or addressee. California did this in 1872. In 1878, in the course of a ruling discussing congressional power to exclude various types of publications from the mails, a U.S. Supreme Court opinion noted:

> Letters and sealed packages . . . in the mail are as fully guarded from examination and inspection, except as to their outward form and weight, as if they were retained by the parties forwarding them in their own domiciles. The constitutional guaranty of the right of the people to be secure in their papers against unreasonable searches and seizures extends to their papers, thus closed against inspection, wherever they may be.

However, Justice Field rejected the position that letters could never be opened by government officials and held that they could be reached on a properly issued warrant "as is required when papers are subjected to search in one's own household." [24]

American law also ensured against unauthorized publication of the contents of letters once they had been delivered. The leading case was *Dennis v. Leclerc*, in 1811, holding that the recipient or holder of a letter has no right to publish it without the consent of the sender. The court in Louisiana rejected an editor's claim that he had a First Amendment right of free press to publish a letter given to him by its recipient. Instead, the court ruled that the need to protect confidential communication by letter required the courts to prevent such unauthorized publication. This ruling was reached wholly apart from any literary or property value in the correspondence: the value asserted was privacy. Justice Story reached a similar conclusion in a federal ruling in 1841, and he commented in his famous treatise on equity jurisprudence that violating private correspondence was "odious": "It strikes at the root of all that free and mutual interchange of advice, opinions, and sentiments, between relatives and friends, and correspondents, which is so essential to the well-being of society, and to the spirit of a liberal courtesy and refinement." Apart from causing great distress to those whose "inviolable secrets" were disclosed, failure to protect such confidences would "compel every one in self defense to write, even to his dearest friends, with the cold and formal severity, with which he would write to his wariest opponents, or his most implacable enemies." To avoid this, Story said, the law will recognize "the implied or necessary intention and duty of privacy and secrecy." [25]

This framework of American law on privacy was a mature and sophisticated system for the first century of national life. In setting a republican and libertarian balance among the values of privacy, disclosure, and surveillance, American law outlawed practices such as religious test oaths for public officials, compulsory testimony by defendants at criminal trials, and federal searches of letters in the mails. In other areas American law set up concepts of reasonableness and adopted procedures for balancing the values of privacy, disclosure, and surveillance in particular contexts. Properly limited and described searches by public officials were upheld by the courts as reasonable, even though homes and other private premises were entered.[26] The courts already began to display tighter standards for search warrants which involved certain types of "moral" crimes on which community opinion was divided, such as cases in the 1850's involving seizure of liquor under state prohibition laws.[27] Citizens had to give personal information to federal census takers, overriding some early objections to the census as an invasion of privacy, and despite the early practice of posting census returns in each district for public scrutiny. The disclosure was accepted because of the confidentiality of data once it was sent to Washington and its unavailability for use in criminal or regulatory proceedings.[28] When new technological developments arrived during this era, American law made effective adaptations to protect the balance of privacy. After the telegraph came into widespread use, in the decade before the Civil War, state statutes were enacted forbidding persons to cut or tap telegraph lines or intercept telegraph messages,[29] and the press reported prosecutions of individuals for such practices.[30] However, original drafts of telegrams filed with clerks for dispatch and the telegraph company's copies written out at the place of destination were not held to deserve the same absolute privilege of privacy as sealed letters in the mails; they had to be produced by telegraph companies for court trials and legislative investigations.[31] Eventually the courts policed both judicial and legislative demands for telegraph messages to ensure that the search was reasonable in its scope and its specific description of the telegrams required, and individuals or business firms would use special telegraph ciphers when they wanted to ensure privacy.[32]

Thus, the notion put forward by legal commentators from Brandeis down to the present—that privacy was somehow a "modern" legal right which began to take form only in the late nineteenth century[33]—is simply bad history and bad law. Pre-Civil War America had a thorough and effective set of rules with which to protect individual and group privacy from the means of compulsory disclosure and physical surveillance known in that era. As shown previously, the opportunities for achieving privacy depend on one's socio-economic status and the type of community one lives in, and even well-to-do Americans had to struggle for their privacy against a prying sensationalist press, American egalitarian curiosity, and strong patterns of social surveillance by various religious and political authorities. Nevertheless, American law controlled surveillance in this pre-technological era in a way that continental regimes in the Roman law–authoritarian tradition did not.

The First Era of Technological Challenge, 1880's–1950

Three technological developments of the late nineteenth century altered the balance between personal expression and third-party surveillance that had prevailed since antiquity. First was the invention of the telephone in the 1880's, and its development into an indispensable instrument of personal, business, political, and governmental life. Now informal and tentative conversation spoken inside the home or office was projected outside it. The near-simultaneous development of telephone tapping made these conversations vulnerable to being overheard and recorded by third parties unknown to the telephone conversationalists. Within ten years after the invention of the telephone the American press featured stories of private telephone tapping to steal stock quotations or newspaper stories, and police listening-in during criminal investigations.

The second technological innovation was the invention in the 1870's of the microphone and of the dictograph recorder in the 1890's. These devices enabled third parties to listen to room conversations from considerable distances away and to preserve them on permanent wax recordings. Such microphone eavesdropping also came into active use before World War I. The age of hidden microphones had begun.

The third technological development was the invention of what was then called "instantaneous photography." Prior to that time, subjects had to sit still for minutes for the photographer to prepare his plate. In the 1880's the Kodak camera perfected dry-plate, fixed-focus photography. Amateurs could now make candid snapshots of people and events, enabling man's physical state, expressions, and actions to be captured on permanent film without his prior consent. By the late 1880's and early 1890's there were complaints about unauthorized publication of photographs in the press and for commercial advertising, as well as the use of concealed cameras by detectives for surveillance work. In 1902 *The New York Times* complained that "kodakers lying in wait" to photograph public figures had become a "wanton" invasion of privacy that demanded legal control.[34]

Each in its own way, these three technological advances brought the capacity for invading privacy into the *informal* arenas of conversation and action. Law could no longer protect privacy of conversation and "free communion" solely by guarding the physical site from physical invasion or by guarding physical records from unreasonable seizure. The new developments demanded that American law define what rights of privacy were inherent in personal acts and conversations themselves. Yet, as will be shown, American law never came to grips effectively with this first technological challenge between the 1880's and the 1950's.

CONSTITUTIONAL-LAW ATTEMPTS TO CONTROL SURVEILLANCE

Public-law responses to the first wave of technological innovation must be understood in terms of two distinct periods of constitutional and political philosophy. Between 1880 and 1937 the Supreme Court majority's endorsement of laissez-faire economic concepts and its hostility to government "interference" in business affairs led to a "propertied privacy" outlook among the Justices. Owners of private businesses were held to be entitled to strike their own bargains in labor relations or pricing, as part of their private liberty to contract. Businesses were held to be immune from general governmental regulations unless their enterprises were "affected with a public interest." This status was very narrowly defined by the courts. Owners of public-accommodation facilities, such as railroads and restaurants, were held to be free to set policies of racial or religious exclusion in their private establishments. Executive agencies and new regulatory commissions were seriously hampered in their attempts to investigate improper business practices by judicial decisions holding many investigations illegal as "fishing expeditions" into "private records" and "private affairs." No "sacrifice of privacy" was to be permitted, the Supreme Court held in an early ICC case, unless a "specific breach of law" was being investigated. Legislative investigations were similarly limited; a congressional inquiry into the suspicious collapse of a land-pool company in which the United States was a principal creditor was held invalid in 1880 as an "inquiry into the private affairs of the citizen."

The leading search-and-seizure decisions of this era were also business and property cases. *Boyd v. United States* in 1886 was the Supreme Court's landmark ruling linking the Fourth Amendment's protection against unreasonable search and seizure to the Fifth Amendment's guarantee against self-incrimination, to give joint protection to "the sanctity of a man's home and the privacies of life." This case held unconstitutional a provision in the Federal Customs Act requiring a person to produce his business papers in court when goods had been seized as contraband or else have the charges of fraudulent importing taken as "confessed" and forfeit the goods. At this time it was solely in support of business values and property rights that American courts used the "liberty of silence" concept of the First Amendment. For example, state statutes requiring railroads to furnish employees with written statements of the reasons for discharge—an attempt to protect employees from penalty for union membership or activity—were struck down by state courts in the 1880's and the early twentieth century as violating the railroad corporation's "sacred" "liberty of silence." [35]

While "propertied privacy" was receiving such broad and decisive protection in the courts between 1880 and 1937, especially on First, Fourth, and Fifth Amendment grounds, the concepts of personal privacy and privacy of communication were treated with singular narrowness. This was especially true of the key issues raised by new methods of physical surveillance. In the *Olmstead* case of 1928, a five-to-four majority of the Supreme Court held that a federal agent's use of wiretapping on the phones of a leading West Coast bootlegger during prohibition was not a search and seizure covered by the Fourth Amendment. Chief Justice Taft stressed that no "tangible material effects" had been obtained by "actual physical invasion" when wires were tapped from outside the homes and offices of defendants. The Fourth Amendment, he said, "cannot be extended and expanded to include telephone wires, reaching to the whole world from the defendant's house or office." And since defendants had voluntarily projected their voices, the Court held that no issue of self-incrimination was presented under the Fifth Amendment.[36] From papers of the Justices who decided the *Olmstead* case, it is known that Chief Justice Taft, a strong supporter of prohibition, was determined to use the *Olmstead* case to make sure that law-enforcement officers would not be hindered by "bleeding hearts." He also saw the case as part of his struggle against the "dangerous" liberal positions advocated on constitutional issues by Holmes, Brandeis, and Stone.[37] If the first wiretapping case had centered on a corporation's telephone in a federal criminal anti-trust case or a state business-fraud investigation, and if telephone conversations between attorney and client had been involved, the Taft-led majority might have seen a tangible governmental surveillance of the communication process, and a "seizure" of something of constitutional value. As it was, the requirement of physical trespass and the "intangibility" of speech were read into the Fourth Amendment, while Brandeis' brilliant dissenting argument supporting a constitutional right to privacy was rejected. The most harmful aspect of the *Olmstead* ruling for the future was its either-or approach to wiretapping. The Court could have held that a telephone tap was sufficiently like a physical search to require that the government satisfy the rule of *reasonableness*, measured by Fourth Amendment standards of probable cause, specificity, and limitation of scope as adapted to the special elements of wiretapping. Had they done so, the Court could have set standards for government use of both taps and bugs.

Though the Court's majority did not adopt this position, Chief Justice Taft stated that Congress could always enact legislation to make wiretap evidence inadmissible in criminal trials. In 1933 Congress did forbid wiretapping in prohibition cases—but that was the last time Congress enacted any statute specifically dealing with government wiretapping.

Equally important in leaving wiretapping and electronic eavesdropping uncontrolled in this period was the failure of the Supreme Court to develop effective doctrines to control police misconduct when there *were* actual entries, physical intrusions, and seizures of tangibles. One complication was the Court's treatment of the law of arrest in relation to that of search and seizure. The Court had held that government officers could never conduct a search solely for evidence of crime, even under a warrant describing particularly what was sought. Searches were supposed to be only for illegal goods, such as stolen property or property that the individual had no right to possess (diseased cattle, untaxed liquor, sawed-off shotguns, narcotics, and the like). This rather sharp restriction of the law-enforcement official's capacity to secure evidence had little meaning in practice, however, because officers making a lawful arrest were allowed to search the premises thoroughly, without a search warrant, and any evidence of crime they unearthed was admissible in court. As a result, police officials usually did not bother to obtain search warrants; they simply got arrest warrants and did their searching after they made the arrest at a person's home or office. Sometimes they did not even bother to get arrest warrants. While the courts might condemn such conduct as illegal, the doctrine that illegally obtained evidence was still admissible evidence in most states denied judges the one remedy—exclusion of evidence—that courts could effectively use against the police. Thus the police went on with their improper practices, without judicial control over government wiretapping and eavesdropping even when there had been illegal entries to plant microphones or tap the telephone instrument itself.

In the late 1930's the "propertied privacy" era in public law came to an end. The elements of "propertied privacy" had been used as a major shield by business in the early 1930's, to resist the New Deal's economic measures and New Deal attempts to investigate business activity. David Lawrence, for example, had attacked congressional investigations of business lobbying and federal collection and use of information from private businesses, calling them direct threats to the right of privacy. "To the judiciary alone," Lawrence wrote, "can the citizen now make his final appeal" to restore "the right of privacy" in America.[38] However, when the Supreme Court upheld the major federal and state New Deal programs, it declared that the judiciary would not substitute its judgment on the necessity or wisdom of economic measures for that of the elected branches. It also upheld broad rights of investigation by elected agencies into private affairs that affected public interests. These decisions ended the immunity of "propertied privacy" that business had enjoyed for five decades in American constitutional law. Now the only major limit left on government economic authority was the reasonableness of the measure and the requirement of procedural due process. The result was that no federal economic regulatory statute or federal legislative or executive investigation into business affairs has been held unconstitutional since 1937.

Though the "propertied privacy" doctrine had been profoundly limited by the Supreme Court, the Justices did not yet have a new theory of constitutional privacy for personal and group privacy in the post-1937 era.[39] In terms of the relation of privacy to constitutional options, the situation in the 1950's was as follows.

First, the Court had not considered whether the First Amendment provided any right to privacy. First Amendment cases had given protection to active public speech, to press, to the right of assembly, and to rights of religious conscience. Some expressions in First Amendment cases had stated that government could not require individuals to "confess by word or deed" a principle contrary to their religious tenets, but only in this sense (involving compulsory flag-salute laws) could it be said that the Court had implied a right to "silence." When the term "privacy" did appear in First Amendment cases, it had been as a description of the householder's interest in quiet enjoyment of his premises—particularly freedom from the raucous blast of sound trucks or door-to-door salesmen. Privacy was thus a passive virtue that the Court invoked in order to place *limits* on active freedom of speech.[40]

There had been one case in 1952, involving the use of recorded music and advertisements by a municipal company inside its buses, that had raised the issue of whether the citizen had a "liberty" right of privacy. The Court felt that no free-speech or due-process right was violated by the company's broadcasting. Justice Douglas dissented, arguing that to force a "captive audience" riding the buses to listen to broadcasting violated the citizen's right to privacy under the due-process clause of the Fifth Amendment. "[E]ven in his activities outside the home," Douglas wrote, "he has immunities from controls bearing on privacy." Compelling a person who must use public conveyances to listen to broadcasts invades privacy beyond the risks of noise and contact properly assumed by travelers. "The right of privacy should include the right to pick and choose," Douglas said, and this applied to entertainment, propaganda, and philosophies while persons were in public conveyances.[41] (It is worth noting, however, that so many Washington residents kept protesting against the bus broadcasts that several advertisers dropped away and, in 1953, the system was abandoned by Capitol Transit.)

Secondly, despite the link that the *Boyd* case had made in 1886 between the Fourth and Fifth Amendments, the privilege against self-incrimination in the Fifth Amendment had come to have little value for defining constitutional privacy rights. In 1896 the Court had decided that the privilege could be claimed only when a witness feared criminal prosecution, and not to protect reputation or private affairs from community disapproval.[42] From then on, for better or worse, the privilege had become characterized by the general public as a right given by a liberty-loving (and "game"-minded) society to persons who had either committed illegal acts or had involved themselves in situations that suggested guilt to reasonable observers. With such a negative context, and with silence carrying the overtones of self-protection, the privilege against self-incrimination was not a firm foundation on which to raise a new structure of constitutional privacy.

This left the Fourth Amendment as the Court's basic constitutional tool for defining privacy rights in the post-1945 setting of surveillance technology. The Court had allowed itself to become hopelessly mired in technicality. In terms of federal eavesdropping by microphone or federal wiretapping, the *Olmstead* doctrine required physical trespass before a search would be held to have occurred.

In 1942 a six-to-three decision of the Supreme Court refused to reconsider the *Olmstead* decision in a case involving eavesdropping on room conversations by federal officers by means of a wall microphone from an adjoining room. The Court stressed the fact that there had been no trespass onto the victim's property and thus no intrusion as defined by the Fourth Amendment.[43] And in 1952, in the *On Lee* case, the court held that police could arrange to have one party to a conversation secretly record it and use the recordings as evidence in federal trials.[44] There had been *no* case in the Supreme Court down to the 1950's in which proof of a physical trespass by law-enforcement officers had been shown and federal eavesdropping thereby established. In the area of federal-state relations the Court had held that evidence illegally obtained by state officials could be used in federal trials as long as the federal officials had not participated directly in the illegal search; state wiretap or eavesdropping recordings could therefore be the basis for convicting defendants in federal trials.

As far as guaranteeing American citizens "national" privacy rights against direct state invasion, *Wolf v. Colorado* had held in 1949 that the "security of one's privacy against arbitrary intrusion by the police—which is at the core of the Fourth Amendment—is basic to a free society . . . and as such enforceable against the States through the Due Process Clause." However, the Court held that *states* did not have to exclude evidence obtained by illegal search and seizure (as the federal rule provided). Exclusion was only one of many remedies that states were free to adopt to give force to the right of privacy. Under this rule, for example, the Court's majority upheld the conviction of a California man for bookmaking even though evidence used against him had been obtained by trespassing on his property, placing a microphone in his bedroom, and listening to the room and telephone conversations of the defendant and his wife. California's rule admitting illegally obtained evidence prevailed, since the police invasion of the defendant's bedroom, though "shocking" to the Court, was not so shocking as to require excluding the evidence.[45]

The Court's situation can be more easily understood if we notice the types of Fourth Amendment claims that the Court found itself confronting in the 1940's and 1950's. From the days of the *Boyd* case until the 1930's the Court's Fourth Amendment cases were concerned primarily with liquor-prohibition cases (between 1919 and 1933) and cases with a property-rights, regulation-of-business setting; in the latter cases, privacy claimants were businessmen and corporations contesting the scope and power of investigations, regulations, and prosecutions. By the 1940's and 1950's, however, business Fourth Amendment cases were rare in the Supreme Court. Most cases now involved professional criminals of the gambler-racketeer variety, "regular" crimes of the murder-rape variety, and persons being investigated or prosecuted for alleged Communist activity. While courts are supposed to apply constitutional limitations regardless of the particular defendants, the "law enforcement" and "internal security" context of these cases did not provide an auspicious launching platform for enunciating a new constitutional right to privacy. Thus American constitutional law was ineffective in the late 1940's and 1950's, just when the new instruments of surveillance technology came into widespread use.

COMMON-LAW ATTEMPTS TO CONTROL SURVEILLANCE

The failure of American law to develop doctrines to bring technological surveillance under constitutional control was accompanied by a similar failure on the part of American common law. At the beginning of the 1800's, most personal interests of privacy were being protected by the common law largely under traditional tort or contract doctrines. In his famous treatise on torts, published in 1879, Judge Thomas Cooley spoke of the right "to be let alone" as a personal immunity.[46] Several state courts had spoken of a right of privacy during the late 1800's in cases involving intrusion by the owner of a house into a guest's room for purposes of sexual assault; the introduction of a young unmarried man by an attending doctor at a birth in a private home, assumed by the mother to be a medical assistant; and the attempt of a promoter who took a photograph of an actress on stage in tights to use the picture for advertising purposes without her consent.[47] In 1891 the United States Supreme Court held that a person bringing an action for personal injuries against a railroad could not be forced to submit to a surgical examination; the Justices quoted Cooley's right "to be let alone," and noted that "inviolability of the person is as much invaded by a compulsory stripping and exposure as by a blow." [48] Despite these decisions protecting interests of privacy under such common-law actions as trespass, assault, deceit, and contract, a call for a new right of privacy arose during the 1890's and early 1900's, spurred primarily by the growth of mass-circulation newspapers which specialized in exposés of the private lives of public figures.

The issue was highlighted in a famous article in 1890 by E. L. Godkin, editor of the New York *Evening Post* and a noted civic reformer.[49] Godkin traced the development of man's desire for privacy from the days of communal life in wigwams to the stage of civilization of 1890, when he saw the desire of both rich and poor for private houses and the separation of rooms within dwelling houses to demonstrate "the ambition of nearly all civilized men and women . . . [to decide] for themselves how much or how little publicity should surround their daily lives." When Anglo-American law recognized a man's house as "his place of repose," this was "but the outward and visible sign of the law's respect for his personality as an individual, for that kingdom of the mind, that inner world of personal thought and feeling in which every man passes some time, and in which every man who is worth much to himself or others, passes a great deal of time." Though the importance attached to privacy "varies in individuals"—some persons finding it painful to have their private lives exposed and others enjoying the publicity—those who do seek and need privacy "are the element in society which most contributes to its moral and intellectual growth."

Godkin saw "curiosity" as the chief enemy of privacy in modern societies. While curiosity was socially healthy in some of its aspects, and only mildly harmful in its older "Paul Pry" form of oral gossip (which reached only small circles of people and could be ignored), the development of mass-circulation, sensation-seeking newspapers had transformed curiosity into a marketable commodity. The once despised and socially censured Paul Pry had become a financially rewarded and socially approved professional dealer in gossip. Now, what an individual said or did privately was reported in lurid detail to thousands of people.

Godkin was frankly puzzled about what law could do when the boundaries of libel had not been violated. He doubted whether juries would be willing to award damages for "mere wounds to [a man's] feelings or his taste." The only remedy he could envisage was public disapproval of press misconduct, but with "pecuniary reward" being the great "incentive" of that age, Godkin believed neither law nor opinion would be likely to protect the sensitive man's claim to privacy.

To achieve control of press invasions of privacy without depending on the rise of an "anti-commercial" public opinion was the task undertaken by Samuel Warren and Louis Brandeis in the *Harvard Law Review* for December, 1890.[50] This classic article began by portraying the common law as a system that had evolved steadily, by judicial decision, from protection of the physical person and tangible property to protection of man's "sensations," "emotions," and "spiritual nature." From early actions for trespass and battery, it had moved to such concepts as nuisance, slander and libel, and intangible property rights.

However, several new developments required that a "next step" be taken to protect the right "to be let alone." The primary threat was press invasion of privacy through publication of personal information and gossip, a trend which was disturbing the "solitude and privacy" men required in "advancing civilization." Along with press gossip went the publication of private portraits without authorization, obtained through the new invention of "instantaneous photography." In the cluster of "recent inventions and business methods" requiring legal control was a brief reference to "mechanical devices" which "threaten to make good the prediction that 'what is whispered in the closet shall be proclaimed from the house-tops.' "

Warren and Brandeis felt that the common law already secured "to each individual the right of determining, ordinarily, to what extent his thoughts, sentiments, and emotions shall be communicated to others." This right was illustrated most clearly in the protection which common law gave to the authors of literary and artistic compositions and private letters to forbid unauthorized publication. The eighteenth- and nineteenth-century English rulings upholding such rights had been based "nominally" on "protection to property," but they were really, Brandeis and Warren held, enforcements of an individual's privacy, based on his right to "an inviolate personality." This right to privacy under common law included "a principle which may be invoked to protect the privacy of the individual from invasion either by the too enterprising press, the photographer, or the possessor of any other modern device for recording or reproducing scenes or sounds."

Over the next sixty years a majority of the states (including four by legislation) adopted the common-law principle of an individual right of privacy.[51] Nearly 300 right-to-privacy cases were decided between 1890 and 1950 (and these were only the cases that produced appellate rulings). In addition, there was a remarkable outpouring of law-review articles, text discussions, and press coverage of the common-law right-of-privacy issue in these decades.[52]

Yet the common-law right-of-privacy action exerted no significant impact on new physical-surveillance instruments. Between 1890 and

1950 there were no cases of common-law recovery against police eavesdroppers, even when they had acted without any legal authorization or
had listened for private and illegal purposes, such as extortion. And of
the 300 right-of-privacy cases reported in this period, only two involved
actions against private persons for use of surveillance techniques. In
1931, the Kentucky Court of Appeals upheld a suit against several
persons who had tapped the plaintiff's telephone line and had taken
shorthand notes of conversations. In the second instance, a Georgia
court in 1939 allowed a woman to recover damages for the distress
caused her when the Coca-Cola Company of Atlanta had its agents place
a listening device in her hospital room to check on her claim in a negligence action.[53]

Why was the common-law right not used more widely in the surveillance situation? First of all, the victim of a photographic invasion of
privacy by the press knows by the publication of the photo that his privacy has been invaded: the photo provides unquestionable proof of the
act about which he is complaining. On the other hand, many victims of
private or governmental surveillance were not aware of a wiretap or microphone installation; or if they were, often lacked proof of its use or of
the identity of the person who had ordered the surveillance. Even if they
had such evidence, the victim was often reluctant to bring a court action
and thereby give general publicity to what was usually a private matter.
Ironically, a desire to protect one's remaining privacy provided a prime
motive for failing to bring an action against physical surveillance for invasion of privacy. In contrast, the press situation was normally one in
which the harm of general publicity had already taken place; the lawsuit
usually gave the victim a chance to publicize his side of the issue or to
express his protest in "public" through the court action, as well as the
chance to seek damages or injunctive relief.

Second, because the common-law remedy originated as a property-
rights action, it did not adapt easily to the most common type of private-
eavesdropping situation: where the owner of property or the telephone
subscriber ordered surveillance to advance his property or family interests. When factory owners used telephone tapping or dictaphone listening on their property to investigate theft or learn of labor-union activity;
when owners of hotels, restaurants, or stores put in listening or watching
devices to check on employee or guest behavior; or when the telephone
subscriber ordered his or her own wire tapped in marital "misconduct"
matters—in all these situations it was never clear under the common-law
concept whether the action was an improper invasion of the privacy of
the factory worker, employee, guest, wife, or the like, or a legally proper
vindication of the property rights of the owner.

Third, the concept of "injury" was stretched to its thinnest in the
eavesdropping situation. If someone made money by using the name or

portrait of a celebrity without his consent, or if there were an injury to the reputation of a person by publication of facts portraying him in a false light, juries could accept these as injuries for which damages were due. The same was true when "rough shadowing" of a person injured his reputation or when physical intrusion into the home caused mental distress. But it required a greater willingness than seemingly existed in the 1890–1950 period for public opinion to see enough harm to award damages when there was only a listening to conversation or a disclosure in a "private" marital dispute or business fight.

Fourth, as to the application of the common-law right to law enforcement, it was apparent that Warren and Brandeis had in mind private rather than official invasions of privacy. In trespass actions against police in the 1790–1850 period, when persons' homes or businesses had been searched and articles had been seized, juries were willing to order the property to be restored when the search had been unauthorized or unreasonable in scope, even though such action sometimes halted prosecution. But common-law actions against police who eavesdropped without authority asked juries to give money damages to persons who were often unsavory figures in the community; yet damages are hardly ever assessed against policemen who are overzealous in pursuing criminal types. Perhaps even more important in restricting the usefulness of the common-law right was the fact that the same public attitude indicated in the government-eavesdropping situation also came into play when private detectives acted on behalf of clients in private law-enforcement situations—such as investigations of thefts, false insurance claims, and selling of business secrets. The introduction of the law-enforcement context changed the whole balance of values in the privacy situation, even when *private* law enforcement was involved.

Fifth, the movement begun by the Godkin and Warren-Brandeis essays was essentially a protest by spokesmen for patrician values against the rise of the political and cultural values of "mass society." For the patricians, the gossip press, commercial advertising, and exposure of the doings of the socially prominent were aggressive and unjustified intrusions by publishers pandering to "mass" curiosity and tastes. Conservative traditionalists among the patricians, such as Samuel Warren and Brooks Adams, fused concern over the immunities of high society with anger at press muckraking of political and social scandals, though this was one instrument which brought the widespread business and governmental corruption of the era under minimum public controls. Liberals among the patricians, such as Godkin and Brandeis, joined a concern over the privacy of the socially prominent with a fear that the artistically sensitive or intellectually unpopular would be harmed by press intrusions —long a minority position in dominant American culture. Thus, from both ideological sides of the patrician protest, the underlying rationale of the right-of-privacy movement was to call for restraints on commercial invasions of privacy for reasons that ran counter to the dominant spirit of American society between the 1890's and the 1950's. Thus it was far from accidental that the common-law right had its only real impact as a *successful* legal action in the situations in which someone had made money out of another person's reputation or misfortune. Beyond this, the more traditional actions (trespass, breach of confidence, business secrets, and the like) could have been invoked just as successfully as the privacy action by complaining parties, or the courts could have denied recovery in right-to-privacy actions because of conflicting interests, such as free press, or by finding that there had been implied consent to publicity.

Sixth, because the values were patrician claims, it would have taken the force of positive legislation, and the educational effect on public opinion of passing such legislation, to win acceptance of an enforceable right to freedom from private technological surveillance. The Warren-Brandeis article seemed to promise that judicial balancing of interests in private-surveillance situations could provide effective relief. This was an illusory promise, and probably deflected social concern which might otherwise have been directed at creating a clear legislative response.

This discussion is not intended to minimize the value of the Warren-Brandeis approach between 1890 and 1950 as a path-breaking contribution to modern conceptions of privacy as a legal right of the individual. The common-law movement produced a rich stream of articles and judicial opinions analyzing why privacy is important to American society, what constitutes a proper claim of personal privacy, and how to weigh the right to privacy against competing social interests, such as publication of facts about public affairs. In this sense the Warren-Brandeis discussion established legal sensitivity to privacy as an interest independently defined, not treated as a dependent adjunct of property or liberty. But as an instrument for providing legal protection against improper surveillance of personal or group privacy, the common-law right simply did not develop into a meaningful remedy in its first sixty-five years. The seed was there, but in this era the warmth of public support to nurture it was lacking.

The Second Era of Technological Challenge— 1950 to the Present

Given the failure of American law to cope effectively with the first wave of technological pressure on privacy, it might be assumed that the arrival of the new devices of the electronic age would have left American society in total disarray. But American society has come to realize that privacy is at the heart of liberty in the modern state, and dominant American attitudes toward civil liberties and civil rights have undergone enormous changes in the past decade. This fact has been reflected at many levels of American society and on many legal fronts, but nowhere more drastically than in the United States Supreme Court. Therefore it is important to note the development of new Supreme Court doctrines that are likely to change the entire context of American law on privacy and surveillance in the 1970's.

To move forward toward a new concept of constitutional privacy, and to do so in a manner reflecting the philosophical and institutional realities of the American judicial process, the Court had to accomplish three things in the past decade. First, it had to develop a positive theory of privacy, based on identifying the interests or functions of privacy in contemporary American society. The negative implications of the Fifth Amendment privilege and the narrow definition of the Fourth Amendment had to be replaced by a concept which established privacy as part of both the values and the process of democratic living.

Second, it had to find the means of discarding the basic judgments that had supported the *Olmstead-Goldman* position: the need for physical trespass; the requirement of "tangible" things as the object of a search; and the underlying assumption that placing electronic eavesdropping or tapping under constitutional control would automatically mean denying *all* eavesdropping power to law-enforcement agencies.

Third, the Court had to find and demonstrate the need for national standards and remedies in the privacy field, since changes in police mores required the kind of national public attention available only through both federal and state actions.

Where the Supreme Court would be able to go once it had accomplished these three goals was another question. But until these three steps were taken, the Court simply could not cope with the problems of privacy in the electronic age. It is clear that the Court began carrying out just these steps between 1957 and 1967, and has moved to the threshold of a comprehensive new position with the *Griswold* decision of 1965.

The Court has identified and upheld since 1957 a series of new privacy interests under the First Amendment and the due-process clause. The right of "associational privacy" was enunciated in NAACP v. *Alabama* in 1958, holding unconstitutional efforts by Alabama to require the NAACP to turn over its membership and officer lists in order to be admitted as an out-of-state corporation. Writing for a unanimous Court, Justice Harlan declared: "This Court has recognized the vital relationship between freedom to associate and privacy in one's associations. . . . Inviolability of privacy in group association may in many circumstances be indispensable to freedom of association, particularly where a group espouses dissident beliefs." [54] Exposure of names, given the history of reprisals and public hostility in Alabama when NAACP names had been made public in the past, created too great a pressure on the associational-privacy rights at stake. In a series of NAACP cases from then on[55] the Court has consistently defended "associational privacy" not only against direct government pressure but also against "indirect" social sanctions linked to government action. Such freedoms, the Court stated in the *Button* case, "need breathing space to survive." It is important to note that the basic principle of "associational privacy" has been reiterated, even though found not to be of paramount influence, in several cases since 1958 involving internal-security issues.[56]

Another privacy interest the Court has identified and expressed, though more tentatively, is "political privacy." The *Watkins* ruling in 1957 on pertinency requirements for congressional questioning speaks of the individual's "personal interest in privacy"; it notes the Court's duty "to insure that the Congress does not unjustifiably encroach upon an individual's right to privacy nor abridge his liberty of speech, press, religion, or assembly." [57] However, the broadest statement to date of a right of political privacy came in the Frankfurter-Harlan concurring opinion in the *Sweezy* case, involving questions put to a scholar and guest lecturer at the state university by a state official investigating alleged subversive activities in New Hampshire. The Court's duty here, held Frankfurter and Harlan, is to balance "two contending principles—the right of a citizen to political privacy, as protected by the Fourteenth Amendment, and the right of the State to self-protection." Discharging that duty, the two Justices concluded: "[T]he inviolability of privacy belonging to a citizen's political loyalties has so overwhelming an importance to the well-being of our kind of society that it cannot be constitutionally encroached upon on the basis of so meagre a countervailing interest of the State . . . [as shown here]." [58]

The next privacy interest that the Court has developed is the right to anonymity in public expression. The leading case, *Talley v. California*, in 1960, involved an ordinance requiring that the name and address of those who prepare or sponsor handbills appear on them. After noting the important role that anonymous handbills, pamphlets, and books had played in early English and American political life, the Court cited the NAACP anti-disclosure rulings and noted that here, too, forced disclosure could inhibit peaceful and important discussion of public affairs. Though the word "privacy" was not used in this ruling, its policy aspects are clearly present.[59]

There are several other privacy interests that the Supreme Court has identified. There is *privacy of the body* ("inviolability of the person"), recognized since the *Botsford* case in 1891, given a public-law definition in *Rochin* and in *Breithaupt*, and recently revitalized on the private-law side again in a 1964 case which applied "reasonableness" privacy limits to the scope of medical examinations that could be required in federal negligence actions.[60] There has also been a recognition of a right to *privacy of counsel* in several federal court-of-appeals rulings. The United States Court of Appeals for the District of Columbia ruled in 1951 that the right to private consultation with counsel guaranteed by the Fifth and Sixth Amendments was violated when the FBI tapped telephone conversations between a defendant and her lawyers after she had been indicted. Another court-of-appeals ruling in 1953 held that the presence of a secret agent of the government who overheard conversations between an accused and his counsel violated the right to private consultation. The Supreme Court may well have adopted this approach itself, judging from the *Massiah* case of 1964. Here federal agents persuaded a man under indictment on a narcotics charge to install a radio transmitter in his car so that federal agents could overhear conversations between the cooperating witness and a defendant on bail for the same indictment. The Court held that the incriminating statements overheard by the listening device were inadmissible in evidence because they were made without the protection of counsel. If there is a right to have counsel in such a circumstance, it seems to follow that government could not eavesdrop on that conversation.[61]

There is also a growing use by the present Court of the Fifth Amendment's privilege against self-incrimination in ways that strengthen the case for a constitutional right to privacy from unreasonable surveillance or compulsory disclosure. The Court's recent rulings on interrogation of suspects while in police custody—stressing the "individual's right to choose between silence and speech" [62]—seem to place an immovable block against the kind of electronic monitoring of prisoners' conversations with visitors, confidential advisors, and other contacts that has been used widely by police forces in the past decade. Even more important was the Court's ruling in 1966, in the *Schmerber* case, that the privilege against self-incrimination protects persons accused of crime from having to "provide the state with evidence of a testimonial or communicative nature . . . whatever form [the communications] might take." The majority opinion stated that lie-detector tests were just such testimonial statements. "To compel a person to submit to testing in which an effort will be made to determine his guilt or innocence on the basis of physiological responses, whether willed or not, is to evoke the spirit and history of the Fifth Amendment." [63] Though the *Schmerber* case involved taking a blood sample from a person suspected of drunken driving in an automobile accident, and the Court upheld such a test by a five-to-four vote as a reasonable measure that was not "testimonial compulsion," its doctrine is likely to contribute to the definition of the individual's "right to silence" whenever the means of disclosure or surveillance do penetrate the inner precincts of the mind and spirit. The majority's reference to the lie-detector situation suggests what is in their minds.

In 1965 the Supreme Court took a major first step toward enunciating a new constitutional doctrine of privacy. In *Griswold v. Connecticut* a seven-to-two majority invalidated a Connecticut law forbidding the dissemination of birth-control information as a violation of a right to marital privacy. The opinion for the Court by Justice Douglas spoke of "zones of privacy" created by "various guarantees" of the Bill of Rights, citing the First, Third, Fourth, Fifth, and Ninth Amendments, and by previous cases decided by the Court involving privacy elements in such guarantees. The Court stated that the Connecticut law "operates directly on an intimate relation of husband and wife . . . a right of privacy older than the Bill of Rights." [64]

The *Griswold* case produced sharp disagreement within the Court as to which sections of the Bill of Rights justified a new constitutional right of privacy broader than the traditional Fourth and Fifth Amendment approaches. Justice Clark was content to join the Douglas opinion without amplifying his own views. Justice Goldberg's concurring opinion —written for himself, Chief Justice Warren, and Justice Brennan— was based on the view that the Fourteenth Amendment's due-process clause protected those rights in the Federal Bill of Rights that were, as the Court had said earlier, "so rooted in the traditions and conscience of our people as to be ranked as fundamental." The right of privacy, stated Goldberg, was a fundamental right, and it could be protected even though it "is not guaranteed in so many words by the first eight amendments." This was particularly true because of the Ninth Amendment to the Constitution, which states that "The enumeration in the Constitution, of certain rights, shall not be construed to deny or disparage others retained by the people." While he emphasized that he was *not* asserting that the Ninth Amendment "constitutes an independent source of rights" or that the Fourteenth Amendment applies the Ninth Amendment to the states, Goldberg declared: "[T]he Ninth Amendment shows a belief of the Constitution's authors that fundamental rights exist that are not expressly enumerated in the first eight amendments and an intent that the list of rights included there were not exhaustive." This, Goldberg felt, was just what the Court had been doing for decades in its interpretation of which "fundamental personal liberties" are included in the Fifth and Fourteenth Amendments' guarantees of "liberty" and "due process." In his view, the "right of privacy in the marital relation" was such a personal liberty, one "retained by the people— within the meaning of the Ninth Amendment."

The concurring opinion by Justice White accepted the right of marital privacy as fundamental, but maintained that the Court must still balance the privacy right with the state's justification for invading it. Applying such a balancing process, White felt that Connecticut had not shown that any legitimate social interest of the state, particularly the policy against illicit sexual relationships, was being served by the ban on the use of contraceptives by married persons. For this reason the statute had to be invalidated as a "sweeping" intrusion of liberty rights without due process of law.

Justice Harlan's concurrence stated that the proper inquiry for the Supreme Court was whether the statute violates basic values "implicit in the concept of ordered liberty," not because of any "radiations" from specific provisions of the Bill of Rights. The concept of due process for Harlan was independent of radiations and called for judicial measurement of "ordered liberty" by use of "the teachings of history, solid recognition of the basic values that underlie our society, and wise appreciation of the great roles that the doctrines of federalism and separation of powers have played in establishing and preserving American freedoms." This was not unfettered personal choice by the judges, as the dissenters maintained, but the assigned role of the judiciary under the due-process-of-law standard of the Constitution.

Justice Black's dissent took two positions of major importance to the idea of a developing right of privacy. First, he denied that any right to privacy was contained in the Bill of Rights. "There are, of course, guarantees in certain specific constitutional provisions which are designed in part to protect privacy at certain times and places with respect to certain activities." But there is no general right to privacy, nor any constitutional provision forbidding laws which "might abridge the 'privacy' of individuals." "I like my privacy as well as the next one," Black commented, "but I am nevertheless compelled to admit that government has a right to invade it unless prohibited by some specific constitutional provision."

The second main point of Black's dissent was a protest against the way in which the majority had imported a right of privacy into the Constitution, through the majority's finding that privacy was a fundamental personal liberty included within the meaning of the due-process clause. Black had frequently called on the Court to apply literally and concretely the guarantees of the first eight amendments as the rights of liberty protected against state action by the Fourteenth Amendment. To do otherwise, Black felt, let the judges write their own notions of liberty into the Constitution rather than the notions of the framers of the Constitution. This position Black reaffirmed in the *Griswold* case. The term "privacy," Black warned, "is a broad, abstract and ambiguous concept" and leaves the Court free to strike down laws that it finds to interfere unduly with "privacy." Black noted that the Ninth Amendment had been passed not to broaden the powers of the Supreme Court or the federal government, but to limit the federal government to expressly given powers or to those raised by necessary implication. For a century and a half, Black observed, "no serious suggestion was ever made that the Ninth Amendment, enacted to protect State powers against federal invasion, could be used as a weapon of federal power to prevent state legislatures from passing laws they consider appropriate to govern local affairs."

Justice Stewart's dissent stated clearly his belief that the Connecticut law was "uncommonly silly" and "obviously unenforceable" but that it does not violate the United States Constitution. Stewart noted: "I can find no such general right of privacy in the Bill of Rights, in any other part of the Constitution, or in any case ever before decided by this Court."

The *Griswold* case, as Justice Black noted to his dismay, represented the creation of a constitutional right to privacy comparable to that first advocated as a torts claim by Warren and Brandeis in 1890. A majority of the Court has now held that "privacy" is part of constitutional liberty. But what types of activity are included in "privacy," which parts of the Bill of Rights are the *primary* shapers of privacy standards (the First Amendment? Fourth? Fifth?), and what kinds of governmental and social interests will be held to justify limitation of "privacy" are all questions that the *Griswold* ruling leaves to later decisions.

Civic reaction to the *Griswold* ruling was quite favorable. A survey of editorial reactions showed that the declaration of a constitutional privacy right was considered vital to the present American era, and that the decision was correct in viewing privacy as a right that Americans consider fundamental to their way of life. There was some criticism of the Ninth Amendment idea in the Goldberg opinion on both historical and practical grounds, and some concern that the Court was again striking down legislative judgments and substituting its "own opinions." But the dominant reaction among editors, matched by the comments of labor, civil-liberties, religious, and business spokesmen, was that a constitutional right of privacy was a welcome and appropriate doctrine for our times. The fact that the Court declared it in a case involving a statute that a great majority of Americans regarded as unwise and degrading no doubt helped to foster a favorable public reaction; had the context been a law-enforcement or internal-security search, the reception probably would have been shaded differently. The most widespread quality to the civic reaction was a note of "let's see where this right to privacy leads in the future." The ultimate civic judgment was being reserved for future applications of the concept.

The thesis that the Court's concept of privacy has shifted from a "propertied" and "ownership" base to a "personal liberty" base is strengthened by the Supreme Court's refusal to strike down business regulation or equality measures on privacy grounds. Thus owners of motels and stores were not able to maintain a constitutional right of privacy in the choice of clientele when faced by the equal-accommodations rules of the Federal Civil Rights Act of 1964.[65] The Court has also found ways to resist enforcing state prosecutions of civil-rights demonstrators who intruded onto the property privacy of owners who refused to serve Negroes in their establishments.[66] This reluctance to uphold state trespass and disorderly-conduct prosecutions of civil-rights demonstrators must be contrasted with the Court's willingness to uphold state and municipal measures limiting noisy sound trucks or door-to-door solicitations.

Thus, if we look at leading cases in the liberty area decided by the Supreme Court in the past decade, we find that the Justices, intuitively rather than explicitly, have been laying out many of the basic elements of a functional definition of constitutional privacy. The functions of autonomy, evaluation, release, and limited communication have each been protected under the new cases, and the Court has dealt with each of the four basic states of privacy: solitude, intimacy, anonymity, and reserve. In this functional theory of constitutional privacy for the person and the group, privacy is not a "negative" concept at all; it has been perceived as a protection of the positive needs of individuals and organizations in our society. And as these needs have been threatened by scientific and social pressures of the post-1945 world, the Supreme Court has begun to respond.

The second step the Court had to take to prepare the way for a new constitutional doctrine of freedom from unreasonable surveillance was to undermine the bases of the *Olmstead-Goldman* doctrines. This has now been done in two of its three crucial elements. On the need for physical entry or intrusion, the Court held in 1961 that a "spike mike" which penetrated into the common wall between the apartment of the defendant and an adjoining apartment and was being used by police officers constituted a trespass by electronic eavesdropping which, without a warrant, violated the Fourth Amendment. In another case, in 1964, the Court reversed a conviction when the police only stuck a listening device into the wall to the depth of a thumb tack. In these cases, the Court indicated that the technical rules of property and common law on trespass could be applied to "formal" entries, and there was even a suggestion that physical entry might not be necessary at all for an intrusion, as defined by the Fourth Amendment.[67] At the same time the Court stated in several cases that conversations could be the object of search and seizure, and therefore, assuming an intrusion, the "intangible" basis for excluding electronic eavesdropping from the Fourth Amendment had been undercut.[68]

In 1963 the Court had an opportunity to re-examine the entire electronic-eavesdropping question in the *Lopez* case.[69] This involved the use of a radio transmitter concealed on the person of a federal official to whom the defendant had offered a bribe. A majority of the Court refused to reverse the earlier precedent of *On Lee v. United States*, a 1952 ruling that had upheld such recording or broadcasting of the conversation by one participant in it.[70] The majority felt that the party being recorded was speaking voluntarily and directly to the person doing the recording and thereby ran the risk that what he was saying would be repeated, or testified to in court.

Whatever the approach to privacy of communication, it is plain that electronic eavesdropping by an open participant in a conversation is different from third-party eavesdropping, and that the third-party situation is the more insidious and far-reaching threat to personal and group privacy today. Thus the *Lopez* case was not the best vehicle for a reconsideration of the *Olmstead-Goldman* doctrine. However, the reconsideration contained in Justice Brennan's dissent, supported by Justices Goldberg and Douglas, has great value as a discussion of the possible bases for a ruling that would overturn *Olmstead*.

Brennan framed the central issue as whether the Fourth Amendment (or the Court's supervisory power in federal criminal trials) provides the basis for excluding "the fruits of surrepititious electronic surveillance by federal agents." He ticked off the unsound assumptions of the *Olmstead* ruling: that the person who talks on the telephone "intends to project his voice to those quite outside," and that this intention somehow extends to third-party eavesdropping by the government; that only the seizure of tangible objects secured by physical trespass was encompassed by the Fourth Amendment; and that it would be dangerous or even improper for the Supreme Court to exclude evidence from trials unless a federal statute or "the letter of the Fourth Amendment" were violated. Brennan showed that the Court's rulings in that past decade had sapped each of these three positions of any real vitality, and that the general application of the Fourth Amendment by the Court to physical searches had been in sharp contrast to the "illiberal" interpretation of *Olmstead*. Recognizing that the Court had long been troubled by the "frightening" advances in surveillance technology—the dangers had been noted with alarm in majority and minority opinions throughout the 1940's, 1950's, and early 1960's—Brennan felt that the explanation for the Court's reluctance to overrule *Olmstead* must lie at a deeper level, in "two factors not often articulated in the decisions."

The first of these was the assumption that a ruling holding electronic eavesdropping to be within the reach of the Fourth Amendment would require a complete ban on wiretapping and microphoning, since electronic searches were so general, so "inherently indiscriminate," and so obviously a quest for "mere evidence," and since, without notice to the suspect, there could never be a reasonable search under Fourth

Amendment standards. Thus, a major tool of serious law enforcement would be completely outlawed. This point had troubled Chief Justice Warren enough to gain his concurrence with the majority in the *Lopez* case, rather than joining Brennan, Douglas, and Goldberg in dissent. It also may have influenced the other member of the Court's usual five-man liberal majority, Hugo Black—though Black's position in unreasonable-search-and-seizure cases had usually been narrower than that of his liberal colleagues. To meet such underlying difficulties, Brennan suggested that no conclusion about the inherent unreasonableness of electronic eavesdropping was required by a reversal of *Olmstead*. Several ways to limit warrant controls might be found which would make electronic eavesdropping and tapping constitutionally reasonable. At least, it was "premature" to assume the contrary to be true. While the issue was obviously hypothetical and while the Court might decide that electronic eavesdropping *was* inherently unreasonable, Brennan felt that this possibility was not inevitable and should not be a ground for preserving *Olmstead*.

The second "significant though unarticulated premise" of the *Olmstead* doctrine was that placing electronic eavesdropping under constitutional standards (or outlawing it) would threaten a host of other investigative techniques on which successful law enforcement rests—the use of informers, undercover agents, shadowing, and even plainclothes detectives. To this argument Brennan replied that the risks of being overheard or watched in those situations were risks "probably inherent in the conditions of society. . . . But as soon as electronic surveillance comes into play, the risk changes crucially. There is no security from that kind of eavesdropping, no way of mitigating the risk, and so not even a residuum of true privacy. . . . Electronic surveillance, in fact, makes the police omniscient; and police omniscience is one of the most effective tools of tyranny."

So far, Brennan had been showing the inadequacy of the *Olmstead* premises and the unnecessary policy assumptions that might be supporting its retention. "But to state the case thus is to state it too negatively," Brennan continued. He devoted the remainder of his dissenting opinion to "the positive reasons for bringing electronic surveillance under judicial regulation." Here Brennan showed that the magnitude of the problem had "grown enormously in recent years," that empirical studies had proved how widespread private and public use of tapping and bugging had become; that the danger of faking recordings had been presented; that these "terrifying" facts had led several states to enact regulatory legislation; and that there had been no proof that "stiff warrant requirement for electronic surveillance would destroy effective law enforcement." Since these facts might be considered grounds for legislative rather than judicial intervention, however, Brennan had to return to *constitutional* positions.

To do so, Brennan drew on opinions in two post-1957 cases which had recovered and restated the "liberty" foundations of search-and-seizure provisions. Both the majority and minority opinions in *Frank v. Maryland,*[71] a 1959 ruling on the need for warrants in public-health-inspection searches, had stated at length the fact that most of the classic British and American search cases had involved "liberty" issues. At stake had been government efforts to control seditious ideas and publication of critical books, or to enforce tax or custom measures that were resisted on grounds relating to rights of political representation in the taxing process. Protecting homes against unreasonable searches was therefore part of protecting civil liberties, free expression, and political rights of opposition, not just "criminals" or "property users." The same ground had been discussed and deepened in a 1961 ruling, *Marcus v. Search Warrant.*[72]

Drawing on the recovery of this stream of history wedded to the Fourth Amendment, Brennan wrote in his "positive" presentation in *Lopez:*

> Electronic surveillance strikes deeper than at the ancient feeling that a man's home is his castle; it strikes at freedom of communication, a postulate of our kind of society. . . . [F]reedom of speech is undermined where people fear to speak unconstrainedly in what they suppose to be the privacy of home and office.

Brennan also picked up the right-to-anonymity and associational privacy cases of the 1950's and early 1960's. "The right of privacy is the obverse of freedom of speech in another sense. This Court has lately recognized that the First Amendment freedoms may include the right, under certain circumstances, to anonymity. . . . Electronic surveillance destroys all anonymity and all privacy; it makes government privy to everything that goes on."

In a closing paragraph Justice Brennan warned that the Court's general decisions on protection of privacy against physical intrusions had "been outflanked by the technological advances of the very recent past." Unless the Court rises to the new challenge, he warned, "we shall be contributing to a climate of official lawlessness and conceding the helplessness of the Constitution and this Court to protect rights 'fundamental to a free society.'"

A third sign that the Supreme Court has been gathering momentum for the declaration of a new right to privacy from unreasonable surveillance is the recent flow of cases on the search-warrant standards of the Fourth Amendment. Before the past decade, search-warrant requirements had little major effect on police practices, though the presence of the warrant requirement did result in occasional reversals of convictions in the federal courts and in those states excluding illegally obtained evidence. As the Deputy Police Commissioner of New York City candidly told a *New York Times* reporter in 1965, before the Supreme Court held that illegally obtained evidence could no longer be admitted in any state trial, "nobody bothered to take out search warrants. . . . [T]he feeling was, why bother? Well, once that rule was changed, we knew we had better start teaching our men about [search warrants]." [73] Not only has the Court held, in the *Mapp* ruling of 1961, that the fruits of illegal searches and seizures cannot be used in evidence; it has also emphasized the availability of damage suits under the Civil Rights Act against the police who engage in illegal searches and the cities or states for whom they work.[74] Moreover, the Court has handed down a series of important decisions defining with greater precision and with more rigorous standards exactly what evidence of crime and probable cause to search is needed for law-enforcement officials to get a warrant, what degree of specificity is needed in describing the things to be seized, what the duties of the magistrate or judge are in passing upon warrant applications and similar matters.[75] This development makes the prospects for putting scientific surveillance under a court-order system more hopeful than in the former "why bother" eras. There have been similar rulings by state courts, notably the case of *People v. McCall*, decided in 1966 by the New York Court of Appeals, which reversed the conviction of three defendants in a narcotics case because there had not been a sufficient factual basis for the issuance of the wiretap warrant under which defendants' telephone conversations had been intercepted by the police.[76]

Thus, the Court seems on the brink of a landmark ruling defining a comprehensive, positive right of privacy from unreasonable surveillance. The rising concern over surveillance devices, alongside continued inaction by Congress on electronic eavesdropping, increases the likelihood that such a ruling will come soon.

The search for new public-law controls over misuse of surveillance devices has been matched by new vitality in the private-law field. Between 1958 and 1964, decisions in three cases upheld common-law recovery for wiretap or microphone invasions of privacy, the cases being spread geographically from West Virginia to Ohio and New Hampshire.[77] In addition, the press has disclosed a dozen other pending damage suits for electronic invasions of privacy beginning in other state courts in 1964–66.[78] This suggests that intrusion into privacy by listening devices—always *legally* encompassed by the common-law right of action —is now beginning to become an actively asserted and judicially encouraged area of litigation, based on a new social attitude toward the morality of eavesdropping for private purposes.

The West Virginia case, in 1958, involved a listening device installed by a landlord in the apartment of a female tenant and connected to a speaker unit in the landlord's office. The plaintiff alleged that the device was used for seven months to listen to her confidential conversations, and that this practice constituted a violation of her right to privacy. The landlord contended that no right to privacy was recognized in West Virginia, that the conversations had not been published or repeated, and that there was no allegation that the tenant had suffered any special damages. The Supreme Court of West Virginia reversed a lower-court dismissal of the suit, holding that the right to privacy would be recognized in West Virginia; that the injury to privacy came not in publication but in the intrusion itself; and that special damages did not have to be alleged to present a valid cause of action in a privacy suit. "To hold otherwise," the court noted, "under modern means of communication, hearing devices, photography, and other technological advancements, would effectively deny valuable rights and freedoms to the individual." [79]

A similar landlord-tenant case was decided by the Supreme Court of New Hampshire in 1964. A landlord in Gilford, New Hampshire, had installed a listening device in the bedroom of a house that he rented to the plaintiffs, who were husband and wife. Hidden wires had been run from the microphone to the landlord's own house, adjacent to the rented dwelling. The husband and wife alleged that the discovery of the listening device had caused them great distress, embarrassment, and severe mental suffering. As in the West Virginia case, the New Hampshire court ruled that the common-law right of privacy would now be recognized in their state and that the plaintiffs were entitled to recovery for the intrusion on their solitude. This intrusion did not have to be physical, the court noted, and eavesdropping on the bedroom conversations of a married couple was clearly a situation "that would be offensive to any person of ordinary sensibilities." The court explained that recent social trends underscored the necessity for protecting innocent persons from such intrusions.

> If the peeping Tom, the big ear and the electronic eavesdropper (whether ingenious or ingenuous) have a place in the hierarchy of social values, it ought not to be at the expense of a married couple minding their own business in the seclusion of their bedroom who have never asked for or by their conduct deserved a potential projection of their private conversations and actions to their landlord or to others.

The use of parabolic microphones and sonic-wave devices to "pick up conversations in a room without entering it" indicated that defining and protecting privacy was especially important for the law.[80]

The Ohio case, decided in 1963, presented a different issue. A wife legally separated from her husband (though not yet divorced) and living alone had a separate telephone installed in her new apartment residence. She informed the telephone-company representative that she was separated and getting a divorce, that this was her own apartment, that she was now paying her own bills, and that she was independently employed. Shortly after a telephone was placed in her apartment, her husband requested the telephone company to install in his house an extension telephone to her line. The company complied, and the line was put in simply by making a wire adjustment in the central telephone office so that calls to the wife's phone rang automatically on the extension in the husband's house. No notification was given to the wife of the extension line and no visit to her premises was necessary to accomplish the hook-up. On hearing suspicious noises on the line, as though someone were listening, the wife notified the telephone company. After several checks of the line, the company informed the wife of the extension. On her complaint, it was disconnected at once, but she brought an action against the telephone company for rendering material aid to the husband in invading her privacy. Her complaint noted that she had been having telephone conversations not only with her friends but also with her attorney about her pending divorce action and property settlement, and she alleged mental distress and nervous reactions as a result of the eavesdropping.

The Ohio Court of Appeals reversed a lower-court ruling dismissing the suit against the telephone company. The appeals court held that, whatever the rule when husband and wife lived together, a separated wife could charge her husband with an invasion of her privacy when he had an extension placed on her line in this manner. And, the court held, the telephone company had been given sufficient information about the independent status of the wife to justify holding the company responsible for aiding in an unlawful use. The "personal integrity" of the wife "deserves the protection of the law" in this instance.[81]

The landlord-eavesdropping cases, because they have such a clear tenant-right-of-property context, are innovative not in their doctrinal basis, but only in the fact that plaintiffs are now coming forward to sue landlords when listening devices are discovered. And while the Ohio case is significant in holding the telephone company liable for failure to check sufficiently to protect the wife's privacy right as an independent subscriber, the court seemed to suggest that the husband and the company might not have been liable if the special conditions of independence and notification had not been present. This qualification underscores the fact that no common-law actions have yet grappled with the harder but vital cases in which a private-law right of privacy is claimed against the owner of premises on which the eavesdropping victim is only a temporary guest, visitor, customer, or employee. This is the area where the common-law right needs most to be expanded, and some of the development ought not to be difficult. For example, the property right the guest in a hotel acquires as a licensee ought to be sufficient to support a damage suit against hotel managements that are using built-in listening devices for a variety of "house-detective" and voyeuristic purposes. The principle ought to fit also whenever the owner of premises open to the public (from stores to hotels and restuarants) installs listening or watching devices in places that social custom regards as offering privacy from direct owner surveillance, such as the toilets in places of public accommodation.

The case becomes harder when the owner of factories or offices installs surveillance devices. The tradition of allowing owners to maintain private police forces and to carry out their own investigations of crime (or any other activity) has become a powerful one in recent decades. Yet there is no logical or social reason to treat privacy-requiring areas, such as rest rooms, any differently than places of public accommodation. Thus, while employers may have proprietary rights to use surveillance devices in stockrooms, loading areas, and over the assembly line, there ought to be a common-law right to recovery in situations such as the one in which an American Telephone and Telegraph Company supervisor installed a camera device in a ladies' rest room to apprehend the person guilty of writing offensive messages on the walls.

In short, the most important area requiring expansion of the common-law right of privacy is the kind of situation in which most of us spend the greater part of our time—at work, in shopping, in travel, and in public-accommodation facilities. To protect privacy only in the home or apartment is to shelter what has become, in modern society, only a small part of the individual's daily environmental need for privacy.

A final point to observe in charting new developments in the private-law area is that many of the state statutes passed recently to control electronic eavesdropping provide a private right of action against violaters of the prohibition. In Pennsylvania a person whose telephone conversations are tapped is given a right to sue for "treble damages" the wiretapper and anyone who uses the recordings. The damages are set at a minimum of $100 plus attorney's fees. Illinois provides an even broader right of private action against any electronic eavesdropper, his employer or superior, or any landlord or building operator who assists in the eavesdropping enterprise. It is no defense under any of these statutes that the eavesdropper's property rights are involved or that police agents who eavesdropped were investigating suspected criminals. But though these statutes were passed in 1957, there have been no reported private-damage suits under them as yet, despite the likelihood that private-eye and police eavesdropping have not vanished from Chicago, Philadelphia, and other places where eavesdropping was known to flourish in the pre-1957 period. There is no doubt that if more attention were drawn to the availability of this private-damage recourse, labor leaders, corporate officers, and private parties to marital actions would begin to bring suits against police and private investigators.

LEGISLATIVE RESPONSES IN THE 1960'S

While judicial developments in the 1960's were creative and promise to be even more so in the future, legislative responses to the challenge of new technology at both state and federal levels were disappointing. As of 1967, only ten states had enacted laws forbidding employers to require polygraph tests as a condition of employment. Less than a dozen states had enacted effectively drawn and clear statutes on the wiretapping-eavesdropping problem. At the federal level there was no legislative action on either the eavesdropping or the polygraph problem.

Since there were many signs from editorial, political, and civic-group spokesmen that dominant American opinion was alarmed about technological invasion of privacy, concerned about increased organizational and governmental power through surveillance, and wanted action to protect individual and group interests in the area, what explains the lack of significant legislative response? It may be that privacy, like such matters as church-state boundaries in America, is so charged with competing values and engenders such passionate commitments from partisans on each side that the normal give-and-take adjustment of the legislative process breaks down, producing heated discussion but no compromises that lead to action. In this context, again as in such issues as church-state relations, public demand for action tends to produce alternative governmental action. This may be judicial intervention, as has already been noted. It may also produce increasingly broad use of executive authority (as with the Johnson Administration's activity in setting new executive rules for electronic eavesdropping and the Defense Department directive on use of the polygraph). Still another response that often operates when legislation fails to evolve is the change in government practices brought about by legislative investigation, exposure, pressure, and negotiations with executive agencies. As with the segregation problems in the 1940's and 1950's, legislative inaction followed by intervention to the limits of executive, judicial, and informal authority may finally force legislative intervention. What legislative actions are desirable and necessary to protect vital aspects of privacy is one major theme of the next chapter.

CHAPTER FOURTEEN

Restoring the Balance of Privacy in America

IT HAS BEEN a long journey since the discussion of new threats to privacy with which this book opened. Yet the most difficult and treacherous ground of all—policy judgment—still remains to be crossed. In one sense, the whole intellectual odyssey thus far has been a toughening-up exercise for this final effort. The explorations of surveillance technology and techniques, public reactions to these pressures, the functions that privacy serves for individuals and society, and the concept of privacy in American law—all these have been attempts to acquire a firm understanding of privacy in contemporary America. With such a basic understanding, the hard problems of balance and choice can be met; without such knowledge, both the public and legal specialists might be tempted to seek simplistic formulas which will neither control intrusive technology nor set a proper balance of privacy.

A Restatement of Themes

To begin, let me restate the main conclusions that have been presented, since it is on these foundations that I shall rest my analysis of the "forces" and "choices" that confront us.

1. A technological breakthrough in techniques of physical surveillance now makes it possible for government agents and private persons to penetrate the privacy of homes, offices, and vehicles; to survey individuals moving about in public places; and to monitor the basic channels of communication by telephone, telegraph, radio, television, and data line. Most of the "hardware" for this physical surveillance is cheap, readily available to the general public, relatively easy to install, and not presently illegal to own. As of the 1960's, the new surveillance technology is being used widely by government agencies of all types and at every level of

government, as well as by private agents for a rapidly growing number of businesses, unions, private organizations, and individuals in every section of the United States. Increasingly, permanent surveillance devices have been installed in facilities used by employees or the public. While there are defenses against "outside" surveillance, these are so costly and complex and demand such constant vigilance that their use is feasible only where official or private matters of the highest security are to be protected. Finally, the scientific prospects for the next decade indicate a continuing increase in the range and versatility of the listening and watching devices, as well as the possibility of computer processing of recordings to identify automatically the speakers or topics under surveillance. These advances will come just at the time when personal contacts, business affairs, and government operations are being channeled more and more into electronic systems such as data-phone lines and computer communications.

2. In the field of psychological surveillance, techniques such as polygraphing and personality testing that probe the intimate thought processes of their subjects have swept into widespread use since World War II. Because they are supposed to offer "scientific" examination of individuals, these techniques have become commonplace in the personnel-selection systems of many corporations, private organizations, and government agencies, and are used for a variety of other purposes as well. At the same time, advances in drug research indicate that we may be approaching the point at which the administration of a drug (with or without the subject's knowledge) may render him a truthful person under questioning; already, arguments in favor of such narco-analysis under new drugs have appeared in police and legal journals. Finally, research in brain-wave analysis establishes that "reading" certain signals of the brain is now possible; if in the coming decades this progresses to the ability to distinguish the more complex messages involved in thoughts and emotions, direct interrogation of the mind may become the "ultimate weapon" in penetration of privacy

3. In the area I have called data surveillance, the rapid pace of computer development and usage throughout American society means that vast amounts of information about individuals and private groups in the nation are being placed in computer-usable form. More and more information is being gathered and used by corporations, associations, universities, public schools, and governmental agencies. And as "life-long dossiers" and interchange of information grow steadily, the possibilities increase that agencies employing computers can accomplish heretofore impossible surveillance of individuals, businesses, and groups by putting together all the now-scattered pieces of data. This danger is augmented by current proposals from some private and government spokesmen who advocate the adoption of a fully-computerized and automatic credit sys-

tem to replace cash transactions, a single-identifying-number system for every person in his dealings with public authorities, and similar "total" computer systems.

4. In each of these areas of surveillance, most of the scientific advances did not arise through efforts to develop instruments for invading the privacy of the citizenry. Rather, they grew out of research to solve broad problems of American society—space travel and communication, medical research, diagnosis and treatment of mental illness, mobile television broadcasts, rapid analysis and use of general data, and a host of similar purposes. Once the scientific advances were made, however, often at levels of cost that only government could supply in the stages of basic research and prototype development, many of the techniques were then adopted swiftly by both government agencies and private interests for purposes of physical, psychological, or data surveillance. The technology we have been discussing has thus been "socially useful" in origin, and potentially "neutral" in relation to privacy. Yet the ease with which the new techniques have been used for penetration of privacy, their relatively low cost in relation to the resources of those wishing to employ these techniques for surveillance, and the ready accessibility of the "parts" or "processes" indicate that existing legal and social rules for policing the borderline between "proper" and "improper" use have proved inadequate. Furthermore, the test psychologists and computer scientists involved in applying the new surveillance techniques have often been so sure of their own purposes and ethics that they have been insufficiently sensitive to the issues of privacy created by the uses of these processes. This preoccupation with scientific solutions to social problems has sometimes tended to place the professionals in various fields in opposition to what they regard as "unscientific" and "emotional" positions asserting "new" claims of privacy.

5. The response of American society to these technological and scientific developments since 1945 has been uneven and often without the consistency that comes with self-consciousness. But the studies of civic reactions to five key problems—subliminal suggestion, electronic eavesdropping, polygraphs, personality testing, and the computer—show steadily growing sensitivity to privacy claims in the press and among national civic groups. Group positions vary, depending on who is doing the surveillance, who is being surveyed, and the purpose for intruding. But so many areas have been affected by the new techniques and so many group interests have been directly threatened that statements deploring the erosion of privacy and the tactics of "Big Brother" have been issuing steadily from every position along the ideological spectrum, from extreme right to radical left. While some might read the record differently, I conclude from the five depth-studies that a "minimum position" in support of privacy is emerging. This unites both liberal and conservative

camps, and awaits only a clear enunciation of basic standards and the development of a creative evaluative process before it becomes a national consensus which can be drawn upon by legislators, judges, and private authorities to deal with the specific problems of privacy under technological pressure.

6. In probing the functions which privacy serves in democratic systems—its psychological, sociological, and political utility—we found that privacy is an irreducibly critical element in the operations of individuals, groups, and government in a democratic system with a liberal culture. For the individual, there is a need to keep some facts about himself wholly private, and to feel free to decide for himself who shall know other facts, at what time, and under what conditions. At the same time, there is an equally powerful need in each person to disclose "personal" or "private" matters to others, as well as a strong impulse to penetrate the privacy of others, not only in terms of his peers and local gossip but also by "eavesdropping" on the activities of leading elites of the society through exposés by the press, government investigations, court trials, etc. While some aspects of this urge for penetration of another's privacy can be considered "voyeuristic" in the personal sense and "populistic" in their political aspect, this is so clearly a fact of behavior, and serves such a key role in a mass society, that its presence must be noted by anyone seriously concerned with privacy norms in our society. There is also a close correlation between the availability of privacy from hostile surveillance and the achievement of creativity, mental health, and ethical self-development, though there is always a shifting standard of balance in these matters and a heavy layer of cultural relativism.

Privacy as a need in organizational life was amply demonstrated in considering the internal affairs of businesses, civic groups, and ideological protest movements. Without time for preparation and internal rationalization of views and differences, private groups cannot fulfill the independent role envisaged for them by the values of a pluralistic, democratic society. Whether to allow such nutritive privacy for a particular group, and how much, are always policy questions for law and government. Thus a scale of privacy depending on the social prestige and assumed social contributions of groups has been a standard feature of our society, with the major religious organizations placed at one end of the scale and "subversive" groups at the other. In addition to the need of individual groups for privacy, there is also a need for privacy in negotiations *between* private groups, such as labor-management bargaining sessions, intercorporate negotiations, and a variety of similar relations in the civic and political sphere.

A core area of privacy is also essential to the successful conduct of democratic government, whether the setting is the private conference of the Supreme Court, meetings of the White House staff with the

President, executive sessions of legislative committees, the conference-committee stage of legislation in Congress, exploratory negotiations with foreign governments, or "frank" sessions behind the scenes at international conferences or at the UN. In situations of all types, privacy is a critical ingredient for the process of accommodation and resolution upon which peaceful settlement of conflicting interests rests. In most instances, the privacy required is a temporary one, and the interests of a democratic society in knowing what its elected and appointed officials are doing can be properly served by pulling back the curtain of privacy after the bargains have been struck and implemented. At that stage, democratic statesmen are held responsible for their acts. Just when the time for disclosure has been reached, and whether privacy is proper at all for a particular process of government, are issues that will receive different answers according to the type of problem, the degree of agreement in the nation on the policies being pursued, the presence of built-in conflicts over privacy created by our separation-of-powers system, and many other factors already discussed. But the need for privacy in democratic government, and the dangers of mislabeling this need by calling it "secrecy," have been the burden of the discussion in this chapter.

7. Finally, in the chapter on privacy and the law, it was seen that concern for protecting privacy has been part of American constitutional law, common law, federal and state legislation, and administrative rules from the very beginning of our national history. A deliberate concept of balancing competing interests was at the heart of American privacy law, as in the "reasonable man" standard for common-law privacy rules and in the federal and state constitutions' ban against "unreasonable" searches. This chapter (and the case studies on civic reactions) showed that the current legal framework is now inadequate to defend the American equilibrium on privacy from new surveillance techniques. However, there has been a strong ferment in American law in the past decade, a beginning of the process necessary to develop in law and social norms what was once assured by physical and technological realities in the older republican society. Despite this recognition that American law is in the process of change, two deep concerns remain: first, that the new legal doctrines should reflect sensitively the needs for both privacy and disclosure; and, second, that major attention should be paid to the role of voluntary, privacy-supporting actions by private authorities and organizations, especially in areas where legal intervention is unlikely or would probably be ineffective.

Developing Criteria for Weighing Conflicting Interests

If privacy is to receive its proper weight on the scales in any process of balancing competing values, what is needed is a structured and rational weighing process, with definite criteria that public and private authorities can apply in comparing the claims for disclosure or surveillance through new devices with the claims to privacy. The following are suggested as the basic steps of such a process: measuring the seriousness of the need to conduct surveillance; deciding whether there are alternative methods to meet the need; deciding what degree of reliability will be required of the surveillance instrument; determining whether true consent to surveillance has been given; and measuring the capacity for limitation and control of the surveillance if it is allowed. Each step is discussed here only briefly; the next section shows how the weighing process would actually be applied to the main problems of privacy and surveillance currently facing American society.

THE SERIOUSNESS OF THE NEED TO CONDUCT SURVEILLANCE

Though surveillance devices are sometimes used for satisfying personal voyeuristic urges and as illegitimate weapons in political or private affairs, the more typical and important use is to solve problems of genuine social importance. Police forces want to solve crimes, corporations to control theft, employers to select more successful employees, educators to identify personality problems in school children, behavioral scientists to observe real-life situations. But if all that has to be done to win legal and social approval for surveillance is to point to a social problem and show that surveillance would help to cope with it, then there is no balancing at all, but only a qualifying procedure for a license to invade privacy. The need must be serious enough to overcome the very real and presently rising risk of jeopardizing the public's confidence in its daily freedom from unreasonable invasions of privacy.

Weighing the seriousness of the need to use surveillance devices might lead American society to deal more frankly than it usually has done with some of its laws against deviant moral or political conduct. For example, we make it criminal to engage in gambling, prostitution, and homosexual solicitation; yet we know that such laws are broken continually by many people who do not regard such activities as immoral. We also know that law enforcement is highly selective, often pursuing the "little lawbreaker" while leaving the more powerful violators untouched. Organized criminal syndicates thrive on providing these services, and too many public officials are corrupted into giving protection to these activities because of public ambivalence toward the acts involved. If the real function of these laws is to hold some social boundaries on such conduct, to prevent it from spreading further than society wishes, we should weigh carefully whether we want to use new surveillance technology in such areas of moral departure. Already police have started installing hidden color cameras and closed-circuit TV in public rest rooms to obtain evidence of homosexual solicitations,[1] have been planting listening devices surreptitiously in such public places as restaurants and motels to investigate prostitution,[2] and have wiretapped for months public telephones where bookmakers place calls.[3] The real question is whether the containment function of our vice laws can justify the spread of surveillance into the large areas of public life that are bound to be involved.

A similar re-examination of need ought to take place over the question of how much public or private employers need to know about the emotions, attitudes, and beliefs of their employees working in ordinary, non-sensitive positions. If our social attitudes toward work are changing as much as they seem to be, if we are coming to believe that objective performance rather than race, color, or religion is our criterion, then judgments about religious, political, and sexual adjustment made covertly by psychologists in the interests of institutional clients may also be found to be unnecessary for selection among applicants and evaluation of the performance of existing employees.

ALTERNATIVE METHODS TO MEET THE NEED: THE BURDEN OF PROOF

Much of life as well as law depends on deciding who has the burden of proof in any situation in which action is to be taken. In deciding whether there are alternative methods less violative of individual and organizational privacy than proposed surveillance devices and processes, the burden of proof that other techniques are not available should be on those seeking authorization. For example, the need to resort to wiretapping or bugging during the course of criminal investigation in modern American society, with our patterns of mobility, swift communication, and so on, is stated as a conclusion by the majority of law-enforcement witnesses before legislative committees.[4] Cases are usually cited in which this was said to have been the fact. But there has never been a detailed presentation by any law-enforcement agency, in terms that the educated public could judge, to prove this view on a crime-by-crime analysis. My own belief, after talking to almost a hundred law-enforcement officials, is that such a case could be made for crimes such as extortion and kidnaping, where the consent of one party (the victim) to the key conversations would be obtainable anyway, and in certain national-security investigations, including the need for positive security checks and offensive intelligence operations. But this case has never been made in public. Until it is, with the opportunity for opponents of eavesdropping to challenge the presentation in the public forum, law-enforcement spokesmen have not proved the positive need for the use of surreptitious listening and watching devices.

The same approach to alternative methods should apply in such matters as personality testing. Record analysis, interviews that stay within decent boundaries of privacy, aptitude and achievement tests (including simulation tests), and on-the-job trial testing seem to provide completely adequate available alternatives to the use of personality tests. There has never been evidence secured under scientific control procedures, in either industry or government, to show that employees selected by personality measures are more successful than those selected without such tests. Nor has there been the slightest proof that employees selected by organizations which do not use personality testing are less effective, successful, or well adjusted than those from companies which have bought the fad of personality testing. The survey that I conducted in 1965 of 208 industrial firms showed that 53.6 per cent were not using personality tests (indicating, happily, a trend away from such use, compared to the 1950's).[5] Among the companies operating without such tests are American Motors, Bristol-Myers, DuPont, Florida Power & Light, A&P, Gulf Oil, Litton Industries, Metropolitan Life Insurance, Northern Pacific Railroad, Pabst Brewing, and RCA, none of which—or the other thousands of companies like them—seem to be centers for emotionally disturbed employees or executives.

To give just one more example, control of petty thefts in industry is a serious problem. Studies have shown that the rising levels of white-collar crime and pilfering have seriously injured industry, with employee thefts amounting to millions of dollars annually for some companies.[6] Yet such techniques as tool and inventory controls, physical inspection of parcels and purses at exit gates, electronic scanning devices that will register certain types of objects, and similar methods, all supplemented by standard investigations of high-loss locations by company investigators (which can include sending in investigators disguised as regular employees), offer adequate alternatives to the periodic polygraphing that has been adopted by some companies in their quest for theft control. The simple proof is that most companies do not use polygraphs, and those firms relying on other security measures, even in high-loss industries, have not been destroyed by their failure to adopt polygraphing.

RELIABILITY OF THE INSTRUMENT

The reliability required of a surveillance device or process will depend on the purpose for which the inquiry is conducted. If acceptance of polygraph reports or narco-analysis as evidence in criminal trials is involved, the courts should take as conclusive scientific tests showing that it is possible for many persons to lie under narco-analysis, or that polygraph readings by average operators are wrong (for example, that they fail to identify lies, or identify as lies testimony that is true) in a significant percentage of trials. When new drugs make it impossible to lie, or computer readings of advanced emotional-sensing equipment increase levels of accuracy to the 95- or 99-per-cent mark, the test of reliability will be met. At that point, however, the issue of admissibility in court would still be subject to inquiry on other grounds.

On the other hand, if intelligence agencies are seeking to choose five men to volunteer for a dangerous mission, or if defectors from a Communist country seek asylum here and want to work for our intelligence agencies, the use of polygraphs or narco-analysis might be justified, even assuming present levels of reliability. Where crucial interests of national security are involved, and issues of judicially determined guilt or innocence are not present, a 75-per-cent accuracy ratio might be sufficient reliability on which to select among candidates or decide whether to trust a report.

As already indicated, no body of data proves that personality tests of any kind, objective or projective, can predict the future performance of individuals in an employment situation in percentages significantly greater than other existing selection methods. Given the fact that the questions used in such tests intrude into otherwise protected areas of personal life and private beliefs, and that preserving an attitude of non-confession toward authorities is a high social goal in American society, the privacy-invading type of personality test fails to meet minimum reliability requirements.

Realistically, the issue of whether a particular surveillance device or technique "works" will be a continuous inquiry, not a one-time test. New types of emotional sensors, and monitors to read their output, are continually being developed, for instance, as are new psychological tests for predicting behavior. A technique might fail the test of scientific validity for decades, then be perfected to accuracy. Therefore a sensible approach would be to think in terms of a scientific threshold that any privacy-invading process must pass before American society should have to reach the next question of whether the process should be permitted even though it *is* wholly scientific. Until such a threshold is passed, both law and social sanctions should require that unproved processes be used only in situations in which individuals freely consent to their use.

THE ISSUE OF CONSENT: EXPRESSED, IMPLIED, OR COERCED?

A central aspect of privacy is that individuals and organizations can determine for themselves which matters they want to keep private and which they are willing—or need—to reveal. Similarly, society can require consent to various general regulations as a condition for receiving government benefits. Furthermore, the needs of social order may require certain levels of exposure and confession even if these are involuntary. Consent is thus to be analyzed in the specific context of the purpose of surveillance and the use to be made of the information so obtained. Neither law nor public pressure should force anyone to have privacy if that person, assuming he is an adult of sound mind, wants to give up his privacy for psychological, commercial, or humanitarian reasons. There is no violation of the right to privacy when persons give general consent to be recorded or watched as part of a scientific experiment, an educational study, a test of a new food or product, or a study of physical or emotional reaction to an entertainment performance; submit to psychological tests for counseling or medical purposes, or to perfect a test; take experimental drugs; give personal data to a private or governmental survey; and the like. This is true as long as the subject is told in advance, the experiment is not one that demeans a civilized society, and there will be no serious harm done to the person. Individuals should be free to take polygraph or personality tests as volunteers for special government missions as long as they will not be penalized if they do not volunteer. Persons should be free, with full consent, to give up their privacy in ways that would be shocking and wholly unacceptable for non-consenters. For example, during 1963 a furor was created by reports that investigators under a National Institutes of Health grant were going to record the conversations of newlyweds in their apartments, to study personal interaction during the early stages of married life.[7] Several Congressmen and editors asked angrily how far the scientific Big Brother would go to penetrate our most sacred retreats. Closer inquiry revealed the following facts: In return for free rent, the couples had agreed in advance to allow recording of conversations in the living room, dining room, and kitchen of the house. No monitoring of bedrooms or bathrooms was involved, and full ground rules were set down as to the hours when the monitoring would be carried out and as to the use to be made of the recordings. This being the case, there was no unreasonable violation of privacy. Indeed, a few moments' reflection about the effect on scientific inquiry of forbidding such volunteer experiments will suggest how unwise intervention by prohibitory legislation would be in this area.

A more difficult problem is deciding when consent is implied by acceptance of a given type of employment or the carrying on of a certain activity. For instance, it is customary for schoolteachers to be visited by principals and division heads to observe classroom performance, just as it has been typical to have ordinary window-glass panels in the doors of classrooms, through which persons in the corridor can see inside. Does the teacher's consent to this customary practice, and the general relation of teachers to administrative supervision, include the right of the administration to install in each classroom loudspeaker boxes which can be switched on silently by the principal to listen to what is going on in that classroom? If the visit could be made in person or from the hall, what difference does it make that the observation will now be unannounced, will be carried out by a mechanical device, and will not disturb the class by a physical intrusion? My answer is that the findings about visibility and conformity discussed earlier indicate such a harmful effect on teacher and student morale, academic freedom, and the sense of personal dignity in schools that these outweigh the benefits of efficiency in observation. One way to convince school administrators who have been using such listening boxes of the need to balance values more sensitively would be to suggest that the school board and the city council should also have a box in the principal's office, to ensure that his standard of performance with teachers, students, and parents is up to the desired levels of excellence.

A harder case is presented when employers, whether private or governmental, require scientific tests that invade privacy for hiring or advancement. When refusal to take the tests means loss of the job, and when the particular type of test becomes a commonplace in the industry or field, a withholding of consent may jeopardize one's basic ability to practice his profession. Moreover, in certain areas of special importance, American law does not allow individuals to consent to waive their rights when there is inequality in the bargaining position, as with statutes outlawing "yellow dog" contracts by which workers promised not to join unions as a condition of employment and continued employment. This suggests that we should examine the nature of consent carefully in each instance, to see how freely given or how coerced the consent is in that context.

Finally, it should be recognized that consent to reveal information to a particular person or agency, for a particular purpose, is not consent for that information to be circulated to all or used for other purposes. The individual may consent to tell things to his teacher or professor that ought not be circulated as part of student records without the student's consent. Information given to life-insurance companies, credit agencies, survey researchers, or government regulatory and welfare agencies ought not to be shared, in ways that identify the particular individual, without notice of the additional use and consent to it. Unless this principle of consent is well understood and accepted as the controlling principle for information flow in a data-stream society, we will be in for serious problems of privacy in the future.

To conclude that consent is not freely given in such circumstances does not mean that such scientific techniques may never be used in these areas. It simply distinguishes true conditions of consent from nonconsent, and carries our analysis to the next stage of inquiry: when can these devices be used without the knowledge or real consent of the subjects, and under what safeguards?

CAPACITY FOR LIMITATION AND CONTROL

Whether or not to authorize the use of surveillance devices or processes must, finally, depend on the specific system proposed for authorization and control of the surveillance. Though there will be variations according to the type of instrument, I would suggest that four basic criteria must be met. First, rules must be set limiting those who may carry out the surveillance. For example, the history of police-force use of eavesdropping is sufficiently stained with misconduct throughout the nation that use of physical surveillance devices at the state level should be strictly limited to district attorneys' offices and state attorney generals' offices, and at the federal level to the FBI and military agencies. Administration of acceptable psychological tests ought to be limited to accredited psychologists specially licensed by state boards of psychology to engage in this practice. Private investigators should be specifically forbidden to engage in physical surveillance with the new listening and watching devices, and owners of property to which the public is invited should be forbidden to install or use secret surveillance, even for safeguarding persons and property, unless notices are prominently displayed to that effect.

Second, detailed regulations should be set for the *scope, duration,* and *operations* of the surveillance. Rules of scope will determine the questions that may be asked and those that are forbidden (on privacy grounds) in psychological and personality examinations, and which questions may not be obtained by government for general data pools. In the case of physical surveillance, rules of scope will determine the types of crime for which surveillance is permitted and the places that may be surveyed. The rules of duration will determine, for example, how long physical surveillance may be carried on (the ideal policy being for short, renewable periods). Rules of operation should specify the way in which the surveillance should be carried out—the type of monitoring equipment to be used and methods of identifying and preserving recordings; the types of tests approved for psychological examinations; the equipment approved for polygraphing and how the results should be read; and others.

Third, some general agency ought to be created to set the standards for surveillance, supervise practices under the rules, investigate compliance, and hear complaints about misconduct. If law-enforcement officials are involved, a system of judicial order should be used, though much more careful rules would have to be set for proving need to use physical surveillance than have prevailed to date under warrant systems.

In the case of personality testing, some combination of public board and private psychologists' association might be established to set standards and hear complaints.

Having set rules for the surveillance itself—who can employ the device or process, how, and under what review authority—the fourth step is to set rules to govern disclosure and use of the information obtained. Use in court—whether in criminal trials or civil cases—ought to be strictly reserved for information gathered in full conformity with the control system; refusal to permit use of evidence obtained in violation of the control system is the simplest and most practical way of building respect for the rules. Beyond this, regulations should be developed for each surveillance process, to insure that the information obtained is used only for the purpose for which it was secured and is seen only by those who must have access to it for that specific purpose. Systems of maintenance and disposal ought to be fashioned to guarantee this protection of privacy, with penalties enforced against unauthorized disclosure or use.

Achieving Control of Surveillance Technology

The preceding discussion suggests five inquiries by which private and public authorities might analyze the conflicting claims of surveillance and privacy when considering whether to authorize new scientific devices or processes. How this analytical process might be applied to leading surveillance issues and where the trends of public opinion and law may take us in the coming decade are the matters we turn to now.

To some observers of our current situation, prohibitory legislation is the ideal and necessary response. Yet if privacy is understood in the broader contexts we have used here, it will be apparent that the shifting equilibrium among privacy, disclosure, and surveillance cannot be captured by legislation alone, nor is legislation necessarily the best first step to achieve control over surveillance techniques in many areas. There are areas in which the stimulation of private authorities to protect rights of privacy will have far more real impact than prohibitory statutes. There are other areas in which there is no real need as yet for legislation, and where hastily enacted statutes might prevent the development of a wise accommodation by private and judicial forces. Legislation may be needed to control some "outlaw" behavior, however, or to stimulate the non-legislative forces and give them the broad moral authority with which to operate. This survey of trends and remedies will begin with the private responses, then turn to possible governmental interventions, executive, legislative, and judicial.

THE ROLE OF PRIVATE FORCES

Five major private forces can play a significant role in establishing the norms of privacy in a democratic society: moral consciousness; scientific counter-measures; intra-organizational rules and decisions; private agreements; and professional ethical standards. There has already been significant activity to strengthen norms of privacy in each of these areas during the past few years, but much more is still needed.

Moral Consciousness. Norms of privacy can change, just as American norms on sexual conduct, race relations, and international participation have changed profoundly in past decades. A close survey of the positions adopted by leading ideological and civic groups toward issues of surveillance and privacy since 1945 indicates that there is now a general identification of privacy with liberty, and that concern over unlimited governmental or private surveillance runs the ideological spectrum from the Daughters of the American Revolution to the New Student Left, and from the *National Review* to the *Nation.* In the 1950's only a few critics were urging restraints on corporate use of personality testing, or on government use of polygraphs for personnel screening; now these and other areas have become matters of deep concern to a large segment of the population. The cry that "Big Brother is Watching" is now raised by any person or group protesting against what he or it considers unfair surveillance. Recent popular exposés, such as Vance Packard's *The Naked Society* and Myron Brenton's *The Privacy Invaders,* and frequent television and press treatments of the new devices have linked the new surveillance technology to questionable currents of commercial, social, and governmental inquisitiveness in post-World-War II America. Anxious articles and editorials about restoring norms of privacy have appeared in business, labor, legal, and academic journals, and many civic groups have adopted policy resolutions deploring erosions of privacy. In addition, the long-range social trends toward urbanization, automation, increasing concentration of employment in large-scale organizations, and the increased growth of government functions—though these stimulate modes of operation that can jeopardize privacy—have already begun to place debates over the protection of privacy at the heart of national thinking about the conditions of freedom in the second half of the twentieth century. Thus our moral concern and our consciousness have been aroused, and have begun to affect the daily choices of individuals as these involve "invasion of privacy" issues. This climate of public opinion may also be ready to support effective action to safeguard privacy if such action can be intelligently framed and effectively presented. Something significant has obviously happened when a President of the United States quotes Justice Brandeis and calls for protection of privacy in a State of the Union message.

Scientific Counter-Measures. Until recently the attention and energies of the scientific community have been directed primarily at the development of more effective instruments for surveillance, intrusion, and penetration. To be sure, there has been classified government research to develop techniques for protecting military and diplomatic privacy from surveillance. In addition some corporations (especially defense contractors) have adopted "floating room" systems to ensure privacy at conferences and there are some jamming and detection devices available on the general market for "bug-protection." But there has not been a major effort to develop new systems for the protection of the average citizen's privacy in telephone communication, room conversations, and private acts.

It may require a congressional or executive-agency investigation to help spur such enterprise, but there is hope that the growing public demand for greater privacy will itself stimulate greater scientific activity, especially by such groups as the telephone companies, electronics firms, and data-processing manufacturers. Many scientific possibilities could be explored. Scramblers could be made available as a general service for telephone subscribers at a reasonable additional cost per month. Special telephone centers could be set up, perhaps using meteor-burst transmissions or other "tap-proof" waves, to which persons could resort to telephone others in similar centers when conversations were of special importance; the telephone company could provide "ground security" for these centers. Even as simple a matter as redesigning the present telephone instrument, to eliminate the empty space in which investigators now drop their bug units so conveniently, would be an impediment to the intruders. Many other possibilities warrant exploration. Whether by persuasion, investigation, or regulatory order, or by the encouragement of competitors who will offer more secure message and data-transmission services than the telephone companies now provide, the progress in scientific counter-measures must be accelerated.

In the area of room eavesdropping, electronic jamming systems could be developed that would be so cheap, efficient, and flexible that, for a cost of $25 or $50 per room, persons and organizations concerned with confidentiality could have such jamming systems built in as part of the regular construction. Already on the market are pocket-size portable jamming devices which protect the bearer from having his conversation picked up electronically with the usual "private-eye" equipment. The fundamental point is that science can do much to safeguard the exercise of privacy if money, intelligence, and commitment are focused on the endeavor.

Sometimes the new technology itself offers ways to protect privacy that were not formerly available. For instance, where personal data (salary level, medical records, former criminal convictions, and the like) are stored on personnel records for computers, the system can be set so that only a person who is given a secret code number can secure such information. The "locks" are thus much tighter, and without files and paper shuffling, access can truly be limited to those, like the company or agency medical officer or the personnel officer, who have a legitimate need for this information.

Intra-Organizational Restraints. Issues of privacy are constantly being resolved by organizational or agency decisions on whether to employ surveillance techniques or devices. "Organizations" here refers to private concerns, such as business corporations, religious groups, universities, labor unions, and voluntary associations.

One basic type of organizational decision involving privacy arises from setting rules of personnel procedure. All large organizations establish rules for hiring personnel, supervising performance, judging fitness for advancement, determining the availability of personnel records throughout the organizational system, and disclosing personnel and intra-agency data to other private or governmental bodies. Whether to use personality tests, polygraphs, and physical surveillance devices, and how to acquire, store, and use information on computers, will be regular and common issues of choice for all these agencies.

Another major decision about privacy is made continually by organizations which acquire large pools of facts and conduct investigations as part of their regular operations. For example, the officers of a newspaper, news magazine, or television station will have to decide whether to employ long-range microphones or cameras to survey celebrities and public officials on the streets or in public places, or to use eavesdropping devices to penetrate closed meetings of private groups. A law firm will decide whether to issue permissive or restrictive instructions to the investigators it employs to gather facts in a pending matter or to evade its responsibility by "leaving it up to the detectives." A market-research agency will be faced with the decision of whether to plant cameras or microphones to secure "authentic" reactions to a new product, performance, or process. In all these situations, the organization confronts decisions in which self-restraint on behalf of the values of privacy collides with increased efficiency for the enterprise through use of new surveillance technology.

This "ethical" issue is one which will be heavily affected—for most organizational leaders—by the attitudes of colleagues in the same field, by the effect using these devices will have on intra-agency morale, and by general editorial and public opinion. If employees and executives have been sensitized by debates over privacy in the mass media to resent the use of secret recording and television monitoring on the job, or the use of polygraphs or personality tests, the organizational leaders may conclude that the economic or efficiency gains are not worth their cost in bad public relations or organizational prestige. Press exposés of organizational practices that invade privacy, legislative investigations of these areas, and similar public spotlights on administrative practices will also have therapeutic effects on the privacy-weighing process within organizations.

A good example of organizational response is the policy established recently by Columbia University to govern the furnishing of data about students to outside inquirers. The growing demands of government and private employers for information, including personal data and matters affecting freedom of expression in classes, plus the shifting of Columbia's records to automated systems, led the University to reconsider its prior policies. Previously the University automatically furnished ten items of information to "any inquirer": the division of the University in which the student was enrolled; his period of enrollment; degrees awarded and dates; home and local addresses; major subject; honors received; verification of signature; confirmation of date and place of birth; name and address of parent or guardian; and statement of good academic standing. But whenever federal investigators presented proper identification, the old procedure allowed them to examine the transcript and academic records of the student.

Under its new policy Columbia University will continue to release the ten items mentioned above to all inquirers. But no person will be allowed to examine a student's academic records or receive a transcript without the student's consent. To avoid harmful delays for students applying to federal agencies for employment, the University will allow students to register in advance, on a special form, their willingness to have their academic records shown to federal officials. Although this new policy does not deal with some vital matters of privacy involved in loyalty-security checks about students—such as what faculty members ought to say about student "attitudes" in class, or the content of their written work—the University has adopted a records policy that puts the decision on release of information in the hands of the individual student.

Private Agreements. American society relies heavily on private bargains which individuals, groups and organizations negotiate among themselves, in economic or social self-government. Private contracts, the collective-bargaining process, government-industry codes, and arbitration systems illustrate this activity. There are already signs of a healthy ferment in this area as far as privacy is concerned. Several labor unions, such as the United Auto Workers and the Communication Workers of America, have raised such strong protests against the use of concealed listening devices on company property that the employers have discontinued their use.[8] Unions have argued that the installation of closed-circuit television cameras to watch workers represents a change in the conditions of work and supervision to which the union must consent;

and in several industries the threat of a strike has led to the cancellation of plans to install such television monitoring. Unions have also taken the question of employer use of physical surveillance devices to arbitration under labor contracts, and there have been rulings holding that television surveillance in the ordinary condition of assembly-line work represented an unreasonable violation of workers' rights to privacy, even when they were working openly on the factory floor.[9]

Other types of private agreement may become activated by the new concern to assert interests of privacy more strongly. Perhaps a guest at a hotel could rely on his contract as a licencee of that facility to sue a hotel management which allowed a private detective to install listening devices or allowed a police official acting without court authorization (in those states requiring such) to do the same. Why shouldn't the contract duty of owners of public accommodation facilities to safeguard the quiet enjoyment of their guests, customers, or clients include the duty not to participate knowingly in surveillance that violates that privacy? And if hotel clerks or waiters in restaurants co-operate in assigning to detectives rooms or tables next to persons who will be subjected to electronic eavesdropping, why shouldn't such conduct, if done with knowledge of the intent of the detectives, be held to constitute a ground for substantial damages?

Professional Standards. Enforcement of professional ethical standards protecting privacy could accomplish a great deal, since techniques of surveillance are widely used by members of professions which deal in the collection and use of personal data. These include doctors, lawyers, accountants, journalists, sociologists, psychologists, political scientists, historians, and anthropologists. The framework for regulation already exists; many of these professions are subject either to self-regulatory ethical codes or to governmental regulation exerted through licensing. Both the internally adopted and the externally imposed codes of conduct are designed to define standards of professional behavior, provide guides for borderline problems, and establish procedures for investigating charges of unethical conduct. Although the sanctions available for breaches of ethics vary widely both in nature and effect, the disciplinary action usually carries some weight in professional life. Indeed, the ultimate sanction to a professional may be a governmental suspension of license to practice. Otherwise, external regulation needs no further consideration here, since the governmental standards are usually either an adaptation of the profession's own ethical code or the product of legislative action, which will be discussed later.

Many of the ethical codes already contain important provisions on preserving confidentiality of information given by clients, requiring tests of scientific validity before employing new techniques or processes, and avoiding types of surveillance or intrusion that violate the principle of

client consent. Such provisions, some of which date back to the Hippo-
cratic Oath and to legal canons from medieval England, were on the
books long before the new applications of science and technology developed in the post-1945 era. But the pressure of the new technology was so
great, and the sensitivity to privacy was often so slight among the professional groups, that the 1945–1965 period was one in which ethical codes
provided little control over immoderate use of surveillance.

This development is well illustrated by the debate among psychologists over the use of personality testing. As a result of rising criticism in
scholarly and popular journals, as well as congressional investigations in
1965, the American Psychological Association and several state groups
have created panels to reassess their ethical codes on testing and privacy.
An entire issue of the *American Psychologist* in 1965[10] was devoted to
the problem. Forums at the national conventions of the American Psychological Association, the American Orthopsychiatric Association and
the New York State Psychological Association in 1966 have considered
the topic. The President's Office of Science and Technology has established a panel on privacy and behavioral research—composed of representatives from the behavioral sciences, law, and the social sciences—to
recommend guidelines for distinguishing reasonable and unreasonable
intrusions into privacy in research conducted or sponsored by the United
States government. An article by Dr. Orville Brim, Jr., and Oscar M.
Ruebhausen, recommending a code for ensuring privacy in such projects,
was published in the *Columbia Law Review*,[11] reprinted in the *American
Psychologist*,[12] condensed in several other scientific and social-science
journals, and has been distributed to members of the field staff of the
National Opinion Research Center, and is sent by the United States
Office of Education to all applicants for grants under USOE's Cooperative Research Program. A major research project on personality testing
has been funded by the Russell Sage Foundation, with the issue of
reasonable and unreasonable intrusions into privacy included in the concerns of the survey. Several leading psychologists are exploring new tests
of psychological strengths for personnel decisions which would eliminate
the main questions objectionable on grounds of privacy—those dealing
with religion, sex, politics, and personal values.

The deepening of responsibility to define and respect boundaries of
privacy in one's own professional activities is by no means limited to the
psychologists. Edward Shils and Margaret Mead have recently criticized
privacy-invading trends among social scientists, including the growing
use of listening and watching devices without the knowledge or consent
of those being "studied." There have been rising debates over the ethical
aspects of invading privacy in survey research, participant-observer projects, community studies, and similar scholarly activities. The issue of
lawyers' use of recording devices with clients, with other lawyers, and in

the employment of private investigators has also been raised under existing provisions of the legal Canon of Ethics by the Special Committee on Science and Law of the Association of the Bar of the City of New York. This ferment promises to increase within the professional groups as public attention is focused on the ethical questions involved.

THE ROLE OF GOVERNMENT ACTION

Development of the five private forces just described should provide important new supports for privacy. But ethical and professional commandments will not always be sufficient to control the conduct of criminal elements, over-zealous government officials, profit-seekers, or insensitive researchers. At this point, governmental action serves to create clear boundary lines of permissible and forbidden conduct and to put fresh moral force behind enforcement of the newly fashioned rules.

Legislative Action to Control Unreasonable Invasions of Privacy. There is good reason to believe that the Supreme Court will soon issue a broad, path-breaking decision on the right to privacy from technological intrusion. However, this expectation ought not to prevent serious legislative debates at the present time. There is no guarantee that the Court will issue a ruling in the near future; the right case might not arise, or the Court might find itself divided internally in a way that would inhibit early declaration of a new position. Furthermore, the specific nature of some issues of technological surveillance calls for detailed control legislation; a judicial opinion drawing a line between constitutional and unconstitutional conduct and relying on exclusion of illegally obtained evidence to compel obedience is not the most promising way of properly balancing the interests of privacy, disclosure, and surveillance. Finally, forsaking a serious attempt to secure legislation in order to pressure the Justices into undertaking an essentially legislative responsibility ignores the separation-of-powers principle. On the other hand, the expression of public policy in new statutes would probably enhance the Court's ultimate role in this area. For these reasons, serious attention should be given now to the legislative possibilities for controlling modern means of invading privacy.

Legislation might well be considered for each of the three areas discussed previously: psychological, data, and physical surveillance. In regard to the first two areas, it may be proper initially to restrict the new controls to the actions of the federal government. The example of the federal government setting its own house in order may do much to persuade (rather than coerce) the states and private organizations to undertake their own reforms. If the example is not followed, Congress can then broaden the statutory coverage and will have the advantage of its previous experience in formulating and enforcing standards. With regard to physical surveillance, however, the situation is different. At present this is the most widespread type of surveillance. Those laws which have been enacted to control it are chaotic and largely ignored. Congress should exercise its full constitutional authority to control as much of this surveillance as possible. It should also encourage the states to reach those actions beyond federal regulatory power.

To explore the directions the necessary statutes might take, I have sketched what seem to me the key concepts that ought to be considered and some of the issues of fact and value that are involved in the choices of policy that I am suggesting.

1. *Psychological Surveillance.* There is a growing need for statutes defining and protecting the government employee's right to freedom from unreasonable invasions of privacy by his employer. It is true that congressional and public pressures have already done much to contain the use of polygraphs and personality tests by federal and state agencies. They are still used without proper justification in some government employment situations, however, and proper control systems have not been devised for those uses that might be justified.

The legislation which should be enacted would have three basic parts. First, the legislature would declare the general right of public employees to be free from unreasonable invasions of privacy. All government officials would be charged to conduct their personnel policies accordingly. This approach would provide a broad standard in the tradition of the common-law right to privacy or the quasi-constitutional approach of anti-trust and regulatory-agency legislation; its broad formulations would give courts and executive agencies maximum freedom to apply the principles of privacy to concrete situations and to deal with future developments in surveillance technology as they appear.

Second, the statute should forbid the use of certain techniques of psychological surveillance, such as polygraph examinations and personality tests. It would provide exceptions for a limited class of cases involving national security and employee assignments of special stress, and would spell out a careful general procedure for determining these situations and conducting the examinations. The regulations recently issued by the Department of Defense for conducting polygraph examinations[13] represent a start in this direction.

Third, the statute could create an independent agency (somewhat along the lines of the Scandinavian Ombudsman) which would be charged with the responsibility of protecting the rights to privacy in the employment relationship. The agency, which should have a bipartisan membership, would be empowered to receive complaints of violations by executive officials, hold hearings, and issue binding decisions. Since a regular executive agency's willingness to control the actions of fellow officials might be somewhat less than wholehearted, a truly independent body is desirable. The statute should allow a government employee to bring a court action for enforcement of the agency's decision by appropriate injunctive relief or to appeal an agency ruling denying his claim.

A statute such as this would be just as applicable and useful at the state level as it is at the federal. It does for the right to privacy what the recently enacted Freedom of Information Law[14] does for the right to publicity—it provides a general principle, specific exceptions to be worked out in practice, and a means of enforcement that does not rest solely on executive self-restraint or intra-executive enforcement.

2. *Data Surveillance.* The effective use of computers calls for rational analysis and painstaking planning. If privacy is to survive, the growth of personal-data processing will necessitate the same high levels of analysis and planning by federal and state legislatures seeking to use computers for large-scale data processing. This means that fresh studies ought to be made of existing confidentiality and non-disclosure requirements for information acquired by government agencies in their regulatory and data-collecting roles. Provisions for confidentiality of information, restrictions on improper circulation, and sanctions against unauthorized use should be written into the basic legislation and administrative rules governing the new law enforcement computer systems.

Similar legislative action is desirable for the government data centers that are rapidly coming into operation at both state and federal levels. The statute could provide that such information must be kept by the agency that collected it and can not be revealed to another government agency or to a private party unless certain conditions are met—national-security or defense needs; general permission in advance from those supplying the information to circulate it freely; specific permission from the supplier for a particular use of the information to be made; and so forth. A process could be established for decision in the executive branch, subject to judicial review, of whether the auxiliary use is proper, has been authorized, and other limitations.

The end sought by such a statute might well develop as an unanticipated dividend from the Freedom of Information Law enacted by Congress in 1966. This Act, designed to make executive records more accessible to the public, set up eight categories of sensitive government information exempt from disclosure. These are defense or foreign-policy secrets authorized to be kept secret by executive order; matters which relate solely to internal personnel rules and practices of an agency; matters specifically exempted from disclosure by statute; trade secrets and other types of commercial information obtained from the public which are privileged or confidential; inter-agency or intra-agency memoranda or letters dealing solely with matters of law or policy which would not be available by law to a private party in litigation with the agency; personnel and medical and similar matters "the disclosure of which would constitute a clearly unwarranted invasion of personal privacy"; investigatory files compiled for law-enforcement purposes except to the extent available by law to a private party; geological and geophysical data concerning wells; and certain reports prepared for regulating or supervising financial institutions. A person denied information can sue the agency in federal court, where the agency has the burden of proof to justify its action. The court can enjoin the agency from continuing to withhold the information if it is not properly withheld under the Act, with power to punish the officials for contempt if they refuse to comply. The reports of the committees that drafted the Act, and the debates in Congress, show that Congress was aware that the Act would provide a basis for safeguarding from disclosure private information about citizens that government has acquired, and that the citizen's right to privacy was a goal of the Act along with the public's "right to know." [15] The Senate Judiciary Committee report stressed that the provision protecting matters whose disclosure would be an invasion of personal privacy "enunciates a policy that will involve a balancing of interests between the protection of an individual's private affairs from unnecessary public scrutiny, and the preservation of the public's right to governmental information. The application of this policy should lend itself particularly to those government agencies where persons are forced to submit vast accounts of personal data usually for limited purpose [such as] health, welfare, and selective service records." [16] The fact that the courts will ultimately pass on the balancing of interests is a major step forward.

The difficulty with the Freedom of Information Act and its state counterparts, however, is that it seems to appoint the government the necessary champion of the citizen's right to privacy. There is no mechanism in these acts by which an individual can challenge in court the willing release by a government agency to the public or to another agency of personal data collected from the individual. Perhaps an amendment to the Act, or a separate piece of state and federal legislation, could provide for such a challenge along the lines of the statute discussed for controlling unreasonable psychological intrusions. Such a statute might contain a broad declaration that information given to the government for a specific purpose may not be used for any other purpose or given further circulation unless the identity of the individual or group supplying the information is completely removed from the data or the supplying source freely consents to the additional circulation. Further exception might be made for a small class of situations requiring either limited or general circulation in the government's discretion. The independent agency previously described might also be assigned responsibility for adjudicating complaints from citizens or government employees about misuse of personal and confidential information. A person might be allowed to challenge the accuracy of information about him in a government dossier, asking whether the source was an improper or tainted one (such as an illegal wiretap) and therefore the information should be struck.

3. *Physical Surveillance: Guidelines for New Wiretapping-Eavesdropping Statutes.* The problem that cries out for legislation most acutely is that of wiretapping, electronic eavesdropping, and optical surveillance. Appeals to the Supreme Court to enter and cut the Gordian knot have been in vain; the Court obviously feels that it can do no more with the ambiguous language of section 605 and has almost pleaded for congressional clarification. Most states are also looking to Congress to take the lead. Thus neither of the two main state models on electronic eavesdropping—the New York statute and the Illinois statute—has been widely accepted in other states. If the current public attention to the problem of unreasonable invasions of privacy by surveillance technology is not to degenerate into a gloomy and dangerous pessimism—a feeling that nothing can be done to control the marvels of gadgetry or that ringing court rulings which do not control government conduct will be the reality of the 1970's—the time is ripe for Congress and the state legislatures to enact a general statutory system controlling physical surveillance by new devices.

The discussion below covers possible federal and state statutes to control physical-surveillance devices and vest a limited power in certain public agencies to conduct electronic surveillance. There would have to be some differences between the federal and state laws because of different governmental powers and responsibilities. The primary difference is that the state laws, enacted under broad state police powers, could apply to all persons within the state's jurisdiction, while the federal statute, in many instances, would restrict only federal officials. Despite these distinctions, each statute would contain four basic elements: prohibitions against unreasonable surveillance by technological devices; exceptions for legitimate private use of surveillance devices; a system of court-controlled use by law-enforcement officials in limited cases; and assorted remedies providing for private and public enforcement of the statutory limitations.

a. *The federal statute.* The federal statute on unreasonable physical surveillance by devices should open with three prohibitions followed, in the next section, by a list of exceptions. First, the statute should protect telephone communication (for which the federal government has basic regulatory responsibility) by making it unlawful for any person, including state or federal officials, to use a device as a means of listening to or recording conversations on a commercial, governmental, or private telephone system without the knowledge and consent of all participants to the conversations. The statute should define the term "device" to cover all known means of telephone tapping and monitoring and should provide a definition of free consent that could be given judicial clarification in particular situations. Second, federal jurisdiction over radio frequencies and their use would support a provision forbidding any person to use radio transmitters for eavesdropping. The third prohibition would make it unlawful for any federal official or his agent to use a device to observe, overhear, or record—without the subject's knowledge and consent—the location, speech, or acts of any person who is in a private place or engaged in a private conversation or activity in a public place. Congress should also consider a provision controlling state and private use of surveillance devices other than those which monitor telephone conversations or rely on radio transmission of conversation; this would cover the common use of microphone and recording devices which operate on standard electric current, batteries, or transistors. Unlike telephone or radio surveillance, these activities lack the requisite interstate character to base federal authority on the commerce clause. However, it can be argued that congressional power arises under Section 5 of the Fourteenth Amendment, which empowers Congress to enforce the citizen's constitutional rights to life, liberty, and property through positive legislation. Under this theory, Congress would regulate state and private interference with the constitutional right to freedom from unreasonable invasions of privacy. As distinguished commentators have noted, recent Supreme Court decisions lay the foundation for such a position.[17] Although the desirable reach of a federal statute is, in the first instance, clearly a policy question, Congress might decide that any system of control over physical surveillance by device which does not reach microphone, tape-recorder, and television-camera surveillance would jeopardize a general statutory protection of fundamental constitutional rights.

While precise definition of these terms might best be left to judicial elaboration, the language suggested here recognizes that people seek, and society has an interest in protecting, certain important moments of privacy in places that our law regards as "public" or "open" areas—streets, park benches, hotel lobbies, restaurant tables. Rather than draw the line between privately owned premises on the one hand and public facilities on the other—a distinction which surrenders far too much terrain to the new surveillance technology—this approach assumes that privacy can be legitimately claimed for certain activities in public as well as private places. For example, persons sitting together on a park bench or walking along the street can reasonably expect to claim privacy from eavesdropping by persons not in normal listening range. Whether optical surveillance beyond the range of normal eyesight should be similarly treated is a harder question but one to which, on balance, the same rule should probably apply. Federal officials and their agents should also be forbidden to use a device to obtain information or data stored in a computer or other data-processing or storing system unless prior consent is obtained from the owner or custodian of the information.

The federal statute's second section would provide some of the exceptions by authorizing the use of surveillance devices in a number of limited instances. These would include the use of devices as aids to impaired physical functions (hearing aids, for instance); in situations where consent for overhearing would be implied (as with marine-band and ham-radio conversations); in research, education, and therapy conducted by federal employees when the individual had given specific consent or a general consent to the experiment that reasonably included the surveillance used; for the physical protection of property from intrusion or to ensure personal safety (TV in elevators, for example) when a notice of surveillance is clearly posted; and for the regular servicing of the communication systems by their operators in a manner that does not intrude unnecessarily into private conversations or communications. A score of clauses might be needed to spell out the necessary exceptions, and these could be expanded—or contracted—as experience with the statute developed. This would *not* include an exception to allow wiretapping or eavesdropping with the consent of one party. This has been the basic charter for private-detective taps and bugs, for "owner" eavesdropping on facilities that are used by members of the public, and for much free-lance police eavesdropping. Allowing eavesdropping with the consent of one party would destroy the statutory plan of limiting the offenses for which eavesdropping by device can be used and insisting on a court-order process. And as technology enables every man to carry his micro-miniaturized recorder everywhere he goes and allows every room to be monitored surreptitiously by built-in equipment, permitting eavesdropping with the consent of one party would be to sanction a means of reproducing conversation that could choke off much vital social exchange.

The third section of the statute would provide a system for the limited use of surveillance by federal law-enforcement officials. The question of the crimes for which physical surveillance might be authorized is one of the key elements to consider here. There are a number of logical positions to choose from: allow physical surveillance for any crime and trust to controls over misuse to provide protection for legitimate privacy; restrict surveillance to serious crimes, drawing the line at felonies or crimes with a minimum sentence of five or more years; restrict wiretapping to serious crimes for which the telephone is of special significance, such as kidnapping and perhaps extortion, and limit microphone eavesdropping to serious crimes involving organized conspiracy for which police work is especially difficult, such as syndicate crime and organized corruption of government officials; restrict physical surveillance to a small list of crimes which society, because of social judgments about the seriousness of the offense, has a special desire to solve or prevent, such as murder, kidnapping, and the like; or pass the decision on this issue to the courts by using a general description such as "in crimes directly imperiling human life." The best procedure would be to hold congressional hearings on this topic and require both federal and state law-enforcement agencies to present their case for allowing surveillance for a particular crime or area of investigation. After such a fresh look at this issue—and it would have to be a close examination that took no claims at face value—Congress could then write the authorization section of the bill. My own initial judgment is that federal technological surveillance should be limited to the FBI and possibly a few other law-enforcement agencies (such as the Secret Service) in the following situations: telephone tapping in kidnapping cases; taps or bugs in espionage and intelligence work and specified crimes involving national security; and physical surveillance when directly necessary to prevent the taking of a life by criminal violence. The CIA and military-intelligence agencies would probably be exempted from the statute when conducting national-security investigations; control over their activities must, realistically, be expected to come from executive and congressional-committee supervision.

Authority to use surveillance devices would have to be obtained by application to a federal district judge in the district where the surveillance by device was to take place. Some provision should be made for surveillance by device for a very short period in emergency situations, if written authorization is obtained from the Attorney General; an application to a district judge would be required within twenty-four hours, to report the use and seek its continuance. Both types of application would have to show, by independent evidence, that a crime for which surveillance by device was allowed by law had been or was about to be committed. The judge would have to be satisfied that the application was supported by a reasonable basis in fact, that all other feasible investigative measures apart from technological surveillance had been attempted or were not possible, and that surveillance by device was therefore essential. He would be required to send his decision, as well as the original application and supporting documents, to the Administrator of the United States Courts. The Administrator would submit an annual report to Congress on the number of applications, types of case, length of surveillance, disposition of investigation, and other facts. Should the Administrator be considered an inappropriate person for this task, the Attorney General could make the annual report. Review by congressional committees would be desirable.

A surveillance order would continue in effect for twenty days and could be renewed by the same judge who had granted it for additional twenty-day periods on a showing of continued need. However, surveillance of public telephones or public premises could be granted only for ten days, renewable for ten-day periods. Each request would have to recite the progress that had been made in the inquiry thus far and would have to justify continued surveillance. A provision might be added making it unlawful for any person knowingly to assist a federal officer in surveillance by device unless the person had been shown a copy of the authorization order.

All records obtained during an authorized surveillance operation, as well as copies of the petitions and orders, would have to be turned over to the Attorney General, registered, and preserved. Destruction should be permitted only by court order. A defendant in a federal criminal trial would be entitled to have the court inquire of the government whether surveillance by device had been used in his case. As a preliminary disclosure in all criminal trials, the law might even require an affidavit by the government stating whether surveillance by device had been used at any time during the investigation of the case; if it had been, the defendant could then challenge the sufficiency of the probable cause for issuing the surveillance order. Though defense counsel would no doubt want to examine all recordings, pictures, and notes taken during an authorized surveillance of his client's acts, it would probably be in the larger interests of society to allow the judge presiding at a criminal trial to examine the surveillance evidence first and strike material not relevant to the defense which would unnecessarily expose the privacy of persons other than the defendant. Information obtained by surveillance through device would be initially disclosed only in judicial proceedings. Until such disclosure, it would be unavailable for use in legislative and executive proceedings. Finally, where surveillance results in proof of crimes other than the one for which it was authorized, the surveillance material should not be available for prosecution of such other offenses unless they are themselves serious enough crimes to have been the basis for an application under the statute.

The federal statute could provide further that state officials might monitor telephone conversations or engage in radio-transmitter eavesdropping if their state has a statute satisfying the minimum federal standards. These would be provisions for surveillance in a limited class of cases, under court order only, by district attorney or prosecutor offices only, and excluding from the state courts any evidence obtained directly or indirectly through violation of the statute. This section should also provide a broad exclusionary rule stating that evidence of conversations or acts obtained by surveillance of privileged communication—husband-wife, attorney-client, religious counselor-congregant, doctor-patient, or psychologist-client—could not be used even though gathered during the course of an otherwise legal surveillance. Though some would leave this to the general rules of evidence, I think that these special areas of limited communication require legislative protection from the new means of surveillance. The statute should also contain a ban on the manufacture and sale of surveillance devices to anyone other than officials legally authorized to conduct surveillances. Other provisions should be added to spell out a procedure for testing the authenticity of surveillance recordings or photographs.

The fourth and final section of the federal statute should provide remedies for violations, perhaps the most crucial section of the statute. Criminal sanctions would be imposed against those violating the statute's policy (probably a one-to-three-year penalty would be appropriate). Evidence obtained directly by or as the fruit of violation would be excluded from both criminal and civil proceedings in federal courts, and a strict anti-disclosure provision would be included. The statute ought to go beyond these remedies, however, to permit both injunctive-relief and damage suits for those whose privacy had been invaded. The injunctive remedy might state that a person who believed his privacy was being illegally invaded by a federal official using surveillance devices could bring a show-cause order in a federal district court to require the official and his agency to cease and desist from maintaining the surveillance. The complainant would have the burden of establishing reasonable grounds for belief that surveillance by device was taking place. The court would then be empowered to examine the federal official and his agency on this issue. If surveillance were being conducted under court order, or if the agency convinced the court that no surveillance was taking place, the show-cause order would be dismissed. Otherwise, the court would order the agency to cease conducting surveillance of the complainant. The damage remedy might provide that any person whose privacy had been invaded by a federal official using surveillance devices in violation of the statute would be entitled to sue that official and the United States government for actual damages, an additional sum of liquidated damages set at $10,000, counsel fees and costs, and, in the jury's discretion, exemplary damages. It would not be a defense to either prosecution or civil suit to assert that the violation was engaged in with the intention of preventing a crime or enforcing the criminal law.

These are the basic features that should be included in a federal surveillance-control statute. But, whatever specific provisions are used, the statute must be based on an honest recognition of the fact that society will not support total bans on official surveillance by device in cases of certain serious crimes or threats to national security. Limited and supervised surveillance by a core group of law-enforcement and national-security agencies is the best way to achieve working sanctions against more widespread use of surveillance devices.

b. *State statutes.* To accomplish the over-all reform projected by this legislative approach, a state statute on unreasonable surveillance by device would be necessary. This could follow the format of the federal statute in many respects; under the general police power of the state, however, each of its prohibitions would be directed against all private persons as well as state officials. While the exceptions for private use might be much the same, the system for law-enforcement authorization would have several important variations. Electronic surveillance by state authorities should be limited to district attorneys' and prosecutors' offices; the record of police departments and the danger of spreading surveillance powers too widely are persuasive grounds for centralizing surveillance power in the hands of the lawyer-staffed and more independent prosecutive offices. Determining which crimes state officials could investigate by physical-surveillance devices would require the same careful legislative investigation of particular crimes as was suggested for the federal statute. It is particularly essential that the list is not extended into morals offenses, political protest, and freedom-of-association areas.

Much as under the federal statute, authorization to utilize the devices would have to be sought from a state judge, and the applications, supporting documents, and orders would go to a chief magistrate or other central judicial authority. Annual reports of surveillance activity could be prepared by the chief magistrate as well as the state attorney general and submitted to the state legislature. Other provisions described in the federal statute—especially the remedies—could be included in the state legislation.

One additional provision that might be considered at the state level would be an independent state agency to coordinate the protection of privacy. The agency might be composed of members chosen by the governor, chief judge of the state's highest court, and president of the state senate, and could be empowered to receive complaints and conduct continuing investigations into the use of surveillance equipment by the state, county, and local agencies. The agency would have subpoena power as well as the power to make on-site inspections. Finally, it would make annual public reports of its findings and could recommend necessary legislative or administrative changes.

These legislative proposals for control of unreasonable psychological, data, and physical surveillance are all well within the existing powers of the federal and state governments. The proposals might be considered separately, or the President and governors might submit omnibus privacy bills that would encompass all of the areas requiring legislative intervention. There are tactical advantages to both area-by-area and the omnibus approach, and it is not necessary here to select one or the other.

One interesting question remains: even though constitutional amendment is not necessary to accomplish any of the above objectives, is an amendment still desirable to delineate a new national policy on a fundamental right? Such an amendment would also provide the basis for direct federal regulation of state police practices and evidentiary proce-

dures and of key private invasions of privacy. There is an attractive quality to this suggestion, especially in terms of the "great debate" over basic
values that a campaign for a constitutional amendment usually fosters.
Yet many conservatives and liberals unite in opposing constitutional
amendments in instances such as this on the ground that it is a procedure which tampers with the growth of American constitutional law
through judicial interpretation and legislative-executive construction. In
the recent school-prayer controversy, for example, many of those who
were not happy with the Supreme Court's ruling on school prayers became convinced that formulation of a new definition of religious freedom and church-state separation would be difficult, that it would be
unpredictable in application, and that the amendment was not worth
the deep conflicts it might generate among leading religious groups. Furthermore, a persuasive argument may be made for the proposition that
the capacity to protect privacy from new technology is contained in existing constitutional provisions.

It is also hard to see what would be gained in real terms by a new
declaration of right by constitutional amendment. The new amendment
might limit itself to a broad statement such as: "The right to privacy of
persons, communication, and association shall not be abridged." Under
this formulation, the courts would still have to determine, much as they
are doing today, what constitutes "abridgement." Or the amendment
might try to delineate the interests involved in the balance between the
right to privacy and the needs of society for disclosure and surveillance.
In this case, it is not likely to do more than apply the probable-cause
and reasonableness concepts in more modern terms, a task which the
courts can perform under existing constitutional doctrines. A constitutional amendment would also leave unanswered the problems of specific remedies and of agencies to apply those remedies; these questions
are crucial to effective protection of privacy in daily life. For all these
reasons, both tactical and substantive in nature, the path of federal constitutional amendment seems to be an unprofitable and unwise diversion.

Inclusion in *state* constitutions of a newly formulated guarantee of
the right to privacy, however, presents somewhat different considerations. Given our tradition of more detailed and more frequently revised
state constitutions, and in light of the "little laboratory" function of
state law, such a guarantee might well be considered.

Finally, it should be recognized that legislative-committee investigation of the use of surveillance technology by government officials offers
special political and educational advantages as a means of protecting privacy short of the actual enactment of legislation. Legislative committees
have the motivation—in the form of a desire to maintain limits on executive power—to compel agencies and law-enforcement officials to disclose publicly what they are doing in the area of surveillance. With sub-

poena power and authority over executive appropriations as their levers, and with aid of the press and television attention usually generated by a significant investigation, legislative committees at the federal and state levels can persuade executive agencies "voluntarily" to abandon improper practices and can ensure that laws enacted to control unreasonable surveillance are respected and enforced by the executive. They can also serve as a protected means of complaint for government employees who feel their rights of privacy are being violated by superiors. Such activity is illustrated by the success of the House Subcommittee on Government Operations (the "Moss Committee") in changing the polygraph practices of the principal federal agencies using this device.[18] Another recent example is provided by the Senate Subcommittee on Administrative Practice and Procedure (the "Long Committee"), which brought an end to some federal surveillance practices by securing promises from federal executive agencies to limit their eavesdropping and wiretapping activities to national-security cases and prompted a Presidential letter to that effect which was sent to the heads of all executive agencies.[19] The Senate Subcommittee on Constitutional Rights (the "Ervin Committee") has received a number of complaints from federal employees and has raised the issues with the agencies involved.[20] One congressional subcommittee, under Representative Cornelius Gallagher, has been created to look into the whole field of government invasion of privacy. Its hearings on possible misuse of information in the proposed Federal Data Center led to reconsideration of the planned approach by executive officials.[21] Joint legislative committees or subcommittees of judiciary committees might be formed at the state level to follow developments in government use of surveillance devices. These could be modeled on the legislative investigations of eavesdropping in the 1950's by the Savarese Committee in New York, the Regan Committee in California, and the Forbes Committee in New Jersey.[22] Of course, support by the press, civic groups, expert witnesses, and the Bar provides necessary ideas and influence for legislative inquiries; thus such committees should be given the closest possible cooperation by those concerned with protection of privacy.

Executive-Agency Protections of Privacy. Sometimes as a matter of responsible administrative planning, sometimes in response to legislative investigations of executive conduct, and sometimes pushed by press and public commentaries, the executive branches at both federal and state levels have turned increasingly in the past five years to developing new executive policies in the areas of physical, psychological, and data surveillance. At the national level, President Johnson has issued an executive directive forbidding the use of electronic eavesdropping by federal agencies in any cases other than national-security investigations, and has required that use in that area be specifically authorized by the Attorney

General. Presidential commissions composed of executive-branch officials and outside experts have been looking into federal use of lie detectors and personality tests, and the standards for behavioral research conducted by government agencies or by private investigators under government funds. The reports of these commissions, though not yet published at the time this book went to press, are known to contain important statements of principle and suggestions for practice that the President and executive agencies could carry into policy. Such execution might even take the form of executive orders that embody most of the principles being suggested in the previous section as desirable legislative interventions. For example, the use of polygraphs by federal agencies could be the subject of an executive order forbidding any general use of such mechanisms for personnel screening, allowing use in a limited class of specially sensitive federal posts, setting standards for questions asked and procedures to be followed in such interrogations, specifying qualifying tests for human polygraph operators and for computer-read systems, and prescribing review authorities within the executive branch, along the lines of the independent agency of the ombudsman type.

It is to be hoped that the President's Committee on Federal Data Policies will do many of the same things in reviewing the present and future data-collection programs of the federal government. The development of such criteria in the federal government might also emerge from the Bureau of the Budget and the General Services Administration, especially to veto requests for unnecessary questionnaires and data collection of federal agencies. At the state level, the New York State Identification and Intelligence System, a computerized base of information about criminal records, has pursued an exemplary policy of discussing such issues with bar associations, civil-liberty groups, and academic experts, and building excellent standards into its data-acquisition and -dissemination procedures. For example, it has been decided that the data pool will not contain family-court subjects, information from grand-jury proceedings, wiretap information, or "unverified tips or rumors." Public officials and agencies seeking information from the sytem will be governed by "specific legal, right-to-know and need-to-know requirements." "Highly-sensitive data will be tagged in the system to insure that its distribution is under the exclusive control of the contributing agency." [23]

There can be no denying that executive agencies face a special dilemma when they must pursue the substantive tasks of government and at the same time place limits on their capacities to accomplish such tasks in the interest of personal and associational privacy. Yet a free society has a right to expect its executive officials to strike just such a fine balance, and the American public has the ultimate weapons with which to compel such policies when they are not willingly adopted.

Judicial Remedies. In the previous chapter I suggested that the Supreme Court stands on the brink of a landmark decision that will over-rule the *Olmstead-Goldman* doctrines and declare that protection of privacy against unreasonable surveillance and improper disclosure by federal or state authorities is a basic constitutional right.

The ideal development of the new doctrine would be for the Supreme Court to rule that *Olmstead* is no longer relevant in its technological assumptions or its legal foundations, and that the constitutional right of privacy requires that government action intruding into such privacy be measured by the requirements of due process. In such a landmark opinion, the constitutional right to privacy from unreasonable surveillance would seem to rest most securely and properly on the First Amendment. It is time for the Court to recover the concepts of "freedom of communion" and "liberty of silence" that Francis Lieber and Justice Story declared to be what the First Amendment meant to the men who wrote it and to their contemporaries. Freedom of communion means, clearly and unquestionably, freedom to speak, debate, and write in privacy, to share confidences with intimates and confidants, and to prepare positions in groups and institutions for presentation to the public at a later point. The right to speak, to publish, to worship, and to associate cannot survive in the modern age of scientific penetration of house, auto, office, and meeting room unless the courts and public mores install a curtain of law and practice to replace the walls and doors that have been swept away by the new instruments of surveillance.

A new constitutional right to privacy from unreasonable surveillance would not have to insulate all activity within a private place from government scrutiny or intrusion. Penetration by government agents, with proper safeguards, for defense of national security or to protect against direct threats to human life might be fair grounds for limiting privacy claims. But the burden would be on those who would prevent freedom of communion to justify their intrusion, not on the individual or the group to show why their right to freedom from surveillance is entitled to judicial protection. If the Court were to write its opinion along these lines, the Justices would probably not try to spell out detailed standards for reasonableness in technological surveillance. Having ruled that such surveillance is constitutionally limited, the Court could await specific cases to test reasonableness in the context of particular state or federal statutes and concrete uses of surveillance under them. Such a technique in the landmark opinion would place on Congress and the state legislatures the responsibility for experimentation with systems of controlled electronic surveillance, with the Supreme Court having fulfilled its role as catalyst for elective-branch responsibility.

At the same time, state supreme courts could well reach similar judgments on the nature of a constitutional right to privacy through interpretations of state constitutions. Much can be expected from tighter state- and federal-court review of the proper basis for warrants in all kinds of police physical-surveillance activity. Extension of the common-law right of privacy to encompass remedies against improper surveillance by owners of property is also a desired development.

As these discussions of private and governmental remedies have indicated, American society now seems ready to face the impact of science on privacy. Failure to do so would be to leave the foundations of our free society in peril.

The problem is not just an American one. Our science and our social development have made us the first modern nation to undergo the crisis of surveillance technology, but the other nations of the West are not far behind. In Britain, France, and Italy, in West Germany, Poland, and the Soviet Union, even in Ghana and Vietnam, the little listening and watching devices have made their appearance and the walls are beginning to dissolve. Throughout the West the computer networks grow, collecting their millions of bits of data, depositing the smallest details of our lives into the unforgetting memory units. Sometimes in the name of Man and sometimes in that of Society, scientists throughout the West are at work to unlock men's minds through drug and brain-wave research.

The setting—the marvels of microminiaturization and circuitry, chemical synthesis and projective psychiatry—is new. But the choices are as old as man's history on the planet. Will the tools be used for man's liberation or his subjugation? In the density, complexity, and tight interrelation of twentieth-century life, can we preserve the opportunities for privacy without which our whole system of civil liberties may become formalistic ritual? Science and privacy: together they constitute twin conditions of freedom in the twentieth century.

NOTES
BIBLIOGRAPHY
AND INDEX

Notes

CHAPTER ONE

1. Edward T. Hall, *The Hidden Dimension* (New York, 1966).
2. Robert Ardrey, *The Territorial Imperative* (New York, 1966).
3. See H. E. Howard, *Territory in Bird Life* (London, 1920); W. C. Allee, *The Social Life of Animals* (Boston, 1958); C. R. Carpenter, "Territoriality: A Review of Concepts and Problems," in A. Roe and G. G. Simpson (eds.), *Behavior and Evolution* (New Haven, Conn., 1958); H. Hediger, "The Evolution of Territorial Behavior," in S. L. Washburn (ed.), *Social Life of Early Man* (New York, 1961); V. C. Wynne-Edwards, *Animal Dispersion in Relation to Social Behavior* (New York, 1962).
4. Ardrey, *op. cit.*, 158–59, 94–100, 178–83.
5. *Ibid.*, 87–88.
6. *Ibid.*, 95.
7. Hall, *op. cit.*, 15, 16–37.
8. *Ibid.*, 120.
9. Hall, *op. cit.*, 13–14.
10. *Ibid.*, 10–14.
11. *Ibid.*, 39–70.
12. *Ibid.*, 17.
13. John B. Calhoun, "A 'Behavioral Sink,'" in E. L. Bliss (ed.), *Roots of Behavior* (New York, 1962), Ch. 22; "Population Density and Social Pathology," 206 *Scientific American*, 139–46 (1962); Hall, *op. cit.*, 21–29.
14. H. L. Ratcliffe and R. L. Snyder, "Patterns of Disease, Controlled Populations, and Experimental Design," 26 *Circulation*, 1352–57 (1962); Hall, *op. cit.*, 175.
15. John J. Christian, "Factors in Mass Mortality of a Herd of Sika Deer (*Cervus nippon*)," 1 *Chesapeake Science*, 79–95 (1960), Hall, *op. cit.*, 17–19.
16. Ardrey, *op. cit.*, 162.
17. F. F. Darling, "Social Behavior and Survival," 69 *Auk*, 183–91 (1952).
18. J. Fisher, "Evolution and Bird Sociality," in J. Huxley *et al.* (eds.), *Evolution as a Process*, (London, 1954).
19. Wynne-Edwards, *op. cit.*
20. Dorothy Lee, *Freedom and Culture* (Englewood Cliffs, N.J., 1959), 31–32.
21. *Ibid.*, 74–75.
22. *Ibid.*
23. Margaret Mead, *Coming of Age in Samoa* (Mentor ed., New York, 1949), 82–85.
24. Livingston F. Jones, *A Study of the Tlingets of Alaska* (New York, 1914), 58.
25. See George P. Murdock, "The Universals of Culture," in E. A. Hoebel, J. D. Jennings, and E. R. Smith (eds.), *Readings in Anthropology* (New York, 1955), 4–5; G. P. Murdock, *Outline of World Cultures* (3rd ed., rev., New Haven, Conn., 1963).
26. There is a large literature on avoidance and social distance. Perhaps the leading work is that of Georg Simmel. See *The Sociology of Georg Simmel*, tr. and ed. by Kurt Wolff (New York, 1950).
27. Robert F. Murphy, "Social Distance and the Veil," 66 *American Anthropologist* 1257–74 (1964).

28. For a discussion of the idea of "self" as present in all societies, though very differently conceived and integrated, see Gardner Murphy, "Social Motivation," in Gardner Lindzey (ed.), *Handbook of Social Psychology* (Cambridge, Mass., 1954), vol. 1, 601–31.

29. Clellan S. Ford and Frank A. Beach, *Patterns of Sexual Behavior* (paperback ed., New York, 1951), 102–104.

30. Murdock, in Hoebel *et al.*, *op. cit.*, 5. See also J. W. M. Whiting and I. L. Child, *Child Training and Personality* (New Haven, Conn., 1953), 84–86, 116.

31. See references and discussion in Sigmund Freud, *Totem and Taboo* (New York, 1950), 27–29, 33.

32. Ford and Beach, *op. cit.*, 92. See also 77–79, 81–83, 196. This is not a characteristic of animal sexual behavior. "A desire for privacy during sexual intercourse seems confined to human beings. Male-female pairs of other animal species appear to be quite unaffected by the presence of other individuals and to mate quite as readily in a crowd as when alone" (*ibid.*, 80).

33. *Ibid.*, 77.

34. *Ibid.*, 77–80.

35. A. R. Holmberg, *The Siriono* (unpublished Ph.D. dissertation, Yale, 1946), 183; quoted in *ibid.*, 78.

36. See, for example, references to the QuKan, in M1, J.25, 3033, Human Relations Area Files, Yale University; W. E. Freeman, "The Family Systems of the Iban of Borneo," in Jack Goody, ed., *Cambridge Papers in Social Anthropology*, No. 1, 1552 London (1958), 52; Aurel Krause, *The Tlingit Indians* (New York, 1956), 112.

37. William J. Goode, *The Family* (Englewood Cliffs, N.J., 1964), 53–54; Beatrice Blackwood, *Both Sides of the Buka Passage* (Oxford, 1935), 22–23.

38. Murphy, *op. cit*, 1274.

39. R. M. Underhill, "Social Organization of the Papago Indians," 30 *Columbia University Contributions of Anthropology*, 119.

40. Dr. Geertz's paper was delivered informally at a seminar on privacy conducted by members of the Center for Advanced Study in the Behavioral Sciences, Stanford, Calif., in 1959. Quoted by permission of Dr. Geertz.

41. Arnold van Gennep, *The Rites of Passage* (Chicago, 1960), 180–83, 183–85.

42. Mead, *op. cit.*, 85.

43. See Georg Simmel, "The Sociology of Secrecy and Secret Societies," 11 *American Journal of Sociology*, 441 (1906); Hutton Webster, *Primitive Secret Societies* (New York, 1908); Camilla H. Wedgwood, "The Nature and Functions of Secret Societies," 1 *Oceania*, 129 (1930); George Schwab, *The Tribes of the Liberian Hinterland* (Cambridge, Mass., 1947); George Harley, *Notes on the Poro in Liberia* (Cambridge, Mass., 1941).

44. See William W. Howells, *The Heathens: Primitive Man, and His Religions* (New York, 1948), Ch. 10; Robert H. Lowie, *Primitive Religion* (New York, 1924); E. Vogt and W. Lessa (eds.), *Reader in Comparative Religion* (New York, 1965).

45. Edwin H. Gomes, *Seventeen Years Among the Sea Dyaks of Borneo* (1911), 204.

46. For an outstanding discussion, see Frederica de Laguna, "Tlingit Ideas About the Individual," 10 *Southwestern Journal of Anthropology*, 180–81, 189 (1954). See also Edward Sapir, "The Life of a Nootka Indian," 28 *Queen's Quarterly*, 232–243, 351–367 (1921).

47. See de Laguna, *op. cit.*, 180.

48. For examples of the "ordeal of privacy," see James, *op. cit.*, 204–205; F. E. Williams, *Orokaiva Magic* (London, 1928), 81–82; Robert H. Lowie, *Indians of the Plains* (New York, 1954); James Swan, *Three Years Residence in Washington Territory* (New York, 1857), 62–63.

49. See, for example, P. Drucker, "The Northern and Central Nootka Tribes," *Bulletin of the Bureau of American Ethnology*, 185 (1951); Swan, *op. cit.*, 61; Elizabeth Colson, *The Makah Indians* (Manchester, Eng., 1953), 48.

50. F. E. Williams, *op. cit.*

51. D. E. Berlyne, *Conflict, Arousal, and Curiosity* (New York, 1960).

52. H. F. Harlow, "Learning Motivated by a Manipulation Drive," 40 *Journal of Experimental Psychology*, 228 (1950).
53. W. McDougal, *An Introduction to Social Psychology* (London, 1908), 49–50.
54. For discussions of the curiosity theme, see Thomas Bulfinch, *Bulfinch's Mythology* (New York, 1947), 80–89; Alexander S. Murray, *Manual of Mythology* (1895), 282–83.
55. Lewis Spence, *An Introduction to Mythology* (New York, 1931), 150.
56. See Robert K. Merton, *Social Theory and Social Structure* (rev. ed., Glencoe, Ill., 1957), 355.
57. John J. Honigmann, *The World of Man* (New York, 1959), 154. Of course there are areas in which some primitive societies set sharp privacy norms that have not been carried over into modern industrial societies. In the culture of the Eskimo, the individual's name is private. To ask it is an intrusion, for to utter the name is to give it life and run risks of sickness and death. Among Australian tribes the new name a youth receives on entering manhood is taboo and must be kept secret. See Freud, *op. cit.*, 33. For an example of the difficulties one anthropologist had in learning names among the Nuer, see E. E. Evans-Pritchard, *The Nuer* (Oxford, 1960), 12–13.
58. For a full treatment of the historical basis of privacy in the West, see Alan F. Westin, *Privacy in Western History* (New York, 1967). See also Edward Shils, "Privacy: Its Constitution and Vicissitudes," 31 *Law and Contemporary Problems* (Spring, 1966), 281.

CHAPTER TWO

1. For writing relating the anti-privacy measures of Soviet totalitarianism to aspects of Russian national character and culture, see Margaret Mead and Elena Calas, "Child-training Ideas in a Postrevolutionary Context: Soviet Russia," in Margaret Mead and Martha Wolfenstein (eds.), *Childhood in Contemporary Cultures* (Chicago, 1955), 179, 190–91; Henry V. Dicks, "Observations on Contemporary Russian Behavior," 5 *Human Relations*, 111, 140, 159, 163–64 (1952).
2. For a discussion of this phenomenon in Communist China today, see P. J. Hollander, "Privacy: A Bastion Stormed," in "Mores and Morality in Communist China," 12 *Problems of Communism* No. 6, Nov.-Dec., 1963, 1–9.
3. See Sidney Hook, *The Hero in History* (Beacon ed., Boston, 1955), 6; R. J. Lifton, *Thought Reform and the Psychology of Totalism* (New York, 1963), 426.
4. For discussion of privacy in terms of democratic political theory, see Hannah Arendt, *The Human Condition* (Anchor ed., New York, 1959), 23–69; H. M. Roelofs, *The Tension of Citizenship: Private Man and Public Duty* (New York, 1957); H. D. Lasswell, "The Threat to Privacy," in R. M. MacIver (ed.), *Conflict of Loyalties* (New York, 1952), 121–40; Clinton Rossiter, "The Pattern of Liberty," in M. R. Konvitz and Clinton Rossiter (eds.), *Aspects of Liberty* (Ithaca, N.Y., 1958), 15–32; Morroe Berger *et al.*, *Freedom and Control in Modern Society* (New York, 1964), 190.
5. Edward A. Shils, *The Torment of Secrecy* (Glencoe, Ill., 1956), 21–22.
6. *Ibid.*, 22.
7. Edward Shils, "Privacy: Its Constitution and Vicissitudes," 31 *Law and Contemporary Problems* (Spring, 196), 281, 283n.
8. For a discussion of British privacy patterns, see Shils, *op. cit.*, 47–57, and H. H. Hyman, "England and America: Climates of Tolerance and Intolerance," in Daniel Bell (ed.), *The Radical Right* (New York, 1963), Ch. 12.
9. On the *Spiegel* case, see Otto Kirchheimer and Constantine Menges, "A Free Press in a Democratic State: The *Spiegel* Case," in G. M. Carter and A. F. Westin (eds.), *Politics in Europe* (New York, 1965), 87–135.
10. For leading works discussing American political culture on which the discussion here has drawn, see R. M. Williams, Jr., *American Society: A Sociological Interpretation* (New York, 1960), Ch. 11; E. E. Morison (ed.), *The American Style*

(New York, 1958); Michael McGiffert (ed.), *The Character of Americans* (Homewood, Ill., 1964); R. E. Spiller and Eric Larrabee (eds.), *American Perspectives: The National Self-Image in the Twentieth Century* (Cambridge, Mass., 1961); Alex Inkeles and D. J. Levinson, "National Character: The Study of Modal Personality and Sociocultural Systems," in Gardner Lindzey (ed.), 2 *Handbook of Social Psychology* (Cambridge, Mass., 1954), 977–1020; David Riesman, *The Lonely Crowd* (New Haven, Conn., 1950); Max Lerner, *America as a Civilization* (New York, 1957). For studies showing the stability of these basic American traits during our history, see Clyde Kluckhon, "Have There Been Discernible Shifts in American Values During the Past Generation?" in Morison (ed.), *op. cit.*, 145–217; Seymour Lipset, *The First New Nation* (New York, 1963), Ch. 3; Lee Coleman, "What Is American? A Study of Alleged American Traits," 19 *Social Forces*, 492–99 (1941).

11. On this theme, see particularly Shils, *op. cit.*, Chs. 4 and 5, and A. F. Westin, "The John Birch Society: Fundamentalism on the Right," in Bell (ed.), *op. cit.*, 239–68.
12. See Shils, *op. cit., passim.*
13. F. L. K. Hsu, *Americans and Chinese* (New York, 1953), 68–93.
14. Kurt Lewin, *Resolving Social Conflicts* (New York, 1948), 18–33.
15. Erving Goffman, *The Presentation of Self in Everyday Life* (New York, 1959).
16. Edward T. Hall, *The Silent Language* (New York, 1959).
17. Edward T. Hall, *The Hidden Dimension* (New York, 1966), 2.
18. On the need for interpersonal intimacy, see H. S. Sullivan, *The Interpersonal Theory of Psychiatry* (New York, 1953), 290.
19. *The Sociology of Georg Simmel*, tr. and ed. by Kurt Wolff (New York, 1950), 402–408. See also the discussion of the stranger in J. S. Plant, *Personality and the Cultural Pattern* (Oxford, 1937), 121–23; Robert Merton, "Selected Problems of Field Work in the Planned Community," 12 *American Sociological Review*, 305 (1947).
20. Georg Simmel, *op. cit.*, 320–29.
21. See Hall, *The Hidden Dimension*, 108–12, 131.
22. While I have chosen to use a functional analysis, various social scientists have written about privacy in terms of "need" theory. Freudian and neo-Freudian theorists have seen a need for privacy as one of the personality traits arising out of the anal or bodily-control stage of libido development. One such analysis puts a "need for privacy and seclusion" among Western social needs such as "acquisition and husbanding of property; methodical orderliness; neatness, punctuality and regularity of procedure, habit, protocol; emphasis on personal hygiene and sensitiveness to dirt, odours and disorder." Russians, with more of an "oral" than "anal" emphasis in child rearing, have been portrayed as lacking in these characteristics, as well as a central need for privacy (Henry V. Dicks, "Observations on Contemporary Russian Behavior," 5 *Human Relations III*, 140 [1952]). See also Karen Horney, *Our Inner Conflicts* (New York, 1945), 73. For writings by social psychologists portraying the need for "seclusion" and "autonomy" among man's social needs or his "higher needs" to achieve "self-actualization," see H. A. Murray, *Explorations in Personality* (New York, 1938), 144–45, 151, 156–58; A. H. Maslow, *Motivation and Personality* (New York, 1954), 212–13, 227, 237. For a similar discussion of the "desire for privacy" as "sufficiently marked to approach the character of a specific instinct" see the work of the political scientist and sociologist Graham Wallas, *Human Nature in Politics* (London, 1908).
23. An excellent statement of this theme in relation to privacy appears in Edward Shils, "Social Inquiry and the Autonomy of the Individual," in Daniel Lerner (ed.), *The Human Meaning of the Social Sciences* (New York, 1959), 114–57.
24. See Goffman, *The Presentation of Self in Everyday Life*, 69–70; Kurt Lewin, *Resolving Social Conflicts* (New York, 1948), 18–33; R. E. Park and E. W. Burgess, *Introduction to the Science of Sociology* (Chicago, 1921), 230.
25. R. E. Park, *Race and Culture* (Glencoe, Ill., 1950), 249.
26. Leontine Young, *Life Among the Giants* (New York, 1966).

27. MacIver (ed.), *op. cit.*, 139.
28. Clinton Rossiter, "The Pattern of Liberty," in Konvitz and Rossiter (eds.), *op. cit.*, 15–17.
29. Goffman, *Presentation of Self*, 56–57.
30. *Ibid.*, 128–82. Goffman suggests that social encounters can be conceived of as theatrical performances in which the individual plays a role whenever he comes into the physical presence of another person. For the individual to mount a successful performance "on stage" he must have "backstage" areas for preparation, rehearsal, rest, and the like, from which the "general audience" is excluded. There, he relaxes among his fellow "actors" until he has to "go on" again, or he goes into his "dressing room" to be alone or among his intimates. This analysis contains a shower of provocative illustrations of the privacy-adjustment process. Certain rooms in the home are frontstage and public; others are backstage and private (*ibid.*, 123). Trade secrets and skills of occupation are considered private, just as performers keep secret the tricks of stage art (*ibid.*, 45, 141–66). When housing conditions enable apartment residents to hear the intimate conversations and noises of neighbors, it is as if the curtain had not come down at the end of the "show" and the audience is seeing a "backstage" area it was never intended to observe (*ibid.*, 119–20). Goffman is careful to note that life is not the same thing as the stage, and that there are too many complexities in human relationships to be captured in the fairly limited situation of performer, fellow performers, and audience. But his suggestive analogy captures the shifting private and public roles that mark the individual's encounters with others in daily life and underscores the crucial function privacy performs in self-expression.
31. This theme has been a major contribution of Robert Merton. See *Social Theory and Social Structure* (rev. ed., Glencoe, Ill., 1957), 342–46; Robert Merton and Bernard Barber, "Sociological Ambivalence," in Edward Tiryakian (ed.), *Sociological Theory, Values, and Sociological Change* (New York, 1963), 91.
32. See Erving Goffman, "On the Characteristics of Total Institutions," in D. R. Cressey (ed.), *The Prison—Studies in Institutional Organization and Change* (New York, 1961).
33. Goffman, *Behavior in Public Places* (New York, 1963), 53.
34. Alan Bates, "Privacy—A Useful Concept?" 42 *Social Forces*, 429, 432–33 (1964). See also Sidney M. Jourard, "Some Psychological Aspects of Privacy," 31 *Law and Contemporary Problems*, 307 (Spring, 1966).
35. Park and Burgess, *op. cit.*, 231.
36. See Franz Alexander, "Observations on Organizational Factors Affecting Creativity," in G. A. Steiner (ed.), *The Creative Organization* (Chicago, 1965), 238.
37. See D. W. Taylor, P. C. Berry, and C. H. Block, "Does Group Participation When Using Brainstorming Facilitate or Inhibit Creative Thinking?" 3 *Administrative Science Quarterly*, 23 (1958).
38. See Frieda Fromm-Reichmann, "Loneliness," 22 *Psychiatry*, 2 (1959). W. C. Middleton, "The Propensity of Genius to Solitude," 30 *Journal of Abnormal Psychology*, 325–32 (1932); Oliver Wendell Holmes, Jr., *Collected Speeches* (Boston, 1913), 22. Einstein wrote "I lived in solitude in the country and noticed how the monotony of a quiet life stimulates the creative mind." Quoted in Milton Rokeach, "In Pursuit of the Creative Process," in Steiner (ed.), *op. cit.*, 67.
39. See Park and Burgess, *op. cit.*, 237.
40. William James, *The Varieties of Religious Experience* (New York, 1902), 31.
41. Alfred R. Lindesmith and Anselm L. Strauss, *Social Psychology* (rev. ed., New York, 1956), 435. For a thoughtful statement of the Catholic position, see the editorial "Technology and Contemplation," 100 *America*, 100 (1958).
42. Simmel, *op. cit.*, 409–16.
43. See the examples in Goffman, *Presentation of Self*, 160–61.
44. Ralph Waldo Emerson, "Friendship," *The Complete Works of Ralph Waldo Emerson* (New York, 1903), 202.
45. See the perceptive discussion in Simmel, *op. cit.*, 326–29.
46. Alan Bates, *op. cit.*, 432. See also Goffman, *Presentation of Self*, 230; Hall, *The*

Hidden Dimension, 108–112.
47. See James Thurber, "The Secret Life of Walter Mitty," in *The Thurber Carnival* (Modern Library ed., New York, 1957).
48. See Sebastian de Grazia, *Of Time, Work, and Leisure* (New York, 1963).
49. M. M. Wood, *Paths of Loneliness* (New York, 1960 ed.); C. E. Moustakas, *Loneliness* (Englewood Cliffs, N.J., 1961); Rollo Brown, *Lonely Americans* (New York, 1929); Percy Burgess, *Who Walk Alone* (New York, 1940); R. E. Byrd, *Alone* (New York, 1938); Charles Kingsley, *The Hermits* (London, 1913); C. C. Bowman, "Loneliness and Social Change," 112 *American Journal of Psychiatry*, 194 (1955); Fromm-Reichmann, *op. cit.*, 1–3.
50. See Eric Fromm, *Escape from Freedom* (New York, 1941); David Riesman, *The Lonely Crowd* (New Haven, Conn., 1950); H. M. Ruitenbeek, *The Individual and the Crowd* (New York, 1964). For a protest against too much privacy in modern urban life, caused by the dissolution of community, see Paul Halmos, *Solitude and Privacy* (London, 1952).
51. Horney, *op. cit.*, 76. See also Fromm-Reichmann, *op. cit.*, 3, on disintegrative loneliness.
52. See, for example, Fromm-Reichmann, *op. cit.*, 6–7; Horney, *op. cit.*, 117.
53. See Fromm-Reichmann, *op. cit.*, 3; Eric Berne, *Games People Play* (New York, 1965).
54. Wilbert Moore and M. M. Tumin, "Some Social Functions of Ignorance," 14 *American Sociological Review*, 787, 792 (1949).
55. See note, 70 *Yale Law Journal*, 1084 (1961).
56. See P. M. Blau, *The Dynamics of Bureaucracy* (Chicago, 1955); Blau and W. R. Scott, *Formal Organizations* (San Francisco, 1962); Melville Dalton, *Men Who Manage* (New York, 1959); Amitai Etzioni, *Modern Organizations* (Englewood Cliffs, N.J., 1964); Etzioni, *A Comparative Analysis of Complex Organizations* (New York, 1961); Walter Galenson and Seymour Lipset, *Labor and Trade Unionism* (New York, 1960); Erving Goffman, *Presentation of Self*; A. W. Gouldner, *Patterns of Industrial Bureaucracy* (New York, 1954); Bertram Gross, *The Managing of Organizations* (Glencoe, Ill., 1964); Seymour Lipset, M. Trow, and J. S. Coleman, *Union Democracy* (Glencoe, Ill., 1956); A. W. Gouldner (ed.), *Studies in Leadership* (New York, 1950).
57. Francis Rourke, *Secrecy and Publicity: Dilemmas of Democracy* (Baltimore, 1961), 104. For criticism of executive claims to privacy, see, for example, Harold Cross, *The People's Right to Know—Legal Access to Public Records and Proceedings* (New York, 1953); Rourke, *op. cit.*; J. R. Wiggins, *Freedom or Secrecy* (New York, 1956); *Second Report by the House Committee on Government Operations*, 85th Cong., 1st Sess., 157 (1957).
58. Robert Luce, *Congress: An Explanation* (Cambridge, Mass., 1926), 12–13.
59. J. P. Frank, *Marble Palace* (New York, 1958), 110–11.
60. Rourke, *op. cit.*, 72.
61. A. A. Berle, Jr., "The Protection of Privacy," 79 *Political Science Quarterly*, 162–68, 164 (1964).
62. See J. W. Bishop, Jr., "The Executive's Right of Privacy: An Unresolved Constitutional Question," 66 *Yale Law Journal*, 477 (1957).
63. For discussion of profit-making by advance information and cases involving the OPA during World War II, the Civil Aeronautics Board, and the Securities and Exchange Commission, see Rourke, *op. cit.*, 34, 50.
64. Adam Yarmolinsky, "Memo on Privacy in Government," June 23, 1965, files of the Special Committee on Science and Law, Association of the Bar of the City of New York.
65. See Cross, *op. cit.*; Wiggins, *op. cit.*
66. Rourke, *op. cit.*, 106.
67. *Ibid.*
68. 13 U.S.C. Sect. 9 (1964).
69. See Internal Revenue Code of 1954, Sect. 6103.
70. *The New York Times*, Dec. 12, 1964.

CHAPTER THREE

1. See *The Sociology of Georg Simmel*, tr. and ed. by Kurt Wolff (New York, 1950), 330–61.
2. Vance Packard, *The Naked Society* (New York, 1964), *passim.*; H. D. Lasswell, "The Threat to Privacy," in R. M. MacIver (ed.), *Conflict of Loyalties* (New York, 1952); Clifton Fadiman, "Please Tap My Wire, I Like It!" *Holiday*, July, 1964, 12, 14; August Heckscher, "The Invasion of Privacy: The Reshaping of Privacy," 28 *American Scholar*, 13 (1959).
3. The correspondence is on file with the Special Committee on Science and Law of the Association of the Bar of the City of New York.
4. Letter from George Gallup to the author, March 17, 1965, on file with the Special Committee on Science and Law of the Association of the Bar of the City of New York.
5. Jourard's articles reporting on self-disclosure experiments are: (with P. Lasakow) "Some Factors in Self-Disclosure," 56 *Journal of Abnormal and Social Psychology*, 91–98 (1958); "Self-Disclosure and Other-Cathexis," 59 *Journal of Abnormal and Social Psychology*, 428–31 (1959); "Healthy Personality and Self-Disclosure," 43 *Mental Hygiene*, 499–507 (1959); (with M. J. Landsman) "Cognition, Cathexis, and the Dyadic Effect in Men's Self-Disclosing Behavior," 6 *Merrill-Palmer Quarterly*, 178–86 (1960); "Self-Disclosure Scores and Grades in Nursing College," 45 *Journal of Applied Psychology*, 244–47 (1961); "Self-Disclosure Patterns in British and American College Females," 54 *Journal of Social Psychology*, 315–20 (1961); "Religious Denomination and Self-Disclosure," 8 *Psychological Reports*, 446 (1961).
6. See, for example, D. E. Berlyne, *Conflict Arousal and Curiosity* (New York, 1960); E. R. Hilgard, *Theories of Learning* (New York, 1956), 430, 475; David Krech, R. S. Crutchfield, and E. L. Ballachey, *Individual in Society* (New York, 1962), 89, 99–100; William MacDougall, *An Introduction to Social Psychology* (Boston, 1921), 61, 322; Gardner Murphy, "Social Motivation," in Gardner Lindzey (ed.), 2 *Handbook of Social Psychology* (Cambridge, Mass., 1954), 617; H. F. Harlow, M. K. Harlow, and D. R. Meyer, "Learning Motivated by a Manipulation Drive," 40 *Journal of Experimental Psychology*, 228, 232 (1950).
7. Richard Rovere, "The Invasion of Privacy (1): Technology and the Claims of Community," 27 *American Scholar*, 416 (1958).
8. See Jack Schwartz, "The 'Hearing Tom' Is Everywhere," *Newsday* (Garden City, N.Y.), Jan. 9, 1965.
9. Goffman, *Presentation of Self*, 235; Simmel, *op. cit.*, 334.
10. See J. C. Coleman, *Abnormal Psychology and Modern Life* (3rd. ed., Chicago, 1964), 403–404; R. M. Dorcus and G. W. Shaffer, *Abnormal Psychology* (4th ed., Baltimore, 1950), 264; J. L. McCartney, *Understanding Human Behavior* (New York, 1956), 150; A. H. Maslow and B. Mittelmann, *Abnormal Psychology* (rev. ed., New York, 1951), 449–53; I. D. Yalom, M.D., "Aggression and Forbiddenness in Voyeurism," 3 *Archives of General Psychiatry*, 305 (1960).
11. Yalom, *op. cit.*, 318.
12. See, for example, *Debonair*, May-July, 1966, 69, 73.
13. For examples, see chapters 6 and 7.
14. See Robert Merton, *Social Theory and Social Structure* (Glencoe, Ill., 1957), 341–53; Simmel, *op. cit.*, 330–61; Hans Zetterberg, "Complaint Actions," 2 *Acta Sociologica*, 179 (1957).
15. Merton, *op. cit.*, 343.
16. *Ibid.*, 375.
17. *Ibid.*, 343–44.
18. See Charles Nordhoff, *The Communistic Societies of the United States* (New York, 1875), 399–418.
19. M. E. Spiro, *Kibbutz: Venture in Utopia* (New York, 1963), xiii, 5, 9, 21, 30–33, 65–69, 203–211, 216, 221, 246.
20. Margaret Mead, "Margaret Mead Re-Examines Our Right to Privacy," *Red-*

book, April, 1965, 15, 16. See also Jane Jacobs, *The Death and Life of Great American Cities* (Vintage ed., New York, 1962), 43, 57–67.

21. In a 1958 opinion, West Germany's highest civil court, the Bundesgerechtshof, recognized the dangers of this type of surveillance and held that it violated Articles 1 and 2 of the Basic Law. The court stated that those articles grant an individual "in his inner personality sphere the freedom and self-determination . . . which is essential to the development of his personality." This freedom includes the right of deciding for himself "whether his words shall be accessible solely to his conversation partner, to a particular group, or to the public, and *a fortiori*, whether his voice shall be fixed on a record." In private conversation the individual expresses his personality and has a right to do so freely, without distrust and suspicion. This expression of personality would disappear if individuals feared that their conversations, even their tone of voice, were secretly being recorded. Men would no longer be able to engage in natural, free discussion. See Opinion of May 20, 1958, Bundesgerechtshof (VI Zivilsenat), 11 *Neue Juristische Wochenschrift*, 1344, 1345 (Ger. Fed. Rep.); *Hearings Before the Senate Subcommittee on Constitutional Rights of the Committee on the Judiciary*, 86th Cong., 1st Sess., pt. 3, 679, n. 12 (1959). (Statement of Professor Helen Silving.)

CHAPTER FOUR

1. The technical discussion in this section is based on the following sources: "A Survey of the Present and Probable Future State of Technology Affecting Privacy," Report No. 1008, June 20, 1963, prepared for the Special Committee on Science and Law of the Association of the Bar of the City of New York by the consulting firm of Bolt, Beranek, and Newman, Inc., Cambridge, Mass., copies of which are on file at the Library of the Association of the Bar; a survey of catalogues and equipment from leading manufacturers of surveillance equipment (see the catalogue citations in the Bibliography); special consultants to the Special Committee on Science and Law (see the list in Acknowledgments); discussions with law-enforcement officials and surveillance specialists; examination of leading police journals; and examination of the literature published in books, technical journals, legislative hearings, and other magazines.
2. See Catalogue No. 61–62, 20 (1961), of Scientific Detection Products Corp., Camden, N.J.
3. See catalogue of C. H. Stoelting Co., Chicago, Ill.
4. See William Shaw, "Applied Electronics . . . Radio Beacon Tails," *Law and Order*, November, 1962, 34–36, 38, 43, 74.
5. See, for example, "Mutemp Sensitizes the Physician's Radio Pill," *The Economist*, June 6, 1964, 1095.
6. See Catalogue No. 61–62, 20 (1961), of Scientific Detection Products Corp., Camden, N.J.
7. See Catalogue No. 300, 116, Criminal Research Products, Inc., Conshohocken, Pa.
8. See *Law and Order*, Dec., 1963, 38.
9. See William Shaw, "An Introduction to Law Enforcement Electronics and Communications, Part III (TV Surveillance)," *Law and Order*, May, 1965, 36–38, 60–61.
10. John M. Carroll, *Secrets of Electronic Espionage* (New York, 1966), 208.
11. By the Lockheed Corp.
12. *Time* magazine, April 22, 1966, 81.
13. See *The New York Times*, Oct. 28, 1958.
14. Distributed, for example, by Burke and James, Inc., Chicago.
15. For example, the "Cambinox" sold by Faurot, Inc., New York.
16. See L. P. Parloto, "The Recording Eye," *Law and Order*, April, 1964, 30.
17. See, for example, Q. O. S. Corporation's advertisement in *Law and Order*,

March, 1959, 32, 48.
18. See *The New York Times*, July 26, 1965.
19. See *Time*, June 21, 1963, 51.
20. See *Electronic Design*, Feb. 15, 1961.
21. See Charles Leedham, "The 'Chip' Revolutionizes Electronics," *The New York Times Magazine*, Sept. 19, 1965, 56–57, 62, 64, 66, 68.
22. See, for example, catalogues of Mosler Research Products, Inc., Danbury, Conn.
23. See *New York Times International Edition*, June 30, 1964.
24. Many of the manufacturers' catalogues or special literature suggest lists of places in which to plant microphones.
25. Distributed by Faurot, Inc., New York.
26. See W. E. Murphy, "Single Channel Monitor Records Twenty-four Hours," *Law and Order*, Jan., 1963, 16–17, 65.
27. See *Product Design and Development*, Jan., 1963, 24.
28. See, for example, "wireless microphone—$225," in 1966 catalogue of W. J. S. Electronics, Hollywood, Calif.; "Tiny Tim FM Voice Transmitter—$137," R. B. Clifton, Miami, Fla.
29. See script of "The Big Ear," televised by NBC on Oct. 31, 1965, 22 (Mittelman's statement).
30. A drawing and description of this device appeared in "Someone Knows All About You," *Esquire*, May, 1966, 101.
31. See catalogue of W. J. S. Electronics, Hollywood, Calif.
32. Carroll, *op. cit.*, 198; see C. H. Stoelting Co. catalogue, Chicago.
33. This was displayed by its developer, Ben Jamil, on the "Tonight Show," NBC, during May, 1966.
34. "Someone Knows All About You," *Esquire*, May, 1966, 101.
35. Carroll, *op. cit.*, 200.
36. See *The New York Times*, May 28, 1960, and June 5, 1960; *Electronics Illustrated*, Jan., 1962, 89–91.
37. Carroll, *op. cit.*, 199–200.
38. See catalogues of any of the surveillance-equipment manufacturers.
39. Distributed by Security Devices Laboratory, Electronics Division of Sargent & Greenleaf, Inc., Rochester, N.Y.; see also "The Law Abiding Safecrackers" in *The Evening Record* (Bergen, N.J.), Jan. 15, 1966.
40. *The New York Times*, Jan. 22, 1966.
41. See "Trans-sentry" equipment distributed by Dee Co., Houston, Texas.
42. See, for example, the 1965 Manhattan Classified Telephone Directory, 880–84: Bondwitt Sound Engineering Co.—"Intrusion Experts"; Confidential Investigation Bureau, Inc., "Counter Industrial Espionage"; and the script of "The Big Ear," televised by NBC on Oct. 30, 1965, 2.
43. See catalogues of Dectron Industries; "When Walls Have Ears, Call a De-Bugging Man," *Business Week*, Oct. 31, 1965.
44. See *The New York Times*, Jan. 22, 1966.
45. See "Wires Tapped? Snoopy Operators? Scramble," 287 *Printers' Ink*, April 10, 1964, 15, and Decatur (Ill.) *Review*, April 17, 1964.
46. Distributed by Delcon Corp., Palo Alto, Calif.
47. Carroll, *op. cit.*, 202–203, 204, 205.
48. *Ibid.*
49. New York *Herald Tribune*, Oct. 7, 1965.
50. See *The New York Times*, April 19, 1958.
51. Carroll, *op. cit.*, 188, 189–90, 92.
52. *Ibid.*, 188–200.
53. See *The New York Times*, May 22, 1963.
54. 26 *Princeton Engineer*, No. 4, Jan., 1966, 26.
55. See *Time*, July 30, 1965, 59; and *The New York Times Magazine*, Oct. 28, 1962, 74, 76, 79–80.
56. See *Popular Science*, May, 1965 (Flying Television Camera, built by the Canadian Armament Research and Development Establishment), and U.S. Industries, Inc., presentation of Elevated Viewing Device, June 30, 1964, Westchester

County Airport, White Plains, N.Y.
57. See A. C. Clarke, "The World of the Communication Satellite," *Astronautics and Aeronautics*, Feb., 1964, 45–47.
58. See *The New York Times*, July 4, 1965.

CHAPTER FIVE

1. See, for example, the report of the Treasury Department's Technical Investigation Aids School, in Boston *Herald*, July 25, 1965, and in "Invasions of Privacy (Government Agencies)" *Hearings Before Subcommittee on Administrative Practice and Procedure of the Senate Judiciary Committee*, 89th Cong., 1st Sess. —hereafter referred to as Long Committee—temporary transcript (1965), 205, 869, 874, 953, 785, and Army Intelligence's eight-week course at Maryland's Ft. Holabird, *ibid.*, 645–46.
2. According to former Treasury agent W. J. Mellin, in 1949, 90 per cent of all wiretappers were old telephone-company men. See W. J. Mellin, "I Was a Wire-Tapper," *Saturday Evening Post*, Sept. 10, 1949, 20.
3. Flyer of Tracer Investigative Products, Inc., Palm Beach, Fla.
4. Flyer of R. B. Clifton Electronic Surveillance Equipment, Miami, Fla.
5. *Los Angeles Times*, Sept. 27, 1962.
6. Arthur Gorlick, "Everything's Bugged as Gumshoes Meet," Long Island City (N.Y.) *Star-Journal*, Sept. 7, 1965.
7. 1964 mailing by Montclair Technical Services, Bloomfield, Conn. I am indebted to R. E. Eyster of New York and New Haven for calling this flyer to my attention.
8. See Memocord ad, for example, in *The New York Times*, July 27, 1965.
9. See the ad in *The New York Times*, Dec. 19, 1963, 15.
10. For example, Feb., 1963, *Diners' Club Magazine*.
11. A description of the growing use of such recorders by lawyers is in "Monitoring Devices and Lawyers," a report of the Special Committee on Science and Law, Association of the Bar of the City of New York, published in 20 *Record of the Association of the Bar of the City of New York*, No. 9 (1965).
12. See, for example, New York *Herald Tribune*, Aug. 12, 1964.
13. Miles Reproducer Co., Inc., letter-leaflet and catalogue sheet, 1964.
14. Ads for American Geloso Electronics, New York.
15. See *The New York Times* "Shopping Guide" for Oct. 30, 1964, and Nov. 14, 1965.
16. Mike McGrady, "You, Too, Can Bug People . . . and Their Phones," Miami *Herald*, Sept. 23, 1965; Gwen Gibson, "Over-the-Counter Bugging Devices," New York *Herald Tribune*, Oct. 14, 1965; "Eavesdropping—Modern Style," *Christian Science Monitor*, Oct. 26, 1965.
17. J. R. Hollinger and J. E. Mulligan, "Build the Shotgun Sound Snooper," *Popular Electronics*, June, 1964, 51, 84; see also ads for surveillance equipment in the Lafayette Radio Electronics Catalogue No. 650, 120; Shure Microphones, Technical Bulletin CA4A, "Ultra-Miniature Ceramic Microphone"; John Meshna, Jr., Surplus Electronic Material, Catalogue No. S-64, offering Sniperscopes, infrared viewers, phone patches, gold-plated "concealed microphone buttons," and other such items.
18. 23 *Popular Electronics*, Oct., 1965, 116.
19. 23 *Popular Electronics*, Aug., 1963, 126, and later issues.
20. San Francisco *Chronicle*, Jan. 25, 1958.
21. New York *Herald Tribune*, Sept. 24, 1961.
22. Denver *Post*, Jan. 17, 1963, 23; March 15, 1963.
23. Miami *Herald*, Dec. 31, 1964; Washington *Post-Times-Herald*, Jan. 7, 1965.
24. Des Moines *Register*, Jan. 29 and Feb. 19, 1959.
25. A large collection of catalogues, ads, and letters from surveillance-equipment

suppliers has been assembled by the Special Committee on Science and Law and is available in its files for examination; material is available from almost all the firms mentioned in the following discussion.

26. C. H. Stoelting Co., "Miniaturized FM Radio Surveillance Equipment for Secret Listening or Transmitting of Intelligence," advertising sheets, Committee files.

27. Azagraph Lecture Guide, Mosler Research Products, Inc., "Surreptitious Listening Methods" (n.d.), Committee files.

28. Solar Research Corp. catalogue.

29. For an earlier example, see Jack E. Rytten, "How to Tap a Telephone," and "Recording and the Police Profession," *Law and Order*, Jan., March, and May, 1955; for recent examples see Paul Bunker, "Twenty-four Hour Monitoring," *Law and Order*, Jan., 1958, 14; William Shaw, "Applied Electronics . . . Radio Beacon Tails," *Law and Order*, Nov., 1962, 34.

30. For recent general discussions of this trend, see Lawrence Stessin, " 'I Spy' Becomes Big Business," *The New York Times Magazine*, Nov. 28, 1965; "When Walls Have Ears, Call a De-Bugging Man," *Business Week*, Oct. 31, 1965; *Wall Street Journal*, Feb. 17 and March 23, 1966; see also, "Business Spies Cost Industry $2 Billion Yearly," San Francisco *Commercial News*, Oct. 14, 1965. The American Management Association held a three-day briefing on "Protection of Intellectual Property Against Industrial Espionage and Theft," in 1965 (see *The New York Times*, March 16, 1965) that featured discussions of electronic eavesdropping.

31. *The New York Times*, May 7, 1965.

32. *Competitive Intelligence: Information, Espionage, and Decision-Making. A Special Report for Businessmen* (Watertown, Mass., C.I. Associates, 1959), 58; see also, Union City (Calif.) *Leader*, July 13, 1966.

33. *Business Week*, Oct. 31, 1964.

34. *The New York Times*, Feb. 6, 1966, Sect. VIII.

35. Dallas *Morning News*, July 24, 1962.

36. W. M. Carley, "Electronic Advances; Air Snoopers Using Eavesdropping Devices," *Wall Street Journal*, April 9, 1963.

37. Miami *Herald*, May 19, 1963.

38. Washington *Post*, Feb. 9, 1963; *The New York Times*, April 22, 1964.

39. Washington *Post*, April 7, 1962.

40. Martin Haver, "The Snoopers," *Man's Magazine*, July, 1960.

41. *Business Week*, Oct. 31, 1965.

42. *Competitive Intelligence* . . . (*op. cit.*), *passim*.

43. Washington *Post*, April 7, 1962.

44. William Shaw, "An Introduction to Law Enforcement: Electronics and Communication," *Law and Order*, July, 1965; reprinted in *Congressional Record*, Sept. 2, 1965, 21916–17.

45. *Time*, Aug. 13, 1965, 42.

46. Los Angeles *Mirror*, Sept. 28, 1960.

47. Samuel Dash, *The Eavesdroppers* (New York, 1959), 272.

48. Detroit *News*, March 28, 1965.

49. Personal interview with the author, 1964.

50. See the reports of speeches to business groups by Clifford Lange of Lange Industries in Van Nuys (Calif.) *News*, April 9, 1965, and Huntington Park (Calif.) *Signal*, Jan. 1, 1965.

51. See Newark *News*, Dec. 5, 1959; AP newsfeature on wiretapping, Jan. 17, 1959; testimony of Harold Lipset, "Wiretapping, Eavesdropping, and the Bill of Rights," *Hearings Before the Subcommittee on Constitutional Rights of the Senate Committee on the Judiciary*, 86th Cong., 1st Sess., 1467–69 (1959).

52. San Jose (Calif.) *News*, May 4, 1964; *Commercial News*, San Francisco, April 30, 1964.

53. The dummy plastic calendars were displayed by J. A. Beirne, President of the Communication Workers of America, at Senate hearings in 1965. See Norfolk

Times-Advocate, June 10, 1965.

54. *Ibid.* For other examples see *The New York Times,* July 7, 1961; Dash, *op. cit.,* 269–70.
55. New York *Post,* Sept. 6, 1960.
56. International Trailer Co. Inc., 133 NLRB #151 (1961).
57. Fresno (Calif.) *Valley Labor Citizen,* July 23, 1965; see also R. J. Farrell, "Exterminating the Electronic 'Bugs,' " New York *Herald Tribune,* March 29, 1964.
58. Los Angeles *Herald-Examiner,* Oct. 21, 1965.
59. *UAW Solidarity,* March, 1965, 4.
60. *Eico, Inc.,* Decision of Arbitrator, 44 LA 563 (1965); *Labor Advocate* (El Paso, Tex.), June 11, 1965.
61. *UAW Solidarity,* March, 1965, 4.
62. *Ibid.,* 4.
63. *The New York Times,* Sept. 25, 1963.
64. *The CWA News,* Oct., 1963, and *UAW Solidarity,* March, 1965, 5.
65. *California Senate Judiciary Committee Report on the Interception of Messages by the Use of Electronic and Other Devices* (Regan Committee), Calif. Legislature, 1957 Regular Sess., 12.
66. Dash, *op. cit.,* 270; W. J. Mellin, "I Was a Wire-Tapper," *Saturday Evening Post,* Sept. 10, 1949, 57; W. J. Keating, *The Man Who Rocked the Boat* (New York, 1956), 240; *The Reporter,* Feb. 10, 1955, 23; R. J. Farrell, "Exterminating the Electronic 'Bugs,' " New York *Herald Tribune,* March 29, 1964.
67. See, for example, Bernard Spindel, "Who Else Is Listening?" *Collier's,* June 10, 1955, 26; Farrell (n. 57, above); Calif. Judiciary Committee, *op. cit.,* 12.
68. Wichita (Kans.) *Beacon,* Feb. 5, 1965.
69. 1962 Hearings on Attorney General's Wiretapping Program, 89.
70. Ben Price, "The Age of the Bugs," Jan. 17, 1959 (AP, Washington, D.C.).
71. See Dash, *op. cit.,* 158–59.
72. Chula Vista (Calif.) *Star-News,* June 3, 1965; National City (Calif.) *Star News,* July 18, 1965.
73. Interview with Clyde Duber, on the NBC television program, "The Big Ear," Oct. 31, 1965, final script, 32.
74. See *Time,* Jan. 23, 1965.
75. *Time,* Jan. 10, 1964, 42.
76. New York *Post,* ("On the Air," by Bob Williams), July 27, 1960.
77. Mike Wallace news report for CBS, Oct. 10, 1964.
78. New York *Journal American,* June 20, 1965.
79. Norfolk *Times-Advocate,* June 10, 1965.
80. Toledo (Ohio) *Blade,* Oct. 21, 1965.
81. San Jose (Calif.) *Mercury,* Oct. 19, 1964; see also, Chicago (Ill.) *Telephony,* July 30, 1966.
82. New York *Journal American,* May 20, 1964.
83. Ft. Pierce (Fla.) *News-Tribune,* March 11, 1964.
84. Cleveland *Plain Dealer,* Aug. 18, 1965; Tampa *Times,* Aug. 26, 1965; Birmingham *News,* Aug. 21, 1965; Springfield (Mass.) *Union,* Sept. 15, 1965. See also cases reported in Cleveland *Plain Dealer,* March 7, 1965, and Springfield (Mass.) *Union,* July 3, 1965.
85. Indianapolis *News,* Dec. 1–2, 1958.
86. See Ed Reid and Ovid Demaris, *The Green Felt Jungle* (Pocket Books ed., New York, 1964), 102 ff.
87. Chicago *Tribune,* July 31, 1965; Chicago *Daily News,* July 31, 1965.
88. *Time,* April 17, 1964, 102.
89. See Myron Brenton, *The Privacy Invaders* (New York, 1964), 15.
90. See FTC Docket No. 7845 (Decision and Order), July 27, 1960, 3, and FTC Docket No. 8560 (Decision and Order), March 12, 1964, 12–13.
91. *The New York Times,* Feb. 6, 1966, Sect. VIII.
92. Martin Haver, "The Snoopers," *Man's Magazine,* July, 1960, 99.
93. Suffern (N.Y.) *Independent,* Oct. 7, 1965.

94. Brenton, *op. cit.*, 181, and *Time*, April 17, 1964; Martin Haver, "The Snoopers," *Man's Magazine*, July, 1960, 99.
95. *The New York Times*, May 7, 1964; Vance Packard, *The Naked Society* (New York, 1964), 85.
96. Packard, *op. cit.*, 87, and Dash, *op. cit.*, 96.
97. Reid and Demaris, *op. cit.*
98. See, for example, *T.V. Guide*, April 24, 1965, 3.
99. Boston (Mass.) *Herald*, June 12, 1966; see also Boston (Mass.) *Evening Globe*, June 16, 1966.
100. *The New York Times*, Sept. 15, 1966.
101. *The New York Times*, Sept. 24-25, 1959; New York *Post*, Sept. 24 and Oct. 29, 1959.
102. *The New York Times*, July 12, 1960.
103. Philadelphia *Evening Bulletin*, Feb. 11, 1958.
104. New York *World Telegram & Sun*, June 6, 1964.
105. Huntington Beach (Calif.) *Pilot*, March 26, 1964.
106. *The New York Times*, Oct. 27 and 28, 1965; New York *News*, Oct. 27, 1965.
107. Bernard Spindel, "Who Else Is Listening?" *Collier's*, June 10, 1955, 26.
108. "Radicals: Waiting for Armageddon," *Newsweek*, April 26, 1965.
109. Baton Rouge *State-Times*, Oct. 10-11, 1961, 23; Dec. 27, 1961; Jan. 18, 1962; Feb. 26, 1963.
110. *Time*, Aug. 4, 1958.
111. *The New York Times*, June 26, 1965.
112. Oklahoma City *Oklahoma Journal*, Oct. 25, 1965.
113. Reading (Pa.) *Times*, May 21, 1964; see Dash, *op. cit.*, *passim*.
114. Philadelphia *Evening Bulletin*, Oct. 12, 1958.
115. *South: The Magazine of Dixie*, March, 1965.
116. York (Pa.) *Gazette and Daily*, Oct. 21, 1964. For other examples, see Chicago *Sun Times*, March 17, 1961; San Antonio *News*, Jan. 26, 1965; San Francisco *Chronicle*, June 9, 1966; San Diego (Calif.) *Tribune*, July 30, 1966.
117. "Hell Breaks Loose in Paradise," *Life*, April 26, 1963, 73-84.
118. See, for example, E. R. Hilgard, *Introduction to Psychology* (3rd ed., New York, 1962), 12, 56, 537.
119. *The New York Times*, Oct. 6-7, 13-14, 1955; F. L. Strodtbeck, "Social Process, the Law, and Jury Functioning," in W. M. Evan (ed.), *Law and Sociology* (Glencoe, Ill., 1961), 151 n.
120. See Miriam Ottenberg, *The Federal Investigators* (Englewood Cliffs, N.J., 1962).
121. *The New York Times*, Sept. 2, 1965; Las Vegas *Review-Journal*, July 14, 1965; Denver *Rocky Mountain News*, April 6, 1965; Washington *Post-Times Herald*, Feb. 20, 1964.
122. *The New York Times*, Oct. 24, 1965; Kansas City (Mo.) *Star*, Oct. 20, 1965; Kansas City (Mo.) *Times*, Oct. 21, 1965.
123. *The New York Times*, Sept. 2, 1965. For discussion of alleged FBI eavesdropping on James Hoffa, see the collection of affidavits, articles, and statements on FBI and Department of Justice surveillance in the Hoffa trial in *Congressional Record*, May 4, 1964, 9674-9706. For the other incidents, see Milwaukee *Journal*, Oct. 20, 1966; *The New York Times*, Dec. 1, 13, 28, 1966.
124. The Levine statements are reported in F. J. Cook, *The FBI Nobody Knows* (Pyramid ed., New York, 1964).
125. *Time*, March 6, 1964, 56.
126. *The New York Times*, May 25, 1966.
127. "Treasury Policy on Wire Tapping," memorandum for Treasury law-enforcement heads, from Arnold Sagalyn, Director, Law Enforcement Coordination, Dec. 17, 1963.
128. W. J. Mellin, "I Was a Wire-Tapper," *Saturday Evening Post*, Sept. 10, 1949.
129. Washington *Post*, Nov. 19, 1963.
130. Ottenberg, *op. cit.*, 162-65.
131. See the statement of Senator Edward Long (D., Mo.), "Big Brother: Snooping

by Internal Revenue Service," *Congressional Record*, July 16, 1965, 16489.

132. Interview by author, Feb. 14, 1964, Washington, D.C.

133. "Treasury Policy on Wire Tapping" (see n. 127, above).

134. Long Committee, 239–40; a list of 42 cities and dates of installation was supplied by IRS Commissioner Sheldon Cohen on July 26, 1965; see, for example, Houston (Tex.) *Chronicle*, Aug. 9, 1965. The estimate of 57 cities in all was in Cohen's testimony (Long Committee, 784).

135. St. Louis *Post-Dispatch*, July 14, 1965.

136. Long Committee, 205, 785, 645–46, 925–26, 800–801, 666.

137. *Ibid.*, 869–99.

138. *The New York Times*, July 15, 1965.

139. Miami *Herald*, Aug. 10, 1965.

140. *The New York Times*, Oct. 24, 1965; Kansas City (Mo.) *Star*, Oct. 17 and 19, 1965.

141. Washington *Star*, July 15, 1965.

142. See Drew Pearson's column, Washington *Post-Times-Herald*, Oct. 29, 1965.

143. Long Committee, April 27, 1965, 284–383, 540, 302–304, 311–26, 610 ff. See also *American Dietaids v. Celebrezze*, 317 F. 2nd 658 (1963). For other recordings of lectures, see Long Committee, 302–309, 819; for another "decoy" case, see 541–42.

144. Appendix to Long Committee, 328–30, 330.

145. See *The New York Times*, Nov. 10, 1964; "State Department Security, 1963–65: The Otepka Case, II," *Hearings Before the Senate Subcommittee on Internal Security, Judiciary Committee*, 89th Cong., 1st Sess., esp. pt. 3 (1965).

146. Los Angeles *Times*, April 21, 1964.

147. Allen and Scott, "Wiretapping a Damoclean Sword Over Heads of Capital Officials," Los Angeles *Times*, April 21, 1964.

148. William Shaw, "An Introduction to Law Enforcement Electronics and Communication," *Law and Order*, July, 1965; see also the National League of Cities survey of police agencies in 1966, in which 68 of 283 police agencies said they were using "electronic eavesdropping equipment" (*Nation's Cities*, Feb., 1966).

149. Boston *Herald*, May 20, 1964; New York *Journal American*, Oct. 29, 1964; Oswego (N.Y.) *Palladium Times*, May 21, 1964; Frankfort (Ky.) *State Journal*, May 17, 1965; Wilkes-Barre (Pa.) *Times Leader News*, March 12, 1965; Phoenix (Ariz.) *Evening American*, Jan. 29, 1965; Witchita (Kans.) *Beacon*, Feb. 5, 1965; Norfolk (Va.) *Ledger-Star*, Dec. 10, 1964; *The New York Times*, Nov. 30 and Dec. 23, 1965; Austin (Tex.) *American*, Sept. 19, 21, 23 and Oct. 1, 1965; Portland (Ore.) *Oregonian*, Oct. 2, 1965; *Oregon Journal*, Oct. 2, 1965; Miami *Herald*, Sept. 1, 1965; Bergen (N.J.) *Evening Record*, Nov. 30, 1965; Carbondale (Ill.) *Southern Illinoisan*, June 26, 1966; Atlanta (Ga.) *Constitution*, Sept. 21, 1966; Garden City (N.Y.) *Newsday*, Aug. 31, 1966; New York *Post*, Sept. 1, 1966.

150. Dash, *op. cit.*, *passim*; Report of the New York County District Attorney's Office, *op. cit.* For some recent examples in the press, see *The New York Times*, Nov. 19, 1964 (murder); New York *Journal American*, May 10, 1965 (robbery); Sacramento *Bee*, Aug. 6, 1965 (extortion); Chicago *Tribune*, Feb. 3, 1965 (narcotics); Miami *Herald*, Sept. 1, 1965 (bribery); Las Vegas *Sun*, July 7, 1966; Costa Mesa (Calif.) *Daily Pilot*, Oct. 6, 1966; New York *Daily News*, June 22, 1966; Titusville (Fla.) *Star-Advocate*, Aug. 18, 1966; Yonkers (N.Y.) *Herald Statesman*, June 9, 1966.

151. Frankfort (Ky.) *State Journal*, May 17, 1965; Portland (Ore.) *Oregonian*, Oct. 2, 1965; *The New York Times*, July 1, 1965.

152. Figures from New York County District Attorney's Office, in files of the Social Committee on Science and Law. I am indebted to District Attorney Frank Hogan, Chief Assistant District Attorney A. J. Scotti, and Chief Inspector Thomas Fay, Jr., for their assistance in this survey.

153. Dash, *op. cit.*, 42, 66, 124, 152, 236, 277; 154, 163–64, 166, 167–68, 221, 239.

154. Scottsdale (Arizona) *Progress*, Jan. 30, 1965.

155. Washington *Post*, Feb. 15, 1965.

156. *The New York Times*, Feb. 25, 1959.
157. *The New York Times*, Nov. 30 and Dec. 23, 1965.
158. Dash, *op. cit.*, 123–28.
159. *Ibid.*, 96-97.
160. *The New York Times*, Oct. 24, 1965.
161. Dash, *op. cit.*, 135–36.
162. *Ibid.*, 153–55.
163. *Ibid.*, 176, 188–90, 213–15.
164. Dash, *op. cit.*, 69–70; New York *Journal American*, May 10, 1965; *The New York Times*, Feb. 5, 1964.
165. *The New York Times*, April 4, 1964; St. Louis *Globe-Democrat*, Jan. 3, 1952. See also, Riverside (Calif.) *Press*, Aug. 11, 1966; Union (N.J.) *Leader*, June 16, 1966; Richmond (Va.) *News-Leader*, Aug. 17, 1966.
166. William Shaw, "Applied Electronics . . . Radio Beacon Tails," *Law and Order*, Nov., 1962.
167. Dash, *op. cit.*, 76–77.
168. Syracuse *Post Standard*, Sept. 8, 1964; *Memo. on Electronic Listening Devices*, Public Safety Building, Syracuse, April 27, 1964, N.Y. State Commission of Correction, Albany, N.Y.
169. Boston *Herald*, June 4, 1959; Denver *Rocky Mountain News*, April 6, 1965; Minneapolis *Tribune*, April 3, 1964.
170. *The New York Times*, Jan. 15, 1965.
171. *Ibid.*, March 3, 1964.
172. "TV for Surveillance," *Law and Order*, Dec., 1964.
173. See *Time*, Nov. 12, 1965.
174. "Camera Surveillance of Sex Deviates," *Law and Order*, Nov., 1963.
175. W. F. McKee, "Evidentiary Problems: Camera Surveillance of Sex Deviates," *ibid.*, Aug., 1964, 72; *Time*, Nov. 12, 1965.
176. Dash, *op. cit.*, *passim*.
177. *The New York Times*, May 7, 1965; Nov. 30 and Dec. 3, 1965; Feb. 17, 1964.
178. See Dash, *op. cit.*; *Irvine v. State of California*, 347 U.S. 128 (1954); *Hearings on Invasions of Privacy (Government Agencies) Before Subcommittee on Administrative Practice and Procedure* (Long Committee) *of Senate Judiciary Committee*, 89th Cong., 1st Sess. (1965); Calif. Senate Judiciary Committee Report on the Interception of Messages by the Use of Electronic and Other Devices, 1957.
179. Dash, *op. cit.*, *passim*.

CHAPTER SIX

1. Lie detectors can be divided into two basic types, those that measure only one bodily change under interrogation, such as the pathometer (galvanic skin reflex), and those that measure several bodily changes, the polygraphs. A newspaper survey in 1954 listed a substantial number of different polygraph machines as being in use at that time: the Keeler Polygraph, the Reid Polygraph, the Lee Psychograph, the Stoelting Cardio-Pneumo Polygraph, the Detectograph, the Reactograph, the B & W Electric Psychometer, and the Darrow Behavior Research Photopolygraph. See New York *Herald Tribune*, Sept. 1, 1954. This discussion will use the term "polygraph" and focus on the Keeler-Reid devices, which have been used most widely and have been subjected to the greatest number of scientific tests. For a historical account of the polygraph's development and technical features, see Fred E. Inbau and John E. Reid, *Lie Detection and Criminal Interrogation* (3rd ed., Baltimore, 1953), 2–141.
2. Ann Ewing, "Lie Detection at a Distance," 88 *Science News Letter*, Aug. 14, 1965, 106; House Committee on Government Operations, *Use of Polygraphs as "Lie Detectors" by the Federal Government*, Report 198, 89th Cong., 1st Sess., March 22, 1965.

3. L. J. Cronbach, *Essentials of Psychological Testing* (2nd ed., New York, 1961); H. J. Eysenck, *Sense and Nonsense in Psychology* (Baltimore, 1962), 175–230.
4. See Cronbach, *Essentials of Psychological Testing*, 465.
5. Office of Strategic Services Assessment Staff, *The Assessment of Men* (New York, 1948).
6. Replies in files of the Special Committee on Science and Law.
7. Several of these companies, though they classified themselves as "non-users," indicated that divisions of their company might have used the tests in the past on a small scale for experimental purposes and had then decided *not* to adopt them. The names of 99 non-user companies appear in our files; 12 companies chose to return the questionnaire anonymously.
8. TABLE 1: WHO IS TESTED (97 COMPANIES)

TYPE OF PERSONNEL	SELECTION	PROMOTION	SPECIAL PERSONNEL PROBLEM	SPECIAL RESEARCH PROJECT
Wage-earning employees	13	13	8	—
Clerical or office employees	28	16	12	—
Professional, technical, or scientific employees	52	25	9	—
Salesmen	58	21	7	—
Management personnel and executives	63	37	14	1

9. TABLE 2: WHO CAN SEE THE RESULTS OF PERSONALITY TESTS (97 COMPANIES)

	Yes	No
Employee or executive himself	31	43
Company psychologist or medical staff	39	21
Personnel staff	75	5
Superiors or supervisors	63	18
Government officers	3	63
Outside credit or rating agencies	1	65
Other firms seeking to hire employees	1	64
Top management only	3	—

10. This account is based on a letter from Civil Service Commission Chairman J. W. Macy, Jr., May 22, 1964, plus Chairman Macy's testimony before the Gallagher Committee, 1965, *op. cit.*, temporary transcript, 94–137, and the Ervin Committee, 1965, *op. cit.*, temporary transcript, 421–55.
11. The information here is contained in two letters from W. J. Crockett, Under Secretary of State for Administration, Dec. 16, 1963, and Feb. 6, 1964, plus the testimony by Mr. Crockett before the Ervin Committee, 1965, temporary transcript, 10–71.
12. Letters from R. K. Davenport, Deputy Under Secretary of the Army for Personnel Management, June 18 and July 24, 1964; J. O. Cobb, Rear Admiral, Deputy Chief of Naval Personnel, June 1 and Oct. 16, 1964; B. W. Fridge, Special Assistant for Manpower, Personnel and Reserve Forces, Department of the Air Force, May 14, 1964; J. P. Goode, Deputy for Manpower, Personnel and Organization, Department of the Air Force, June 23, 1964.
13. Testimony of W. T. Skallerup, Jr., Ervin Committee, 1965, temporary transcript, 384–420.
14. Testimony of L. R. Werts, Administrative Assistant Secretary, Department of Labor, Gallagher Committee, 1965, temporary transcript, 384–58.

15. Testimony of O. A. Singletary, Director, Job Corps, Ervin Committee, 1965, temporary transcript, 348–58.
16. Testimony of J. C. O'Brien, Director, Division of Personnel Management, Department of Health, Education and Welfare, *ibid.*, 456–82.
17. Letter from J. W. Hawthorne, General Manager of the Los Angeles Board of Civil Service Commissioners, June 3, 1964.
18. Letter from T. H. Lang, New York City Personnel Director, July 14, 1964.
19. See the returned questionnaire from J. M. Posegate, Merit System Director, Arizona Merit System Board, July 21, 1964, in files of Special Committee on Science and Law.
20. Letter from C. K. Wettengel, Director of Wisconsin Bureau of Personnel, July 23, 1964.
21. Letter from M. C. Krone, President of the New York State Department of Civil Service, May 22, 1964.
22. Letter to Bevis Longstreth, Secretary, Special Committee on Science and Law, from D. J. Subletter, Secretary and Chief Examiner of the Detroit Civil Service Commission, May 14, 1964.
23. Letter from W. H. Finnegan, Director, Massachusetts Civil Service, April 29, 1964.
24. New York *Herald Tribune*, Aug. 3, 1957; *Police Science*, April, 1961, 50.
25. See New York *Daily News*, May 28, 1963.
26. *National Observer*, April 29, 1963; St. Louis *Post-Dispatch*, Feb. 16, 1962; Minneapolis *Star*, July 23, 1963; *The New York Times*, March 6, 1962; New York *Journal American*, Jan. 23, 1961, and May 27, 1957; and Miami *Herald*, Oct. 7, 1964.
27. Survey conducted by the Special Committee on Science and Law, using clippings of Luce-Romeike Agency, New York (clippings in files of Special Committee).
28. See Oklahoma City *Oklahoman*, April 23, 1964.
29. For the agencies' replies, see the table in Moss Committee's Tenth Report (House Report No. 198, 89th Cong., 1st Sess., 1965), between pp. 36 and 37.
30. *Business Week*, June 18, 1960, 104.
31. *Newsweek*, April 29, 1963, 82.
32. Miami *Herald*, Oct. 15, 1961.
33. See New York *Mirror*, Dec. 6, 1953.
34. See *Reporter*, June 8, 1954, 15; *Wall Street Journal*, Oct. 17, 1961; *Business Week*, June 18, 1960, 105.
35. *Saturday Evening Post*, Nov. 10, 1962.
36. See *Reporter*, June 8, 1954, 15.
37. New York *Daily News*, May 30, 1963.
38. *Business Week*, June 18, 1960, 98, 105–106.
39. Reported by *The Texas Observer*, as quoted in the Feature Press Service, Weekly Bulletin No. 2125, American Civil Liberties Union, Feb. 5, 1962; see also *Time*, March 7, 1960.
40. *Wall Street Journal*, Oct. 17, 1961.
41. Richmond (Va.) *Times Dispatch*, April 14, 1955.
42. Miami *Herald*, Dec. 13, 1963.
43. New York *Daily News*, May 30, 1963.
44. *Los Angeles Times*, April 7, 1963.
45. See Police Department Manual, Orlando, Fla.; International City Managers Association Statement, Jan. 27, 1960; *Law and Order*, July, 1960, 24; *Public Personnel Review*, July, 1962, 197; *The New York Times*, Feb. 11, 1962; *Public Personnel Review*, July, 1962, 192; Miami *Herald*, Aug. 12, 1962; R. O. Arther, "Polygraph Picks Potential Policemen," *Law and Order*, Sept., 1964.
46. *The New York Times*, Jan. 29, 1960.
47. See International City Managers Association printed statement, Jan. 27, 1960.
48. See Denver *Post*, Nov. 22 and 26, 1961.
49. See Los Angeles *Times*, June 26, 1962.
50. *Public Personnel Review*, July, 1962, 192.
51. Chicago *Tribune*, Nov. 22, 1963.

52. "The Lie Detector Era," *Reporter*, June 8, 1954, 10–18; June 22, 1954, 22–29.
53. See Moss Committee Preliminary Study, 89th Cong., 1st Sess., April, 1964, 21, 78.
54. *Ibid.*, see "Table of Agency Replies," following p. 36.
55. From copy of CIA questionnaire.
56. See Washington, D.C., *News*, April 8, 1964.
57. See New York *Herald Tribune*, March 29, 1964.
58. See Moss Committee, Tenth Report, March, 1965, 43 (n. 26 above).
59. Moss Committee Hearings, pt. 2, 88th Cong., 2nd Sess., April 10, 1964, 206, 241.
60. *Ibid.*, Tenth Report, March, 1965, 19.
61. See L. A. Gottschalk, "The Use of Drugs in Interrogation," in Biderman and Zimmer (eds.), *op. cit.*, 96–141; "The Influence of Drugs on the Individual," in S. M. Farber and R. H. L. Wilson (eds.), *Control of the Mind* (New York, 1961), 77–130; C. B. Hanscom, "NARCO Interrogation," *Police*, Nov.-Dec., 1957, 44–50.
62. See G. H. Dessin, L. Z. Freedman, R. C. Donnelly, and F. C. Redlich, "Drug-Induced Revelation and Criminal Investigation," 62 *Yale Law Journal*, 315–47 (1953); J. F. Kubie, "Instrumental, Chemical, and Psychological Aids in the Interrogation of Witnesses," 13 *The Journal of Social Issues*, 44–46 (1957); and L. A. Gottschalk, "The Use of Drugs in Interrogation," in Biderman and Zimmer (eds.), *op. cit.*, 112–17.
63. See Leonard Uhr and J. G. Miller (eds.), *Drugs and Behavior* (New York, 1960); Farber and Wilson (eds.), *op. cit.*, 77–130; and *McGraw-Hill Encyclopedia of Science and Technology* (New York, 1960), 81–82, 16–17.
64. See *The New York Times*, Dec. 28, 1965, 1, 24; see also Biderman and Zimmer (eds.), *op. cit.*, 14–15.
65. See "Brain Monitor Operates Inside Astronauts' Helmet," *Science News Letter*, Aug. 31, 1963, 133.
66. See "Gains Reported in Brain Study," *The New York Times*, Nov. 29, 1964, 80.
67. *Ibid.*
68. See "Intelligence Test Uses a Light Flash," *The New York Times*, Oct. 30, 1965.
69. See "Brain Monitor Operates Inside Astronauts' Helmet," *Science News Letter*, Aug. 31, 1963, 133.
70. See "Gains Reported in Brain Study," *The New York Times*, Nov. 29, 1964, 80, and R. G. Heath, M.D., "Electrical Self-Stimulation of the Brain in Man," 120 *The American Journal of Psychiatry*, Dec., 1963.
71. See "The Eye is Found Clue to Thought," *The New York Times*, Nov. 22, 1964, and E. H. Hess and J. M. Polt, "Pupil Size as Related to Interest Value of Visual Stimuli," 132 *Science*, Aug. 5, 1960, 349–50.
72. See "Chemical Brain Control," 85 *Science News Letter*, April 4, 1964, 214.

CHAPTER SEVEN

1. The photochrome micro-image system was developed by National Cash Register Co. and was displayed at its New York World's Fair pavilion. See *Time*, May 1, 1964, 94.
2. Richard Harwood, "Is Your Name on a Secret Dossier?" Washington *Post*, May 29, 1966.
3. See Myron Brenton, *The Privacy Invaders* (New York, 1964), Ch. 4.
4. See David Sarnoff, "No Life Untouched," *Saturday Review*, July 23, 1966, 22; *Business Week*, Feb. 19, 1966, 110, 113.
5. *Report to the President on the Management of Automatic Data Processing in the Federal Government*, Senate Doc. No. 15, 89th Cong., 1st Sess., March 4, 1965; "Government Electronic Data Processing Systems," *Hearings Before the*

Subcommittee on Census and Statistics of the Committee on Post Office and Civil Service, 89th Cong., 2nd Sess. (1966), 6, 248.

6. *The New York Times*, Nov. 7, 1965, Sect. III.

7. See, for example, Felix Kaufman, "Data Systems That Cross Company Boundaries," 44 *Harvard Business Review*, 141–45, 148–52 (1966); John Diebold, "New World Coming," *Saturday Review*, July 23, 1966, esp. 18; and S. R. Schmedel, "New Computer Systems are Developed to Solve Many Problems at Once," *Wall Street Journal*, March 25, 1966; "Western Union Links Teletypewriter System and Computer Center," *Wall Street Journal*, March 17, 1966; and John Lear, "Whither Personal Privacy," *Saturday Review*, July 23, 1966, 36–37, 67.

8. *Information Sharing: The Hidden Challenge in Criminal Justice*. Brochure of the New York State Identification and Intelligence System.

9. "A National Crime Information Center," *FBI Law Enforcement Bulletin*, May, 1966, 1–6, 22–23.

10. See J. W. Macy, Jr., "Automated Government," *Saturday Review*, Aug. 23, 1966, 21.

11. David Sarnoff, "No Life Untouched," *Saturday Review*, July 23, 1966, 21.

12. About 3.5 million persons belong to American Express, Carte Blanche, and Diners' Club. Officials of these major corporations indicated that membership rolls are presently increasing by 35 to 40 per cent yearly. To this figure can be added local credit-card plans for limited use, such as Bank of America's Uni-Card, Washington D.C.'s Central Charge, and the like. Totaled in with gas-company credit cards, offering increasingly extensive services, the total participation of American families in credit-card plans might well be as high as 20 or 30 million.

13. Described in *Newsweek*, Aug. 2, 1965, 58.

14. See "Next in Banking: Pay Bills by Phone," *Business Week*, Nov. 13, 1965, 82.

15. "A Government Watch on 200 Million Americans?" *U.S. News & World Report*, May 16, 1966; see for example "National Information Center," *Hearings Before the Ad Hoc Subcommittee on a National Research Data Processing and Information Retrieval Center of the House Committee on Education and Labor*, 88th Cong., 1st. Sess. (1963).

16. S. M. Humphrey, "Impact of Computer Developments," *Proceedings of the Association of Computing Machinery*, 17–18 (1959).

17. Paul Armer, "Computer Aspects of Technological Change, Automation, and Economic Progress," the RAND Corporation, Nov., 1965; W. H. Ware, "Future Computer Technology and Its Impact," the RAND Corporation, March, 1966.

18. "Memory Process Puts 645 Million Bits on a Square Inch," *Electronic Design*, Dec. 6, 1966.

CHAPTER EIGHT

1. W. R. Plum, *The Military Telegraph During the Civil War* (1882), Vol. 1, 11, 60–61, 69, 201–02; Vol. 2, 265, 282; Samuel Dash, *The Eavesdroppers* (New York, 1959), 23; *The New York Times*, May 18, 1874; *Congressional Record*, H.R., 43rd Cong., 1st Sess., 2378 (1874).

2. Reproduced from *Scribner's Monthly*, 1889, in M. Wilson, *American Science and Invention* (1960), 270.

3. *The New York Times*, June 30, 1893; Aug. 3, 1894; Oct. 21, 1899; Dec. 22, 1903; San Francisco *Call*, Jan 1, 1899; New York *Herald Tribune*, Jan. 22, 1917; New York *World*, May 19, 1916; Dash, *op. cit.*, 25–26; Meyer Berger, "About New York," *The New York Times*, March 7, 1955; "Wire-Tapping Cases in New York," 113 *Outlook*, May 31, 1916, 234; New York *Herald Tribune*, May 19 and 20, 1916; "How Detective Burns Listened to Dynamiter Plot," 106 *Science American*, 284 (1912); *The New York Times*, Feb. 18, 1912; Jan. 30, 1912; Feb. 28, 1912; Jan. 28, 1912; Feb. 2, 1912; Feb. 18, 1912; March 27, 1912; Dec. 30, 1912; and Feb. 2, 1913.

4. For a full account as of 1952, see Alan F. Westin, 'The Wire-Tapping Problem: An Analysis and a Legislative Proposal," 52 *Columbia Law Review*, Feb. 1952, 165.

5. Dash, *op. cit., passim.*

6. See, for example, testimony of Attorney General Herbert Brownell, Hearings on *Wiretapping for National Security, Before a Subcommittee of the Senate Judiciary Committee*, 83rd Cong., 2nd Sess., 1954 ("less than 200 wiretaps").

7. Don Whitehead, *The FBI Story* (New York, 1956), 272–74; F. L. Collins, *The FBI in Peace and War* (New York, 1962); Frederick Ayer, Jr., *Yankee G-Man* (Chicago, 1957), 11–12, 22–24, 26–27, 50, 92; *U.S. v. Coplon*, 88 F. Supp. 921 (S.D., N.Y., 1950), 185 F. 2nd 629 (2nd Circ., 1950). See the discussion in Westin, "The Wire-Tapping Problem," 169 ff. (See n. 4, above); and see "The Wiretappers," *Reporter*, Jan. 6, 1953, 9.

8. "The Wiretappers," *ibid.*, 11.

9. W. J. Mellin, "I Was a Wire-Tapper," *Saturday Evening Post*, Sept. 10, 1949.

10. See Westin, "The Wire-Tapping Problem."

11. See, for example, *The New York Times*, Feb. 18, 1955; "The Wiretappers," *Reporter*, Dec. 23, 1952, and Jan. 6, 1953.

12. See, for example, Bernard Spindel, "Who Else Is Listening?" *Collier's*, June 10, 1955, 26.

13. See the survey by Guy Richards, "Is Your Telephone Tapped?" New York *Star*, Sept. 27–30, 1948, based on interviews with 18 former FBI agents of ten- to twenty-year service.

14. Such FBI eavesdropping on lawyer-client conversations was disclosed in court in the *Coplon* case, *U.S. v. Coplon*, 191 F. 2nd 749 (D.C. Circ., 1951). Similar conduct was said to have taken place in the Alger Hiss and William Remington cases also. See F. J. Cook, *The FBI Nobody Knows* (Pyramid ed., New York, 1964), 304, 327–29.

15. See Westin, "The Wiretapping Problem," 165–208, and esp. 172–73, for discussion of *Olmstead v. U.S.* (277 U.S. 438, 1928).

16. *Goldman v. U.S.*, 316 U.S. 129 (1942).

17. See Westin, *op. cit.*, 172–74; and 40 Stat. 1017 (1918).

18. 47 Stat. 1381 (1933); and see 56 *Congressional Record*, 10761 (1918).

19. See Westin, *op. cit.*, 174, and see 78 *Congressional Record*, 8822–37, 8842–54, 10304–33, 10968–94, and esp. 10313 (1934).

20. Westin, *op. cit.*, 174; and see hearings pursuant to S. Res. 266, 75th Cong., 1st Sess., 1585–88 (1937).

21. See *Nardone v. U.S.*, 302 U.S. 379 (1937), and *Nardone v. U.S.*, 308 U.S. 338 (1939).

22. Westin, *op. cit.*, 178–81.

23. See *Hearings Before and Report of Subcommittee of the Senate Committee on Interstate Commerce, Pursuant to Sen. Res. 224*, 96th Cong., 3rd Sess. (1940).

24. See 86 *Congressional Record*, Appendix, 1471 (1940), statement of Attorney General Jackson.

25. See H.J. Res. 41, 78th Cong., 1st Sess. (1943); H.J. Res. 304, 283, 273, H.R. Nos. 2079, 2048, 77th Cong., 2nd Sess. (1942); for conflicting views on President Roosevelt's supposed authorization of war-time wire-tapping, see Note, 2 *Stanford Law Review*, 744, 750, n. 42 (1950), and Halfeld, "Justice Department Policies on Wire-Tapping," 9 *Law Guild Review*, 60, n. 34 (1949).

26. Westin, *op. cit.*, 181.

27. *Ibid.*, 169–71, and *U.S. v. Coplon*, 91 F. Supp. 867 (DDC), *rev'd.*, 191 F. 2nd 749 (D.C. Cir. 1951), *cert. denied*, 342 U.S. 926 (1952); *U.S. v. Coplon*, 88 F. Supp. 921 (S.D., N.Y.), *rev'd.*, 185 F. 2nd 629 (2nd Circ., 1950), *cert. denied* 342 U.S. 920 (1952).

28. Westin, *op. cit.*, 189–92.

29. See Sen. Report No. 2700, 81st Cong., 2nd Sess. (1950), and Westin, *op. cit.*, 181.

30. For a list of the 38 states, with their statutes cited, see Westin, *op. cit.*, 181–82.

31. Del. Rev. Code 5232 (1935); N.J. Stat. Ann. Sect. 2:171–1 (1939).

32. For an excellent analysis of the inadequacy of state laws (to 1947), see Rosenzweig, "The Law of Wiretapping," 33 *Cornell Law Quarterly*, 73 (1947).

33. See *People v. Trieber*, 28 Cal. 2nd 657, 171 P. 2nd 1 (1946), and *Commonwealth v. Publicover*, 98 N.E. 2nd 633 (Mass., 1951).

34. *Wolf v. Colorado*, 338 U.S. 25 (1949); *Schwartz v. Texas*, 344 U.S. 199 (1952).

35. *Weeks v. U.S.*, 232 U.S. 383 (1914).

36. *Irvine v. Calif.*, 347 U.S. 128 (1954).

37. *The New York Times*, Feb. 18, 1955; and Dash, *op. cit.*, 83 ff.

38. Ed Reid and Ovid Demaris, *The Green Felt Jungle* (Pocket Books ed., New York, 1964), 102 ff.

39. See *The Reporter*, Dec. 23, 1952; Jan. 6, 1953.

40. See 83rd Cong., 1st Sess. (1953), H.R. 408 by Rep. Celler; H.R. 477 by Rep. Keating; H.R. 3552 by Rep. Walter; H.R. 5149 by Rep. Reed; and A. F. Westin, "A New Law for Wiretappers," *The New Leader*, March 29, 1954, 3; see also *Hearings on H.R. 8644 Before Subcommittee No. 3 of the House Committee on the Judiciary*, 83rd Cong., 1st Sess., May 4 and 20, July 8, 1952.

41. *Hearings on H.R. 8644 . . . (op. cit.)*; see also Report No. 1461, House Committee on the Judiciary, April 1, 1954.

42. See A. F. Westin, "Wire-Tap: The House Approves." *New Republic*, April 19, 1954, 6; see also Report No. 1461 (*op. cit.*), 1–2, 5–6.

43. Westin, "Wire-Tap: The House Approves," 6.

44. *Ibid.*, 7.

45. Among the papers endorsing court-order tapping for national security cases (often with obvious reluctance at the necessity), were the Portland *Oregonian*, April 10 and May 20, 1954; Chicago *Tribune*, April 10, 1954; Dallas *Morning News*, May 18, 1954; *Christian Science Monitor*, April 9 and May 24, 1954; New York *Herald Tribune*, April 10, 1954; Washington *Post*, April 8, 10, 11, 24, and May 18, 1954; Richmond *Times-Dispatch*, April 10, 1954; Boston *Herald*, April 3, 1954; *The New York Times*, April 8, 1954; San Francisco *Chronicle*, March 24, 1955; *Wall Street Journal*, Jan. 19 and Feb. 25, 1955; Chicago *Sun-Times*, April 13, 1954.

46. For an account of these developments, see Westin, "Wiretapping: The Silent Revolution," 29 *Commentary*, April, 1960, 333–40.

47. *Commonwealth v. Chaitt*, 176 Pa. Super., 318 (1954).

48. Pennsylvania House Bill 248 (1955).

49. *Legislative Journal* of Pennsylvania House, June 1, 1955, 1756, letter to the editor of *The New York Times*, Jan. 17, 1955.

50. *Legislative Journal* of Pennsylvania House, 1756–58 (1955).

51. See Dash, *op. cit.*, 239–40, 248, 249.

52. See Philadelphia *Evening Bulletin*, July 25, 1956; see Dash, *op. cit.*, 249, and *Civil Liberties Record*, Oct., 1956, and Nov., 1956, published by the Greater Philadelphia Branch, ACLU; Philadelphia *Evening Bulletin*, July 26, 1956; T. A. McDermott, "I Smashed Philadelphia's Pornography-Prostitution Ring," *True Police Cases*, Feb., 1957, 8; F. J. Lederer, "Exclusive Inside Story of Philadelphia Vice Investigation," *Official Detective Stories*, Feb., 1957, 10.

53. *Legal Intelligences*, Jan. 30, 1957, and Pa. Sen. Bill 97 (1957); Philadelphia *Inquirer*, June 21, 1957; Feb. 27, 1957; and see, for example, John Lofton, "Stop the Listening Toms," ACLU, Pittsburgh Chapter; *Legislative Journal* of Pennsylvania House, June 1, 1955, 1751.

54. Personal interviews by the author.

55. Pa. Act. No. 411, July 16, 1957.

56. *The New York Times*, April 13, 1949; Sect. 552-a, N.Y. Penal Law (April, 1949).

57. A. F. Westin, "The Wire-Tapping Problem," 166–68.

58. Dash, *op. cit.*, 54–56.

59. *People v. Applebaum*, 301 N.Y. 738 (1950).

60. *The New York Times*, Feb. 18 and March 3, 1955.

61. *The New York Times*, Jan. 7, 1955; see also report of A. S. Wechsler, Director

of Licenses, Aug. 7, 1956, 2; and see letter to author from B. J. Nova, Executive Director, Secretary of State (N.Y.), Aug. 9, 1957.

62. See Dash, *op. cit.*, p. 41.
63. Dash, *op. cit.*, 118–19.
64. See *The New York Times*, Feb. 23, 1955.
65. *Ibid.*, April 22, 1956.
66. See the *Interim Report of Joint Legislative Committee to Study Illegal Interception of Communications*, State of New York, Jan. 16, 1957; see *The New York Times*, March 19, 1957.
67. *The New York Times*, April 15, 1958; Nov. 11 and Dec. 24, 1958.
68. See Assembly Bill No. 930 (1957).
69. See Dash, *op. cit.*, 175–80; see also *People v. Tarrantino*, 45 Calif. 2nd 590, 593 (1955); and *Report of the Calif. Sen. Judiciary Committee on the Interception of Messages . . .* , Regular Sess., 12 (1957).
70. Calif. Ann. Codes, Penal Code 653(h) (West, 1956).
71. *Wirin v. Parker*, 48 Calif. 2nd 890 (1957).
72. *Irvine v. State of Calif.*, 347 U.S. 128 (1954), 130–32; see A. F. Westin, "Bookies and Bugs in California," in Westin (ed.), *The Uses of Power* (New York, 1962), 138, 146–47; 338 U.S. 25 (1949).
73. See San Francisco *Chronicle*, Sept. 5, 1954; Opinion No. 54–41, from Office of the Attorney General, State of California, Sept. 4, 1954.
74. *People v. Cahan*, 44 Calif. 2nd 434 (1955).
75. San Francisco *Chronicle*, Jan. 12, 1955.
76. See *Report of the Calif. Sen. Judiciary Committee*, 13 (1957) (n. 69, above); also, Westin, "Bookies and Bugs in California," 155.
77. See San Francisco *Chronicle*, April 25, 1957; *Report of the Calif. Sen. Judiciary Committee*, 28–29 (1957).
78. See Dash, *op. cit.*, 200.
79. See *Wirin v. Parker*, 48 Calif. 2nd 890 (1957).
80. New York *Journal American*, Feb. 13, 1959.
81. Minneapolis *Tribune*, Jan. 20, 1961; Baltimore *Sun*, March 15, 1959.
82. 355 U.S. 96 (1957).
83. See, for example, *The New York Times*, Jan. 3 and 4, 1958.
84. *Pugach v. Dollinger*, 277 F. 2nd 739 (1964).
85. *The New York Times*, Nov. 15, 1961.
86. *Ibid.*, April 15 and 16, 1960; Nov. 16, 1961; Feb. 22 and 23, 1962.
87. *Ibid.*, May 18, 1962.
88. *Pugach v. Dollinger*, 363 U.S. 836 (1960).
89. *Mapp v. Ohio*, 367 U.S. 643 (1960); *Lopez v. U.S.*, 373 U.S. 427 (1963).
90. *Silverman v. U.S.*, 365 U.S. 505 (1961).
91. H.R. Report No. 1215, 87th Cong., 1st Sess. (1961); H.R. Report No. 1898, 87th Cong., 2nd Sess. (1962).
92. "*Wire-Tapping: The Attorney General's Program, 1962*": *Hearings Before the Sen. Judiciary Committee*, 87th Cong., 2nd Sess. (1962). See also "Robert Kennedy Defines the Menace," *The New York Times Magazine*, Oct. 13, 1963.
93. A survey by this author of 70 newspapers in 1958–61 and over 100 between 1961 and 1963 showed that the great majority favored federal legislation to outlaw private taps and bugs, to provide for a court-order system for federal tapping and bugging in national-security and threat-to-life cases, and to allow states to authorize limited tapping and eavesdropping by law-enforcement officials if state court-order controls were enacted.
94. New York *Herald Tribune*, April 5, 1964; *Wall Street Journal*, April 9 and 14, 1963; Chicago *Sun-Times*, June 18 and 20, 1963; other clippings on file at the Association of the Bar of the City of New York.
95. Miami *Herald*, May 19, 1963; *Business Week*, Oct. 31, 1964; Detroit *Free Press*, Sect. B, May 5, 1963.
96. Detroit *News*, March 28, 1965; San Antonio *News*, Feb. 1, 1965; Hollywood (Calif.) *Citizen-News*, Sept. 28, 1965; Chicago *Sun-Times*, June 18–20, 1963.

97. Margaret Mead, "The Human Study of Human Beings," 133 *Science*, 163 (1961); Edward Shils, "Social Inquiry and the Autonomy of the Individual," in Daniel Lerner (ed.), *The Human Meaning of the Social Sciences* (New York, 1959), 114–57.

98. "Questionnaire Relating to Invasions of Privacy," *By the Subcommittee on Administrative Practice and Procedure of the Committee on the Judiciary,* U.S. Senate, 88th Cong., 2nd Sess., 1964.

99. "Invasions of Privacy (Government Agencies)," *Hearings Before the Subcommittee on Administrative Practice and Procedure of the Committee on the Judiciary,* U.S. Senate, 89th Cong., 1st Sess., 1965, Part 1.

100. *Ibid.*, Parts 3 and 4.

101. *Ibid.*, Part 2.

102. *Idem.*

103. *The New York Times*, July 3, July 24, 1966; Alan Barth, "Lawless Lawmen," *New Republic*, July 30, 1966.

104. *The New York Times*, Nov. 28, 1966. Copies of other editorials are in the files of the Special Committee on Science and Law.

105. "Invasions of Privacy," *op. cit.*, Part 5.

106. *Idem.*

107. Copies in the files of the Special Committee on Science and Law.

108. See, for example, *Congressional Record*, July 26, 1965, Temp. Ed. 17591; Feb. 7, 1966, Temp. Ed. 2131.

109. Copies of the editorials are in the files of the Special Committee on Science and Law.

110. *Idem.*

111. *Idem.*

112. *Idem.*

113. William F. Buckley, Jr., "What We Need Is a Law," *National Review*, June 1, 1965, 455.

114. Personal interviews.

115. Personal interview with an official of *Life* Magazine.

116. Copies in the files of the Special Committee on Science and Law.

117. *The New York Times*, July 16, 1965; and personal interview by member of Special Committee on Science and Law.

118. *The New York Times*, Aug. 29, 1965; May 29, 1966.

119. FCC Docket No. 15262, 31 *Red. Reg.* 339 (1966).

120. See catalogues of Dee Co., Houston, Tex.; Tracer, Newport Beach, Calif.

121. Decision No. 69447, Public Utilities Commission, State of California, July 27, 1965, reprinted in *Congressional Record*, U.S. Sen., Aug. 26, 1965, 21193–96.

122. Appendix to Long Committee hearings, 342–43 (see Bibliog. III, "Invasions of Privacy [Government Agencies]").

123. Chicago *Daily News*, Jan. 21, 1966.

124. Hartford *Courant*, Aug. 2, 1965.

125. *People v. Alfinito*, 16 N.Y.S. 2nd 181 (1965). The burden of proof in such proceedings is said to be on the defendant.

126. *People v. Gold*, 46 Misc. 2nd 495 (1965); *People v. McCall*, 17 N.Y. 2nd 152, 216 N.E. 2nd 570 (1966); see also *People v. Cohen*, 24 App. Div. 2nd 900 (1965). For the impact of these rulings on local New York trials, see "Wiretap World Opens a Little," Long Island (N.Y.) *Press*, May 27, 1966.

127. *People v. Grossman*, 257 N.Y.S. 2nd 266 (1965).

128. *People v. Kurth*, 216 N.E. 2nd 154 (1966).

129. Los Angeles *Metropolitan News*, Oct. 27, 1965.

130. *State v. Cory*, 62 Wash. 2nd 371 (1963).

131. See Chicago *American*, July 29, 1965; Chicago *Sun Times*, July 30, 1965.

132. Chicago *Sun-Times*, Aug. 12, 1966.

133. *The New York Times*, Feb. 24, 1966.

134. *Salvador Pardo-Bolland v. U.S.*, 348 F. 2nd 316 (1965).

135. For the Illinois episode, see Chicago *Tribune*, Feb. 6, March 20 and 24, July

7, 1965; Chicago *Sun-Times*, Feb. 15, March 25, June 24 and 29, 1965; Chicago *Daily News*, Feb. 5, March 20 and 25, 1965; on Minnesota see Minneapolis *Star*, Feb. 16, March 5 and 6, April 20 and 22, May 12, 1965.

136. Chicago *Tribune*, March 24, 1965; Chicago *Daily News*, Feb. 1 and 9, March 26, 1965; Chicago *Sun-Times*, Feb. 15, 1965; Minneapolis *Star*, May 12, 1965.

137. De Kalb (Ill.) *Chronicle*, June 29, 1965.

138. Miami *Herald*, Feb. 23, 1966; Providence (R.I.) *Bulletin*, Dec. 7, 1964; Gallup (N.M.) *Independent*, Dec. 11, 1964; *Congressional Record*, 89th Cong., 2nd Sess., 3701–702.

139. Md. Ann. Code, Art. 27, Sect. 125D (1965); Baltimore *Sun*, July 31, 1965.

140. Albany (N.Y.) *Times-Union*, July 11, 1965.

141. Philadelphia *Bulletin*, Sept. 10, 1965.

142. Hollywood (Calif.) *Citizen News*, Nov. 19, 1964; Santa Monica (Calif.) *Outlook*, May 7, 1965; Cleveland *Plain Dealer*, March 7 and 31, 1965; Houston *Chronicle*, March 24, 1965; Huntington Beach (Calif.) *Pilot*, March 26, 1964; Tampa *Times*, Aug. 26, 1965; National City (Calif.) *Star News*, July 18, 1965.

143. Springfield (Mass.) *Union*, Sept. 15, 1965.

144. Los Angeles *Herald-Examiner*, Oct. 21, 1965; Cleveland *Plain Dealer*, Aug. 18, 1965; Birmingham *News*, Aug. 21, 1965.

145. Los Angeles *Times*, Feb. 3, 1966; Austin (Tex.) *American*, Oct. 15, 1965.

146. Rockford (Ill.) *Register-Republican*, June 22 and 23, 1965.

147. Fresno (Calif.) *Valley Labor Citizen*, July 23, 1965.

148. National City (Calif.) *Star News*, July 18, 1965.

149. Washington *Post-Times-Herald*, Jan. 7, 1965. The suit was upheld by the New Hampshire Supreme Court against the landlord's defense that the state did not recognize the common law right of privacy and that the tenants had not alleged that anyone overheard their conversations. *Hamberger v. Eastman*, 206 A. 2nd 239 (1964).

150. Statement of Attorney General Nicholas deB. Katzenbach to the Subcommittee on Criminal Laws and Procedures of the Senate Committee on the Judiciary, March 22, 1966, 7–9 (mimeographed).

151. *The New York Times*, Jan. 11, 1967.

152. See S. 928, introduced by Senator Long of Missouri, *Congressional Record*, 90th Cong., 1st Sess., 1967.

153. *The New York Times*, Jan. 13 and 15, 1967.

154. The poll, conducted by the Mutual Broadcasting Company, is reported in the Appendix to the *Congressional Record*, August 22, 1966, A4417–4418.

155. See, for example, the American Institute of Public Opinion poll #452K dated January, 1950. Of 1548 persons asked, 729 approved the use of wiretap evidence in a court trial, 543 disapproved, 216 had no opinion and 60 did not answer.

156. Edward V. Long, *The Intruders* (New York, 1967), 211–230.

157. Dash, *The Eavesdroppers, op. cit.*

158. G. Robert Blakey, "Aspects of the Evidence Gathering Process in Organized-Crime Cases: A Preliminary Analysis," Unpublished paper submitted to the President's Commission on Law Enforcement and Administration of Justice, Oct., 1966, 48–57.

CHAPTER NINE

1. See F. E. Inbau and J. E. Reid, *Lie Detection and Criminal Interrogation* (3rd. ed., Baltimore, 1953), 111.

2. Burke M. Smith, "The Polygraph," 216 *Scientific American* (Jan., 1967), 25; J. W. Kubis, "Studies in Lie Detection," Report No. RADC-TR 62–205 (1962), United States Air Force. For a reply by polygraph advocates, see John E. Reid and Fred E. Inbau, *Truth and Deception: The Polygraph ("Lie De-*

tector") *Technique* (Baltimore, 1966), 255–57, 264–76.

3. See "Use of Polygraphs as 'Lie Detectors' by the Federal Government," *Hearings Before a Subcommittee of the House Committee on Government Operations*, 88th Cong., 2nd Sess. (1964), Part 1.

4. See, for example, D. G. Ellson *et al.*, *A Report of Research on Detection of Deception*, distributed by the Department of Psychology, Indiana University, 1952.

5. See Kubis, *op. cit.*

6. See Washington *Post*, April 29, 1963.

7. *Christian Science Monitor*, June 3, 1954, and *Reporter*, June 8, 1954, 13.

8. See statement by F. E. Inbau, in "Use of Polygraphs as 'Lie Detectors' by the Federal Government," Moss Committee Hearings, pt. 1, 8.

9. See statement by George Lindberg, *ibid.*, 43.

10. See New Orleans *Picayune*, Aug. 18, 1963.

11. See statement by John Larson, in J. M. Skolnick, "Scientific Theory and Scientific Evidence: An Analysis of Lie-Detection," 70 *Yale Law Journal*, April, 1961, 715, n. 77.

12. For decisions after 1960 see *Aetna Insurance Co. v. Barnett Bros.*, 289 F. 2nd 30 (8th Circ., 1961); *State v. Arnivine*, 67 N.J. Supp. 483, 171 A. 2nd 124 (1961); *U.S. ex rel Sadowy v. Fay*, 189 F. Supp. 150 (S.D., N.Y., 1960), aff'd. 284 F. 2nd 426 (2nd Circ., 1960), *cert. denied* 365 U.S. 850 (1961); *State v. Mottram*, 158 Me. 325, 184 A. 2nd 225 (1962); *State v. Driver*, 38 N.J. 255, 183 A. 2nd 655 (1962); *State v. Chang*, 374 P. 2nd 5 (Haw. 1962); *People v. Boney*, 28 Ill. 2nd 505, 192 N.E. 2nd 920 (1963); *Commonwealth v. Fatalo*, 191 N.E. 2nd 479 (Mass., 1963); *Sheppard v. Maxwell*, 231 F. Supp. 37 (S.D., Ohio, 1964), *rev'd. on grounds*, 346 F. 2nd 707 (6th Circ., 1965); *State v. Sneed*, 98 Ariz. 264, 403 P. 2nd 816 (1965); *McCroskey v. U.S.*, 399 F. 2nd 895 (8th Circ., 1965). Nor are results of a polygraph examination admissible before a grand jury, *People v. Dobler*, 29 Misc., 2nd 481, 215 N.Y.S. 2nd 313 (1961).

13. *Massachusetts v. Fatalo*, 191 N.E. 2nd 479 (1963).

14. For example, *U.S. v. Stromberg*, 179 F. Supp. 278 (S.D., N.Y., 1959); *State v. Lowry*, 163 Kan. 622, 185 P. 2nd 147 (1947).

15. 91 Ariz. 274, 371 P. 2nd 894 (1962).

16. *Conley v. Commonwealth*, 382 SW 2nd 865 (Ky., 1964); *State v. Trimble*, 68 N.M. 406, 362 P. 2nd 788 (1961); *Stone v. Earp*, 331 Mich. 606, 50 P. 2nd 788 (1951). See also *State v. La Forest*, 207 A. 2nd 429 (N.H., 1965), where the question was left open.

17. See *McCain v. Sheridan*, 160 Cal. App. 2nd 174, 324 P. 2nd 293 (Dist. Ct. of Appeal, 1958).

18. See NLRB General Counsel Administrative Rulings Nos. SR-57 and SR-211 (1959), 44 *Labor Relations Reference Manual*, 1359, 45 *Labor Relations Reference Manual*, 1074.

19. St. Louis *Post-Dispatch*, May 19, 1962.

20. For a full review, see Inbau and Reid, *op. cit.*, 259–62 and references cited therein.

21. Lag Drug Co., Inc., and Local No. 743, Warehouse & Mail Order Employees Union, International Brotherhood of Teamsters, Dec. 20, 1962, 11 ALAA Sect. 71,879.

22. General American Transportation Corporation, 31 LA 355.

23. For treatment of about three dozen relevant cases through 1962, see L. M. Burkey, "Lie Detectors in Industrial Relations," 1 *Continuing Legal Education* (Illinois), No. 2, April, 1963, 107–18.

24. See *Wall Street Journal*, April 8, 1965.

25. *Newsweek*, April 29, 1963, 82–83.

26. R. A. Sternbach, L. A. Gustafson, and R. L. Colier, "Don't Trust the Lie Detector," 40 *Harvard Business Review*, No. 6, 133.

27. See Los Angeles *Times*, April 7, 1963.

28. See AFL-CIO publications numbered "DLR 10–29–64 No. 212: A-4" and "DLR 180 (1964): A-6," and printed in *American Federationist*, Nov., 1964, No. 212: A-5.
29. *The New York Times*, Feb. 26, 1965.
30. *Ibid.*
31. See *Wall Street Journal*, April 8, 1965.
32. See "The Attack on Invasion of Employees' Privacy," *Industrial Relations News*, April, 1965, 3.
33. George Meany, 17 *Virginia Law Weekly*, DICTA, No. 24, May 6, 1965, 1–2.
34. *Ibid.*; *Wall Street Journal*, April 8, 1965. For other union activity, see Salisbury (Md.) *Times*, May 4, 1964; letter to the author from Jacob Sheinkman, General Counsel, ACW, Dec. 11, 1963; David Sutor, "The Gray Flannel Couch—The Lie Detector in Business," *U.S. Catholic*, July, 1964, 11; and statement printed in Moss Hearings, pt. 4, 508–509.
35. Mimeographed reprint of the discussion, Sept., 1963 (Chicago), 15; for a different union position, see p. 46.
36. See Mass. General Laws Annotated, 149; General Provisions as to Employment, Sect. 19B.
37. Cincinnati *Enquirer*, June 5, 1964; *Industrial Relations News*, Feb. 6, 1965, 3; and I.R.N. Special Report, April, 1965, 3.
38. See *Christian Science Monitor*, June 4, 1963; Nov. 6–7, 1963.
39. For greater detail on the legislative history of this statute see *Oregon Labor Press*, March 29, April 5, 12, and 19, May 3 and 17, and June 21, 1963; see also the letter in the files of the Moss Committee from E. J. Whelan to W. E. Barnaby, May 21, 1963, discussing the purpose of the measure.
40. See Los Angeles *Times*, April 7, 1963.
41. See *ibid.*, and May 28, 1963.
42. See New Orleans *Picayune*, Aug. 18 and 20, 1963.
43. See Smith-Hurd, Ill. Statues, Annotated, Title 38, Sect. 951 *et seq.*; Session Laws of Ky., 1963, Ch. 78 (S.B. 63); and Session Laws of N.M., Regular Sess., Ch. 225, Laws, 1963, No. 341.
44. See *The New York Times*, March 15, 1961, for Sen. Laverne's remarks citing the Rochester case as an example of the ineffectuality of lie-detector tests.
45. *Ibid.*; also, March 15, 1961.
46. See St. Louis *Post-Dispatch*, Sept. 11, 1962.
47. See *The New York Times*, May 26, 1963.
48. *Ibid.*, April 4 and 5, 1963.
49. See New York *Daily News*, May 30, 1963.
50. *Ibid.*
51. The above points were developed in some detail in a letter from O. M. Ruebhausen to the author, May 5, 1964.
52. S.I. 1189, A.I. 1969; and letter from R. R. Corbett, President of New York State AFL-CIO to E. J. Bloustein, Jan. 29, 1964.
53. See *The Record*, 322–23.
54. See Ill. Rev. Stat. Ch. 110, and 54.I.
55. See "Unions Act on Threats to Privacy," *Business Week*, March 13, 1965, 87–88.
56. The other states are Alaska, California, Hawaii, Massachusetts, Oregon, Rhode Island, and Washington.
57. See Commerce Clearing House Corporation Service memo.
58. See the Indianapolis *Leader*, Oct. 8, 1965, and *Business Week*, March 13, 1965, 87.
59. See Drew Pearson's column in the Washington *Post*, March 1, 1952.
60. See *The New York Times*, Jan. 18, 1952.
61. *Ibid.*, July 2, 1954.
62. See reference in Dwight Macdonald, "The Lie Detector Era," *Reporter*, June 8, 1954, 18.
63. *Ibid.*
64. See Moss Committee, Tenth Report, March 22, 1965, 3.

65. *Ibid.*, 4.
66. *Ibid.*, 3.
67. *Ibid.*, 4–5.
68. See *The New York Times*, April 4, 1963.
69. *National Observer*, April 29, 1963.
70. See *The New York Times*, April 4, 1963.
71. *Ibid.; Saturday Evening Post*, May 4, 1963; *Reporter*, April 25, 1963, 16–20.
72. *Saturday Evening Post*, May 4, 1963.
73. See Moss Committee, Tenth Report, March, 1965, 6–7.
74. *Ibid.*, 29–32.
75. Moss Committee Hearings, pt. 3, April 29, 1964, 303.
76. See, for example, *ibid.*, pt. 2, April 10, 1964, 240.
77. See *ibid.*, pt. 5, May 25, 1964, 514–16, 544.
78. *Ibid.*
79. See Moss Committee draft report, 1966.
80. See, for example, *ibid.*, pt. 1, April 7, 1964, 42–43.
81. *Ibid.*, 7, 38, 43.
82. Moss Committee, Tenth Report, March, 1965, 1, 19–20; also 13, 15, 17, 19, 22, 25.
83. *Ibid.*, 2.
84. See *ibid.*, 45.
85. *Ibid.*, 43–44.
86. See *ibid.*, 10–12, 15–16.
87. See *"Invasion of Privacy"* Hearings of the Special Subcommittee of the House Committee on Government Operations, 1965, discussed in later sections.
88. Moss Committee, Tenth Report, March, 1965, 44.
89. *Ibid.*
90. Cleveland *Press*, June 23, 1964; South Bend (Ind.) *Tribune*, April 9, 1964; Houston *Post*, April 12, 1964; Texarkana (Ark.) *News*, April 28, 1964; Annapolis *Capital*, April 17, 1964; Charlotte (N.C.) *Observer*, April 27, 1964; Washington (D.C.) *Post-Times-Herald*, April 11, 1964; New York *Daily News*, April 8, 1964; Newark (N.J.) *News*, April 13, 1964; Des Moines *Register*, April 9, 1964; Minot (N.D.) *News*, March 3, 1964; and Beverly (Mass.) *Times*, April 15, 1964.
91. Washington (D.C.) *Daily News*, March 19, 1964.
92. See reprint of the memorandum in Moss Committee, Tenth Report, March, 1965, 36–38.
93. Department of Defense Directive No. 5210, July 13, 1965, 48.
94. See Moss Committee draft report, 1966, 3.
95. *Ibid.*, 5. The directive stated that only 18 officials were empowered to give test results to state officers.
96. *Ibid.*, 6.
97. See Moss Committee Hearings, pt. 4, 478, 496.
98. Washington (D.C.) *Daily News*, April 13, 1964.
99. See letter from A. J. Biemiller, Director, AFL-CIO Department of Legislation, to Rep. Gallagher, July 16, 1965, in Gallagher's files.
100. *The New York Times*, Dec. 14, 1965, 35.
101. Col. J. P. Ferguson, Supt. of Delaware State Police, "The Polygraph Knockers," in *The Police Chief*, May, 1962, 26–27.
102. *Law and Order*, Nov., 1964, 46.
103. *The Police Chief*, May, 1961, 41–42.
104. See 144 *Science*, April 24, 1964, 397; H. Bean, "Everybody Is Dishonest," 45 *Life*, 70; Cleve Backster, "Is the Polygraph Profession's Greatest Danger from Within?" mimeographed paper presented at University of Oklahoma, Fifth Annual Polygraph Examiners Clinic, March 9–11, 1964.
105. See Council of Polygraph Examiners, *Newsletter*, Vol. 1, No. 1, April 21, 1964, 2–3; and Vol. 1, No. 2, May 8, 1964, 1, 3.
106. See statement by consultant Norman Jaspan in *Business Week*, Feb. 27, 1960, 109.

107. James Poling, *Readers Digest*, May, 1966, 109–13; Arthur Whitman, *Saga*, March, 1966, 31–32, 63–65, 67.
108. See Lafayette Radio Electronics Catalogue, No. 640, 1964.
109. G. O. W. Mueller, "The Law Relating to Police Interrogation Privileges and Limitations," in C. R. Sowle (ed.), *Police Power and Individual Freedom* (Chicago, 1963), 141.
110. Quoted in J. P. Sisk, "Taking Man's Measure," *Commonweal*, April 15, 1960, 59.
111. Vance Packard, *The Naked Society* (New York, 1964), and Myron Brenton, *The Privacy Invaders* (New York, 1964).
112. Helen Silving, "Testing of the Unconscious in Criminal Cases," 69 *Harvard Law Review*, 683–705 (1956).

CHAPTER TEN

1. See, for example, C. S. Myers, "The Pitfalls of Mental Tests," *British Medical Journal* (1911); Roy Kelly, *Hiring of the Worker* (New York, 1919), was very critical of the claims for the utility of psychological testing made by Hugo Munsterberg, a pioneer in such testing, in *Psychology and Industrial Efficiency* (Boston, 1913).
2. See, for examples of this commentary, "Psychological Testing for Workers: Is Industry Buying a Fad?" *Business Week*, July 19, 1952, 82–86; William H. Whyte, Jr., "The Fallacies of 'Personality' Testing," *Fortune*, Sept., 1954, 117–21; F. D. Duffey, C.S.C., *Testing the Spirit* (St. Louis, 1947); W. C. Bier, S.J., "Psychological Testing of Candidates and the Theology of Vocation," 12 *Review for Religious*, 296 (1953).
3. Kitty Jones, "How 'Progressive' Is Your School?" distributed by America's Future, Inc. (1954). See also the letter distributed by the Psychological Corporation, April 22, 1954, in answer to an attack on the use of the Mooney Problem Check List by the Citizens Educational Council, a right-wing group in Tenafly, N.J.
4. For an example of one liberal complaint against too much questioning of citizens by government and social scientists, including a complaint against personality testing, and a call for "resistance," see M. S. Marshall, "Who Wants to Know?" 75 *School and Society*, 385–89 (1952).
5. "Personnel Selection Tests and Fair Employment Practices," *Test Services Bulletin*, of the Psychological Corporation, Nos. 36–40 (1948–50), 23.
6. W. H. Whyte, Jr., *The Organization Man* (Garden City, N.Y., 1956).
7. *Ibid.*, 189, 191.
8. *Ibid.*, 203.
9. *Ibid.*, 208 ff.
10. *Ibid.*, 221–22.
11. J. L. Otis, "Psychological Espionage," unpublished address, American Psychological Association, 1957.
12. S. W. Gellerman, "A Hard Look at Testing," *Personnel*, May-June, 1961, 9; see also *The New Englander*, March, 1961, 12, 36–37.
13. *The Management Review*, Jan., 1961, 46.
14. J. P. Sisk, "Taking Man's Measure," *Commonweal*, April 15, 1960, 59; see also Vance Packard, *The Pyramid Climbers* (New York, 1962), 282–85.
15. M. L. Gross, *The Brain Watchers* (New York; Signet edition, 1963).
16. John Barton, "Pseudo Psychos," *American Mercury*, Oct., 1956, 5–12.
17. Jo Hindman, "The Fight for Your Child's Mind," *American Mercury*, Nov., 1957, 7–12; Jo Hindman, "Secret *Cum* Files: A Leftist Wedge," *ibid.*, Oct., 1958, 118–26; *Secret Files for Secret Purposes*, Oct., 1958, Educational News Service, Fullerton, Calif.; reprinted 1961.
18. Jo Hindman, "The Fight for Your Child's Mind," *American Mercury*, Nov., 1957.

19. Baltimore *News-Post*, Oct. 14 and Nov. 14, 1958; Baltimore *Sun*, Oct. 15, 1958. For an episode in Arlington, Va., see Washington *Post*, April 3 and 4, 1958; *Secret Files for Secret Purposes*, 4 (see n. 17, above).

20. *Secret Files* . . . , 12, 33; *The Wanderers: A National Catholic Weekly* (St. Paul, Minn.), Feb. 19, March 5, and March 12, 1959.

21. *Congressional Record*, U.S. Senate, Aug. 13, 1958, 15923–27.

22. *The Homiletic and Pastoral Review*, Aug., 1959, 982–87; *Human Events*, Aug. 25, 1958.

23. See *The New York Times*, April 23–25, 1959.

24. Paterson *Evening News*, Nov. 18, 1959; Bergen *Evening Record*, Nov. 20 and 21, 1959; San Diego *Union*, May 7, 1959; Sacramento *Bee*, Jan. 16, 1960; *Secret Files* . . . , 20; *The Southern Conservative* (Ft. Worth, Tex.), reprinted in *Secret Files* . . . , 17–18; Gwynn Nettler, "Test Burning in Texas," *American Psychologist*, 682–83 (1959). For other episodes, see *Minority Report of the Citizens Advisory Committee on Education*, State of California, 1960; Richard Harsh, "Attacks on Personality Testing in the Schools," Los Angeles County Superintendent of Schools, Div. of Research and Guidance, 1962; *Statement Regarding Psychological Testing in the Schools*, Committee on Testing of the Calif. Association of School Psychologists and Psychometricists (1963).

25. Kent (Wash.) *News Journal*, Aug. 10, 1960; Auburn (Wash.) *Sun*, July 14, 1960; Seattle (Wash.) *Post Intelligencer*, July 7, 1960; interview with Dr. Harold Seashore, Psychological Corp., New York, June 29 and July 4, 1964; Long Island (N.Y.) *Kernel*, Feb. 23, 1961; letter from D. S. Bush to M. L. Gross, Oct. 18, 1962.

26. Tom Allen, "Snoopers in our Schools," New York *Daily News*, June 11 and 18, 1961.

27. Mina Wetzig, "Have Personality Testers Gone Too Far?" *Information*, Nov., 1961, 2–9.

28. See Long Island *Kernel*, Feb. 23, 1961, and Bush letter to Gross, Oct. 18, 1962; for the New York situation in 1962, see the article in the Long Island *Press*, March 14, 1962.

29. Described by Sen. Goldwater in his column of Dec. 27, 1963, Los Angeles *Times*.

30. Gwynn Nettler, "Test Burning in Texas," *American Psychologist*, 683 (1959).

31. M. L. Gross, *op. cit.*

32. *Ibid.*, 12 ff.

33. *Ibid.*, 78–79.

34. *Ibid.* These ideas are not collected in one place, but can be found throughout Gross's volume.

35. *Ibid.*, 239–40.

36. Washington *Star*, Nov. 16, 1962; Tampa *Tribune*, Feb. 17, 1963; Louisville *Courier-Journal*, Nov. 4, 1962; for an example of a non-privacy-oriented critique of Gross, see G. W. Thompson *et al.*, "An Empirical Evaluation of the Watchers of Brainwatchers: A Survey of Testers, Tests, and Testing Programs," 3 *Journal of School Psychology*, No. 4 (Summer, 1965), 49–57.

37. *New Republic*, Oct. 1, 1962, 17–20.

38. See *Saturday Review*, Nov. 17, 1962, 70–71; *The New York Times Book Review*, Oct. 21, 1962, 6; Louisville *Courier-Journal*, Nov. 4, 1962; *National Review*, Feb. 6, 1963; Columbus *Dispatch*, Nov. 18, 1962; *The Arizona Republic*, Oct. 21, 1962; New Haven *Register*, Nov. 4, 1962; Bulletin from *Christian Herald*, Sept. 17, 1962.

39. This is printed in *Daughters of the American Revolution Magazine*, June-July, 1963, 514–15; their resolution calling for action was inserted in the *Congressional Record*, Appendix, May 16, 1963, A3126.

40. John Ashbrook (Ohio) introduced H.R. 10508 on March 1, 1962; James Utt (Calif.) introduced H.R. 12114 on June 13, 1962; Henry Schadburg (Wisc.) introduced H.R. 12581 on June 17, 1962; and Edgar Hiestand (Calif.) introduced H.R. 12584 on Aug. 9, 1962.

41. *Congressional Record*, Oct. 10, 1962, 21836–37, 21835.
42. *Ibid.*, 21838–39, 21840–41.
43. *Newsday* (Long Island, N.Y.), March 21, April 24 and 27, May 1 and 3, 1962; Mid-Island *Times*, April 26, 1962; Seattle *Times*, Oct. 1, 1962; Tacoma *News-Tribune*, Aug. 28, Sept. 27 and 28, 1962; Waterford (Conn.) *News*, Nov. 2, 1962; Abilene (Tex.) *Reporter News*, March 18, 1963; "Testing in Boulder Valley Public Schools," a 32-page mimeographed report distributed by the Save America Constitutionally Club, Boulder, Colo., Oct. 30, 1963; Washington *Post*, Sept. 17, 1963.
44. *Advertising Age*, Nov. 26, 1962.
45. S. W. Gellerman, *Personnel*, May-June, 1963; see also, P. E. Jacobs, *The Office*, Jan., 1963.
46. R. S. Barrett, "Guide to Using Psychological Tests," *Harvard Business Review*, Sept., 1963, 138–46.
47. *Business Management*, Sept., 1962; *Chemical Week*, April 20, 1963; *Industrial Relations Newsletter*, Nov., 1962.
48. *Management Record*, Jan., 1963, 29.
49. Sen. Barry Goldwater, "Tax Supported Testing," Los Angeles *Times*, Dec. 29, 1963; letter of Goldwater to Washington *Evening Star*, Oct. 7, 1963; see also Senate Report 553, Oct. 1, 1963, on H.R. 4955, 19.
50. Telegrams to Senators and Congressmen, Oct. 15, 1963, from American Psychological Association. For the action of the New York State Psychological Association in writing to Senators Javits and Keating, see letter of A. V. Williams, Executive Director, N.Y. State Psychological Association, Aug. 31, 1964.
51. APA Telegrams, Oct. 15, 1963.
52. "Statement on Purposes, Implementation, and Proposed Amendment of Title V-A, National Defense Education Act," Office of Education, Department of Health, Education and Welfare, Nov. 4, 1963. For the HEW regulations referred to, see *U. S. Office of Education Policy Bulletin*, NDEA, Series V-A, No. 7, Aug. 9, 1961.
53. The Senate discussion of the deletion appears in the *Congressional Record*, 88th Cong., 1st Sess. (1963), 23309–10, during the debate on Dec. 13.
54. See *The New York Times*, Oct. 31, 1963.
55. Mottram Torre (ed.), *The Selection of Personnel for International Service* (New York, 1963), 81–91.
56. *High Points*, Feb., 1963, 73; for a dissenting viewpoint, see *California Teachers Association Journal*, March, 1963.
57. *Personnel and Guidance Journal*, May, 1963, 824–25.
58. See review of the Gross book by J. L. Holland, of the National Merit Scholarship Corporation, *Columbia University Teachers' College Record*, March, 1963; similar review may be found in *National Education Association Journal*, Dec., 1962.
59. See, for example, note 11, *supra*, this chapter.
60. *The New York Times Book Review*, Oct. 21, 1962, 6. For reviews in psychological journals criticizing Gross's work, but noting the serious issues involved, see 12 *Psychological Reports*, 295 (1963); *Contemporary Psychology*, June, 1963, 228–29; *American Psychologist*, Aug., 1963, 529–33. The privacy issue was not discussed directly in any of these reviews.
61. L. J. Cronbach, *Essentials of Psychological Testing* (New York, 1961), 460, 459–60.
62. *Ibid.*, 462.
63. See the "Ethical Standards of Psychologists," adopted in 1953 and printed, 18 *American Psychologist*, 56–60 (1963). For an account of the APA's development of these standards, see the testimony of Dr. A. H. Brayfield, Executive Director, APA, in temporary transcript of *Hearings on Rights of Government Employees, Psychiatric Exams, and Psychological Tests, Before the Subcommittee on Constitutional Rights of the Senate Judiciary Committee*, 89th Cong., 1st Sess., 1965, 145–46.
64. See the comments of liberal critics reported in "Testing and Discrimination,"

Wall Street Journal, April 21, 1964, and "Jobs and Psychology," *ibid.,* Feb. 9, 1965; also the review of the debate as of 1964 in J. C. Flanigan and R. E. Krug, "Testing in Management Selection: State of the Art," *Personnel Administration,* March-April, 1964, 3–39; also, "Personality Testing; An Invasion of Privacy?" 14 *Industrial Relations News,* No. 30, July 25, 1964; "The Attack on Invasion of Employees' Privacy," *ibid.,* Special Report, April, 1965. For one example of a community controversy in Westchester County, N.Y., over both "sociological" and "psychological" testing in the schools, see *The New York Times,* June 19, 1964; *The Patent Trader* (Mt. Kisco, N.Y.), Aug. 23 and 27, 1964. Groups such as the John Birch Society and the Save America Constitutionally Club, of Boulder, Colo., were active in legal protests. See Abilene (Tex.) *Reporter News,* March 18, 1963; "Testing in Boulder Valley Public Schools," mimeographed report, distributed by the Save America Constitutionally Club. See for example, also, "To Amend the Education Law, in Relation to Prohibiting Psychological Tests of Children Without Parental Consent," New York State Assembly Introductory No. 1701, by Mr. Russo, filed Jan. 8, 1964. See also "Critics of Psychological Tests—Basic Assumptions—How Good," *Psychology in the School,* Jan., 1964; see S. R. Hathaway, "MMPI; Professional Use by Professional People," 19 *American Psychologist,* 204 (1964); "Psychological Tests and Public Responsibility," (a symposium), 20 *American Psychologist,* 123 (1965); "The President's Column," 17 *News-Letter of the Division of Clinical Psychology"* (Winter, 1964).

65. See the discussions of these complaints in the testimony before the Ervin and Gallagher committees, discussed later in this chapter, pp. 259 ff.
66. Testimony of George Meagher, Gallagher Committee, 1965, temporary transcript, 147–48.
67. See the Monthly Staff Reports of the Ervin Committee for May 2, June 1, July 2, and September 3, 1966.
68. Russell Baker, "The Big Brain Invasion Goes On and On," *The New York Times,* Sept. 10, 1964.
69. James Ridgeway, "The Snoops: Private Lives and Public Service," *New Republic,* Dec. 19, 1964, 13–17; *Christian Century,* Dec. 23, 1964. See "A Communication," *New Republic,* Jan. 9, 1965, 28–30—reply of Dr. J. E. Gordon, Associate Professor of Psychology and Social Work at University of Michigan, to Ridgeway article.
70. The Illinois Commission ordered Motorola to pay the applicant $1,000, but did not order him to be hired or rule the test to be improper. Motorola said it would continue using the test because it did not regard it as in any way discriminatory as to race, and would appeal the Commission ruling to the courts (*Wall Street Journal,* Feb. 9, 1965).
71. "Mental Exams Said Firing Tool at Kelly," San Antonio (Tex.) *News,* June 11, 1965; report of the Board of Directors, San Antonio Civil Liberties Union, June 7, 1965.
72. *Occupational Hazards,* Aug., 1965, 29.
73. Joan Zola, "Adventures of a Test Taker," *National Review,* Jan. 12, 1965, 21–23.
74. See the "Monthly Staff Report to the Senate Subcommittee on Constitutional Rights," beginning Oct., 1964, and going through 1966, especially the report for Dec. 1, 1964, 2–3.
75. *Congressional Record,* March 29, 1965, 6054.
76. *Ibid.,* May 17, 1965, 10287.
77. *Ibid.,* April 28, 1965; March 29, 1964, 6054.
78. The discussion reported here appears in the *Testimony of Charles F. Luce Before the Gallagher Committee,* 288–392.
79. The Peace Corps testimony appears in Gallagher Committee, 1965, temporary transcript, 229–47.
80. Memorandum from the Peace Corps Office, Teachers College, Columbia University, to the author, Feb. 15, 1965.
81. See reprint in 21 *American Psychologist,* May, 1966, 409.

82. Newark *Star-Ledger*, Sept. 23, 1965; Miami *Herald*, Sept. 24, 1965.
83. Ervin Committee, 1965, temporary transcript, 126–81.
84. *Ibid.*, 204–31. For a defense of the MMPI by Dr. W. G. Dahlstrom, see 564–610.
85. *Ibid.*, 493–538.
86. *Ibid.*, 256–97.
87. Gallagher Committee, 151–220; Ervin Committee, 77–123; Gallagher, 138–50; Ervin, 611–42; Ervin, 358–83.
88. See ACLU Bulletin No. 2269, June 13, 1966, and the Bergen (N.J.) *Record*, May 16, 1966, A-8.
89. ACLU Bulletin No. 2269, 1.
90. ACLU Bulletin No. 2269, 2.
91. Ervin Committee, 72–76.
92. See "Monthly Staff Report to the Senate Subcommittee on Constitutional Rights," June 1, 1966, a, 3.
93. See, as samples from my clippings of editorials, Augusta (Me.) *Kennebec Journal*, June 21, 1965; Hamilton (Ohio) *Journal-News*, July 7, 1965; Pendleton (Ore.) *East Oregonian*, June 10, 1965; Circleville (Ohio) *Herald*, April 12, 1965; Norfolk *Virginian Pilot*, June 7, 1965; Houston *Post*, June 13, 1965; Washington *Star*, May 4, 1965; see also a UPI feature, "Band of Congressmen Fighting Government's Personality Tests," Nov. 16, 1965, release.
94. *Time*, June 18, 1965; *Newsweek*, June 14, 1965.
95. See, for example, Louisville (Ky.) *Labor News*, June 5, 1965; *Federal Times*, June 23, 1965.
96. See, for example, *Christian Century*, April 7, 1965.
97. J. J. Kilpatrick, "Gallagher Stymies 'Big Brother,' " Washington *Evening Star*, July 1, 1965.
98. Charles Alex, *How to Beat Personality Tests* (New York, 1966), reviewed by James Ridgeway, *New Republic*, Feb. 26, 1966, 31–32.
99. *The New York Times*, Feb. 5, 1966; Feb. 8 and 9, 1966.
100. Miami *Herald*, Dec. 11, 1965.
101. *The New York Times*, May 25, 1966.
102. Letter from J. W. Macy, Jr., to D. F. Hornig, Director, Office of Science and Technology, May 18, 1966.
103. *The New York Times*, Feb. 9, 1966; *Congressional Record*, April 5, 1966, 7365; *ibid.*, Jan. 12, 1966, 99–100.
104. Quoted in *Newsletter*, Division of Clinical Psychology of the American Psychological Association, Vol. 17 (Winter, 1964), "The President's Column," 1–4.
105. S. R. Hathaway, "MMPI: Professional Use by Professional People," 19 *American Psychologist*, 204–10 (1964).
106. The creation and work of this committee are described in R. F. Berdie, "The Ad Hoc Committee on Social Impact of Psychological Assessment," 20 *American Psychologist*, 143–46 (1965).
107. This committee's formation and work is described in "Ethical Practices in Industrial Psychology: A Review of One Committee's Deliberations," 19 *American Psychologist*, 174–82 (1964).
108. J. R. Barclay, "The Attack on Testing and Counseling: An Examination and Reappraisal," 43 *Personnel and Guidance Journal*, 6–16 (1964).
109. R. A. Katzell, "A Psychologist Examines Violations of Privacy," 17 *Virginia Law Weekly*, DICTA, No. 4 (1964).
110. 20 *American Psychologist*, 123–46 (1965); 146 *Science*, Dec., 1964, 1695–97.
111. 20 *American Psychologist*, 126 (1965).
112. *Ibid.*, 130; see also O. M. Ruebhausen and O. G. Brim, Jr., "Privacy and Behavioral Research," 21 *American Psychologist*, 423–37 (1966).
113. Samuel Messick, "Personality Measurement and the Ethics of Assessment," 20 *American Psychologist*, 136–42 (1965).
114. For another significant symposium article, see R. F. Berdie, "The Ad Hoc Committee on Social Impact of Psychological Assessment," *ibid.*, 143–46.
115. *Columbia Daily Spectator*, Nov. 19, 1965.

116. See the letter by J. W. Hamblen to 151 *Science*, March 3, 1966, 1174.
117. See M. Maruyama, *Science Digest*, Jan., 1966, 70–75.
118. *Saturday Review*, Feb. 5, 1966, 61–70.
119. See "Image Worries Psychologists," Los Angeles *Times*, Jan. 31, 1966.
120. See the press comments cited earlier in the report of the Congressional hearings, plus those cited in the Special Issue of *American Psychologist*, Nov., 1965, cited below.
121. 20 *American Psychologist*, Nov., 1965, 857–993.
122. *Ibid.*, 857.
123. The 15 firms were: Psychological Corporation; BFS Psychological Associates; Science Research Associates; The Personnel Psychology Center; The Personnel Laboratory, Inc.; Klein Institute for Aptitude Testing; Case & Co.; James N. Farr Associates; Harless & Kirkpatrick Associates; Booz, Allen & Hamilton; Dale, Elliott & Co.; The McMurray Co.; Walter V. Clarke Associates; Warner Brothers Co. The replies are in the files of the Special Committee on Science and Law.
124. "Privacy of the school" has been invoked recently in developing federal-state relations over federal aid to education and civil-rights compliance activities. For examples of refusals by several dozen cities to administer questionnaires to students on "equal educational opportunities" as requested by the U.S. Office of Education, see Bergen (N.J.) *Record*, Oct. 11, 1965.
125. Samuel Messick, "Personality Measurement and the Ethics of Assessment," 20 *American Psychologist*, Feb., 1965, summarized in 146 *Science*, 136–42 (1965).
126. See also O. G. Brim, Jr., "American Attitudes Toward Intelligence Tests," *American Psychologist*, Feb., 1965, summarized in 146 *Science*, 125–30 (1965); D. A. Goslin, "The Social Consequences of Predictive Testing in Education," paper delivered at the Conference on Moral Dilemmas of Public Schooling, University of Wisconsin, May 12–14, 1965; O. M. Ruebhausen and O. G. Brim, Jr., "Privacy and Behavioral Research," 65 *Columbia Law Review*, 1184 (1965).

CHAPTER ELEVEN

1. See *The New York Times*, Sept. 13, 1957; three other accounts of the Vicary press conference relied on here are Marya Mannes, "Ain't Nobody Here But Us Commercials," 17 *Reporter*, Oct. 17, 1957, 35–37; "Talk of the Town," *The New Yorker*, Sept. 21, 1957; and "Ads You'll Never See," *Business Week*, Sept. 21, 1957, 30–31.
2. Vicary had been in the news a few years earlier with the disclosure of his theory that the eye-blink rate of women slowed up considerably in pleasant supermarkets, demonstrating that they were shopping in a kind of hypnotic trance. Photographing the blink rate was supposed to enable merchandisers to test degrees of effectiveness in packaging the food displays.
3. See, for example: *The Wall Street Journal*, Sept. 13, 1957; *Broadcasting Telecasting*, Sept. 16, 1957; *Business Week*, Sept. 21, 1957, 30–31; *Newsweek*, Sept. 23, 1957, 70; *The Sunday Bulletin* (Phila.), Sept. 29, 1957; *The Christian Century*, Oct. 2, 1957, 1157; 71 *Scholastic Teacher*, 17 (1957); *Saturday Review*, Oct. 5, 1957, 20; *Reporter*, Oct. 17, 1957, 35–36; *Science News Letter*, Oct. 26, 1957; Fred Othman, "Eerie Business, This," Washington *Daily News*, Nov. 8, 1957; *Christian Science Monitor*, Nov. 12, 1957; New York *Daily News*, Dec. 19, 1957; "Perils of Subliminal Projection in Elections" ("Washington Scene," by George Dixon), Washington *Post and Times Herald*, Dec. 19, 1957; 3 *IUD Digest* (Winter, 1958), 136–39; *New York Times Magazine*, Jan. 12, 1958, 22, 59; *The New York Times*, Jan. 23, 1958 (editorial); *The Sunday Star* (Washington), Feb. 9, 1958, A-31; *Life*, March 31, 1958, 102–14.
4. *Newsday* (Garden City, N.Y.), referred to in *Christian Science Monitor*, Jan. 6, 1958.

5. "Talk of the Town," *The New Yorker*, Sept. 21, 1957.
6. Phyllis Battelle, " 'Invisible' Advertising," New York *Journal American*, Sept. 17, 1957.
7. "Smudging the Subconscious," 40 *Saturday Review*, Oct. 5, 1957.
8. See *Advertising Age*, Dec. 1957, and a brochure printed by PRECON, Process and Equipment Corp., 4918 Canal St., New Orleans 19, La., entitled "The Big Story of 1958: Subliminal Communication," Oct., 1958.
9. *The New York Times*, Dec. 4, 1957.
10. *Christian Science Monitor*, Feb. 17, 1958.
11. *The New York Times*, Nov. 14, 1957.
12. "Ban on Subliminal Ads, Pending FCC Probe is Urged," *Advertising Age*, Nov. 11, 1957, 1, 121.
13. See Bills H.R. 10802 (Feb. 18, 1958), 85th Cong., 2nd Sess., and H.R. 1998 (Jan. 9, 1959), 86th Cong., 1st Sess., and David Wise, "House Bill Would Ban TV Ads You Can't See," New York *Herald Tribune*, Jan. 25, 1959.
14. See Bill H.R. 11363 (March 12, 1958), 85th Cong., 2nd Sess.
15. Letter from E. William Henry, FCC Chairman, to author, July 9, 1964, 7–8.
16. See *Public Hearing Before N.J. Commission to Study Subliminal Projection, Created Under Assembly Resolution No. 33 (1958) and Reconstituted Under Assembly Concurrent Resolution No. 6 (1959)*, April 8, 1959, 10, 11, xvii.
17. *The New York Times*, March 13, 1958.
18. *Advertising Age*, Jan. 27, 1958, 107.
19. *The New York Times*, March 7, 1957.
20. *Wall Street Journal*, March 7, 1958.
21. *Advertising Age*, Dec. 16, 1957, 93.
22. Letters from T. L. Davis, General Manager, WAAF, to author, Feb. 13 and March 17, 1964.
23. W. H. Kallis, "The Phantom of the Soap Opera," *Public Relations Journal*, March, 1958, 6.
24. *Wall Street Journal*, March 7, 1958.
25. *Ibid.*
26. *Christian Science Monitor*, Jan. 6, 1958.
27. *Wall Street Journal*, March 7, 1958.
28. *Television Age*, Feb. 10, 1958, 23, cited in letter by D. H. Ocheltree to the Editor of *Christian Science Monitor*, March 6, 1958.
29. "The Big Story of 1958: Subliminal Communication," Oct., 1958, 34, PRECON, Process and Equipment Corp.
30. *Life*, March 31, 1958, 113.
31. *Christian Science Monitor*, April 25, 1958.
32. *Public Hearing before N.J. Commission to Study Subliminal Projection Created Under Assembly Resolution No. 33 (1958) and Reconstituted Under Assembly Concurrent Resolution No. 6 (1959)*, 60A–61A.
33. *Advertising Age*, July 28, 1958: *Subliminal Communication*, Institute of Practitioners in Advertising (London, 1958), 6.
34. *Advertising Age*, Sept. 15, 1958.
35. *Christian Century*, Nov. 9, 1957.
36. *The New York Times*, Aug. 10, 1958.
37. *Ibid.*, May 16, 1958.
38. Aldous Huxley, *Brave New World Revisited* (Harper Torchback ed., 1965), 63–69, quotations at 69 and 90.
39. *Wall Street Journal* and *Playboy* (Aug., 1958) cartoons are reproduced in "The Big Story of 1958: Subliminal Communication," Oct., 1958, 26–27, PRECON, Process and Equipment Corp. The *Consumer Reports* cartoon is in the issue of Jan., 1958, 9.
40. E. S. Aarons, "The Communicators," 14 *The Magazine of Fantasy and Science Fiction*, June, 1958, 52–53.
41. *Advertising Age*, Dec. 23, 1957, 3.
42. Quoted by Gay Talese, "Most Hidden Hidden Persuasion," *The New York Times Magazine*, Jan. 12, 1958, 59, 60.

43. *Advertising Age*, June 16, 1958, 85.
44. *Ibid.*, Dec. 2, 1957, 22.
45. *Christian Science Monitor*, April 25, 1958.
46. Gay Talese, "Most Hidden Hidden Persuasion," 22.
47. See letter by R. A. Fryer to Editor of *Christian Science Monitor*, Dec. 4, 1957.
48. Gay Talese, "Most Hidden Hidden Persuasion," 22.
49. Apart from that experiment, however, the BBC has never included subliminals or subaudials in their program. Letter from Kathleen Haacke (Secretariat, BBC) to Prof. E. J. Bloustein (N.Y.U. Law School), Feb. 14, 1964.
50. *Life*, March 31, 1958.
51. *Ibid.*
52. *Advertising Age*, Feb. 10, 1958.
53. *The New York Times*, Dec. 4, 1957.
54. *Christian Science Monitor*, April 7, 1959.
55. See the remarks of Dr. Livingston Welch, reported in St. Louis *Post-Dispatch*, Feb. 5, 1958.
56. See the comments of Dr. Richard P. Barthol, in *The Nation*, Nov. 15, 1958, 357.
57. St. Louis *Post-Dispatch*, April 27, 1959.
58. *The Nation*, Nov. 15, 1958, 358.
59. See, for example, the testimony of Dr. Z. A. Piotrowski, Clinical Professor of Psychology, Jefferson Medical College of Philadelphia, in *Public Hearing Before N.J. Commission to Study Subliminal Projection* . . . , Trenton, April 8, 1959, 11.
60. See *Advertising Age*, Nov. 11, 1957.
61. *The New York Times*, Jan. 15, 1958.
62. "Use of 'Subliminal Perception' Advertising by Television Stations," FCC, 52308, FCC 57-1289, Public Notice, Nov. 27, 1957.
63. Communications Act Amendments of 1960, Public Law 86–752, 86th Cong., 1st Sess., 74 Stat. 889.
64. See *Broadcast Sponsorship Identification Rules Amended*, FCC Report No. 4627, 35186 Public Notice-B, May 6, 1963; *Applicability of Sponsorship Identification Rules*, FCC 63–409, 34174 Public Notice, May 6, 1963; and *Report and Order*, FCC 63–408, 34173, Docket No. 14094.
65. Letter from E. William Henry, FCC Chairman to author, July 9, 1964, 6, 8.
66. This seems to have been the case in California. See Calif. Sen. Bill No. 1100, "An Act to add Sect. 5295 to the Business and Professional Code, relating to Subliminal Radio and Television Messages," referred to Committee on Business and Professions, March 31, 1959; Calif. Sen. Bill No. 1386, Los Angeles *Times*, April 1, May 4, June 10, and Dec. 18, 1959.
67. *Wall Street Journal*, March 7, 1958.
68. For a personal account by Vicary of his troubles, see *Advertising Age*, Sept. 17, 1962.
69. *Wall Street Journal*, March 12, 1958, and "The Big Story of 1958; Subliminal Communication," Oct., 1958, PRECON, Process and Equipment Corp.
70. The PRECON Patent is No. 3,060,795, Oct. 30, 1962. Corrigan, *et al.*, "Apparatus for producing visual stimulation." The Patent Office refused to discuss the basis of its earlier rejection of the PRECON application on the ground that once a patent is issued, the Patent Office may not deal with "matters arising out of the grant." Letter to the author from E. L. Reynolds, Acting Commissioner of Patents, Feb. 10, 1964.
71. Letters from S. M. Hassanein, President, Skouras Theatres Corp., Feb. 18, 1964; Archie Weltman, Secretary and General Counsel, Loew's Theatres, Inc., Feb. 18, 1964; Morris Goldschlager, Legal Dept., American Broadcasting-Paramount Theatres, Inc., Feb. 17, 1964.
72. Letters were received from Ted Bates and Co., Feb. 13, 1964; Batten, Barton, Durstine and Osborn, Feb. 19, 1964; Friend-Reiss Advertising, Inc., Feb. 14, 1964; Benton and Bowles, Feb. 20, 1964; Compton Advertising, Inc., Feb. 19, 1964; and Diener and Dorskind, Feb. 12, 1964.
73. Quoted in letter from A. M. Frothingham, General Counsel, Ted Bates and

Co., to the author, Feb. 13, 1964.

74. Letter from H. C. Pollack (Diener and Dorskind) to the author, Feb. 12, 1964.

75. A. W. Rose, "Motivation Research and Subliminal Advertising," 25 *Social Research* (1958), 283.

76. See R. N. Haber, "Public Attitudes Regarding Subliminal Advertising," 23 *Public Opinion Quarterly* (Summer, 1959), 291–93.

77. "Remote Control Hypnosis," *Time*, July 2, 1965, 37.

CHAPTER TWELVE

1. New York *Post*, April 16, 1961.

2. See *The New York Times*, Jan. 1, 1962, for the remarks of Dr. Hamming at 1962 meeting of American Association for the Advancement of Science (symposium), "Man and the Computer."

3. E. C. Berkeley, "The Computer and Wrongdoing," May, 1963, 7.

4. See Bergen (N.J.) *Evening Record*, March 21, 1963; Robert Gannon, "Big Brother 7074 Is Watching You," *Popular Science*, March, 1963, 86–88, 206–208.

5. *Time*, "1410 Is Watching," Aug., 1963, 53.

6. David Bergamini, "Government by Computers?" *The Reporter*, Aug. 17, 1961, 21.

7. R. N. Freed, "Your Computer . . . ," *Management Review*, 1962. For another and later article on this theme, see M. R. Wessel, "Legal Protection of Computer Programs," 43 *Harvard Business Review*, 97–106 (1965).

8. For a general account of this episode, see Charles R. Foster, "A Question on Religion," Case No. 66, Inter-University Case Program Study (1961). For specifics see *The New York Times*, Nov. 23, 1956; Dec. 13, 1957; July 8, Aug. 2 and 9, Nov. 22, Dec. 13, 1957; Aug. 2, 1957 (letter to editor from Stanley Lichtenstein). For Census Bureau responses to the privacy protests, see Foster, *op. cit.*, Appendix, II, 18–19. See the letters from Lawrence Fuchs and Paul Blanchard, *The New York Times*, Aug. 19 and Aug. 6, 1957. See Foster, *op. cit.*, 14–15, and *ibid.*, Appendix I, 17 (Population Association of America, University of Michigan Survey Research Center, Alfred Politz Organization, and assorted business groups supported the census proposal). *The New York Times*, July 19, 1957. See also, Foster, *op. cit.*, Appendix, I, 17 for data on Protestant reactions; also, *ibid.*, 10, 18, 11; also, *The New York Times*, Dec. 13, 1957, and Aug. 24, 1966; and Foster, *op. cit.*, 13–16.

9. Personal interviews.

10. David Bergamini, "Government by Computers," *The Reporter*, Aug. 17, 1961, 24.

11. *Newsweek*, July 27, 1964, 32.

12. *U.S. News and World Report*, April 11, 1966, 38.

13. *Time*, Aug. 20, 1965, 41.

14. *The New York Times*, Sept. 27, 1964. For details of the system beyond those published in the press, see "Feasibility Report and Recommendations for a New York Identification and Intelligence System," Systems Development Corporation Report, TM-LO–1000/600/00 (Nov. 1, 1963).

15. "Electronic Lawman," *The National Sheriff*, Nov.-Dec., 1963, 24.

16. Personal interview.

17. *The New York Times*, Aug. 25, 1965; Feb. 5, 1966.

18. Quoted in *"The Federal Paperwork Jungle": Hearings Before the House Subcommittee on Census and Government Statistics*, Committee on Post Office and Civil Service, 86th Cong., 1st Sess., 212 (1964)—hereafter Olsen Hearings. For statistics on "administrative and regulatory reporting" rather than that required of individuals and organizations, see 323.

19. *Ibid.*, 272. See also the similar statement by a Commerce Department witness at 278.

20. *Use of Electronic Data Processing Equipment in the Federal Government*, House

Report No. 858, Committee on Post Office and Civil Service, 88th Cong., 1st Sess., 1963; these examples are given at 17. Also note statement of Census Bureau spokesman on opportunities for collection of inter-agency data due to computerization, 342.

21. See *The New York Times*, June 20, 1964; "Independent Offices Appropriations, 1965," Hearings before the Subcommittee of the Senate Committee on Appropriations, 88th Cong., 2nd Sess, pt. 2, 1079–89 (1964).
22. *Use of Electronic Data Processing Equipment* . . . , House Report No. 858, 1963 (*op. cit.*), 22.
23. Reprinted in Olsen Hearings, 1964, 251–52.
24. *Ibid.*, 123, 139, 198, 199, 642, 640, 644.
25. See a description of these in J. L. Buckley, "Central Index File—Europe," *Law and Order*, Feb., 1964, 50–53.
26. *The Nation*, Sept. 7, 1964, 84.
27. See Olsen Hearings, 1964, 267–68, 491–92; also, "The Paperwork Jungle," speech of Rep. Arnold Olsen, Chairman, Subcommittee on Census and Government Statistics, Feb. 8, 1964, and letter from Rep. Olsen, May 13, 1964, in files of Special Committee on Science and Law.
28. *Newsweek*, Aug. 2, 1965, 58.
29. See S. H. Brooks and I. R. Whiteman, "Transportation," *Data Processing Yearbook*, 1962–63 (Detroit, 1963), 177.
30. See *The New York Times*, July 10, 1966, Sect. III, 1, 41.
31. *Ibid.*, Aug. 1, 1966.
32. *Ibid.*, July 24, 1966.
33. *Wall Street Journal*, July 13, 1964.
34. See *The New York Times*, Sect. II, May 23, 1965.
35. *Ibid.*, July 17, 1964.
36. Quoted in J. L. Buckley, "Computers, Automation, and Security," *Law and Order*, March, 1965, 58.
37. *Use of Electronic Data Processing Equipment* . . . , House Report No. 858, 1963 (*op. cit.*), 17; see also, J. L. Buckley, "The Future of Computers in Security and Law Enforcement," *Law and Order*, Pt. 1, Aug., 1965; Pt. 2, Sept., 1965.
38. T. C. Rowan, "Computer Technology and Social Change," paper delivered at the American Orthopsychiatric Association Annual Meeting, 1964.
39. See quotations in John Lear, "Whither Personal Privacy," *Saturday Review*, July 23, 1966, 36, 41.
40. *Ibid.*, 41.
41. See *Congressional Record*, May 11, 1964, 10143–45.
42. See *The New York Times*, April 15, 1966; "The Dossier Banks," *Wall Street Journal*, May 16, 1966; *U.S. News and World Report*, May 16, 1966, 56–59. See also Richard Harwood, "Is Your Name on a Secret Dossier?" *Washington Post*, May 29, 1966.
43. S. P. Wagner, "Records and the Invasions of Privacy," 40 *Social Science*, 38–45 (1965); reprinted in *Congressional Record*, May 18, 1965, 10442–45.
44. D. N. Michael, "Speculations on the Relation of the Computer to Individual Freedom and the Right of Privacy," 33 *George Washington Law Review*, 270–286 (1964).
45. *The New York Times*, June 20, 1964; see also *Time*, July 30, 1965, 59.
46. *Saturday Review*, July 23, 1966.
47. *Newsweek*, July 25, 1966.
48. Fletcher Knebel and C. W. Bailey, 2, *Convention* (New York, 1964)—see 136–37, 234.
49. Eugene Burdick, *The 480* (New York, 1964).
50. *Hearings of the Special Subcommittee on Invasion of Privacy of the House Committee on Government Operations*, 89th Cong., 1st Sess. (1965), temporary transcript, Vol. II, 6, 79–80, 69–71; Vol. V, 4, 24–25, 42–43, 50–55.
51. See Statistical Evaluation Report No. 6, Office of Statistical Standards, Bureau of the Budget, hereafter cited as Dunn Report.

52. *Ibid.*, Appendix 3, 3, 21, 16.
53. *U.S. News and World Report*, May 16, 1966, 56–58; Washington *Post*, June 13, 1966; Warren (Ohio) *Tribune-Chronicle*, May 31, 1966.
54. See *Congressional Record*, June 1, 1966, 11453–54.
55. See Long Committee, temporary transcript, 1612–50.
56. See Dunn Report, *op. cit.*, 4, 25.
57. See Long Committee, temporary transcript, 1644. Another ambiguous point creating concern appeared in Appendix C of the Dunn Report (p. 4) and involved the apparent assumption of responsibility by a national data center for utilizing all of the standards of safeguards used by each government unit contributing data, i.e., to protect that particular data from access unwarranted under the contributing bureau's own standards.
58. Long Committee, temporary transcript, 1613.
59. *Ibid.*, 1628, 1631, 1633.
60. *Ibid.*, 1636 ff.
61. *Ibid.*, 1634, for example; 1613, 1649.
62. "The Computer and Invasion of Privacy," *Hearings Before a Subcommittee of the Committee on Government Operations*, 89th Cong., 2nd Sess. (1966), 65, 96.
63. *Ibid.*, 94, 132–33, 142.
64. *Ibid.*, 76.
65. *Ibid.*, 315. This dialogue did start in 1967, partly as a result of Congressman Gallagher's suggestion. In addition to various conferences of legal, social-science, government, and computer experts held in the winter and spring of 1967, a general session on "The Computer and Privacy" was held at the American Federation of Information Processing Societies Convention on April 18.
66. "Report of the Task Force on the Storage of and Access to Government Statistics," Bureau of the Budget, Oct., 1966.
67. See the hearings on S. 3779, held on Sept. 23 and Oct. 3, 4, and 5, 1966, by the Senate Subcommittee on Constitutional Rights (to be printed in 1967).
68. Monthly Staff Report to the Senate Subcommittee on Constitutional Rights, Jan. 5, 1967.
69. See the list of sponsors printed with S. 3779, 89th Cong., 2nd Sess. (1966).

CHAPTER THIRTEEN

1. For a description of privacy in a series of leading Western societies from the Greek city-state to the American republic, see Alan F. Westin, *Privacy in Western History* (New York, 1967).
2. Michel-Guillaume de Crèvecoeur, *Letters from an American Farmer* (1782).
3. Joseph Story, *Commentaries on the Constitution of the United States*, 2 (2nd ed., 1851), 591, 597, 600.
4. Francis Lieber, *On Civil Liberty and Self Government* (1853), viii, 44–47, 71–75, 224.
5. J. Holbrook, *Ten Years Among the Mail Bags* (1855), xviii.
6. Lieber, *op. cit.*, 103–105, 224–25.
7. A. J. Beveridge, 4 *The Life of Marshall* (1919), 313–19; Note, "The Constitutional Right to Anonymity," 70 *Yale Law Journal*, 1084, 1085 (1961).
8. Story, *op. cit.*, 608.
9. *Ibid.*, 608–609.
10. Lieber, *op. cit.*, 45, 46–47, 44.
11. T. G. Cooley, *A Treatise on Constitutional Limitations* (1868); citations here are to the 4th ed. (1878), 367, 373, 378, 375, n. Cooley sharply criticized the search powers of federal agents under the revenue laws; indeed, Cooley's section on unreasonable searches resembles a draft of Bradley's later opinion in the *Boyd* case (see below).

12. For examples of these trespass actions, see *Grumon v. Raymond*, 1 Conn. 40 (1814); *Sanford v. Nichols*, 13 Mass. 286 (1816); *Reed v. Rice*, 25 Ky. (2 Marsh) 45, 19 Am. Dec. 122 (1829); *Anonymous*, 13 Am. Dec. 31 (Ala., 1821); *Halsted v. Brice*, 13 Mo. 171 (1850); *Humes v. Taber*, 1 R.I. 464 (1850). For cases applying these doctrines against private searches by creditors, see *Hobbs v. Griggs*, 13 Serg. & R. 417 (Pa., 1825); *Bell v. Clapp*, 10 Johnson 263 (N.Y., 1813); and *Robinson v. Richardson*, 79 Mass. (13 Gray) 454 (1859).

13. *Anonymous*, 13 Am. Dec. 31 (Ala., 1821); *Larthet v. Forgay*, 2 La. Ann. 524, 46 Am. Dec. 555 (1847).

14. Lieber, *op. cit.*, 76.

15. *Commonwealth v. Lovett*, 4 Clark 5 (Pa., 1831). For other eavesdropping prosecutions, see *State v. Williams*, 2 Overt. 108 (Tenn., 1808); *Commonwealth v. Mengelt*, 1818, quoted in *Commonwealth v. Lovett*, 4 Clark 5 (Pa., 1831); *State v. Pennington*, 3 Head 299 (Tenn., 1859).

16. Joseph Story, *Commentaries on Equity Jurisprudence* (2nd ed., 1839), 711. See also *Greenleaf on Evidence* (4th ed., 1848), 320.

17. Joseph Story, *Equity Jurisprudence*, 1 (1836), 223. On trademarks, also see *ibid.*, 223.

18. Benjamin Hawkins to Thomas Jefferson, in Julian Boyd (ed.), *The Papers of Thomas Jefferson*, 3 (Princeton, N.J., 1952), 69.

19. See Leonard White, *The Federalists* (New York, 1948), 80–81.

20. *Ibid.*, 81.

21. Quoted in Wigmore, *op. cit.*, VIII, 809.

22. *People v. Philips*, N.Y. Ct. Gen. Sess. 1813, abstracted in 1 West L.J. 109 (1843).

23. *Corps v. Robinson*, 2 Wash. C. C. 388 (1809); *Mills v. Griswold*, 1 Root 383 (Conn., 1792); *Calkins v. Lee*, 2 Root 363 (Conn., 1796); *Sherman v. Sherman*, 1 Root 486 (Conn., 1793), in which a doctor's testimony obtained in medical confidence was compelled in a divorce action based on adultery; N.Y. Rev. Stat. 1828, 406 (pt. 3, c. 7, Art. 9, Sect. 73); and Wigmore, *op. cit.*, 820.

24. 1 Stat, 232, 236 (1792), Sect. 16; California Penal Code, Sect. 618; and *Ex parte Jackson*, 96 U.S. 727 (1878).

25. *Dennis v. Leclerc*, 1 Mart. (O.S.) 297 (La., 1811). For a different result by a New York court, see *Hoyt v. Mackenzie*, 3 Barb. Ch. 320 (N.Y., 1848); *Folsom v. Marsh*, 2 Story 100 (C.C., 1841), Fed. Cas. No. 4, 901; Story, *Equity Jurisprudence*, 220–22.

26. Though personal rights are "sacred and inviolable," a Massachusetts court noted in 1838, and the guarantees against unreasonable search and seizure are to shield citizens from "the effects of arbitrary power," they are "not an exemption from the just operation of criminal laws." The Fourth Amendment "only guards against *unreasonable* searches and seizures" (*Banks v. Farwell*, 38 Mass. [21 Pick.] 156, 159, [1838]). See also *Commonwealth v. Dana*, 43 Mass. (2 Metc.) 329 (1841); *Stone v. Dana*, 46 Mass. (5 Metc.) 98 (1842).

27. In the 1850's many states passed liquor prohibition laws in response to the temperance movement's campaign against drink as a major cause of pauperism, crime, and immorality. Most states moved to "take the profit out of the trade" by providing for seizure and destruction of all liquor being kept for sale by other than excepted categories of persons, producing a rush of searches and seizures in the prohibition states during the 1850's and a host of challenges to the right of the officers to search and seize. Many judges adopted unusually strict standards for liquor search warrants. Such rulings threw out cases for defects in the warrant in not reciting which buildings would be searched or what classes of liquors were being sought, and declared the provisions for searches and seizures in some prohibition laws to be unconstitutional because they did not require the officers to designate the specific individuals who intended to sell the liquor the officers wanted to seize. The result was that far more liquor seizures were returned to their owners, far more complainants in liquor cases won trespass actions, and far more defendants went free than in any other class of search and seizure cases

in the 1850's. See *State v. Staples,* 37 Me. 228 (1854); *State v. Spenser,* 38 Me. 30 (1854); *Mallett v. Stevenson,* 26 Conn. 428 (1857); *Fisher v. McGirr,* 67 Mass. (1 Gray) 1, 61 Am. Dec. 381 (1854); *State v. Gurney,* 33 Me. 527 (1852); *State v. Spiritous Liquors,* 39 Me. 262 (1855); *McGlinchy v. Barrows,* 41 Me. 74 (1856); *Jones v. Fletcher,* 41 Me. 254 (1856); *Guenther v. Day,* 72 Mass. (6 Gray) 490 (1856); *Kent v. Willey,* 77 Mass. (11 Gray) 368 (1858).

28. See objections in Congress, 1 *Annals of Congress,* 1077–78, remarks of Rep. Samuel Livermore of New Hampshire, Jan. 25, 1790, and U.S. Bureau of Census, "Bureau of the Census, Fact Finder for the Nation" (Washington, D.C., 1957), 3.

29. See W. Scott and M. Jarnagin, *Treatise Upon the Law of Telegraphs* (1868), Appendix, 457–507.

30. See Samuel Dash, *The Eavesdroppers* (New York, 1959), 23.

31. The highlights of the story can be found in Thomas Cooley, "Inviolability of Telegraphic Correspondence," 18 *American Law Register* (N.S.) 65 (1879) and Henry Hitchcock, "The Inviolability of Telegrams," 5 *Southern Law Review* (N.S.) 413 (1879).

32. See *Congressional Record,* 46th Cong., 2nd Sess. (1880), 937; *Ex parte Brown,* 72 Mo. 83, 37 Am. Rep. 426 (1880); *Ex parte Jaynes,* 12 Pac. 117 (Calif. 1886); *U.S. v. Hunter* . . . , F. Rep. 712 (N. Dist., Miss., 1882).

33. See, as examples, Hofstader and Horowitz, *The Right of Privacy* (New York, 1964), 15; E. Adams, "The Right of Privacy and its Relation to the Law of Libel," 39 *American Law Review,* 37 (1905); L. Nizer, "The Right of Privacy: A Half Century's Development," 39 *Michigan Law Review,* 526 (1941); S. Warren and L. D. Brandeis, "The Right to Privacy," 4 *Harvard Law Review,* 193 (1890).

34. Warren and Brandeis, "The Right to Privacy"; for popular advertisements during the 1880's offering the latest "Kodaks" for private investigation purposes, including one "detective" camera built into a bowler hat, for secret photographs, see advertisement in *Scribner's Monthly,* for 1889 (the Hawk Eye Detective and Combination Camera) sold by the Boston Camera Company for $15 (reproduced in M. Wilson, *American Science and Invention* [1960], 270); T. K. Derry and T. I. Williams, *A Short History of Technology* (1960), 678. For an earlier prescient article on future legal problems from photography, see J. A. J. "The Legal Relations of Photographs," 8 *American Law Register* 1 (1869); *The New York Times,* Aug. 23, 1902.

35. *Wallace v. Georgia, C. & N. Ry.,* 94 Ga. 732 (1894); *Atchison, Topeka & S.F. Ry. v. Brown,* 80 Kans. 312 (1909); *St. Louis, S.W. Ry. v. Griffin,* 106 Tex. 477 (1914).

36. 277 U.S. 438 (1928).

37. See Walter Murphy, *Wiretapping on Trial* (New York, 1965).

38. David Lawrence, "The Lost Right of Privacy," 33 *American Mercury,* 12–18 (1936).

39. For an interesting case showing this lack of a general theory, see *Sibbach v. Wilson & Co.,* 312 U.S. 1 (1941).

40. *West Va. Bd. of Ed. v. Barnette,* 319 U.S. 624 (1943); *Kovacs v. Cooper,* 336 U.S. 77 (1949); *Breard v. Alexander,* 341 U.S. 622 (1951).

41. *Public Utilities Commission v. Pollak,* 343 U.S. 451 (1952).

42. *Brown v. Walker,* 161 U.S. 591 (1896).

43. *Goldman v. U.S.,* 316 U.S. 129 (1942).

44. *On Lee v. U.S.,* 343 U.S. 747 (1952).

45. *Wolf v. Colorado,* 338 U.S. (1949); *Irvine v. Calif.,* 347 U.S. 128 (1954).

46. *Cooley on Torts* (2nd ed., 1888), 29.

47. *Newell v. Whitcher,* 53 Vt. 589, 39 Ann. Rep. 703 (1880); *DeMay v. Roberts,* 46 Mich. 160, 41 Ann. Rep. 154 (1881); *Manola v. Stevens,* N.Y. Sup. Ct., described in *The New York Times,* June 14, 18, and 21, 1890. See also *Moore v. Rugg,* 44 Minn. 28, 20 Ann. St. Rep. 539 (1890).

48. *Union Pacific Ry. v. Botsford,* 141 U.S. 250 (1891).

49. E. L. Godkin, "The Rights of the Citizen—IV: To His Reputation," 8 *Scribner's*, 58 (1890).
50. S. Warren and L. D. Brandeis, "The Right to Privacy," 4 *Harvard Law Review*, 193 (1890).
51. For a good account of this development, see W. Prosser, "Privacy," 48 *Columbia Law Review*, 383 (1960).
52. For a full account of these developments, see Prosser, "Privacy," 386–89.
53. *Rhodes v. Graham*, 238 Ky. 225, 37 S.W. 2nd 46 (1931); *McDaniels v. Atlantic Coca-Cola Bottling Co.*, 60 Ga. App. 92, 2 S.E. 2nd 810 (1939).
54. *NAACP v. Alabama*, 357 U.S. 449 (1958).
55. *Bates v. Little Rock*, 361 U.S. 516 (1960); *Louisiana ex. rel. Gremillion v. NAACP*, 366 U.S. 293 (1961); *Gibson v. Fla.*, 372 U.S. 539 (1963); *NAACP v. Button*, 371 U.S. 415 (1963).
56. *Uphaus v. Wyman*, 360 U.S. 72 (1959); *Konigsberg v. State Bar of California*, 353 U.S. 252 (1961); *Communist Party v. Subversive Activities Control Board*, 367 U.S. 1 (1961); *Cohen v. Hurley*, 366 U.S. 117 (1961).
57. *Watkins v. U.S.*, 354 U.S. 178 (1957).
58. *Sweezy v. New Hampshire*, 354 U.S. 234 (1957), 265.
59. *Talley v. California*, 362 U.S. 60 (1960).
60. *Union Pacific Ry. v. Botsford*, 141 U.S. 250 (1891); *Rochin v. California*, 342 U.S. 165 (1951); *Breithaupt v. Abram*, 352 U.S. 432 (1957); *Schlagenhauf v. Holder*, 379 U.S. 104 (1964).
61. *Coplon v. U.S.*, 191 F. 2nd 749; *Caldwell v. U.S.*, 205 F. 2nd 879; *Massiah v. U.S.*, 377 U.S. 201 (1964).
62. For example, *Escobedo v. Ill.*, 378 U.S. 478 (1963), and *Miranda v. Arizona*, 86 S.C. 1602 (1966).
63. *Schmerber v. California*, 86 S.C. 1826 (1966).
64. *Griswold v. Connecticut*, 381 U.S. 479 (1965).
65. See *Heart of Atlantic Motel, Inc. v. U.S.*, 379 U.S. 241 (1964); *Katzenbach v. McClung*, 379 U.S. 294 (1964).
66. See, for example, *Hamm v. City of Rock Hill* (No. 2) and *Lupper et al. v. Arkansas* (No. 5), 13 L. Ed. 2nd 300 (1964).
67. *Silverman v. U.S.*, 365 U.S., 505 (1961); *Clinton v. Virginia*, 377 U.S. 158 (1964).
68. *Wong Sun v. United States*, 371 U.S. 471, 485–86 (1963); *Silverman v. United States*, 365 U.S. 505 (1961).
69. *Lopez v. U.S.*, 373 U.S. 427 (1963).
70. *On Lee v. U.S.*, 343 U.S. 747 (1952).
71. 359 U.S. 360 (1959).
72. *Marcus v. Property Search Warrant*, 367 U.S. 717 (1961).
73. *The New York Times*, April 28, 1965.
74. *Mapp v. Ohio*, 367 U.S. 643 (1961); *Monroe v. Pape*, 365 U.S. 167 (1961).
75. *United States v. Ventresca*, 380 U.S. 102 (1965); *Stanford v. Texas*, 379 U.S. 476 (1965); *Aguilar v. Texas*, 378 U.S. 108 (1964); *Jones v. United States*, 362 U.S. 257 (1960).
76. *People v. McCall*, 17 N.Y. 2nd 152, 216 N.E. 2nd 570 (1966).
77. *Roach v. Harper*, 143 W. Va. 869, 105 S.E. 2nd 564 (1958); *Le Crone v. Ohio Bell Telephone Co.*, 120 Ohio App. 129; 201 N.E. 2nd 533 (1963); *Hamberger v. Eastman*, 206 A. 2nd (N.H.) 239 (1964).
78. Clippings in files of Special Committee on Science and Law.
79. *Roach v. Harper*, 143 W. Va. 869, 105 S.E. 2nd 564 (1958).
80. *Hamberger v. Eastman*, 206 A. 2nd (N.H.) 239 (1964).
81. *Le Crone v. Ohio Bell Telephone Co.*, 120 Ohio App. 129, 201 N.E. 2nd 533 (1963). For an earlier ruling in this case, see *Le Crone v. Ohio Bell Telephone Co.*, 114 Ohio App. 299, 182 N.E. 2nd 15 (1961).

CHAPTER FOURTEEN

1. Kyler, "Camera Surveillance of Sex Deviates," *Law and Order*, Nov., 1963, 16; *Time*, Nov. 12, 1965, 59–61.
2. *The New York Times*, Feb. 5, 1964.
3. Samuel Dash, *The Eavesdroppers* (New York, 1959), 69–70.
4. See, for example, the statements of Frank Hogan and Daniel Sullivan in *Hearings on S. 2183 and S. 1495, Before the Senate Committee on the Judiciary*, 87th Cong., 2nd Sess. 173, 195–98 (1962).
5. See the description of this survey in Ch. 6, pp. 136 ff.
6. *Business Week*, Feb. 27, 1960, 109; *ibid.*, June 18, 1960, 98, 105.
7. New York *Herald Tribune*, Sept. 28, 1963.
8. *UAW Solidarity*, March, 1965, 4.
9. Eico, Inc., 44 *Labor Arbitration*, 563 (1965).
10. 20 *American Psychologist*, 123–46 (1965).
11. O. M. Ruebhausen and O. G. Brim, Jr., "Privacy and Behavioral Research," 65 *Columbia Law Review*, 1184 (1965).
12. 21 *American Psychologist*, 432–37 (1966).
13. *The New York Times*, July 21, 1965.
14. Act of July 4, 1966, 80 Stat. 250.
15. See, for example, *Congressional Record*, daily edition, House of Reps., June 20, 1966, 13007–28.
16. "Clarifying and Protecting the Right of the Public to Information and for Other Purposes," Report No. 1210, Senate Committee on the Judiciary, 88th Cong., 2nd Sess., 7 (1964).
17. See, for example, the letter of Archibald Cox in *The New York Times*, Sept. 14, 1966, p. 42, cols. 5–7, citing *Katzenbach v. Morgan*, 384 U.S. 641 (1966); *U.S. v. Guest*, 383 U.S. 745 (1966); and *S. Car. v. Katzenbach*, 383 U.S. 301 (1966).
18. See *Hearings on the Use of Polygraphs as "Lie Detectors" by the Federal Government Before a Subcommittee of the House Committee on Government Operations*, 88th Cong., 2nd Sess. (1964).
19. See *Hearings on Invasions of Privacy (Government Agencies) Pursuant to S. Res. 39 Before the Subcommittee on Administrative Practice and Procedure of the Senate Committee on the Judiciary*, 89th Cong., 1st Sess. (pts. 1–4) (1965); *The New York Times*, July 16, 1965.
20. See *Hearings on Psychological Tests and Constitutional Rights Before the Subcommittee on Constitutional Rights of the Senate Committee on the Judiciary*, 89th Cong., 1st Sess. (1965).
21. See *Hearings on the Computer and Privacy Before a Subcommittee of the House Committee on Government Operations*, 89th Cong., 2nd Sess. (1966); *The New York Times*, July 28, 1966; *ibid.*, July 27, 1966.
22. See *N.Y. State Joint Legislative Comm. to Study Illegal Interception of Communications Rep.*, Legis. Doc. No. 53 (1956); *Cal. Senate Judiciary Comm., Report on the Interception of Messages by the Use of Electronic and Other Devices* (1957); *Hearings of the N.J. Joint Legislative Comm. to Study Wiretapping and the Unauthorized Recording of Speech* (1956) (unpublished transcript).
23. *Information-Sharing: The Hidden Challenge of Criminal Justice*, New York State Identification and Intelligence System (1965), 9, 11.

Bibliography

I. THE FUNCTIONS OF PRIVACY

Alexander, Franz. "Observations on Organizational Factors Affecting Creativity," in G. A. Steiner (ed.), *The Creative Organization*. Chicago, 1965.

Allee, W. C. *The Social Life of Animals*. Boston, 1958.

Arendt, Hannah. *The Human Condition*. Anchor ed., New York, 1959.

Ardrey, Robert. *The Territorial Imperative*. New York, 1966.

Barclay, Dorothy. "Supervision Without Snooping," *The New York Times*, Nov. 1, 1959, Sect. VII.

Bates, Alan. "Privacy—A Useful Concept?" 42 *Social Forces*, 429 (1964).

Berger, Morroe, *et al. Freedom and Control in Modern Society*. New York, 1964.

Berle, A. A., Jr. "The Protection of Privacy," 79 *Political Science Quarterly*, 162–68 (1964).

Berlyne, D. E. *Conflict Arousal and Curiosity*. New York, 1960.

Berne, Eric. *Games People Play*. New York, 1965.

Bishop, J. W., Jr. "The Executive's Right of Privacy: An Unresolved Constitutional Question," 66 *Yale Law Journal*, 477 (1957).

Blackwood, Beatrice. *Both Sides of the Buka Passage*. Oxford, 1935.

Blau, P. M. *The Dynamics of Bureaucracy*. Chicago, 1955.

———, and W. R. Scott. *Formal Organizations*. San Francisco, 1962.

Bossard, J. H. S. *The Sociology of Child Development*. Rev. ed., New York, 1954.

Bowman, C. C. "Loneliness and Social Change," 112 *American Journal of Psychiatry*, 194 (1955).

Brown, Rollo. *Lonely Americans*. New York, 1929.

Bulfinch, Thomas. *Bulfinch's Mythology*. New York, 1947.

Burgess, Percy. *Who Walk Alone*. New York, 1940.

Byrd, R. E. *Alone*. New York, 1938.

Calhoun, J. B. "A 'Behavioral Sink,' " in E. L. Bliss (ed.), *Roots of Behavior*. New York, 1962. Ch. 22.

Carpenter, C. R. "Territoriality: A Review of Concepts and Problems," in A. Roe and G. G. Simpson (eds.), *Behavior and Evolution*. New Haven, Conn., 1958.

Chapin, Barbara. "Shh . . . The Need for Do-Nothing Quietude," *Recreation* (Nov., 1964), 437.

Chapman, Dennis. *The Home and Social Status*. London, 1955.

Christian, J. J. "Factors in Mass Mortality of a Herd of Sika Deer (*Cervus nippon*)," 1 *Chesapeake Science*, 79–95 (1960).

Coleman, J. C. *Abnormal Psychology and Modern Life*. 3rd ed., Chicago, 1964.

Coleman, Lee. "What Is American? A Study of Alleged American Traits," 19 *Social Forces*, 492 (1941).

Colson, Elizabeth. *The Makah Indians*. Manchester, Eng., 1953.

Cowgill, D. O. *Mobile Homes: A Study in Trailer Life*. Washington, D.C., 1941.

Cross, Harold. *The People's Right to Know: Legal Access to Public Records and Proceedings*. New York, 1953.

Cuming, Luella. "Getting Along Together: Neighborhood Social Awareness," *Family Circle* (June, 1965), 62.

Dalton, Melville. *Men Who Manage*. New York, 1959.

Debonair, May-July, 1966, 69. Advertisements for electronic eavesdropping equipment.

Dicks, Henry V. "Observations on Contemporary Russian Behavior," 5 *Human Relations III*, 140 (1952).

"Do You Violate Your Teen-ager's Privacy?" *Parents' Magazine*, 48 (1960).

Dorcus, R. M., and G. W. Shaffer. *Abnormal Psychology*. 4th ed., Baltimore, 1950.

Drucker, Philip. "The Northern and Central Nootka Tribes," *Bulletin of the Bureau of American Ethology*, 185 (1951).

Emerson, R. W. "Friendship," *The Complete Works of Ralph Waldo Emerson*. New York, 1903.

Erikson, Eric. *Childhood and Society*. Rev. ed., Boston, 1964.

Etzioni, Amitai. *A Comparative Analysis of Complex Organizations*. New York, 1961.

———. *Modern Organizations*. Englewood Cliffs, N.J., 1964.

Evans-Pritchard, E. E. *The Nuer*. Oxford, 1960.

Fadiman, Clifton. "Please Tap My Wire, I Like It!" *Holiday* (July, 1964), 12.

Ford, C. S., and F. A. Beach. *Patterns of Sexual Behavior*. Paperback ed., New York, 1951.

Frank, J. P. *Marble Palace*. New York, 1958.

Freeman, W. E. "The Family System of the Iban of Borneo," in Jack Goody, ed., *Cambridge Papers in Social Anthropology*, No. 1 (London, 1958), 1552.

Freud, Sigmund. *Totem and Taboo*. Vintage ed., New York, 1960.

Friedenberg, E. Z. *Coming of Age in America*. New York, 1965.

Fromm, Eric. *Escape from Freedom*. New York, 1941.

Fromm-Reichmann, Frieda. "Loneliness," 22 *Psychiatry*, 1 (1959).

Galenson, Walter, and Seymour Lipset. *Labor and Trade Unionism*. New York, 1960.

Geertz, Clifford. Paper on Indonesian societies in Bali and Java, delivered at a seminar on privacy at Center for Advanced Study in the Behavioral Sciences, Stanford, Calif., 1959.

van Gennap, Arnold. *The Rites of Passage*. Chicago, 1960.

Getzels, J. W., and P. W. Jackson. *Creativity and Intelligence: Explorations with Gifted Students*. New York, 1962.

Goffman, Erving. *Behavior in Public Places*. New York, 1963.

———. "On the Characteristics of Total Institutions," in D. R. Cressey (ed.), *The Prison—Studies in Institutional Organization and Change*. New York, 1961.

———. *The Presentation of Self in Everyday Life*. New York, 1959.

Gomes, Edwin H. *Seventeen Years Among the Sea Dyaks of Borneo*. 1911.

Goode, W. J. *The Family*. Englewood Cliffs, N.J., 1964.

Gouldner, A. W. *Patterns of Industrial Bureaucracy*. New York, 1954.

——— (ed.). *Studies in Leadership*. New York, 1950.

de Grazia, Sebastian. *Of Time, Work, and Leisure*. New York, 1963.

Green, A. W. "The Middle Class Male Child and Neurosis," *American Social Review*, 31–41 (1946).

Greenberg, S. M. (ed.). *The Encyclopedia of Child Care*. New York, 1954.

Gross, Bertram M. *The Managing of Organizations*. Glencoe, Ill., 1964.

Hall, Edward T. *The Hidden Dimension*. New York, 1966.

———. *The Silent Language*. New York, 1959.

Halmos, Paul. *Solitude and Privacy*. London, 1952.

Harley, George. *Notes on the Poro in Liberia*. Cambridge, Mass., 1941.

Harlow, H. F., M. K. Harlow, and D. R. Meyer. "Learning Motivated by a Manipulation Drive," 40 *Journal of Experimental Psychology*, 228 (1950).

Hearings Before the Senate Subcommittee on Constitutional Rights of the Committee on the Judiciary, 86th Cong., 1st Sess., esp. pt. 3, 679, n.12 (1959).

Heckscher, August. "The Invasion of Privacy: The Reshaping of Privacy," 28 *American Scholar*, 13 (1959).

Hediger, H. "The Evolution of Territorial Behavior," in S. L. Washburn (ed.), *Social Life of Early Man*. New York, 1961.

Hilgard, E. R. *Theories of Learning*. New York, 1956.

Hollander, P. J. "Privacy: A Bastion Stormed," in "Mores and Morality in Communist China," 12 *Problems of Communism* (Nov.-Dec., 1963), 1.

Holmberg, A. R. "The Siriono." Unpublished Ph.D. dissertation, Yale University, 1946.

Holmes, Oliver Wendell, Jr. *Collected Speeches.* Boston, 1913.

Honigmann, J. J. *The World of Man.* New York, 1959.

Hook, Sidney. *The Hero in History.* Beacon ed., Boston, 1955.

Horney, Karen. *Our Inner Conflicts.* New York, 1945.

House Report 157. *Second Report by the Committee on Government Operations,* 85th Cong., 1st Sess. (1957).

Howard, H. E. *Territory in Bird Life.* London, 1920.

Howells, William W. *The Heathens: Primitive Man and His Religions.* New York, 1962 ed.

Hsu, F. L. K. *Americans and Chinese.* New York, 1953.

Hyman, H. H. "England and America: Climates of Tolerance and Intolerance," in Daniel Bell (ed.), *The Radical Right.* New York, 1963.

Inkeles, Alex, and D. J. Levinson. "National Character: The Study of Modal Personality and Sociocultural Systems," in Gardner Lindzey (ed.), *Handbook of Social Psychology* vol. 2. Cambridge, Mass., 1954.

Jacobs, Jane. *The Death and Life of Great American Cities.* Vintage ed., New York, 1962.

James, William. *The Varieties of Religious Experience.* New York, 1902.

Jones, Livingston F. *A Study of the Tlingets of Alaska.* New York, 1914.

Jourard, Sidney. "Healthy Personality and Self-Disclosure," 43 *Mental Hygiene,* 499–507 (1954).

———. "Religious Denomination and Self-Disclosure," 8 *Psychological Reports,* 446 (1961).

———. "Self-Disclosure and Other-Cathexis," 59 *Journal of Abnormal and Social Psychology,* 428–31 (1959).

———. "Self-Disclosure Patterns in British and American College Females," 54 *Journal of Social Psychology,* 315–20 (1961).

———. "Self-Disclosure Scores and Grades in Nursing College," 45 *Journal of Applied Psychology,* 244–47 (1961).

——— (with M. J. Landsman). "Cognition, Cathexis, and the Dyadic Effect in Men's Self-Disclosing Behavior," 6 *Merrill-Palmer Quarterly,* 178–86 (1960).

———. "Some Psychological Aspects of Privacy," 31 *Law and Contemporary Problems,* 307 (Spring, 1966).

——— (with P. Lasakow). "Some Factors in Self-Disclosure," 56 *Journal of Abnormal and Social Psychology,* 91–98 (1958).

Kingsley, Charles. *The Hermits.* London, 1913.

Kirchheimer, Otto, and Constantine Menges. "A Free Press in a Democratic State: The *Spiegel* Case," in G. M. Carter and A. F. Westin (eds.), *Politicals in Europe.* New York, 1965.

Kluckhon, Clyde. "Have There Been Discernible Shifts in American Values in the Past Generation?" in E. E. Morison (ed.), *The American Style.* New York, 1958.

Krause, Aurel. *The Tlingit Indians.* New York, 1956.

Krech, D., R. S. Crutchfield, and E. L. Ballachey. *Individual in Society.* New York, 1962.

de Laguna, Frederica. "Tlingit Ideas About the Individual," 10 *Southwestern Journal of Anthropology,* 180 (1954).

Landis, P. H. *Adolescence and Youth.* New York, 1952.

Lasswell, H. D. "The Threat to Privacy," in R. M. MacIver (ed.), *The Conflict of Loyalties.* New York, 1952.

Lifton, R. J. *Thought Reform and the Psychology of Totalism.* New York, 1963.

Lee, Dorothy. *Freedom and Culture.* Englewood Cliffs, N.J., 1959.

Lerner, Max. *America as a Civilization.* New York, 1957.

Lewin, Kurt. *Resolving Social Conflicts.* New York, 1948.

Lindesmith, A. R., and A. L. Strauss. *Social Psychology.* Rev. ed., New York, 1956

Lipset, Seymour. *The First New Nation.* New York, 1963.

———, M. Trow, and J. S. Coleman. *Union Democracy.* Glencoe, Ill., 1956.

448   *Bibliography*

Lowie, Robert H. *Indians of the Plains*. New York, 1954.
Luce, Robert. *Congress: An Explanation*. Cambridge, Mass., 1926.
McCartney, J. L. *Understanding Human Behavior*. New York, 1956.
McDougal, W. *An Introduction to Social Psychology*. London, 1908.
MacDougall, William. *An Introduction to Social Psychology*. Boston, 1921.
McGiffert, Michael (ed.). *The Character of Americans*. Homewood, Ill., 1964.
MacIver, R. M. (ed.). *Conflict of Loyalties*. New York, 1952.
Maslow, A. H. *Motivation and Personality*. New York, 1954.
──────, and B. Mittelman. *Abnormal Psychology*. Rev. ed., New York, 1951.
Mead, Margaret. *Coming of Age in Samoa*. Mentor ed., New York, 1949.
──────. "Margaret Mead Re-Examines Our Right to Privacy," *Redbook* (April, 1965), 15.
──────, and M. Wolfenstein (eds.). *Childhood in Contemporary Cultures*. Chicago, 1955.
Merton, Robert K. "Selected Problems of Field Work in the Planned Community," 12 *American Sociological Review*, 305 (1947).
──────. *Social Theory and Social Structure*. Rev. ed., Glencoe, Ill., 1957.
──────, and Bernard Barber. "Sociological Ambivalence," in Edward Tiryakian (ed.), *Sociological Theory, Values, and Sociological Change*. New York, 1963.
Middleton, W. C. "The Propensity of Genius to Solitude," 30 *Journal of Abnormal Psychology*, 325 (1932).
Moore, Wilbert, and M. M. Tumin. "Some Social Functions of Ignorance," 14 *American Sociological Review*, 787 (1949).
Morison, E. E. (ed.). *The American Style*. New York, 1958.
Moustakas, C. E. *Loneliness*. Englewood Cliffs, N.J., 1961.
Murdock, G. P. *Outline of World Cultures*. 3rd ed., rev., New Haven, Conn., 1963.
──────. "The Universals of Culture," in E. A. Hoebel, J. D. Jennings, and E. R. Smith (eds.), *Readings in Anthropology*. New York, 1955.
Murphy, Gardner. "Social Motivation," in Gardner Lindzey (ed.), *Handbook of Social Psychology* vol. 2. Cambridge, Mass., 1954.
Murphy, R. F. "Social Distance and the Veil," 66 *American Anthropologist*, 1257–1274 (1964).
Murray, A. S. *Manual of Mythology*. London, 1895.
Murray, H. A. *Explorations in Personality*. New York, 1938.
Myrdal, Alva. *Nation and Family*. London, 1935.
Nordhoff, Charles. *The Communistic Societies of the United States*. New York, 1875.
"Note." 70 *Yale Law Journal*, 1084 (1961).
Packard, Vance. *The Naked Society*. New York, 1964.
Park, R. E. *Race and Culture*. Glencoe, Ill., 1950.
──────, and E. W. Burgess. *Introduction to the Science of Sociology*. Chicago, 1921.
"Population Density and Social Pathology," 206 *Scientific American*, 139–48 (1962).
Ratcliffe, H. L., and R. L. Snyder. "Patterns of Disease, Controlled Populations, and Experimental Design," 26 *Circulation*, 1352–57 (1962).
Riesman, David. Introduction to E. Z. Friedenberg, *The Vanishing Adolescent*. Boston, 1959.
──────. *The Lonely Crowd*. New Haven, Conn., 1950.
Riffle, M. A. *The Personality of the Young Child*. New York, 1955.
Roe, A., and G. G. Simpson (eds.). *Behavior and Evolution*. New Haven, Conn., 1958.
Roelofs, H. M. *The Tension of Citizenship: Private Man and Public Duty*. New York, 1957.
Rokeach, M. "In Pursuit of the Creative Process," in G. A. Steiner (ed.), *Creative Organization*. Chicago, 1965.
Rossiter, Clinton. "The Pattern of Liberty," in M. R. Konvitz and Clinton Rossiter (eds.), *Aspects of Liberty*. Ithica, N.Y., 1958.
Roth, H. Ling. "The Natives of Borneo," 21 *Journal of the Anthropological Institute*, 112.
Rourke, Francis. *Secrecy and Publicity*. Baltimore, 1961.
Rovere, Richard. "The Invasion of Privacy: Technology and the Claims of Com-

munity," 27 *American Scholar*, 416 (1958).
Ruitenbeek, H. M. *The Individual and the Crowd*. New York, 1964.
Sapir, Edward. "The Life of a Nootka Indian," 28 *Queen's Quarterly* (1921).
Schiff, E. J. "Children Have a Right to Privacy," *The P.T.A. Magazine* (June, 1962), 26.
Schwab, George. *The Tribes of the Liberian Hinterland*. Cambridge, Mass., 1947.
Shils, Edward A. "Privacy: Its Constitution and Vicissitudes," 31 *Law and Contemporary Problems*, 281 (Spring, 1966).
———. "Social Inquiry and the Autonomy of the Individual," in Daniel Lerner (ed.), *The Human Meaning of the Social Sciences*. New York, 1959.
———. *The Torment of Secrecy*. Glencoe, Ill., 1956.
Simmel, Georg. "The Sociology of Secrecy and Secret Societies," 11 *American Journal of Sociology*, 441 (1906).
———. *The Sociology of Georg Simmel*. Tr. and ed. by Kurt Wolff. New York, 1950.
Spence, Lewis. *An Introduction to Mythology*. New York, 1931.
Spiller, R. E., and Eric Larrabee (eds.). *American Perspectives: The National Self-Image in the Twentieth Century*. Cambridge, Mass., 1961.
Spiro, M. E. *Kibbutz: Venture in Utopia*. New York, 1963.
Sullivan, H. S. *The Interpersonal Theory of Psychiatry*. New York, 1953.
Swan, James. *Three Years' Residence in Washington Territory*. New York, 1857.
Taylor, D. W., P. C. Berry, and C. H. Block. "Does Group Participation When Using Brainstorming Facilitate or Inhibit Creative Thinking?" 3 *Ad Science Quarterly*, 23 (1958).
"Technology and Contemplation" (editorial), 100 *America*, 188–189 (1958).
Thurber, James. *The Thurber Carnival*. (Esp. "The Secret Life of Walter Mitty.") Modern Library ed., New York, 1957.
Underhill, R. M. "Social Organization of the Papago Indians," 30 *Columbia University Contributions of Anthropology*, 119 (1939).
Vogt, E., and W. Lessa (eds.). *Reader in Comparative Religion*. New York, 1965.
Wallas, Graham. *Human Nature in Politics*. London, 1908.
Webster, Hutton. *Primitive Secret Societies*. New York, 1908.
Wedgwood, C. H. "The Nature and Functions of Secret Societies," 1 *Oceania*, 129 (1930).
Westin, A. F. "The John Birch Society: Fundamentalism on the Right," in Daniel Bell (ed.), *The Radical Right*. New York, 1963.
———. *Privacy in Western History*. New York, 1967.
Whiting, J. W. M., and I. L. Child. *Child Training and Personality*. New Haven, Conn., 1953.
Wiggins, J. R. *Freedom or Secrecy*. New York, 1956.
Williams, F. E. *Orokaiva Magic*. London, 1928.
Williams, R. M., Jr. *American Society: A Sociological Interpretation*. New York, 1960.
Wood, M. M. *Paths of Loneliness*. New York, 1960.
Wynne-Edwards, V. C. *Animal Dispersion in Relation to Social Behavior*. New York, 1962.
Yalom, T. D. "Aggression and Forbiddenness in Voyeurism," 3 *Archives of General Psychiatry*, 305 (1960).
Yarmolinski, Adam. "Memo on Privacy in Government," June 23, 1965. In files of Special Committee on Science and Law.
Young, Leontine. "A Child's Right to Privacy," *McCall's* (March, 1966), 57.
———. *Life Among the Giants*. New York, 1966.
Zetterberg, Hans L. "Complaint Actions," 2 *Acta Sociologica*, 179 (1957).

II. THE NEW TECHNOLOGY

Advertisements in Manhattan Classified Telephone Directory, 1965, 880–84, and for the following:
    "Conductor tape" (electronic), *Product Design and Development* (Jan., 1963), 24.
    Miniature cameras, *Law and Order* (Dec., 1963), 38.
    Miniature ceramic microphone, *Design News*, Jan. 9, 1963, 40.
    "Sniperscope," by Q.O.S. Corp., *Law and Order* (March, 1959), 32, 48.
"Brain Monitor Operates Inside Astronauts' Helmet," *Science News Letter*, Aug. 31, 1963, 133.
Brenton, Myron. *The Privacy Invaders*. New York, 1964.
Business Week, Feb. 19, 1966, 110.
Carroll, John M. *Secrets of Electronic Espionage*. New York, 1966.
Catalogues of the following companies:
    Criminal Research Products, Conshohocken, Pa. Catalogue No. 300.
    Dee Co., Houston, Tex.
    Delcon Corp., Palo Alto, Calif.
    Mosler Research Products, Inc., Danbury, Conn.
    Scientific Detection Products Corp., Camden, N.J. Catalogue No. 61–62 (1961).
    Security Devices Laboratory, Electronics Division of Sargent and Greenleaf, Inc., Rochester, N.Y.
    C. H. Stoelting Co., Chicago. Ill.
    W.J.S. Electronics, Hollywood, Calif. Catalogue for 1966.
"Chemical Brain Control," 85 *Science News Letter*, April 4, 1964, 214.
Clarke, A. C. "The World of the Communications Satellite," *Astronautics and Aeronautics* (Feb., 1964), 45–47.
Cronbach, L. J. *Essentials of Psychological Testing*. 2nd ed., New York, 1961.
Derrick, C. D. "Interrogation by Hypnosis," *The Police Chief* (March, 1959), 26–29.
Dessin, G. H., *et al.* "Drug Induced Revelation and Criminal Investigation," 62 *Yale Law Journal* (Feb., 1953), 315–47.
Diebold, John. "New World Coming," *Saturday Review*, July 23, 1966, 18.
Electronic Design, Feb. 15, 1961. (Transmitter in tooth.)
Electronics Illustrated (Jan., 1962), 89–91. (Surveillance by microwave beams.)
Estabrooks, G. H. *Hypnotism*. New York, 1957.
Evening Record (Bergen, N.J.), Oct. 30, 1964.
Ewing, Ann. "Lie Detection at a Distance," 88 *Science News Letter*, Aug. 14, 1965, 106.
"The Eye Is Found Clue to Thought," *The New York Times*, Nov. 22, 1964.
Eysenck, H. J. *Nonsense in Psychology*. Baltimore, 1962.
"Flying Television Camera," *Popular Science* (May, 1965).
"Gains Reported in Brain Study," *The New York Times*, Nov. 29, 1964.
Gottschalk, L. A. "The Use of Drugs in Interrogation," in A. D. Biderman and H. Zimmet (eds.), *The Manipulation of Human Behavior* (New York, 1961), 96–141.
"Government Electronic Data Processing Systems," *Hearings Before the Subcommittee on Census and Statistics of the Committee on Post Office and Civil Service*, 89th Cong., 2nd Sess. (1966).
"A Government Watch on 200 Million Americans?" *U.S. News & World Report*, May 16, 1966.
Hanscom, C. B. "NARCO Interrogation," *Police* (Nov.-Dec., 1957), 44–50.
Harwood, Richard. "Is Your Name on a Secret Dossier?" *Washington Post*, May 29, 1966.
Heath, R. G. "Electrical Self-Stimulation of the Brain in Man," 120 *American Journal of Psychiatry*, 571–577 (Dec., 1963).
Herald Tribune (N.Y.), Oct. 7, 1965.
Herman, Lawrence. "The Use of Hypno-Induced Statements in Criminal Cases,"

25 *Ohio State Law Journal*, 1–59 (1964).

Hess, E. H., and J. M. Polt. "Pupil Size as Related to Interest Value of Visual Stimuli," 132 *Science*, Aug. 5, 1960, 349–50.

House Report 198. *Use of Polygraphs as "Lie Detectors" by the Federal Government.* House Committee on Government Operations, 85th Cong., 1st Sess., March 22, 1965.

Humphrey, S. M. "Impact of Computer Developments," *Proceedings of the Association of Computing Machinery*, 17 (1959).

Information Sharing: The Hidden Challenge in Criminal Justice. Brochure of the New York State Identification and Intelligence System, 1966–67.

"Intelligence Test Uses a Flash Light," *The New York Times*, Oct. 30, 1965.

Kaufman, Felix. "Data Systems That Cross Company Boundaries," 44 *Harvard Business Review*, 141–45, 148–52 (1966).

Kubie, J. F. "Instrumental, Chemical, and Psychological Aids in the Interrogation of Witnesses," 13 *Journal of Social Issues*, 44–46 (1957).

"The Law Abiding Safe-crackers," *Evening Record* (Bergen, N.J.), Jan. 15, 1966.

Lear, John. "Whither Personal Privacy," *Saturday Review*, July 23, 1966, 36.

Leedham, Charles. "The 'Chip' Revolutionizes Electronics," *The New York Times Magazine*, Sept. 19, 1965, 56.

McGraw-Hill Encyclopedia of Science and Technology (New York, 1960), 81–82, 16–17.

Macy, J. W., Jr. "Automated Government," *Saturday Review*, Aug. 23, 1966, 21.

"Monitoring Devices and Lawyers," a report of the Special Committee on Science and Law, Association of the Bar of the City of New York, 20 *Record of the Association of the Bar of the City of New York*, No. 9 (1965).

Murphy, W. E. "Single Channel Monitor Records Twenty-four Hours," *Law and Order* (Jan., 1963), 16.

"Mutemp Sensitizes the Physician's Radio Pill," *The Economist*, June 6, 1964, 1095.

"A National Crime Information Center," *FBI Law Enforcement Bulletin* (May, 1966), 1.

"New Computer Systems Are Developed to Solve Many Problems at Once," *Wall Street Journal*, March 25, 1966.

Newsweek, Aug. 2, 1965, 58.

The New York Times: April 19 and Oct. 28, 1958; May 28 and June 5, 1960; May 22, 1963; July 4 and 26, 1965; Nov. 7, 1965, Sect. III; Dec. 28, 1965, 1, 24; Jan. 22, 1966.

The New York Times Magazine, Oct. 28, 1962, 74 ("voice prints").

"Next in Banking: Pay Bills by Phone," *Business Week*, Nov. 13, 1965, 82.

Orne, M. T. "The Potential Use of Hypnosis in Interrogation," in A. D. Biderman and H. Zimmet (eds.), *The Manipulation of Human Behavior* (New York, 1961), 169–215.

Parloto, L. P. "The Recording Eye," *Law and Order* (April, 1964), 30.

Princeton Engineer, Vol. 26, No. 4 (Jan., 1966), 26 (infrared light devices).

"Remote-Control Hypnosis," *Time*, July 2, 1965.

Review (Decatur, Ill.), April 17, 1964.

Sarnoff, David. "No Life Untouched," *Saturday Review*, July 23, 1966, 22.

Senate Document No. 15. *Report to the President on the Management of Automatic Data Processing in the Federal Government*, 89th Cong., 1st Sess., March 4, 1965.

Shaw, William. "Applied Electronics . . . Radio Beacon Tails," *Law and Order* (Nov., 1962), 34 ff.

———. "An Introduction to Law Enforcement Electronics and Communications, Part III (TV Surveillance)," *Law and Order* (May, 1965), 36.

"Someone Knows All About You," *Esquire* (May, 1966), 101.

Subliminal Communications. Institute of Practitioners in Advertising, London, July, 1958.

"A Survey of the Present and Probable Future State of Technology Affecting Privacy." Report No. 1008, prepared for the Special Committee on Science and Law by Bolt, Beranek, and Newman, Inc., Cambridge, Mass., June 20, 1963.

Time: June 21, 1963, 51; July 30, 1965, 59; April 22, 1966, 81.
Uhr, L., and J. G. Miller (eds.). *Drugs and Behavior.* New York, 1960.
Vernon, M. D. *The Psychology of Perception.* Baltimore, 1962.
"Western Union Links Teletypewriter System and Computer Center," *Wall Street Journal,* March 17, 1966.
"Wires Tapped? Snoopy Operators? Scramble," 287 *Printers' Ink,* April 10, 1964, 15.

III. THE STRUGGLE FOR CONTROLS

"Ads You'll Never See," *Business Week,* Sept. 21, 1957, 30–31.
AFL-CIO publications: DLR 10–29–64 No. 212:A-4 and DLR 180 (1964):A-6, printed in *American Federationist* (Nov., 1964), No. 212:A-5.
Alex, Charles. *How to Beat Personality Tests.* New York, 1966.
Allen, Tom. "Snoopers in Our Schools," *New York Daily News,* June 11 and 18, 1961.
Arthur, R. O. "Polygraph Picks Potential Policemen," *Law and Order* (Sept., 1964).
The Assessment of Men. Office of Strategic Services Assessment Staff. New York, 1948.
"The Attack on Invasion of Employees' Privacy," *Industrial Relations News* (April, 1965)—special report.
Ayer, Frederick, Jr. *Yankee G-Man.* Chicago, 1957.
Backster, Cleve. "Is the Polygraph Profession's Greatest Danger from Within?" Paper presented at Fifth Annual Polygraph Examiners Clinic, Univ. of Oklahoma, March 9–11, 1964.
Baker, Russell. "The Big Brain Invasion Goes On and On," *The New York Times,* Sept. 10, 1964.
Barclay, J. R. "The Attack on Testing and Counseling: An Examination and Reappraisal," 43 *Personnel and Guidance Journal,* 6–16 (1964).
Barrett, R. S. "Guide to Using Psychological Tests," *Harvard Business Review* (Sept., 1963), 138–46.
Barton, John. "Pseudo Psychos," *American Mercury* (Oct., 1956), 5–12.
Battelle, Phyllis. " 'Invisible' Advertising," New York *Journal American,* Sept. 17, 1957.
Berdie, R. F. "The Ad Hoc Committee on Social Impact of Psychological Assessment," 20 *American Psychologist,* 143–46 (1965).
Bergamini, David. "Government by Computers?" *Reporter,* Aug. 17, 1961, 21.
Berger, Meyer. "About New York," *The New York Times,* March 7, 1955.
Bier, W. C., S.J. "Psychological Testing of Candidates and the Theology of Vocation," 12 *Review for Religious,* 296 (1953).
"The Big Ear." Final script of NBC television program, Oct. 31, 1965.
"The Big Story of 1958: Subliminal Communication." Brochure published by PRE-CON, Process and Equipment Corp., 4918 Canal St., New Orleans, La., Oct., 1958.
Brean, H. "Everybody Is Dishonest," 45 *Life,* Nov. 24, 1958, 70.
Brenton, Myron. *The Privacy Invaders.* New York, 1964.
Brim, O. G., Jr. "American Attitudes Toward Intelligence Tests," *American Psychologist* (Feb., 1965); summarized in 146 *Science,* 125–30 (1965).
Brooks, S. H., and I. R. Whitman. "Transportation," *Data Processing Yearbook,* 1962–63 (Detroit, 1963), 177.
Buckley, J. L. "Central Index File—Europe," *Law and Order* (Feb., 1964), 50–53.
———. "Computers, Automation, and Security," *Law and Order* (March, 1965), 58.
———. "The Future of Computers in Security and Law Enforcement," *Law and Order,* Pt. 1, Aug., 1965; Pt. 2, Sept., 1965.
Bunker, Paul. "Twenty-four Hour Monitoring," *Law and Order* (Jan., 1958), 14.
Burdick, Eugene. *The 480.* New York, 1964.
Burkey, L. M. "Lie Detectors in Industrial Relations," 1 *Continuing Legal Education* (Ill.), No. 2 (April, 1963), 107–18.

"Business Spies Cost Industry $2 Million Yearly," San Francisco *Commercial News*, Oct. 14, 1965.

California Senate Judiciary Committee Report on the Interception of Messages by the Use of Electronic and Other Devices, Calif. Legislature, Regular Sess., 1957.

"Camera Surveillance of Sex Deviates," *Law and Order* (Nov., 1963).

Carley, W. M. "Electronic Advances; Air Snoopers Using Eavesdropping Devices," *Wall Street Journal*, April 9, 1963.

Catalogues of the following companies collected in files of Special Committee on Science and Law:
Mosler Research Products, Inc.—Azagraph Lecture Guide.
Solar Research Corp.
C. H. Stoelting Co., Chicago, Ill.

Catalogues and flyers of the following companies:
R. B. Clifton Electronic Surveillance Equipment, Miami, Fla.
Lafayette Radio Electronics, Catalogue No. 640 (1964).
Miles Reproducer Co., Inc. (1964).
Montclair Technical Services, Bloomfield, Conn. (1964).
Shure Microphones, Technical Bulletin CA4A.
Tracer Investigative Products, Inc., Palm Beach, Fla.

Clarifying and Protecting the Right of the Public to Information and for Other Purposes. Report No. 1210, Sen. Committee on the Judiciary, 88th Cong., 2nd Sess. (1964).

Collins, F. L. *The FBI in Peace and War*. New York, 1962.

Competitive Intelligence: Information, Espionage, and Decision-Making: A Special Report for Businessmen. C. I. Associates (Watertown, Mass.), 1959.

Cook, F. J. *The FBI Nobody Knows*. Pyramid ed., New York, 1964.

1 *Council of Polygraph Examiners Newsletter*, Nos. 1–2, April 21 and May 8, 1964.

"Critics of Psychological Tests—Basic Assumptions—How Good," *Psychology in the School* (Jan., 1964).

Cronbach, L. J. *Essentials of Psychological Testing*. 2nd ed., New York, 1961.

Dash, Samuel. *The Eavesdroppers*. New York, 1959.

Dixon, George. "Perils of Subliminal Projection in Elections," Washington *Post* and *Times Herald*, Dec. 19, 1957.

"The Dossier Banks," *Wall Street Journal*. May 16, 1966.

Duffey, F. D., C.S.C. *Testing the Spirit*. St. Louis, 1947.

"Eavesdropping, Modern Style," *Christian Science Monitor*, Oct. 26, 1965.

"Electronic Lawman," *The National Sheriff* (Nov.-Dec., 1963), 24.

Ellson, D. G., *et al.* "A Report of Research on Detection of Deception," Dept. of Psychology, Univ. of Indiana, 1952.

"Ethical Practices in Industrial Psychology: A Review of One Committee's Deliberation," 19 *American Psychologist*, 174–82 (1964).

Farrell, R. J. "Exterminating the Electronic 'Bugs,' " *New York Herald Tribune*, March 29, 1964.

"Feasibility Report and Recommendations for a New York Identification and Intelligence System." Systems Development Corporation Report, TM–LO–1000/600/oo (Nov. 1, 1963).

"The Federal Paperwork Jungle." *Hearings Before the House Subcommittee on Census and Government Statistics, Committee on Post Office and Civil Service*, 86th Cong., 1st Sess. (1964). ("Olsen Committee," temporary transcript.)

Ferguson, Col. J. P. (Supt. of Delaware State Police). "The Polygraph Knockers," *The Police Chief* (May, 1962), 26–27.

Flanigan, J. C., and R. E. Krug. "Testing in Management Selection: State of the Art," *Personnel Administration* (March-April, 1964), 3–39.

Foster, C. R. "A Question on Religion." Case No. 66, Inter-University Case Program Study (1961).

"1410 Is Watching," *Time* (Aug., 1963), 53.

Freed, R. N. "Your Computer . . . ," *The Management Review*, 1962.

"Gallagher Stymies 'Big Brother,' " Washington *Evening Star*, July 1, 1965.

Gannon, Robert. "Big Brother 7074 Is Watching You," *Popular Science* (March,

1963), 86–88, 206–208.

Gellerman, S. W. "A Hard Look at Testing," *Personnel* (May-June, 1961), 9.

Gibson, Gwen. "Over-the-Counter Bugging Devices," New York *Herald Tribune*, Oct. 14, 1965.

Goldwater, Barry. "Tax Supported Testing," Los Angeles *Times*, Dec. 29, 1963.

Gorlick, Arthur. "Everything's Bugged as Gumshoes Meet," Long Island City (N.Y.) *Star-Journal*, Sept. 7, 1965.

Goslin, D. A. "The Social Consequences of Predictive Testing in Education." Paper delivered at Conference on the Moral Dilemmas of Public Schooling, Univ. of Wisc., May 12–14, 1965.

Gross, M. L. *The Brain Watchers.* New York, 1962.

Haber, R. N. "Public Attitudes Regarding Subliminal Advertising," 23 *Public Opinion Quarterly* (Summer, 1959), 291–93.

Halfeld, D. M. "Justice Department Policies on Wire-Tapping," 9 *Law Guild Review*, 57–69 (1949).

Harwood, Richard. "Is Your Name on a Secret Dossier?" Washington *Post*, May 29, 1966.

Hathaway, S. R. "MMPI: Professional Use by Professional People," 19 *American Psychologist*, 204 (1964).

Haver, Martin. "The Snoopers," *Man's Magazine* (July, 1960).

"Hell Breaks Loose in Paradise," *Life*, April 26, 1963, 73–84.

Hilgard, E. R. *Introduction to Psychology.* 3rd ed., New York, 1962.

Hindman, Jo. "The Fight for Your Child's Mind," *American Mercury* (Nov., 1957), 7–12.

———. "Secret *Cum* Files: A Leftist Wedge," *American Mercury* (Oct., 1958), 118–26.

Hollinger, J. R., and J. E. Mulligan. "Build the Shotgun Sound Snooper," *Popular Electronics* (June, 1964), 51, 84.

"How Detective Burns Listened to Dynamiter Plot," 106 *Scientific American*, 284 (1912).

"How Good Are Personality Tests, Anyway?" *Administrative Management* (Oct., 1962).

Huxley, Aldous. *Brave New World Revisited.* New York, 1958.

"Image Worries Psychologists," Los Angeles *Times*, Jan. 31, 1966.

Inbau, F. E., and J. E. Reid. *Lie Detection and Criminal Interrogation.* 3rd ed., Baltimore, 1953.

"The Influence of Drugs on the Individual," in S. M. Farber and R. H. L. Wilson (eds.), *Control of the Mind* (New York, 1961), 77–130.

"Information Sharing: The Hidden Challenge of Criminal Justice." New York State Identification and Intelligence System, 1965.

"Invasion of Privacy." *Hearings of the Special Subcommittee on Invasion of Privacy of the House Committee on Government Operations,* 89th Cong., 1st Sess. (1965). ("Gallagher Committee," temporary transcript.)

"Invasions of Privacy (Government Agencies)." *Hearings Before the Subcommittee on Administrative Practice and Procedure of the Senate Judiciary Committee,* 89th Cong., 1st Sess. (1965).

"Jobs and Psychology," *Wall Street Journal*, Feb. 9, 1965.

Kallis, W. H. "The Phantom of the Soap Opera," *Public Relations Journal* (March, 1958).

Katzell, R. A. "A Psychologist Examines Violations of Privacy," 17 *Virginia Law Weekly*, DICTA, No. 4 (1964).

Keating, W. J. *The Man Who Rocked the Boat.* New York, 1956.

Kelly, Roy. *Hiring of the Worker.* New York, 1919.

Knebel, F., and C. W. Bailey, II. *Convention.* New York, 1964.

Kubis, J. W. "Studies in Lie Detection." Report No. RADC-TR 62–205 (1962), United States Air Force.

Lear, John. "Whither Personal Privacy," *Saturday Review*, July 23, 1966, 36, 41.

Lederer, F. J. "Exclusive Inside Story of Philadelphia Vice Investigation," *Official Detective Stories* (Feb., 1957), 10.

McDermott, T. A. "I Smashed Philadelphia's Pornography-Prostitution Ring," *True Police Cases* (Feb., 1957), 8.
MacDonald, Dwight. "The Lie Detector Era," *Reporter*, June 8, 1954, 10–18, and June 22, 1954, 22–29.
McGrady, Mike. "You, Too, Can Bug People . . . and Their Phones," Miami *Herald*, Sept. 23, 1965.
McKee, W. F. "Evidentiary Problems: Camera Surveillance of Sex Deviates," *Law and Order* (Aug., 1964), 72.
"Man and the Computer." Symposium at meeting of American Association for Advancement of Science, 1962.
Mannes, Marya. "Ain't Nobody Here but Us Commercials," 17 *Reporter*, Oct. 17, 1957, 35–37.
Marshall, M. S. "Who Wants to Know?" 75 *School and Society*, 385–89 (1952).
Mellin, W. J. "I Was a Wire-Tapper," *Saturday Evening Post*, Sept. 10, 1949.
"Mental Exams Said Firing Tool at Kelly [Air Force Base]," San Antonio (Tex.) *News*, June 11, 1965.
Messick, Samuel. "Personality Measurement and the Ethics of Assessment," 21 *American Psychologist* (May, 1966), 136–42.
Michael, D. N. "Speculation on the Relation of the Computer to Individual Freedom and the Right of Privacy," 33 *George Washington Law Review*, 270–86 (1964).
Miniature microphones. Advertisement in *The New York Times International Edition*, June 30, 1964.
Minority Report of the Citizens' Advisory Committee on Education, State of California, 1960.
Mueller, G. O. W. "The Law Relating to Police Interrogation Privileges and Limitations," in C. R. Sowle (ed.), *Police Power and Individual Freedom*. Chicago, 1963.
Munsterberg, Hugo. *Psychology and Industrial Efficiency*. Boston, 1913.
"National Information Center." *Hearings Before the Ad Hoc Subcommittee on a National Research Data Processing and Information Retrieval Center of the House Committee on Education and Labor*, 88th Cong., 1st Sess. (1963).
National Training Center of Lie Detection. Advertisement in *Law and Order* (Sept., 1965), 52.
Nettler, Gwynn. "Test Burning in Texas," 13 *American Psychologist*, 682 (1959).
Otis, J. L. "Psychological Espionage." Unpublished address to American Psychological Association, 1957.
Ottenberg, Miriam. *The Federal Investigators*. Englewood Cliffs, N.J., 1962.
Packard, Vance. *The Naked Society*. New York, 1964.
———. *The Pyramid Climbers*. New York, 1962.
"Personality Testing: An Invasion of Privacy?" 14 *Industrial Relations News*, No. 30, July 25, 1964.
"Personnel Selection Tests and Fair Employment Practices," *Test Services Bulletin* (of the Psychological Corp.), Nos. 36–40 (1948–50).
Plum, W. R. *The Military Telegraph During the Civil War*. 1882.
"The Polygraph's Enemies," *Law and Order* (Nov., 1964), 46.
"Protection of Intellectual Property Against Industrial Espionage and Theft," *The New York Times*, March 16, 1965.
"Psychological Testing for Workers: Is Industry Buying a Fad?" *Business Week*, July 19, 1952, 82–86.
"Psychological Tests and Public Responsibility" (a symposium), 20 *American Psychologist*, 123 (1965).
Public Hearings Before a New Jersey Commission to Study Subliminal Projection, Created Under Assembly Resolution No. 6 (1959), April 8, 1959.
"Radicals: Waiting for Armageddon," *Newsweek*, April 26, 1965.
Reid, Ed, and Ovid Demaris. *The Green Felt Jungle*. Pocket Books ed., New York, 1964.
Reid, John E., and Fred E. Inbau. *Truth and Deception: The Polygraph ("Lie Detector") Technique*. Baltimore, 1966.
"Remote-Control Hypnosis," *Time*, July 2, 1965, 37.

Richards, Guy. "Is Your Telephone Tapped?" New York *Star*, Sept. 27–30, 1948.
Ridgeway, James. "The Snoops: Private Lives and Public Service," *New Republic*, Dec. 19, 1964, 13–17.
"Rights of Government Employees, Psychiatric Exams, and Psychological Tests." *Hearings Before the Subcommittee on Constitutional Rights of the Senate Judiciary Committee*, 89th Cong., 1st Sess. (1965). ("Ervin Committee," temporary transcript.)
"Robert Kennedy Defines the Menace," *The New York Times Magazine*, Oct. 13, 1963.
Roper, Elmo. "How Powerful Are the Persuaders?" 40 *Saturday Review*, Oct. 5, 1957, 19.
Rose, A. W. "Motivation Research and Subliminal Advertising," 25 *Social Research*, 271–84 (1958).
Rosenzweig, Margaret L. "The Law of Wiretapping," 33 *Cornell Law Quarterly*, 73 (1947).
Rowan, T. C. "Computer Technology and Social Change." Paper delivered at the annual meeting of American Orthopsychiatric Association, 1965.
Ruebhausen, O. M., and O. G. Brim, Jr. "Privacy and Behavioral Research," 21 *American Psychologist* (May, 1966), 423–37, and 65 *Columbia Law Review*, 1184 (1965).
Rytten, J. E. "How to Tap a Telephone," and "Recording and the Police Profession," *Law and Order* (Jan., March, and May, 1955).
"Secret Files for Secret Purposes." Educational News Service, Fullerton, Calif. (Oct., 1958; reprinted 1961).
Shaw, William. "Applied Electronics . . . Radio Beacon Tails," *Law and Order* (Nov., 1962), 34.
———. "An Introduction to Law Enforcement Electronics and Communication," *Law and Order* (Mar., April, May, June, July, 1965).
Shils, Edward. "Social Inquiry and the Autonomy of the Individual," in Daniel Lerner (ed.), *The Human Meaning of the Social Sciences*. New York, 1959.
Silving, Helen. "Testing of the Unconscious Criminal Cases," 69 *Harvard Law Review*, 683–705 (1956).
Sisk, J. P. "Taking Man's Measure," *Commonweal*, April 15, 1960, 59.
Skolnick, J. M. "Scientific Theory and Scientific Evidence: An Analysis of Lie-Detection," 70 *Yale Law Journal* (April, 1961), 715.
Smith, Burke M. "The Polygraph," 216 *Scientific American*, Jan. 5, 1967.
Spindel, Bernard. "Who Else Is Listening?" *Collier's*, June 10, 1955, 26.
2 *Stanford Law Review*, 744, 750, n. 42 (1950). (Note regarding conflicting views on President Roosevelt's supposed authorization of wiretapping in World War II.)
"State Department Security, 1963–65: The Otepka Case, II." *Hearings Before the Senate Subcommittee on Internal Security, Judiciary Committee*, 89th Cong., 1st Sess. (1965).
Statement Regarding Psychological Testing in the Schools. Committee on Testing of the California Association of School Psychologists and Psychometricists (1963).
Sternbach, R. A., *et al.* "Don't Trust the Lie Detector," 40 *Harvard Business Review*, No. 6 (Nov.-Dec. 1962), 133.
Stessin, Lawrence. " 'I Spy' Becomes Big Business," *The New York Times Magazine*, Nov. 28, 1965.
Strodtbeck, F. L. "Social Process, the Law, and Jury Functioning," in W. M. Evan (ed.), *Law and Sociology* (Glencoe, Ill., 1961), 151, n.
Subliminal Communication. Institute of Practitioners in Advertising, London, 1958.
Sutor, David. "The Gray Flannel Couch—The Lie Detector in Business," *U.S. Catholic* (July, 1964), 11.
Talese, Gay. "Most Hidden Hidden Persuasion," *The New York Times Magazine*, Jan. 12, 1958, 59.
"Talk of the Town," *The New Yorker*, Sept. 21, 1957.
"Testing in Boulder Valley Public Schools." Mimeographed report distributed by

the Save America Constitutionally Club, Boulder, Colo., Oct. 30, 1963.

"Testing and Discrimination," *Wall Street Journal*, April 21, 1964.

Thompson, G. W., *et al.* "An Empirical Evaluation of the Watchers of Brain-watchers: A Survey of Testers, Tests, and Testing Programs," 3 *Journal of School Psychology*, No. 4 (Summer, 1965), 49–57.

Torre, Mottram (ed.). *The Selection of Personnel for International Service.* New York, 1963.

"Unions Act on Threats to Privacy," *Business Week*, March 13, 1965, 87–88.

Use of Electronic Data Processing Equipment in the Federal Government. House Report No. 858, Committee on Post Office and Civil Service, 88th Cong., 1st Sess. (1963).

"Use of Polygraphs as 'Lie Detectors' by the Federal Government." *Hearings Before a Subcommittee of the House Committee on Government Operations*, 88th Cong., 2nd Sess. (1964). ("Moss Committee.") Preliminary Study, April, 1964; Tenth Report, March, 1965.

Wagner, S. P. "Records and the Invasions of Privacy," 40 *Social Science Journal* (Jan. 1965), reprinted in *Congressional Record*, May 18, 1965, 10821–25.

Wessel, M. R. "Legal Protection of Computer Programs," *Harvard Business Review*, 97–106 (1965).

Westin, A. F. "Bookies and Bugs in California," in Westin (ed.), *The Uses of Power* (New York, 1962), 138.

———. "Wire-Tap: The House Approves," *New Rerpublic*, April 9, 1954, 6.

———. "Wiretapping: The Silent Revolution," 29 *Commentary* 333–340 (April, 1960).

———. "The Wire-Tapping Problem," 52 *Columbia Law Review*, 165 (1952).

Wetzig, Mina. "Have Personality Testers Gone Too Far?" *Information* (Nov., 1961), 2–9.

"When Walls Have Ears, Call a De-Bugging Man," *Business Week*, Oct. 31, 1965.

Whitehead, Don. *The FBI Story.* New York, 1956.

Whyte, W. H., Jr. *The Organization Man.* Garden City, N.Y., 1956.

"Wiretap World Opens a Little," *Long Island* (N.Y.) *Press*, May 27, 1966.

"The Wiretappers," *Reporter*, Jan. 6, 1953, 9.

"Wire-Tapping Cases in New York," 113 *Outlook*, May 31, 1916, 234.

"Wiretapping, Eavesdropping, and the Bill of Rights." *Hearings Before the Sub-committee on Constitutional Rights of the Senate Committee on the Judiciary*, 86th Cong., 1st Sess. (1959). ("Ervin Committee," temporary transcript.)

"Wiretapping for National Security." *Hearings Before a Subcommittee of the Senate Judiciary Committee*, 83rd Cong., 2nd Sess. (1954).

Zola, Joan. "Adventures of a Test Taker," *National Review*, Jan. 12, 1965.

IV. PRIVACY IN AMERICAN LAW AND POLICY

Adams, E. L. "The Right of Privacy and Its Relation to the Law of Libel," 29 *American Law Review*, 37 (1905).

Beveridge, A. J. *The Life of Marshall.* New York, 1919.

Boyd, Julian (ed.). *The Papers of Thomas Jefferson.* Princeton, N.J., 1952.

"The Constitutional Right to Anonymity," 70 *Yale Law Journal*, 1084, n. (1961).

Cooley, Thomas M. "Inviolability of Telegraphic Correspondence," 18 *American Law Register* (N.S.), 65 (1879).

———. *A Treatise on Constitutional Limitations.* Boston, 1890.

Crèvecoeur, M.-G. de. *Letters from an American Farmer.* 1782.

Dash, Samuel. *The Eavesdroppers.* New York, 1963.

Derry, T. K., and T. I. Williams. *A Short History of Technology.* New York, 1960.

Godkin, E. L. "The Rights of the Citizen—IV. To His Reputation," 8 *Scribner's*, 58 (1890).

Greenleaf, Simon. *A Treatise on the Law of Evidence.* 4th ed., Boston, 1848.

Hitchcock, Henry. "The Inviolability of Telegrams," 5 *So. Law Review* (N.S.), 413 (1879).

Hofstader, Samuel H., and George Horowitz. *The Right of Privacy.* New York, 1964.

Holbrook, James. *Ten Years Among the Mail Bags.* Philadelphia, 1855.

J.A.J. "The Legal Relations of Photographs," 8 *American L. Reg.,* 1 (1869).

Lawrence, David. "The Lost Right of Privacy," 33 *American Mercury,* 12–18 (1936).

Lieber, Francis. *On Civil Liberty and Self-Government.* London, 1853.

Murphy, Walter. *Wiretapping on Trial.* New York, 1965.

Nizer, L. "The Right of Privacy: A Half Century's Development," 39 *Michigan Law Review,* 526 (1941).

Prosser, W. "Privacy," 48 *Columbia Law Review,* 383 (1960).

Scott, W., and M. Jarnagin. *A Treatise Upon the Law of Telegrams.* Boston, 1868.

Story, Joseph. *Commentaries on Equity Jurisprudence.* 2nd ed., Boston, 1830.

———. *Commentaries on the Constitution of the United States.* 2nd ed., Boston, 1851.

Warren, S., and L. D. Brandeis. "The Right to Privacy," 4 *Harvard Law Review,* 193 (1890).

White, Leonard. *The Federalists.* New York, 1948.

Wigmore, John H. *A Treatise on the Anglo-American System of Evidence in Trials at Common Law,* Vol. 8. 3rd ed., Boston, 1940.

Wilson, M. A. *American Science and Invention.* New York, 1954.

Index

Alan F. Westin

Born in New York City in 1929, Alan F. Westin is both a lawyer and a political scientist. A member of the District of Columbia Bar, he has taught at Harvard, Yale, and Cornell universities, and is now Professor of Public Law and Government at Columbia University and Director of the Center for Research and Education in American Liberties of Columbia University and Teachers College. His books include *The Anatomy of a Constitutional Law Case, The Supreme Court: Views from Inside, The Uses of Power, An Autobiography of the Supreme Court, Freedom Now!: The Civil Rights Struggle in America,* and *Views of America.* His writings have appeared in *The New York Times Magazine, Saturday Review, Commentary, The Nation, Harper's, American Heritage, The New Republic, The New Leader, American Political Science Review, Journal of Politics,* and the law reviews of Harvard, Yale, and Columbia universities. Professor Westin is a member of the National Board of Directors of the American Civil Liberties Union, the National Civil Rights Committee of the Anti-Defamation League, and the Commission on Law and Social Action of the American Jewish Congress. A frequent participant on television programs dealing with constitutional, political and foreign-policy topics, Professor Westin has appeared on *Open End, Open Mind, Court of Reason,* and other discussion programs. The theme of invasion of privacy has been a central concern of his writing for more than a decade. His articles since 1952 on wire-tapping have been leading ones in this field and he has given expert testimony before several Congressional committees looking into invasion of privacy. The work on which this book is based was done between 1962 and 1966 under the auspices of the Special Committee on Science and Law of the Association of the Bar of the City of New York, under a grant from the Carnegie Corporation. Professor Westin lives in Teaneck, New Jersey, with his wife and three children.